Otto Bauer (1881–1938)

Historical Materialism Book Series

The Historical Materialism Book Series is a major publishing initiative of the radical left. The capitalist crisis of the twenty-first century has been met by a resurgence of interest in critical Marxist theory. At the same time, the publishing institutions committed to Marxism have contracted markedly since the high point of the 1970s. The Historical Materialism Book Series is dedicated to addressing this situation by making available important works of Marxist theory. The aim of the series is to publish important theoretical contributions as the basis for vigorous intellectual debate and exchange on the left.

The peer-reviewed series publishes original monographs, translated texts, and reprints of classics across the bounds of academic disciplinary agendas and across the divisions of the left. The series is particularly concerned to encourage the internationalization of Marxist debate and aims to translate significant studies from beyond the English-speaking world.

For a full list of titles in the Historical Materialism Book Series
available in paperback from Haymarket Books, visit:
https://www.haymarketbooks.org/series_collections/1-historical-materialism

Otto Bauer (1881–1938)

Thinker and Politician

Ewa Czerwińska-Schupp

Translated by Maciej Zurowski

Haymarket Books
Chicago, IL

First published in 2016 by Brill Academic Publishers, The Netherlands
© 2016 Koninklijke Brill NV, Leiden, The Netherlands

Published in paperback in 2018 by
Haymarket Books
P.O. Box 180165
Chicago, IL 60618
773-583-7884
www.haymarketbooks.org

ISBN: 978-1-60846-817-1

Trade distribution:
In the US, Consortium Book Sales, www.cbsd.com
In Canada, Publishers Group Canada, www.pgcbooks.ca
In the UK, Turnaround Publisher Services, www.turnaround-uk.com
All other countries, Ingram Publisher Services International, ips_intlsales@
ingramcontent.com

Cover design by Jamie Kerry of Belle Étoile Studios and Ragina Johnson.

This book was published with the generous support of Lannan Foundation
and the Wallace Action Fund.

Printed in Canada by union labor.

10 9 8 7 6 5 4 3 2 1

Library of Congress Cataloging-in-Publication data is available.

† To my late husband, Walter Schupp, for everything that has been, and still is beautiful in my life.

∵

Otto Bauer in 1931

Contents

Introduction to the English Edition

Let us for a moment go back to the history of the 1960s and 1970s leftist social movement. Those years revealed a profound crisis of ideological and political values – a crisis that deeply affected the exponents of West European radical Social-Democratic groups, liberalising Eurocommunist factions of the Communist movement, and European and American leftist intellectuals. It found expression in the growing strength of various endeavours: First, critiques of the programmatic line of Social-Democratic Parties – such as their eclecticism, ideology of the 'people's party', lack of revolutionary theory, and state monopoly capitalism – and demands for structural reforms towards internal party democracy.[1] Second, the Eurocommunists' attempt to adjust socialist ideology to the needs of the modern industrial state.[2] Third, the appearance of intellectuals and groups of radical youth under the banner of the 'new left', casting doubt over the theoretical, methodological, and ideological value of Marxism and its practical consequences, such as the principles of party organisation and forming alliances. These movements demanded the transformation of societies through their ideological and cultural realms.[3]

---

1 See *JUSO-Jahrbuch 1968–69*, Bonn 1970, p. 41, and *Handbuch für die Jungsozialistenarbeit*, Bonn 1971, p. III/1.

2 The expression 'Eurocommunism' was first used by the Yugoslavian journalist, France Barbieri, in 1975, and shortly after by the Italian journalist, Arrigo Levi, and by the Catholic philosopher, Augusto Del Noche. The Italian, Spanish, French, Swedish, British, and Greek Communist parties were eventually dominated by the Eurocommunist trend, as were – not entirely logically due to their geographical locations – the Japanese and Australian Communist parties. The tendency, whose adherents were ideologically rather than organisationally linked, was characterised by its open approach towards Marxism and other ideological orientations, its critical attitude towards the Soviet model of socialism and the Leninist party concept, its demand for autonomy and equality of Communist parties, and its postulates for a democratic path to socialism and a pluralist-democratic model of socialism in economy and politics. Compare Leonhard 1980.

3 Originally, the 'new left' represented an intellectual current. It emerged at the turn of the 1950s and 1960s mainly among academics (philosophers, sociologists, and economists), publicists, and writers drawing on neo-Marxism, existentialism, and social psychoanalysis. Under the influence of the student protests and French 'gauchism' of 1968, it transformed into a political movement. Representatives of the 'new left' included, among others, C. Wright Mills, Herbert Marcuse, Wilhelm Reich, and Theodore Roszak in the United States, André Gorz, Jean-Paul Sartre, Paul Sweezy, Charles Bettelheim, and Ernest Mandel in France, Oskar Negt and Rudi Dutschke in West Germany, and Rossana Rossanda in Italy. The strengths of the new left were

These critiques of the conception of socialist revolution and the repressive nature of the power apparatuses in the countries of 'really existing socialism', as well as rejections of the proletariat as the driving force of history, were linked to the quest for a so-called 'third way' between capitalism and socialism. And although the Western left was ideologically diverse, it was united in one intention: the desire to lead society onto a path that would overcome the deficiencies of both systems. Consequently, the winning tendency was the one that endeavoured to work out a theoretical model of society that would match the realities of the post-industrial age. In this tendency were underlying causes of a growing interest, in the 70s and 80s, with a current known as Austromarxism, which had played a significant role in the international workers' movement before World War II (namely, from 1904–38).

In my 1991 book of the same name, I referred to this trend as 'the tendency of mediation'. In the theoretical realm, its mediation pertained to the relationship between Marxism and the most important philosophical, social, and political tendencies of the turn of the nineteenth and twentieth centuries; at a practical level, it concerned choosing a path between reformism and Bolshevism. I also wish to highlight an undeniable achievement of Austromarxism: its representatives managed to work out theoretical and political concepts that transcended the interpretations of Marxism common among the groups of the Second International, i.e. the right around Eduard Bernstein, the centre around Karl Kautsky, and the left around Vladimir Lenin. The political thought of Austromarxism, especially the works of Otto Bauer and Max Adler, were unified in one central idea: its ambition to overcome the divide between Social Democracy and Communism, embodied in its purest form by Bauer's concept of 'integral socialism', the idea of a process of mutual learning and dialogue.[4]

---

its sharp critique of the economic and political structure of the capitalist state, exploitation, social inequality, racism, colonialism, war, and consumerist ideals, and its demand for the democratisation of social relations in both capitalist and socialist countries. Its weaknesses were its inability to work out tools for winning a broad social base and confining itself to the actions of small extremist groups.

4   The theoretical views of Austromarxism and the activity of Austrian Social Democracy from 1868–1934 were the subject of my interests in the following works: *Austromarksizm w teorii i w praktyce. Studium myśli filozoficznej i społeczno-politycznej* (*Austromarxism in Theory and Practice. A Study of its Philosophical and Socio-Political Thought*, Poznan 1986); *Nurt mediacji. Austromarksizm i jego recepcja w Polsce* (*The Tendency of Mediation. Austromarxism and its Reception in Poland*, Poznan 1991); *Filozof i demokrata. Studium myśli społeczno-politycznej Otto Bauera (1881–1938)*, Vol. 1 (*Philosopher and Democrat. A Study of Otto Bauer's Socio-Political Thought*, Poznan 1998); *Utracona demokracja. Studium myśli społeczno-politycznej*

The Socialist Party of Austria that rose from the ashes of the Social-Democratic Workers' Party (SDAP) after World War II decidedly broke with its roots. This was challenged by many socialists – including Oskar Pollak, who demanded that the gains of Austromarxism, especially Bauer's, be preserved.[5] The intellectual leader of pre-war Social Democracy fell into oblivion. Meanwhile, his former party comrades Karl Renner, Adolf Schärf, and Oskar Helmer – who, admittedly, had already renounced Bauer's political course before 1934 – adopted political positions in the Second Republic close to those of the Austrian People's Party (ÖVP). This trend persisted until the end of the 1970s. Only the year 1978 saw a change in direction when Austria's socialist party was captured by the general wave of Austromarxist revival. At the party congress in the same year, Bruno Kreisky introduced Bauer's conception of social democracy into the programme.[6]

The renaissance of Bauer's views and Austromarxism began with a debate inspired by Norbert Leser's 1968 monograph, *Zwischen Reformismus und Bolschewismus. Der Austromarxismus als Theorie und Praxis* (*Between Reformism and Bolshevism. Austromarxism as Theory and Practice*), which is regarded as a standard reference work on Austromarxism to this day. The argument put forward by the author – a historian, political scientist, and philosopher at Vienna University – provoked numerous controversies among scholars of Austrian Social-Democratic history. Many found it difficult to agree with Leser's theses, which allocated the blame for the defeat of the Social-Democratic party in 1934 one-sidedly to Bauer and the political line he had adopted. Not only

---

Otto Bauera (1881–1938), Vol. 2 (*The Lost Democracy. A Study of Otto Bauer's Socio-Political Thought*, Poznan 1998); and *Otto Bauer. Studien zur sozial-politischen Philosophie* (*Otto Bauer. A Study of Socio-Political Philosophy*, Frankfurt 2005), which was based on the aforementioned Polish publications, *Philosopher and Democrat* and *The Lost Democracy*. It is worth mentioning that Bauer himself did not refer to Austromarxism as an exclusively Austrian current, but rather as an 'international ideological trend of the Marxist centre, which constituted, based on scientific analysis, a specific party policy which aimed to preserve a centrist position "between reformism and Bolshevism" and maintain a union of revolutionary work for the future and practical reformist work in the here and now' (our translation) – see Bauer 1927, p. 549. Boudin was the first to use the term 'Austromarxism' in 1908. Leon Trotsky popularised it after 1918 in his critique of the political movement.

5 See Hindels 1981, p. 5.

6 At the time, Kreisky expressed sentiments close to the old leader's views: 'We socialists aspire to a classless society in which relations of domination and privileges have been overcome, and which rests on the fundamental values of freedom, equality, equal rights, and solidarity' (our translation) – Hindels 1981, p. 7. Kreisky had enjoyed a warm relationship with Bauer, whose last disciple he had been. The party moved to the left when he became its leader.

did they criticise Leser's method of illuminating facts, they also accused him of a gross subjectivism and personal animosity towards Bauer. In addition, two works glorifying the leaders of the pre-war SDAP further ignited the argument about Austromarxism's legacy: Viktor Reimann's *Zu gross für Österreich. Seipel und Bauer im Kampf um die erste Republik* (*Too Big For Austria. Seipel and Bauer in the Struggle for the First Republic*, 1968) and Otto Leichter's *Otto Bauer. Tragödie oder Triumph* (*Otto Bauer. Tragedy or Triumph*, 1970). The ultimate fruits of this debate were the 1975–80 publication of Bauer's collected works, around 300 tomes and articles dedicated to this current's theory and practice written from 1970–2014 by Austrian, German, Italian, French, American, Russian, Yugoslavian and Polish authors, numerous international conferences and seminars, and a discussion on the continued relevance of Bauer's programme conducted in the pages of the socialist press.[7] In the 1970s, journals such as *Problemi del socialismo* and *Mondoperaio*, for instance, published writings by Italian Communist Party members drawing parallels between the Weimar Republic, the First Republic in Germany, and the contemporary socio-political crisis in Italy; the authors attempted to find convergent positions between Bauer and Antonio Gramsci.[8] In light of a party-internal crisis, the student movement, criticism from the Young Socialists in the SPD and attacks from the 'new left', the West German socialists revised the form of their old ideological superstructure, appealing to the experience of 'red Vienna'. The socialist left, mainly in West Germany, Austria, and Italy, looked to the Austromarxists' works to find a base for the concept of social democracy, the theory of the balance of class forces, and justifications for the dissimilar economic structures in highly developed countries and the USSR and Asian countries. Note that Austromarxism also

---

7   There were the following events and publications, among others: a 1976 Berlin conference organised by left socialists from Bremen University, Detlev Albers, Volker Gransow and Michael Krätke, concerning strategic premises for the West German workers' movement – with respect to social partnership, the conference harked back to Bauer's proposals; three conferences on Otto Bauer in Vienna in 1978, 1979, and 1981; a 1982 seminar entitled 'Nostalgia or Austromarxist renaissance' in Paris; celebrations of Bauer's 100th birthday in Budapest; a 1984 conference on Otto Bauer's and Austromarxism's contribution to the development of democratic socialist theory and practice, organised on the initiative of Horst Heimann and Thomas Meyer, editors of *Zeitschrift für sozialistische Politik und Wirtschaft* (*Journal for Socialist Politics and Economy*). For extensive assessments of the reception of Bauer's works and actions, see Butterwegge 1990, pp. 17–31; Saage 2009, pp. 59–62; and Hanisch 2011, pp. 387–93.

8   A collection of Austromarxist texts, edited by Marramao and introduced by Mozetič, met with vivid interest in the Eurocommunist camp.

became attractive to Christian theorists at that time. The idea of collaboration between the church and the state propagated by Franz König harked back
directly to Bauer's position on the necessity of co-operation between political
and church leaders in denouncing exploitation and social injustice, as well as
in defending social rights and mass access to culture. These ideas were seen
as constituting the foundation for a moral renewal of contemporary capitalist
societies.

At this point, I would like to retract some statements I made in the introduction to the Polish and German editions of this book concerning 'Austromarxism
as a closed chapter'. Works on this political current continue to be published
to this day, the best examples being an outstanding biography by the Austrian
historian, Ernst Hanisch, *Der grosse Illusionist. Otto Bauer 1881–1983* (*The Great
Illusionist*, 2011) and Olaf Leiße's *Der Untergang des österreichischen Imperiums. Otto Bauer und die Nationalitätenfrage in der Habsburger Monarchie* (*The
Decline of the Austrian Empire. Otto Bauer and the Nationalities Question of the
Habsburg Monarchy*, 2012). To the extent this was possible, I have incorporated
works that appeared after my Polish and German publications, as well as books
and articles published from 1984–2014 that I had been previously unaware of,
into the scope of the present work.

Their protagonist, Otto Bauer, was a true authority in the international workers' movement in his lifetime. He entered the history of political movements
as the ideological leader of Austrian Social Democracy in the First Republic; co-founder and prime mover of Austromarxism from 1906–38, state func-
tionary, influential theorist, and one of the leaders of three internationals –
the Second International, the International Working Union of Socialist Parties
('Second and a half international'), and Labour and Socialist International,
respected parliamentarian, outstanding speaker, editor of socialist newspapers
and journals, and teacher at the 'workers' college'. No less respected were his
theoretical contributions as a historian, sociologist, philosopher, Sovietologist,
political thinker, and author of texts on economics. He wrote 47 monographs
and around 4,000 articles – his written publications amount to more than
10,000 printed pages. The articles Bauer wrote for the *Arbeiter-Zeitung* newspaper and *Der Kampf* monthly journal informed readers extensively on national
and international political events and acute questions in the international
workers' movement and his party, and at the same time crucially influenced
public opinion.[9] All of this suggests that in the eyes of contemporary socialists

---

9 Bauer began writing aged 24 in 1904 and continued to write until the end of his life. That the
   magazines *Przedświt* and *Robotnik* continually translated his writings into Polish testifies to

and ordinary SDAP members, it was Bauer, not other outstanding Social Democrats such as Karl Renner or Max Adler, who embodied the system of values that crucially shaped Austromarxism. For the same reasons, the international workers' movement considered the SDAP to be Bauer's party. For many intellectuals of his time, Bauer was an exemplary humanist, yet also an exceptionally multi-faceted human being full of tensions and contradictions.[10] His inner conflicts came to light in both his theoretical concepts and his political actions. Bauer still appears as an extraordinary phenomenon today: a thinker and politician whose political errors and contradictions were visible and widely criticised, but who still fascinated his contemporaries. This peculiar position that Bauer occupied in his contemporaries' consciousness inspired me to address in this book a number of questions regarding Bauer's role in the SDAP and the international workers' movement, as well as the content and scope of his theory.[11]

What further inspired me to write this book was my belief that the solutions Austromarxism offered to theoretical and practical questions concern-

---

the interest in his work. The Polish Socialist Party (PPS) published his books, which had a vivid impact on the debates and views of PPS theorists. Mieczysław Niedziałkowski in particular had great sympathies for Bauer. Compare Śliwa 1980, p. 53. The theoretical works of the PPS theorists placed an emphasis on those elements of Austrian Social-Democratic theory and politics in which the search for a 'third way' between Communism and Social Democracy was manifest. Under their influence, there emerged in Poland, especially on the left of the PPS, a narrow understanding of Austromarxism. The PPS left regarded Austromarxism mainly as a trend that put forward positions divergent from those that were commonly accepted in Social-Democratic parties.

10   According to the biographer, Ernst Hanisch, Bauer appeared to be an intelligent, exceptionally talented person who possessed rich knowledge in many areas, a loner burying himself in work, almost devoid of any private life, prone to depression, soft and conciliatory, yet violently temperamental. See Hanisch 2011, p. 13 and p. 139.

11   I must abstain from elaborating on the relevant literature due to its scope. The extensive literature on Bauer available contains books, unpublished dissertations, assessments of individual questions and political actions, and contributions of a historical, sociological, or economic character. The 1980–88 works of the following publicists – published primarily in the journals *Die Zukunft, Wiener Tagebuch, Weg und Ziel, Die Neue Gesellschaft,* and *Zeitgeschichte* – deserve to be mentioned: Raimund Löw, Josef Hindel, Ernst Wimmers, Norbert Leser, Ernst Hanisch, Helmut Konrad, and Herbert Steiner. For some of the most important works on Bauer, see (a) books: Hanisch 2011; Leser 1968; Butterwegge 1990; Reimann 1968; Leichter 1970; Braunthal 1961; Steiner 1967; Duczyńska 1975b; Löw 1980; Albers 1983; Böhm 2000; Goller 2008; Leiße 2012; Albers 1985b; Fröschl and Zoitl 1985, and (b) unpublished dissertations: Böhm 1974; Volpi 1977; Kende 1977; and Rudziński's typescript, *Socjalizm integralny.*

ing the democratic system deserve to be remembered. Likewise, the negative experiences of this movement, which resulted from internal contradictions and inconsistencies in Bauer's thought and actions that often led to dangerous political outcomes, might serve as an effective warning today.

The subject of this book is a critical and analytical assessment of Bauer's socio-political thought and the politics of Austrian Social Democracy, which helped shape this thought and which, in turn, was shaped by it. The term 'socio-political thought' has a specific meaning here. Its objective reference points are questions arising in the social and political realms of philosophy. Leaving aside the essential characteristics of this subject area due to their richness and diversity, let us just note that the social-philosophical realm on which we are focusing will give us the opportunity to assess Bauer's reflections upon society, the laws and mechanisms of its development, trends of social change, the driving forces behind historical and social processes, and so on, while the realm of political philosophy will provide us with insights on his political views.

One may sum up the main objectives of this work as follows:

- to define the cognitive and practical value of solutions for socio-political and economic problems of the democratic political order proposed by Bauer and other Austromarxists. The overarching theme that links these proposed solutions within the framework set by Austromarxism is the question of democracy and the values associated with it;
- to highlight the differences between the philosophical, social, and political concepts developed by Bauer and those proposed by the classical Marxists, orthodox Marxists, and particularly Lenin and the practical manifestation of his concepts, Bolshevism;
- to determine the extent to which the defeat suffered by Austrian Social Democracy in 1934 was due to erroneous political decisions, and to what degree it resulted from its uncritical adaptation of Marxist theoretical and philosophical premises that history had already proven wrong.

I will furthermore reconstruct Otto Bauer's theoretical, philosophical, economic, sociological, and socio-political concepts. Despite the multi-layered nature of his writing, these areas of Bauer's work have a relatively autonomous character and do not form a homogeneous system. Particularly the political, but also the economic ideas contained therein are rooted in the contemporary socio-historical situation. I therefore found it appropriate to depict them in light of the political developments in the SDAP, the international workers' movement, and the socio-historical processes in Austria and Europe at the time. However, the scope of available material has placed certain restrictions on me. I will therefore eschew thorough assessments of other exponents of Austromarxism and their views. Similarly, the positions of European Social Democracy's key ideologues will be taken into account only marginally for a number of reasons. First, the similarities and differences between the positions of individual Austromarxists, especially their political outlook, have already been the subject of my work, *Nurt Mediacji* (*The Trend of Mediation*). Second, Bauer's theory and practice was far more influenced by political events in Austria and in Europe than by debates conducted in the international workers' movement. The final reason is practical yet crucial: a detailed comparison of Bauer's solutions with the reflections of Europe's Social-Democratic leaders would exceed the scope of this book and strain the reader's attention.

With the exception of the first chapter, the present work is structured thematically rather than chronologically. It consists of eight chapters.

The first chapter contains a biography of our protagonist and serves as an outline of the history of Austromarxism as a political movement. It gives a summary of Bauer's theoretical journey towards Marxism and his emergent conception of a democratic transformation of the capitalist system as a task for the working class. Special attention will be paid to Bauer's relationship to Austromarxism and his role within that current. I will depict his most important achievements as a writer, as well as the results of his political activity in parliament and the three internationals. I will also attempt to trace how the events of World War I and the dramatic revolutions in Germany, Austria, and Russia turned Bauer into a socialist pragmatic.

From a philosophical point of view, Bauer's interpretation of Marxism, which was embroiled in the contradictions of the positivist and neo-Kantian schools of thought, emerges as the main question. The model of scientific knowledge based on these premises was crucial for Bauer's attitude towards the content of Marx's theory, and the naturalist and scientistic perspective he adopted determined his view of basic historiosophical problems such as determinism and freedom in history, the role of objective and subjective factors in the social process, the status of ethical values, and the interdependence between historical and ethical necessity and between consciousness and the economy. These questions will be addressed in the second chapter.

Bauer's deterministic conception of history, clearly apparent in his historiosophical ideas, also manifested itself in his economic thought. The subject of his reflections were prognoses that emerged in the course of his polemics with Rosa Luxemburg, and were based on Rudolf Hilferding's theory of 'organised capitalism'. It is worth highlighting the nature of Bauer's economic analysis of the structure of capitalism. It served as a justification for the evolutionary theory of history and, in practice, reformist politics. One cannot overestimate its significance for the strategic objective of Austrian Social Democracy in the period before World War I – i.e. to maintain the *status quo* of the monarchy. We will investigate these questions in the third chapter.

The notion of preserving the Austro-Hungarian Empire prevailed in numerous works of Bauer's on the so-called 'national question'. Bauer worked out a cultural theory of the nation that informed his proposals for solving the nationalities question in the multinational Habsburg state. In the period before World War I, he advocated national-cultural autonomy for the Slavic peoples, and towards the end of the war the concept of Austria's *Anschluss* (annexation) to the German Reich. Both solutions, which we will assess in the fourth chapter, testified to the German nationalism prevalent in Austrian Social Democracy.

Regarding subject matter, my work will depict Bauer's political thought within two areas. The first consists of questions linked to the fulfilment of Social Democracy's programmatic goal, that is, the realisation of socialism. The theory of parliamentary-democratic revolution occupied a central place here: it was based on the premise that the legal institutions of the capitalist state, especially parliament, could be utilised for the purposes of the proletarian struggle for socialism. This premise determined Bauer's position on the dictatorship of the proletariat, the workers' and soldiers' councils, and programmatic drafts to win the middle classes for the revolution. In practice, the strategy based on this premise resulted in a politics of defending Austria against socialist revolution and, as a consequence, the strengthening of counter-revolutionary forces. Bauer's attempts to save democracy at a time when the conservative camp was consolidating itself, contained in the Linz programme and his concept of 'integral socialism', were divorced from reality from the outset. I will introduce the problems outlined here in the fifth chapter and elaborate them further in the sixth. In those chapters I will demonstrate to what extent Bauer's absolutising parliamentary democracy as a value determined his evaluation of the bourgeois state and its forms. His vision of democracy also shaped projects to democratise social and political life, defined his attitude to coalition policies, and ultimately determined his model of a socialist order.

The weaknesses inherent in the theory of a 'third way' to socialism and corresponding strategy for the working-class movement became particularly apparent during periods of parliamentary crisis caused by World War I and as the gradual fascisisation of Austria ensued. I will identify them within the second subject area (chapters 7 and 8) when introducing Bauer's views and assessments concerning the causes of World War I and his fear of the outbreak of World War II. The central issue at stake in this part of my work is fascism.

For Austrian Social Democracy, to assess this phenomenon was to create the basic outline for a modification of its strategy and tactics. A recurring theme in Bauer's thinking on the subject is the necessity of co-operation between Social Democrats and Communists for the sake of defending democracy. Bauer and the SDAP leadership were guilty of downplaying the threat of fascism, as their strategy was founded upon a misrecognition of the socio-political situation. The results were that Austromarxism was exposed and compromised as a political theory, accompanied by the defeat of the party, and the demise of democracy in Austria.

The work you are holding in your hands is based on the German edition, but it has been revised and expanded by insights drawn mainly from literature published from 1990–2014. I have rectified inaccuracies and mistakes spotted by reviewers of the German edition. For this, I would like to thank the critical remarks of Dr Uli Schöler, Dr Gerald Mozetič, and Dr Mark E. Blum. The overly arbitrary nature of my opinions and judgements with respect to Bauer, the SDAP leadership, and their political work consequently underwent some moderation, and I have removed some of them. Indeed, I have arrived at the conclusion that it is not the business of an analyst of philosophical, social, and political thought to rather liberally pass political judgement, much less so if they are a foreigner and lack the qualifications of a political scientist. Naturally, this does not mean that the book is entirely free of such opinions. Compared to the original Polish text, the German and English language editions contain shorter passages on such matters that have been competently and thoroughly studied by Austrian and German authors, especially historians, prior to the release of my work. I make use of their insights and refer to them where I do not see the need to rehearse existing accounts of Austria's political history for the sake of studying Bauer's thought.

As the author of the present text, I do not claim the right to pass general judgement over Bauer's work and the politics on which he had a determining influence. I merely offer the reader one of many possible analyses and inter-pretations of the Austrian socialist's key theories and strategical and tactical concepts. I strove to make use of all materials available to me in Austria, Germany and Poland. Primarily, I drew on all of Bauer's works that dealt with the areas under discussion, as well as consulted an extensive collection of publications on the social and political history of the First Republic. No ori-ginal archive materials of Bauer's have been saved, as they were confiscated by Vienna police along with the handwritten manuscript of his unfinished work, *Rationalisierung-Fehlrationalisierung*, during the events of February 1934. His very extensive theoretical, journalistic, and epistolary work, in contrast, has been preserved.

The sources for my book were Bauer's[12] and other Austromarxist writings, a selection of their articles, speeches held in parliament and at party congresses, documents of their work in the three internationals, letters, diaries, and memoirs, SDAP programmes, protocols of SDAP congresses and conventions of the Second International and Labour and Socialist International. Of no lesser importance were the works of the classical Marxists, representatives of different Marxist trends – Kautskyism, revisionism, and Leninism, among others – and those who were opposed to Marxism, e.g. positivism, neo-Kantianism, and normativism. Studies and articles on the history of Austria, Europe, Austrian Social Democracy and the international workers' movement formed a separate group.[13] The biography is complemented by contemporary literature dealing with the respective areas of study. I collected these materials in the Social-Democratic archive of Bonn – Bad Godesberg, and in the following Austrian archives: Adler-Archiv, Allgemeines Verwaltungsarchiv, Archiv der Republik, Haus-, Hof und Staatsarchiv, Arbeiterkammer, Verein für Geschichte der Arbeiterbewegung; and in the libraries of Bonn, Leipzig, Heidelberg, Warsaw, Krakow and Vienna.

Three questions require explanation. When depicting the system of Bauer's social and political thought, I endeavoured to point out how his way of thinking and the resulting inconsistencies in his ideological and political decisions were conditioned. The reason for this was my wish to avoid 'pigeonholing' Bauer by simply falling back on the readily available model of three main currents

12   Bauer's extensive legacy of writing varies in quality. Besides his significant theoretical treatises, there are occasional writings that are primarily of political and propagandistic value. What further complicates his work is the fact that he merged scientific with journalistic language, as well as occasionally, in the heat of the moment, entirely eschewing scientific discourse in favour of revolutionary pathos.

13   Some of the most valuable publications on Austromarxism as a political movement are the works of Austrian and German historians and political scientists. Their analyses of the history of Social Democracy in the First Republic take a broad spectrum of phenomena and social processes of this period into account, placing them within the political context in Austria at the time. Of particular interest are the works of Zöllner, Pollak, and Brügel on the history of Social Democracy against the background of Austrian history; those of Botz, Tallos, Neugebauer, Konrad, Panzenböck, and Hanisch on nationalism, Austrofascism, and the *Anschluss* question; Leser and Glaser on Austria's political and intellectual culture; Konrad and Mommsen on the national question; Mozetič on Austromarxism's social theory; and Fischer, Mattl and März on economic questions and the economic policies of Austromarxism. Note that Austromarxism did not meet with any great interest in Poland. Polish publications on the subjects are: Sobolewski 1956; Rudziński 1956; the chapter on 'The Austromarxists' in Kołakowski 2005; and my aforementioned writings.

within the workers' movement. To understand why one should refrain from classifying him in this manner, one must become aware of the special trait of his political views – that is, their evolution from the left to the right, contrary to their stereotypical categorisation as centrist. The second question pertains to terminology. I have consciously retained terms from the era under discussion – especially those such as class struggle, bourgeoisie and proletariat, which are typical of the period and are generally recognised in relevant literature. I am aware that to counterpose the bourgeoisie to the workers' party is somewhat vague – after all, part of the bourgeoisie belonged to the electorate of the SDAP, and some were members of that party.

The third question is somewhat delicate. A comprehensive monograph on Bauer will inevitably contain paragraphs and even chapters that parallel published work of Austrian and German authors. I have therefore decided upon a rule that is, in my view, fairly clear. Where I refer to already existing insights, I will confine myself either to roughly sketching out the issue at hand, or else – that is, in most cases – analysing it anew by addressing the relevant literature in an affirmative or polemical fashion.

The nature of this book was, to some degree, influenced by the events of the 1980s, including in Poland: the devaluation of Marxism as ideology and social theory, the political defeat of Eurocommunism, and the demise of 'really existing socialism'. Attempts to build bridges between the Eastern and Western blocs based on Bauer's thought have been rendered futile, as these two worlds became politically and economically alike. Likewise, Bauer's proposals to bring two ideologically different parties together have not proved any more useful. This book is therefore intended as a historical work – which does not mean, however, that all questions and problems addressed here have lost their relevance.

Every work to which one has dedicated many years of research – I studied Bauer and Austromarxism mainly from 1978–2003 – contains an element of subjectivity and emotional baggage. I have attempted to keep these to a minimum. To follow the good example set by Ernst Hanisch,[14] I ought to add that I have been, and continue to be, a moderate Social Democrat since my teenage years. My political sympathies are reflected in my studies of Austromarxism and can also be found in this publication.

Ewa Czerwińska-Schupp
Vienna, 2014

---

14   In his Otto Bauer biography, *Der grosse Illusionist*, Hanisch states at the beginning that he has never been a socialist. See Hanisch 2011, p. 14.

Foreword

It is with great satisfaction that I have accepted the honour to write the Foreword to Ewa Czerwińska's work on Otto Bauer. After all, I have supervised the author for over twenty years, for the most part during her scholarship at the Philosophical Institute of Vienna, where I was a Professor of Social Philosophy from 1980 until my retirement in 2001. Ewa Czerwińska devoted herself intensely to a subject I had first addressed in my 1968 monograph, *Der Austromarxismus in Theorie und Praxis (Austromarxism in Theory and Practice)*, and gradually, through many intermediate stages and publications, progressed to this present book. It earned her a postdoctoral qualification and, subsequently, a tenured professorship at the University of Poznan, from which she originated and to which she always remained close. The book thus became the crowning glory of her scientific work. Despite my role as her mentor and protector, she researched her chosen subject independently – and, despite my influence upon her, arrived at her own conclusions that were not always in accordance with mine. Naturally, the fact that she also adopted a generally critical stance towards the object – or rather, subject – of her research, Otto Bauer, is not primarily the result of her close scientific and personal relationship to me. Rather, the subject matter itself quite naturally forced such a stance to the point where certain conclusions became inevitable – anybody devoting him- or herself to the material with the same degree of intensity would have arrived at rather similar judgements.

In any event, the author's present work is the most comprehensive, and probably most in-depth, analysis of Austromarxist theory and practice published since my own 1968 book, *Zwischen Reformismus und Bolschwismus (Between Reformism and Bolshevism)*. Of course, it does not cover the whole scope of its subject matter, Austromarxism, but instead focuses on Otto Bauer's personality and work. However, since it was Otto Bauer (and Otto Bauer *alone*) who was at the centre of Austromarxism between the wars – and to some extent, also prior to World War I – to discuss him is also to discuss the politics he inspired and orchestrated, namely, Austromarxism.

In the first place, the author assesses Bauer as a scientist who penned groundbreaking work in Marxist theory. Aside from the effect they had within the realms of Marxist theory, these contributions are interesting in and of themselves. This is particularly true of Bauer's debut, the 1907 tome, *The Question of Nationalities and Social Democracy*. When he was only in his mid-twenties, the book made him famous virtually overnight, and granted him the status of a leading Social-Democratic thinker, brilliant intellectual and, above all, writer. The definition of the nation presented by Bauer in this masterpiece is, in my opinion, still superior to all other such attempts. When Bauer defined the nation as 'the totality of human beings bound together by a community of fate into a community of character', he coined a formula that had universal value, but applied especially to the Austrian nation formed in the Second Republic – even if Bauer neither realised it nor approved of it, his thinking being steeped in German nationalist categories, and the time being not yet ripe for this notion. This was a sign that a theory, if correct and good in its own right, can subsequently prove itself in light of realities not yet recognised at the time of its inception. Bauer's definition occupies a rational middle ground between romantic concepts of the nation and those based on objective criteria, such as language and territory, as developed by Lenin and Stalin. Suffice it to say, this merit of Bauer's perspective did not mean the nationalities concept that he and Karl Renner had worked out and introduced into the programmes of Austrian Social Democracy was successful in practice. That is to say, it could not stop the decline of the old Austria, the collapse caused by its unresolved national problem. Indeed, to observe the discrepancy between theory and practice in this case is literally to study a classic example of how an intrinsically sensible theory can fail in light of present conditions and obstacles.

Unfortunately, concerning nearly all of Bauer's other theories, not only the inability to put them into practice doomed them to failure. In most cases, the theories were erratic and lacking in and of themselves. As Bauer was not merely a theorist, but *de facto* leader of his party in the interwar period, he was permanently tempted to justify his practice ideologically. More often than not, he succumbed to the temptation. Hence, it is impossible to strictly distinguish between his theories and theorems, which invoked Marxism, and the designated practice they guided – and much less to maintain such a distinction. Just as I experienced before she herself did, Ewa Czerwińska is often under the impression that, for Bauer, the framework of Marxism provided a screen onto which he could project his political practice, as well as a means of rationalising beliefs he held quite independently of it. Bauer conducted his politics under the auspices of this framework, which he did not deduce from factual reality, but which he treated as a self-evident premise to be merged and acquainted with factual reality.

According to a dictum that was passed down but remains unverified, from early on Victor Adler referred to Bauer as the 'talented misfortune of the party', thus painting a picture that would only later prove tragically valid. In this context, I recall the noteworthy remark of a social-democratic Federal Assembly member named Jakob Brandeis, whom I met decades ago in Bad

Hofgastein. When I asked him how he evaluated Otto Bauer in hindsight, he paused to think, smiling mischievously. Finally, he replied, 'there is not one error that he did not commit'.

Indeed, it is not just a case of individual mistakes and errors of judgement in Bauer's life that one cannot ignore with the best will in the world. Even if one approaches the matter the other way round, it is difficult to make out theories that stand the test of experience – the latter, according to Marxist interpretation, being the criterion for the veracity of any theory.

Otto Bauer offered wrong answers to the most obvious questions, as well as to the least obvious ones. In fact, he put his prejudices, which he always dressed up in Marxist fashion, in the way of sober analysis. To begin with the most glaring issue: Bauer developed a completely unrealistic perspective for the location and stage of his activities – Austria – that was rooted in his own wishful thinking. He neither predicted nor advocated Austrian independence, conceiving instead the construct of an 'all-German revolution'. His German nationalism and unswerving faith in the revolution, which he invariably postponed but never dropped from the agenda, prevented him from approving of Austria as an independent state or deeming its restoration desirable. Bauer's supporters, such as the likes of Oscar Pollak and Karl Czernetz, held on to his all-German perspective even in British exile. As an emigrant in Sweden, Bruno Kreisky was the first to envision and advocate Austria's independence and restoration as a positive goal, before it became an objective of the Allied forces as decreed in the Moscow declaration of 1 November 1943.

To move on from the most to the least obvious: Bauer's assessment of the development of Bolshevism and his resulting perspective for democratic socialism were misjudged and illusory. This was especially the case in his work, *Zwischen zwei Weltkriegen?* (*Between Two World Wars?*), in which he developed the notion of 'integral socialism'. History would expose his concept of rapprochement, even reunification, of Social Democracy and Bolshevism as precisely the 'tragic illusion' that the publicist Julius Braunthal, a close associate and comrade of Bauer's, posthumously described it as in his Bauer biography.

These two examples of gross misjudgement with respect to pressing issues justify the question as to whether Otto Bauer also committed grave, perhaps even fatal, errors with respect to the focus of his politics; namely, the domestic politics of interwar Austria, thereby contributing to the demise of democracy in the country. Of course, this negative contribution was neither intentional nor borne out of ill will, as was the case with Social Democracy's bourgeois political enemies, who bear the chief responsibility for the demise of Austrian democracy. Certainly, it is possible to adopt a position on the failure of Social Democracy that the Austromarxist publicist and warhorse, Alfred Magaziner, defended against my critique in a televised debate: he argued that the political situation in the First Republic had been an 'uncontrollable' (and therefore hopeless) state of affairs. Whatever Bauer and other leaders may have done, or refrained from doing, it would not have changed the fatal ending for democracy and for Austria in any way, shape or form. From 1918 to 1927 (at the latest), the situation was so severe that even the best political strategy could not have steered Austria back to any promising course. If we adhered to this interpretation of historical events and their context, it would indeed become superfluous to investigate possible errors and their sources, as avoidable mistakes would only be superseded by unavoidable ones.

This pessimistic and deterministic perspective, however, is itself an after-effect of the optimistic determinism that Bauer maintained for too long. For him, the historical necessity of socialism was certain up until the point when development brushed aside not only socialism, but also democracy itself. To counter the determinist perspective held by Bauer and Magaziner, which merely underwent a transformation from confidence in victory to doom-and-gloom fatalism, one might cite Wilhelm Ellenbogen's statement from his memoir, *Die Katastrophe der österreichischen Sozialdemokratie* (*The Disaster of Austrian Social Democracy*), which I edited: 'Perhaps the party would have not experienced any fundamental break at all had it handled the democracy question correctly'.

What, then, did the wrong approach to democracy, which led to such devastating results, consist of? Put in a concise formula, it is possible to say that under Otto Bauer's towering influence, the Austrian Social Democratic movement remained in opposition for too long, confident in its victory and succumbing to the illusion that its victory in the upcoming elections was secure anyway – and apart from that, capitalism would decay and collapse under its own contradictions. Holding on to this twofold perspective, which would guarantee the victory of the proletariat and its party, the Social Democrats in 1931 and even 1932, closed their minds to any kind of agreement that still might have been able to somehow prevent the demise of democracy and build a united front against National Socialism. By the time Bauer realised that the alternative was no longer 'capitalism or socialism', but 'democracy or fascism', it was too late. At that stage, under the pressure of Mussolini and the Heimwehr, the bourgeois opposing party was no longer interested in a peaceful solution – especially as the Social Democrats acquiesced in Dollfuss's violation of the constitution without a fight, not even attempting to get Dollfuss to concede by means of a general strike or mass demonstration.

In his written defence, *Der Aufstand der österreichischen Arbeiter* (*The Uprising of the Austrian Workers*), Bauer admitted to miscalculations, yet did not deconstruct their base: his historical determinism and corresponding perspective of collapse. He identified the passive acceptance of Dollfuss's constitutional breach as his gravest mistake. And indeed, what good were the superfluous and ambiguous deliberations from the 1926 programme of Linz, formulated with potential bourgeois resistance against majority-backed socialist rule in mind? Clearly, the party was not prepared to make use even of a self-evident and frequently invoked right to self-defence and put its words into practice when facing a much more straightforward case, the violation of common constitutional law. Akin to the German Social Democrats and other democratic forces in Germany, Austrian Social Democracy cannot be spared from the reproach that it passively surrendered the foundations of democracy without even the slightest attempt at resistance.

The failure to act in 1933, however, had a long prehistory. Was the party's paramilitary organisation, the Republikanische Schutzbund, really intended as a combat formation – or was it only a bluff serving to intimidate the opponent and pacify the party's supporters? Because the latter was the case, this mechanism, which had served its purpose up until 1927, lost its effectiveness after the bloody events of 15 July 1927. Even prior to the violence that unfolded during that year, the imperial general Theodor Körner made a remark that would be fully vindicated by future events as he withdrew from the Schutzbund: 'You cannot fight a war with an army of pacifists'. The Social Democrats had the option to disarm one-sidedly – since there was no general political and military disarmament – and morally and politically capitalise on this voluntary sacrifice. Or else, become serious about the fight they had been threatening – at least when there was a need for self-defence, which was plainly the case in 1933. Because the Social-Democratic leadership could not decide one way or the other, the struggle against the bourgeois enemy was already politically lost before the military struggle could begin.

The real fault on the part of the Social-Democratic leadership, and Otto Bauer, was that they persuaded themselves, and the masses who trusted them, that they possessed a concept for struggle and the will to fight. In reality, these two necessary elements for a successful defence were missing, giving lie to the revolutionary pathos that the party continued to extol.

What is more, there is every reason to question Otto Bauer's fundamental understanding of democracy – as opposed to the conception of democracy on which Karl Renner based his tactical and strategic considerations and which remains impressive even to this day. Bauer's, by contrast, hardly possesses qualities that correspond to a contemporary, pluralist definition of democracy.

Thus, Bauer's treatise, 'Die Zukunft der Sozialdemokratie' ('The Future of Social Democracy'), published in the December 1931 edition of *Der Kampf*, boasted a statement that exceeded its original purpose of assessing Social Democracy's possible future development and touched upon the roots of Bauer's conception of democracy:

> We are democrats and socialists. However, we are not petty-bourgeois vulgar democrats, who counterpose democracy to socialism, put democracy over socialism, and are prepared to jeopardise or even surrender all the socialist elements that the revolution has won for the sake of democracy. We are democrats for the sake of socialism.

According to Bauer, democracy is not intrinsically legitimised as majority rule, but is subordinated to and legitimised by socialism. Hence, democracy becomes a means to a predetermined end. However, this also means that the order can be reversed: socialism can be introduced before democracy if the historical circumstances demand it. That is why Bauer could interpret and accept Russian Bolshevism as 'despotic socialism' without great difficulty – in the hope and belief, of course, that the process of democratisation would be developed later on. With respect to this, Karl Kautsky – in whose footsteps Otto Bauer walked until he discovered and began to justify 'despotic socialism' – was a better Marxist and democrat. He did not capitulate to the illusion that a dictatorship with terrorist features would ever turn into a democracy. What is more, he maintained the idea that Bolshevism would collapse, which, for the time being, eclipsed the Marxist perspective of capitalist collapse.

Thus, we can only conditionally consider Bauer a flawless democrat. Not only based on how we perceive democracy today, but even in terms of how his contemporaries, Karl Renner and Hans Kelsen, distinguished it. Rather, we should regard him as a democrat who adhered to democracy primarily or exclusively because, most of the time, it appeared to him as the safest road to socialism. It is no accident that there is not a single paragraph in Bauer's collected works where the author positively refers to the continued existence of a multi-party system in a future socialist society. Bauer did not openly state what he, as a consistent Marxist, was compelled to think: that the basis for the existence of different parties would disappear with the demise of antagonistic classes. To preserve the liberty and creativity of the responsible individual was a different issue for Bauer, who was a humanist and defender of the classical legacy of the Enlightenment. This attachment to individual freedom was precisely what separated him from Bolshevism in spite of all appearances. Suffice it to say, he also hoped that individual freedom, like democracy, would be restored in the Soviet Union.

With respect to the essential questions, Ewa Czerwińska and I agree despite minor differences. In view of the publication of this important text, I naturally took the liberty to further develop and add my own ideas about Otto Bauer and the brand of socialism he inspired. What today separates us all from Otto Bauer's thought, regardless of our various backgrounds, is the way in which he did not claim the historical necessity of socialism as a matter of course, but also the manner in which he employed the term 'socialism' as a complete alternative to the existing bourgeois capitalist society. In his text, *Der Weg zum Sozialismus* (*The Road to Socialism*), which was republished several times, Bauer was only able to outline the socialist society of the future in the most vague terms. Regardless, he still assumed that this society would be not only economically efficient, but also more social than the existing society. Bauer was no advocate of state socialism or mere nationalisations. He even brought himself to make a statement that would be proven right many times in the future: 'Nobody is worse at managing industrial enterprises than the state'. It is also no accident that his framework of dividing company management into representatives of three groups – employees, consumers, and regional authorities – was not adopted anywhere. The Yugoslavian model for which the Yugoslavian chief ideologue, Edvard Kardelj, claimed Marxist authenticity – consisting of a development planning framework plus workers' self-management – was the closest arrangement to that proposed by Austromarxism. However, it was even less efficient than the centrally managed economies of 'really existing socialism'.

The judgements passed by both the author and myself have frequently been reproached for their contradictory line of argument, which one moment criticises from the left, and the next from the right. But is not every critique on a contradictory personality and contradictory politics therefore condemned, in turn, to reflect the contradictory nature of its object – in this case, the historical object of thought and action, Otto Bauer – and culminate in aporia?

This kind of aporia remains in any case, since no-one can tell with certainty whether policies other than those enacted by Otto Bauer and his great foe, Ignaz Seipel, would have led to different, better results. May we, in this and other cases, therefore cease to investigate the sources of such errors on historical positions and actions because we lack definitive certainty of judgement? With this in mind, Ewa Czerwinska's and my own criticisms of Otto Bauer and his theoretical constructs are not a case of knowing it all with the benefit of hindsight. Rather, they form part of a continuation of the immanent critique already conducted by contemporaries such as Karl Renner and Hans Kelsen, which was confirmed by historical experience. Of course, even if he merely proved to be an *ignis fatuus* in the end, Otto Bauer still remains one of the most fascinating phenomena in Austrian history and of international socialism.

Prof. Norbert Leser
Vienna, 2014

Acknowledgements

As the author of this text, I feel obliged to a number of people and institutions to whom I owe immense gratitude. Without your invaluable help, the book and its English edition would not have been possible.

My warmest thanks go especially to my late husband, the Viennese lawyer, Dr Walter Schupp. I am grateful to him not only for his attentive proofing of the German text and his patient listening, but particularly for his insights into the intellectual and political history of Austria and our exchange of ideas. Without his intellectual support, my research over several decades would not have been possible.

I am also grateful to my late academic supervisor Dr Seweryn Dziamski, under whose direction I worked at the Institute of Philosophy in Poznan for many years. I owe a lot to his knowledge, experience, and benevolent criticism, as well as his encouraging words, which were always full of trust in me.

I am particularly grateful to friends who helped to draft the first Polish edition of my book. They were its first, extremely patient readers – Dr Danuta Sobczyńska, Dr Seweryn Dziamski, and Dr Andrzej Papuziński.

I am equally grateful to those who reviewed the book – Dr Leszek Kołakowski, Dr Michał Śliwa, Dr Seweryn Dziamski, Dr Bernard Piotrowski, Dr Klaus Müller, Dr Gerald Mozetič, Dr Mark E. Blum and Dr Uli Schöler. Their perceptive advice helped to prepare the English-language edition of the book, remove inaccuracies, and lend a clearer shape to the text.

During my work on Austromarxism, the chair of philosophy of the social sciences at the University of Vienna, Norbert Leser, has assisted me with advice for 30 years. I thank him kindly for helping me to obtain two state scholarships in his department and inviting me to participate in conferences and seminars that he organised.

The translator of this edition, Maciej Zurowski, deserves his own, special thanks.

I have to thank Sebastian Budgen, editor and head of Brill's *Historical Materialism* series, who initiated and guarded the English-language edition of this book. I would like to express my deep gratitude for our pleasant co-operation.

The institutions that I had the opportunity to work with also greatly contributed to this edition. Immeasurable help was offered by the library of the Archive of Social Democracy in Bonn, the library of the Arbeiterkammer in Vienna, the National Library, and the Institute for the Danube Region and Central Europe in Vienna and its archives, which supported and awarded my research project,

Die verlorene Demokratie. Otto Bauer. Theorie und Praxis in 1997. I would like to express my heartfelt gratitude to the staff at these institutions.

I am equally obliged to the administration of the Friedrich-Ebert-Stiftung in Bonn and the Austrian ministry of science, research, and economics in Vienna for granting me the scientific scholarships that made it possible for me to collect source material and specialised literature.

Last but not least, I am profoundly grateful to the Austrian Science Fund in Vienna (FWF), which contributed financially to the translation and publication of this book. For helping to choose me for the grant and their friendly co-operation, I want to thank Scientific Fund employees in Vienna, Sabine Abdel-Kader and Doris Haslinger, from the bottom of my heart.

Ewa Czerwińska-Schupp

Illustrations

FIGURE 1   *Otto Bauer around 1920*
PHOTOGRAPHER: ALBERT HILSCHER OTTO BAUER. ÖSTERREICHISCHE
NATIONALBIBLIOTHEK, INVENTORY NUMBER: PF 737 E1 OR H 680/1

FIGURE 2   *Otto Bauer*
ÖSTERREICHISCHE NATIONALBIBLIOTHEK, INVENTORY NUMBER:
LW 75202-B.

FIGURE 3   *Mass demonstration in front of Parliament on the occasion of the proclamation of the First Republic of German Austria, 12 November 1918*

FIGURE 4   *State Secretary Otto Bauer along with companions at the Westbahnhof train*
station just before his departure to Weimar, 23 February 1919
PHOTOGRAPHER: RICHARD HAUFFE. ÖSTERREICHISCHE
NATIONALBIBLIOTHEK, INVENTORY NUMBER: 427.103-B.

FIGURE 5   *Austrian Chancellor Karl Renner signs the Treaty of St. Germain at the castle of*
St. Germain in 1919
ÖSTERREICHISCHE NATIONALBIBLIOTHEK, INVENTORY NUMBER:
S 646/69

FIGURE 6   *Karl Renner, First President of the 2nd Republic, around 1949*
ÖSTERREICHISCHE NATIONALBIBLIOTHEK, INVENTORY NUMBER: SIM 21

FIGURE 7   *Otto Bauer (left) with Alexandre Marie Bracke-Desrousseaux during the Social
Democratic Party Congress in Vienna, October 1929*

FIGURE 8   *Otto Bauer in 1931*
PHOTOGRAPHER: ALBERT HILSCHER. ÖSTERREICHISCHE
NATIONALBIBLIOTHEK, INVENTORY NUMBER: H 680/2

FIGURE 9   *Max Adler*
ÖSTERREICHISCHE NATIONALBIBLIOTHEK, INVENTORY NUMBER: 196.809-B.

FIGURE 10 *Ignaz Seipel at his desk*
ÖSTERREICHISCHE NATIONALBIBLIOTHEK, INVENTORY NUMBER: 211240 C.

FIGURE 11   *Otto Bauer in front of Vienna's City Hall around 1930*
ÖSTERREICHISCHE NATIONALBIBLIOTHEK, INVENTORY NUMBER:
NB 535298-B.

FIGURE 12   *SDAP poster for the National Council elections on 9 November 1930 (text: "Not civil war / peace / and / work / vote social democratic")*

ÖSTERREICHISCHE NATIONALBIBLIOTHEK, INVENTORY NUMBER: E10/353

FIGURE 13   *Protection League (Schutzbund) march in Eisenstadt, 1932; Otto Bauer standing
in the middle on the bleachers*
PHOTOGRAPHER: ALBERT HILSCHER. ÖSTERREICHISCHE
NATIONALBIBLIOTHEK, INVENTORY NUMBER: NB H 1308/4

FIGURE 14   *National Socialist rally in front of the Karlskirche in Vienna on 12 November 1932*
PHOTOGRAPHER: LOTHAR RÜBELT. ÖSTERREICHISCHE
NATIONALBIBLIOTHEK, INVENTORY NUMBER: RÜ ZK 182/2

FIGURE 15   *Homeguard (Heimwehr) positioned in front of the Burgtheater, 12 February 1934*
PHOTOGRAPHER: FRANZ BLAHA. ÖSTERREICHISCHE NATIONALBIBLIOTHEK,
INVENTORY NUMBER: E2/6

FIGURE 16   *Marching Home Guard unit. Photographer: Lothar Rübelt.*
ÖSTERREICHISCHE NATIONALBIBLIOTHEK, INVENTORY NUMBER: RÜ Z 1282

FIGURE 17   *Flyer announcing Otto Bauer and Julius Deutsch's escape in 1934. (Text: "Workers!*
The leaders of the Social Democratic Party: Dr. Otto Bauer – Dr. Deutsch – drove your
comrades to the barricades. They let you down and fled by car! While your comrades
put their lives at risk in senseless revolt, the "leaders" were already safe at the other
side of the border.")
ÖSTERREICHISCHE NATIONALBIBLIOTHEK, INVENTORY NUMBER:
PLA16318199

FIGURE 18 *Dollfuss with Gombos and Mussolini, signing the Rome Protocols on 17 March 1934*
ÖSTERREICHISCHE NATIONALBIBLIOTHEK, INVENTORY NUMBER: PF 5465
C(36)

FIGURE 19 *Warm welcome for Hitler in Vienna, 1938*
ÖSTERREICHISCHE NATIONALBIBLIOTHEK, INVENTORY NUMBER: S 60/41

FIGURE 20   *Speech of Kurt von Schuschnigg to the Bundestag, 24 February 1938. Photographer:*
Albert Hilscher.
ÖSTERREICHISCHE NATIONALBIBLIOTHEK, INVENTORY NUMBER: H 4810/1A

FIGURE 21 *Hitler in Vienna, 15 March 1938. Photographer: Albert Hilscher.*
ÖSTERREICHISCHE NATIONALBIBLIOTHEK, INVENTORY NUMBER: H 4827/3

Volk von Österreich!

Zum ersten Male in der Geschichte unseres Vaterlandes verlangt die Führung des Staates ein offenes Bekenntnis zur Heimat.

Sonntag, der 13. März 1938

ist der Tag der Volksbefragung.

Ihr alle, welchem Berufsstand, welcher Volksschichte Ihr angehört, Männer und Frauen im freien Österreich, Ihr seid aufgerufen, Euch vor der ganzen Welt zu bekennen; Ihr sollt sagen, ob Ihr den Weg, den wir gehen, der sich die soziale Eintracht und Gleichberechtigung, die endgültige Überwindung der Parteienzerklüftung, den deutschen Frieden nach innen und außen, die Politik der Arbeit zum Ziele setzt, — ob Ihr diesen Weg mitzugehen gewillt seid!

Die Parole lautet:

„Für ein freies und deutsches, unabhängiges und soziales, für ein christliches und einiges Österreich! Für Friede und Arbeit und die Gleichberechtigung aller, die sich zu Volk und Vaterland bekennen." Das ist das Ziel meiner Politik.

Dieses Ziel zu erreichen, ist die Aufgabe, die uns gestellt ist und das geschichtliche Gebot der Stunde.

Kein Wort der Parole, die Euch als Frage gestellt ist, darf fehlen. Wer sie bejaht, dient dem Interesse aller und vor allem dem Frieden!

Darum, Volksgenossen, zeigt, daß es Euch ernst ist mit dem Willen, eine neue Zeit der Eintracht im Interesse der Heimat zu beginnen; die Welt soll unseren Lebenswillen sehen; darum, Volk von Österreich, stehe auf wie ein Mann und stimme mit

ja!

Front-Heil! Österreich!

Schuschnigg

Verleger: Vaterländische Front (Werbedienst); für den Inhalt verantwortlich: Dr. Fritz Bock; alle Wien I, Am Hof Nr. 4

FIGURE 22 *Call for a referendum by the Fatherland Front, 13 March 1938*
ÖSTERREICHISCHE NATIONALBIBLIOTHEK, INVENTORY NUMBER: S 350/10

FIGURE 23 *Graves of Friedrich Adler, Engelbert Pernerstorfer, Viktor Adler, Karl Seitz and Otto Bauer in the Zentralfriedhof of Vienna*
PHOTOGRAPHER: BRIGITTA ZESSNER-SPITZENBERG. ÖSTERREICHISCHE NATIONALBIBLIOTHEK, INVENTORY NUMBER: 432.520A(B)

Otto Bauer and His Time

During the night between 3 to 4 July 1938, Otto Bauer died in the Rue Turgot in Paris.[1] He was only 57 years old. His close friend and long-time editorial assistant of Vienna's *Arbeiter-Zeitung*, Otto Leichter, who was called to Bauer's deathbed by his wife Helene, wrote: 'There was no doubt to anyone who was able to spend Bauer's last months with him that he died of a broken heart in the truest and saddest sense'.[2] Bauer passed away believing that he was responsible for the defeat of the party and unhappy about his forced emigration and separation from his native country. He was also distressed over the fate of his comrades and the new party, the Revolutionary Socialists of Austria, after Hitler's *Anschluss* (annexation of Austria). His death came during an unfavourable period for the workers' movement: the threat of war was becoming increasingly likely, the masses were disillusioned with bourgeois democracy, the totalitarian system of the USSR had consolidated itself, and divides within

---

1   This chapter was originally written for Polish readers who were scarcely familiar with Otto Bauer and the political background in Austria from 1889–1938. Hence, this English-language edition only contains an abridged version. I believe that it serves as (1) an introduction to further factual analyses, and (2) a summary of the extensive materials about Bauer's works and political activity, as well as the politics of the SDAP, which are scattered across many German-language studies and sources. I based this chapter on biographical and historical sources including: Ackermann 1969; Botz 1978; Bauer 1961; Braunthal and Peiper 1975; Böhm 1974; Kulemann 1979; Leichter 1970; Mozetič 1983 and 1987; Leser 1968; Singer 1979; Reimann 1968; Weinzierl 1984; protocols of the SDAP congresses, conferences of the Labour and Socialist International bureau, Bauer's speeches and letters, and, finally, my earlier works. In preparation for the English-language edition, I was able to include details about Bauer's life and political activity drawing on the outstanding and challenging Otto Bauer biography by Ernst Hanisch, *Der große Illusionist* (*The Great Illusionist*) of 2011. I wholeheartedly recommend this work, which is written in a lively and accessible prose.

2   Leichter 1970, p. 14. Based on the memoirs of Leichter and doctor and writer Richard Berczeller, Hanisch states that Bauer suffered a heart attack in his office on 2 July 1938. He did not want to go to the doctor because, as a notorious chain smoker, he feared that he would be banned from smoking entirely. On 3 July, he began to feel better and had supper with Fritz Adler's family. That night, however, his condition weakened, and he had trouble breathing. His wife Helena called a doctor and their friends Theodora and Lidiê Dan, who sent Bauer to a Russian doctor. When the doctor arrived, he found Bauer dead in his bed. Likewise, Leichter arrived at the hotel after Bauer's death – see Hanisch 2011, pp. 373–4.

the Social-Democratic movement were widening. Moreover, there was a lack
of developed organisational principles and tactics for the workers' struggle
against fascism. Bauer's funeral on 6 July 1938 at the Père Lachaise Cemetery
in Paris, which commenced with a rendition of the Internationale, turned into
a demonstration of workers' solidarity.[3] Many renowned activists of the international labour movement, party comrades, and hundreds of workers were
present. As an homage to Bauer and his legacy, his ashes were placed next to
the urns of the Paris Commune fighters, then wrapped in a red flag, covered in
red flowers, and passed to two young Austrian socialists.[4] Speeches were held
by Léon Blum, who represented the French Socialist Party, Friedrich Adler, a
friend and colleague of Bauer's, Gustav Richter (Joseph Buttinger), the chair
of the Revolutionary Socialists of Austria, and Louis de Brouckère, the chair
of the Labour and Socialist International. Blum's words were a fitting résumé
of the aspirations that had defined the entire life of the departed theorist
and politician: 'Each and every one of us feels that Bauer was cut from the
same cloth as leaders such as Jaure, Guesde, and Vaillant: always illuminating action through theory, always invigorating theory through action'.[5] He did
not merely want to be a socialist in parliament. Rather, he viewed his duties
as issuing the guidelines of historical materialism when investigating socialist
transformation and utilising the results to determine the strategy and tactics
of the workers' party. They served to improve the economic and political situation of the proletariat and allied groups and, ultimately, herald the victory
of socialism. Even the illegal periodical of the Communist Party of Austria,
which was hostile towards Social Democracy, printed a note after the funeral,
attesting to Bauer's undisputed authority as an ideologist and theorist of the
SDAP.[6]

Otto Bauer was born on 5 August 1881 in Vienna. He was the first-born son of a
wealthy textile factory owner and merchant in north Czechia, Philip Bauer, and
his wife Käthe (born Greber). At that time, Otto's family, including his sister
Ida, who was a year younger than him, lived in the Jewish district, Leopold-
stadt, and later changed its residence several times. The roots of his father's

---

3   Weinzierl 1984, p. 11.
4   See 'Zum Tode Otto Bauers', RS Korrespondenz in Diaries and Memoirs.
5   Ackermann 1969, p. 6.
6   'Bauer stamped his personality on an entire period of the Austrian workers' movement ... To
    honour Otto Bauer's work critically, to overcome his errors critically remains a task for us. The
    greatness of this task testifies to the greatness of the man who departed from us'. *Weg und Ziel*
    7, p. 249.

family were based in Czechia, where Bauer's Jewish grandparents originated.[7] According to Braunthal, Otto grew up in an atmosphere that was conducive to his predisposition: free from material worry, pampered by his mother who dedicated her entire time to the family, and his father, who was known for his jovial personality and liberal views.[8] The atmosphere at home was one of ideological tolerance,[9] mainly due to Bauer senior, who was a member of a Masonic lodge.[10] The family read the works of German and French writers and philosophers with pleasure and cultivated an interest in theatre and the arts. His father's illness was the reason as to why Otto frequently changed schools, attending schools in Vienna and Meran. He finished grammar school in Reichenberg. In all schools, he was the best in class.[11] In this period of his life, he had three passions: the study of German culture and history, foreign languages (he had a good command of Latin and Greek, knew Czech from early childhood, spoke French and English fluently, learned Serbo-Croatian for his studies of the history of the Balkans, and later learned Russian in a prisoner-of-war camp), and sports (particularly alpine hiking, which would remain his hobby for the rest of his life).[12] When attending grammar school, he began to take an interest in socialist literature. He wrote a letter to Kautsky on 19 May 1904, and *Anti-Dühring, The Communist Manifesto*, and *Capital* were discussed among his circle of friends.[13]

In accordance with his father's will, which would entrust Otto with the management of the factory, he took up law studies at Vienna University in the winter

---

7   Their three sons quickly assimilated and took up respectable social positions. Ludwig was an acclaimed Viennese lawyer. The inspiration behind Bauer's interest in socialism, Karl, was a well-known merchant. Otto Bauer's father Philip was the owner of a textile factory in Warnsdorf. See Braunthal 1975, p. 3.

8   Ibid.

9   As an adult, Bauer defended the freedom of religion and remained respectful towards it. He did not quit the Jewish religious community of Austria, the Israelitische Kultusgemeinde, out of respect for the religion of his ancestors and his solidarity with Jews. See Hanisch 2011, pp. 50–7.

10   'He belonged to the Friedrich Schiller lodge of Vienna' (our translation). Hanisch 2011, p. 22.

11   As Hanisch writes, 'Bauer was blessed with an outstanding mind – inquisitive, hungry for knowledge, and linguistically gifted' (our translation). Hanisch 2011, p. 29.

12   See Singer 1979, p. 106.

13   The youthful fascination with the classics of Marxism reflected, above all, a moral indictment of capitalist social relations, a loss of faith in the values of bourgeois culture, and an affirmation of the intellectual freedom of the individual as understood by Kant. In reference to Marx's prognoses of social development, Bauer hoped for the victory of socialism based on the realisation of this idea.

semester of 1900–1.[14] At the turn of the century, Vienna was not only a centre of the scientific, cultural, and political life of the Austro-Hungarian monarchy, but also a significant focus of the socialist movement led by Victor Adler since 1889.[15] The policies enacted by Franz Joseph I of Austria and the governments of Eduard Taaffe, Count Kasimir Felix Badeni and Ernst Koerber turned the Habsburg monarchy into a modern capitalist state economically, and a constitutional state in the administrative realm. The convergence of the aims of monarchic state power and the interests of Social Democracy was typical of that state. The former was favourable to political circles that desired stronger links between Austria-Hungary and Germany; in the broadest sense, it was also well disposed towards the advocates of federalism, who aimed to divide the monarchy into multiple federal states. The Social Democrats, meanwhile, aspired to preserve the unity of the multinational state. Each of these parties had different expectations concerning electoral reform. The Emperor hoped to empower the government and empire, while the Social Democrats hoped to strengthen the working class. Yet both found it important to recognise parliament as the platform of political and economic decision-making. It was precisely the SDAP's overestimation of the significance of parliament that later led to its downfall: it misread legal measures as guaranteed victories for the working class. At the turn of the nineteenth and twentieth centuries, however, Victor Adler's tactics corresponded with the consciousness of the proletariat at the time. They involved the unification and reinforcement of the workers' move-

---

14   Bauer's years of study were characterised by his titanic diligence and distinctly ascetic lifestyle, which he would maintain for the rest of his life. He was a rather unsocial, radical teetotaller who seldom forged friendships and kept people at a distance, which many interpreted as conceit. As Hanisch confirms, Bauer enrolled in Roman and German law, history of Austrian law, and philosophy, and additionally, history of economy in the second semester and political economy and general statistics in the third. He had an academic gap year from 1902–3 in order to do his military service. Upon returning to university, he focused his attentions on national economics, political economy, and Austrian commercial law. See Hanisch 2011, pp. 68–9. In later years, Bauer broadened these interests by his own extensive studies, which was reflected in his work.

15   The unification of the workers' movement in Austria took place at the Hainfeld congress from 31 December 1888–1 December 1889, in which delegates from socialist groups of various nationalities participated. In accordance with the programme authored by Victor Adler, acquiring universal suffrage was regarded as the ultimate objective of the class struggle. Accordingly, the question of revolution was postponed indefinitely. Sheer numbers testify to the strength of the labour movement at the time: 150,000 members, 540,000 trade union members, one million votes, eight seats in parliament. See Abendroth 1965, p. 74.

ment, the struggle for political and social reforms within the legal framework of the existing state, and a politics of compromise with the bourgeoisie and aristocracy. Adler's goal was to transform the empire into a democratic multinational state. His means to this end were the struggle for universal suffrage, the consolidation of the party's position by legal means, and, later, winning the majority of seats in parliament. According to the Social Democrats, the prerequisites for the victory of socialism in the distant future were the development of class consciousness and greater historical maturity of the masses, their will to transform the constitutional order, and advanced economic conditions. The party wanted a peaceful revolution that would preserve the democratic and cultural gains of the capitalist state. The political trajectory and interpretation of socialist ideology suggested by Adler at the 1901 congress secured the SDAP support from the working class and the sympathies of the progressive intelligentsia. Its electoral victories garnered the attention of students – in parliament, the SDAP came second to Karl Lueger's Christian Social Party, which represented the bourgeoisie, petty bourgeoisie, and peasantry.

At Vienna University in the early 1890s, the philosopher Max Adler founded the Free Association of Socialist Students and Academics, which counted the future Austromarxists, Karl Renner and Rudolf Hilferding, among its members.[16] In 1894, this group merged with the academic debating society Veritas, in which Adler and Ernest Pernersdorfer were also involved. Under the influence of the Social Democrats, the Free Association became a powerful centre for self-education. In 1894–5, its members began to collaborate with the academic historians Ludo Hartmann and Karl Grünberg, with whom they founded the Sozialwissenschaftlicher Bildungsverein (Social Sciences Education Society). Bauer joined both organisations. He was not only motivated by moral considerations when joining the socialist movement. His study of Marxism, *Capital* in particular, persuaded him that Marx's historical materialism was theoretically correct and illuminated the path for historical and social development.[17] He joined the so-called Bernstein debate and defended Marx's basic premises against the attacks of revisionists. Three legacies inspired his Marxist positions on the socio-economic phenomena of the time: the philosophy of Kant; the methodological premises of positivism and scientism; and the Austrian school of political economy, including the views of Eugen Böhm-Bawerk, whose seminar he participated in.

---

16   Haussmann gives dates with respect to the beginnings of the socialist movement at Vienna University – see Haussmann 1979, pp. 180–2.

17   Compare Mozetič 1987, p. 23.

Bauer's philosophical and social worldview became more sophisticated after he joined the educational society Die Zukunft, the first workers' school of Vienna founded in 1903. Its co-founders Max Adler, Karl Renner and Rudolf Hilferding (who were some 10 years Bauer's senior), and its later members Gustav Eckstein, Friedrich Adler, Wilhelm Ellenbogen, Robert Dannenberg, Anton Hannak and Bauer created the intellectual and ideological tendency that later became known as Austromarxism. Most of them were from bourgeois families, mainly within the Jewish intelligentsia, while Renner and Hannak hailed from peasant backgrounds. Actively participating in workers' school and party organisations, they also intended to overcome the workers' scepticism towards intellectuals in the socialist movement.[18] Their aim was to fuse the original ideas of Marxism with philosophical, sociological, economic and legal theories and political positions which were dominant within bourgeois ideology: positivism, naturalism, social Darwinism, legal normativism, the heritage of the Austrian school of national economics, reformism, and syndicalism. German nationalism played a role in their attempts to merge these concepts to a degree. It was most evident in their reluctance to integrate any scientific and political systems that had originated from outside the remits of German culture. At least, not without first melting them in the polemical fires and then remoulding them to suit German national consciousness. Their standpoint, which became the cornerstone of Social-Democratic political practice, was in fact a collection of theories linked solely through the affirmation of socialism, which was conceived abstractly as a synthesis of general humanist values. The fact that the founders of this school actively participated in the struggles of the workers' movement influenced the theoretical concepts they adhered to. Amongst Austromarxists, there was a certain division of labour, which affected the subject of research. Max Adler focused on philosophical, ideological and ethical matters; Hilferding attended to economic problems; Renner concentrated on law, the state order and sociology; and Bauer dedicated himself to sociological, historical and socio-political aspects, as well as

---

18   They represented the third generation of Marxists, who were immersed in the classics of
      Marxism, as well as the popularising works of Kautsky. It is questionable as to whether
      Kautsky really belonged to the Austromarxist tradition, as Trotsky argued – see Trotsky
      2011, pp. 229–30. Kautsky was a member of the Austrian Social Democrats until he departed for Zurich in 1880, yet he never abandoned his close co-operation with Victor Adler. His
      evaluation of Bolshevism, sympathy for the Mensheviks, and concept of socialist revolution met with the full recognition of the Vienna group, although he had no organisational
      ties to it.

philosophy and economy. After Adler's death in 1918, Bauer determined the ideological and programmatic course of the SDAP.

The influence of contemporary Vienna on their theories cannot be overestimated. The young 'Viennese Marxists', as Karl Vorländer called them later, came of age in an atmosphere of subservience to the house of Habsburg, which was saturated in clericalism, anti-Semitism, and nationalism. In this climate, national tolerance had its limits: the superiority of the German nation had to be unconditionally recognised. All of them were students of liberal-reformist bourgeois teachers.[19] Still, they let themselves be carried away by the new *zeitgeist*, i.e. the unconventional literary currents of the early twentieth century (Hermann Bahr, Hugo von Hofmannstahl, Arthur Schnitzler, Karl Kraus, Robert Musil), music (Anton Bruckner, Gustav Mahler, Arnold Schönberg), architecture (Otto Wagner, Joseph Hoffmann, Adolf Loos) and painting (Gustav Klimt, Joseph Maria Olbrich, Kolo Moser and Egon Schiele among others). This was all an expression of their rebellion against traditional ideas and values.

The beginning of the Viennese socialists' scientific activity was marked by the publication of the first volume of *Marx-Studien* by Max Adler and Rudolf Hilferding, which was dedicated to Victor Adler (the publication of this tome coincided with the end of the Social Democrats' long campaign for universal suffrage, which had persisted from 1889–1907). It contained the group's programmatic manifesto, as well as Max Adler's 'Kausalität und Teleologie im Streite um die Wissenschaft' ('Causality and Teleology in the Struggle for Science'), Renner's 'Die soziale Funktion der Rechtsinstitute, besonders des Eigentums' ('The Social Function of Legal Institutions, Particularly Property'), and Hilferding's 'Böhm-Bawerks Marx Kritik' ('Böhm-Bawerk's Critique of Marx'). The latter posed a challenge to positivism, neo-Kantianism, the psychological school of economics, and especially interpretations of Marxism held in so-called orthodox circles that were indebted to naturalism, scientism and Darwinism. Even if the authors had originally intended their concepts as antidotes to revisionism, they nonetheless testified to the birth of a new theoretical direction within the Second International.

The Austromarxists believed that Marx's development stage of capitalism belonged in the past. Applying methods and analyses derived from historical

---

19   An expert on this period, Norbert Leser, argues: 'Austromarxist cultural and intellectual life was not only characterised and inspired by a revolutionary Marxist and pseudo-religious, messianic element, but also by a classical pathos for education, which drew on the stock of German classicism and romanticism. It is apparent in almost all exponents of Austromarxism' (our translation). Leser 1986, p. 1986.

materialism to the needs of contemporary society, they argued that new theoretical problems had arisen. Their openness to ideas alien to Marxism and their willingness to assimilate them gave their variation of Marxism a more modern appearance than could be said of Kautsky's canonical interpretation. Generally speaking, the philosophical and historiosophical hallmarks of Austromarxism were its sociological-historical conception of social reality, an evolutionary conception of historical progress and its categories, and epistemological, axiological and ideological pluralism. Influenced by positivism, scientism and Kantianism, its adherents viewed Marxism as a sociological and scientific theory that had not yet developed on ontological and ethical levels. Moreover, in spite of Marxism's revolutionary premises, they believed that the subjective factor had no place or justification. Their critique of naturalism stressed the importance of consciousness, ethics and culture in socio-political transformations. While agreeing that the Marxian method of explaining social phenomena and processes was imperative, they established its correctness not on the grounds of dialectics, but rather on Kant's method of transcendental criticism (Max Adler, Bauer) or, alternatively, inductionism (Renner). The Austromarxists' interests centred around the neo-Kantianism of the Baden and Marburg schools, Ernst Mach's empirio-criticism, Sigmund Freud's psychoanalysis, Hans Kelsen's pure theory of law, Böhm-Bawerk's theory of marginal utility, the works of Eduard Bernstein and Vladimir Lenin, the historical works of Karl Lamprecht and Karl Grünberg, and the sociological theories of Ferdinand Tönnies, Georg Simmel and Max Weber. Alfred Pfabigan's harsh criticism that Austromarxism reflected the intellectual poverty of Austrian philosophy at the turn of the nineteenth and twentieth centuries is problematic given its far-reaching influence.[20] The period bore numerous fruits, e.g. the psychoanalytical theories of Sigmund Freud and Alfred Adler, Ludwig Wittgenstein's philosophy of language, the analytical philosophy of the Vienna Circle, and the work of unconventional thinkers such as Otto Weininger and Fritz Mauthner. The Austromarxists also creatively aided the development of the Baden and Marburg schools' neo-Kantian ideas. They crucially contributed to epistemology, the role of ideas and the conscious will in the historical process, the inseparable connection between the historical and ethical necessity in history, and the criterion of separation between natural science and social science (M. Adler, Bauer). Moreover, they re-evaluated Mach's empirio-criticism (F. Adler, Ellenbogen) and criticised vulgar materialism and revisionism.

---

20   See Löw, Mattl and Pfabigan 1986, p. 103.

The socialist movement at the time was characterised by a lack of distinction between its leaders' theoretical and practical commitment. This phenomenon was particularly palpable in Austria. The Austromarxists actively participated in party affairs and organised self-education activities. They were especially close to Victor Adler and his reformist policies. Not for nothing did Yvon Bourdet's characterise Austromarxism as the unity of theory and practice – a feature that Bauer proudly emphasised during the 1927 party congress. As I pointed out in *Nurt mediacji* (*The Current of Mediation*), it was a very specific unity: the theory did not always fully take reality into account, and the practice often resulted in the opposite of what the authors expected. Although Victor Adler was not an advocate of Bernstein, he concurred that it was necessary to eschew the revolutionary road to power and concentrate on strengthening the workers' movement. He adhered to a deterministic view of the social process and believed in the inevitable self-destruction of capitalism, i.e. the advent of socialism by virtue of the 'iron laws of history', which Social Democracy could only accelerate. The material basis for this were social policies raising the living standard of the working class, the Social-Democratic parties' electoral successes, particularly in Germany, and the swelling ranks of parties and trade unions.[21] The Austrian socialists scrutinised the fate and strategies of their German sister party, whose congresses they attended before becoming organisationally and theoretically independent (1869–89). Later, they continued their co-operation, e.g. via the Karl Kautsky edited journal, *Die Neue Zeit*. They also had contacts with socialists in other countries: Antonio Gramsci (Italy), Paul Lafargue, Eduard Vallante, Hubert Lagardelle and Alexandre Bracke (France), Georgi Plekhanov, Pavel Axelrod, Julius Martov, and Theodor Dane (Russia), Emil Vandervelde (Netherlands), Hermann Grenich (Switzerland), the Geneva Socialist Association, the workers' parties of Belgium, Denmark, Poland, Bulgaria, Romania, Australia and the United States.[22]

Before World War I, Austromarxism was chiefly an intellectual and ideological movement. After 1918, it became more clearly political, largely so due to the influence of its real leader, Bauer. His involvement in the communal, cultural and educational policies of the socialist government left a lasting impression on Austria's cultural and political life. Indeed, it gave birth to an entirely new and hitherto unknown spirit in conservative, bourgeois Vienna.

---

21 In the Reichstag elections of 1890, the SPD won 1,427,298 votes (about 20 percent). From 1898–1912 the number of votes doubled, and in 1912 it even went up to 4,250,329 (34.8 percent). The number of trade union members rose from 680,000 in 1900 to 2.6 million in 1912. Compare Waldenberg 1976, p. 26.

22 Compare Seidel 1982, p. 9.

With respect to social policy, the Austromarxists advocated progress in various spheres of the sciences and arts. They fought for social legislation, general access to culture, and the reform of the educational system, including through sports. They succeeded in raising the political consciousness of poor social layers and changed their lifestyles. From the outset, Austromarxism as a political movement polarised opinions, depending on the political faction, different interpretations of Marx's doctrine, and the strategic objectives of the respective parties and social groups.[23] The left of the international workers' movement (Lenin, Trotsky) berated Austromarxism for its right deviationism, pacifism, and politics of compromise towards the bourgeoisie. Conversely, the parties of the right and the Catholic press denounced it as Austro-Bolshevism, Julius Deutsch and Otto Bauer as despots, and Friedrich Adler as a murderer.[24]

As Bauer acknowledged in his memoirs, he spent the best years of his life in the circle, Die Zukunft, where he enjoyed a close friendship with Karl Renner, 11 years his senior. They managed to preserve their friendship despite later quarrels and political slander, including when they parted ways during World War I, as Renner was a strong advocate of war imperialism.[25] Bauer held Max Adler in high esteem. He shared his vision of a new culture and new man, and

---

23   Specialist literature from 1970–2014 contains divergent views on Austromarxism. To list them all would exceed the limits of this work; instead it is practical to cite the main currents only. Up until the collapse of the Eastern bloc, Soviet and East German researchers, as well as the Polish author Marek Sobolewski, referred to Austromarxism as a variant of revisionism, an opportunistic movement that combined radical slogans with the renunciation of any revolutionary perspective. In Western history, two interpretations prevail; the only point they have in common is that they regard Austromarxism as part of the Marxist centre of the Second International. The first interpretation claims a theoretical unity of this intellectual tendency existed between the years 1901–14; the second views the war years as a transitional period between the first (1903–14) and second (1918–39) development stages of Austromarxism, based on its positions on World War I, the October Revolution, and the transitional stages between different political and social formations. My view is doubtlessly a minority position: I deny the ideological and theoretical unity of Austromarxism from its very inception. Austromarxism's attitude to theory and practice is another controversial point – there are three distinct responses to this matter. The first claims unity, the second claims separation, and the third denies that the former proponents of Austromarxism can be considered part of this current after becoming supporters of other political trends.

24   See Lenin 1993, p. 38; Trotsky 2011, pp. 229–30; *Das Neue Reich*, p. 198; Kaff 1931. Böhm comments on this in Böhm 1974, p. 35.

25   In 1930, Bauer published an article dedicated to their friendship in *Der Kampf*. The theoretical and tactical differences between the two friends escaped the attention of their comrades.

endorsed his belief in the historical mission of the proletariat. Nevertheless, he criticised Adler's inclination for Hegelian ways of thinking, his inability to recognise the real balance of class forces, and his abstraction from the politics of the day.[26] Although Adler was, from the very start, more radical than the rest of the group, he exercised friendly restraint when criticising Bauer's personality and activism. Similarly, when Hilferding opposed Bauer's support for Austrian union with Germany after World War I, this did not affect their personal relationship. Political differences, which were already perceptible during the early periods of Austromarxism, intensified during World War I. Max Adler assumed a leftist position, Renner positioned himself on the right, and Bauer oscillated between the two wings depending on political struggles.[27] These divisions did not affect their organisational ties. All Austromarxists supported the idea of party unity that Bauer had inherited from Victor Adler.

The integral component of the preservation of the multinational state, had already become manifest in Bauer's early articles and treatises. As is evident in his letter to Kautsky of June 1904, he dedicated himself to the study of economic history and economic crises, questions on tariff protection, and colonial policy at the age of 23. The results were published in the form of nine texts in *Die Neue Zeit*. His article, 'Marx' Theorien der Wirtschaftskrise' ('Marx's Theories of Economic Crisis'), in which he defended Marx's theory of value against the polemics of the Austrian School of Economics, was strongly approved of by Kautsky. Before the age of 24, Bauer had already earned a reputation as an outstanding speaker and teacher in self-education courses.[28]

In the memoirs of his colleagues, the young Bauer is described as a rationalist who understood reality in theoretical terms, but also as a romantic who was emotionally committed to the economic, social, and intellectual liberation of the proletariat. This conflicting nature would later be reiterated to explain the lifelong contradiction between his thoughts and practice. Even during the early days, Bauer attracted the attention of scientists who had few sympath-

---

26   See Bauer 1961.

27   Trotsky unfairly dismissed Adler's left position as 'literary opposition'. Adler was primarily a man of theory rather than practice. He was one of a few to come out in opposition to revisionism as early as the 1901 party congress in Vienna. He foresaw revisionism's deleterious effects for the workers' movement, such as its 'growing into' the political and legal structures of bourgeois society. Compare Löw, Mattl and Pfabigan 1986, p. 66.

28   He was often referred to as Victor Adler's 'prodigy' and 'great discovery'. 'When I joined the socialist movement in the autumn of 1905', wrote Julius Braunthal, 'Otto Bauer's reputation as its most erudite and sharp thinker was already established. He was 24 years old at the time' (our translation). Braunthal 1964, p. 79.

ies for Social Democracy. Some of them, such as the anti-Marxist Ludwig von Mises, predicted a political future for him.[29] Sigmund Freud, whom Bauer knew personally, did not agree with this flattering prophecy: he viewed him as a scientist and advised him against taking up politics altogether.[30] Yet Bauer did not merely want to be a theorist and analyst. He considered it his duty to transform social reality, not just interpret it. His main reasons for championing socialism were axiological rather than economic or social. For him, socialism embraced the prospect of a moral and intellectual rebirth of individuals and societies. In his first major essays, he remained faithful to this moralistic perspective: In 'Marxismus und Ethik' ('Marxism and Ethics', 1906) and 'Geschichte eines Buches' ('History of a Book', 1907), which contained his commentary on Marx's *Capital*, he defended the evaluative orientation of socialism. For Bauer, socialism was principally an ethical goal, a form of social coexistence that would allow for the full realisation of all major human values. He held on to this until the end of his life, regarding it as his obligation to provide a basis for how this ideal, which he approached from a Kantian perspective, could be integrated into Marx's laws of social development. In the aforementioned works, he attempted to provide a foundation for socialism that was reliant on the premises of Kantian ethics. He overcame his propensity for Kantianism between 1916 and 1920, yet he continued to perceive universal moral rights as the roots of democratic ideals and humanist values. His writing, which he continued even in times of political failure and after his party was defeated, was imbued with social optimism. This was manifest in his unswerving faith in the continuity and linearity of social progress and his belief in the victory of socialism.

Bauer joined the SDAP when he began his studies in the winter semester of 1900–1. At the time, the unresolved nationalities question was the central problem in Austrian Social-Democratic politics. Nationalities conflicts, Czech separatism in particular, led to the intensification of German nationalism, but also restrained economic development within the empire and caused serious disruptions to parliamentary life. Indeed, the Hainfeld programme of 1889 entirely ignored the nationalities question, advocating instead the general principles of internationalism and the abolition of national privileges. Bauer dismissed this as a 'naive cosmopolitanism'.[31] Victor Adler eschewed the national question at party congresses, as he feared a surge in Slavic nationalist sentiments and a

---

29   As to Ludwig von Mises's characterisation of Bauer, compare Mozetič 1987, p. 7.

30   See Singer 1979, p. 106.

31   Bauer 1996, p. 417.

consequent disintegration of the party. His was a far-sighted politics: the federal party structure, enforced in 1897 by strong centres of opposition especially
in Czechia and Poland, weakened the stability of the workers' movement. The
party leadership held the view that the preservation of vast economic territories was in the interest of the proletariat. Hence, leaving aside the class aspect
of the national question, the programme it adopted in Bern in 1899 demanded the transformation of Austria-Hungary into a federal state of autonomous
peoples, defended the inviolability of the borders of the monarchy, and *de
facto* rejected the right of nations to self-determination. This programme soon
found theoretical support in Renner's 1902 concept of exterritorial national-
cultural autonomy.[32] Bauer addressed this concept in several articles in *Der
Kampf* in 1907–8 – 'Die soziale Gliederung der österreichischen Nationen' ('The
Social Structure of the Austrian Nations'), 'Unser Nationalitätenprogramm und
unsere Taktik' ('Our Nationalities Programme and Tactics'), and 'Massenpsyche
und Sprachenrecht' ('Mass Psychology and Linguistic Right') – and in his most
substantial work, *The Question of Nationalities and Social Democracy*, which
Victor Adler had encouraged him to write. When the latter text was first published in 1907 in the second volume of *Marx-Studien*, it earned the 26-year-old
author deserved fame and international recognition.[33] Based on the reception
of Karl Lamprecht's *Die deutsche Geschichte (German History)*,[34] Bauer's text
was a departure from the widespread belief among Social Democrats (such as
Jean Guesde and Rosa Luxemburg) that the national idea was but a bourgeois
prejudice. What is more, it attacked canonical sociological theories by Ferdin-
and Tönnies, Georg Simmel, and Rudolf Stammler, and challenged the Social
Darwinists. One of Bauer's achievements was that he applied Marx's method of
historical and economic analysis – he was unjustly accused of having borrowed
the form of presentation from Marx's *The Eighteenth Brumaire of Louis Napo-*

---

32   See Renner 1902.

33   This work was translated into many languages. Parts of it were published in Polish in 1908,
     enticing great interest from theorists in the Polish Socialist Party (PPS). In the 1920s, the
     programme of national-cultural autonomy inspired Kazimierz Domosławski, Zygmunt
     Dreszer, and Tadeusz Hołówko, while the Austrian idea of federalisation found the support
     of Bolesław Limanowski and Mieczysław Niedziałkowski. Leon Wasilewski maintained
     the idea of national assimilation. Echoes of the cultural interpretation of the nation
     contained in *The Nationalities Question and Social Democracy* can be found in the work
     of Tadeusz Rechlewski, Bronisław Siwik, M. Niedziałkowski and L. Wasilewski. I wrote
     on the differences between Austrian and Polish socialist conceptions in Czerwińska 1991,
     pp. 437–59.

34   Bauer wrote its sections as part of a dissertation in 1905 and added further parts in 1906.

leon – to explain processes of nation forming, the causes of nationalities conflicts, and the important role of national interests in the life of modern societies.

Even though he was overburdened with teaching and publishing work, Bauer finished his studies with outstanding results. In 1906, he received the doctorate in canon from Vienna University.[35] During this period, Bauer met Helena Gumplowicz-Landau at a meeting at the Café Central. She was married to a lawyer, Max Landau, and was 10 years older than Bauer.[36] By that time, she had already authored many treatises in economic sciences and was an influential activist in the Polish Social Democratic Party of Galicia, a territorial organisation of the SDAP. Her open but critical mind and vivid temperament put a spell on Bauer – he married her in 1920.[37] The couple had no children, but their choice turned out to be right for both: in spite of Bauer's affairs, she remained his closest partner in intellectual work and party activism until the end of his life.[38]

In 1907, the government decided on a new electoral procedure, fearing that Austria had the potential to see a revolutionary uprising comparable to the 1905 disturbances in Russia. Following this, the first democratic parliamentary elections were held in May 1907. The result was a significant electoral success for the Social Democrats: their mandates went up from 10 (1901) to 87,

---

35   In the Polish and German editions of this book, I erroneously stated that he graduated 'sub auspiciis Imperatoris' (under the eye of the Emperor of Austria) – the highest possible honour for achievement in Austria at the time. Erich Hanisch corrected this in his Otto Bauer biography, writing that Bauer received the mark 'excellent' in two PhD exams, and 'satisfactory' in a third. In order to graduate 'sub auspiciis Imperatoris', it was necessary to receive 'excellent' marks in all three exams. See Hanisch 2011, p. 72.

36   See Singer 1979, p. 112. Helene came from Krakow, studied economic sciences in Vienna and Zurich, and graduated with a PhD. When she met Bauer, she already had three children.

37   I am taking the opportunity to correct the year of the wedding, which I previously stated as 1914 in the Polish and German editions of this work. My mistake, also made by many others, resulted from a fact explained by Hanisch: they moved in together in an apartment in Kasernengasse 2/3/13 (known as Otto-Bauer-Gasse today), and lived there as an unmarried couple until 1920. Helena was only divorced in 1918. See Hanisch 2011, pp. 35–6.

38   As Hanisch states, the 45-year-old Bauer fell in love with a very attractive Jewish woman named Hilde Marmorek (born Hofmann) in the mid 1920s. She was 11 years younger than he, and he kept the affair secret for a long time. It was revealed when Mr and Ms Marmorek headed to Bern at the same time as him in 1934. After her husband's death in the United States in 1943, Hilde married the well-known Social-Democratic journalist Jacques Hannak in 1945. In 1948, she returned to Vienna by Hannak's side. See Hanisch 2011, pp. 38–9.

meaning that they became the strongest political group in parliament, and they remained so until 1912. The parliamentary group of the Social Democrats consisted of four fractions: German, Czech, Polish and Italian, as well as two Slovenian and Ukrainian representatives. Hence, there was a pressing need for a secretariat to coordinate all the work and ensure that the different national fractions advocated a common standpoint in parliament. In a move designed to demonstrate his recognition of Bauer's contribution to Social-Democratic theory, Victor Adler suggested that the 26-year-old take up the post of secretary of the parliamentary group. He held this function until the outbreak of World War I. As parliamentary group secretary, Bauer was the initiator of the Bodenbach party school founded in 1910. In addition to his work in parliament, he engaged in plenty of party activism. From 1911–33, he attended all party congresses, from 11 November 1911, he was a member of the SDAP leadership, and in 1914 he commenced his activity on the platforms of the Second International. In 1918, he became the parliamentary representative for the Social Democrats. During the second legislative period (1923–5), he was a member of about 30 committees. Among other functions, he was the chair of the constitution committee and foreign policy committee, and a member of the central, finance, legal, trade and military committees. From 1919–33, he held more than 130 speeches in parliament, speaking with a passion that lent his words great suggestive power. In his presentations on 'Lebensmittelteuerung und Wohnungsnot' ('Rising Food Prices and Housing Shortage', 1911) and 'Wirtschaftskrise und Arbeitslosigkeit' ('Economic Crisis and Unemployment', 1913), he decried the deficiencies of a social security system that led to economic stagnation, low efficiency in production, especially in agriculture, a housing shortage, and growing unemployment. It is not difficult to understand why Bauer's appearances provoked indignation and turmoil in the ranks of the parliamentary right, as well as earning him the resentment of representatives of the aristocracy and bourgeois-peasant parties (the Christian Socials and Greater Germans).

Bauer combined his activity in parliament and party duties with his journalistic and publishing work. In 1907, he co-founded the central theoretical organ of the SDAP with Renner and Adolf Braun. The monthly journal, *Der Kampf*, was dedicated to the theory and immediate issues of the Austrian workers' movement.[39] The journal gave him the opportunity to publish 152 theoretical articles under the monikers Karl Mann, Heinrich Weber, as well as his own name. From

---

39   Compare Bauer 1961, p. 14. The first issue of the journal was published in September 1907, after which monthly editions continued until 1934. When the party was banned, Bauer relaunched the journal in Berne. After his emigration to Paris in 1938, the journal continued to be published as *Der sozialistische Kampf* right up until Bauer's death.

1911–34, he was also editor-in-chief for a socialist daily paper, the already established *Arbeiter-Zeitung*, initially just of the trade union section but later also the politics pages.[40] His colleagues fondly remembered the atmosphere of integrity and responsibility that Bauer created. He was wont to appear at the editorial office after midnight to discuss the contents of the upcoming edition with Friedrich Austerlitz. His friendliness towards all colleagues and tireless enthusiasm earned him respect. Upon leaving the editorial office, he normally wrote an article for the next edition at home before going to bed.[41] Each of his texts was a spirited reaction to the matters of the workers' movement or the situation at home and abroad. Bauer commented on the aspirations, tasks, and tactics of the party, social and political events, the economic situation and foreign policy; he polemicised against the opponents of Social Democracy. The *Arbeiter-Zeitung* exerted tremendous influence when it came to forming and raising Austrian working-class consciousness.

In the period leading up the outbreak of World War I, tense relations between Austria and Serbia, as well as the threat posed by Tsarist Russia, became increasingly frequent topics of discussion at leadership conventions. The main questions were: how should the workers' party respond if tensions escalated, and would it be possible to exploit the war situation to commence revolutionary action? Victor Adler, who had always been negatively inclined towards strikes and revolutionary insurrection, admitted that the party had not discerned any programme of war prevention and felt entirely at the mercy of the political goals of world imperialism. The question of armed proletarian struggle to achieve socialism was, as it were, a marginal one. Despite its revolutionary rhetoric, the party leadership felt that Austria-Hungary could be transformed into a bourgeois-democratic, multinational state, and it should not exceed this expectation. Using the national movements to stage an insurrection against the ruling classes was therefore out of the question. The Social Democrats, including Bauer, supported the Austrian-German alliance because they feared an expansion of imperial Russia. They did not foresee the fatal consequences it would have for Austria-Hungary: the power of the state was reinforced, and the Germans insisted on intervening in the Balkans conflict by military means. In contrast to the German Social Democrats, the dissolution of parliament prevented the Austrian Social Democrats from declaring a firm position with respect to the international conflict. However, news articles from this period

---

40   See Singer 1979, p. 113.

41   During this period, Bauer was additionally burdened for family reasons. His mother died
      in 1913, and the health condition of his father, who he was looking after, worsened.

prove that they endorsed the government's military measures.[42] Bauer did not share Victor Adler's attitude to the war, nor did he agree with his pessimistic assessment of the strength of the Austrian workers' movement. He agreed with the German and Austrian Social Democrats, however, that the working class of a beleaguered country had the right of self-defence, even if it countered its class interests.[43] This perspective was dominant among the activists of the Second International – Jean Jaurès, Édouard Vaillant and Georgi Plekhanov all took similar positions. Lenin, Rosa Luxemburg, Karl Liebknecht and other left participants who argued for instrumentalisation of the war to transform the state order were a distinct minority. The conflict in the Balkans plainly demonstrated for Bauer that imperialist aims and conflicting interests of Austria and Russia would lead to a war that would alter the borders of Europe and undermine the foundations of the Austro-Hungarian empire. His letter to Kautsky is evidence that he did not believe the war could be stopped by initiating a revolution.[44]

A few days after the outbreak of war, Bauer was drafted to the Galician front as lieutenant and soon became company commander. He participated in Austria-Hungary's victorious battles of Komarów, Rava-Ruska, and Przemyśl.[45] The letters he sent to his party comrade, Karl Seitz, and his then-partner, Helene, in the period from 27 August–23 September 1914, testify to his courage and fighting spirit. However, they were also an attempt to absolve himself of guilt for participating in the imperialist war that he had earlier described as a threat to the development of the international workers' movement, and initiated by the interests of big capital.[46] Bauer felt justified, as he now thought the war against imperial Russia, the bulwark of reaction in Europe, was in the interest of the entire working class and would accelerate its liberation. During the battle on the fringes of Krakow, where the Austrians had retreated from Russian attacks, Bauer became a Russian prisoner-of-war.[47] He spent almost

---

42 See Austerlitz 1914 and 1914b.

43 Consequently, Hindel's claim that Bauer opposed the party's policy of 'homeland defence' is unjustified. See Hindel 1981, p. 13. During this period, Bauer did not join Friedrich Adler's left wing of the party, which in a letter of 7 August 1914 regarded the defence theory as a war objective of the Social Democrats.

44 Letter from Otto Bauer to Karl Kautsky, 3 January 1913.

45 The exact dates of these battles can be found in Botz 1978, p. 32.

46 See Singer 1979, p. 104.

47 See Bauer 1980v, pp. 1035–6. On 22 November, Bauer received orders to hold the line at all costs. During the Russian attack on the evening of the next day, he remained with only four other soldiers while the rest deserted. His conduct on the front was rewarded with

three years in captivity in the POW camp of Berezovka-Troitskosavsk (renamed Kyakhta after 1935) at the Mongolian border. He found his captivity hard to endure. This much is evident from his letters, which betray his longing for party comrades, feelings of isolation, and desperation for information about current affairs. Bauer dedicated his free time to honing his language skills – he learned Russian, among other languages, but also studied mathematics. As a POW, he wrote his only comprehensive philosophical treatise, *Das Weltbild des Kapitalismus* (*The Worldview of Capitalism*). Taking Kantianism to task, the text explained the historical origins and development of modern philosophical ideas from a Marxist point of view. After the outbreak of the Russian Revolution, Bauer was free to leave the POW camp due to the efforts of Victor Adler and intervention by Hjalmar Branting, chair of the Scandinavian committee of the Socialist International.[48] Instead of returning to Vienna, however, he was resettled to Petrograd, where he spent four weeks.[49] During this time, he drew closer to the Mensheviks, which had an impact on his later analyses and perspectives for the development of Russia, his attitude to the dictatorship of the proletariat, and his concept of the mass party. He also followed the Bolsheviks with great attention and attended the meetings of workers' and soldiers' councils. In his 1917–18 correspondence with Kautsky, his change in perspective on the October Revolution and proletarian dictatorship was noticeable. Highlighting the momentousness of the social and political transformations in Soviet Russia, he distanced himself from Kautsky's charges against the Bolsheviks, later summarised by Kautsky in *Dictatorship of the Proletariat* (1918) and *Marxism and Bolshevism: Democracy and Dictatorship* (1918).[50] For instance, Kautsky criticised the Bolsheviks for building socialism in an economically and culturally backward country while restricting political rights and liberties.[51] How greatly the October Revolution had impressed Bauer was also evident in the

---

the Military Service Cross, Third Class. For more about Bauer's conduct in combat and attitude to war, see Botz 1978, p. 32, compare Hanisch 2011, pp. 80–6.

48 Letter from Victor Adler to Hjalmar Branting, 7 May 1917, quoted after Botz 1978, p. 34, compare Singer 1979, p. 113.

49 According to Löw, Bauer was at all times a prisoner, yet he was granted permission to visit the library and study. He was also allowed to go to town when accompanied by a detective. He moved in with a Polish socialist, Peter Lapiński, who was a follower of Martov. Furthermore, he met Martov himself and visited his family, his sister Lydia, and her husband Bogdan almost every day, looking after their daughter, who was ill with tuberculosis, with great self-sacrifice. See Löw 1980, p. 10; compare Leichter 1970, p. 311.

50 See Bauer 1980l, p. 1040; Bauer 1980m, p. 1044; Bauer 1979l, p. 549.

51 Lydia Dan successfully beseeched the war minister, Boris Savinkov. In September 1917, Bauer was classed as a war cripple and designated for a prisoner exchange – see Löw 1980,

first article he wrote upon his return to Austria on 10 October 1917: 'Die Russische Revolution und das Europäische Proletariat' ('The Russian Revolution and the European Proletariat') reflected on the course and meaning of the revolution.

Upon returning to Vienna, Bauer resumed party activity. His stay in Russia had radicalised his political views. He changed his evaluation of the war and adjusted his perspective on the role of the workers' party in the capitalist state. Concurrently, he mitigated his stance on the dictatorship of the proletariat. It was also at this time that he no longer hoped that the Austro-Hungarian Empire would be salvaged. He now expected its demise, the emergence of new states in Europe, and the potential eruption of a proletarian revolution in Austria. A cycle of articles in *Der Kampf* expressed these sentiments.[52] His positions prompted strong objections from Renner – it was the first time their friendship was in jeopardy. In his wartime works, *Österreichs Erneuerung* (*Austria's Renewal*, 1916) and *Marxismus, Krieg und Internationale* (*Marxism, War and the International*, 1917), Renner sought to prove the necessity in preserving vast economic territories and cast doubt on the possibility of an autonomous existence for the states of Austria-Hungary. He argued that the German-Austrian working class should resist potential Slavic revolutions to defend its own economic and political interests. In 1917, Bauer joined the left wing of the party, which had vigorously reprimanded the pro-war dispositions of the party right. His critique had no influence upon the policies of the SDAP and the government. Later, the so-called 'Declaration of the Left' was drafted under Bauer's authority.[53] A programme that denounced the politics of compromise with bourgeois parties, it urged the party leadership to ardently work to end the war. The introduction of the programme assured its readers that the left did not wish to jeopardise the unity of the party, but hoped to make it more democratic and ideologically tolerant. The programme was more of a wish list than a real proposal for an alternative politics.

Several factors provided a fertile breeding ground for increased anti-war sentiments in Austria-Hungary: the prolonged war, the defeat of the Austro-Hungarian army on the front, news about the outbreak of revolution in Russia passed on by soldiers, and a poor supply of food and medication in the crown lands. This mood was apparent at the Vienna workers' anti-war demonstration

---

p. 11. Victor Adler welcomed him back with great joy. It was at the time he saw Bauer as his successor. See letter from Victor Adler to Karl Kautsky, 14 November 1917.

52   See Bauer 1918.

53   At the time, Friedrich Adler was in prison for his assassination of Prime Minister Karl von Stürgkh.

on 28 November 1916, Friedrich Adler's assassination of Prime Minister Karl Stürgkh on 21 October 1916, and the strike in January 1918. In the crown countries, which had recognised the rule of the Habsburgs at the outbreak of the war, separatist movements, such as the Polish separatist movement and the Czech movement under the leadership of Tomáš Masaryk, rose to the surface. As far as outside political observers were concerned, the days of the dynasty were soon to come to an end. Only two forces did not accept the historical inevitability of the monarchy's demise: the government and the right wing of the Social Democrats, which constituted the majority of the party. Ernest von Koerber's government introduced a programme for the autonomy of Austro-Hungarian countries, and, prior to that, passed an act that allowed Galicia to separate. These solutions were too little, too late. There were no parties left that might have been interested in them. The same fate was bestowed on Charles I of Austria's manifesto of 17 October 1918, by virtue of which all nations of the monarchy were to be granted extensive autonomy. Karl Renner's 'Mitteleuropa' ('central Europe') project, which had been an official objective of Social-Democratic politics since 1916, was based on similar premises. The goal was to build a league of nations from the North Sea to the Aegean Sea. A democratic constitution would guarantee equal economic and cultural development for all member states. Bauer's left minority viewed this project sceptically, introducing in 1917 a programme which guaranteed the right of nations to self-determination. This programme was more concerned with the German minority in Austria than it was with Slavic states. From October to November 1918, independent governments emerged in Czechoslovakia, Poland and Hungary, and with Charles I's resignation on 11 November 1918, the existence of the monarchy was brought to an end. The most obvious reasons for its demise were wartime defeats and national liberation efforts, though there were further contributing factors under the meniscus: the bureaucratised mechanism of power in the constitutional monarchy, which only functioned by virtue of the law of inertia, miscalculations in foreign policy, the military shortcomings of the army, the elderly form of Emperor Franz Joseph I. Furthermore, parliamentarism was still weak in Austria.

As the empire was in its death throes, German-speaking delegates of the strongest political parties – the Christian Social Party, the Greater German People's Party, and the SDAP – convened the Provisional National Assembly and founded the first coalition government, the State Council, on 21 November 1918. This was done in order to curb riots on the part of workers, who demanded the establishment of a democratic state power, an end to the war, and the eradication of restrictions in the factories. However, the individual parties had opposing interests that could not be brought into accord. The liberal politician, Josef Redlich, wrote: 'Adler demands the republic, the Christian Socials demand the monarchy, and the Greater Germans demand annexation to the German Reich' (our translation).[54] During the first cabinet meeting, Victor Adler maintained that the coalition was a historical necessity, and that parliament had to be recognised as an instrument of struggle for power and socialism. Moreover, he voiced anxiety about the fate of the German nation in Austria, claiming that it would face annexation by Germany if it did not found its own state as soon as possible. His fear at the time was unjustified. The German Reich, after all, faced the same fate as the Habsburg Empire, with revolutionary uprisings spreading over Germany. Nonetheless, his fear possibly reflected the vivid aversion of the working class towards Prussian Germany. On 12 November 1918, the Provisional National Assembly decided upon a constitution in which German Austria was declared a constituent part of the German Republic. The purpose of this was to prevent a further escalation of workers' demonstrations.[55] The constitutional decision to grant popular determination of public rights, however, did not settle the question of state order, the extent of mass participation in state power, and the role of the workers', peasants' and soldiers' councils that had existed since 1917. On the day before the proclamation of the republic, Victor Adler died, leaving his legacy to Bauer. From that moment, Bauer was the factual, if not formal, leader of the SDAP. He also assumed the leadership of the parliamentary fraction and took over Adler's role as chair of the foreign ministry. Additionally, he became the chair of the socialisation committee in March 1919.

Bauer became the *de facto* leader of the party at a time when its entire political line to date, as well as the politics of Austromarxism at large, was put to

---

54   'Adler verlangt die Republik, die Christlichsozialen die Monarchie, die Deutsch-Natio-nalen den Anschluss an das Deutsche Reich' – Weinzierl 1982, p. 12. The coalition divided responsibilities among parties according to geographical locations: the Social Democrats maintained their influence in the cities, while the Christian Social Party focused on maintaining theirs in the countryside. One consequence of this division of labour was that circa 500,000 members of the rural proletariat remained out of reach for the SDAP and were not taken into consideration when it came to social legislation. This strengthened the bourgeoisie in the countryside.

55   The Communist Party of Austria (KPÖ) – a party that emerged out of the Left Radicals around Paul and Elfriede Friedländer, Russian prisoners of war, and radical youths – attempted to seize the moment during the proclamation of the republic and win over the protesting workers to the idea of establishing a soviet republic. However, it was too weak organisationally, numerically, and politically. Its long-time party leader, Johann Koplenig, in Koplenig 1963, p. 118, confirms this. The KPÖ was not represented in the National Assembly or in the regional assemblies, the *Landtage*.

the test. In the autumn of 1918, Austria, particularly Vienna, was gripped by a revolutionary wave. The situation was contradictory: radical splinter groups of the working class urged the party leadership to take power and introduce the dictatorship of the proletariat. Meanwhile, the leaders of the SDAP, a party among whose ranks the necessity of revolutionary transformation had been repeatedly evoked since 1889, assumed a critical distance to the events. In fact, they deployed all means at their disposal to prevent a proletarian revolution. While Victor Adler feared revolution despite considering its outbreak inevitable in 1918, Bauer and Friedrich Adler, who had educed the trust of the working class through reformist successes, actively attempted to convince the proletariat that revolution in Austria had no purpose and was doomed to fail. Bauer's standpoint was characterised by a strong pragmatic perspective that outweighed theoretical considerations. The political decision for the reformist path, for parliamentary democracy, and against a dictatorship of the proletariat was based on an actual estimation of the social balance of power.[56] Vienna in particular was revolutionary, yet the rural provinces were under Christian Social influence and were hostile towards revolution, and the Communist Party of Austria and radical left groups were isolated. Unlike the Russian proletariat, who had nothing to lose when faced with an analogous situation, the majority of the Austrian working class did not want to jeopardise the gains of reformist policies. To assume that the Austrian workers would leave the revolutionary ranks when faced with difficult times was therefore justified.

The line of Bauer's foreign policies was wholly dominated by the desire to maintain the national unity of Germans in the face of social revolution (from 21 November 1918 until 26 July 1919, he was foreign secretary). During the peace negotiations of Saint-Germain in May 1919, the Austrian peace delegation led by Chancellor Renner bore witness to a disaster. The victorious powers found Austria-Hungary guilty of initiating the war, and as a result imposed war reparations, and drew new borders meaning the loss of territories in which Germans were the majority, such as Bohemia, Moravia, South Tyrol, and parts of Carinthia and Styria. During this arduous time, Bauer's primary objective was to regain these territories. In the *Arbeiter-Zeitung*, he protested against the decision to blame the new Austrian state for the foreign policies of the monarchy.[57] However, he dedicated most of his attention to the question of an Austrian *Anschluss* to Germany, which had been ignored in the treaty. Bismarck's 'lesser German solution' of 1871, in which Austria had been excluded from

---

56   I will consider this more extensively in point 1.2 of Chapter 5.

57   See Botz 1978, p. 32.

the empire, did not correspond with the preference of the German-speaking parts of Austria's population. The national consciousness of the society was torn. They were Austrians, yet they considered themselves German. This was accompanied by the notion that German culture was superior to other cultures within the empire. While nationalist tendencies and the demand for *Anschluss* were especially pronounced in the Greater German camp, they were far from unknown in the Christian Social Party and the SDAP. Victor Adler was among the advocates of unification, and Bauer continued the legacy in considering *Anschluss* the central question of his foreign policy. He envisioned the creation of a body of German states with centrally administered foreign and financial policies and continued autonomy in domestic questions. Bauer stressed three aspects of the *Anschluss*: national, economic, and political (revolutionary). The working class of Austria, which did not desire close links to Prussian Germany, was largely hostile to this idea. It had strong reservations about the SDAP's efforts for reunification, such as its official recognition of the request for *Anschluss* on 6 June 1917, and repeated appeals for *Anschluss* in the national programme of the left in January 1918. Bauer was fully aware of these sentiments, and he knew that the party leadership had misgivings about the unification question. What is more, he expected that the victorious countries would resist any such attempts. As early as October 1918, an active propaganda campaign in favour of *Anschluss* began. Bauer published a series of articles illustrating its historical necessity in the *Arbeiter-Zeitung*, attempting to seduce the workers as well as the party majority to his positions. As Viktor Reiman ironically commented, 'for the first and last time, his willingness to act was greater than his habit of cautiously evaluating all possibilities'.[58] Yet Bauer's efforts failed. It is true that the 1 November 1918 plenum of the SDAP declared the *Anschluss* demand an official aim of the party, and Bauer's Berlin talks with the German Chancellor, Friedrich Ebert, culminated in a secret arrangement concerning *Anschluss* on 2 February 1919. However, these plans were never put into practice due to the opposition of the Entente powers. Of all countries, France protested most vehemently against the agreement, fearing a surge in German power and a potential reconstruction of the German super-state. Czechoslovakia also opposed the project. Equally remarkable is the fact that the *Anschluss* found no support from the German government, which in its political calculations considered the Austrian question of secondary importance.[59] Consequently, the French Prime Minister, Georges Clémenceau, had no

---

58   Reimann 1968, p. 284.

59   Among those who spoke out against an *Anschluss* was also the Chancellor, Paul Hirsch,

qualms enforcing a ban on *Anschluss* in the Treaty of Saint-Germain and eras-
ing the word 'German' from the state name and constitution. Equally, Bauer's
attempts to reclaim Austria's lost territories failed: South Tyrol;[60] the whole
of the crown land Craniola, a territory disputed by Yugoslavia; and territories
inhabited by 3.5 million Sudeten Germans, which Czechoslovakia incorporated according to the Treaty of Saint-Germain. Austria's economic instability
and political isolation in the early years of the republic, which allowed the victorious powers unlimited room for manoeuvre, validated the failure of Bauer's
foreign policy. Austria suffered great territorial and diplomatic losses during
Bauer's time in office as foreign secretary. Beside South Tyrol and the German-
speaking territories of Czechoslovakia, South Carinthia and South Styria were
also at stake. A plebiscite in Vorarlberg concerning union with Switzerland
resulted in 80 percent of the votes cast against Austria, even if the annexation was not accomplished and the territory remained Austrian. In addition,
relations with Germany and Italy were tense, and the tariffs union with Liecht-
enstein, which had been in place since 1852, was dissolved.[61] Embittered by his
political defeats, Bauer tendered his resignation to the chair of the National
Assembly on 25 July 1919. He explained the motivation behind his decision in
more detail in the pamphlet, *Acht Monate auswärtiger Politik* (*Eight Months of
Foreign Policy*, 1919).[62] The ratification of the contract of Saint-Germain, which
extinguished any hope for unification with Germany, coincided with Bauer's
resignation from government and election as chair of the SDAP parliamentary
club.

On 16 February 1919, the first democratic National Assembly elections took
place. Winning 72 seats, the Social Democrats saw a victory over the Christian
Social Party (69 seats) and Greater German Party (26 seats). In the coalition government formed by the SDAP and the Christian Social Party on 15 March 1919,

---

who acted on behalf of the Prussian government. See letter from Ludo Hartmann to Otto
Bauer, 24 June 1919; compare Reimann 1968, p. 284.

60   On 8 July 1919, Prince Borghese refused to participate in the negotiations on behalf of the
Italian government.

61   When characterising Bauer in his role as state secretary for foreign affairs, Hanisch writes
that Bauer was lacking diplomatic experience, knowledge of conventions, a sense of
situation that characterised the aristocrats holding this office at the time, and, finally, the
kind of presence that is useful in this position. See Hanisch 2011, pp. 149–50.

62   After Bauer's resignation, Karl Renner took over the Ministry of Foreign Affairs as its
Chancellor. On 5 July 1920, he initiated an agreement with the Soviet Union together with
the Christian Social Party in order to secure Austria's neutrality in the East-West conflict.
Compare Haas 1982, p. 5.

the Social Democrats assumed three important areas of responsibility: Karl Renner became Chancellor, Otto Bauer became Foreign Minister, and Julius Deutsch became Defence Minister. In addition, the Social Democrats chaired most offices in Vienna – Karl Seitz, for instance, became mayor. Fearing that the revolutionary fervour might grow and a soviet republic be installed, as had just occurred in neighbouring Hungary and Bavaria in March and April respectively, the Social Democrats and Christian Socials made joint efforts to expand democracy, introduce social security legislation, and improve the living conditions of all working people.[63] On 14 March 1919, the National Assembly formed a socialisation committee chaired by Bauer and the prelate Ignaz Seipel, who would later become one of Bauer's most loathed political opponents. Thereafter, Bauer established a socialisation programme. Its fundamental idea was the gradual socialisation of highly developed production branches, large estates, and forests and pasture land in return for an adequate compensation.[64] The programme was so far from being radical that it even found the support of Seipel and bourgeois circles who hoped it would stifle the revolutionary mood of the working class. The bourgeois camp did not overestimate the implications of Bauer's demand to build industrial councils. It was aware that these would not shake the foundations of the capitalist economic structure. In the spring of 1919, parliament passed a range of socialisation laws, which largely continue to apply in Austria. High taxes imposed upon the wealthy were used for the development of social welfare, cultural and educational institutions, and housing. The socialists' local government policies, which benefited not only the working class, but also officials and parts of the peasantry, gained the workers' support. Given the situation of the working masses in the Hungarian and Bavarian republics, which had been crushed by counter-revolution,

---

63   Hans Hautmann offers useful information on social changes heralded by the bourgeois
      revolution. Among these were the 'dismissal and, finally, expulsion of the last monarch
      from the country, the dismissal of all members of the ruling dynasty by virtue of the
      Habsburg law of 3 April 1919, the abolition of all aristocratic privileges, the removal of the
      military caste and disappearance of the old imperial army, the dissolution of any bodies
      based on political privilege such as the House of Lords, the abolition of class and census
      suffrage in the regions and communes, and the restoration and expansion of civil liberties'
      (our translation). Hautmann 2007, p. 95 and p. 97.

64   In 1919, Bauer popularised this programme in a series of ten articles in the *Arbeiter-Zeitung*.
      They were republished as a collection entitled *Der Weg zum Sozialismus* (*The Road to
      Socialism*) in the same year. The fact that there was great interest in this programme across
      the Second International is evidenced by the fact that 12 editions were published within
      two years. Most of them were translated into different languages.

they were justified in considering Bauer's politics of preventing revolution far-sighted. The author of the socialisation programme himself was more sceptical in evaluating the chances of its fulfilment than the enthusiastic workers, who joined the party *en masse* (it had 500,000 members at the time). Bauer feared the economic weakness of the state and the consolidation of capitalist forces as threats to the endurance of his reforms. His fears would soon be confirmed: the emboldened position of the Christian Social Party in the countryside and the Social Democrats' concessions to capitalist circles meant that the socialisation question waned in practical importance after August 1919. Its political effects, however, met the expectations of the SDAP leadership: not only did it avert the danger of revolution, but it also increased the workers' trust and belief in the effectiveness of SDAP leadership policies. These circumstances affirmed Bauer in his belief that the peaceful, democratic, so-called 'third way' to socialism was an optimal solution under Austrian circumstances.

In fact, the political situation of 1919 revealed that the chosen strategy and tactics were based on a poor assessment of the actual situation. As early as 8 January 1919, the chief of police, Johann Schober, presented a list of key measures for the struggle against Bolshevism at a cabinet meeting. The Social-Democratic politicians were not fully aware that the Christian Social Party's willingness to form a coalition government had sparked the revolutionary insurrection and shaken the socio-political foundations of the postwar period. After the fall of the Bavarian and Hungarian soviet republics on 2 May and 1 July 1919 respectively, the danger of revolution in Austria had already been contained. The bourgeois bloc in parliament gradually began to exclude the Social Democrats from government. The first step in this direction was made when a cabinet based on proportional representation replaced the coalition government. After an interpellation submitted by delegates of the Greater German Party on 10 June 1920, co-operation between the SDAP and the Christian Social Party in this cabinet was relinquished. The second step was made when the constitution drafted by Hans Kelsen was adopted on 1 November 1920.[65] The Social-Democratic leaders, including Bauer, supported this draft because it legitimised the coalition between the SDAP and the Christian Socials. It would serve the Social Democrats as a platform for the co-operation between the working class and peasantry. The SDAP leadership was wrong to expect that the

---

65   Hans Kelsen (1881–1973) was an Austrian state and law theorist, the founder of legal
      normativism and the 'pure theory of law'. He drew on the normative method, a peculiar
      choice with regards to law, and assumed a dualism of being and ought. Consequently, any
      judgement in the realm of legal theory was abandoned, and law was abstracted from socio-
      historical and psychological foundations.

constitution would yield positive results for its strategic goals. The Austrian parliamentary tradition was very weak, and the system of social partnership still immature. In July 1920, Bauer anticipated an outbreak of social conflicts and optimistically hoped for a reinvigorated co-operation between the bourgeois bloc and the Social Democrats. He hoped that this would culminate in new socio-political reforms to the advantage of the industrial working class, which was a crude miscalculation.[66] Because Lower Austria had been constitutionally targeted as an autonomous land, Social-Democratic influence was limited to the capital and Christian Social and Greater German influence was fortified in the provinces. At the July 1920 party congress, Bauer stated that Austria could not be a socialist oasis in capitalist Europe. This was a legitimate argument, yet it also demonstrated the vulnerability of the workers' party under changing socio-political circumstances.

The elections held on 17 October 1920 according to the new constitution, which the Christian Social Party won, validated the SDAP's impotence. No longer looking to compromise with the socialists, its leaders formed a cabinet of officials under the authority of Michael Mayr.[67] In this situation, the Social Democrats had no choice but to join the opposition along with the Greater Germans, whose support the SDAP fought for in vain. The only common ground between these two parties was their agreement on the *Anschluss* question, which was now obsolete. The Greater Germans had a different electoral base – the aristocracy, big capital, and part of the bourgeoisie – and cultivated a monarchist and nationalist orientation. During this period, Bauer did not doubt for a second that the chosen tactic was correct, that power could be recaptured, and that the parliamentary majority could be won. These prognoses were not entirely unsubstantiated: after the 1923 elections, when the Social Democrats increased their number of seats in parliament by six mandates, the party was but 300,000 votes short of exercising power on its own. However, the domestic situation made the realisation of Bauer's goal impossible. It was characterised by growing unemployment, hyperinflation, and increasing political apathy. Furthermore, society was increasingly polarised due to dispossession of parts of the petty bourgeoisie, which tilted the balance in favour of big capital. Conflicts between the paramilitary formations of different parties were not unusual.

---

66   See Bauer 1920.

67   In these elections, the Christian Socials won 79 mandates, the Social Democrats won 62, the Greater Germans 18, the Peasant Party 6, and independents 1 – see Zöllner 1979, p. 502.

After the SDAP had joined the opposition, three problems were decisive for Bauer as the principle architect of the party's theoretical and strategic line: (1) defending the economic and social interests of the working class during the period of crisis and hyperinflation; (2) winning the parliamentary majority by gaining influence in the countryside; and (3) building a platform on which all wings of the socialist movement could communicate. The third question was bound to the necessity of a theoretical perspective justifying the adoption of concepts that were, according to the theoretical tradition of the Second International, contradictory: democracy and dictatorship, peaceful and revolutionary ways to socialism. These were the questions with which Bauer and the SDAP were preoccupied from 1920–6.

The phenomena dissected by Bauer in his 1921 pamphlet, *Volkswirtschaftliche Fragen* (*Questions of Political Economy*) – progressive devalorisation of the crown since 1918, rising food prices (a threefold increase from July to October 1921), and unsuccessful attempts to get international credit – led to riots in Vienna from 1921–2 and witnessed the fall of two cabinets: Michael Mayr's on 21 June 1921 and Johann Schober's on 30 May 1922. The government crisis allowed the most intelligent adversary of Social Democracy, the prelate Ignaz Seipel, to come to power.[68] Seipel was a prime example of the Christian-Social Party's 'Vienna trend'. His anti-democratic and pro-monarchy politics were driven by two interlinked objectives: to overcome the crisis in Austria, and to establish a strong bourgeois state without the parliamentary influence of Social Democracy. On 4 November 1922 in Geneva, Seipel effected a signed agreement between Austria and the governments of France, England, Italy and Czechoslovakia, by virtue of which Austria received 650,000 Krones in credit to save its economy. However, the agreement bore two adverse conditions for Austria. First, Austria would be banned from seeking *Anschluss* for the next 20 years. Second, state finances would be subject to the control of the commissary general of the Entente countries. The ratification of the Geneva protocols in parliament on 27 November 1922 garnered the Social Democrats' passionate resistance. As the conference in Geneva was in progress, Bauer made a presentation about Austria's political and economic situation, 'Der Genfer Knechtungsvertrag und die Sozialdemokratie' ('The Enslaving Contract of Geneva and Social Democracy') at the party congress on 14 October 1922. It contained a draft for a budget overhaul by means of so-called self-help, i.e. the voluntary self-taxation of the working class and bourgeoisie. It is not for nothing that this

---

68   Seipel had already entered the political stage during World War I, when he was a follower of Heinrich Lammasch.

draft was seen as problematic. Bauer was accused of negligence of political conditions. The proletariat would not be able to bear a higher tax burden, and the bourgeoisie would certainly not voluntarily agree to it. At the party congress in June 1923, Bauer acknowledged that Social Democracy had not succeeded in convincing society to share the cost of overcoming the crisis. Nonetheless, the Social Democrats scored a partial victory in the struggle against the 'restructuring programme' of Geneva, whose consequences hit the working class and civil servants first and foremost. The controversial points of the programme were erased, and the positions of the party leadership resulted in an increase in votes by 23 percent in the 1923 elections (the Christian Social Party was one mandate short of absolute majority).[69] As an aside, Seipel's policies, although they did not solve unemployment nor even temporarily benefit the poorer social classes, nevertheless stabilised the currency and spared the country from economic collapse.

The growing support of the electorate in the 1923 elections did not result in the victory of Social Democracy just yet. Only 68 socialists were granted seats in parliament, while the Christian Social Party was awarded 82. The SDAP leadership, proud of maintaining organisational unity and swelling party ranks, was convinced that their strategy would lead to winning the parliamentary majority and peaceful radical change in the forthcoming years. The actual political situation, however, was not that advantageous. Beside a strong bourgeois bloc and a decidedly right-wing government that had abolished all social and political revolutionary successes of the working class, tensions between the city and the countryside and a poor economic situation for workers prevailed. The middle class, which, due to Social-Democratic policies which aimed to benefit the petty bourgeoisie, had previously bolstered the ranks of the SDAP in 1919, changed sides and joined the Christian Social camp in the wake of inflation. The party's strategy was based on a misreading of the political situation. Bauer's stubborn adherence to his political strategy, which he could in no way implement, solidified the character of the SDAP leadership's policies and led to defeat.

Bauer created the main pillars of these politics based on his experiences in Russia and the revolutionary period in Austria. His writings from 1919–24 – such as *Weltrevolution* (*World Revolution*, 1919), *Der Weg zum Sozialismus* (*The Path to Socialism*, 1919), *Bolschewismus oder Sozialdemokratie?* (*Bolshevism or Social*

---

69   Löw has a different view on this, claiming that the Social Democrats relinquished the possibility of winning the middle classes by showing too much tolerance towards suggestions from the bourgeois camp. Compare Löw 1980, p. 32.

Democracy, 1920) – attracted great interest abroad. Elaborating a so-called
'third way' to socialism, all of these works negated the Bolshevik revolutionary model, which Bauer rejected for theoretical, moral and tactical reasons. He
envisioned a parliamentary democratic and social revolution, and hoped that
the objective laws of capitalist development would lead to a transformation
of capitalism into socialism. This would gradually lead to the domination and
intellectual hegemony of the working class within the democratic state. In his
texts, Bauer attached great importance to the qualitative differences between
the conditions of struggle in Western democracies and those in semi-feudal
Russia. In spite of the different positions of the Russian and Austrian peasantry, the experience of the Soviet revolution drew Bauer's attention to the
alliance between workers and peasants. Since its inception, Social Democracy
had attempted to secure the support of the working class in the big industrial and commercial territories, leaving the peasantry to the influence of the
Christian Socials. Consequently, it did not have any agrarian programme, and
policies concerning the confiscation of large estates did not elicit the interest
of Austrian peasants. After all, they were large estate holders by virtue of the
1848 law, and unlike the Russian peasants, they did not yearn for land. Hence,
the Social Democrats had little chance of overcoming the distrust of the clerical
peasantry. For them, the only possibility was to win the agrarian proletariat. In
order to achieve this, the SDAP needed a reform programme that could acquire
tangible economic and social gains. The SDAP's lack of faith in the possibility and endurance of a worker-peasant alliance was a further disadvantage for
Social Democracy. While Bauer was also sceptical about such an alliance, he
recognised the necessity of looking into the agrarian question in view of the
upcoming elections. In 1921, he published 'Leitsätze zur Agrarpolitik' ('Principles of Agrarian Policy') in *Der Kampf*, which contained the foundations for
a discussion in the SDAP. In 1924, he summoned the convention of the agrarian
committee, which was to design a complex agrarian programme (it was only
published in 1926). With reference to collections of legal acts, he prepared a
comprehensive sociological and historical study of the Austrian agrarian structure: *Der Kampf um Wald und Weide* (*The Struggle for Forests and Pastures*,
1925). Aside from comprising a history of the distribution of land, usage rights
of forests and pastures in Austria, and the independence struggle of Austrian
peasants – held in high esteem by experts – it contained the agrarian programme of Social Democracy. The two basic premises of this programme were
thus: stages between different economic formations last a very long time, and
capitalist and socialist elements coexist in agriculture. This was not an attractive programme for people in the countryside: it did not promise anything more
to land-owning peasants than what they had already received in the past, which

was the socialisation of large estates and the right to preserve their exclusive property. Nor did it have anything to offer the rural poor, since it did not provide any social welfare legislation similar to that enjoyed by the working class. It is therefore unsurprising that Bauer's attempt to engage with the peasantry was ultimately unsuccessful.

In the years 1921–6, Bauer enthusiastically joined Friedrich Adler, the delegates of the British Independent Labour Party (ILP) and the Independent Social Democratic Party of Germany (USPD) in their efforts to facilitate a rapprochement of the centrist Social-Democratic parties that had drifted apart after 1918. Together with Friedrich Adler, he attempted to rebuild the International. One expression of this aspiration towards unity was the founding of the International Working Union of Socialist Parties, the so-called Vienna International, at the Vienna convention from 22–7 February 1921. Because its ideological orientation lay somewhere between the Socialist and Communist internationals, the organisation, which united 20 parties from 13 countries, was also known as the 2½ International. Bauer's voice was decisive in determining its programmatic line. The main statements focused on the struggle against imperialism and counter-revolution, the two-stage revolution as outlined by the Austromarxist doctrine (the political revolution first, then gradually the economic and social revolutions), and the establishment of diplomatic and economic ties with Soviet Russia. At the time, Bauer was convinced that the mutually opposing methods of Social Democrats and Communists could somehow be reconciled with the common interest of the international workers' movement. He believed that a common theoretical approach to the class struggle could be drafted. This turned out to be impossible, as the rift within the international workers' movement deepened even further. The lifespan of the Vienna International was a mere two years, its demise coinciding with the dissolution of the USPD and the defeat of the ILP. The relative insignificance of its successes testified to the weakness of centrist and leftist tendencies in Social Democracy. Bauer, still dedicated to the idea of unification, initiated a convention of the executives of all three internationals in Berlin from 2–5 April 1922 – yet the meeting did not result in an agreement. He was an active participant in the founding congress of the Labour and Socialist International (LSI), in Hamburg from 21–25 May 1923, where he gave a programmatic talk – Bauer belonged to the bureau and executive of the LSI. In his presentation, he made it clear that he preferred the free play of forces and parliamentary means of class struggle, pleading for the gradual realisation of socialism under the conditions of a bourgeois-democratic republic.

The real political muscle of the SDAP was systematically weakened when the party joined the opposition upon Bauer's advice in 1920. In turn, the power

structures of the Christian Social and Greater German coalition were consolidated and enlarged. By and by, the coalition abolished democracy and worked
towards the establishment of an autocratic state. Bauer, Braunthal and Seitz
evidently misjudged the direction in which state policies were heading. The
party leadership nursed the illusion that every increase in mandates meant that
the working class would soon inevitably seize power; despite the fact that the
economic and political situation of the proletariat had worsened every year
from 1921–5, while the offensive of the domestic enemies of democracy grew
stronger.[70]

The new economic and social conditions forced the SDAP leadership to
revise its programme, which had been untouched since the Vienna party congress of 1901. Significant changes were undertaken at the party congress in
Linz from 30 October–2 November 1926. The tactical groundwork was laid for
the party to continue operating under conditions of the counter-revolutionary
and fascist advance. This basis was only established through fierce argument,
exposing the brittle tensions of party leaders who had been so carefully maintaining a united front to the working class. As it now emerged, party unity had
been but a myth – a myth that Bauer himself firmly believed in at the time.
The cause for the argument between the party right, left, and centre was a
divergence of opinion as to whether Marx's theses and prognoses still applied
in changed economic and political circumstances. To be precise, the question
was how much of his revolutionary doctrine could be preserved in view of the
reformist practice. Bauer's position at the party congress in Linz was a difficult one. He wanted to prevent a split in the party at all costs. Hence, when
the right wing around Renner wanted to erase the demand for a dictatorship of
the proletariat from the programme, while the left around Max Adler wished to
preserve it, Bauer suggested a compromise. It received the majority of votes at
the congress. The motion contained the concept of 'defensive violence', which
permitted the working class to use force only if the bourgeois parties strayed
from the democratic path.[71] Ignoring the creeping decline of democracy in Austria, which had been an ongoing process since the early 1920s, the draft declared
it the vital condition for social upheaval. Certainly, this decision came a few
years too late and could not achieve a serious change of SDAP policies. Even
if the party leadership was not fully aware of it, this was mainly because the
integration of reformism into the organs of the state had progressed to such a

---

70   During these years, the unemployment rate rose fivefold. Meanwhile, real income de-
      creased by 25 percent, and social welfare for workers was reduced.
71   See Berchtold 1967, p. 253.

degree that the Social Democrats were unable to tackle even obvious symptoms of democracy's degeneration. One such problem was the armed paramilitary units deployed by the bourgeois parties, especially the wave of terror unleashed by the Heimwehr (Home Guard) after 1923, which grew more severe after 1925. The head of government, Ignaz Seipel, deemed the debate of Linz to be another political manoeuvre rather than a genuine threat. Nonetheless, Bauer had more in mind than mere tactics when establishing the 'theory of defensive violence' – he intended to bridge the gap between reformism and revolutionary socialism. While he already entertained the idea at that time, he would go on to elaborate it theoretically in his last book, *Zwischen zwei Weltkriegen* (*Between Two World Wars*), thus establishing integral socialism, a theory now associated with his name.

In light of the enthusiasm and faith expressed in Linz, the Austrian working class once again provided its trust, despite suffering from mass unemployment (in 1927, the unemployment rate in Vienna was 33 percent higher than in 1923 and 116 percent higher outside of Vienna), a lack of compliance with social legislation in the factories, and power abuses on the part of officials and police.[72] Its faith was beneficial for the SDAP, which won its all-time largest share of the vote at 42 percent in the 24 April 1927 elections. This was also due to the party's electoral agitation, which focused on the protection of rent controls. Although the elections meant three additional seats for the Social Democrats (71 mandates in total) and a bitter defeat for the Christian Social Party (which lost nine mandates), this did not change the dynamics in parliament.[73] The lone Social Democrats faced the united opposition of conservative forces: the Christian Socials, the Greater Germans, the Rural Federation supported by the army under the leadership of Carl Vaugoin, and loose paramilitary organisations such as the Heimwehr and the Frontkämpfervereinigung (Front Fighters' Union). The Social Democrats were only able to counter the military organisations of the bourgeois bloc with the poorly armed Republikanischer Schutzbund (Republican Protection League), which was established in 1923 to defend the constitution of the republic. As Friedrich Adler pointed out, this organisation was only meant to be a defensive measure from its inception, preserving the progress of the revolutionary period before the bourgeois counterrevolution.[74]

---

72   Compare Leichter 1964, p. 28.

73   Compare Zöllner 1979, p. 509.

74   See Adler 1923, *Rede auf der Sitzung der Roten Garde*, in the archival sources in the references section.

In a sense, this adverse balance of forces, which neither the leadership nor the rank-and-file membership of the party were ever fully aware of, had already dictated the defeat of Social Democracy from the beginning. However, it was a great surprise for party leaders in 1927. While it had been an electorally successful year, it nonetheless saw the defeat of the party's strategic line and a crisis for democracy. The beginning of the crisis was marked by a skirmish between the Republican Protection League and the Front Fighters' Union on 23 January 1927, where the eight-year-old Josef Grössing and the disabled war veteran Matthias Csmarits were killed. In response to the acquittal of the perpetrators on 14 July 1927, the workers of Vienna staged a demonstration the following day, and there was a case of arson at the Palace of Justice. This fierce epidemic of workers' protest can be attributed to the following: the SDAP's defensive attitude regarding the acquittal of the killers; poverty and unemployment in the ranks of the proletariat in spite of the economic upturn; lenient court sentences in murder cases where the victims were left-wingers; and the SDAP's inability to take advantage of its electoral successes. In the course of fighting between the protesters and police under the command of Johann Schober, 89 people lost their lives – among them, five members of the SDAP executive and four police officers. 491 were injured.[75] The day became a milestone on the path towards the authoritarian state order as desired by Chancellor Seipel, who, according to Renner, counted on 'the idea of murdering citizens as political principle'.[76] The freedom to protest had been infringed, and the time had truly arrived for the ideas of Linz to be put into practice. Yet the SDAP leadership with Bauer at its helm limited itself to a one-day general strike and a statement proposing that the Social Democrats participate in the government coalition, which was not a timely suggestion in consideration of the political situation. The SDAP also refused to arm protesters.[77] 15 July exposed the flaws of the party leadership, its lack of will and decisiveness to make use of the spontaneity of the working masses. Adding insult to injury, the protestors were reprimanded for breaking party discipline at the October 1927 party congress.[78] Furthermore, the party's poor engagement with the masses

---

75   At the time, Bauer, Karl Seitz and Julius Deutsch engaged in talks with the chief of police, Johann Schober. See Leichter 1964, p. 53.

76   Our translation, cited after Braunthal 1976, p. 21.

77   In 1927, the party had 600,000 members and 1.5 million voters. Because of the prevailing belief in its own strength, it thought itself safe and did not expect that the government would use force.

78   See *Protokoll des sozialdemokratischen Parteitages von 1927* under 'Documents, programmes, protocols' in the references section.

and insufficient response to the popular mood became apparent. However, the defeat of the workers' movement did not shatter Bauer's faith that the party's strategy was correct.[79] During Bauer's indictments against the government in parliament and at the October congress, he did, however, admit to two mistakes with a deep sense of guilt: he regretted abandoning the mobilisation and neglecting to mobilise the Schutzbund in order to protect the demonstrations. However, he was not fully convinced that the constitution had been broken. In his public speeches, his fear of provoking a civil war prevailed.[80] At the time, he petitioned against driving a harder political line, arguing at odds with historical realities. He claimed that the strength of the workers' party had grown in opposition, and that fascism did not constitute a threat. In his political naiveté, he even went so far as to call for the disarmament of political parties, which proved he underestimated the power of the police and military of the bourgeois state. It is difficult to say with certainty whether Bauer was aware of the contradictions between his way of thinking and his political practice, and to what extent. Faced with an urgent possibility of further bloodshed, the intellect triumphed over the will, which proved the SDAP's loyalty to state institutions. In practice, it also meant victory for Seipel and a reinforced Heimwehr. As Renner observed, Bauer's decisions were coloured by his 'strength of character, his earnest, unbending adherence to his convictions'.[81]

In late 1927, a wave of repression against the working class, which had been protesting against the restriction of civil liberties and social legislation, heightened further. After the events of 15 July, the public expected that para-military organisations would be disarmed, yet the opposite took place. With increasing frequency, squads were involved in skirmishes that jeopardised the normal functioning of the state. In their trust in the power of the mass party, the SDAP leaders failed to recognise the growing counter-offensive of bourgeois forces and restricted themselves to criticising government policies in parlia-ment. They rejected the February 1927 proposal of the KPÖ, which offered to support the SDAP in the forthcoming elections considering the growing fas-cisisation of the country. The SDAP did not want to endanger party unity by associating with a party that was irrelevant in Austria.[82] The sole issue that the leaders of the respective party wings – Renner, Bauer and Max Adler –

---

79   At the conference of the metal industry federation, Bauer explained that the position of
      the party was determined by its recognition of the balance of forces in Europe – i.e. the
      lack of revolution.

80   See e.g. Bauer 1976k, pp. 698–729.

81   Our translation, quoted from Braunthal 1976, p. 23.

82   1927, the KPÖ had 3,000 members – see Burian 1974, p. 21.

agreed on was their negative assessment of fascism as a counter-revolutionary and anti-democratic movement. However, their views on potential anti-fascist strategies were wildly divergent. Renner merely considered a coalition with the Christian Socials, underestimating both the power of the organisation and the intrinsically different interests it represented. Bauer solicited for a 'wait and see' policy, while Max Adler argued for violent measures, a mobilisation of the revolutionary forces of the proletariat and co-operation with the Communists. However paradoxical this may sound, groups on the centre and left of the Christian Social Party had a more realistic view of the danger posed by Austria's fascisisation than did the SDAP.

The danger of a fascist victory in Austria was made more acute by the economic and political consequences of the world crisis from 1929–31. It hit Austria particularly hard: industrial production fell by 39 percent compared to the previous year (and by 47 percent by 1934), while foreign trade decreased by 47 percent. The debt of domestic industries rose due to government investment in international bank credit in the Balkans, which only exacerbated the economic crisis. The critical situation of the banks reached its peak with the bankruptcy of Austria's largest bank, the Creditanstalt, on 16 June 1931. The working class was hit the hardest by the fall of real income by 30 percent and rise of unemployment by 25 percent (44.5 percent among industrial workers) compared to the years 1924–8.[83] Young people were pushed into a particularly desperate situation.[84] From 1929–36, Bauer was the only Social-Democratic politician to investigate the economic crisis. He made an effort to explain the causes of crisis and analyse its consequences for different economic groups. Based on his studies of the development of capitalism after the war, Bauer authored two works, *Kapitalismus und Sozialismus nach dem Weltkrieg. Bd. 1 Rationalisierung – Fehlrationalisierung* (*Capitalism and Socialism after the World War, Vol. 1: Rationalisation – Mistaken Rationalisation*, 1931) and *Zwischen zwei Weltkriegen* (*Between Two World Wars*, 1936), the latter of which was published during his emigration to Bratislava. In these two studies, Bauer illustrated the impact of the development of productive forces and relations of production on the process of capital and concentration of agriculture. He recognised the aftereffects of these changes, i.e. the social dynamics within organised capitalism.

---

83   Compare Maderthaner 2004, p. 61.

84   In 1918 after the fall of the monarchy, German-speaking public servants and teachers who returned to Austria filled the ranks of the unemployed, as the situation of the middle classes grew worse. The First Republic saw a consistent rise of the unemployment rate: 160,000 in 1923; 276,000 in 1927; 500,000 in 1930–1; 770,000 in 1934. See Löw, Mattl and Pfabigan 1986, p. 32.

The crisis exaggerated anti-democratic sentiments among the representatives of big capital, aristocratic landowners, petty bourgeoisie and peasantry. Carl Vaugoin, head of government since April 1931, inflamed the anti-democratic political direction. The Catholic Church, too, advocated a ban on Social Democracy from the political stage – it believed a Christian corporate state without Social Democracy or civil war were the only two alternatives.[85] In the face of a real threat of fascisisation in 1931, which neither Bauer nor Renner fully acknowledged, Seipel offered the SDAP the chance to form a coalition government on 19 June 1931. He suggested Bauer for the post of vice chancellor despite not holding him in great esteem as a politician. The leading politicians of the SDAP – Bauer, Renner, Seitz and Robert Dannenberg – rejected this offer for ideological reasons, thus squandering the last opportunity to change Austria's domestic and foreign policies and preserve the social gains of the revolutionary period. With full confidence in working-class resistance, they merely convened the fourth congress of the Labour and Socialist International (LSI) in Vienna from 25 July–1 August 1931. Bauer drafted the resolution adopted by congress. It announced the necessity for the working class of Western European countries, mainly Germany and Austria, to take revolutionary measures in order to avert the danger of fascism. When designing this resolution, Bauer began from a false premise. Because he believed that the German proletariat would not allow for the fascisisation of its country, he envisaged the working class as leading the struggle against National Socialism. Furthermore, he hoped that the German workers would co-operate with the government and thus prevent Adolf Hitler from taking power.[86]

In view of the marginal practical significance of the resolution passed at the fourth LSI congress, the SDAP leadership announced in 1932 that it was prepared to form a coalition government with the bourgeois parties. Although with 72 of 165 seats the Social Democrats were still the most substantial force in parliament, basic premises for a coalition government were non-existent: right-wing groups were in control of the bourgeois parties, and on 6 May 1932 Karl Buresch's powerless government resigned. Engelbert Dollfuss, who represented the right wing of the Christian Social Party, was entrusted with forming a new government. On 25 May 1932, a government consisting of the Christian Socials, the Landbund and the Heimatblock, which was backed by the Heimwehr, was formed.[87] The support of the Heimwehr, whose leader Emil Fey became

85   See Schöpfer 1929.
86   See Bauer 1976o, p. 164.
87   The Landbund (countryside alliance) emerged out of the German-Austrian Peasant Party

vice chancellor, was imperative for Dollfuss because the new government was
formed with a majority of only one vote. Dollfuss had remained faithful to his
promise to the Heimwehr and the forces of big capital that he would transform
Austria into an authoritarian state.[88] In the new corporate state, ideologically
based on the papal encyclical, *Quadragesimo anno*, bourgeois democracy was
completely annihilated. A number of repressive measures led up to the fall
of democracy: a ban on regional elections; restrictions on the freedom of the
press and independence of the judiciary on 7 March 1933; the dissolution of
parliament effected by Dollfuss and the police on 15 March 1933; a ban on the
operations of the Schutzbund on 30 March 1933; the arrest of KPÖ leaders and
the liquidation of their party on 26 May 1933, the ban of the NSDAP in June 1933;
the weakening of the position of the SDAP in the self-governing social security
bodies from February 1933 onward; and the abolition of industrial councils

---

formed in 1920. Its base was the protestant peasantry. The Landbund stood out among
national parties because it was ideologically homogenous and put forward its own slate.
It also took up coalition work with parties that wished to preserve parliamentary democracy – in the First Republic, this meant co-operation with the SDAP, as well as the Christian Socials and Greater Germans. The Landbund was hostile to the Heimwehr and NSDAP.
It quickly identified its participation in the Dollfuss government, which pursued an openly
anti-democratic politics, as a mistake. Consequently, it left the political stage in 1933.

88   Ulrich Kluge identified five development stages of the First Republic:

1918–29:   consolidation of the bourgeois parties at home after a transitional revolu-
           tionary period;
1929–33:   the state-presidential stage;
1933–4:   the stage of constitutional and social corporate order;
1934–6:   an autocratic state based on the corporate constitution coupled with the
           Heimwehr's immanent extremism;
1936–8:   an autocratic state sketchily based on the corporate constitution in coalition
           with Austrian National Socialism.

Compare Kluge 1984. According to Gerhard Botz, an expert on Austria's period of fascisisation, one can distinguish four phases of the Austrian *Ständestaat* (corporate state):

I.   Phase of the late parliamentary government (May 1932–March 1933);
II.   Phase of the authoritarian semi-dictatorship and increasing fascisisation (until
       January 1934);
III.   Phase of the developed semi-fascist authoritarian dictatorship (until October 1935
       or mid 1936);
IV.   End phase of partial de-fascisisation and bureaucratically ossified corporatism.
       Compare Botz 1984, p. 320.

in state enterprises on 23 November 1933 and the Arbeiterkammer (workers' chamber) in December 1933, followed by the dissolution of the latter on 27 June 1938.

The solutions offered by Bauer and his comrades during this year, which was so decisive for the Austrian workers' movement, did not meet the expectations of party members and sympathisers. While the working class staged spontaneous demonstrations to protest against the dissolution of parliament, the party leadership could not agree on proclaiming a general strike. At that time, the SDAP was bigger than the Social Democratic Party of Germany, had greater social weight, had preserved its unity, and did not have to consider the influence of the KPÖ. The only objective justification for the political passivity of its leadership was the fact that the SDAP's electoral support base was concentrated in Vienna, Lower Austria and Styria since industrial areas, unlike in Germany, were dispersed across the entire country. Provinces averse, even actively hostile, to the socialists surrounded these territories. Even so, the working class was more internally consolidated and better armed in March 1933 than would be the case a year later, as Bauer confirmed in *Der Aufstand der österreichischen Arbeiter* (*The Uprising of the Workers of Austria*, 1934). Indeed, 1934 saw workers build barricades in an act of desperation to save the remains of a dying democracy. The fall of democracy was largely due to political rather than economic factors. Among them were a weak parliamentary practice, the ossification and bureaucratisation of political parties, offers of co-operation being rejected, the personal charisma of politicians of an authoritarian proclivity, the SDAP leadership's erratic assessment of possibilities to evoke support from the middle classes, the political ambitions of the church, and, not least, the Social Democrats' excessive willingness to compromise, a tendency which dominated in Bauer's positions. In 1933, he fought for a coalition government, and in order to achieve such co-operation, he even amended his official, if not actual, position concerning *Anschluss*. Bauer's suggestion to the Christian Social Party to wage a common struggle against fascism in March 1933 led to discord within the SDAP.[89] Dollfuss rejected the offer, yet this did not stop Bauer from believing in the potential of an understanding until January 1934 and attempting to convince the chancellor of co-operation – he was prepared

---

89   As Butterwegge states, the autumn of 1933 saw the formation of a partyist left for the first time since the end of the war. Under the leadership of Ernst Fischer and Ludwig Wagner, it criticised what it regarded as 'Austromarxist fatalism', defensive methods of struggle, fear of foreign intervention and compromise with the government. At the SDAP congress in 1933, the left was a minority. It dropped its resolution, which called for active struggle, not least in order to preserve party unity. See Butterwegge 1990, pp. 463–5.

to pay the price of concessions and endure the corporate state.[90] In March 1933, Dollfuss took up negotiations with Hitler. Bauer feared an alliance of Christian Socials, the Heimwehr and the NSDAP against Social Democracy, as well as civil war, and urged to resolve the conflict peacefully. Like many fellow Austrian politicians, he was taken by surprise: after failed negotiations with Hitler, the Dollfuss government's foreign policies took a sharp turn when it sought Benito Mussolini's support in April 1933. As a condition, the Italian Duce demanded that Dollfuss establish a fascist dictatorship and end the Marxist peril. Swiftly reacting to this request, the Heimwehr, which had strong bases in Upper Austria, Tyrol, Styria, Vorarlberg and Burgenland, increased search operations for weapons, which led to the destruction of printing presses and demolition of Social-Democratic party offices. The party's emergency congress, which convened in October 1933, proved politically irrelevant due to the divisions within the party. The right wing with Renner as its principle spokesman regarded the struggle against the Heimwehr and NSDAP as political suicide. The left, while sharply criticising the compromising stance in Bauer's address to congress, did not display much fighting spirit either. It justified its concessions and willingness to settle the conflict constitutionally by insisting on the need to preserve party unity.[91] A psychologically vital factor was the fact that the party considered the Dollfuss government to be a 'lesser evil' in comparison to Hitler's assumption of power in Germany, while the Communists thought of both dictatorships as equally destructive. The goals that the party set itself at the emergency congress were unrealistic. Faced with the fascisisation of the country and a moribund democratic life, it demanded that popular representation be reconvened, jobs created for 200,000 unemployed, freedom of assembly, coalition, and the press reintroduced, and fascist hit squads disarmed.[92] An important novelty: all delegates pleaded for an autarkic, neutral Austria and wished to remove the demand for *Anschluss* from the party programme. The latter was merely of propagandistic and moral importance given the balance of forces in Europe. For the case that the government adopted a fascist constitution, banned the activities of the SDAP and trade unions, and established a 'provisional administration' in Vienna, the congress resolved to proclaim a general strike. Bauer distanced himself from the resolution in his speech. Given the economic and political crisis, he did not think that a strike would have any chance of success. He blamed the defeat of the workers' movement in Austria

---

90   Contrary to the interests of the working class, Bauer endorsed Dollfuss's ambitions in a series of 1933 articles in the *Arbeiter-Zeitung*.

91   Jedlicka and Neck 1975, pp. 365–8.

92   See Bauer 1978c, p. 695.

on the German workers' movement, and still did not believe that the government would outlaw the Social-Democratic party.

In January 1934, Fey announced a ban on the SDAP.[93] Mussolini sent an emissary to Austria to convince the Dollfuss government of the need for a final confrontation with the Social Democrats.[94] On 10 February 1934, the illegal KPÖ issued a leaflet calling for a general strike and change of government. The leader of the Christian trade unions, Leopold Kunschak, identified the threat of imminent civil war, appealing in vain to the Social Democrats to resist fascism together.[95] The workers felt betrayed by their party. Since 1933, the period of greatest unemployment, only 40 percent of those without work had been receiving unemployment assistance, which was further reduced. In addition, their political rights had been confiscated. On 12 February, the Schutzbund engaged in open struggle against the forces of the Heimwehr, police and constabulary without prior communication with the SDAP. The insurgents found themselves in a dire situation. Fearing unemployment, they were leaving the barricades in the mornings to go to the factories, they were lacking arms, food and medication, and the combat operations were inadequately coordinated. In his memoirs, Wilhelm Ellenbogen wrote that Bauer felt personally responsible for the failure of the SDAP's political line, the lonely struggle of the Schutzbund, and the death of hundreds of people.[96] He recognised the bloody end of the Social-Democratic movement of the First Republic as his own failure and a tragedy from which he would not recover until his death. His bad conscience was made worse by the fact that he had fled Austria on the second day of the uprising, fearing arrest.[97] On his day of departure, Bauer joined Deutsch and headed for the outskirts of Vienna to meet the Schutzbund fighters, yet they were unable to pass the police cordon. As Hanisch states, Bauer and Deutsch boarded a car on the 13 February 1934 and, guarded by Ernst Paul and Joseph Plely, crossed the Austrian-Czechoslovakian border heading for Bern.[98]

---

93   He would assume leadership of the ministry of defence and police in February.

94   See *Secret letter exchange between Mussolini and Dollfuss* in Letters.

95   See *Rede L. Kunschak vom 9. Februar 1934 im Gemeinderat Wien* in Archival sources.

96   See Ellenbogen 1983, p. 120.

97   Hanisch explains Bauer's behaviour by way of a panic attack. See Hanisch 2011, p. 305.

98   See Sporrer and Steiner 1983, p. 60; Braunthal 1976b, p. 12; Hanisch 2011, p. 305. Steiner states that from 1934–8, about 2,000 people found refuge in Czechoslovakian territory (Schutzbund fighters, socialists, Communists). The Social Democratic Party of Czechoslovakia largely provided financial support. During the Stalinist period, many of them were accused of espionage and arrested. In 1936–7, a significant percentage of them went to Spain and enlisted with the International Brigades. See Steiner 1984, pp. 535–40.

Upon emigrating, Bauer and Deutsch founded the Foreign Office of Austrian Socialists (ALÖS) with Bauer as chair.[99] It served to support the families of fallen Schutzbund members and the illegal socialist movement forming in Austria financially. Out of this emerged a party, the Revolutionary Socialists of Austria (RS).[100] The *Arbeiter-Zeitung* and *Der Kampf*, both relaunched by Bauer, were the advisory organs of this movement, and the first issue of the *Arbeiter-Zeitung* was published as early as 25 February 1934. Bauer greeted the initialisation of the new party with enthusiasm and without attempting to act as a decisive influence in this organisation. He perceived himself to be a defeated leader: although the young party considered him a moral authority, he demanded that it – if not consistently until the end – issue a new general line and disassociate itself from the mistakes of Austromarxism.[101] His study from this period, *Die illegale Partei* (*The Illegal Party*), offered a new system of judgement, a critical assessment of the old party, and a draft for illegal work close to the Bolshevik model.[102] The necessity to change the forms of internal party life, educate members, and establish conspiratorial methods of action took centre stage. The text not only testified that Bauer re-evaluated the old doctrine and expanded his political consciousness, but also contained a revolutionary message. Bauer advocated that the dictatorship of the proletariat be rehabilitated under the existing balance of social forces and the approach to the Communist movement be modified.[103]

Bauer had already attended to the question of drafting a new strategy for the international workers' movement in the early 1930s. However, only when analysing his experiences and mistakes in exile did he conclude that united action of different working-class tendencies alone had the potential to overcome fascism. The concept of 'integral socialism' as outlined in Bauer's text, *Between Two*

---

99   Upon immigrating to Czechoslovakia, Bauer severed his ties with Renner, who had rejected his proposal to collaborate with the illegal movement. In 1934, Bauer vigorously criticised one of Renner's articles from the *Neue Wiener Tagblatt*, in which Renner had endorsed Hitler's annexation of Austria.

100   Among its members were Oscar Pollak, Manfred Ackermann, Otto Leichter, Joseph Buttinger, Rosa Jochmann, Roman Felleis, Karl Holoubek, Fritz Rauscher and Karl Seiler.

101   In 1934, he wrote to the Revolutionary Socialists from Bern: 'There is no doubt that we committed mistakes ... I can confess to my mistakes even more because I do not incriminate anybody else. For I am more responsible for the mistakes that have been committed than anybody else' (our translation) – Singer 1979, p. 125. See also Braunthal 1976n, p. 14.

102   It was posthumously published by Friedrich Adler in 1938.

103   Bauer appealed to an established reality: back in Austria, the representatives of the former party left had argued in favour of a united front with the Communists as early as 1934.

World Wars, was based on a positive, but also idealistic and wishful assessment of the trajectory of social transformation and the construction of socialism in the Soviet Union. Bauer did not approve of the general drift to the right of parties that belonged to the Labour and Socialist International, nor did he share their concerns about co-operating with the Third International. Admittedly, his proposal of co-operation between the two tendencies had little hope of success. The Communists were optimistic that the world economic crisis would initiate the world revolution and fall of capitalism, thus proving the Social-Democratic strategy wrong. Indeed, they laid the blame for the social and political consequences of fascism on the LSI parties. In 1924, they had coined the memorable phrase 'social fascism' to describe Social Democracy. The conference of the LSI international from 13–16 November 1935 rejected mutual participation with the Communist International in support of the workers' struggles in Spain. They also refused Bauer's suggestions to instigate contact between the respective executive and form a united struggle against fascism out of fear of a potential German attack against the Soviet Union.[104] To justify this, it evoked concern that broader social layers might change sides and join the fascist camp. Bauer was ambiguous on the controversies between Social Democrats and Communists. On the one hand, at the LSI conferences he attempted to convince its leaders to initiate co-operation with the Comintern. On the other, he feared that the LSI might lose its ideological identity and organisational unity.

After Hitler's invasion of Czechoslovakia and the dissolution of the ALÖS, Bauer was forced to leave Bern. In May 1938, he took a plane to Paris alongside the leader of the KPÖ, Johann Koplenig.[105] At the time, Julius Deutsch, Otto Leichter, Oscar Pollak and Joseph Buttinger were already staying in Paris, and the Foreign Office of Austrian Socialists was founded upon their initiative. At the party congress in Brussels, the Revolutionary Socialists decided to entrust Bauer with the leadership of the RS.[106] In Paris, Bauer founded a new journal, *Der sozialistische Kampf*, with three issues produced under his direction. Two days before his death, he participated in a meeting between confidants in the Montmartre district. As Berczeller remembered, the hoary and apathetic

---

104   Compare Löw 1980, p. 205.

105   Bauer went to Paris with great reluctance. Leichter remembered those moments as follows: 'As we drove from Brussels to Paris in early April, I sensed this deep sadness in him. I tried to distract by hinting at the beauty. "It is not as beautiful as home", Bauer said (...) "You will see it again", I tried to console him. "I will never see my home again", he replied, "do you really believe I could pick up where I left off on 12 February 1934?"' (our translation) – see Leichter 1970, p. 15.

106   See Weinzierl 1984, p. 10.

Bauer looked old for his 57 years.[107] Nevertheless, he did not stop writing and publishing until his final hours. His last two articles were grief-stricken moral demands. In 'Nach der Annexion' ('After the Annex'), he called for a critical instead of reactionary approach to Austria's *Anschluss*: a common struggle against fascism alongside the working class of Germany. 'Ich appelliere an das Gewissen der Welt' ('I Appeal to the Conscience of the World'), which he wrote just hours before his death, was dedicated to the 300,000 Austrian Jews and mass deportations to Dachau concentration camp. He pleaded to save those who were targeted by the fascist terror.

The material presented in this chapter contains only the most important events in Bauer's vast theoretical and political activity and political direction of the SDAP. Readers will find that the following chapters examine these themes in more detail, yet we will sometimes need to reacquaint ourselves with this basic chronology – after all, it is impossible to abstract the philosophical, social, and political concepts of a dedicated socialist from his practical actions.

---

107   See Leser and Berczeller 1977, p. 140.

CHAPTER 2

The Materialist View of History

1   Scientistic Marxism

Leszek Kołakowski rightly referred to the period of the Second International (1899–1914) as the 'golden age' of Marxism.[1] During this period, the doctrine was received in a spontaneous fashion. It was referenced and fiercely discussed by many branches of the social sciences, and, ultimately, was not spared criticism. It was also during this time that two contradictory interpretations of Marx and Engels's thought took shape, leaving aside certain sub-varieties. This resulted from divergent ways – controversial to this day – in which determinist and activist elements, i.e. the two spheres of phenomena and processes (the objective and subjective spheres), were linked together.[2] So-called objectivist interpretations of Marxism, which developed mainly under the influence of naturalism, scientism and positivism, were based on the premise that social realities are subject to their own autonomous, inevitable laws of development. These laws were treated as extensions of the laws of nature. The significance of conscious and purposeful human action was minimised or eliminated from the historical process. Instead, an emphasis was placed on material factors, especially economic aspects. This was reflected in how modes of consciousness were viewed as external to being, and the relationship between objective and subjective conditions was conceived of mechanically, as moving in one direction only. The opponents of the 'naturalists' – not just revisionists, but equally

---

1   Kołakowski 1978, p. 355.
2   Numerous Marxists from the period of the Second International noticed the inherent contradiction between the determinist and activist elements in Marx's thought. The determinist aspect concerns Marx's economic prognosis that capitalism would inevitably develop towards communism and his vision of capitalism's decline, which was linked to his theory on crises of overproduction. The activist aspect concerns the conscious participation of the oppressed classes in the destruction of capitalism. The attempts of these Marxists to link the two elements together were motivated by their aspiration to defend the economic interpretation of theory without denying the driving force of collective action. Resulting from this, Marxist theorists were caught up in contradictions and inconsistencies. However, many of them favoured one of the two aspects. This spawned two distinct interpretations of Marxian theory: an objectivist and an activist interpretation. Please note that this outline is a conscious simplification of the problem.

ethical socialists and so-called revolutionary Marxists – rightly objected to this interpretation of Marxism. In their view, it reduced Marxian theory to a historical automatism, and in political practice it strengthened so-called *attentist* attitudes in the workers' movement.[3]

In contrast, the Marxists who advocated an activist standpoint – also known as the humanist perspective – stressed the relative independence of the sphere of consciousness from the economic structure. Most overstated subjective factors in the historical process, particularly ethical and political factors, which they ultimately separated from the socio-economic foundation.[4]

The emergence of these two primary models of understanding Marxism can be attributed to the fact that the theorists of the Second International took two opposing positions in relation to their 'masters'.[5] The first approach was characterised by a relatively unreflective attitude towards the adopted doctrine, which they considered self-contained, unified, and self-sufficient. The advocates of this interpretation believed that Marxism encompassed a comprehensive worldview, held a ready set of questions and indisputable answers that explained all phenomena of natural and social life, and produced its own scientific criteria and methodological tools. Karl Kautsky, Georgi Plekhanov, Rosa Luxemburg, Vladimir Lenin and Joseph Stalin, among others, were in this group.

In comparison, the second stance was characterised by a certain distrust as to the durability and correctness of the solutions offered by Marx and Engels, and an openness towards questions and problems posed by other intellectual currents. It took an instrumental approach towards Marxist theory, albeit in the positive sense of the term. Characteristically, Marxism was treated as a base that supplied analytical methods and tools to conduct research in various fields of the social sciences, e.g. philosophy, sociology, history, economy, and politics. Marx's theory as such was not deemed of interest as a separate subject of study. The likes of Eduard Bernstein, the ethical socialists, the Austromarxists, Antonio Labriola, Antonio Gramsci, and the 'young' György Lukács represented this approach to the founding doctrine. While naturalistic interpretations of Marxism generally went hand in hand with the previous stance, activist interpretations were associated with the latter. However, one cannot apply

---

3   The politics of passively waiting for events to unfold automatically.

4   For the representatives of both determinist and activist interpretations, the following idea of Marx was unclear: consciousness always means conscious being, since it is based on our active life process, which is accomplished in specific socio-historical conditions.

5   See Kołakowski 2005, 511.

this rule to all Second International theorists, the case of Otto Bauer being exemplary in this regard.

Not unlike Gramsci and Lukács, Bauer stood for a tendency that aspired to creative interpretations of Marxism – yet his method of reading the philosophical content of Marx's theory was closer to the 'naturalists' than to their 'activist' opponents. Bauer dedicated relatively little room to the reception of Marxism in his works; it only featured in a sporadic and rudimentary fashion within his literary output.[6] To a certain degree, his lack of philosophical education was decisive in this. Before we move on, we should be clear that as a thinker Bauer was not of the same stature as Max Adler or the neo-Kantians. The influential non-Marxist philosophical currents of his time set the limits of his philosophical horizon. There was another factor no less crucial to Bauer's idiosyncratic reception of Marxism.[7] He was mainly interested in sociological and historical depictions of social reality, and especially the possibility of using historical analysis, based on historical data, for researching the origins and development of social phenomena; for gaining insight into the laws and internal mechanisms of socio-economic processes; and for explaining the structural evolution of societies. Thus, Bauer only sporadically took interest in strictly philosophical questions – his sole philosophical work was *Das Weltbild des Kapitalismus* (*The Worldview of Capitalism*), published in 1924, which he wrote as a prisoner of war in Russia from 1916–17 (it was published in an anniversary edition in honour of Karl Kautsky's 70th birthday). It is impossible, then, to identify philosophical thought as an autonomous strand of research in Bauer's work. While it appears on the margins of his historical and sociological works, it does not form a coherent or even loosely connected whole.[8] Nor does it contain a meta-theoretical layer. There was, however, a distinct turning point in Bauer's reflections on Marxism. In the first phase, he reflected upon the scientific status of Marxism, interpretations of philosophical materialism, dialectics, epistemology and

---

6 Bauer wrote on Marxism mainly on the occasion of anniversaries, and, even then, not very much: his first and most important work in this respect is the study 'Marxismus und Ethik' ('Marxism and Ethics', 1905–6). Further relevant texts are the article 'Die Geschichte eines Buches' ('History of a Book'), published in 1908 for the 40th anniversary of *Capital*, the article 'Marx und Darwin', published in 1909 for the 50th anniversary of Marx's preface to *Critique of Political Economy*, and the article 'Marx als Mahnung' ('Marx as a Warning'), published in 1923 for the 40th anniversary of Marx's death. As to the works of other Marxist theorists, only Karl Kautsky's *The Economic Doctrines of Karl Marx* attracted his interest – see Albers 1985, pp. 69–70.

7 This question will be discussed comprehensively later.

8 Albers also notes this aspect in Bauer's work: see Albers 1983, pp. 98–9.

ethics from a scientistic, positivist and Kantian point of view. Following his
watershed moment in 1916, he critically reviewed the theoretical and philosophical perspectives of the past during the second phase.

To discuss Bauer's reception of Marx, one needs to consider the scientific
context with due regard to Austrian specifics, as well as the social and political conditions in which Marxism found itself at the turn of the twentieth
century. An important circumstance was the lack of familiarity with the revolutionary form of Marxism in Austria,[9] which can be traced back to a number
of reasons. The workers' familiarity with the writings of Marx and Engels, for
instance, had all but vanished.[10] Christian Social and nationalist groups exerted a strong influence. The workers' movement was organisationally divided
for a prolonged period. Furthermore, no independent theory emerged in the
Austrian Social-Democratic movement up until 1904. It therefore adopted the
theoretical and political assumptions of German Social Democracy, the most

9   Referring to Austromarxism as 'revisionism of a special type', Alfred Pfabigan writes: 'In
     order to understand this "revisionism of a special type", we need to take a brief look at the
     conditions for the reception of Marxism in the Austrian workers' movement. In Austria,
     these conditions were rather unfavourable. Marx and Engels's thought evolved largely in
     Great Britain, which was socially at a higher level, and rested on a foundation that was
     alien to the culture of the Danube Monarchy: an advanced, industrialist way of thinking.
     I only want to mention some aspects of this mode of thinking, which was an important
     precondition for socialist thought and missing in Austria. The Enlightenment never fully
     prevailed in this country, utopian socialism was a marginal phenomenon, no materialism
     that argued in a scientific manner existed, and the writings of classical political economy
     were largely unknown. The same is true for classical German philosophy ... Especially for
     Hegel it was not necessary to perish in 19th century Austria, he was already a "dead dog"
     when he was still alive' (our translation) – Pfabigan 1990, p. 47 and Pfabigan 1990b, p. 53.
10   See Pfabigan 1990, p. 47. Ernst Hanisch also supports this in his article, 'Die Marx-Rezep-
     tion in der österreichischen Arbeiterbewegung' ('The Reception of Marx in the Austrian
     Workers' Movement'). Hanisch writes: 'Only a small number of workers had a more intim-
     ate knowledge of Marx and Engels' (our translation) – Hanisch 1978, p. 120. In the same
     article, however, Hanisch argues: 'Nonetheless, Marx was an established name for the
     majority of Austrian workers: as the creator of "scientific socialism", as a genius, as a sym-
     bol' (our translation) – ibid. Discussing the lack of reception of Marx and Engels's works
     in the Austrian labour movement, Hanisch points out that the SDAP's daily newspaper,
     Arbeiter-Blatt, printed the *Communist Manifesto* on 7 June 1868. Furthermore, from 1869
     onwards, the leaders of both groups in the workers' movement – the 'radicals' and the
     'moderates' – as well as circles of educated workers were familiar with Marx's *Capital* and
     Engels's *The Condition of the Working Class in England*. In addition, Marxism was popular-
     ised by workers' calendars in a form that was understandable to them. See Hanisch 1978,
     pp. 93–121.

important of which included an evolutionary interpretation of the historical process and resulting reformist orientation. Almost all Austromarxists, most of whom held PhDs from the University of Vienna, were influenced by its bourgeois professors. Followers of Johann Friedrich Herbart and Friedrich Jacob dominated the philosophy department there, but unlike in France, there was no strong materialist tradition. The works of 'itinerant preachers', such as Karl Vogt, Jacob Moleschott and Ludwig Büchner, were known in Austria, yet they did not provoke any major interest, and the synthesis of philosophical materialism and dialectics was neither understood nor accepted. Likewise, the influence of German idealism was minor – among German philosophers, only Kant commanded respect and attention. Hegel was regarded as a dangerous irrationalist and mystic. Furthermore, there was strong resistance against the neo-Kantian methodology and its dichotomous understanding of the sciences – i.e. the differentiation between nomothetic and idiographic sciences made by the Baden School. The Austrian conception of Marxism, within which neither philosophical materialism nor materialist dialectics were granted a right to exist, evolved in this intellectual climate. In the fields of ontology and epistemology, Kantianism and empirio-criticism, respectively, had become prevalent.

The limited reception of Marxism in Austria was conditioned by objective circumstances and, in a sense, historically justified. During the period of the Second International, only a few elements of Marx's theory were subjected to factual analysis, as his early writings did not appear until the 1920s. However, it also resulted from the programmatic task that the Austromarxists had set themselves. They had no desire to prove the legitimacy and correctness of historical materialism in the way earlier generations had done. Rather, they wanted to utilise Marx's findings and method for their own research in the areas of philosophy, law, economy and history. In doing so, they were aware that any further development of Marxism would involve confronting its basic theoretical and philosophical assumptions with the latest findings of hard science and explanations offered by other currents of intellectual culture. For it was not Marxism, but positivism, scientism, social Darwinism, naturalism and Kantianism that defined perceptions of social and historical reality at the time. Of no less importance were the insights of formal sociology (Ferdinand Tönnies, Georg Simmel and Max Weber), which were thriving particularly in Germany.[11]

---

11   The concepts of society and social ties contained in Ferdinand Tönnies's *Community and Society* (1887) and Georg Simmel's *Sociology. Inquiries into the Construction of Social Forms* (1908) met with lively interest in scientific and Marxist circles. See Tönnies 2003 and Simmel 2009.

In view of the growing importance of the 'Bernstein debate', the Austrian socialists were faced with a dilemma: they could either subscribe to the thesis of
a 'scientific crisis' of Marxism, popularised particularly by the neo-Kantian or
positivist-oriented revisionists, or take to Marxism's defence. Few of those who
chose the latter option were fully aware of Marxism's distinct theoretical and
methodological features, which is why they felt that drawing on notions, methods and criteria of scientificity developed by the social sciences up until then
would be the correct way to proceed. The essential advantage of their approach
was that they could fall back on age-old scientific and philosophical traditions
that had accompanied the birth of Marxism. Indeed, at the turn of the twentieth century, it was not at all self-evident that Marxism was part of European
philosophical culture.

Another crucial question that prompted both interest and controversy in
the Marxist camp was the relevance and adequacy of Marx's theory to the
political practice of Social Democracy, which was changing during the era of
monopoly capitalism. Under the new economic and social conditions (concentration of capital, increasing stratification of the working class and changes in
the class structure of society) and political circumstances (newly legal activity
of working-class parties, rising membership and growing trade-union ranks),
Social Democracy left behind its formative years. Spontaneous mass demonstrations were already of the past, and the Social-Democratic parties focused
on defending reformist gains. They did not stand in the way of the process
through which the working class was gradually integrated into the existing
socio-political structures. Their main objective was to transform the capitalist state into a socialist state by democratic means. At the turn of the century,
this position found a particularly acute expression in revisionism, which gave
a theoretical grounding to earlier attempts at combining Marxism with non-
Marxist currents in the social sciences. Based on empirical research, it furthermore put the main theses of historical materialism into question – rightly so,
as history would show. For the practice of the workers' movement, revisionism
meant abandoning the revolutionary principles of Marx's theory and strengthening reformist politics based on a temporary acceptance of the bourgeois-
democratic state – despite its simultaneous verbal and ideological negation.
The strong influence of revisionism on the workers' movement shaped the
worldview of Social-Democratic parties at the beginning of the twentieth century: its foundation was non-revolutionary Marxism and the reformist orientation of workers during the 'golden age' of capitalism in the 1890s.[12]

---

12   Bauer rightly recognised that this worldview met the expectations of the progressive

The Austrian interpretation of Marxism mainly grew out of opposition to revisionism. Its essence – as mentioned in the first chapter – was a modification of the theoretical and philosophical premises of Marxism, which was achieved by contrasting its conclusions with the findings of scientism, positivism, naturalism and neo-Kantianism. This process enabled the Austrians not only to settle scores with the revisionists, but also to overcome the weaknesses and limitations of orthodox Marxist theory. As a result of their investigations, two different – yet not wholly opposing – models of interpreting Marx and Engels emerged. Anti-naturalist and anti-positivist elements outweighed scientistic elements in Max Adler's model, while positivist and scientistic aspects characterised Friedrich Adler, Karl Renner and Otto Bauer's approaches. It is worth noting in passing that the Austromarxists regarded themselves as legitimate heirs to Marx and their theories as creative advancements of his doctrine. They knowingly overlooked the fact that their paths were, in truth, divergent, and that the right wing headed by Karl Renner had moved fairly close to revisionism. The fact that they took a stand against revisionism was motivated more by ideology than by theory. At least at the level of proclamation, their intervention allowed them to maintain the revolutionary character of the party. One could observe an interesting phenomenon in the process, which Alfred Pfabigan described: the Austrian socialists debated the views of Bernstein, Ignaz Auer, and Ludwig Woltmann – but not their own, as they were anxious not to cast doubt on the ideological unity of the party.[13]

Let us, however, focus on Bauer's interpretation of Marxism, whose point of departure was, likewise, its references to revisionism. Bauer assumed a position that was not entirely consistent: he repeatedly asserted his hostility towards revisionism, describing it as vulgar Marxism, yet without offering any interpretation of that term.[14] At the same time, he tended to minimise the significance of Bernstein's theoretical critique by claiming that it did not concern Marx's system as a whole, but merely abstract formulas and generalities. Nor was he, on

---

intelligentsia and academic youth. He wrote: 'As the bourgeois intelligentsia no longer had to provide arguments for the suppression of the workers' movement by force, but aimed to win over the working class, to pacify the socialist movement, and eliminate its revolutionary character, it now scorned the vulgar old criticism of Marx. It recognised the historical achievement and scientific importance of Marxism, but at the same time, of course it sought to detach socialism from its previous revolutionary ideology. The neo-Kantianism which was dominant in the universities provided it with arguments and methods' – Bauer 1978d, p. 51.

13   See Pfabigan 1985, p. 41.

14   See Bauer 1979f.

the other hand, fully convinced whether one could deny the scientific and historical legitimacy of Bernstein's intervention. A remark he made on the fortieth
anniversary of Marx's death testifies to this: 'What today appears to be a crisis
of Marxism is nothing but the painful process of adjusting socialism to a fundamentally revolutionised world' (our translation).[15] He only perceived revisionism as a threat to certain areas of political practice, fearing it could lead to a
loss of faith in socialism among the masses and transformation of parties from
revolutionary to reformist – the latter, *nota bene*, was already a *fait accompli*.
This was partly why he pointed to the fundamental difference between revisionism and Marxism at the 11th party congress in Innsbruck in 1911: revisionism
viewed social gains and the path of reform as the foundation for a transition
from capitalism to socialism, whereas Marxism argued that the concentration
of capital itself paved the way for its socialisation, and that the growing contradictions between classes must necessarily culminate in a decisive struggle.[16]
Bauer disassociated himself from revisionism in numerous statements, yet this
did not prevent him from approving of Victor Adler's reformist tactics.

In contrast to the revisionists, however, Bauer did not regard Marx's theory
as outmoded or erratic.[17] He conceded that some of Marx's theses no longer
fully applied to existing socio-historical conditions, but, in his view, this did
not mean that the doctrine itself was deficient. He was in favour of generally
remaining faithful to Marx's ideas, yet he considered Marxism itself to be an
open-ended system still capable of providing cognitive and methodological
directives to meet the needs of socio-economical and political analysis of reality. In his social philosophy, Bauer put forward the slogan of 'Marx overcoming Marx', although he discerned a certain distrust in the party ranks towards
posing problems in new ways. He was mainly concerned with utilising Marx's
historical method to research new socio-political phenomena. To him, historical materialism (which he just as often referred to as 'the materialist view
of history') represented, more than anything, a science of the laws of social
development, as well as a method for studying the driving forces behind the
evolution of societies. He also understood it as a methodological postulate for
examining forms of intellectual life in their dependence of the economic structure. From a political point of view, Bauer added that the value of historical

---

15   'Was heute eine Krise des Marxismus zu sein scheint, es nichts anders als der schmerzhafte
     Prozeß des Anpassung des Sozialismus an eine vom Grund aus umgewälzte Welt' – Bauer
     1980i, p. 50.
16   See Bauer 1978, p. 50.
17   See Heimann 1985, p. 131.

materialism lay in indicating the ways and means to change the existing socio-economic order; it was also an instrument to which Social Democracy had to refer if it endeavoured to make socialism a reality.[18]

Bauer was particularly absorbed in the question about the scientific nature of Marxism. Before we engage in any further discussion, we should understand that Bauer's view of Marxism was defined particularly by positivism and scientism. According to Bauer, Hermann Cohen had already posed the crucial opening question: what is Marxism – a science or an ideology? The reply that it was both a science and an ideology was difficult to accept for Bauer and other Marxists informed by the intellectual climate of the time. However, the widespread belief that it was a science prompted the question as to what scientific model it was based on, while also pointing to a more general query: what criteria does knowledge need to fulfil in order to be considered scientific?

It is worth stressing that, when addressing this issue, Bauer did not address essential questions about the relationship between social reality and nature, theory and empirical evidence, and deductive and inductive approaches. They appeared, however, in his observations on the economic development, class structure and national question. Bauer took a critical stance towards Karl Menger's scientific model, which was widespread among Austrian scientists at the time.[19] It was based on the method of abstraction and deduction, operating on the premise that the categories established by a particular theory decisively shape the process and results of acquiring knowledge. In his own attempt to define a model of scientific knowledge, Bauer drew on a historical method suggested by the historian Karl Grünberg, who had developed it harking back to J.S. Mill's position. Its core principle was to examine diagnosed social conditions in order to draw conclusions about their causes, i.e. it was the science

---

18   Hence, as Detlev Albers convincingly argued, Bauer put special emphasis on two principles: (1) the development of Marxism as a social science and guide for practical action; and (2) the role this theory played in revolutionising the political consciousness of the proletariat and maintaining the unity of the workers' movement. See Albers 1985, pp. 77–8.

19   Karl Menger (1840–1921) – founder of the Austrian school of political economy. He was interested not in the production of goods, but in their exchange. He placed an investigation into the formation of prices in the exchange process at the centre of his analysis and viewed prices as the result of individual evaluations of the usefulness of exchanged goods on the market. Menger understood economy as a network of bundled markets and economic activity as a result of actions by individual economic subjects. Main works: *Grundsätze der Volkswirtschaftslehre* and *Untersuchungen über die Methode der Sozialwissenschaften und der politischen Ökonomie insbesondere* (*Principles of Economics and Research into the Methods of Social Science, particularly Political Economy*). See Menger 1981 and 1985.

of deducing from descriptive studies, which, in turn, would serve as the basis for an inductively accomplished synthesis. The greatest direct influence upon Bauer's concept of science, however, was J.S. Mill, especially his distinct view on the correlation between theory and empirical evidence, deduction and induction. The scientific theory of Ernst Mach was of no lesser importance. Under the influence of positivism, Otto Bauer agreed that knowledge only bore phenomenal characteristics. Experience, which one must read independently of any class and social determinants, is its only source: 'Science is nothing but the collecting, organising, and processing of experience' (our translation).[20] Like Ernst Mach, Bauer assumed that scientific results represent a set of approximately adequate facts, and that the researcher's subjective goal determines their degree of adequacy. Because he also recognised Mach's principle of 'economy of thought', Bauer treated theory as a quicker, economic way of recording empirical data. Sharing the position of the positivists and Kantians, he advocated ontological reductionism, and, accordingly, demanded a strict separation of science and philosophy.

Let us note at this point that Bauer also applied the principle of eliminating ontological and value judgements from science within the field of Marxism. Consequently, he adopted a solution that aimed to extract 'pure' and 'applied' science from Marx's theory very much in line with Bernstein's approach. In other words, he viewed socialism as a fact, value, goal, and ideal. Of course, Bauer did not agree with the Machian empirio-critical method in one respect. He sharply protested against its inherent tendency to deny science its autotelic value and reduce it to a means to an end. Instead, he defended the autonomy of science and its right to seek truth. This position manifested itself in his negation of Lenin's postulate for a partification (*partiinost*) of science.[21]

Crucially, Bauer was interested in the mode of being, adopted premises, and the role of science primarily with respect to the scientific status of the humanities, among which he also placed Marxism. His arguments were part of a debate that was taking place in German philosophy and sociology. The key question was whether the methodological premises of a homogeneous model of science built on naturalist foundations were legitimate.

In the argument between the positivists and the Baden school of neo-Kantians, Bauer sided with the former, though not resolutely so.[22] He was inspired by

---

20   'Alle Wissenschaft ist nichts anderes, kann nichts anderes sein als Sammlung, Ordnung, Bearbeitung von Erfahrungen' – Bauer 1980i, p. 49.

21   See Haug 1985, pp. 69–70.

22   For more on Bauer's contradictory relationship with positivism and empirio-criticism, see Goller 2008, p. 70.

Max Adler's insights, especially his criterion of isolating humanist phenomena and his category of lawfulness (*Gesetzmäßigkeit*), and wanted to integrate them into his position. His aim was to formulate a unified theory that could explain natural and social phenomena, while simultaneously taking into account their specific characteristics. At the outset, Bauer considered the paradigm of natural sciences as the only correct model for acquiring scientific knowledge. He stressed the importance of basing social science on the conceptual framework and methods of the hard sciences. For him, this was the only approach that could approximate the degree of precision and certainty associated with the natural sciences and therefore guarantee objective results. Nonetheless, one should refrain from classifying Bauer as an advocate of natural-scientific reductionism. In his statements, he frequently cited the differences between natural sciences and sociology: according to him, they consisted of their varying degrees of accuracy. Of Marx's works, he held *Capital* in particularly high regard and argued that it embodied a prime example of social science. Marx's special achievement, in Bauer's view, lay in the fact that he defined the material premises of social conditions and formulated objective laws of social development. Hence, the author of *Capital* had built a model for the social sciences that approximated the ideal of the natural sciences.

This begs the question: on what premise did Bauer base his judgement? Bauer regarded the Marxian method – which, according to him, was fundamental to the scientificity of his system – as the essence of Marxism.[23] He referred to this method as the 'materialist view of history' or 'economic historicism'. He substantiated his high opinion thus: not only did the method explain the tendencies of social development; it also provided a methodological apparatus, i.e. a means of interpreting concrete socio-political situations and structural changes in relation to general laws. For Bauer, however, it was not just a historical method; he believed that both Hegel and Marx had employed a technique on par with the mathematical natural sciences. For him, Hegel and Marx's greatest achievement was that they had expanded the remits of applied natural sciences to social science. Bauer went a step further and drew a parallel between Marx's and Darwin's respective methods. According to him, their theories differed only in terms of their fields of research. What Bauer had in mind in this instance was undoubtedly the methodological approach: in this

---

23   Both Detlev Albers and Alfred Pfabigan have noted this fact, although neither took any particular position on it. Let us therefore stress that reducing Marxism to a method was an unjustified simplification, given that Marxism contains a complete view of the development of class societies, and thus a theory of economic formations. See Albers 1985, p. 78; compare Pfabigan 1977, pp. 42–3.

respect, both theories fulfilled the requirements of modern science. However, his ongoing quest for a unified and universal means of gaining knowledge was another positivist trait in his reading of Marx.

According to Bauer, Marx adopted two core methodological principles from scientism and positivism. The first principle, phenomenalism, negates the notion that objects have a hidden essence. The second, empiricism, entails a strict refusal to recognise facts that are not established through experience; it furthermore contains an imperative to generalise findings in accordance with the principles of logic. Bauer believed that Marx's method proceeded from describing social conditions to then stating their regularity and intersubjective verifiability, and, lastly, to formulating laws. From this, Bauer concluded that Marx, following the example set by Mills, linked induction with deduction. He particularly emphasised the significance of the inductive method for substantiating claims that had the characteristics of general laws. However, in this regard, his approach was not entirely consistent. His criticism of Renner's attempt to replace the deductive method of *Capital* with an inductive one demonstrated this.[24] As if to further highlight his inconsistency, he himself employed Marx's deductive method for economic analyses. Bauer failed to adequately recognise the distinctiveness of Marx's principle of rising from the abstract to the concrete (for the sake of accuracy, it should be noted that he wrote about it himself).[25] Likewise, he did not sufficiently appreciate Marx's aspiration to investigate phenomena accessible to observation by means of abstract theoretical categories from outside the sphere of empirical reality.

A reading of Bauer's writings might create the impression that he viewed the reality of nature and social reality as one body. The naturalist position was reflected in his belief that the evolution of humankind constituted but one stage in the evolution of nature. In his text 'Marx and Darwin', which was heavily informed by a Darwinian perspective, Bauer concluded that the cultural development of humanity was a continuation of evolution in nature. However, this text is not a very representative source for evaluating Bauer's position. His other works do not allow us to lump him in with the Social Darwinist current.[26] Bauer did not ignore the complexities at the point of

---

24   See Bauer 1980s, p. 260.

25   Alfred Pfabigan would most certainly not agree with my assessment. According to him, Bauer was the first of socialist theorists to recognise the significance of the Marxian method, 'from the abstract to the concrete', although he interpreted it in a critical cognitive sense. See Pfabigan 1977, p. 43.

26   According to Richard Weikart, Social Darwinism can be understood as an ideology that views nature as based on competition and uses the Darwinian concept of struggle for

interception between the world of nature and the world of humans, nor did he disregard the qualitative differences that separate natural and social realities.

Bauer clearly stressed the elements that distinguish humankind in nature: our ability to gain knowledge about ourselves and our innermost need to subordinate nature. Like Max Adler – and later Lukács and Gramsci, who continued this line – he was looking for intrinsic connections linking both spheres of reality that constituted a unity and a whole without concealing the immanent differences. Thus, Bauer concluded that there was an ontological dependency between the laws of nature and social laws. He found the link between the two in the universal validity of the causality principle, which allowed one to discover consistent laws of natural and social life. Assuming that social phenomena were causally determined, Bauer suggested that a deterministic causality principle reigned in the sphere of human action. However, we must not infer that he eliminated objectives and values from the historical process. To substantiate his perspective, he referred to the category of 'social causality' first introduced by Adler.[27] Much like Adler, he followed a Kantian approach when deducing social causality from the formal psychological characteristics of consciousness. He assumed *a priori* socialisation of individual consciousness, yet, unlike Adler, he did not develop this approach any further.[28] True to his under-

---

survival as a basis for social theory (see Weikart 1993, p. 469). In its early stages, Social Darwinism emphasised individual competition, yet from the 1860s onwards, its advocates stressed the collective struggle in order to justify racism, eugenics and imperialism. Since the 1870s, Darwinism was hugely popular in liberal academic scientist circles, i.e. among philosophers, sociologists, theologians, economists and historians. Bauer was not the only Social Democrat fascinated by Darwin's theory of evolution. It was also echoed in Karl Kautsky's and Ludwig Woltmann's ideas. We should also remember that the two founders of Marxism, Karl Marx and Frederick Engels, approved of Darwin's teachings. See Engels 1983, p. 551, and Marx 1985, p. 232.

27   I dealt with this category more extensively in Czerwińska 1991, pp. 160–1. Guided by methodological assumptions close to Max Adler's, Wilhelm Dilthey's successor at the University of Berlin, Alois Riehl, challenged the Baden School's differentiation between nomothetic and idiographic sciences. This differentiation was based on the opposition between generalising and individualistic understanding, as well as the opposition between causal and teleological modes of explanation. Riehl assumed that the individual was a manifestation of the general, and that there are general causal relationships in both types of science. At the same time, Adler and Riehl agreed with the neo-Kantians that the notion of general laws was a feature of consciousness superimposed on nature and history.

28   According to Max Adler, causality in nature differs from causality in society insofar as the former has a mechanical character, whereas according to the latter, the assessment process is an integral component of the causal process.

standing of the social sciences – i.e. Marxism – Bauer ascribed the significant purpose of combining two opposed concepts to the causality principle: first, the scientistic-positivist belief in the impartiality of science, and second, Marx's demand to establish science as the basis for action.

Other questions raised in Bauer's earlier writings concerned philosophy, dialectics, and epistemological theory in Marxism, though they merely formed a collection of passing remarks. Bauer's interpretation of the philosophical content of Marx's theory was defined by his view of science and the fact that he applied it to Marxism. The author of *The Question of Nationalities and Social Democracy* understood that social theory was more closely related to philosophy than to natural science and could not eschew basic philosophical questions concerning the essence of the world and the meaning of the succession of phenomena. Even so, he placed these questions beyond the realm of science, given that they reached, or even exceeded, the limits of experience. Using the philosophical and methodological premises of positivism and scientism, he interpreted Marx's historical materialism as an empirical science that approached the precision of prognoses and analyses in the natural sciences.

Bauer emphasised the objectivist and naturalist qualities of historical materialism. At the same time, he denied that one could base ontological and evaluative assumptions on historical materialism, which he reduced to a sociology modelled on the natural sciences. He commented:

> Marx's social doctrine is an exact science. It is thus not a critique of knowledge nor a philosophy ... In principle, Marxian social theory needs guidance from philosophy just as little as, for instance, mechanics or astronomy.[29]
>
> our translation

Bauer's view of sociology as an exact science that draws on research practices analogous to the natural sciences emerged, firstly, from his polemical examination of Wilhelm Dilthey's thesis, according to which it was impossible to establish a scientifically grounded sociology. Dilthey questioned the adequacy of a sociological approach and its ability to solve the questions it posed. Secondly, Bauer criticised Georg Simmel, who negated sociology's basis in naturalism. At the same time, Bauer's reductionist understanding of Marxist sociology

---

29   'Marx Gesellschaftslehre ist eine exakte Wissenschaft. Sie ist also keine Erkenntniskritik, keine Philosophie. (...) An sich bedarf die Marxsche Gesellschaftstheorie der Belehrung durch die Philosophie ebenso wenig wie etwa die Mechanik oder die Astronomie' – Bauer 1979f, p. 188.

as a pure doctrine, devoid of any basic assumptions, had far-reaching consequences. That is to say, it led him so far as to disregard the internal connection
between Marx's philosophical materialism and his theory of social development.

In this context, Bauer's aversion to Kautsky's interpretation of Marx's social
theory becomes understandable, given that Kautsky's reading gave emphasis
to its origins in historical materialism. To Bauer, materialism entailed the positivist directive of basing the research of social phenomena and processes on
empirical foundations. His defence of Marxism against the pitfalls of materialism was analogous to that of other Austromarxists, who equally reduced materialism to its natural-scientific dimension and denied it a right to exist philo-
sophically.[30] According to Pfabigan, their position was inspired by the neo-
Kantian Friedrich Albert Lange. Lange's work *History of Materialism and Critique of its Present Importance* (1866), which was popular in Social-Democratic
circles, reduced materialism to natural sciences and rejected its metaphysical
content.[31]

Let us briefly recap. Bauer's notion of the interrelationship between science and philosophy was rooted in the scientistic postulate of an opposition
between science and ideology (*Weltanschauung*). According to this view, it
was unacceptable to deduce one's conception of the world from science –
consequently, there was no relationship between scientific practice and the
ideological implications of science. It is therefore understandable why Bauer
negated the ideological nature of socialism: he considered the choice of *Weltanschauung* to be a private matter. Bauer thought that every participant in the
workers' movement accomplished their own interpretation of ideology;
according to him, the foundation for any kind of democratic socialism was 'the
free self-determination of the working class in choosing an intellectual current
from among those competing for its verdict' (our translation).[32] It should be
noted here that the claim about Marxism's ideological neutrality was a pillar
of Austrian Social Democracy, serving its political aim to win people of various
views and beliefs to the idea of socialism. That the party agreed to integrate
trends into Marxism that represented divergent theoretical and philosophical

---

30   For Friedrich Adler, the concept of materialism was synonymous with the experience of
      modern natural science – see F. Adler 1918, p. 137. For Max Adler, it constituted a realistic
      positivism, i.e. a restriction of science to the causal examination of reality. See M. Adler
      1964, p. 83.

31   See Pfabigan 1977, pp. 42–3.

32   'Die freie Selbstbestimmung der Arbeiterklasse in der freien Wahl der um ihr Urteil
      ringenden Geistesströmungen' – Bauer 1980q, p. 199.

assumptions was closely linked to its political practice. This way, it could legit-imise Social Democracy's collaboration with bourgeois parties.[33]

Bauer frequently identified philosophical materialism with a specific method: that of investigating phenomena and processes in their movement and development, i.e. in their interrelationship. However, he did not think of the interrelationship between phenomena and processes as a dialectical con-tradiction. At the time of Austromarxism's inception, dialectical materialism was understood as neither a characteristic nor a self-evident method of Marx-ism. Even Bauer, under the influence of Karl Lamprecht, had a negative stance towards it, which was certainly aided by his faint knowledge of Hegel's works. Among Austromarxists, only Max Adler fully appreciated the significance of Hegel's philosophy for Marxist theory, while others considered it irrelevant. In his defence of the role of dialectics in Marxism, Adler eschewed its ontological implications and reduced it to a method of gaining insight into the sphere of consciousness. His critique of Engels's and Lenin's notions of dialectics resul-ted from his ontological and epistemological assumptions – for Adler, being was merely a product of thought, while the critique of scientific knowledge was a critique of consciousness. Bauer held Hegel's insights in low esteem, stress-ing that the Hegelian triad of development was a speculative construct that bore no relationship to reality in either nature or society. Consequently, when Bernstein accused Marx of abandoning the empirical method of inquiry and instead applying Hegelian *a priori* development schemes to historical reality, Bauer defended Marx against Bernstein's claims.

As the above account makes abundantly clear, Bauer believed that Marx's theory contained no philosophy, value theory, or epistemology. From 1904–16, he demanded that Marxism be complemented with Kantian epistemo-logy. In Austromarxism, this was a particular hobbyhorse of Max Adler's, and Bauer highly valued his attempts to merge Marxism with transcendentalism.[34] However, he did not create an epistemology of his own, and some of his passing remarks betray a flawed understanding of the epistemological problems in Kant and Marx. In light of Bauer's own insights, it is worth noting his surpris-ing results when he attempted to defend the scientific character of Marxism employing a method of transcendental critical philosophy. Rather than recog-nising the laws of social development formulated by Marx as empirical laws, he conceived of them as transcendental regularities that could be investigated due to *a priori* conditions of human knowledge. Initially, he assumed, along with

---

33   See Pfabigan 1977, p. 51.
34   See Bauer 1961, pp. 228–36.

Max Adler, that the process of gaining knowledge occurred through the agency of a supra-individual consciousness expressed in *a priori* socialised individual consciousness. He soon revised his position and declared that there were *a priori*, socio-historically divergent cognitive forms: 'There not only exists a social *a priori* of human knowledge in general, but ... also a special social *a priori* of each historical epoch, each social order, and each class' (our translation).[35] Bauer interpreted the Kantian approach as historical and credited himself with building a bridge from Kantianism to Marxism. This 'achievement' of Bauer's, which was devoid of any scientific value, did not meet with the slightest interest from Marxist theorists or Social Democrats.

From 1916–17, the years during which he wrote *The Worldview of Capitalism*, Bauer began to critically examine Kantianism, its socio-historical determinants, and its limitations. In 1924, in the preface to the second edition of his text, *The Question of Nationalities and Social Democracy*, he wrote: 'It was only in the context of later studies that I learned to grasp critical philosophy as itself a historical phenomenon, thereby overcoming my Kantian childhood malady and at the same time also revising my methodological viewpoint'.[36] In *The Worldview of Capitalism*, Bauer, following Marx's directive to investigate the historical evolution and social conditioning of philosophical ideas, attempted to explain why the bourgeois intelligentsia and Marxists were both appealing to Kant.[37] He pointed out how economic and philosophical knowledge was conditioned by socio-economic and historical factors. The economic and political decline of liberalism was followed by a period of organised capitalism. In the field of philosophy, scientific materialism was superseded by positivism and relativism. Scientific knowledge was no longer a goal in itself: it was utilised to build capitalism, make socio-economic life more efficient, and thus facilitate capitalism's free development. For this purpose, it took lawmaking as its reference point, understood as the legislative parliamentary practice that passes laws to secure the effectiveness of economic enterprise. The new worldview triumphed over mechanical materialism; when faced with the demise of the latter, a generation of Marxists still clinging to intellectual categories typical of early capitalism at the turn of the nineteenth century resorted to Kant.

---

35 'Es gibt also nicht nur ein *Sozialapriori* der menschlichen Erkenntnis überhaupt, sondern ... auch besondere *Sozialapriori* jeder Geschichtsepoche, jeder Gesellschaftsordnung, jeder Klasse' – Bauer 1961, p. 232.

36 Bauer 1996, p. 7.

37 This being Marx's notion, in *The Holy Family*, that the history of ideas is intrinsically conditioned by the history of production. See Kołakowski 2005, p. 125.

In the aforementioned text, Bauer employed Marx's methodological postulate mainly to interpret the philosophy of the eighteenth and nineteenth
centuries.[38] He was especially preoccupied with the historical origins of scientific materialism and the reasons why it had replaced philosophical idealism
during the early period of capitalism. He considered the following as the most
important factors in this development: philosophical interest transformed into
an aspiration to investigate the scientific laws of the development of the world
and subordinate them to the needs of the flourishing capitalist mode of production; traditional social structures were destroyed and atomised societies created; the third factor was the development of the relationship between society
and nature, based on the principle of the free interplay of forces. Consequently,
Bauer associated the progress of modern capitalism with the origins of modern natural science and the related philosophical systems: positivism, scientism, and materialism. According to his one-sided interpretation, the laws of
the capitalist market alone determined the new worldview. The author argued
that changes in production relations and property rights determined changes
in philosophical thought, as did the character of international economic relations and modifications to the organisation of the working process. Among
these changes were a shift from idealism to materialism and from universal-
ist approaches to individualism, a transition from a quantitative to qualitative
interpretations of phenomena, and a shift from causal to teleological ways of
thinking. Concerning the interrelationship between social being and social
consciousness, Bauer – and we will elaborate on this shortly – attributed a
decisive role to the former. This inevitably led him to overstate the degree to
which the economic base determined thought structures. Bauer concluded his
treatise by stating that materialism constituted the 'last dogmatic system of
capitalism', bound to be annihilated alongside capitalism's demise.[39] In *The
Worldview of Capitalism*, he once more identified the critiques of mechanistic
materialism proposed by positivism and Marxism with a complete rejection
of materialism of any kind. He maintained that science and philosophy were
radical opposites – a judgement rooted in scientism.

---

38   Hanisch argues that Bauer's work is 'the result of an impressive intellectual effort and
      extensive knowledge of the history of philosophy, but it is reductionist. Philosophical
      thought is mechanically traced back to the socio-economic conditions' (our translation) –
      Hanisch 2011, p. 22.
39   Bauer 1976f, p. 931.

2   Historiosophical Reflections

Bauer's adopted naturalist and scientistic perspectives had an effect on his historiosophical views. Before we examine them, it is worth noting that Bauer was a historian who, inspired by Marxism, broke away from merely presenting the history of dynasties, wars, ideas, and 'great men', i.e. the traditional Austrian way of history writing.[40] His treatises linked the analysis of economic life with the history of human action (i.e. mass movements), although he did not develop a clear concept of history. For him, the history of humankind was no more than the history of class struggles. Bauer applied historical materialism, which he understood as a methodological guideline, to investigate the ways in which various forms of spiritual life – ideological consciousness in particular – were determined by the development of the economic structure. This being the case, he paid little attention to some fundamental questions of historical materialism: the nature of social laws; their relation to the laws of evolution in nature; and the question of progress in history. Nor was he – in contrast to Max Adler – interested in the rationality and purposiveness of the historical process as a subject of independent reflection. In fact, he tried to evade references to philosophical traditions altogether. This was particularly true for the historiosophy of Hegel, which was incomprehensible to him. Of the broad range of issues that historical materialism addressed, he only took interest in two problems intrinsically linked to the Social Democrats' party-political practice: firstly, the question of dependency between economics and consciousness, which Bauer often identified as ideology. Secondly, the view of class struggle as an objective law and driving force behind historical development. Bauer's conclusions can be put down to two opposing claims. One of them was linked to naturalism and evolutionism; the other was based on the Marxian premise of social change as revolutionary process.

The two claims might be summed up thus:

– The economic factor is predominant in the historical process, significantly reducing its arbitrary and contingent character. This economic factor is genetic and primarily functional with regard to social and individual consciousness.
– The direction that the social process takes is decisively influenced by the struggle of classes that strive for social and political liberation.[41]

---

40   Hanisch investigates the differences between the Viennese school of history and Bauer's historical method in detail. See Hanisch 2011, pp. 181–91.

41   When advocating this interpretation of the socio-historical process, Bauer was certainly

Bauer started from Marx's well-known dictum that people make their own history, albeit in material conditions not of their own choosing. This thesis prompted questions about the ways in which human activity was determined by pre-existing material conditions (and to what extent), the scope of human influence, and the degree to which humans could give purpose and direction to the evolution of society. Like Friedrich Adler, Bauer was one of the Austromarxists who adopted a deterministic, monist position, i.e. he regarded the unity and general determinacy of natural phenomena and the social world as an ontological principle.[42] He drew two conclusions from the assumption of a general determinacy: both types of regularity had a causal character, and, what is more, the causal relationship was unequivocal. Bauer was therefore convinced that the laws of social development could be grasped as tightly as the laws of physics. Referring to *Capital*, he claimed: 'Thus, Marx gave us the first mathematical law of motion of history' (our translation).[43] Bauer fully accepted the historical-materialist thesis that the social process was self-contained and immanent. He also believed that it proceeded according to objective and consistent laws. Naturally, he did not link his determinism to a dialectical theory of development. On the contrary, he eliminated any dialectics from the historical process, veering towards an evolutionist interpretation. In most of his writings, he reduced the Marxian relationship between base and superstructure to a one-way concurrency: 'As the scientific and social living conditions of humans change, so do their modes of thought, their customs, their moral values, the sciences, art, and religion' (our translation).[44] Bauer conceived of the productive forces

---

not fully aware that the key theses of his analysis were contradictory. As I have stressed earlier, not even Marx could avoid this paradox, and his faithful students perpetuated the incoherence of this doctrine. This also applies to the theories of Bauer and Kautsky, although the theses that Bauer adopted were not as blatantly contradictory.

42   Of all Austromarxists, Friedrich Adler placed the strongest emphasis on the biological necessity of the historical process. Indeed, he assumed that it constituted a plain extension of the laws of nature. See F. Adler 1918b, p. 62.

43   'So gibt uns Marx das erste mathematische Bewegungsgesetz der Geschichte' – Bauer 1979f, p. 937. Bauer's familiarity with the works of Marx was somewhat tenuous. Presumably, he used many of Marx's concise expressions without looking into their essence. When passing judgement on *Capital*, he referred to the preface of *Critique of Political Economy*, where Marx wrote that the material upheaval of the economic conditions of production could be measured with the precision of hard science. As P. Śpiewak rightly points out, the Marxists' attempts at establishing a social science based on the model of the natural sciences were harshly criticised by Antonio Labriola, Antonio Gramsci and Georges Sorel – see P. Śpiewak 1977, pp. 48–50.

44   'Mit den wissenschaftlichen und sozialen Lebensbedingungen der Menschen verändert

and objectively existing relations of production as the base, which in his view were determined by changes in production and the exchange of goods. The superstructure, for him, consisted of intellectual achievements and the legal and political system. As already mentioned, he did not agree that there was a dialectical relationship between the two sides of the socio-economic process, instead stressing their mutual dependency.

These reflections reveal a grave inconsistency in Bauer's theory that is worth examining more closely. The inconsistency relates to questions of the mutual relationship between objective and subjective factors of history, where the philosopher took a position close to that of the anti-naturalists. He summarised the relationship between the objective and subjective sides of Marxism in a formula that went beyond the confines of what was accepted by orthodox Marxists. Taking issue with their positions, he emphasised: 'To simply counterpose subjective and objective factors is worlds away from Marxist dialectics. One needs to understand that the qualities of the subjective factor result from objective factors no less than objective factors result from subjective actions'.[45] It is not difficult to explain the position that Bauer took here. Because he agreed that transformations in the economic structure constituted the sole determinant of social development, he logically assumed that the human spirit obeyed material conditions. This assumption was, as it were, a sort of plea for the automatism of history. Inevitably, it led to the affirmation of attentist attitudes in the workers' party, which ran counter to the implicit objective of the Social-Democratic movement, namely that of revolutionary upheaval. To overcome this dilemma, Bauer made a remarkable attempt to link deterministic-economic elements with activist elements (note that both are intrinsic to Marx's theory). Bauer's line of argument accentuated the following components:

1. The consciousness-forming constituents of the economic base, the productive forces, have no purely material character. Rather, they are forces of nature that humans consciously instrumentalise in order to satisfy their needs. Human thought is an inalienable part of technological processes. Economic relations must always be read as social relations. Let us note here that Bauer's

sich ihre Denkweise, verändern sich die Sitten die moralischen Werte, die Wissenschaft, die Kunst, die Religion' – Bauer 1976j, p. 491.

45   'Man ist von marxistischen Dialektik weltenweit entfernt, wenn man den subjektiven und den objektiven Faktor einander unvermittelt gegenüberstellt, statt die Qualitäten des subjektiven Faktors ebenso als Resultate objektiver Faktoren zu begreifen wie die objektiven Faktoren als Resultate subjektiven Handelns' – Bauer 1980ee, p. 739.

privileged treatment of the role of consciousness did not at all imply inde-terminism concerning the economic sphere.[46]

2. Economic relations are not forces that influence humans mechanically – economic regularities merely illuminate the main tendencies of historical development. The way in which this developmental process evolves (and how quickly) depends on the activities of individual social groups and classes.[47] Bauer highlighted the role of mass movements, which is why he adopted a position close to the anti-naturalists on this subject, arguing in favour of relatively autonomous social consciousness. This position also jus-tified his view of the class struggle as the decisive driving force behind social change.

3. Needs and ideas are conditioned by the mode of production and can only be realised in the material sphere of human actions, even if they act as external forces in relation to social being. Not individuals, but the masses are carriers of ideas.

Bauer thus understood the socio-historical process as a permanent and pro-gressive development of forces of production and related economic conditions that develop in the course of our conscious struggle to dominate nature for the sake of satisfying our needs. This process, according to Bauer, is synonym-ous with the evolution of humankind itself. If individuals actively participate in the collective social production of goods through their own productive activ-ities, then not only can they grasp the prevailing laws and regularities, but they can also use the knowledge acquired to help shape their own history. The question arises as to whether Bauer considered the subjective and objective factors of history equally significant. Since he assumed – analogously to Marx and Kautsky – that economic factors were predominant and determined social and political factors, he evidently did not give equal weight to both subject-ive and objective factors. It is no accident that Bauer invariably appealed to so-called objective conditions to justify his and his party's anti-revolutionary stance. Even so, Bauer's critics unjustly accused him of construing Marxism in

---

46   Gerald Mozetič passes the same judgement – see Mozetič 1987, p. 115.

47   According to Bauer, historical materialism discovered the laws of social development and signposted a way to achieve the goals of the practical order, which led to a particular social politics. However, historical materialism is based on applied theory in practice, rather than just being a theoretical hypothesis. According to Bauer, Marxism does not, in and of itself, contain any ideological claims because it is an economic theory of society. It is here that the scientist perspective of separating theory from practice and science from social interests becomes obvious.

the spirit of automatism and historical fatalism.[48] Much like the late Kautsky, Bauer viewed any fatalistic understanding of the laws of historical materialism very sceptically. He criticised theories that argued that the downfall of capitalism was inevitable. Indeed, he viewed crises as virtual opportunities for the capitalist economy to renew itself.[49] Yet merely to assume an ontological law of the general determinacy of phenomena and processes is not tantamount to presuming that the historical process is subordinated to a vaguely specified destiny. Neither is it synonymous with writing all subjectivity out of history.

Bauer reiterated a well-known thesis from the works of philosophers such as Giambattista Vico, Johann Gottlieb Fichte and G.W.F. Hegel and economists like Adam Ferguson and Adam Smith. Marx's thought mirrored this thesis: the general determinacy of phenomena does not enable us to strictly predict any consequences that human actions may have. More than once, Bauer stressed that history was often the result of an unconscious interplay of human actions, albeit with humans functioning as members of society, rather than as individuals. He sharply criticised bourgeois historiosophy for its individualism and elitism, particularly its emphasis on so-called great men in history. In his own text, *Revolutionäre Kleinarbeit* (*Revolutionary Detail Work*, 1928), meanwhile, Bauer ascribed the ability to comprehend historic lines of development to outstanding individuals, while denying that the masses possessed such a quality. Similarly, he believed that only outstanding individuals were capable of utilising acquired knowledge to give direction to historical events. The role of great men was to lead mass movements, yet the subject of the historical process was always the masses themselves. At most, leaders can channel the energy of the masses, but they cannot trigger it, for it matures spontaneously in the course of historical development. It was not Louis Bonaparte who changed history, but the peasant masses who were insufficiently informed about the socio-political situation and the aims of the battles they fought. They therefore supported Bonaparte against their objective class interest.[50] Actually existing social classes, groups, and layers that could be captured by empirical research, not groups that merely exist as theoretical categories, carried the collective

---

48   Leser 1979, p. 31. Compare Kulemann 1979, p. 260.

49   Kulemann writes about this too (Ibid.). Among Austromarxists, Max Adler and Karl
      Renner both rejected the theory of the inevitable collapse of capitalism – they took
      different premises as their starting point. Adler presumed the priority of the subjective
      over the objective factor, while Renner based his notion regarding the endurance of
      capitalism on his belief that the working class was immature and had not developed a
      proletarian class consciousness.

50   Bauer 1976m, p. 588.

subject, according to Bauer. That is why he – unlike the other representatives
of Austromarxism, Max Adler and Karl Renner – did not define the working
class as a term, but pointed to subjective and objective economic, sociological and political factors which determined the position of a class in society.[51]
The most crucial among these factors, according to Bauer, were the position
of a class within the production process and distribution of goods, its numbers, strength, intensity and degree of organisation, level of education, political
activity, and, ultimately, its ability to conceive an ideology.[52] In the 1926 Programme of Linz, Bauer drew on two distinct meanings of the term 'working
class'. He used it more narrowly to denote the large-scale industrial proletariat
(this use can also be found in the writings of Marx, Engels, Lenin and Luxemburg), and more broadly to encompass all waged workers.[53] Interestingly, he
did not comment on the diversification of the working class into various layers. In my view, there was an ideological reason for this: the effort to preserve
before the proletarian masses the notion of a united labour movement. Nor did
Bauer explore the preconditions for the formation of classes. Like other Marxists of his time, he focused his attention on the 'class for itself', i.e. a class that
is conscious of its distinct interests, develops its own ideology, and builds its

---

51   Max Adler regarded social classes as a socio-historical category. By this, he meant a group
     of humans conscious that they form an interest group; their position in the social struc-
     ture is defined by their participation in the social process of production – see M. Adler
     1925, pp. 63–5. Karl Renner used the term as follows: 'Individuals of the same or related
     social status, whom we at first conceive individually, are driven together by the similarity
     of their conditions. They gradually learn to self-perceive as a community, and finally estab-
     lish a common organisation. In order to differentiate them, we call them social groups,
     and, as soon as they come into hostile conflict with each other, *social classes*' (our trans-
     lation). Original: 'Individuen gleicher oder verwandter sozialer Stellung, vorerst jedes für
     sich erfasst, werden durch die Gleichartigkeit der Lage zusammengetrieben, lernen sich
     allmählich als Gemeinschaft fühlen und geben sich zum Schluss eine gemeinsame Organ-
     isation. Wir nennen sie unterscheidend *soziale Gruppen* und sobald sie gegeneinander in
     feindselige Abgrenzung geraten, *soziale Klassen*' – Renner 1952, p. 111. Renner's definition
     had a subjective psychological character and did not comprise economic criteria.
52   Bauer 1976c, p. 346.
53   The term 'working class' is unclear in Marx's work. Kołakowski noticed this, and, according
     to Andrzej Flis, so did Stanisław Ossowski, Bertell Ollman and Sidney Hook. Hook writes:
     'Marx uses the term "class" ambiguously ... In some instances, the criterion of differenti-
     ation is the role in the production system exercised by a group. In others, it is the group
     members' entire way of life – including their culture and tradition – their source or level
     of income, profession, or, in case of unemployment, the lack of any profession' (our trans-
     lation) – compare Flis 1990, p. 30.

own apparatuses such as parties and trade unions. It becomes obvious here that Bauer reduced the meaning of the subjective factor to the concept of social consciousness, and he considered political consciousness its most significant type. He thoroughly analysed its development as an indispensable component of the class struggle, and, furthermore, deemed it one of the most crucial factors of the revolutionary process. Like Kautsky, and Marx too, Bauer conceived of the transformation of a 'class in itself' into a 'class for itself' as a gradual and lengthy process, which nonetheless pointed in one direction only. He regarded the conflict of economic interests and its extrapolations (political, cultural, and national interests), class struggles, and knowledge of the laws and tendencies of social evolutionary development as determinants of this process. According to Bauer, the formation of this type of consciousness was traceable to processes in the economic structure of societies – yet at the same time, he stressed that it evolved in the course of the historical process. He distinguished between four stages of development in that process:

1. During the first stage, an occupational notion of solidarity emerges; this occurs during the initial phase of working-class organisation at the level of different economic branches.
2. The second is a transitional stage between occupational and class solidarity. The proletariat achieves it during its volatile struggle against other classes. As with the previous one, this stage is devoid of historical self-consciousness. It is worth noting that Bauer merely spoke of the tendency of the working class of one particular nation state to unite. Because of the scramble for the labour market under capitalism, he regarded international solidarity as problematic.
3. Thirdly, the organisational stage of the working class in parties and trade unions struggling for economic and social reforms within the legal and institutional framework of the capitalist state. During this stage, the working and middle classes are too weak to seize state power. Hence, they depend on finding advocates of their ideology among all progressive forces in society. It is here that Bauer underestimated how alien ideologies might negatively affect proletarian class consciousness.
4. During the final stage, the working class understands that the conflict between their interests and those of other social groups and classes is irreconcilable; it demonstrates that it is prepared to wage a struggle for economic and political state power.

Bauer's reconstruction of historical stages within the development of proletarian political consciousness was significant to the theory of revolution, of which 'education towards socialism' was a component. For Marx, the proletariat's achievement of revolutionary consciousness was synonymous with the emergence of self-knowledge and therefore with the historical process itself, for in practice, the recognition of the sources of oppression meant its abolition. Lukács wrote about this in a similar vein.[54] Nonetheless, many leading theoreticians of the Second International – Kautsky, Plekhanov, Lenin, Karl Vorländer and Gramsci among them – were sceptical as to whether the political and revolutionary maturity of the working class could develop spontaneously. Even before Bernstein's appearance, history demonstrated, firstly, that the economically exploited and politically disenfranchised proletariat did not develop a revolutionary consciousness. Secondly, that a deteriorating situation resulted in apathy, while an improved situation increased the workers' susceptibility to reformist and anti-revolutionary slogans. Bauer held the opinion that the proletariat left to itself was incapable of achieving a level of theoretical consciousness, i.e. consciousness of the laws and mechanisms that determined social development, and the capitalist formation in particular. Hence, Bauer stuck to the judgement also made by Kautsky, Lenin and Gramsci that consciousness needed to be brought into the ranks of the working class 'from the outside'. Despite that, he did not endorse their method of engaging in agitational activity. Bauer also came out against the notion that it was the task of the bourgeois intelligentsia (Kautsky, Plekhanov, Vorländer and Gramsci) or party bureaucrats (Lenin) to raise revolutionary consciousness. He rightly feared that the propaganda war would degenerate into a scramble for political leadership or personal gain. Together with Max Adler, Bauer developed his own concept for spreading revolutionary consciousness among the working masses, drawing on ideas of education from Immanuel Kant, Johann Herder, and Wilhelm von Humboldt. The task of raising 'new man' (a term coined by Max Adler) would be entrusted to educational and cultural institutions, and the intelligentsia, party members, and workers would participate in their efforts. Interestingly, the Social Democrats seemed to use the terms 'theoretical consciousness', 'revolutionary consciousness', and 'socialist consciousness' interchangeably, as if they were one and the same – nor were Bauer and the Social Democrats of his time aware of any problems with the idea of introducing socialism 'from without'. It is worth remembering that this question was far from obvious in light of Marxian theory. One may conclude from Marx's assertion that 'social being determines social consciousness' that only socialist relations of production can facilitate the development of socialist consciousness. Hence, one can hardly

---

54   See Lukács 1971, p. 76.

expect such consciousness to evolve in a capitalist social formation, unless as an artificial intellectual construct. The only knowledge one can carry into the working class is the explanation of the reasons for its oppression and the mechanisms of historical evolution as revealed by Marxism.

In his outstanding historical study *Der Kampf um Wald und Weide* (*The Struggle for Woods and Pastures*, 1925), Bauer ascribed the emergence of social classes and polarisation of capitalist society to the antagonistic structure of capitalist relations of production – circumstances that would inevitably lead to social revolution. The mode of existence in capitalist societies was the class struggle, its objective necessity determined by conflicts in people's material sphere of life. Bauer regarded the contradiction between divergent economic interests as the driving factor behind human activity; he also considered the national component, although he viewed this as less essential. Furthermore, he looked into other elements of the class struggle – that is, elements of the primordial (biological, geographical, demographical) kind. Much like Karl Renner, he took his cue from Social Darwinism, interpreting the class struggle as a form of the individual's fight for survival within social structures. Bauer believed that the proletarian struggle against the bourgeoisie followed the pattern of natural processes – a viewpoint that left no room for a dialectical perspective of development. On what, then, is the mechanism behind proletarian struggle against the bourgeoisie based? Bauer strictly ascribed it to the economic base, linking capitalism's phases of boom to the economic and political victories of the proletariat – and economic collapse to the failure of the class struggle. The claim that the class struggle had no continuous character and did not gradually intensify served as the Social-Democratic party's argument to justify political defeats.

The Austrian socialists believed that the working class had to wage an economic and social struggle for emancipation in order to defend its interests. The specificity of the Austromarxist concept concerned the means and methods: the struggle between the right-wing majority, which pleaded for the unity of classes, the centre, which favoured parliamentary means of struggle, and the left, which advocated the armed insurrection, intensified during World War I (we will investigate this question more closely when discussing political thought). In this debate, Bauer consistently argued that methods depend on the objective conditions of struggle. While insisting that the working class should use democratic means into the 1920s, he changed his mind in view of the fascisisation of Austria, conceding that the proletariat must employ revolutionary methods if it is to defeat the fascist dictatorship.

Bauer authored sharp analyses of the class struggles in Austria, including the struggle of the peasantry against aristocratic landowners since the fourteenth century, the bourgeoisie against the aristocracy, the petty bourgeoisie against the bourgeoisie during capitalism's transition from its liberal to its monopolistic phase, and the proletariat against the bourgeoisie during the early days of imperialism. His study led to the following conclusions: the history of class struggle determines the course of history in general. The class struggle constitutes the basis for historical progress, as every class struggling for its emancipation and against the outmoded, decrepit elements of the existing system strives to obtain a higher level of rationality, morality and culture. Therefore, the class struggle always has the features of a struggle for values. True to his scientistic perspective, Bauer, like Max Adler, assumed a position of axiological determinism, according to which the dissemination of values – rather than conflicting material interests – was the source of progress. The author of *The Struggle for Power* borrowed the idea that historical progress had a continuous and unidirectional character from positivism. In its struggle against the bourgeoisie and for its liberation, the proletariat was the successor of all progressive classes in history. Bauer believed that the struggle of the working class represented the final and highest stage of class struggle. The proletariat stood for a classless society that would return freedom to the individual. It was therefore the only class whose sectional interest was consistent with the common interest. Socialism was, according to Bauer, not only a necessity, but also an ethical goal to which the labour movement ought to aspire.

Much like Marx, Bauer never gave up faith in the coming of a proletarian revolution and the victory of socialism. He emphasised its historical necessity at every opportunity, not least for propagandistic value. Drawing on Marx, he pointed to three tendencies that indicated that socialism was coming: the concentration of capital; the increasing power of capital; and the numerical rise of the proletariat. However, he viewed the victory of socialism as much more than just a consequence of objective historical tendencies – his theory merged deterministic and voluntaristic elements. Bauer stressed that social will must be present as much as a historically founded tendency. The will would release mechanisms that constituted a precondition for historical change. According to Bauer, the will did not spontaneously develop as a correlation of a particular social position. Rather, it was based on recognising that the goal of the struggle represented an objectively significant moral value. If the socialist idea were to become a material force that captured the masses, it had to unite a historical and moral order in itself. This subject brings us to our discussion on the relationship between Marxism and ethics.

3 Marxism and Ethics

Bauer and the Austromarxists' views were characterised by a specific approach to ethics that developed at the turn of the nineteenth and twentieth centuries. Two opposing perspectives on evaluative assumptions and theses in Marxist theory influenced it. The first was that of Marburgian neo-Kantians, as the ethical socialists were also called. The second was the perspective coined by Kautsky, author of the 1906 paper *Ethics and the Materialist Conception of History*. Notably, anarchist attempts to propagate a 'socialism without ethics' in the 1870s – see Mikhail Bakunin's *Catechism of a Revolutionary* – and the Marxists' neglect of the ethical question, which remained apparent into the 1890s, both fed into the notion that Marx had wholly abandoned the axiological perspective.[55] For the Social-Democratic movement, however, the ethical legitimacy of socialism was of fundamental ideological and practical importance. That is why the neo-Kantian project of uniting the philosophies of Kant and Marx at an ethical level was welcomed in Social-Democratic circles.[56] Nevertheless, it provoked a sharp reply from Kautsky, who took to defending the axiological neutrality of socialism. Both positions – Kautsky's and the neo-Kantians' – will be the subject of closer investigation. The reasons for this are, firstly, that the Marburgian perspective strongly influenced Bauer's views on the place of ethics in Marxism, and secondly, because Bauer's proposition evolved in response to Kautsky's negative stance towards moral theory.

The Marburgians – Hermann Cohen, Karl Vorländer, Rudolf Stammler, Ludwig Woltmann, Franz Staudinger, and Conrad Schmidt – espoused the view that Marx had not entirely thought through his basic axiological assumptions. Their doubts as to whether it is possible to integrate individual aspirations into a system of class goals, or of society as a whole, were not wholly unjustified. The Marxist ambition to liberate humanity through revolutionary violence was also met with resistance. The Marburgians all agreed that Marxism contained no imminent theory of values that might justify the necessity of socialism. In and of itself, the historical inevitability of socialism as derived from the assumptions of Marxist theory says nothing about its moral value. It is not clear why

---

55 It is not the subject of this work to decide if, and to what extent, such a perspective is immanent in Marxism. However, I am inclined to the view that an evaluative orientation is a fundamental component of the Marxian theory of socio-economic progress.

56 At the turn of the nineteenth and twentieth centuries, numerous articles about the socialist position on ethics and the relationship between the theories of Marx and Kant were published. On the 100th anniversary of Kant's death in 1904, the role of his philosophy was particularly emphasised.

the working class should aspire to socialism in the name of society as a whole. According to the ethical socialists, it was impossible to prove the historical and moral necessity of socialism based on Marx's theory of social development. Historical materialism could only provide empirical knowledge about reality and thus serve as a basis for prognoses concerning social development. In his paper *Ethics of Pure Will*, Hermann Cohen went so far as to claim that it is impossible to deduce an ethical ideal from the empirical notion of society employed in Marx's work. Cohen proposes to introduce a transcendental understanding of society in parallel to a reality-based conception and thus establish the ideal transcendentally.[57] Let us note in advance that Bauer integrated these elements into his concept drawing on Cohen.

According to Cohen and other neo-Kantians, Marx committed two fundamental errors. His first error was the way in which he understood the relationship between economics and consciousness.[58] Because of this, he (1) downplayed the realm of ideas as an independent driving force of social life, (2) traced back ideas to the material conditions of human life in historical-materialist fashion, and (3) conceived ideas in the spirit of positivism and ascribed to them a psychological or social colouring. In their critique of Marx, the neo-Kantians asserted that ideas such as the good in man, justice, and freedom, had transcendental features, i.e. they were purely moral principles with regulative power.[59] Marx's second fundamental error was linked to the fact that he, fol-

---

57   There are pre-established, transcendental social bonds at the basis of a society thus conceived, which, in turn, are determined by the sphere of common moral goals. This double approach to conceiving of society means that there also exists an ethical society aside from the society made up of producers of consumer goods: i.e. a human community that has free, autonomous, natural goals. While the former view is determined by economic principles, the latter is based on a formal moral principle rooted in the idea of humaneness as a goal in itself – see Cohen 1910, p. 223.

58   In neo-Kantianism, Rudolf Stammler attempted to reverse the Marxian relationship between economics and law. See Stammler 1896 and 1920.

59   Karl Vorländer writes: 'The transcendental ideology leads to a system of cognition that is not a principle, but which is indeed an indicative target towards which one can plan' (our translation). Original: 'Die transzendentale Ideenlehre führt auf eine *Systematik* der Erkenntnis, die zwar kein Prinzip ist, von dem sich das Besondere ableiten kann, wohl aber ein Richtziel, auf das hin *projektiert* werden kann' – Vorländer 1955, p. 374. One might add the following: a social history of origins, or else the reality of an idea, cannot be found, because being and the ideal are two different forms of appearance: one is an objectivation of nature; the other is an objectivation of the mind. Being is a fact that is accessible to scientific experience, while the ideal is a fact that is accessible to philosophic realisation. The opposition between the two is a permanent factor in integrally conceived

lowing Hegel, negated the dualism of *Sein* (being) and *Sollen* (ought), i.e. what is and what ought to be. Furthermore, he suspended the opposition between causal and teleological perspectives on which the socialist idea as a principle of objective must be based. A consequence of the Marxian idea was that the scope of the causal principle was illegitimately applied to the sphere of morality, where, according to the ethical socialists, the teleological principle applied. Based on their own assumptions, the Marburgians attempted to reconcile the opposition between the two methods drawing on a core thesis of their philosophical system, namely the ontological unity of subject and object. Because of this, they viewed both principles as general laws of human consciousness. Moreover, they regarded the principle of causality as a method of regulating scientific cognition, and the teleological principle as one of practical cognition. In their understanding, the two principles were not only reconcilable, but also complementary, as they pertained to different realms of existence. Cohen based this argument on the claim that the real play of forces and moral ideas are types of pure consciousness – hence, there was no basis to differentiate between the two as Marxism had done.[60] From these claims, Cohen – and later his disciples – drew a far-reaching conclusion: if one adequately modified historical materialism (i.e. idealistically), one could merge it with the viewpoint of Kantianism without contradictions. Thus, it would become possible to rectify Marxism's fundamental error, i.e. the lack of an independent and creative role for ethical ideas. For this purpose, it is sufficient to complement Marxism with Kant's ethical ideal.

Before we continue, let us note that the Marburgians' efforts to employ Kantian ethics to justify socialism played the most crucial role in Bauer's ethical considerations. In their view, the neo-Kantians attempted to invoke Kant's theses that prefigured socialist ideas and demonstrated unity in the mode of thought. The Marburg School's most passionate proponent of uniting the theories of Kant and Marx was Karl Vorländer, who was closest to the Social-Democratic movement among neo-Kantians.[61] Vorländer viewed Kant as the

---

experience. Maria Szyszkowska interestingly depicts the neo-Kantian critique of Marxism in Szyszkowska 1970, pp. 78–87.

60   See Cohen 1921, p. 39.

61   The author of a series of lectures about socialism at the University of Münster in 1914, co-author of the Social-Democratic Party of Germany's Görlitz programme of 1912. He dedicated a separate text to the relationship between the theories of Kant and Marx – see Vorländer 1926. In another text, he observed: 'The way of liberalism, in the true sense of the word, leads not just historically, but also logically to Marx' (our translation) – Vorländer 1920, p. 46.

forerunner of German socialism. For them, Kant's and Marx's ideals of the state, the democratic ideals contained in their respective theories, and their negative attitude towards colonialism, militarism, and privileges grounded in birthright – i.e. landed property – testified to a substantial convergence in their thinking.[62] However, his argument carried far more weight on an ethical level. In fact, Vorländer thought that the Marxian 'association, in which the free development of each is the condition for the free development of all' was analogous to the Kantian 'community of men of free will' as a goal in and of itself. This convergence provided sufficient reason to seek principles for the socialist movement in Kant's ethics. They were impossible to deduce from the materialist view of history, which was limited to analysing economic phenomena and explaining the world in terms of cause and effect. Kantian ethics, in contrast, accepted reason – defined by its general and objectively valid requirements – as a foundation for morality. It stressed the universality and timelessness of ethical principles.

In accordance with Kant, the Marburgians assumed that morality had a universal, timeless character and encompassed all human beings. At the same time, they argued that the socialist idea must be based on morality conceived in this way. That is to say, the question on how far the system of the future would live up to their requirements – i.e. general justice, equality, and freedom – could only be answered with reference to universal and general ethical ideas that could not be relativised. These ideas defined the general validity of moral values and made for a paradigm according to which a desired social model could be shaped. Hence, the Marburgians concluded that the pursuit of socialism must rest on conscious, rational will, meaning it had to be a postulate of practical reason. The idea of socialism, then, was purely regulatory: 'The social ideal is merely a formal method with which to govern and judge the empirically intruding material of historical justice and social will according to the communal idea. This idea serves as the fundamental law of human purpose' (our translation).[63] For the Marburgians, one question mattered the most: why should socialism be the one crucial goal of social struggle and objective of moral aspiration? Their answer was, essentially, that socialism ought to be considered an aim in and of itself, because it represented an ethical ideal. It could also serve as a basis for a social order that had overcome the contradiction

62 Compare Kołakowski 2005, pp. 556–7.
63 'Das soziale Ideal bezeichnet lediglich eine formale Methode, den empirisch sich aufdrängenden Stoff des geschichtlichen Rechtes, des sozialen Wollens nach dem Gemeinschaftsgedanken als dem Grundgesetz der menschlichen Zwecke zu leiten und zu richten' – Stammler 1896, quoted from Vorländer 1926, p. 132.

between sectional and common interests, and granted the same degree of freedom to every individual (the Kantian ethical community of a 'purposeful state',
a *Zweckstaat*). Vorländer, Woltmann and Conrad Schmidt were all convinced
that the formula of the categorical imperative was congruent with the central
idea of socialism.[64] The moral necessity of socialism, argued the Marburgians,
was a duty placed upon us by the categorical imperative. This duty was not
subject to the passage of time, as it was rooted in autonomous reason. Socialist morality could not be taken as a given, nor could it be adopted once and
for all, but was a system of values that had to be continuously fought for. The
formalism implicit in the neo-Kantians' conception excluded the possibility of
establishing a general ethical law through gradual moral transition. Ethical values were merely goals for the socialist movement to orientate itself towards –
they possessed the quality of postulates only in the Kantian sense. The question as to how they should be obtained (indeed, their complete fulfilment was
impossible) was of little interest to the Marburgians. As can be seen in their
statements, they did not believe that the fight of the working class to bring
about a new socio-economic system would decide over the demise of capitalism and arrival of socialism. Rather, this would occur when the people became
conscious of their longing for freedom and collective respect of justice. According to the Marburgians, the socialised ownership of the means of production
would provide the legal foundation to regulate co-operation between human
beings in socialism. In contrast to Marx's position, though in accordance with
the idealist basic assumptions of their own system, they did not view socialisation as the core of the new system, but as a tool to change consciousness.[65]

---

64   Schmidt writes: 'It is quite clear that this type of ethical-social idealism, which is otherwise
      completely independent of Kant's specifically rationalist moral philosophy, and whose
      principle ultimately derives from the freedom and development interest of the species,
      is not necessarily – as one would think – a cloud-cuckoo-land outlook that puts its trust
      in the sheer persuasive appeal of the ideal' (our translation) – Vorländer 1926, p. 167.
      According to Woltmann, the socialist idea, 'same rights and duties regardless of sex and
      ancestry', corresponds to Kant's idea of a general legislation that embodies the highest
      moral principle – see Woltmann 1974, p. 116.
65   Compare Szyszkowska 1970, p. 87. Hans-Jörg Sandkühler, a German philosopher at the
      University of Bremen, criticised the ethical position of the neo-Kantians sharply: 'To sac-
      rifice a historical perspective in favour of an anthropological or metaphysical restitution
      of reason as substance is not without consequences: it involves limiting ethics to a formal
      transcendental theory of morality. (...) The material abstractness of the "categorical imper-
      ative", which is inadequate for the political requirements of socialism, makes clear that
      neo-Kantian ethics, as a theory of ought, was unable to fulfil its purpose as a complement
      to Marxism because it insufficiently considered Marxism' (our translation) – Sandkühler

Marburgian neo-Kantianism made an impact upon Marxist theory due to the writings and speeches of the founder of revisionism, Eduard Bernstein. While the idea of merging Marx and Kant was alien to him, he certainly shared the neo-Kantians' view that it was necessary to distinguish between being and ought. Bernstein criticised Marx from this standpoint, claiming that there was a descriptive and axiological incoherence to Marx's theory, i.e. it presented socialism as an impartial science, yet also a moral ideal that social movements were striving to accomplish. In Bernstein's view, the contradiction between science and practice that arose on the ground of this theory was a result of the legacy of utopian thought, but, above all, a consequence of the adopted materialist worldview. Frankly, Bernstein was not convinced of the validity of Marx's combination of factual claims and value judgements – as a scienticist, he did not accept value judgements as an *immanent* component of the historical process. Furthermore, he found the Marxian theory of socialism as a historical necessity unconvincing. According to Bernstein, this 'necessity' was, in fact, the result of Marx's unjustified adoption of Hegelian schemata of social development. He rejected this 'necessity': in Bernstein's interpretation of historical materialism, the emphasis was on the role of consciousness (knowledge of the mechanisms of social and historical development), will (interests), and ethics (moral knowledge) in the historical process.

The degree of acceptance that the positions of Bernstein and the ethical socialists enjoyed in intellectual circles and among Marxists, prompted the stalwarts of Marxist orthodoxy – Kautsky, Franz Mehring, and Plekhanov – to investigate the question of ethics in Marxism thoroughly. Voicing his convictions in *Ethics and the Materialist Conception of History*, Kautsky in particular regarded it as a matter of duty to defend the monistic and materialist character of Marx's theory.[66] Kołakowski, Waldenberg and Rudziński already subjected the interpretation of ethics that he accomplished in this text to closer ana-

---

1974, p. 42. Of course, Sandkühler is correct in saying that the marriage of Kantian ethics and Marxism is theoretically useful to explain the ethical foundations of Marx's theory. Let us note, however, that Marx did not create any ethics as such. Moreover, his analysis of formations clearly indicates that his adopted perspective uncompromisingly linked historical with moral progress. Marx sacrificed the concept of alienation that was present in his early work. The texts of the Marxist theorists of the Second International – the period during which neo-Kantianism took hold – confused, rather than clarified, the question of values in Marxism. It is no surprise, then, that scientists from various philosophical and theoretical backgrounds disagree on this controversial point to this day.

66   See Kautsky 1910.

lysis.[67] I will therefore focus my attention on the elements that became causes of disagreement in the polemic between Kautsky and Bauer.

Kautsky did not acknowledge that a transcendental world might exist beside the empirical world. Nor did he, like the neo-Kantians and Austromarxists, think of the epistemology of values as a philosophical question. Rather, he thought that it was only possible to solve the question of value judgement by researching the real historical and social process. Kautsky negated the dualism of being and ought, arguing that by investigating the causal relationship, the question of morality could be resolved in the sphere of experience. In other words, it was necessary to find out why humans make one moral choice instead of another under given conditions. Hence, he considered the descriptive-genetic explanatory mode as the only correct approach to the value question. As is well-known, Kautsky only granted the status of a science to descriptive ethics, while placing normative ethics entirely outside the scientific realm. Like the Austromarxists, he was sceptical about the scientificity of normative reflection, even if their starting points were different: Kautsky assumed the unity of knowledge on values and facts, whereas the Austromarxists held the opposite view.

For Kautsky, the socio-historical process was an extension of the processes occurring in nature. He therefore believed that early forms of morality could be found in the animal world. Darwin demonstrated that the struggle for survival among social animals and humans produced drives and instincts that regulated relationships between humans in communities and served the survival of the species. Basing his theory on Darwin's findings, Kautsky transferred the social drive from the animal world directly onto the world of humans, thus tracing the roots of morality back to the natural essence of humanity. However, his line of argument was certainly not free of naturalistic simplifications. Indeed, Kautsky assumed that the struggle for survival guaranteed the continuation of human history, which depended on three fundamental innate drives that originated in the animal world: the self-preservation, reproductive, and social drives. The emergence of the social drive, which was decisive for the development of morality, originated in the earliest forms of organisation based on animal and human struggle for survival. Material conditions forced humans to adopt moral norms to regulate social life (Kautsky draws a veil of silence over the fact that normative agreements might have preceded these moral norms). One might conclude from Kautsky's contemplations that moral law is rooted in the social

---

67   Compare Kołakowski 2005, pp. 382–6; Waldenberg 1976, pp. 144–6; Rudziński 1975, pp. 48–
       65.

drive, which, essentially, is of the same character as the self-preservation and reproductive drive. Kautsky wrote:

> Because the moral law is the universal instinct, of equal force to the instinct of self preservation and reproduction, thence its force, thence its power which we obey without thought, thence our rapid decisions, in particular cases, whether an action is good or bad, virtuous or vicious; thence the energy and decision of our moral judgement, and thence the difficulty to prove it when reason begins to analyse its grounds. Then one finally finds that to comprehend all means to pardon all, that everything is necessary, that nothing is good and bad.[68]

One may notice that Kautsky did not attempt to explain here, or anywhere else in *Ethics*, the criteria upon which to judge actions. Nor did he disclose the principles humans should adopt so that their actions might be morally condoned. One can therefore assume that he preferred standards of action beneficial to human development. He was not convinced that behavioural norms had a transhistorical or universal character, a quality he attributed only to biological factors. Moral norms, in contrast, depended on the mode of production and technological progress. According to Kautsky, they were determined by the class structure of society.

Kautsky reiterated Marx's idea: economic development goes hand in hand with intensifying class contradictions, leading to the emergence of a new social class. Its victory in the class struggle is synonymous with the formation of a new morality. Even so, this new morality does not set, according to Kautsky, any new objectives; its role is limited to negating the existing morality. Goals of action cannot be deduced from ethical ideals since such a position would presuppose an extra-empirically existing ideal. As to the relationship between consciousness and social being, Kautsky also championed a Marxian perspective. He looked at three aspects of this relation: ontological (consciousness as

---

68   'Weil das Sittengesetz ein tierischer Trieb ist, der den Trieben der Selbsterhaltung und
       Fortpflanzung ebenbürtig, deshalb seine Kraft, deshalb sein Drängen, dem wir ohne Über-
       legen gehorchen, deshalb unsere rasche Entscheidung in einzelnen Fällen, ob eine Hand-
       lung gut oder böse, tugendhaft oder lasterhaft; deshalb die Entschiedenheit und Ener-
       gie unseres sittlichen Urteils, und deshalb die Schwierigkeit, es zu begründen, wenn die
       Vernunft anfängt, die Handlungen zu zergliedern und nach ihren Gründen zu fragen.
       Dann findet man schließlich, dass alles begreifen alles verzeihen heißt, dass alles not-
       wendig, nicht gut oder böse ist' – Kautsky 1906, pp. 63–4, compare Kautsky 1909, pp. 97–
       8.

a product of social being); objective (consciousness as a reflection of material conditions of existence); and functional (ideas and values disseminated at a certain level of social development are determined by the class structure). Consequently, he assumed that goals grew out of the historical process itself. Individuals could judge their actions as good or bad, but the objective value of such a judgement depends on whether their actions corresponded to norms and goals established by the practice of the class at the time. With reference to the revolutionary potential of the class, Kautsky regarded the struggle of the proletariat and its class consciousness as the most important ethical factors in the historical process. Furthermore, although Kautsky was an advocate of moral relativism, he viewed the goals of the proletariat from the perspective of axiological universalism: the class interest of the proletariat determined universal human values and goals in the long term. Therefore, science (Marxism) decided what goals were adequate under existing conditions, and the class struggle decided how these goals were to be achieved. The socialist idea contained a vision of the liberation of the proletariat, yet this necessity, according to Kautsky, had no moral value. As Kołakowski and Rudziński pointed out, the theory outlined above in no way explained why that which is historically necessary should be desired by the people, nor why it is morally justified.[69]

The theses developed in *Ethics and the Materialist Conception of History* triggered an immediate reaction on the part of Bauer and Max Adler (in an article in 1906). The Austromarxists concurred with Kautsky that all social developments, including all moral developments, were determined by changes in the realm of production and technology – yet they did not accept this as a sufficient solution to the ethical question. Quite rightly, they accused Kautsky of anthropologism with respect to his conception of the animal world. Criticising the limitations of historical materialism, they observed that, even though it helped to gain knowledge about changes in social practices, it could only demonstrate changes in the content of values and point to the reasons for the withering away of old values and the birth of new ones. Hence, Kautsky merely revealed that the emergence and change of moral norms and ethical ideals were socio-historically determined. Yet the real ethical problem starts beyond these genetic observations. As Adler wrote: 'The material conditions do not produce the ethical ideal; they only give it historical content. They determine how it will be implemented'.[70] For the Austromarxists, the primary

---

69   See Kołakowski 2005, p. 385, and Rudziński 1975, p. 65.
70   'Die materiellen Bedingungen schaffen also nicht das sittliche Ideal, sondern sie geben

reference point was the opposition between being and ought, rather than the coexistence of different values in society. They aptly pointed out that an ethics that contented itself with describing modes of moral behaviour did not offer any criteria for moral behaviour. The mere observation that humans make one choice or another under certain conditions did not say whether that choice was right or wrong. Bauer and Adler's critique of Kautsky revealed another important contradiction: on the one hand, Kautsky deduced a moral ideal from the class struggle. Yet at the same time, he recognised the interaction of frequently opposed moral ideals, all of which were rooted in the position of the respective classes. This left open the question as to which of these ideals one should endorse if there were no objective criteria for judging their validity.

To illustrate the poverty of naturalist ethics and to prove the necessity of normative ethical reflection in Marxism, Bauer constructed the example of an unemployed worker who contemplates whether he has the right to become a strikebreaker when his family's livelihood is under threat. When individual interest conflicts with class interest, Bauer argued, Kautskyan arguments – such as 'the struggle for existence triggers social drives from which the moral law emerges', 'the proletariat is a force that enters the stage of history embodying the highest morality, as well as the future', or 'socialism will come by virtue of the necessary laws of social development' – did not help to determine the worker's moral duty. In Bauer's opinion, Kautsky's theory did not offer a justification for a proletarian ethics. This led the Austromarxist to pose a more general and fundamental question: did the theory of socialism contain a valid criterion for moral judgement? Could Marxism ethically justify socialism at all? Here, Bauer brought another important element into the open: if Marxism was to serve as a theory for the conscious change of reality, then it had to contain normative judgements pointing to objective criteria by which the validity of actions might be judged. He solved this problem in a Kantian spirit, drawing on a simplified form of the Marburgians' arguments.

As mentioned earlier, Bauer, inspired by Kantianism, argued in favour of a dualism between being and ought and the differentiation between the knowledge of values and the knowledge of facts.[71] The latter belonged to the sphere

---

ihm nur den geschichtlichen Inhalt, sie entscheiden über die Art seiner Realisierung' – M. Adler 1913, p. 135.

71   In *Marxismus und Ethik* (*Marxism and Ethics*, 1906), he wrote: 'The matter of imperatives belongs to the historian's field of research – in this, the materialist conception of history is the guideline of research. Even there, however, Kant turns to the formal law of morality. His task is completely different from that of a historian. Because he operates in a different

of experience and science – and, according to Bauer, '[t]here is no such thing as a science of ought'.[72] Max Adler took a similar view, arguing that Marxism was a casuistic science.[73] According to him, such a model of science did not offer any ethical justification of politics, nor did it set any guidelines for practical action. Marx's analysis of changes in moral consciousness merely demonstrated the relativity and historical changeability of ethical phenomena, while not saying anything about the justification for moral behaviour. In short, Marxism was ethically neutral and did not contain any moral guidelines. For Bauer, it was only possible to solve the moral question by adopting the formalism of the moral ideal. Hence, insights of Kant's practical philosophy that substantiated the formal correctness of ethics and offered a basis for moral judgement were, in his view, of crucial importance to Marxism. The Kantian categorical imperative, as a formal norm constituting the necessary condition for every rule, allowed for the judging of which norms functioning in society were correct.[74] Bauer notably directed his adoption of the Kantian solution against the ethical relativism favoured by the bourgeoisie of his time. In this context, it also had an ideological function: it demonstrated that Marxism, complemented by Kantianism, offered the working class a clear and indisputable criterion for moral judgement. Bauer argued that Kant had provided the normative groundwork for a proletarian ethics – although for him, this was not synonymous with solving the most important question that faced the workers' movement. The real problem was to figure out how Kant's categorical imperative could be utilised as an efficient instrument of political action in the proletarian struggle for

---

field, he does not meet with the materialist conception of history at any point. For Kant, it is necessary to discover the formal law of all ought, whatever his subject matter' (our translation) – 'Die Materie der Imperative gehört zum Forschungsgebiet des Historikers, hier ist die materialistische Geschichtsauffassung Leitfaden der Forschung. Kant aber wendet sich auch hier wieder der formalen Gesetzlichkeit des Sittlichen zu. Seine Aufgabe ist eine ganz andere als die des Historikers und er kann, da er sich auf einem anderen Gebiet bewegt, mit der materialistischen Geschichtsauffassung in keinem Punkte zusammenstoßen. Für Kant gilt es, die formale Gesetzlichkeit alles Sollens, welches immer seine Materie sein mag, zu entdecken' – Bauer 1979e, pp. 880–1.

72   'Eine Wissenschaft vom Sollen gibt es nicht' – Bauer 1979e, p. 874.

73   See M. Adler 1978, pp. 76–7.

74   Kautsky was not fully content with Bauer's solution. In his reply, he conceded that his ethics did not offer a criterion to unite contradictory interests, i.e. individual and collective interests. However, he far from agreed with Bauer that the problem could be solved by a formal principle. Rather, he thought that one had to investigate the social causes of conflict, and, furthermore, assess the possibilities of a solution by drawing on scientific insights gained from earlier experiences. See Kautsky 1983, pp. 48–9.

socialism. Bauer did not strive for originality in addressing this question. Noting that the problem had already been solved convincingly by the Marburgian neo-Kantians, he simply reiterated their statements. Essentially, they claimed that the content of the categorical imperative was congruent with the content of the socialist ideal: during the struggle for socialism, the working class aspired to attain the goals set by Kantian ethics. However, it would be wrong to conclude that Bauer adopted the Marburgian ethical position in its entirety. What he had in common with the neo-Kantians was the notion of a dichotomy between the formal and material elements in ethics, and the ethical justification for socialism, including the claim that values had the status of transcendental ideas. On whether there was a historical necessity to socialism, however, Bauer took a different view. He rightly noted that the Marburgian concept lacked a unifying element between the universal, super-temporal ideal and reality – it was the price at which they had abandoned the dualism of being and ought at their very point of departure. Bauer started with the same assumption, yet unlike the neo-Kantians, he was too weak a philosopher to realise that it was impossible to integrate formally defined goals into social life. He believed that it would be enough for the working class to recognise that the crown of historical development indicated by Marx, the socialist state order, embodied the Kantian ideals. This way, it would discover in Kantian ethics the principles towards which the socialist movement should orientate itself in the class struggle. Bauer did not wish to acknowledge two problems. Firstly, for Marx, communism was a condition that society would usher in. Rather than being an ideal according to which reality would be shaped, it was a real movement that would abolish the capitalist system due to the objective laws of historical development. This also included ideas to the extent that the masses identified with them. Secondly, Kant's ethics affirmed the ideals of enlightenment humanism and did not have a specifically socialist content. Moreover, their formalist perspective bore no relation to the fundamental assumptions of historical materialism. Bauer's was a proverbial attempt to unite fire and water: two different perspectives based on different premises and different theoretical and philosophical assumptions. His attempt to provide the foundations for a normative ethics in Marxism was not particularly fruitful.

Let us consider another important element in Bauer's theory: his desire to incorporate Kantianism into Marxism was linked to a judgemental interpretation of socialism. He regarded the socialist order as twofold: sociological (a classless society of producers) and axiological (a social order that grants individuals general and equal participation in social, political, and cultural life). Bauer gave absolute priority to the latter dimension. However, he did not assume that the socialist order would emancipate humans completely. In this respect, his judgement was close to Marx's: as long as the economic compulsion to work persisted, there could be no talk of full freedom.[75] Bauer referred to a Hegelian motive that was also present in Marx: freedom as a prerequisite for the realisation of subjectivity. Socialism was, according to this concept, not just a political order under which social and class inequality had been abolished, the division of labour had vanished, and a prosperous society indulging in consumer goods (*à la* Lafargue) had emerged. It was also a socio-political order that returned freedom to the individual – that is, freedom in a Kantian sense in the sphere of ethics, and freedom as a democratic ideal in the sphere of politics:

> We must counter Prussianism with a different state idea that is genuinely, radically opposed to it: a socialism rooted in the individual's urge for freedom, originating in the self-activity of the masses, and aiming for the self-government of all working people … Nothing is more essential to German socialism than an element of true democracy with individualistic roots, which seeks its realisation in the English notion of industrial self-government, i.e. social transformation through the self-activity and self-education of the masses.[76]
>
> our translation

Bauer, like many socialists of his time, faced a serious dilemma: how could one preserve the culture and democratic achievements of an earlier period, while at the same time supporting the proletariat's struggle to shake off its socio-political yoke? Marx's theory, which made a point of the necessity of revolutionary violence, was at odds with the basic premise of its ethical standpoint, i.e. the defence of individual freedom. A solution to this dilemma was contained in the 'third' way to socialism, the key component of the Austromarxist notion of revolution. We will investigate this in the fifth chapter.

---

75   Marx 1959, p. 820.

76   'Wir müssen dem Preußentum eine andere, ihm wirklich radikal entgegengesetzte Staatsidee entgegenstellen: einen Sozialismus, dessen Wurzel der Freiheitsdrang des Individuums, dessen Quelle die Selbsttätigkeit der Masse, dessen Ziel das selfgovernment aller Werktätigen ist. (…) Nichts tut dem deutschen Sozialismus dringender not als ein Einschlag jener echten, aus individualistischer Wurzel entsprossenen Demokratie, die im englischen Gedanken des industrial selfgovernment der sozialen Umgestaltung durch die Selbsttätigkeit und Selbsterziehung der Masse, ihre Verwirklichung sucht' – Bauer 1976c, pp. 356–7.

CHAPTER 3

A Contribution to the Theory of Imperialism

Even as a student, Bauer took an interest in economics. In these early days, he initiated a polemic against the founders of the Austrian School of national economy.[1] He would return to these topics throughout his entire life. As a theorist, he felt compelled to investigate the degree to which the levels of development achieved by capitalism could potentially facilitate the victory of socialism. As a pragmatist, he had to consider what consequences imperialist policies would have for the working class. Many of his texts were dedicated to observations on the nature of imperialism and its perspectives, its ramifications for the proletariat, and the problem of crises.[2] Although it is difficult to assess to what extent this was intentional, his analyses became part of an argument about the breakdown (*Zusammenbruch*) of capitalism that was

---

1   As Hanisch states in *Der große Illusionist* (*The Great Illusionist*), Bauer studied economics under the tutelage of the second-generation Austrian School, Friedrich von Wieser, and Eugen von Böhm-Bawerk. When participating in a seminar by Böhm-Bawerk, he defended Marxian economics against his teacher's critique. See Hanisch 2011, p. 67.

2   These included the following articles among others: *Marx Theorie der Wirtschaftskrisen* (*Marx's Theory of Economic Crises*, 1905), *Über britischen Imperialismus* (*On British Imperialism*, 1907), *Krise und Teuerung* (*Crisis and Inflation*, 1907/8), *Österreich und der Imperialismus* (*Austria and Imperialism*, 1908), *Der Staat und die Kartelle* (*The State and Cartels*, 1908/9), *Das Finanzkapital* (*Finance Capital*, 1909/10), *Theorien über den Mehrwert* (*Theories of Surplus Value*, 1909/10), *Die Akkumulation des Kapitals* (*The Accumulation of Capital*, 1913), *Kapitalvermehrung und Bevölkerungswachstum* (*Capital Increase through Population Growth*, 1914), and *Die Wirtschaftskrise im Ausland und in Österreich* (*Economic Crisis in Austria and Abroad*, 1924). In addition, he authored the following works: *Die Teuerung. Eine Einführung in die Wirtschaftspolitik der Sozialdemokratie* (*Inflation. An Introduction to the Economic Policies of Social Democracy*, 1910), *Großkapital und Militarismus. Wem nützen die neuen Kriegsschiffe?* (*Big Capital and Militarism. Who Benefits from the New War Ships?*, 1911), *Volkswirtschaftliche Fragen* (*Questions of Political Economy*, 1921), *Die Wirtschaftskrise in Österreich. Ihre Ursachen – ihre Heilung* (*The Economic Crisis in Austria. Its Causes and its Cure*, 1925), *Zollfragen in der Lebensmittelindustrie und die Stellungnahme der Arbeiterschaft hierzu* (*Tax Problems in the Food Industry and the Response of the Working Class*, 1928), *Kapitalismus und Sozialismus nach dem Weltkrieg. Band 1 Rationalisierung – Fehlrationalisierung* (*Capitalism and Socialism after the World War. Volume One – Rationalisation and Misrationalisation*, 1931), *Zwischen zwei Weltkriegen. Die Krise der Weltwirtschaft, der Demokratie und des Sozialismus* (*Between Two World Wars. The Crisis of the World Economy, Democracy and Socialism*, 1936), *Einführung in die Volkswirtschaftslehre* (*Introduction to Political Economics*, 1956).

being waged within European Social Democracy. The crisis theory of capitalist economy was a part of that debate.

There were three sources for Bauer's theory of imperialism.[3] Marx's *Capital* served as an inspiration, though it was not the most crucial one. From *Capital*, he borrowed Marx's conceptual framework and research technique, i.e. he utilised the abstract-deductive method to theorise accumulation and analyse business cycles.[4] Moreover, he employed Marxian guidelines to investigate the historical course of phenomena and processes of social life, as well as Marx's functional-genetic explanatory model. Some elements, however, played a far more prominent role in Bauer's economic thought than the analyses contained in *Capital*: above all, his fascination with the theory of 'organised capitalism' that Rudolf Hilferding outlined in *Finance Capital* (1910).[5] Secondly, his criticisms of Rosa Luxemburg's conclusions, which he elaborated on in detail in *Accumulation of Capital* (1913).[6] Challenging Luxemburg, Bauer specifically attempted to demonstrate how wrong she had been in her judgement of the following factors:

– The character of the symptoms that accompany imperialism in the following spheres: economic (monopolisation, cartelisation, the role of bank capital), social (unemployment, impoverishment of the proletariat), and political (role of the state, militarisation);
– Limits to the development of the capitalist mode of production;

---

3   Grzegorz Kotlarski wrote: 'In the second half of the 19th century, the word "imperialism" appeared in scientific literature that explained new practical and economic phenomena of capitalism ... The term "imperialism" (Latin: *imperialis* – powerful) has English origins. In the beginning, it was used to describe a protest movement of those who advocated Great Britain's colonial policies. It was directed against the activities of the changing government cabinets, which it deemed not energetic enough, to protect the interests of colonial officials. Later, after the reforms of William Ewart Gladstone, "imperialism" referred to the consolidation politics of the British Empire. In the 1890s, it became part of the political jargon and synonymous with the politics of conquest and colonial expansion. The leading ideologues of imperialism were Benjamin Disraeli, Cecil Rhodes, and Otto Bismarck' – Kotlarski 1987, p. 142.

4   The fact that he employed the abstract-deductive method, and appealed to Marx as its pioneer, is testimony to the incoherence in his thinking. As mentioned at the beginning of the second chapter, Bauer believed Marx's method to be inductive. The reasons for this kind of inconsistency remain unclear. One can only assume that the interpretation of Marx's method present in Bauer's philosophical thought was heavily shaped by the influence of scientism.

5   See Bauer 1980c, pp. 377–99.

6   See Bauer 1986 and 1979h.

–   The crisis-prone character of the capitalist economy and factors that might
    revive it.

We shall briefly preface our reconstruction of Bauer's views on numerous
related economic problems (including tendencies in the development of the
world economy, the accumulation of capital, business cycles, possibilities of
overcoming crises, and the economic transition from capitalism to socialism).
The following general remarks are, arguably, the key to Bauer's entire observations on imperialism.

–   In economic analyses, Bauer adopted two distinct stances. Firstly, that of
    a theorist addressing a number of questions: the direction in which cap-
    italist imperialism was developing and its economic, social, and political
    consequences, the roots of crises and possibilities to prevent and counteract
    the outbreak of crises. Bauer's second stance was that of a dedicated parti-
    cipating observer who studied empirical reality, described the negative con-
    sequences of imperialism for the Habsburg monarchy, explained crises in
    Austria-Hungary (later just Austria) and sought emergency economic meas-
    ures to stop them. This internal conflict of Bauer as an economist inevitably
    shaped his analytical model. He divided his observations into purely theor-
    etical studies on the one hand, and investigations that served the everyday
    politics of the party – or were subordinated to the author's political views –
    on the other.
–   In Bauer's economic studies, his political viewpoint determined his eco-
    nomic position. His analyses were not always inventive, and occasionally
    they were erroneous. One should not treat this appraisal as a significant
    objection, given that Bauer was not a professional economist.[7] He was,
    however, an attentive observer of capitalism's developmental tendencies,
    and of the ways in which these tendencies changed the character of the state.
    He was also familiar with statistics concerning crises before 1914 and from
    1918–31, and knew the state of the European and world economies well.[8] The
    value of his analyses, which were insightful and meticulously supported by

---

7   Bauer's posthumous work, *Einführung in die Volkswirtschaftslehre* (*Introduction to Political
    Economy*, 1956), in which the author discussed the main categories of Marxian economics,
    testified to his profound knowledge of political economy.
8   Bauer's wide knowledge in these areas and erudition in economic literature are genuinely
    impressive. He was familiar with the more important economic theories, and the condition
    of the economies of Europe – especially Germany, Great Britain, and the Balkans – North
    America, and South America.

data, is most certainly a historical one, although some of Bauer's prognoses appear prophetic and relevant even today. In his historical period, it was not simply Bauer's insights that mattered, but primarily the goals they were to serve, which were crucial to discussions within the circles of European Social Democracy. As mentioned earlier, one of Bauer's goals was to refute Luxemburg's theory with his hypothesis of a 'self-defensive' capitalist economy – to be sure, an outmoded idea in today's economic science. Another was the defence of Austria's national interest, which involved the preservation of Austria's sovereignty and independence through protectionism. These goals also influenced Bauer's ideas on the transition from capitalism to socialism. What is more, they shaped his views of how the socialist state model would function in the economic sphere, i.e. as part of a centralised planned economy.

1   Imperialism as a Necessary Stage of Capitalism

With the exception of Max Adler, a determinist view of history was typical for Austromarxists. According to this perspective, socialism would emerge due to the objective laws of historical development, while Social-Democratic politics could only accelerate this historical moment. Informed by the anticipation of capitalism's inevitable breakdown, this view was popular in the Second International, but controversial in German Social Democracy in particular. According to Zenona Kluza-Wołosiewicz,[9] its roots are in Marx's theory of accumulation. Marx drew the widely recognised conclusion that there is an immanent tendency in capitalism to develop growing contradictions, which are detrimental to development and ultimately lead to its demise.[10] According to Marx, capitalism's fundamental contradiction is the concentration of the means of production in the hands of a small group versus the social character of production itself, and its inevitable consequence is a socialist revolution in which the proletariat becomes capitalism's gravedigger. For ideological rather than scientific reasons, Marx did not question the inevitability of revolution anywhere in his work. However, it is possible to find remarks warning against a mechanic interpretation of the developmental tendency of capitalism, and even doubts over Marx's own prognosis of a progressive centralisation of production.[11]

---

9   See Kluza-Wołosiewicz 1963, p. 78.

10   See Marx 1990, p. 929.

11   See Marx 1959, p. 246. One has to agree with Paul M. Sweezy when he says of Marx's eco-

The reasons as to why Marx's disciples, who lived in a different economic and social reality – capitalism had entered its imperialist phase – considered it their prime task to verify (or falsify) Marx's prognosis about the direction of capitalist development are obvious. Even then, signs were looming that Marx might have been mistaken about the route capitalism would take, which was synonymous with the demise of revolutionary theory – a pillar of the Marxian system. At the turn of the nineteenth and twentieth centuries, Bernstein's argument about the breakdown of capitalism polarised Marxist circles. Part of the controversy concerned questions surrounding crises: there were opponents of the theory of capitalism's inevitable breakdown on one side, and passionate proponents on the other. Bernstein, Mikhail Tugan-Baranovsky, Conrad Schmidt, Wolfgang Heine and Max Schippel represented the former camp, while Kautsky, Louis Boudin, Heinrich Cunow and Rosa Luxemburg were stalwarts of the latter. The dispute regarding the breakdown of capitalism, which was raging between the opposing camps from 1899–1913, raised a number of questions. Its importance for the workers' movement cannot be overestimated. Indeed, the revolutionary perspectives and strategy that Social-Democratic parties would choose depended on the conclusions drawn here.

At a factual and theoretical level, both sides in this debate based their arguments on economics. But even if Marx's economic theory provided reference points for both, their conclusions were nonetheless diametrically opposed. In a nutshell, the essence of the argument was as follows: orthodox Marxists (1) defended the proposition that production and property would be concentrated and centralised, followed by a concentration of property in commerce and agriculture; (2) emphasised how the negative impact of the monopolies and cartels intensified class antagonisms: (3) drew attention to the increasing polarisation of capitalist society into two basic social groups – capitalists and workers; (4) upheld the concept that the capitalist state has a class character; and (5) provided evidence that the theory of the impoverishment of the proletariat was still relevant. The revisionists took the adverse view on all questions. Hence their belief that capitalism had strong 'self-defensive' powers was matched at an economic level by the concept of capitalism's 'growing into socialism'. From this, they drew the practical conclusion that revolution is destructive and had to be abandoned.

As time moved on – especially following the outbreak of World War I – the controversy surrounding the breakdown of capitalism waned in importance for

nomic theory that 'nowhere in his work is there to be found a doctrine of the specifically economic breakdown of capitalist production' – Sweezy 1964, p. 192.

German Social Democracy, instead giving way to arguments concerning questions of militarism and attitudes towards war. The scarce interest in further discussion resulted not least from the fact that many former advocates of Marxist orthodoxy, Kautsky and Cunow among them, had now adopted revisionist positions. The situation in Austria was different. In the works of Austrian Social Democracy – with the exception of those of Hilferding – the rationale of an inevitable breakdown of capitalism lived on until the demise of the monarchy and the advent of economic decline. For the sake of accuracy, it is worth adding that Henryk Grossman claimed as late as 1929 that the law of capitalist breakdown was 'the fundamental law that governs and supports the entire structure of Marx's thought'.[12] This does not mean that it is impossible to find positive remarks about capitalism's endurance and ability to reform in the works of Austrian socialists from 1908–18. Bauer's writings, for instance, offer many descriptions of the self-defence mechanisms that capitalism had developed. Nevertheless, the Austromarxists dogmatically clung to the theory of capitalist breakdown up until 1918, which served the purpose of maintaining the faith of the working class in the imminent victory of socialist revolution. Let us draw attention to another significant difference between German and Austrian Social Democracy, both of which participated in the breakdown debate. In Germany, the positions were sharply divided between resolute critics and apologists. The Austrian Marxists, meanwhile, combined elements of both affirmation and denial of capitalist imperialism. One expression of this was their argument that the capitalist mode of production had set the foundations for a socialist economy. This notion, which the Austrian socialists made an effort to highlight, even provided the basic outline for Hilferding's theory of imperialism. It also defined Bauer's understanding of the development tendencies of the capitalist economy.[13]

Bauer's point of departure for his theory of imperialism was the analysis of the development of capitalist formation.[14] It began with a reference to the

---

12   Grossman 1992, p. 127.

13   Bauer had already dealt with the formation and development of modern capitalism in his first major work, *The Question of Nationalities and Social Democracy* (see Bauer 1996). He dedicated many articles that were published in the pages of *Die Neue Zeit* to specific problems, i.e. colonial, military, customs, and inflation policies. For a collection of these articles, see Bauer 1979, pp. 758–1048.

14   Christian Butterwegge does not share my view: 'Impressed by Hilferding's reflections, Bauer took the market behaviour of cartels, syndicates and trusts – rather than the conditions under which they arose – as a starting point' (our translation) – Butterwegge 1990, p. 86.

main contradiction in capitalist production – i.e. the opposition between the social character of production and capitalist property relations – and the main goal of the capitalist mode of production, the extraction of profit. The fundamental difference between capitalism and earlier formations, which produced to satisfy consumer needs, is its constant striving to increase surplus value. According to Bauer, capitalism passes through three stages: the manufacture capitalism of the sixteenth and seventeenth centuries, the liberal capitalism of the eighteenth and nineteenth centuries, and imperialism, which begins to blossom in the 1890s.[15] All three stages are inevitable and historically necessary, i.e. the changes that take place have an immanent and objective character. When describing the first stage, Bauer undertook a comparative analysis of imperialism and 'early capitalism'. He pointed out the similarities and differences in an engaging fashion, concluding that imperialism represents a regression to the capitalism of manufacture, albeit at a higher stage of economic development. In doing so, he was naturally not concerned with the mode of production or market activity, but with the role of the state as a regulator of production. He considered the second stage, liberal capitalism, as a transitional stage characterised by the extreme liberalism that found its full expression in the physiocratic maxim, *laissez-faire*, and a corresponding economic programme. Capital served as an economic means for state power at the time, and the role of the state was limited. In the economic sphere, it defended the interests of its citizens by introducing tariffs to protect the domestic market. In some economic branches (traffic, steel and energy), it applied protectionist policies. In domestic politics, its role was limited to maintaining the social peace, and in foreign affairs, facilitating peaceful relations to other states. As Hanisch pointed out, Bauer, when analysing liberalism, raised an interesting question concerning the difference between the economic and political liberalism of the Austro-Hungarian monarchy and the liberalism of the whole of Europe. According to Hanisch, Bauer established that Austrian liberalism was detrimental to broad sections of society, since (1) it was orientated towards German peoples, confining Slavic countries to the margins, (2) its driving force was the elite of the German population, (3) it owed its economic and political position to violence and corruption, and (4) it preferred Jews in the economy, whose activities led to the crisis and ultimate demise of liberalism in the monarchy.[16]

For Bauer, three tendencies were decisive in the transition of capitalism to its third, imperialist stage: cartelisation with simultaneous tariff protection, out-

---

15   See Hanisch 1985, p. 195.
16   See Hanisch 1985, p. 196.

flow of capital into economically less developed regions, and the merging of
national capitals.[17] These tendencies were preceded by an increased concentration of industrial and bank capital.[18] Deriving these ideas from Hilferding's
Finance Capital, Bauer referred to three of its core theses and drew conclusions
that were just as one-sided as Hilferding's.[19] He adopted the following points
from Hilferding:

- Firstly, the thesis that individual enterprises will merge and become joint
  stock companies, cartels and trusts with simultaneous strong involvement of
  the banks. Much like Hilferding, he was convinced that capitalists advance
  from being production managers to shareholders over the course of this
  process.[20] One consequence of the interrupted connection between the
  ownership of capital and production management is a change in property
  relations. Company profit is superseded by a new category – 'founder profit'
  (*Gründergewinn*). It is a factor of accelerated accumulation accompanied
  by capital concentration and centralisation, which occurs at the expense of
  smaller enterprises (which are eliminated). This process is encouraged by
  the credit policy of the banks, which favour high interest rates, and therefore
  favour corporations and support the establishment of industry monopolies.
- Secondly, the thesis of industrial and bank capital merging into finance
  capital.[21] This type of capital possesses greater financial powers than the
  sum of capitals of all individual entrepreneurs. Consequently, bank capital
  seizes industrial capital. Along with Hilferding, Bauer committed an error:
  he believed this tendency to be permanent. Both disregarded the antagon-

---

17   Compare Lederer 1965, p. 375. Until 1908, Bauer was convinced that it was impossible for
      Austrian capitalism to develop towards imperialism. In his later writings, he aptly poin-
      ted to the role of German capital in the emergence of Austrian imperialism. German
      protective tariffs at the beginning of the twentieth century made the import of Austrian
      agricultural goods to Germany difficult. After the 1905 trade agreement between Germany
      and Austria, German exports to Austria doubled by 1914, while Austrian exports to Ger-
      many remained constant.

18   See Bauer 1980b, p. 170.

19   According to Kluza-Wołosiewicz, Hilferding's *Finance Capital* (1910) met with greater
      interest in Russia than it did in Germany. The Russian labour movement brought it to
      Poland. There are also echoes of Hilferding's theory in the imperialism analyses of two
      Polish authors: Jędrzej Moraczewski and Oskar R. Lange. See Kluza-Wołosiewicz 1963,
      p. 259.

20   See Hilferding 1981, pp. 204–7. Compare Bauer 1976q, p. 847.

21   Hilferding writes: 'I call bank capital, that is, capital in money form which is actually
      transformed in this way into industrial capital, finance capital' – Hilferding 1981, p. 225.

istic forces and increasing financial autonomy of big corporations. Hence, Bauer – like Hilferding – drew the dubious conclusion that the combined interests of all entrepreneurs could be consolidated into a central cartel, complete with a newly established world bank controlling and administering all production according to a plan. From this, they unjustifiably further concluded that there was an intrinsic tendency of the world economy to transform into a socialised planned economy.[22]

– Thirdly, the belief that a new organisational form of economic life is created by the policies of the cartels, which strive for a monopoly position on the world market. These policies intensify the struggle against small-scale enterprise, which is economically compelled to integrate in order to survive, even if it can only do so in this modified form.[23] As a result of this struggle, only big industrial monopolies can survive in the market.[24] Neither Hilferding nor Bauer hesitated to draw a far-reaching conclusion from these analyses: the cartels would displace small- and medium-sized enterprises from the market and thus 'introduce' a regulative factor to economic life.[25]

On the grounds of economic science, Bauer regarded the development tendencies of imperialism outlined above as inevitable and objective. This is not to say that he failed to see their negative consequences, especially their social effects. The centralisation of production and capital might have a positive effect on technical and economic progress by increasing labour efficiency, yet, according to Bauer, under capitalism this is not synonymous with progress. Technological development increases exploitation and unemployment, as capitalists are not interested in the social implications, but only in the economic effects of new technology, i.e. the maximisation of profits. Another negative phenomenon of centralisation is the constraint on democracy in economic life: it allows a tiny group of powerful capitalists who own the instruments of economic and political power to rise to the top.

---

22   See Bauer 1976q, p. 849.

23   Lenin, Trotsky and Luxemburg were also convinced that a process of ever more profound global economic integration was taking place.

24   Bauer interchangeably referred to this phase of capitalist development as 'monopoly capitalism', 'organised capitalism', or 'state capitalism'.

25   Bauer had already developed these three theses in his article 'Das Finanzkapital' ('Finance Capital') – see Bauer 1980c, pp. 377–87. One can find a similar viewpoint in the works of Bernstein at the end of the nineteenth century. Lenin subjected it to criticism in 1901 when he attempted to prove that monopolies would further intensify the contradictions of capitalist economy. See Lenin 1964, pp. 213–16.

In addition to these negative side effects of capital concentration and centralisation, Bauer identified two mutually linked features of imperialism that deepen the problem. Thus far, we have insufficiently touched upon these features: imperialism's international nature and its expansionism. Admittedly, Bauer did not mention them separately in his work, but he clearly recognised that they were connected to other questions. Firstly, he linked the international character of imperialism to the changing roles of the bourgeois state and great economic spheres, and secondly, he linked its expansionism to colonialism and militarism.

Bauer aptly observed that the development of the world economy, which transcends the borders of 'national economies', leads to a more intense struggle between cartels and syndicates for the economic and political sphere of influence. Indeed, the battle of monopolies is a battle of states. For under imperialism, a unification of the interests of finance capital and the state apparatus takes place, which comprises the following realms: the protection of one's own raw material, commodity and labour markets; the export of commodities abroad (in order to postpone the ripening contradictions of the accumulation process at home); and finally, the scramble for international markets and colonies. Bauer shared Hilferding's opinion that the economic role of the state becomes stronger under imperialism, claiming that the state provided the foundations of a national economy.[26] At the same time, he came out in favour of maintaining or creating big state organisms. He argued that only a big (i.e. independent and strong) state can act as a regulator of socio-economic life, and that only such a state can assert itself in the struggle for economic and political hegemony on the international stage.[27] In defence of the validity of his viewpoint, Bauer appealed to the work of the bourgeois economists Albert Schäffle, Gustav von Schmoller and Adolf Wegner, who regarded countries with vast geographic areas and large populations as autarkic and considered big enclosed state territories to be independent economic units.[28]

Bauer emphasised another consequence of the unification process in the global economy that results from the struggle of monopolies and states for

---

26   See Bauer 1975b, p. 695; compare p. 703. In *Zwischen zwei Weltkriegen* (*Between Two World Wars*), Bauer alternatively uses the terms 'dirigist economy' and 'planned economy' to describe the dependence between the economy and the state – see Bauer 1976q, p. 107.

27   Rosa Luxemburg shared this view – see Luxemburg 1976, p. 129. In Austromarxism, Karl Renner developed the theory of establishing large economic sectors. See Renner 1916, pp. 112–17.

28   Lederer also wrote on this subject. See Lederer 1956, p. 406.

spheres of influence: the subordination of less economically developed countries to economically stronger national units. Expansionism is therefore an inherent characteristic of imperialism; its framework only maps out the limits of capital accumulation. In special cases, the territory for capital expansion might be domestic insofar as a country contains regions where the capitalist economy is not yet fully developed. In other cases, economies of neighbouring countries that are characterised by a low concentration of capital and low levels of technology are subjected to expansion. Above all, however, non-capitalist territories are targeted. Bauer exposed the power-hungry face of imperialism, yet he also argued that imperialist states would conquer colonies peacefully by introducing trade and replacing barter with commodity production, which would happen with the consent of native populations. He realised that the influx of capital and cheap industrial materials into colonies revolutionises existing production relations, which, in turn, changes their social and political structures. Bauer clearly held a negative view of these processes, and his attitude to colonialism was unequivocally hostile. In his speeches against colonial policy, he considered two viewpoints: that of the population of the conquered country, and that of the working class of the aggressor countries.[29] The consequences for the colonies are economic exploitation, economic imbalance, the ruin of peasants and small artisans who then fill the ranks of the unemployed, and the deterioration of the living conditions of society's poorer layers. Politically, colonialism means that existing political structures are subordinated to the aggressors for the sole purpose of protecting the capitalist economy. For all social classes (with the exception of the ascendant national bourgeoisie), this means increasing political oppression. It is a natural tendency of subjugated countries to strive for political and economic independence. Hence, national liberation struggles under the leadership of the local bourgeoisie commence. The national bourgeoisie is interested not only in shaking off the yoke, but also in creating its own capitalist economy.[30]

Like many German Social Democrats – e.g. Kautsky, Bernstein, Luxemburg and Schippel – Bauer regarded militarism as an integral component of expansionism. In contrast to the German theorists, however, he barely investigated the militarisation of the economy. It was not so much the economic consequences of militarism and expansionism that interested him, but their social implications. Two of his comments on the role of militarisation in the economic

---

29   See Bauer 1979d, pp. 828–43.
30   See Bauer 1976q, pp. 837–40.

cycle and development of capitalism are notable. Firstly, he rejected Schippel's thesis about the counter-crisis effect of militarisation.[31] He pointed out that armaments and an increase in military and navy spending lead to higher taxation, thus reducing the social capacity to consume and making it more difficult to overcome crises.[32] Secondly, he proved that all positive effects of the developing armaments industries (acceleration of capital accumulation, economic upturn, expansion of the manufacturing base, increased demand for human labour, guaranteed security of favourable capital investment, reduced unemployment, and improved material conditions for the working class) only last for a short period of time, as militarism has a tendency to expand automatically. This expansion drastically exceeds the initial goals and motives of competing countries. It inevitably leads to war between the major powers, resulting in the ruin of the capitalist economy.[33]

2   The Socio-Political Context of Bauer's Observations on Imperialism

If one wants to fully comprehend Bauer's statements from 1907–13 concerning the necessity of maintaining colonialism, militarism, and a vast state territory, one should not forget that his motives were not only scientific, but also political. He was chiefly concerned with two things: firstly, the political and economic interests of the Habsburg monarchy and the implications of imperialist policies for the working class; secondly, and consequently, the stance of the Social-Democratic party towards potential dangers unleashed by the development of imperialism.

The very notion of creating vast, economically autarkic state territories was geared towards the protection of a relatively autonomous production sector. Above all, however, the intention was to safeguard the consumer market of the Austro-Hungarian monarchy, whose preservation Bauer passionately defended up until 1917. Arguably, this standpoint predetermined his negative attitude towards Friedrich Naumann's project, *Mitteleuropa* (Central Europe), which the German section of the SDAP and the Hungarian Social Democrats

---

31   In German Social Democracy, Max Schippel founded the theory of overcoming crises by increasing the unproductive consumption of the state. He viewed the development of militarism as its most favourable form. See Schippel 1888.

32   See Bauer 1975c, pp. 780–90.

33   Bauer shed light on the relationship between fascism and imperialism in his later work in the 1930s, which contained a theory of fascism based on the theory of imperialism. I will investigate this in Chapter 8.

endorsed.[34] The project was based on the changing role and function of the state in the era of imperialism. It was essentially an economic argument for establishing a union of Middle European states (Germany, Austria-Hungary, Bulgaria and Turkey), which was a political project directed against British, French and Russian capitalism.[35] Bauer objected to the *Mitteleuropa* project for national reasons. He feared that the course of development implied in the name would lead to the establishment of a trust which would destroy the domestic economic sector.[36]

For the same reason, he viewed the effects of colonialism upon the economy of Austria-Hungary negatively. That is to say, he believed that colonial policy was an obstacle for domestic economic development: increased armament and navy spending was not conducive to the development of the domestic labour market. The latter was additionally jeopardised by cheaper labour in the colonies. According to Bauer, the import of cheap products, which increased the wage earner's purchasing power, was the only form of colonisation beneficial for the working class of the aggressor country. Convinced that colonisation policies were not a necessary condition for the development of capitalist production, Bauer formulated his credo as follows: 'Even if imperialism is not a means to facilitate accumulation in the first place, it nonetheless serves as a means to further expand its limits and make it easier to overcome crises that are periodically caused by overaccumulation' (our translation).[37] Incidentally, Bauer's standpoint had no practical influence upon the policies of the SDAP.

---

34   Friedrich Naumann (1860–1919) – a German liberal, publicist and politician. Founder of the periodical *Die Hilfe*.

35   It concerned the necessity of creating vast economic territories which would guarantee the capitalist system unlimited production.

36   Hilferding and Kautsky advocated a similar position on this question. See Hilferding 1915. Compare Kautsky 1916, p. 11.

37   'Ist also der Imperialismus nicht ein Mittel, die Akkumulation überhaupt zu ermöglichen, so ist er doch ein Mittel, ihre Grenzen weiter zu spannen und die Überwindung der Krisen, die periodisch aus der Überakkumulation entstehen, zu erleichtern' – Bauer 1979g, p. 1039. Bauer's critique was part of a wider discussion conducted in the international labour movement at the Amsterdam (1904) and Stuttgart (1907) congresses. The attitude of the Social-Democratic parties toward the colonial policies of the imperialist countries was the topic of debate. While the Social Democrats conceded that any ambitions to conquer hitherto independent states ought to be abandoned, they were unsure about maintaining already existing colonies. They wondered, for instance, whether it might be necessary to preserve the colonies for the continued functioning of the world economy. If economically backward countries were granted a free and independent development, would that constitute a threat to capitalism?

The Austrian delegate in the committee for colonies at the Stuttgart International Socialist Congress (18–24 August 1907), Engelbert Pernerstorfer, pleaded for an expansive colonial policy.[38] At the same time, the Austrian Social Democrats voiced their opposition to a resolution that denounced the methods of colonisation. Indeed, in 1917, the party leadership supported the government's colonial policies. Bauer had already been aware since 1910 that the scramble for new sales markets, new raw material markets, and cheap labour in the colonies would lead to the outbreak of war between highly developed countries. He warned of the potential consequences of war for the Austro-Hungarian monarchy: defeat and demise. Taking a long-term view, Bauer claimed that in the case of military conflict, Germany would strive to incorporate German-speaking territories to secure an additional reservoir of raw materials and cheap labour for the armaments industry.[39] In this context, he wrote: 'The collapse of Austria presupposes the triumph of imperialism in the German Empire, in Russia, in Italy ... The Austrian workers cannot place their hopes in German, Italian, and Russian imperialism, which is the enemy of their brothers abroad and the victory of which would diminish their own power at home'.[40] From this, he drew the following conclusion: during the epoch of imperialism, the working class is probably not interested in the demise of the monarchy because that would result in the defeat of the proletariat on an international scale. Bauer strikingly exposed an additional feature of German imperialism, namely a nationalism that linked the project of capitalist expansion with the pan-German idea. Its ideologues strove to break the resistance of the German working class against the economic policy of conquest by suggesting that the latter amounted to a struggle for national liberation. Exposing its predatory face, Bauer argued that the fight against German nationalism and its real aim – a world war – should be waged as a workers' struggle against imperialism.[41]

For Bauer, a committed Social Democrat, the most significant part of his research into imperialism was the economic and socio-political consequences of expansionism and militarism for the working class. Of course, this is not to say that his analyses were devoid of more general assessments of imperialism's economic and social effects. On the contrary, Bauer avoided the one-sided conclusions so characteristic of many socialist authors – Kautsky and Lenin, for instance – and depicted the results of the new epoch of capitalist development with a healthy dose of sobriety. He argued that many economic phenomena,

---

38   See Pernerstorfer 1907, p. 112.

39   See Lederer 1956, p. 387; compare p. 391.

40   Bauer 1996, pp. 403–4.

41   See Bauer (alias Heinrich Weber) 1909, p. 538.

which accompany capital concentration and centralisation, are fundamentally important for the harmonious growth of the capitalist economy. Developments such as the export of capital surplus, rationalisation of the manufacturing process, technological progress, and replacing free competition with monopoly market control increase productivity and work intensity. Bauer felt that these processes were positive. He viewed the demise of many branches of commercial production and their consequences – the destruction of small trade resulting from the concentration of capital – as an inevitable side effect of internal development tendencies within capitalism. On the other hand, it is crucial to understand that Bauer did not quietly ignore the negative social and political effects of imperialist policies. More than once, he pointed out that they aggravate class antagonisms and lead to a widening of the economic gap: a small group of capitalists becomes wealthier at the expense of the working masses; petty owners are declassed and join the ranks of contract workers. They also result in falling levels of consumption among the population, declining wages, and rising levels of unemployment. The weakening of democratic structures – a result of the growing interventionism of the bourgeois state, the reinforcement of its instruments of power (the police and army) and their deployment in the service of capital – posed, in his view, a serious danger to social life. An expanded army – as he argued in opposition to Schippel – does not bear any benefits for the working masses at all. Rather, it becomes a machine to strangle their resistance, a barrier to their economic, political and social emancipation.[42]

Bauer's merit as far as raising awareness of imperialism's consequences, however, lay not in his general observations, but in his attempt to demonstrate how monopoly policies helped shape the standard of living for the working class. His earlier judgements from the years 1906 and 1907 are not entirely reliable, which resulted from the fact that data on the development of imperialism was sparse and could not provide a base for objective assessment in the early stages of his research. In his later work, Bauer revealed to the working class the dangers and ostensible benefits of capitalism's development towards imperialism.[43] On the one hand, the period of capital circulation is shortened due to intensified production, and the import of cheap food supplies from the colonies improves the purchasing power of labour. On the other, the positive consequences of capital outflow are neutralised by tariff policies that serve to

---

42   Schippel's analysis concluded that the army of the bourgeois state can be converted into a people's army. Hence, the progress of militarisation can be considered as a way of 'growing into' socialism.

43   Karl Renner and Max Adler also wrote about this – see Renner 1915; compare Adler 1915.

protect the development of highly organised branches of production, prices set by monopolies, and indirect taxes. Reinforcing his argument, Bauer stated that the development of industrial monopolies reduces contradictions between the interests of industrial capitalists and landowners as the demand for protective tariffs unites both classes. He borrowed this line of argument from Hilferding, who had established a thesis closely linked to underconsumption theory: unlike capitalists, the working class is only interested in the development of the domestic market. The two classes thus assume a mutually hostile stance. With the intention of defending Austria's national interests, Bauer concluded thus from Hilferding's observations: under imperialism, the working class must reject the position of classical Marxism on protective tariffs,[44] as they are outdated and only support policies that protect the domestic market.[45] He justified the struggle of the proletariat for changes in tariffs policies as follows: 'While the profit interests of the enterprises are at odds with the public interest of the national economy, the interest of the working class coincides with the interests of national economic progress. [...] In the struggle against the tariffs policies of the propertied classes, the working class is the champion of national economic progress' (our translation).[46] He also associated the protection of the domestic market with the socio-economic benefits that were in line with the policies of the party, which hoped to end the increasing hardship of the working class. Interestingly, for Austrian Social Democracy – unlike Social Democracy in other European countries – the controversial question as to whether there could be talk of pauperisation of the proletariat did not play a decisive role in any period. In the SDAP, the theory of pauperisation was rejected. Only Adler drew attention to the phenomenon of relative pauperisation in his article 'Zur Revision des Parteiprogramms', and protested against the rejection of pauperisation theory at the Vienna Congress of 1901.[47] Bauer consistently championed the view that the development of imperialism does not lead to

---

44   About the tariff question, Marx shared Ricardo's position. In 1849, he was not of the opinion that free trade and tariff policies were of great importance for the working class. Marx and Engels advocated free trade.

45   See Bauer 1979k, pp. 113–15.

46   'Während die Profitinteressen der Unternehmen dem Gesamtinteresse der Volkswirtschaft widerstreiten, fällt das Interesse der Arbeiterklasse mit dem Interesse des volkswirtschaftlichen Fortschritts zusammen ... Im Kampfe gegen die Zollpolitik der besitzenden Klassen ist die Arbeiterklasse die Sachwalterin des volkswirtschaftlichen Fortschritts' – Bauer 1975b, p. 700.

47   See Adler 1901.

pauperisation in a physical sense but in a social sense: it increases the dispar-
ity between the consumption levels of the propertied classes and workers. As
one of the few Second International theorists, he was aware that an increase
in the consumption of labour power – the result of an intensification of labour
linked to technological progress – requires an increase in the means of subsist-
ence for its social reproduction. This additionally depresses the living standard
of the working masses. In *Die Teuerung* (*Inflation*, 1910), he furthermore wrote
about the socio-economic consequences of cartelisation and the disruption of
balance between industrial and agricultural production, arguing that it leads
to an upsurge in food prices and the growing impoverishment of the working
class. As Pfabigan noted, Bauer was convinced that the capitalist order cannot solve the problem of price hikes – it only disappears under socialism.[48]
That is why, as early as 1911, Bauer issued a call demanding that the struggle
against price hikes be linked to the revolutionary struggle, bearing in mind
that this slogan only had propagandistic value, which was surely his intention. In this stage of his life, Bauer had not mapped out a vision for revolution
yet.[49]

3   The Question of Crises in the Capitalist Economy

When analysing imperialism, Bauer was preoccupied with the capitalist economy's susceptibility to crises. Crucially, the following questions related to this
problem:

- Is the cyclical return of crises an objective economic law, i.e. a feature of
  capitalism that is inherent and inevitable?
- What economic and social consequences do crises leave in their wake,
  especially for the working class?
- What is the role of crises in creating the foundations of the new social
  order? Does the imperialist stage of capitalist development itself create the
  conditions for it to be replaced with socialism? If so, should the proletariat
  wait for that historic moment, and if not, what tasks for the proletariat does
  the new situation pose?

---

48   In 1911, a massive demonstration against unacceptable price rises took place in Vienna. It
      was suppressed by the police in a bloody fashion, leading to four deaths and hundreds of
      injuries. Three hundred participants were arrested.
49   See Pfabigan 1985, p. 41.

Behind these doubts was, in fact, a much more fundamental issue: in the background, the dilemma of revisionism was looming, albeit in a modified form. If the development of capitalism had taken a different direction from that envisioned by Marx, and if capitalism had created self-defence mechanisms, could one then continue to uphold the theory of its destruction by a socialist revolution, or should revolution be abandoned for good? If the theory were to be abandoned, then it could only be replaced with a concept that might reassure the masses that the workers' party had not broken with Marx.

At the outset of further discussion, let us note that Bauer viewed crises as an inevitable phenomenon of capitalist economy.[50] Concurrently, he claimed that capitalism acquired powers of regenerating itself and would not fall before the world revolution. He disagreed with the revisionist idea that crises progressively decrease in frequency, scope and duration.[51] Furthermore, he questioned whether crises have a tendency to transform into a great global crisis, as the revisionists claimed. Bauer believed that two types of crises occur during the contemporary development phase of imperialism: conjunctural crises, which periodically result from the global crisis, and structural crises, which are local and rooted in the conditions of the respective countries.[52] He viewed each type of crisis from a different perspective: for Bauer, conjunctural crises were a theoretical problem, which is why he addressed them in the debate among European Social Democracy. In contrast, he analysed structural crises as a pragmatist looking for temporary solutions in Austrian conditions.

3.1 Conjunctural Crisis and the Theory of Overcoming Crises

Bauer based his theory of the business cycle on an analysis of the global crisis from 1929–31, even if it contained elements of his earlier thought from 1913. His own assessment of the Austrian structural crisis provided the foundations. It was also the source of numerous erroneous assumptions, the most significant of which were his overestimation of the role of (1) monopolies, (2) the demographic factor, and (3) 'slips' in the rationalisation process.

Like Marx, Bauer conceived of the crisis as a disturbance in the process of capital accumulation.[53] As Marx further explained, this is caused by three

---

50   See Bauer 1979c, p. 794. Compare Bauer 1976l, p. 639.

51   Kautsky held similar views on this – see Kautsky 1902, p. 136. This led to the thesis of capitalism being in a state of 'chronic depression' that only socialism could cure.

52   See Bauer 1976l, p. 639.

53   Many authors believe that the classics of Marxism did not produce a coherent or unified theory of crisis and the business cycle. See Sweezy 1964, pp. 207–8. Compare Kluza-Wołosiewicz 1963 p. 172, and Barczyk and Kowalczyk 1985, p. 106. Indeed, Marx named

factors: the contradiction between the strong productive forces of the economy and the low purchasing power of the population; the anarchy of capitalist economy; and the falling rate of profit. The falling rate of profit in particular is, according to Bauer, fundamental, as it is an objective law of capitalist economy and therefore causes crisis as an inevitable phase within the business cycle.[54] Hence, Bauer treated the crisis of 1929 as a normal and unavoidable occurrence. He was convinced that this economic meltdown, like the previous one, represented a self-regulatory element and driving mechanism of capitalism. Analysing the causes of the crisis, he arrived at the following conclusions: World War I compromised the global economic balance. Following that, new global divisions gave rise to, on the one hand, closed economic sectors, and, on the other, intensified competition between the imperialist countries for markets and spheres of influence abroad. In Bauer's eyes, the crisis of 1929 was a crisis of overproduction, and the causes of such economic disturbances – Marx was equally convinced of this – are the falling rate of profit and a simultaneous rise of surplus value. That is, a situation in which consumption cannot keep up with the surplus of production capital. Thus, Bauer rejected a theory popularised by the works of J.S. Mill and Jean-Baptiste Say, which remained alive in bourgeois economics until the days of John Maynard Keynes: namely that, in the long term, it is impossible to glut the capitalist market, as there is no disturbance in the C–M–C circulation of commodities. All income from the sale

---

a number of real causes of crisis in different volumes of *Capital*, including the contradiction between levels of production and consumption, disparities in the development of different branches and sections of production, and the falling rate of profit. See Marx 1972, pp. 414–15; compare Marx 1959, pp. 483–4. This triggered a wave of criticism among thinkers inside and outside the socialist camp. Among the first to attack Marx's crisis theory were – according to Kluza-Wołosiewicz 196, p. 172 – Bernstein and Mikhail Tugan-Baranovsky. See Bernstein 1899, pp. 66–82, compare Tugan-Baranovsky 1923, p. 197.

54   After World War I, Social Democrats pointed to the falling rate of profit as a cause for the breakout of crisis. Bauer was therefore not alone in claiming this. I shall use the opportunity to make two corrections. Firstly, many economists incorrectly think of Bauer as the author of the claim that crisis does not constitute an inevitable phase of the business cycle because periods of boom and depression are crucial for the cycle. They also wrongly accuse Bauer of providing with this thesis – which, *nota bene*, he never put forward – a basis for Hilferding's theory of crisis-free cycles. See Mendelson 1959, p. 96. Compare Sweezy 1964, pp. 447–8. Secondly, Hilferding's theory of 'organised capitalism' did not exclude the possibility of crisis in the first phase, i.e. before a central cartel that totally controls all production is established. Hilferding himself had doubts that such a cartel would be created.

of commodities produced, according to this theory, is invested into purchasing articles of consumption and furthers the means of production.[55]

Having investigated the capitalist economy's susceptibility to crises, Bauer felt obligated to raise further interesting economic questions. Do, for instance, other causes for the disruption of the economy accrue from the fundamental contradiction between production and property relations? Is it possible to counteract the emergence of overproduction – and if so, how? Can the development of imperialism lead to a modification of the business cycle? In other words, the question was whether the capitalist mode of production could protect itself against crises upon entering the stage of imperialism.

I will preface Bauer's answer with an important comment. Bauer, who had authored *The Explanation of Imperialism*, embarked on his own distinct path when discussing the problems of overproduction and crises under imperialism. He made no concessions to positions that were popular in Social Democracy, and which were mainly advocated by German theorists at the time. True, his theory contained echoes of fashionable explanatory models of crises, such as the theory of disproportionality between different economic branches and sectors, low consumption levels among the masses, and the theory of 'organised capitalism'. But if the solutions he offered were not always satisfactory – an objection one could raise against most of the theories of his period – they were at least innovative. Most of all, Bauer avoided the kind of one-sidedness that characterised other voices in the debate on crises from 1901–14. Tellingly, two opposing camps emerged from this debate, which went on to defend their positions passionately for almost 15 years:

- Bernstein, Tugan-Baranovsky, and especially Hilferding, among others, represented the first camp. These authors explained crises as resulting from disproportion between individual economic branches and looked to the centralised planned economy of the monopolies and banks for countermeasures.
- The second camp counted among its protagonists Jean Charles Sismondi, John Atkinson Hobson, Schippel, Kautsky, Luxemburg, and the Russian *Narodniks*. They ascribed the troubles of capitalism to the underconsumption of the masses, suggesting either the introduction of high wages or the flight to foreign markets in order to overcome them.[56]

---

55 Jean-Baptiste Say developed this theory in *A Treatise on Political Economy* – see Say 2000. Bauer criticised it in Bauer 1979c, p. 791.

56 I am fully aware that the division depicted here is a gross simplification. However, the

Displaying an acute sense of intuition in contrast to the theorists of either camp, Bauer identified a fact that had remained unnoticed in the debate among Social Democrats. The relationship between individual economic branches and sections, as an aspect of the social process of production, is not separate from the social capacity to consume – the two are interdependent. This concept was decidedly novel: Bauer drew on both theories (disproportionality and underconsumption) to explain the causes of crisis, arguing that capitalism's possibilities of self-defence lay in overcoming its tendencies to issues such as disproportion and underconsumption. However, Bauer attributed a greater role to the regulatory properties of the consumer market than he did to a balanced relationship between the two departments of social production.[57]

When formulating his conception of saving capitalism from crisis, Bauer took his critique of Rosa Luxemburg's theory as a starting point. He had criticised her text, *The Accumulation of Capital*, as early as 1913.[58] Let us therefore briefly reiterate the theory that Bauer considered to be Luxemburg's most theoretically misguided – and therefore dangerous – for the Social-Democratic movement. Like Marx, Luxemburg thought that capitalism's real goal was not to cover society's consumer needs, but constant profit maximisation. At one point, however, she did not concur with Marx: she instead questioned his view that there could be unlimited capital accumulation, arguing that the end of capitalism is inevitable when it meets its limits in the form of closed borders. She did not attach any major importance to the evolution of the domestic market, as she believed that its capacity to absorb capital was limited – the cause of recurring crises in highly developed countries. Crucially, Luxemburg cited the existence of non-capitalist countries as a core prerequisite for any further capital accumulation. Hence, she assumed that capitalism meets its limits of development and collapses the moment it absorbs and transforms the last non-capitalist elements. Kautsky put forward a similar viewpoint, according to which the existence of agricultural countries was an imperative for the development of capitalism. For Kautsky, their transformation into industrial nations implies the end of the system.[59]

Bauer far from accepted these suppositions. As readers will remember, he rejected the theory of overcoming crises by expanding foreign markets through

---

protagonists of both camps did share a basic idea, while their more detailed analyses were very different. To dissect the problem in detail would go beyond the scope of this book.

57   Production is divided into two major departments: the first is the department of means of production (I); the second is the department of articles of consumption (II).

58   The relevant article appeared in *Die Neue Zeit* on 7 and 14 February 1913.

59   See Kautsky 1910, p. 222, and Kautsky 1911.

the conquest of colonies. As far as Bauer was concerned, Luxemburg made a fundamental error. She believed that her premise of constant consumption on the part of the working class under conditions of expanded reproduction was an indisputable axiom. This led her to the erroneous conclusion that capitalist markets in themselves could not realise surplus value.[60] What is more, if one accepts her claim that capital accumulation is impossible in closed systems, then only exporting commodities to non-capitalist countries can save the capitalist economy. However, the capitalist economy does not exclude the possibility of importing raw materials from these countries. Bauer based his main proposition on one conclusion he had drawn from his critique of Luxemburg's theory: the accumulation of capital is possible, even necessary, in isolated capitalist countries.[61] Attempting to identify the prerequisites of capital accumulation in a closed system, he cited two indispensable, mutually dependent conditions:

1. The necessity of a proportionate development of the two departments of production (I and II). When making this argument, he drew on Hilferding's theory of 'organised capitalism'.
2. The demographic factor: growth and drops in population must be proportional to the development of the productive forces, i.e. proportional relations between the productive forces and the consuming power of society must be maintained.[62]

To substantiate his position, Bauer appealed to Marx's schema of expanded reproduction. From this schema, it follows that crises are a consequence of imbalance between the production value of the first (I – means of production) and second (II – articles of consumption) departments of production. When investigating the causes of imbalance, however, Bauer did not conform to the analysis provided by Marx, who rejected the interpretation of the cycle as a phenomenon of the money sphere. Like Hilferding, he instead argued that the imbalance of prices in different departments of production was decisive, yet did not go into detail about the causes of this imbalance.[63] In his study

---

60 Bukharin drew attention to this error of Luxemburg's in Bukharin 1972, pp. 166–7.
61 See Bauer 1986, p. 108. Note that Bauer stressed political and national factors when defending this: in the period leading up to the fall of the monarchy, it was a matter of preserving its national sovereignty, and in the period of the First Republic, a question of confirming its development capacities.
62 See Bauer 1980f, pp. 887–8.
63 Hilferding emphasised the influence of technological progress upon the disproportional-

of the capitalist economy, Bauer did not so much foreground the importance of production as he highlighted the significance of the market. Differing from Marx, he did not link changes in the rate of profit with the price of commodities (which, according to Marx, was a derivative of the organic composition of capital). His premise resulted in a contradictory thesis: it is enough to regulate prices in order to expand production infinitely.[64] Bauer presumed that the sphere of circulation is the most important sphere for the capitalist economy and must therefore be controlled. According to him, this seemed a very easy task: it would be enough to establish a balance between the first and second departments of social production. Bauer was certainly unaware of the writings of Cunow and Lenin, who had both demonstrated that the first department is relatively independent from the second, and had pointed to the source of this independence.[65] When analysing the correlation between the two departments, Bauer concluded that the pace at which the manufacture of the means of production develops merely depends on mass consumption, this being in contrast to the production of articles of consumption. One can find a substantial amount of further incorrect conclusions. Let us briefly look at two of them, keeping in mind that they are worthless from an economic point of view:

1. A huge amount of commodities manufactured in the first and second departments can be consumed. That is because the surplus value extracted in both departments only increases at a rate at which its consumption matches population growth. Hence, the workers' capacity to consume only grows at the same rate as their numbers. The capacity of the whole of society to consume precisely reflects the increase of surplus value. The tendency to maintain this balance is inherent to the capitalist mode of production because the accumulation of capital 'adjusts' to demographic growth – this,

---

ity between the departments of production: in branches of industry with a high organic composition of capital, investments are the highest. Hence, the expansion of their production base requires longer periods. Supply cannot keep up with demand, which inevitably leads to price rises (thus to higher profits) and attraction of capital. This, in turn, gives rise to excessive capital accumulation and overproduction, which surpasses the demand for commodities from industry branches with a low organic composition of capital.

64   See also Mattl 1985, p. 94.

65   See Cunow 1903. Compare Lenin 1972, pp. 155–6. As the economist Lev Mendelson acknowledged, the disproportionality between the development of the first and second departments under conditions of expanded reproduction is permanent, and reflects the contradiction between production and consumption. See Mendelson 1959, p. 60.

precisely, is its self-regulating mechanism.[66] The limits of accumulation are determined by the supply of labour power.[67]

2. Surplus value cannot be exported abroad because that would effectively inhibit production in both departments – foreign investments make accumulation impossible (Bauer did not take all possibilities of foreign investment into account, including the purchase of raw materials and labour power at lower prices than at home). Policies that accelerate the development of the domestic market are in the interest of the proletariat.[68]

Alas, one cannot conclude from Bauer's comments on the mechanisms of the capitalist economy whether or not he believed it possible to completely abolish this phenomenon under capitalism. Like Hilferding, he assumed that it would only become possible to avoid crises once the anarchy of the capitalist economy was abolished and a planned economy introduced.[69] As mentioned earlier, Bauer thought that the regulating organs of the economy – monopolies, cartels, banks, and the state that assumes control over economic life – already fulfilled this function to some extent.[70] As they eliminate disproportions between the individual branches by changing the business cycle, they moderate crises.[71]

---

66 See Bauer 1986, p. 106.

67 Compare Haussmann 1979, p. 229. In 1929, Bauer claimed in his speech to the trade union congress that the crisis in Austria would be overcome in eight years, as the relation between population growth and mortality rates would change for the better during this period. To support his statements, Bauer drew up a scheme of expanded reproduction. According to this scheme, the accumulation rate mechanically depends on the population growth rate and the complex growth rate of constant capital (the accumulation rate was purportedly unchanging, constant capital would grow by 10 percent and variable capital by 5 percent). As Sweezy states, Henryk Grossman drew on Bauer's scheme when performing his complex calculations. They led him to the opposite conclusion to that of Rosa Luxemburg: due to the lack of surplus value, capitalism would collapse after 34 years.

68 As Robert Haussmann observes, Bauer's views on this concerned the Austro-Hungarian monarchy. In Czechia and Lower Austria, the proportion of the industrial working class in relation to the total number of employed reached its peak at the beginning of the twentieth century. People married late, the birth rate declined, and the market boasted an excessive supply of commodities. In other parts of the monarchy – Galicia, Dalmatia and Carniola – the process of capital accumulation was slow and birth rates high. Given the weakness of foreign trade, the development of the domestic market was the only possible way to industrialise the country. See Haussmann 1979, pp. 229–30.

69 See Bauer 1980, p. 55.

70 See Bauer 1980b, p. 174.

71 Hilferding described this tendency in a more transparent manner than Bauer: 'As long

This reasoning was based on two arguments, the first of which was pure speculation and was not backed by any evidence: if, for instance, cartels co-operate in setting monopoly prices, this amounts to regulating the movement of prices. The second argument was essentially the same misguided premise that also misled Hilferding: money originates in the act of exchange, the percentage rate being the result of the supply of money capital and demand for it. From this it follows that banks set money supply and percentages arbitrarily. In this manner, they also control and regulate production levels. Alas, Bauer's judgement was incorrect.

3.2   Structural Crisis and Ways of Overcoming It

Bauer paid particularly strong attention to analysing the crises that occurred in Austria from 1921–33. Alluding to the additional crisis that Engels distinguished in his work – also known as transitional crisis – he concluded that two types of crises had occurred in his country: conjunctural and structural. The latter, according to Bauer, resulted from the specific conditions and relations

---

as capitalist production is superimposed upon widespread production for use and non-capitalist, artisanal commodity production intended for a local market, the full impact of crises is felt only by the capitalist superstructure. They affect branches of production where sales may be brought almost to a standstill because the circulation which is absolutely indispensable for the turnover of goods in society is provided by handicraft production or by domestic production ... As capitalist production develops handicraft and domestic production are largely destroyed. The impact of a crisis is now felt by a system of production, the contraction of which is limited by the necessity of satisfying social needs on a much larger scale, both absolutely and relatively ... Changes in the character of crises are also bound to follow the advance of capitalist concentration. The ability of an enterprise to survive increases with its size ... Along with the concentration of firms the scale on which production can be maintained also increases' – Hilferding 1981, pp. 289–90. Kautsky and Luxemburg took an opposing view to that of Hilferding and Bauer, claiming that the effect of the monopolies, which aim for total domination of all branches of production by eliminating competition, intensifies the anarchy of the capitalist economy and accelerates the crisis. See Kautsky 1899, pp. 146–7; compare Luxemburg 2004, pp. 137–8. The practical conclusions that Bauer drew from this analysis should also be mentioned in passing. From his point of view, a balance between the supply and demand of commodities was an ideal situation for the working class (and, according to him, Germany had achieved such conditions). However, the fact that demand depends on the supply of labour power should have led him to the following conclusion: a disproportion between the extent of accumulation and the number of workers results in labour emigration (Russia, Austria-Hungary), which divides the proletariat. A state of balance is the most beneficial for the working class: it has fewer reasons to rebel, so its organisation, unification, and consciousness-raising can proceed smoothly.

in Austria-Hungary. In his analysis, he focused on the causes that led to a structural crisis in Austria (especially in the years 1921–2), while being less interested
in its course and consequences.[72] Speaking as a dedicated politician rather than
as a theorist, Bauer appealed to fact to reveal the complexity and diversity of
factors that decisively influenced the recession of the Austrian postwar economy. He included the following causes: (1) economic – Austria's loss of economic territories, resulting in a smaller material, domestic and labour market,
the outflow of foreign capital and the weakness of domestic capital, the introduction of protective tariffs on commodities exported from Austria; (2) demographic – decline in population and changes in its structure; (3) political – the
necessity of paying war reparations; (4) technological-administrative – poor
work organisation, low efficiency and quality of work due to insufficient technological progress, and the introduction of new scientific solutions.[73] I will
allow myself to disagree with Siegfried Mattl, according to whom Bauer overlooked an important aspect when explaining the causes of structural crisis. In
Mattl's view, Bauer neglected the policies of domestic banks, which orientated
towards exporting capital to Eastern Europe instead of promoting domestic
production, this being unfavourable to Austria.[74] In fact, Bauer did notice this
aspect – yet his analyses led him to conclusions which were not entirely correct:
that the process of work rationalisation can provide a foundation for preventing crises, and that technological development is only possible in vast economic territories. Notably, the second conclusion had political undertones and
served to buttress an idea propagated by Bauer: that of annexing the German
part of Austria to the German Empire.

After the fall of the monarchy, Bauer had doubts as to whether a country as small as Austria could survive, which served as one of his reasons for
demanding the annex. Nonetheless, he was against the idea of Austria becom-

---

72   The labour market of the First Republic had the characteristics of a semi-colony: in
      the best year, the unemployment rate was at 8.3 percent. The official statistics served
      to conceal the dramatic situation in the industry, where the unemployment rate was
      at 30 percent in 1927. Compared to the period before the war, the investment ratio
      had gone down. Not before 1929 did the total industrial output reach the levels of 1913.
      Already in 1929, however, the crisis affected steel production and the paper and tex-
      tile industries – in 1930, production in these branches fell by 50 percent compared to
      the year before. In 1933, industrial production decreased by 38 percent compared to
      1928, and unemployment affected 33 percent of those capable of work. See Weber 1984,
      p. 38.

73   See Bauer 1976l, pp. 639–40.

74   See Mattl 1985, p. 83.

ing dependent on other European countries. His comments on the causes of structural crisis from 1921–2 became the foundation for the Social-Democratic party's economic recovery programme for Austria, which it introduced in 1922 when debating the government on the results of the 'Geneva Convention' (also known as Upper Silesian Convention). The Social Democrats, Bauer in particular, protested against the economic and political dependency that resulted from the convention, as well as dreaded (justifiably) the consequences of the 'recovery programme' for the poorest layers of the population. The minister of finance, Dr Spitzmüller, had worked out a programme drawing on the economic thought of Keynes: economic recovery would be brought about by increasing the demand for investments (i.e. developing the municipal economy and introducing public works financed by the state budget), and overcoming the crisis by utilising inflation policies.[75]

In those days, Bauer was critical of Keynes's theory.[76] Because of the country's small size and economic weakness, he did not believe that it could be put into practice in Austria. In October 1921, he formulated his own programme for saving the Austrian economy. It drew on the theory of cyclical crises, and also on Hilferding's notion of the state as a force that accelerates the process of overcoming crisis. As mentioned in the first part, this programme was effectively a suggestion to win financial means by taxing wealthier social groups and foreign bank accounts held by Austrian citizens. In addition, a state front of public works – comprising road, water supply line, railroad and postal service works – was to be set up and financed by domestic loans. For all their differences, both programmes noticeably contained a common element: they placed emphasis on stimulating investment by the state for the purpose of creating a labour market that might help to overcome the crisis.[77] The government reacted negatively to the demand that the costs of crisis be shared across all social classes, and it

---

75   John Maynard Keynes (1883–1946) – a British economist, finance expert, politically dedicated publicist, initiator of the International Monetary Fund and the International Bank for Reconstruction and Development. He advocated a politics of strong intervention of the capitalist state into economic life in order to prevent crises. In his theory, he stressed the role of investment in maintaining the balance of capitalist economy (employment rates depend on demand, and demand depends on investment rates).

76   He strongly protested against one element of this theory in particular: the proposition to prevent crises by regulating the value of money in relation to gold, thus attempting to maintain the balance between the conjuncture and tariffs. Bauer thought Keynes's theory had a political character: in his view, it served to defend Britain's financial independence from the United States. See Bauer 1976h, p. 253.

77   It is worth mentioning that the foundations of the economic regeneration project, i.e. the creation of a labour market in the sense of anti-cyclical economic policies conducted by

rejected the Social Democrats' financial plan *tout court*. By doing so, it disassociated itself from the prospect of co-operating with the Social Democrats on economic questions.[78]

As noted earlier, the 'Geneva regeneration' that the government introduced resulted in the anticipated stabilisation of the economy, yet at the same time, as the Social Democrats had feared, it deepened the polarisation of society. The costs of overcoming the crisis were shared unequally, hitting the poorest layers of society – including pensioners, disabled war veterans, and the unemployed – hardest.

3.3   Rationalisation Crisis

In this passage, I will not content myself with Bauer's view of the conjunctural and structural crisis because that would not exhaust the subject. What is more, Bauer's opinion on crises changed somewhat in 1931. This evolution was conditioned by the threat of fascisisation in Western European countries, as well as – indirectly – by his hopes for a democratic development in the Soviet Union. In his 1931 work *Kapitalismus und Sozialismus nach dem Weltkrieg Bd. 1 Rationalisierung – Fehlrationalisierung (Capitalism and Socialism after the World War, volume 1 – Rationalisation and Misrationalisation)*, Bauer referred to the crisis of 1929 as a rationalisation crisis, i.e. a crisis of economic and technological progress.[79] The main question that arose here pertained to the causes of degeneration and errors in the rationalisation process. He offered one answer: the capitalist mode of production itself is to blame, as it contains the inherent contradiction between capital and labour. To defend his thesis, he pointed out that entrepreneurs strive to reduce costs rather than reduce the social costs of production. This is consistent with the practice of claiming public subsidies financed by tax money that is equally common today. Bauer just as sharply denounced the negative consequences of rationalisation such as unemploy-

---

the state, were laid by Gunnar Myrdal in Sweden, and – interestingly – in 1933 by Otto Bauer in his work *Arbeit für 200.000 (Work for 200,000)*. In 1927, Bauer and Renner pleaded for state concessions to enterprises in the name of the party leadership; they believed that in this way it was possible to stimulate the economy and reduce unemployment. In the SDAP, Johann Schorsch warned that such an intervention might bring 'technological unemployment' in its wake, yet his opinion was not taken into consideration – see Mattl 1985, p. 90.

78 Hans Kernbauer demonstrated the negative consequences of government policies for the economy and state finances in Kernbauer 1990, pp. 324–5.

79 Bauer intended for this work to be a study in four volumes, but only the first was published. It was not very well received in Austria, and criticism was strong. See Chaloupek 2009.

ment, the expansion of industrial bureaucracy, and occupational diseases resulting from more intensive labour. He drew the following conclusion:

> The social order can only be rationalised in the struggle of the working
> class against the capitalists. If, when, and in what ways the working class
> will be able to accomplish the rationalisation of the social order, however,
> will depend on the successful construction of socialism in the USSR on the
> one hand, and democracy asserting itself in Europe on the other.[80]
>
>   our translation

It is no wonder that Bauer was impressed by the centralised, state-owned Soviet
economy of the 1930s, which allowed the country to master crises caused by
the external tensions of capitalist economies. His positive judgement of the
Soviet economy was undoubtedly a result of his personal beliefs, but citing
Russia as an example also served as a foundation for a broader thesis: in a
socialist economy, crises disappear, and this process will go hand in hand
with full rationalisation. This is the key to a question that will conclude the
issue.

4   Socialism and the Theory of 'Organised Capitalism'

Like Marx, Bauer assumed that objective conditions for building the socialist
order are achieved when the concentration and centralisation of capital is at
its highest levels. At the time when he established his theory, the Social Democrats were guided by the notion that imperialism would naturally develop
towards planned capitalism. Bernstein and Hilferding in particular highlighted
this thesis, although they arrived at fundamentally different conclusions. Bernstein demonstrated that capitalism had already laid the social foundations for
socialism (i.e. the concentration of production accelerated its socialisation, the
process of capitalism's 'growing into' socialism was permanent and uninterrup-
ted, and the class struggle was waning). Hence, calls for revolutionary action
were no longer substantiated or justified. While Bauer agreed with the eco-

---

80   'Die Rationalisierung der Gesellschaftsordnung kann nur errungen werden im Klassen-
      kampf der Arbeiterklasse gegen die Kapitalisten. Aber ob und wann, auf welchen Wegen
      und mit welchen Mitteln die Arbeiterklasse die Rationalisierung der Gesellschaftsord-
      nung durchzuführen vermögen wird, wird abhängen einerseits von dem Gelingen des
      sozialistischen Aufbaues in der Sowjetunion, andererseits von der Behauptung der Demo-
      kratie in Europa' – see Bauer 1931.

nomic arguments of the far more revisionist Bernstein, he did not accept his radical thesis. He was much closer to Hilferding's perspective, fully subscribing to his insights and conclusions.[81]

It would go beyond the scope of this book to discuss Hilferding's theory exhaustively. Let us nevertheless look at some of his observations. According to Hilferding's analysis, the development of capitalism sharply aggravates class antagonisms, leading to a bipolar social structure of a new type that consists of the financial oligarchy and the working class. Because administration is separated from production and property, production was socialised. From these observations, Hilferding concluded that the domination of finance capital over industrial capital is the highest development stage of capitalism, and the initial stage of socialist socialisation.[82] Hilferding identified political consequences in this inner tendency of capitalist development: the socialist elements in the capitalist state and society would automatically become stronger. In other words, one should view socialism as the result of a gradual evolution of 'organised capitalism', given that capitalism 'as such' is working towards its own abolition. One should not attempt to accelerate this moment because 'in all forms of society based upon class antagonisms the great social upheavals only occur when the ruling class has already attained the highest possible level of concentration of its power'.[83] The financial oligarchy would soon find itself in a similar situation, and then it would suffice if the organised labour movement simply took power under its party leadership. It is worth noting that Hilferding's concept – unlike the views of the revisionists – does not exclude the possibility of revolution. However, it places a stronger emphasis on the smooth progression of socialisation in the socialist state – after all, it is argued, capitalism has already laid the foundations in the shape of a planned economy.[84] Hilferding's vision of the economic future of the world contained the establishment of a main cartel that would regulate the whole of production and a world bank appointed to administer finance. The activity of these institutions would lead to the abolition of

---

81   Peter Rosner engagingly and transparently discusses the theory of Hilferding's contained
      in *Finance Capital*. He critically examines it and demonstrates how it affected the political
      practice of Austrian Social Democracy and the socio-political development in Europe. See
      Rosner 1987, pp. 11–35.

82   See Hofmann 1971, p. 186.

83   Hilferding 1981, p. 369.

84   In Poland, Oskar Ryszard Lange was a proponent of 'organised capitalism'. All the same, he
      did not endorse the conclusion of a 'growing into socialism' that Bernstein, Schmidt and
      Renner had drawn from it, subjecting their theories to sharp criticism. See Lange 1929,
      p. 70.

commodity and money exchange in the socialist economy – their goal was not to maximise profits, but to expand production.[85]

Bauer adopted Hilferding's statements with minor reservations, to which I shall return later.[86] He was convinced that the Soviet Union had assumed the role of a central planner and accomplished economic transformations in the spirit of socialism.[87] This explains why he attached so much importance to rationalisation processes in the USSR and obsessively clung to the idea that only the world revolution could end capitalism for good. This clearly distinguished him from the revisionists. What he had in common with them, however, was his belief that there could be no question of a sudden transition from capitalism to socialism in the economy. As late as 1928, he defended the model of a mixed economy whereby economic decisions are made by representatives of cartels and the government at joint conferences (I will discuss this in more detail in Chapter 5).[88] Bauer prefigured the so-called convergence theory that would become popular in the 1970s and whose proponents would include John Kenneth Galbraith, Walter Bickingham, Pitrim Sorokin and Raymond Aron. Its key concept alluded to a convergence between capitalism and socialism thanks to the scientific-technological revolution. Convergence theory also recommended the creation of a mixed socio-economic system that unites positive elements of both economic models.

To conclude my observations, I would like to cite another interesting comment of Bauer's. Although he believed that the process of rationalisation would eventually lead to a socialist economy – a fashionable idea among Social Democrats at the time – another popular view was alien to him: the idea that the economic goal of socialism would be production for the market, but not for profit. According to Bauer, socialism would not raise the standard of living by modifying the distribution of surplus value (which must be used for accumu-

---

85   The works of Luxemburg and Bukharin also contain the notion of moneyless exchange in the socialist economy.

86   See Bauer 1931. Bauer broke with the notion of 'growing into socialism' of the capitalist economy under the impression of Nazi Germany's armament policies in the mid-1930s. Note, however, that this work of Bauer's contained original studies of the problems concerning cycles in agriculture, cycles in the production of gold, cycles in the war economy, the influence of the credit system upon the modification of the course of cycles, and the relationship between profits, prices, and wages. Furthermore, it boasted his own formulation of the 'law of the rate of profit'. Michael R. Krätke discusses these questions comprehensively and transparently – see Krätke 2008, pp. 173–8.

87   See Bauer 1976p, p. 117.

88   Compare Mattl 1985, p. 95. See also Bauer 1976q, p. 375.

lation, technological development, and educational purposes), but by raising work productivity. The latter, in turn, can be achieved by intensifying the social division of labour. With this thesis, Bauer consciously contradicted Marx's assumption that abolishing the division of labour was an important condition for implementing the socialist order.

To summarise, it would certainly not be a misrepresentation to say that Bauer's economic thought – which contained many errors, but also many interesting insights and conclusions – was barely relevant to the policies of the SDAP. For the workers, it was incomprehensible and often went directly against their immediate interests – for instance, concerning wage increases. I have tried to highlight the strong and weak points in his line of thinking when depicting its individual elements. What is more, Bauer's economic observations did not receive as much attention in the Second International as the respective works of Kautsky, Luxemburg, Lenin, Tugan-Baranovski, Hilferding, and others. The decisive factor was that Bauer's economic theory evolved at the wrong time to make much of an impact. The years from 1896–1913, in contrast, were a time of intense debate about the economic future of capitalism. They were followed by a period during which more critically important issues, such as the outbreak of World War I, the fascisisation of Europe, and the imminent outbreak of World War II, were at the centre of attention.

Although I will refrain from an overall judgement of the historical importance of Bauer's economic theory, I have nonetheless identified far-reaching trains of thought that are reflected in today's global economic situation. Among them are the rise of global capital and the web of international money transfers; the subordination of political and social structures to the logic of circulation and accumulation of capital; the weakening of national economies, and the formation of decision-making centres. It is also worth citing the negative results of technologisation that Bauer warned of in *Rationalisierung-Fehlrationalisierung* (*Rationalisation and False Rationalisation*, 1931), namely phenomena such as the rise of mass unemployment and the creation of a consumer society in which the media pushes uniform needs, values, and views. To use Marcuse's terminology: a one-dimensional society.[89]

---

89   See Bauer 1931, pp. 815, 837.

CHAPTER 4

The National Question

1   The Nation and National Culture

Prior to the outbreak of World War I, the national question was a pressing concern for Austrian Social Democracy. Quarrels and national conflicts not only jeopardised the existence and stability of the Austro-Hungarian monarchy, they also made it more difficult to achieve the primary objective Social Democracy had set for itself: maintaining the unity of the working-class movement in a multi-ethnic state. As Austrian activists and leaders of the European labour movement became aware, it would be impossible to design a coherent and realistic nationalities programme if arguments insufficiently discussed by the classical Marxists remained unsolved.[1] Among these were, for instance, the essence of the nation, traits that constitute a nation, and the relationship between society, nation, and state. In his early work, *The Question of Nationalities and Social Democracy* (1907), Bauer attempted to solve these, as well as related issues. He intended the text as a draft for a Social-Democratic political programme on the nationalities question under the Habsburg monarchy.[2] In way of a preliminary study, Bauer's text also contained remarkable sociological theory, which granted it a place in the canon of classic contributions on the so-called 'national question'.[3]

---

1   The classical Marxists did not codify a definition of the nation. It is possible to conclude from their texts on the Jewish question, pan-Slavism, colonialism, and the right of oppressed nations to independence that they conceived of the nation as a product of economic, social, and political relations rooted in territory and language. In their positions on the national question, the classical Marxists instead favoured social revolution and the class interest of the proletariat in the struggle for social and political liberation.

2   Bauer's observations on the essence of the nation, its constitutive factors, and determinants in the process of nation formation were the first Marxist interpretations of the national question on a European scale. The book consists of four thematic units: (1) the nation as a concept, (2) the nation state, (3) the multi-ethnic Habsburg state, (4) the nationalities programme of Social Democracy.

3   The text provoked controversy among Marxists when its author was still alive, and it continues to do so today. Kautsky and Stalin immediately rebuked it. Bauer's theory of the nation also provoked vivid debate in the Polish socialist camp. Mieczysław Niedziałkowski was directly influenced by it, while Leon Wasilewski evaluated it critically. See Kautsky 1917, 2009 and 2010; Stalin 1913 and 2003; Niedziałkowski 1926 and 1943; and Wasilewski 1929. For testimony

Bauer was mindful of the difficulties and limitations he would face when formulating the premises of his theory of the nation, as a medley of divergent ideas as to what actually made a nation apprised the social consciousness of the period. In addition, hard science – biology and psychology in particular – was still relatively undeveloped. He drew inspiration from two sources: Karl Lamprecht's *Deutsche Geschichte* (*German History*, 1891–1908) and the works of Marx, namely *The Eighteenth Brumaire of Louis Napoleon*. Drawing on the analytical method of historical materialism, Bauer created a concept of the nation that was sharply antagonistic towards the idealist conceptions within romantic nationalist ideology, racist constructs with biological inclinations, and empirical as well as psychological theories (his concept was saturated with psychologism, despite claims to the contrary).[4] Bauer also criticised the anti-Semitism present in German and Austrian Social Democracy and polemicised against those who declared, like Kautsky and Werner Sombart, that a nation was defined by common language and territory.[5] He observed that there existed not only distinct nations that spoke a common language, but also conquered nations that preserved their distinct nationality while embracing the language of the invader. Bauer found that it was not possible to grasp the essence of a nation merely by listing traits commonly associated with the term. When making use of the theoretical sources and basic methodological premises of Marxism to develop his concept, he defied orthodox Marxism and its fundamental object-subject opposition. The category of nationality that he introduced was based on social practice in the broader sense, thus continuing the line of logic

---

as to the different ways in which Bauer's theory of the nation was interpreted, see Konrad 1981, Mozetič 1987, Przestalski 1981, Śliwa 1980 and Wiatr 1973.

4 See Kołakowski 2005, p. 297, and Leser 1968, p. 253. Rooted in romantic ideologies, idealist theories appealed to metaphysical notions of the national soul, frequently accrediting an exceptional mission in human history to the nation (*Volksgeist*, the influence of Herder and Hegel) – Bauer described these as national spiritualism. Racist theories based on Darwin and Weismann's research suggested the existence of a mysterious reproductive substance. In empirical theories, the nation was understood as a complex of traits such as language, territory, law, morals, religion, economy, and so on; Stalin and Kautsky both conceded to this. Psychological conceptions equated the existence of the nation with a national sense of belonging. According to these, the peasantry was outside of the nation as late as the nineteenth century. Bauer pointed out that after Kant, such psychological approaches lacked any scientific basis.

5 Kautsky did not believe that Jews constituted a nation since they possessed neither territory nor a common language – they were linked merely through religious and group ties. In contrast, Sombart thought that Jews belonged to an entirely different race. See Kautsky 2009 and 2010, and Sombart 1909.

in Marx's *Capital*. The most valuable aspect of his theory was his departure from
positivist conceptions of the relationship between humans and their environment. In his analysis of individual factors that make up nationalities – such as
economic conditions, political organisation, and culture – he put culture first.
Because he deduced culture from practical human actions, his theory was not
only descriptive, but also possessed an axiological dimension: national values
and national culture played a vital role in the process of nation-forming.

1.1   *The Essence of the National Character*

The essence of a nation – or, to use Bauer's phrase, national community – is
determined by a set of interacting social phenomena. This complex is specifically determined by various factors. Of these, he deemed the national character to be the most vital: 'The nation is the totality of human beings bound
together by a community of fate into a community of character'.[6] The fact that
Bauer conflated the nation with the national character had significant implications for his entire concept, as it shifted the emphasis from the material world
onto the sphere of consciousness. What, then, exemplifies the essence of the
national character, and why did Bauer ascribe central importance to this category as a qualifier of the nation?

For Bauer, everyday experience is already a good index of the similarities and
differences between historically constituted nations. Similar geographical and
demographic conditions, the type of economy, and the forms in which political life is institutionalised bind them together. Differences between nations,
on the other hand, are usually manifest in disparities of territory and language,
as well as different customs, traditions, ideas, diverse mentalities and modes of
experiencing the world, and in the production of material and intellectual culture. That neither similar living conditions nor a shared territory and language
can always erase national differences in the spheres of law, morals, aesthetics,
science and religion inspired Bauer to seek the constitutive characteristics of
the nation in the sphere of consciousness. This decisive criterion constituted a
'community of character'. The community of character, according to him, was
nothing but the intersubjective sphere of social consciousness that reflected a
common mentality, a mode of experience, a way of passing judgement, in short:
all that is crucial for the unity of humankind. Bauer understood the concept of
character in its enormity. It was a complex of physical and intellectual human
attributes, although he thought that physical characteristics were of secondary significance. He established that intellectual and physical traits evolved

---

6   Bauer 1996, p. 117.

through an individual's participation in a variety of social relationships and dependencies. These, in turn, defined specific types of social relations such as class, professional and national relations. It was therefore justified to speak of class character, professional character, and national character as categories that were not mutually exclusive. A German worker, for instance, displayed traits that are typical of Germans, but also characteristics he shared with workers from different countries.

Bauer was conscious of the ambiguity and fluidity of the concept of national character. 'A community of character', he declared, 'links the members of a nation together in a particular era, but it by no means links the nation of our era with its ancestors two or three thousand years ago'.[7] The concept requires further elucidation as science only distinguishes individual types of national character. Bauer rejected perspectives that exemplified the behaviour of individual citizens to illuminate the essence of these types.[8] This is understandable given the concept of community that Bauer as a sociologist introduced. This approach to research neglected two substantial facts for him: (1) that the community of character is manifest in all, not just specific, actions; and (2) that actions are determined by real, historically distinct social relations. When analysing the distinct national characters of the English and French and their evolution, he focused on differences rooted in national history in the broader sense. According to Bauer, French culture was shaped by the Royal court, whereas in England, the aristocracy and urban patriciate were the enforcers of culture. Hence the divergent status of the ruling classes and their inherent traits such as aesthetics, taste, lifestyle, and intellectual culture subsequently becoming appropriated as standard by other social classes. The two countries, Bauer argued, produced different types of political conventions: English political thought was characterised by traditionalism and a penchant for patriotism, the result of a power struggle waged by the peerage. In this case, the ideology of an emerging class incorporated that of a class in the process of leaving the historical stage. In contrast, France was distinguished by a propensity to revolutionary upheavals, a result of the ruling dynasty's assertion of its power. Here, the new schema of ideas rigorously disassociated itself from the past system. Based on his analysis, the author concluded that the confines of the term 'national character' were extraordinarily broad. In his view, it encompassed state and social life, institutional forms, and the accomplishments of

---

7 Bauer 1996, pp. 20–1.
8 According to Bauer, Sombart committed this error when claiming that the essence of the
   Jews' national character was defined by their propensity to abstract thinking. See Sombart
   1909, p. 128.

science, philosophy, poetry and culture. Crucially, Bauer viewed the essence
of the national character as primarily determined by cultural heritage. The
provenance of the national character, on the other hand, was a matter of secondary importance for him.

However, the question remains as to why a particular type of national character arbitrates a strictly defined range of common behavioural patterns and
bonds in the sphere of consciousness. Furthermore, what trait of the national
character affords it priority over professional or class character? The answer
is in how the national character manifests itself in concrete human actions,
and for these, the 'direction of will' (*Willensrichtung*, a category he introduced
under the influence of Max Adler) is significant. According to Bauer, every
rational human being makes conscious decisions in the struggle to satisfy their
needs. As cogitative subjects, humans regulate the shape of social phenomena,
yet at the same time, their being is determined by reality. Every external stimu-
lus triggers a specific type of behaviour, one particular action instead of another.
Defending the monist-determinist perception of society, Bauer was prepared to
accept that general determination prevailed in the world of social phenomena.
Clearly inspired by Max Adler's neo-Kantian disquisitions, Bauer believed that
this was rooted in the fact that the individual's will was an expression of the
a priori collective will. The collective will, as a form of human consciousness,
is subject to the determination process. Individuals form a nation through a
unified will. This becomes apparent in the fact that people of the same nation
make the same, or at least very similar, choices. When finding themselves in
similar situations or being subject to similar factors, they draw on the same
system of values:

> The will expresses itself even more directly in decision-making. A Ger-
> man and an Englishman act differently in different circumstances and
> approach the same work in different ways. They choose different pleas-
> ures when they wish to enjoy themselves, prefer different lifestyles and
> satisfy different needs when they share the same level of prosperity. These
> traits are certainly constitutive of the essence of the national character.[9]

In relation to the world of humans and nature, Bauer regarded the will as
the creative force. Consequently, the national character decided the type of
actions directed towards other humans and nature (nature being understood as
a social category in the Lukácsian sense). In Bauer's estimations, this 'direction

9   Bauer 1996, p. 99.

of will' was a comprehensive law conditioned by physical and intellectual attributes that were characteristic of all members of a nation. He believed that these evolved in the course of the common struggle for survival and through inheritance of socially acquired traits and cultural assets. In other words, the character of the individual is forged by the same natural and socio-historical factors, yet will as expressed through practical actions is the final instance that determines the nature of the national character. The unified will is the enduring, objective characteristic of the national character.

There was another remarkable aspect to the conception of the national character suggested by Bauer. It became conspicuous whenever he left the terrain of metaphysical observations and dedicated his attention to the empirical reality bound to the existence of concrete nations. Bauer warned of a fetishistic approach towards the national character, i.e. of treating it as an independent historical driving force. He stated that the national character as such did not lead to the emergence of a nation. On the contrary, the existence of a nation provided the foundations for an emerging national character.[10] The national character, for him, was an empirical truth. Its form was the product not only of historical influences and inheritance of cultural assets, but also of material living conditions, the development of productive forces, and relations of production. In Bauer's view, national consciousness, whose materialisation was a historical process and subject to various conditions, played an active role in recognising this.

1.2 *The Peculiar Quality of National Consciousness*

National consciousness – the specific feeling of commonality and otherness in relation to other nations – is, according to Bauer, a form of social consciousness. It is not the source, but the aftereffect of a process of national integration that can last for centuries. The nature of the actual national bonds which emerge between individuals in a strictly defined historical situation defines the degree to which individuals integrate. Bauer particularly emphasised the inconstant nature of national affinity. This was because, for Bauer, national affinity was rooted in an ever-changing, evolving commonality of historical fate. He perceived the commonality of historical fate as an emotional and psychological community – or, in other words, an enduring structure of emotions and consciousness (which is related to the aforementioned conception of national character). The above observation is fundamental for understanding Bauer's interpretation of the term 'national consciousness'. National affinity – which,

---

10   Compare Moringer 1978, p. 156.

according to Max Adler, has a transcendental character – is understood as a spiritual, psychological type of affinity. It develops due to actions in which humans are emotionally involved. 'It is not the similarity of fate, but only the shared experience and suffering of a fate, the community of fate, that produces the nation'.[11] In this sense, some critics were validated in asserting that Bauer was himself inclined towards a psychological theory of the nation, even though he had set out to oppose it.[12]

When defining the essence of national kinship, Bauer neglected, or at least diminished, the role of elements such as emotional attachment to a territory, state, or even blood ties. This is further evidence that, as previously stated, physical ties between individuals were only of secondary value for Bauer. Cultural factors evidently took precedence. Bauer identified culturally constituted intellectual culture – emotional and psychological bonds, legal ties, common customs, religion, language, literature and the arts – as the essence of national affinity. National consciousness unambiguously reflected national affinity, giving expression to the objectivised system of intellectual and cultural achievements of a society organised as a nation. From this perspective, Bauer challenged subjectivist conceptions of national consciousness, i.e. notions according to which the subjective feeling of belonging to a nation was a sufficient criterion for an individual's nationality. To explain the process of emerging national affinity and consciousness, he appealed to science as the one form of social consciousness that utilises objective criteria in analysing and describing social phenomena.

Bauer stressed how slowly the developing process of national consciousness unfolds, highlighting its historical variability and its psychological and socio-historical prerequisites. According to him, the so-called 'law of inertia', which inhibits all that appears external, new, or alien, slows this process down.[13] Bauer's analysis of the socio-historical prerequisites for the origins of national consciousness made numerous conclusions that converged with Marxism. He suggested that the content of national consciousness, expressed in the products

---

11   Bauer 1996, pp. 100–1.

12   See Lenin 1977, p. 398; compare Kozyr-Kowalski 1974, p. 327.

13   Bauer distinguished different 'levels' of consciousness induced by the law of inertia. He cited the consciousness of a peasant and that of a modern bourgeois as examples, while emphasising a common trait, namely their conservative inclinations. Bauer viewed their will to preserve the status quo as based on divergent foundations. He argued that the peasants' conservatism had psychological roots in their attachment to the behavioural patterns and norms inherited from their ancestors. For the bourgeois, conversely, class position and the struggle to preserve it were paramount.

of a given country's intellectual culture, illustrates the historically changing objective material conditions of social being. Moreover, the composition of national consciousness expresses the interests of the economically strongest (ruling) class, given that the same historical and economic process that fabricates the basis of class relations also underlies emerging national relations.[14] Due to the exclusion of certain classes from the national community, national consciousness either had a feudal or bourgeois character in early, pre-capitalist stages of national development. Hence, Bauer correctly observed that the lack of national consciousness might be due to a class's objective existence on the fringes of a nation. For him, a further crucial requirement for the development of national consciousness was general access to cultural assets. His ratification of this criterion *per se* reflected a perceptive observation: classes and social layers with limited access to culture displayed lower levels of national consciousness. Capitalism managed to conquer this obstacle, giving rise to two new phenomena: steadily growing national consciousness in the ranks of the proletariat and the increasing dominance of national affinity over class solidarity. Bauer was inclined to believe that in the modern capitalist state, national affinity assumed an increasingly harmonious character and was stronger than class bonds. If we consider contemporary struggles for national independence, history seems to confirm this tendency.

As an aside, Bauer's text contained a particular thesis according to which all forms of social consciousness were subject to national determination. From this, it would logically follow that science is also subject to such determination. All the same, Bauer did not deny the objective existence of science as a supra-national form of acquiring knowledge in his other works. This incoherence reflected the intellectual contradictions in which the young Bauer was embroiled. The purpose that he himself ascribed to science – i.e. to explain the foundations of judgement in national categories and assess them critically – was ample evidence that he was aware of its objective status.

---

14   Bauer associated the emergence of national consciousness with the advancing process of capitalisation of social and political relations. He claimed that this shift occurs, stage by stage, as society's means of production are revolutionised. However, he was often mistaken and he did not consider increasing exploitation. To offer an example, he argued that the import of goods from Czechia lowered wages for German workers and had other negative effects: in economic terms (Germans had to pay the costs of economic inequality), and in the sphere of consciousness (the national divide sharpened).

1.3   *Thinking in the Categories of National Values*

In Bauer's view, humans are not only passive observers and recipients of history, but actively participate in its construction. Similarly, they are subject to the effects of culture passed down through generations, while at the same time ardently transforming it. This is the reasoning behind Bauer's argument that individuals are active products of their nation, including its historical defeats and victories, material conditions, and intellectual culture created over the course of centuries. The vital element for the role of the individual in the world is the will. The individual will, which establishes the scale and hierarchy of values, is subject to two types of determination: intellectual and emotional. According to Bauer, humans follow two opposing value systems: a rationalist and a national one:

> National evaluation and rationalist evaluation are both rooted in human nature. The former is ultimately based on the fact that the human being, bound to the nation by a causal relationship, is the product of his nation. The latter is based on the fact that the human being is a being that sets itself goals and chooses means, a being that orders itself within the natural and causal context through conscious action. Both forms of evaluation arise from the nature of the human, both are equally ineradicable, both are found in every human being, struggle with each other in every individual.[15]

Bauer captured the fact that the sphere of values is the real subject activity of humans that orients itself towards other people as well as nature. Thus, nature loses its substantiality as something external to humans: instead, it becomes matter continuously in flux according to human needs. In relation to nature, humans are guided by reason – they are progressive and revolutionary. With regards to their fellow humans and under the leverage of national traditions, however, they are governed by emotions and become conservative.[16] Bauer did not believe that these two value systems often manifested themselves simultaneously.[17] Essentially, he thought that in the course of human history, the national system of values had been dominant.

---

15   Bauer 1996, p. 127.
16   Przestalski also wrote about this, adding that Oskar Lange produced a similar theory in the 1950s. See Przestalski 1981, p. 213.
17   He referred to the work of Gotthold Lessing as an example of rationalist value judgement and nationally conditioned value judgement interpenetrating and determining one another. In his analysis, Bauer erroneously deduced that Lessing attempted to liberate

In his further observations on the value question, Bauer particularly focused on the national conditionality of judgements and ethics. When individuals evaluate their actions through the prism of the nation, they either subordinate their own system of values to the national interests, or alternatively submit to the complex of values, norms, and judgements produced by a nation. Bauer attached greater importance to the second interpretation, arguing that the evolution of a national culture was strongly affected by tradition. The practical expression of this was a sentimental and declamatory glorification of German bourgeois culture in his writings.[18] As an aside, Bauer did not inquire into the essence of values, nor did he consider investigating them scientifically. He simply took their existence as a given, claiming they, like the realm of culture in its entirety, were objective and subject to historical change in the course of social evolution.

This led him to another substantial idea, namely that values had a class character. Values promoted at any given moment in the course of historical development are, according to Bauer, synonymous with the values of the dominant social class. The existing social order serves to protect certain national values, and it is simultaneously committed to values that serve to perpetuate the rule of the powerful classes. Bauer accused the ruling classes of demoting national values to a mere tool of class struggle by employing trickery: to defend their interests, they construe any resistance of the oppressed against the existing social order as an assault on the national tradition. Bauer added that value judgement depends on the goals that individual classes have set themselves. In the age of anti-absolutist and anti-feudal struggles, the bourgeoisie aspired to rationality. It assumes a conservative bias, frequently citing the need to defend national values, during the period of high capitalism. The class struggle gives rise to the following: rationalist thinking characterises classes that fight for social and economic liberation, while appeals to national traditions and conservatism typify the ideology of the ruling classes. The development of capitalism produces a new social class, the modern proletariat. Having been excluded

German culture from French cultural influences to restore and preserve the values of his own nation. However, he aptly observed that Lessing's work accommodated the interests of the rising German bourgeoisie, which rejected French court culture without having yet established its own ideology.

18   Bauer was convinced of the superiority of German culture over the cultures of other nations. Mommsen points out that by categorising every new cultural achievement as an achievement of the German nation, Bauer was also hiding national motives behind his humanist and emancipatory deliberations. See Mommsen 1979b, p. 212; compare Mozetič 1987, pp. 225–6 and Hanisch 2011, p. 95.

from cultural assets for hundreds of years, after all, it emerges free from tradition. In place of the rigid and obsolete, it creates a new ideology. According to
the law of historical progress, Bauer argued, national values have to give way to
the values of the proletariat. The first reason for this is that the idea of socialism embodies the highest supranational and universal human values.[19] The
second, which deserves particular scrutiny, is that socialist and national ideas
are not mutually exclusive, as will be elaborated on later. Without delving too
deeply into this, it is important to note that the reality of the multi-national
monarchy was very different from Bauer's idealised perception. For the workers of many nations – especially Polish and Czech workers – nationalist and
pro-independence rhetoric bore more truth than proletarian internationalism
and socialism.

1.4   *Cultural and Natural Community*

Bauer challenged the theory of the nation commonly accepted in contemporary sociology. In particular, he criticised empiricist positions and the naturalist
current. The former, in his opinion, were particularly salient in the writings of
Italian sociologists. They were also present in Stalin's renowned essay on the
subject. Definitions of the nation offered in these texts were based on chronic-
ling common assets such as ancestry, territory, language, customs, morality, law,
religion, and the past. In Bauer's view, although these elements were important
to various degrees, merely listing such idiosyncrasies revealed little about the
essence of the nation. He pointed to the main difficulty that rears its head when
this factor theory is applied to living, changing organisms such as the nation.
The problem relates to structuralising individual components and the nature
of their mutual relationships (those who follow contemporary sociological literature will be aware that this problem remains contested).

The crucial point of Bauer's research was to find a concept that would
overcome this problem. For this purpose, he developed a definition of the
nation that harked back to the Kantian concept of community, which Bauer
borrowed from Max Adler's texts, and Ferdinand Tönnies's understanding of
the same term.[20] Claiming that the 'community' was the original source of

---

19   The Second International turned the notion of socialism as the embodiment of universal
      values into a dogma.

20   See Adler 1978. In *Community and Society*, Tönnies introduced the concept of 'community'
      to denote the nation and the concept of 'society' to denote the state. For this purpose,
      he distinguished two types of regulation: internal (linked to the emergence of social
      bonds and based on the community of mindset and fate) and external (which emerges
      due to the effects of legal norms, customs and language). Tönnies based the concept of

all social relations,[21] Bauer made it the central concept of his sociological observations.[22] He emphasised: 'The nation is not a sum of individuals; rather, each individual is the product of the nation; the fact that they are all the product of the same society makes them a community'.[23] The essence of community is that the individuals who sustain it are tied together by psychological social bonds. Drawing attention to the importance of psychological social bonds for the existence of social structures, Bauer, like Adler before him, accentuated their formal elements. With reference to Adler's category of 'socialised man', he assumed the transcendental existence of social bonds. That is to say, social bonds are not forged as a mere result of interpersonal relationships, but appear only with the *a priori* socialisation of individual consciousness, which in social life unifies subjects in all their diversity. In this sense, the existence of social bonds involves the ontological, transcendental uniformity of the subject-world. Following Adler's critical theory of consciousness, Bauer defined the society-nation as a distinct phenomenon of socialised man. The existence of the nation, he argued, could not be explained with reference to the outward form of human nature or, as conceived of by Rudolf Stammler, by appealing to an external law. Bauer adopted a transcendental interpretation instead. Accordingly, he criticised the individualistic theories, particularly the atomistic model, which defined the society-nation as a collection of individuals linked by a net of

---

community on the former and that of society on the latter regulation. Pawlak summed up Tönnies's distinction as follows: 'The community is made up of individuals equipped with a natural, spontaneous will (Wesenswille), while a society consists of members who possess a purposeful, rational will (Kürwille). In the community, people are tied together emotionally – their mutual relations are benevolent, harmonious, based on tradition and religion. A community fully engulfs the personality of each member. In society, the basis for co-operation is individual interest, agreement, calculation, public opinion' (our translation) – Pawlak 1979, p. 85. Bauer voiced reservations that he would attribute an alternative meaning to these categories. Nonetheless, his convictions overlapped with those of Tönnies. His differences can be put down to a transcendental interpretation of social bonds. Finally, Bauer did not employ the concept of community consistently. When differentiating between nation and class, for instance, he used the term 'community' to epitomise the nation and the term 'society' to mean social class. In spite of this, he frequently understood the class as a community and its social institutionalisation in the form of trade unions and political parties as society. Compare Mozetič 1987, p. 223.

21   Bauer 1996, p. 111.

22   To prove the consistency of his theoretical and methodological revelations, he associated this with two categories, although he often used them interchangeably: society and nation. It is worth noting that the two concepts are not synonymous in sociological literature.

23   Bauer 1996, p. 110.

reciprocal relationships. 'The nation', he wrote, 'does not exist by virtue of a formal convention, but is – logically, not historically – anterior to every formal convention'.[24] According to his premise, the introduction of external regulation (language, legal and moral norms) was immaterial in terms of the genesis of the society-nation, since 'external regulation is the form of social collaboration between individuals united by the community'.[25] Affinity, conversely, emerged because of the internal, *a priori* socialisation of human nature.

Having established his classification of the nation on a transcendental basis, Bauer then attempted to define it. The result of his analysis was that the nation always represented a unity between the community of nature and the community of culture. The following observations will illustrate (1) the evidence on which Bauer based his definition of the nation, and (2) what the proposed definition means from Bauer's perception.

Beginning his inquiries with the theory of heredity, Bauer criticised not so much the insights of Darwin and Weismann, but the practicability of biological and naturalist theory for investigating social phenomena. In his view, heredity theory sought the origins of the nation in specific organic matter, i.e. in a biological seed passed down from generation to generation (germplasm). Bauer referred to positions based on Darwin and Weismann's theories as 'national materialism'. It was his belief that the positive role of biologism rested on one simple accomplishment. That is, it challenged the legitimacy of spiritualist and idealist theories, which suggested the existence of a mysterious spirit permeating the nation, revealing itself in all activities and forms of consciousness that the nation produces. That aside, he did not believe that 'national materialist' theories had any explanatory value. Moreover, he objected to them because they capitulated to a biological and race-anthropological determinism that he rightly regarded as an early stage of racist theories.[26] When drawing on the theory of heredity, Bauer modified its scope and range. He did so in opposition to Social Darwinism, but also sought a possible transition to historical materialism within hereditary theory. The hereditary process, in his view, encompassed two mutually dependent processes: (1) the inheritance of physical and intel-

---

24   Bauer 1996, pp. 110–11.

25   Bauer 1996, p. 111.

26   According to these theories, causal relationships have one sole form: if A occurs, then B is its strictly defined consequence. Bauer referred to this causality as 'substantial' or natural. He explained it as follows: although the same processes occur in the natural and human-made worlds, and although phenomena are linked in a chain of cause and effect, different kinds of causality apply in the two spheres: these being natural and social causality respectively (these categories have already been explained).

lectual (biological and socially conditioned) traits, and (2) the acquisition of cultural gains and values. For Bauer, contemporary natural sciences could not really explain in detail the mode of acquiring social traits such as courage, humility, discipline, or loyalty. He argued that these traits were a result of living conditions, lifestyles, education, and social environment. Hence, he suggested that personality traits of successive generations reflected bygone social conditions and modes of production. Investigating the nation as a community of nature required taking into consideration not only its genetic material, but also the transformation of relations of production and exchange.

As Bauer observed, the material conditions for the reproduction of social life already belong to the sphere of social phenomena, which are characterised by an extensive diversity. These conditions define what traits successive generations inherit. Bauer's analysis had enormous implications: he recognised that biological theories could never provide an adequate description of the social prerequisites for human subject activity. Hence, he protested the inclusion of the nation in the biological natural realm of reality. If the nation is conceived as a literal, biological entity, then the national community of nature becomes a community of descent based on blood kinship. Such a community is, at least in its purest form, no more than an abstract concept that never existed in human history. One main tendency of the community of nature is the steadily expanding degree of differentiation. It leads 'an originally unified people' to 'split into different nations. This is a general law: every nation whose cultural community is based exclusively on common descent faces the threat of differentiation'.[27] Clans and tribes can unite to form a nation only on the basis of an identical intellectual culture that provides identity. Bauer was explicit on this: 'A mere community of nature without a community of culture may as a race be of interest to anthropologists, but it does not form a nation. The conditions of the human struggle for existence *can* also produce the nation via the means of the community of nature, but they *must* always do so via the means of the community of culture'.[28] One can only separate these two types of community in theory. That is why, according to Bauer, the nation will always represent a unity of the community of culture and the community of nature. The belief that they condition each other formed the basis for Bauer's definition of the nation.

His definition was also cultural, entrenched in Herderism and German Romanticism. It attached greater importance to the inheritance of cultural

27   Bauer 1996, p. 39.
28   Bauer 1996, p. 106.

assets than to the heritage of natural traits.[29] The heritage of cultural assets, for Bauer, is the most decisive factor for a nation's durability. Consequently, tradition, whose significance Bauer strongly accentuated, encapsulates the idea of the nation. The values passed down through cultural tradition define the national character to a great extent. This process occurs gradually. The first step is childhood and youth, the period in life when humans are the most receptive, yet also the most passive. The second step is the maturing period: the individual rejects certain established standards and helps to introduce new values. When discussing the inheritance of cultural assets, Bauer touched on an important matter: he noticed that certain elements of intellectual culture are eliminated through the process, while new elements are born.[30]

To return to the pre-eminence of the community of culture over the community of nature in Bauer's theory of the nation, it should not be overlooked that this contained three wholly different implications. The first implication is summarised as follows: that which is non-material, intellectual, or spiritual determines what is natural. The second and third implications were politically inclined: the second is best understood as the endeavour to solve class antagonisms by appealing to the concept of a 'culture nation' (*Kulturnation*), a term still used by the Social Democratic Party of Germany. The third implication was an argument for accepting the hegemonic status of the cultural element. According to Bauer, its impact should set the limits of national sovereignty. The author was fully conscious of the third implication; after all, he intended for a theory of the nation that would solve the nationalities question in the Austro-Hungarian Empire. His theory was palpable in the principle of national and cultural autonomy for all nations of the empire. It embodied the centrifugal and centralist ambitions of the monarchy, as well as of Austrian Social Democracy, which allied with the monarchy on the nationalities question.

Bauer's cultural theory of the nation was castigated for its abstraction from economic conditions. This was unjustified insofar as Bauer allowed plenty of room for the inclusion of material factors in moulding national conscious-

---

29   One can find the same cultural approach to the national question in Schlesinger 1950, and in Poland in Chałasiński 1966, Horwitz 1907, Luxemburg 1976, Niedziałkowski 1922, Ossowski 1967, Siwek 1921, Wasilewski 1929 and Znaniecki 1952.

30   It is difficult to concur with Przestalski's statement that Bauer 'ascribes considerable autonomy and independence of social relations to this idea, assuming that a specific form of social consciousness, once established, becomes permanent, its continued existence secured once and for all ... What is being negated here is the thesis that consciousness is socially determined' (our translation) – Przestalski 1981, p. 217. Bauer's theory implied a diametrically opposed situation.

ness. Indeed, he suggested that economic transformation, the development of a commodity money economy under feudalism and the development of capitalist production in particular, were the very foundations of nation forming, as were the accompanying changes in the societal structure. He viewed the process of nation forming as a long-lasting historical phenomenon.

Bauer's definition of nationhood provoked a wave of criticism from Marxists. Kautsky, Stalin, Pannekoek and Joseph Strasser, among others, argued against it.[31] Although I have examined the contents of these polemics in another text,[32] it is worth offering a succinct analysis of the debate between Bauer and Kautsky, as well as Stalin's denunciation of Bauer's position. In the course of his polemic with Bauer, Kautsky claimed that a community based on a shared historical fate included not all members of society, but only one class, one social layer, one municipality, one guild, one political party, or one state. He directed his criticism against the concept of the nation as a community of character, pointing to the empirical diversity of individual character traits. In view of the language difficulties in the multi-ethnic state, he identified language as a national principle and designated it as a nation-forming component. Bauer wholly rejected this, responding that Kautsky had not understood his concept of a community of fate: after all, Bauer argued, it rested on transcendental foundations. Moreover, Kautsky had mistakenly equated *common* with *equal* fate. To recognise the *a priori* character of social bonds meant to admit to their primary existence in relation to their historical forms in empirical reality. Language was not a determinant of community because it was a cultural product and instrument of communication, i.e. the means of a secondary order. It was not possible to elevate it to a national principle, as examples of divided nations that shared the same language were historically verifiable. The same goes for nations that had adopted the language of an occupying power or of the territory they inhabited. According to Bauer, language conflicts served as a pretext to conceal economic and class antagonisms. Stalin's critique, by contrast, allied heavily with the factor theory Bauer rejected. Stalin interpreted the nation as a mosaic of traits such as language, territory, economic life and culture, and if one of these assets was missing, one could not speak of a nation. What is more, he accused Bauer of omitting these factors in his analyses. The principle difference between Bauer's and Stalin's positions was that Bauer classified certain traits, for example national character and culture, as imperative for the essence of the nation. Arguably, Bauer's intention was entirely defensible. In formulat-

---

31   See Kautsky 2009, Pannekoek 1912, Stalin 1913 and Strasser 1912.

32   See Czerwińska 1991, pp. 326–8.

ing a broad notion of the national character, he demonstrated that it permeated through all forms of human activity determined by socio-economic living conditions. His model contained all the elements that Stalin mentioned, but also additional prerequisites for nation forming. Bauer was perceptive enough to stress that features such as national character, national consciousness, and culture were the specific traits of a nation that determined whether it would endure.

1.5   The Determinants of Modern Nation-Forming

The concept of the nation served Bauer to interpret the history of contemporary European nations. Using the example of the German nation to conduct his analysis of the premises of nation forming, he investigated the processes that lead to the emergence of conscious national communities. Furthermore, he studied class contradictions that limited the capacity of these communities and ways to overcome them. Bauer examined three aspects of the nation-forming process: cultural, economic and class-related. Seen from this perspective, the analysis of a nation's history becomes an analysis of the trajectory in which a socio-economic construct evolves. The transition from a 'lower' to a 'higher' stage of the nation is thus conceived of as a general law of historical evolution and criterion of progress.

According to Bauer, it is possible to distinguish between two stages in the history of a nation. The first is bound to the emergence of tribal organisations and nomadic communities. These communities are self-contained political entities whose members form a homogeneous unity through blood bonds, social relations based on common ownership of the means of production, customs inherited from their ancestors, moral values and language. In this pure, primordial form of the nation, social life is characterised by the participation of all members in shaping the politics, law, and morality of their community – i.e. they all have an equal say in the creation of an intellectual culture in the broadest sense. Bauer put forward an interesting hypothesis: according to him, the communities of ancient Greeks, Romans and Celts that emerged in the primitive epoch were based on a different type of association from those that emerged in class societies. As agriculture and sedentary lifestyles replaced nomadic ways and Germanic tribes mixed with the populations of the conquered lands (Celts and Slavs), the original clan community of the Germanic people fell apart. At the end of this process, their community of culture disappeared. At the same time, the end of this process marked a break in the nation's history. Although Bauer referred to this elemental culture as primitive, he did not undervalue its importance for the German nation-forming process. He even reasoned that German community collapsed due to the division of labour and property the moment social relations based on opposed economic interests took shape. The genesis of modern nation forming coincides with class differentiation and the emergence of private ownership of the means of production. The rise of the ruling classes marks the beginning of the second stage in a nation's history – a stage that continues to the present day.

Compared to the earlier form of the nation, the new feudal nation was fundamentally different inasmuch as it had a class structure. The feudal nation was a community of the ruling classes, the knighthood and aristocracy. The integration process in the feudal era merely unified landowners into a community of culture: 'The unifying moment that linked the nation together, however, was no longer that of a common culture handed down from a common ancestral people, but that of a new community of culture'.[33] From this, Bauer concluded that the German nation in the age of feudalism was not a continuation of the Germanic clan nation. All high intellectual culture – a product of knighthood – was based on the French model. Moreover, Bauer stressed that the preservation of the nation in this form was only possible due to the exploitation of the peasantry. In the middle ages, the peasants were the largest group among the 'tenants of the nation' (*Hintersassen der Nation*) – i.e. popular masses excluded from creating and receiving cultural assets and condemned to form isolated local communities.

The sharp divide that had separated the propertied classes from the popular masses lessened with the inception of the capitalist mode of production and emergence of a modern political system, the bourgeois nation state. As Bauer observed, commodity economy and the political changes initiated by the bourgeois revolutions played an enormous function in the transition from feudalism to capitalism. In these revolutions, the national idea was an element of integration for the nation. Here, Bauer agreed with Kautsky: the capitalist mode of production and exchange and the changes in the economic apparatus of society were the factors of integration that assembled the nation as a fully conscious, united entity. The confluence of the nation occurred not least on account of the socio-political changes heralded by the development of modern capitalism, but it was also due to the establishment of an education system, standardisation of the language, and political gains such as universal suffrage, parliamentary democracy, and freedom of assembly and association. Another uncontested gain of capitalism was its tendency to overwhelm impediments to supranational integration. However, in the era of modern capitalism, the masses are, according to Bauer, part of the nation only to

---

33   Bauer 1996, p. 48.

the extent that they submit to the framework set by the culture of the propertied classes.[34] For Bauer, the most important phenomenon engendered by
the development of capitalism was the emergence of an internationally organised labour movement. This movement anticipated the political emancipation of the proletariat by augmenting its position to the national class and
hegemon. To what degree the working class becomes the leading force in the
process of national integration depends upon the degree to which its class
priorities intersect with the interests of the nation. The process of integration will be finalised in a proletarian state in which culture is accessible to
all.

In his account, which also delineated the communities of culture in more
detail, Bauer also illustrated the history of the nation. During the first stage,
there is a clan community of culture, the clan nation. During the second, the
feudal nation unites a narrowly confined elite of landowners into a community
of culture. In the capitalist nation – the third stage – economic and political ruling classes define the essence of the community of culture. This community,
however, exhibits a stronger tendency to national affinity based on education
and politics than the fragmented local communities of the feudal epoch. The
final stage is the solidaristic community of the future, the socialist nation.
Unlike all earlier communities, it is based on the equal and universal participation of all citizens in national culture. Bauer did not foresee any potential
processes of disintegration in socialist societies.

Bauer's analysis also contained a differentiation of nations rooted in the
Hegelian tradition popularised by Engels, distinguishing between historic and
non-historic nations.[35] The introduction of these categories remained associ-

34   According to Bauer, the confines of the bourgeois community of culture are transparent:
     it encompasses the court nobles, landowners, high officials, the prosperous bourgeoisie,
     and the newly emerged independent urban professions. See Bauer 1996, p. 69.
35   Engels justified the differentiation between historic and non-historic nations by citing the
     difference between civilisation and barbarism. He equated civilisation with the develop-
     ment of industry, capitalism, and the rise of the bourgeoisie, while identifying barbarism
     with economic backwardness, feudalism, and peasant culture. See Engels 1977. The the-
     ory of non-historic nations was also present in Ferdinand Lasalle's work: he remarked that
     the French had a justified historical and cultural mission with regards to the Algerians,
     as the British had towards India. See Bernstein 1892, p. 30. Butterwegge stated: 'Bauer's
     adopted differentiation between "non-historical" and historical or cultural nations, which
     corresponded with his Greater Germanism and implied a German-Austrian cultural mis-
     sion with respect to the Slavic peoples, was ambiguous to say the least. Indeed, his book
     was cited by the German Social Democratic leadership to justify its approval of war credits
     for World War I' (our translation) – Butterwegge 1981, p. 131.

ated with the question of the so-called political nation, i.e. a national community contained in its own state (among Austromarxists, Karl Renner stressed the political aspect of nations).[36] Bauer described those that were already on the cusp of forming capitalist relations of production and displayed a fully developed social structure, especially its own propertied class, as historical nations. For example, Germany, Italy, Poland and Hungary all constituted historical nations because they lacked their own native upper classes; Bauer viewed Czechia, Slovakia, Serbia and Romania as still being non-historical nations in the nineteenth century. As Marx had done in *The Communist Manifesto*, Bauer argued that the late nineteenth century had seen a change in circumstances: capitalism had created the conditions for the development of national cultures, leading to a revival of nations 'without history'.

To further demonstrate the process of rebirth of non-historical nations, Bauer analysed the last two hundred years of Czechia's development. He cited five factors which contributed to the emergence of a mature Czech nation: (1) The development of a domestic ruling class accompanied the development of capitalism and weakened the influence of the German bourgeoisie. Bauer noted that the 1848 bourgeois revolution in Austria had also been a national revolution. National revolutions, he concluded, were a driving force in the genesis of nations. The leading role in the process of national integration fell to the Czech bourgeoisie. (2) The Czech bourgeoisie adopted the liberal and humanist slogans of the French enlightenment. (3) The development of the national education system and language allowed broad popular layers to participate in national culture. (4) The proletariat became increasingly class-conscious. (5) In the course of struggle against the German ruling class, the intelligentsia became politically conscious and increasingly solidaristic with other classes. Chiefly, Bauer did not see the intelligentsia as an intrinsic agent of the national idea. Rather, he believed that it did not possess the necessary material and political strength to accomplish the project of national unification. Due to these factors, the Czech people, who had previously lacked any political or administrative tradition for hundreds of years, rose up and fortified themselves as a historic nation in possession of a nation state.

---

36 Renner 1964, p. 11. It has to be emphasised that the terms 'nation' and 'nationality' are rather diffuse in Bauer's *The Nationalities Question*. Particularly in relation to the opposition between community and society that Bauer had described when defining the essence of the nation, it is fair to say that he did not apply the term 'nation' consistently to the 'stately nation' ('historical nation'). Moreover, he used 'nationality' to denote two different things: (1) belonging to a nation, and (2) an ethno-cultural community that lacks political rights and constitutional guarantees ('non-historical nation').

With final regards to the historical forms of the nation and its prerequisites, it is worth mentioning that Bauer, in his historiosophical position on the rebirth of peoples, once again referred to the role of culture in the process of nation forming. He alluded to the specific cultural mission of historic nations in relation to non-historical nations.[37] As Bębenek demonstrates, this notion originated in Hegelian historiosophy.[38]

1.6   *The Nation as a Real Community of Culture in a Future State*

In the course of his reconstruction, Bauer distinguished three basic types of national community of culture (while identifying the four different types of nation): (1) the clan community; (2) the antagonistic class society; (3) the solid-aristic community of the future, i.e. the socialist society. Bauer's classifications had an unambiguously evaluative character: his criterion was access to national culture and possibilities of participation. The choice of this decisive factor logically resulted from the author's overall conception.

According to the criteria Bauer had established, the clan order, in which all members were carriers of society's material and intellectual culture, repres-ented an exemplary form of the nation. It lost this form in the feudal age, as class contradictions intensified. The popular masses were excluded from the national community, and any possibility of participating in the political and cultural life of the nation was confiscated from them.[39] According to Bauer, the process of integration in the feudal and early capitalist eras only unified a nar-row social group into a community of culture, namely the propertied classes. The cultural assets only became the property of the whole nation as the cap-italist system evolved. Yet in Bauer's view, this system also excluded the pos-sibility of fully realising the nation. It erected material barriers that prevented the nation's various classes and social layers from equally participating in its gains. Bauer argued that it would only become a nation again under a social-ist constitution: in the future state, the socialisation of the means of produc-tion, social character of labour, and final abolition of inequality and privileges would facilitate participation in culture. Without dissecting Bauer's views on these matters – after all, this would also necessitate investigating Marx's rel-

---

37   Bauer was particularly concerned with the cultural mission of the German nation towards the Slavic peoples. See also Butterwegge 1990, p. 131 and Hanisch 2011, p. 98.

38   See Bębenek 1987, p. 35.

39   It is certainly remarkable that Bauer's analysis bypassed slaveholder society. He thought of it as irrelevant and not clearly distinguishable in the evolution of the nation. This view can be attributed to the fact that slavery had never been dominant among the nations that he analysed.

evant theories – the aforementioned statements contained three portentous insights: Firstly, the participation of the masses in culture helps to integrate the masses into the nation. Secondly, whether the nation prevails depends on whether the liberated classes cultivate the assets of the old culture. Thirdly, the cultural education of the masses will be as inseparable from the socialist order as the public appropriation of the means of production. Bauer thought that the socialisation of labour was the most important element in the transformation process. The Polish philosopher and cultural critic Stanisław Brzozowski had similar ideas: a nation could only become a self-contained cultural community if it first became a community of labour. The liberation from reified labour, an essential factor in satisfying intellectual needs and fostering the development of culture, would lead to the realisation of a complete, real nation.

Based on this, Bauer established that the proletariat was the executer of the national idea and the driving force of progress in the realm of culture. He was deeply convinced that only the rule of the working class would create the conditions for a nation in the full sense of the term, as it would strengthen the development towards an intellectually unified civilisation. Bauer believed that the task of the modern proletariat was to build a socialist state and conquer national culture for the benefit of the entire nation. Bauer's initial sentiments were: 'The international struggle is a means that we must use to realise our national ideal'.[40] He therefore disagreed with Luxemburg and Lenin, who argued that the national movement was an obstacle for the class struggle. They feared that nationalism would spread if the proletariat pursued cross-class objectives. In response, Bauer suggested that the consolidation of proletarian social consciousness had a class character and a simultaneous national essence.

Viewed with the benefit of historical hindsight, the veracity of his further statements is questionable. Bauer claimed that the position of the proletariat within the class hierarchy had far-reaching implications for its position on the nationalities question. The proletariat, he proposed, would only support the national idea if national aspirations for independence coincided with the struggle for class liberation. Bauer frequently emphasised the class character of the national struggle for sovereignty, pointing to the integral connection between class divisions and divisions within the nation. This belief was widely held in the Second International. If the proletariat succeeded in abolishing class antagonisms, this would also end national oppression. This was the only convergence of Bauer's views with the official position of the Second International.

---

40   Bauer 1975, p. 32.

Bauer staunchly focused on the interpenetration of different cultures and consequent emergence of an international culture.[41] Unlike Kautsky, though, he did not believe that increasingly fluid cultural boundaries would eliminate distinct national characteristics. According to the Marxian view, the nation would lose its value with the victory of socialism and realisation of a classless society. Numerous socialists, including Luxemburg and Jean Guesde, concluded that the concept of the nation was a bourgeois myth. For many, the socialist idea also contained what Bauer referred to as a 'naive cosmopolitanism' (Bauer's term) inherited from humanist enlightenment philosophy. Bauer believed differently: for him, proletarian internationalism was not synonymous with cosmopolitanism. In his mind, socialist ideology had to rest upon the foundations of every respective nation's cultural traditions. In defiance of common formulas, he declared that socialism would not only preserve national identity, but it would even strengthen and develop it.[42]

All of Bauer's observations had a corresponding point of reference: the realm of culture. On this basis, he attempted to explain the development of the national character, the genesis and determination of national consciousness, and the role of value judgement in the process of nation forming. What is more, he aspired to distinguish the objective bonds which tied individuals to a nation and examine restrictions which interfered with the integration of the whole nation. Bauer's belief that the participation of all citizens in national culture was the fundamental condition for the existence of a nation in the full sense still informs contemporary theories on the nationalities question.[43]

Bauer's undeniable merit was his challenge to many stereotypical concepts of the nation to which socialists adhered during the Second International period. Equally valuable was the simple truth that every nation possesses an intrinsic value and has its own unique dynamics of development. Bauer's belief in the longevity and identity of nations based on culture is still viable in European consciousness.

---

41   This was directly opposed to Lenin's position. Lenin opposed national culture as bourgeois nationalism and advocated for a consistently democratic and socialist international culture. See Lenin 1963, pp. 246–7.

42   Kołakowski, Mozetič, Kulemann, and many other Austrian authors have also mentioned this. See Kołakowski 2005, p. 298; Mozetič 1987, p. 225; Kulemann 1979, p. 127.

43   It is worth mentioning the following Polish scientists in this regard: Cackowski 1974; Kozyr-Kowalski 1974; Wiatr 1973.

2   The Nationalities Question in the Austro-Hungarian Monarchy

As we have seen in the previous chapter, Otto Bauer placed great emphasis on the integral link between the process of nation forming and the cultural realm in the broadest sense. The cultural theory of the nation focused on the role and value of a society's intellectual culture and tradition. It was based on a strong belief that class antagonisms and social contradictions are reduced when a nation matures, and are entirely abolished under socialism when broad social layers are able to participate in national culture. These elements provided the foundation for Bauer's programme to solve the nationalities question under the Habsburg monarchy. It is entirely justified to claim that until 1918, all of Bauer's observations on the national problem were subordinated to the political aims of Social Democracy, i.e. they served to resolve the ferocious conflicts between the nations incorporated into Austria-Hungary. From the 1880s onwards, they manifested themselves more sharply.

National conflicts were an element inseparable from political life under the Habsburg monarchy since its inception, even if in the times of centralist abso-lutism, the causes were different from those in the era of constitutional fed-eralism. During the first period, the so-called Hungarian question – i.e. the struggle surrounding Hungarian independence – was prevalent. The second revolved around the decentralist and separatist aspirations of Poles, Slovaks, Italians, Croats and South Slavs. To be sure, the lands ruled by the monarchy were granted autonomy in the 1861 constitution: tasks of self-administration were delegated to local parliaments. At the same time, the position of the aris-tocracy and wealthy bourgeoisie, which was overwhelmingly of German des-cent, was strengthened in their respective territories. Contrary to the expect-ations entertained by liberal politicians in the empire, the introduction of dualism in 1867 – i.e. the establishment of Austria-Hungary – did not end national conflicts. Rather, it only strengthened the central powers in the two divided states. The ruling nations tried to keep the less developed nations eco-nomically and politically subordinated, and – understandably – encountered resistance from the latter. National struggles sharpened particularly in the 1890s.

A closer look at the fundamental issues underlying these conflicts reveals that socio-economic and political reasons were prevalent. However, one should not minimise psychological and emotional factors either. Let us remember that at the turn of the nineteenth and twentieth centuries, Austria-Hungary made up a territory of 260,242 square miles and comprised a population of 51 million – among them, two million Germans, 10 million Hungarians, nine mil-lion Czechs and Slovaks, seven million Croats and Slovenes, six million Poles, three million Ukrainians, and one million Italians.[44] It was a state that comprised territories of varying levels of economic development. Industrialisation was accomplished particularly in Lower Austria, Styria, Silesia, Bohemia and Moravia. In the other parts of the country, especially Hungary and Galicia, industrial development was low – above all, large-scale land ownership was an impending factor, taking up some 45 percent of the land surface. As monopolies formed, small and medium-sized businesses could not compete with big German enterprises. These countries provided a basis for raw materials and a supply of cheap labour. Particularly in Bohemia, Moravia and Galicia, where a strong bourgeoisie emerged in the 1880s, the dependency on German capital was viewed not only from an economic, but also from a national perspective. In all countries ruled by the crown, increasing exploitation went hand in hand with political subjugation: an anti-democratic system of government whose political, military and administrative posts were staffed mainly by Germans, alongside discrimination in education and against national languages and cultures. Another source of conflict between the peoples was socio-economic differences between ruling and subordinated countries. They affected the working class first and foremost – the relatively good conditions enjoyed by Czech workers employed in German-speaking territories were an exception to the rule. The German-Austrian workers formed the 'labour aristocracy' of the empire – which, incidentally, significantly influenced the national policies of the SDAP leadership. Their income was a fifth higher than the income of workers in the other countries, they were better educated, and they had better developed organisational structures in the trade unions.[45] Furthermore, they were very receptive to petty-bourgeois ideology, part of which was German nationalism. Opposing economic interests, competition between German workers and those of other nationalities, and rampant nationalism made an emergence of class consciousness and a united struggle of the Austro-Hungarian proletariat impossible; the effect was that differences within the class concurred with national differences. At the end of the nineteenth century, anti-Semitism and conflicts between competing local nationalisms, skilfully fostered by the Christian Social Party, threatened the peace between the peoples of the monarchy.

There is much to suggest that national conflicts were indeed among the main reasons for the longstanding division within the Austrian workers' party from 1866–89. Both factions – the moderates under the leadership of Heinrich

---

44   Kreisler 1970. Rauscher depicts the roots of national conflicts under the Habsburg monarchy in an interesting fashion – see Rauscher 1995, pp. 45–6.

45   Compare Mommsen 1963, p. 88.

Oberwinder and the radicals under Andreas Scheu – were clear that the socio-economic and political interest of the working class required energetic consolidating action. As a condition for the success of such action, however, a position had to be formulated to finally reconcile national interests and resolve issues concerning nationalism and the working class. This question also remained fundamental and acute for the Social-Democratic movement that united in Hainfeld. Notably, this movement claimed to be Marxist from its inception – hence, the Austrian socialists consistently attempted to base their solution to the national question on socialist theory. Under Austrian conditions, this attempt was bound to fail. This requires some explanation.

One question in particular springs to mind: did the classical Marxist texts and the positions of the Second International contain any theoretical solutions in the interest of the working class that could be practically implemented in a multi-national state?

For Marx and Engels, the problem of specifically national working-class interests did not really exist.[46] When they were active, nationalism was not a significant factor of political life, and they did not pay much attention to it.[47] They located the source of national conflict in the class character of the bourgeois state. In their view, free competition – i.e. free trade, the emergence of a world economy, and standardisation of the forms of production – would level differences and antagonisms between the peoples during the period of capitalist development. These contradictions would then be abolished entirely with the unification of the proletariat and its seizure of power. Marx and Engels deemed the socialist revolution the real means for the emancipation of the working class and oppressed nations. To be precise, the classical Marxist texts viewed the solution to the national question as depending upon the solution to the social question. They regarded national struggles not as an independent factor of history, but as an integral component of the class struggle. Let us note, however, that Marx's – but particularly Engels's – conception of the national problem led them to champion nations that they believed were carriers of historical progress. For them, large economic and political organisms were progressive.[48] Because they believed that these organisms were the focus of revolutionary energy, they projected their desire for socialist revolution upon them and expected them to provide the catalyst. Their thesis that the world revolution was an objective consequence of historical development and would

---

46   Helmut Konrad offers more details about the classical Marxists and the national question
      in Konrad 1976, pp. 6–17.

47   Compare Leichter 1976, p. 78.

48   See Konrad 1977, p. 195.

unite all of human civilisation was irreconcilable with the trend in establishing small independent nation states.[49]

It should come as no surprise, then, that Marx and Engels only took a marginal interest in the problems of the Habsburg state.[50] In two articles,[51] Engels took up an ambiguous position on the national struggles in Austria. In his 1848 article, 'Der Anfang der Endes in Österreich' ('The Beginning of the End in Austria'),[52] he described the monarchy as a bulwark of reaction and national oppression, predicting its imminent fall due to the oppressed nations' growing hatred of their German tyrant. A year later in *Democratic Pan-Slavism*,[53] he denied so-called non-historical nations the right to exist as political entities, claiming that they lacked the economic, geographic, historical, and political conditions for an independent political existence.[54] This position could be interpreted as Engels's approval of the subjugation of less developed nations and condemnation of their emancipatory ambitions.

Marx and Engels's conception of the national question determined the views of Second International theorists. Their leaders – including Karl Kautsky, Jules Guesde and Rosa Luxemburg – feared that highlighting the national question would divert attention away from class antagonisms. Like the classical Marxists, they assumed that the national question would inevitably disappear once the social question had been solved, and that socialist revolution would decide this in the near future. Many Second International activists disregarded progressive aspects of the emergent national identities, and many had

---

49   'Naturally, in full accordance with the Victorian stereotype, civilisation was identified with Western civilisation, whose main pillars were the United States and the "advanced countries" of Europe' – Walicki 1995, p. 155.

50   In 1860, Marx regarded Austria as a dam against the flood of Russian imperialism. He wrote: 'The sole factor that has justified Austria's existence as a state since the middle of the 18th century, [has been] its resistance to Russian progress in the East – a helpless, inconsistent, cowardly but tough resistance' – Marx 1982, p. 131. Apart from Konrad 1976, pp. 9–14, Hanisch explains the attitude of the classical Marxists toward the nationalities question as follows: 'From the 1840s onward, Marx and Engels were convinced that the monarchy had to be smashed. The "great nations" that lived in the territories of the Habsburg empire – the Poles, the Hungarians, the Italians – had to constitute themselves as independent republics' (our translation) – Hanisch 1978b, p. 339.

51   Helmut Konrad cites these in Konrad 1976, pp. 9–11.

52   Engels 1975, pp. 530–6.

53   See Engels 1977, pp. 362–78.

54   According to Konrad, Engels's negative view of the Czech and Yugoslavian positions during the 1848 revolution led to his change of mind – he went on to refer to them as counter-revolutionary.

no idea how to link the idea of internationalism with the principle of national self-determination.[55] For some Social Democrats, the sheer link between the national principle and the notion of statehood was incomprehensible. Not infrequently, they assumed that historical development would lead to the 'absorption' of smaller nations by larger ones and stressed the significance of assimilation processes – Rosa Luxemburg, for instance, attempted to prove the emergence of supra-national states. Only Lenin warned the leaders of the International that the development of capitalism would awaken the national consciousness of all classes and unite them in their ambition to found nation states. However, his warnings were dismissed.

The positions put forward by the classical Marxists and their successors in the Second International were not particularly helpful for the Austrian Social Democrats for solving the tense relations between the Austro-Hungarian nations. The political situation demanded a programme for present circumstances, and socialism still seemed a long way off in the late nineteenth century. From its inception, the Austrian Social-Democratic movement aimed to create a unified organisation that represented the interests of the whole Austro-Hungarian working class and maintained this unity. Hence, the formulation of a pragmatic national programme was fundamental to the movement's existence and effectiveness. Because socialist theory did not offer the Austro-marxists any models to follow, they considered it their task to deal with the so-called Austrian problem on their own. Indeed, Social-Democratic circles – strictly speaking, Renner and Bauer – proposed the most interesting solutions to Austria-Hungary's national question in the early twentieth century. For our purposes, Bauer's theory and its consequences for the policies of the SDAP is the key issue. Given that it grew out of the Social-Democratic movements' political practice and, in turn, co-determined this practice, it seems appropriate to preface our detailed assessment with an outline of the national question in the politics of the SDAP.

2.1   Social Democracy and the National Question

Authors such as Mommsen, Konrad, Leser, Kulemann and Rauscher all offer thorough accounts of this question.[56] Hence, it appears unnecessary to write the history of the national question in the policies of the SDAP anew – even more so because the main focus of this sub-chapter is not the national ques-

---

55   Compare Mommsen 1963, p. 202.
56   See Mommsen 1963 and 1979b; Konrad 1976 and 1977; Leser 1968; Kulemann 1979; and Rauscher 1995.

tion as such, but rather Bauer's approach to it. Our reconstruction will therefore refer to the aforementioned researchers' key conclusions and will be limited to a brief exposition of the Social Democrats' stance. Embroiled as they were in ideological and tactical difficulties, the Social Democrats had not yet taken up a unified position on the national question in the 1860s–70s.[57] Documents from the first congresses of the workers' organisations testify to the conflict of opinions.[58] Likewise, during the period of unification, the Social Democrats were in doubt as to whether they should simply dismiss the national question as a bourgeois chimera and instead campaign for internationalism, or else seek a solution within the existing constitutional framework. The founder of the movement, Victor Adler, was aware of this dilemma. He resisted any debate on the national question in the party as best he could, wary that it might lead to a split in the labour movement.[59] Adler agreed with Kautsky that the national question could be reduced to a language problem and therefore had to be transferred from the economic and political onto a cultural terrain. Adler underestimated the underlying socio-economic and political reasons for national conflicts. Nor did he recognise the degree of tensions that existed between workers of different nationalities. In the programme of the unifying Hainfeld congress, the Social Democrats consequently argued for maintaining the status quo of the monarchy – a policy that Adler and Kautsky had authored. On Adler's inference, there was conspicuous silence around the national question, which had been bypassed in favour of a strong focus on the struggle for universal suffrage. The resolution proclaimed at congress defined the party as international, yet did not define internationalism more closely. The party

---

57   The moderates advocated a compromise with the liberal and national parties, while the
        radicals aimed to maintain independent political action and internationalism.

58   The Manifesto to the Working People of Austria, which had been formulated by the fifth
        Vienna workers' congress on 10 May 1868, called upon the solidarity of workers of all
        Austro-Hungarian nations and assured them that the time of national divisions was over.
        The April 1874 party congress in Neudörfl adopted a diametrically opposite position: the
        resolution approved of separatist national organisations and adopted the right of nations
        to self-determination. The programme adopted at the congress in Wiener Neustadt (13–
        15 August 1876), conversely, was a backward step when compared to the progressive parts
        of the 1874 programme: it attempted to unite the workers around the slogan, 'the workers
        of Austria fight, but they do so within the framework of the existing constitution' – see
        Berchtold 1967, p. 199. The 'programmatic resolution' of 1877, which contained a common
        position of all national organisations on universal suffrage, represented a compromise of
        sorts. For more on the programmes mentioned here and the national programme of Bern,
        compare Kulemann 1979, pp. 120–6.

59   Compare Konrad 1977, p. 138.

settled for stating that 'The Social Democratic party of Austria is an international party. It condemns the privileges of nations just as much as it condemns the privileges of birth, property and descent, and it declares that the struggle against exploitation must be just as international as exploitation itself'.[60] It was decided to solve the national question through a formally conceived principle at a forthcoming party congress. Indeed, few Social-Democratic politicians at the time believed in the necessity of equal rights between nations. They took the claims contained in the congress programme, according to which absolute impoverishment would soon affect the workers and middle classes of all Austro-Hungarian nations to the same extent, at face value. This situation, they thought, would lead to greater international solidarity among workers, and to workers and the petty bourgeoisie rejecting the nationalist mindset.[61] The party leadership attempted to downplay the fact that nationalism had long infiltrated the ranks of these social groups and become a general social problem. By then, it was playing an ever-greater role in the politics of the state.

The unity of the SDAP brought forth by the Hainfeld programme had a formal rather than programmatic character. It never took shape in reality. Austrian Social Democracy – which was principally German – drew on the blueprints of German Social Democracy. It bypassed the traditions of the Czech Social-Democratic movement and it did not incorporate the experience of Social-Democratic organisations in Bukovina or Eastern Galicia, which had built on progressive peasant movements. Only during the period of consolidation did the national centres refrain from infringing on the leading role of Austrian Germans in the labour movement. The party-internal process of nationalisation involving the Poles, Czechs, South Slavs, Italians and Ukrainians was eating away at the SDAP from its inception. Separatist ambitions were particularly strong in the Czech fraction.[62] As early as 1878, the Czech socialists founded the Czech Social Democratic Workers' Party with reference to the national principle (it obtained full independence on 27 December 1893). Thus, they opened the door for more and more intense quarrels within the party. The Czechs started the process of national federalisation: their resolution on a federal party structure was passed at the sixth congress of the SDAP in 1897.[63] The federal

60   Berchtold 1967, p. 138.

61   See Konrad 1976, p. 48.

62   Berchtold 1967, p. 138.

63   By act of this resolution, the Austrians, Germans, Czechs, Poles, Slovenes and Russian sections of the party became independent national political organisations. Coordination of political activity was to be secured by a common governing body with headquarters in Vienna, which consisted of delegates from the individual national administrations,

division did not just weaken the workers' movement of the monarchy; it also led to tense relationships between the Slavic parties and the German-Austrian party, with the latter attempting to preserve its privileged position. Suffice it to say, this state of affairs was not beneficial to resolving the national question. While the parties pushed it into the background, it became manifest in the trade-union movement, despite the fact that the unions were organised according to trades rather than the national principle.[64] Subsequent congresses of the Second International in Amsterdam (1904), Stuttgart (1907) and Copenhagen (1910) sided with the SDAP leadership in defending centralism in the labour movement. Regardless, the disintegration process in the trade unions deepened.[65]

Fearing that national quarrels might erupt into the open and consequently lead to a terminal breakdown of already weak organisational structures, the SDAP leadership made the last attempt in the history of the monarchy to draft a complex national programme.[66] This took place at the congress in Bern from 24–29 September 1899. The SDAP leadership and the Slovenian socialists presented two drafts to delegates. The leadership proposed to grant territorial autonomy, but preserve a centralised state, whereas the Slovenian draft demanded cultural autonomy according to the territorial principle.[67] The adopted programme reconciled both positions in that it conceded national and cultural autonomy according to the territorial principle, yet within the framework of a federal state. In fact, the decision to adopt this principle was synonymous with sacrificing the right of nations to self-determination to preserve unity and the inviolability of imperial borders. The resolution did not define the authority of local parliaments and state council more closely, and it was difficult to conclude

---

joint representation in the state council, and biannual congresses. See SDAP 1897, p. 7; Wasilewski 1907, p. 71.

64   At the 1896 trade union congress, the Czechs demanded an independent secretariat with headquarters in Prague. Although their demand was rejected at the time, national trade unions were operating in Czechia and Moravia as early as 1906. Compare Mommsen 1963, p. 396.

65   Compare Zimmermann 1976, p. 373.

66   It is discussed in detail in Konrad 1977, pp. 198–200.

67   See Berchtold 1967, p. 145; SDAP 1899, p. 75; and Kelles-Krauz 1903, p. 276. According to Rauscher, 'The demand to replace the old crown lands with nationally demarcated, autonomous administrative units and transform Austria into a democratic federative state of nationalities was not new. Nor was the rejection of an official language. The concept of ethnic federalism originated from the time of the 1848–9 revolution. Moreover, this decidedly moderate political programme meant that Austrian Social Democracy was affirmative of the imperial concept' (our translation) – Rauscher 1995 pp. 46–7.

from it where the limits of federalism ended and central authority began.[68] It was assumed that the working class, which was numerically the strongest and enjoyed universal suffrage, would automatically secure the decisive vote in the administrative bodies. The electoral system at the time, which unambiguously privileged the propertied classes, made politics in the interests of the working class impossible from the outset. The programme envisioned a modern bourgeois state based on democratic foundations. Commenting on it, Kulemann rightly notes that it misconceived the link between the national question and the struggle for socialism.[69] It is easy to explain why that was the case: as mentioned earlier, many Social Democrats failed to acknowledge progressive aspects of national liberation struggles. Therefore, they did not establish a link between national and social revolutions. Moreover, the project of national and cultural autonomy did not imply that fully independent centres of state power would be established. Rather, the intention was to appoint national organs of self-administration with tasks within the spheres of culture and education. Hence, workers' struggles in the respective countries were understood not as attempts to seize political power, but as struggles for access to the cultural sphere against the national bourgeoisie. Mommsen writes: 'This national consciousness was in essence apolitical, not state-oriented'.[70] The situation was, as it were, a closed circle: Austria-Hungary was a patchwork of many nations held together by the emperor, imperial court, state power and army. Given this state of affairs, real bonds to link peoples that did not identify with the state could only be created at a cultural level. History proved that this was too weak a factor in the face of Austrian realities to preserve cultural ties through the state or save the socialist movement from splitting.

Neither the two drafts introduced in Bern nor the suggested solution became reality. Meanwhile, the Slavic peoples of Austria far from relinquished their struggle for equal rights and separation. Contemporary political events, such as the Russian revolution of 1905 and the annexation of Bosnia and Herzegovina, only aggravated the situation. The Czechs refused to give up their efforts for equal language rights in public offices, schools for national minorities, and the right to appoint their own representatives in the state council.[71] They did

---

68   See Mommsen 1963, p. 107.

69   See Kulemann 1979, p. 124. The Polish and Ukrainian socialists, who regarded the suggested solution as a regression towards positions predating the Hainfeld period, opposed the Bern programme.

70   Mommsen 1963, p. 317.

71   In 1905, Czech and German-Austrian Social Democrats stood separately for state council elections for the first time.

so despite the fact that their separatist aspirations were condemned at the 1910 congress of the Second International in Copenhagen. The liquidation of the common party in 1911, then, only officially confirmed the split between regional organisations that had long been a *fait accompli*. Already, in 1905, the trade unions had been decentralised into national departments. Victor Adler's grand achievement, the unification of the Austrian workers' movement, fell apart – even though this time, unlike in the Hainfeld period, the Social Democrats had a theoretical understanding of the national question, which was essentially contained in the work of Renner and Bauer. Their studies offered concrete – in Renner's case, no less than detailed[72] – reform programmes for the constitutional foundations of the state; thus, national conflicts in the monarchy were at least partially reduced, if not entirely pacified. Moreover, they laid the theoretical groundwork for Social-Democratic nationality policies. I will return to them later to evaluate to what extent the conditions for their implementation were present.

2.2 *Bauer's Position on the So-Called Nationalities Question*

2.2.1 Position on National Conflicts

Bauer's stance on the national conflicts and decentralist aspirations of the Slavic peoples was unambiguously negative. Not only was this an expression of solidarity with the party leadership's official line, but it also had an emotional and psychological underpinning: Bauer was motivated by his fascination with German culture and attachment to the monarchy, in whose continued existence he believed and whose *raison d' état* he defended.

Bauer wrote *The Question of Nationalities* ... during the period when Austrian monopoly capitalism entered its imperialist phase. The propertied classes of Austria and Hungary intensified their oppression of classes and nations, for the economically weaker peoples served as cheap labour and ensured sales markets as long as they were kept in their place. The bourgeois nationalist parties – the Greater Germans and Christian Socials – bore witness to a rebirth of nationalism at the turn of the nineteenth and twentieth centuries. Nationalism, which had previously resonated, particularly among ethnic German workers, now appealed to the workers of other nations in Austria-Hungary. Bauer thought that nationalisms were on the rise because a flourishing capitalism had aggravated social contradictions. He emphasised the class character of national

---

72   Karl Renner developed them in the following works: Renner 1902, 1913, 1914, 1916, 1917, 1964, and 2005. For our purposes, Renner's conceptions are secondary. I will only deal with them to the extent that their impact upon Bauer's programme necessitates it.

struggles: while the bourgeoisie resorts to national values to preserve the existing social structures of capitalism, he argued, the working class turns them into a constituent part of its struggle for emancipation.[73] However, this apt observation did not have the slightest influence upon Bauer's fundamental political position on the nationalities question. As previously alluded to, Bauer did not unambiguously advocate utilising the nationalities conflicts in the struggle for socialism. Nor did he, up until 1918, explicitly cite the right of nations to self-determination.[74] For him, the pivotal goals were the abolition of national subjugation and alleviating the nationality conflicts that stood in the way of conducting effective Social-Democratic reform policies.

However, this did not mean that Bauer blindly disregarded the ambitions of subordinated nations to rebuild their state structures. Indeed, he took the possibility of an armed Polish and Ukrainian uprising into account. More than once, he warned Germans and Hungarians that national consciousness might grow among so-called non-historical peoples. He frequently appealed to the Poles, Czechs, and South Slavs to give up nationality policies that aimed for a breakdown of the monarchy. Bauer was convinced that preserving a huge national economic organism would serve the interests of the proletariat and all peoples of Austria-Hungary. In his view, it was the foundation for a fruitful class struggle, and it served as the basis for the nationalities policies of Social Democracy:

But those who long for a disintegration of Austria as the fulfilment of their national hopes now know how fragile this hope is. Every considered per-

---

[73] When evaluating the role of classes as carriers of the national idea, Bauer did not manage to avoid premature judgements. In 'Deutschtum und Sozialdemokratie' ('Germanness and Social Democracy'), he demonstrated that the bourgeoisie had betrayed the national principle, and that the only 'true national politics' was being conducted by the working class. To prove this, Bauer invoked a rather facile argument: the workers' struggle to improve their material conditions leads to increased population growth and therefore to the growth of the German nation. This thesis drew on sociological theories of Darwinian origins that were popular among Social Democrats at the time and tended to overestimate the role of the demographic factor in the life of nations. Along with his belief that the greatness of a people could be measured by the greatness of its culture, this argument of Bauer's betrayed his Germanophile outlook.

[74] Saage argues: 'With his major study on the nationalities question in the Habsburg monarchy, [Bauer] laid the foundations for the right of nations to self-determination. He thus established the positions of Social Democracy after World War I with regard to both the relationship of the multi-ethnic state to the nations and the question of Anschluss to the German empire' (our translation) – Saage 2009, p. 52. In my view, this is a bit of a stretch.

son must strive to find a workable form of coexistence for the nations within the given state framework. No one can be allowed to withdraw from the struggle for a solution to the Austrian nationalities question by consoling himself with the belief that a great transformation in world politics will produce a solution to the national questions within this empire ... The workers, too, are unreasonably attributed an irresponsible catastrophist politics when called upon to place their hopes in the disintegration of this empire.[75]

It is also for political reasons that Bauer, like Renner, thought of the decentralist aspirations of the nations as senseless: he was sure that the emergence of new nations would prompt a lengthy struggle between Austria and Russia. This served as the basis for an erratic political prognosis. Bauer did not regard the independence movements of the peoples as such as a threat. Rather, he feared a potential clash between German and Turkish imperialism in the Balkans – or else, in case of an armed Polish uprising, Russian military intervention, which might spread into territories enclosed in Germany and Austria. This could have developed into a hotbed of war involving the whole of Europe.

It is necessary to add that under conditions of 1907, Bauer did not expect the demise of the monarchy and rise of independent nation states. He cited the following factors to substantiate his position: (1) The peoples of Austria-Hungary are economically and politically too weak to survive and defend themselves in independent states; (2) The industrial bourgeoisie is interested in preserving the monarchy. This is because of its economic and financial connections; (3) Because of the influence of the church and the power of tradition, the bourgeoisie and the peasantry endorse the multinational state.

Let us attempt to explain the reasons for Bauer's positive attitude towards the monarchy and his aversion to the decentralist politics of the Slavic peoples. The fact that he did not like the Slavs is of lesser importance. It is fair to assume that his views were crucially influenced by the classical Marxists' beliefs in the endurance of vast national territories and the revolutionary role of the consolidated working class. Bauer's commitment to the internationalist idea also had some significance. However, it is also important to note a factor that has already been mentioned on several occasions: namely his fascination with Germany's achievements and culture.[76]

---

75   Bauer 1996, p. 403.
76   Compare Mozetič 1987, p. 226. Mozetič evaluates Bauer's position as a manifestation of German nationalism. Although I do not share his harsh judgement, I concede that Bauer

When defending the nationalities policies of Social Democracy at party congresses, Bauer passionately argued against the Czech separatists who demanded national trade unions. The issue of federal structures had been settled in 1897, yet the argument about local trade unions continued. Like Renner and Friedrich Adler, Bauer regarded Czech separatism as a great danger for the workers' movement in the monarchy and opposed splitting up the unions. He based his argument on the common economic interests of the international working class, the necessity to preserve a centralised financial sector and unity of administration, and the need to pursue a common social politics. In 1910, when the breakup of the unions was a long accomplished fact, Bauer defended the territorial principle against Czech demands to base the trade-union movement on the personal principle.[77] He regarded the territorial principle as the last effective means to preserve the unity of the proletarian movement.

In this context, Bauer's position on the Polish question in the monarchy is remarkable. He did not attach any importance to Polish independence within the context of Austro-Hungarian politics. Nor did he fear a war between Austria and Russia over Poland's independence. Although he was critical of Luxemburg's thesis that Poland's economy was insufficiently autarkic, her suggestion to concede national-cultural autonomy to solve the Polish question was where their positions overlapped. Luxemburg envisioned autonomy within the framework of a Russian state that would arise from the ruins of the Tsarist Empire. For Bauer, autonomy would be granted in Russia, Poland and Austria. This solution to the Polish question was consistent with Bauer's nationalities programme. Its essence was to concede national-cultural autonomy to the nations of Austria-Hungary and suppress their pursuit of state independence.

2.2.2 The Programme of National-Cultural Autonomy

Bauer drew the basic premises of this programme from some of Renner's texts, where the author had declared that autonomy was a prerequisite for

---

often underlined the leading role of the German nation and its cultural mission in Europe. His proclivity to link the class struggle of the proletariat with German national interests is documented in many of his texts. It is also noticeable in articles in which he analyses German-Czech relations and Czech national demands. Concerning these, Bauer endorsed the linguistic demands of the Czechs.

77   The personal principle, which was counterposed to the territorial principle, was the subject of much argument in the Austrian Social-Democratic movement. Not the individual's place of residence, but subjective identification with national ties and descent was to decide over one's nationality.

the transformation of the monarchy into a democratic multinational state. His proposition was based on four key premises:

1. The nation is, above all, a community of culture; the unity of economic and social interests plays a secondary role for the nation.
2. The nation has no significance for the process of state formation. This thesis served to justify the introduction of the personal principle as a distinguishing criterion of the nation.[78]
3. The development of capitalism leads to the formation of vast state and economic territories. Hence, the existence of small nation states is an anomaly.
4. The nationalities question is solved gradually in the course of the fundamental democratisation of the legal system and state order.

Renner paid particular attention to issues concerning the legal system and state order. He incorporated an outline for a two-dimensional federalism into his proposal: the state would be sub-divided into provinces of greater ethnic homogeneity and communities based on the personal principle (according to this principle, all citizens of a given nationality belonged to that nation irrespective of where they lived). The community would serve the protection of minority rights – to be sure, Renner primarily had the rights of dispersed Germans across non-German territories in mind.[79] In his vision, ethnically homogeneous autonomous territories would simultaneously constitute a basic element of the federal state and the federation of national states. The national association as a whole would preserve its right to full cultural autonomy, representation in the national administration, and self-administration by virtue of its statehood. The autonomy principle rested on three premises: unity of organisation; distribution of legal responsibilities; and type of federalisation. It is significant that Renner, contrary to his premise, considered the unity of economic and social interests to be a foundation for creating autonomous countries. One might rightly accuse him of introducing the personal alongside the territorial prin-

---

78   Compare Konrad 1976, p. 90.
79   He explicitly wrote about this in 'Grundlagen und Entwicklungsziele' ('Foundations and Development Aims'): 'We do not want to divide or dominate anybody – we want the national aspect to be separated from the political aspect; Whether dualism, trialism ... pentarchy ... or chiliarchy ... from a national standpoint, they are all the same to us. Nonetheless, all Germans between Bodenbach and Oršava ought to form a legally recognised cultural co-operative that has the sovereignty to impose individual taxation, and the power to build primary schools, secondary schools, and high schools wherever the Germans want and need them' (our translation) – Renner 1906, p. 239.

ciple through the backdoor. However, the serious mistake about his concept was the following: Renner took for granted that individual countries pursued the same economic and political interests as the monarchy and that state unity should therefore be preserved as the only favourable solution. As Helmut Zimmermann correctly observes, this led to the following conclusion: 'Reducing matters to cultural autonomy not only allowed for existing economic conditions to persist, but also perverted relations between different national groups of workers into open economic hostility' (our translation).[80] It is worth highlighting that Renner's model only contained an ostensible equality of nations – the principles of proportion and independence were limited to cultural questions such as language, the development of the education and school system, science and art. They did not apply, for instance, to political public life, i.e. the appointment of official posts.[81] It is also noteworthy that there was no mention of the interrelationship between the national struggle and the class struggle. Renner assumed that democratic reforms in the bourgeois multinational state would stave off the hunger for socialism for an extended period. As late as 1918, when there was no longer any chance to preserve the monarchy, he compulsively defended the draft for national-cultural autonomy (even as president of the Second Austrian Republic, he had still not come to terms with the loss of Austria's territorial outline).

The unifying element between Bauer's socio-political thought and Renner's scheme was their belief that political democracy would solve the national question.[82] Parliament would become a tool for reform beneficial to the quarrelling peoples of the monarchy. This was rooted in the idea that constitutional guarantees of national equality would convince the nations to relinquish their demands and mutually accept their respective national goals. Moreover, Bauer and Renner believed that institutional and democratic forms of social life would allow Austria-Hungary to reduce the nationalities question to the cultural sphere. Four points related to Renner's ideas guided Bauer's conception of national-cultural autonomy. Firstly, he advocated a separation of state and nation. Secondly, he proposed the exterritoriality principle as a means to determine nationality. Thirdly, he wanted to limit autonomy to the cultural sphere. Fourthly, his thinking was steeped in Greater German categories, coupled with a concern that the German nation might be slavicised.

---

80   Zimmermann 1976, p. 385.
81   See Kann 1973, p. 6.
82   Compare Mommsen 1963, p. 202.

However, the two conceptions of autonomy were not fully congruent. Renner's proposition was based on research of the legal and institutional relations between peoples. Bauer, conversely, took an analysis of the economic and political conditions of different classes as a starting point.[83] He arrived at an astonishing conclusion: the economic interests of all Austro-Hungarian social classes, especially those of the propertied classes, militated for the introduction of autonomy in Austria-Hungary; all classes had an objective interest in it.[84] From this, Bauer concluded that autonomy should be adopted into the programmes of all nations, classes, and parties that had a stake in the continued existence of Austria. Bauer wanted his postulate to be understood in this way: the bourgeoisie defends the multinational state in the name of its economic and political interests, and the proletariat should equally support it to protect its own interests. Not only did Bauer disregard the conflict of interests between classes in any capitalist state, he also ignored the response of oppressed nations. Hence, his judgements missed the historical truth, namely that the Czech and Polish bourgeoisie and the Czech industrial proletariat were sceptical of the notion of autonomy.

According to Bauer's premise, the Social-Democratic movement had to act within the existing constitutional framework. He therefore regarded the struggle for autonomy as a central objective of Social-Democratic nationalities policy. Bauer believed that conceding autonomy might relieve tensions within the working class and facilitate united struggle within the given legal framework. Bauer wrote:

> [T]he state should limit itself to the protection of those interests which are a matter of indifference in national terms, but are common to all nations. Thus, national autonomy, the self-determination of nations, necessarily becomes the constitutional programme of the working class of all nations within the multinational state.[85]

The slogan, 'national autonomy is a necessary goal of the proletarian class struggle',[86] succinctly expressed his confidence in the continued ability of

---

83   Compare Zimmermann 1976, p. 389. Hanisch writes that Bauer broadened Renner's conception by giving it a wider historical, theoretical, and political context – see Hanisch 2011, p. 101.

84   Compare Kulemann 1979, p. 128.

85   Bauer 1996, pp. 255–6.

86   Bauer 1996, p. 258.

the nations to survive without the necessity for revolutionary transformation of the existing state.

The question arises as to what Bauer meant by national-cultural autonomy. Much like Renner, he conceived of the autonomous association as possessing its own state structures, i.e. a parliament, government, state budget, culture and education. The state authority would exercise self-administration. Each federal state would preserve national and administrative unity as part of a federation with a common fiscal system. Their official language would be German. Administrative tasks, the central economy, and the military would be left to the individual federal states. The state ought to guarantee its citizens the free development of national culture, education, institutional forms, and social life.[87] This concept of national-cultural autonomy, however, excluded political autonomy. It was assumed that states would not strive for independent national statehood if they were granted national gains within a multinational structure. According to Bauer and Renner, national-cultural autonomy would be based on the exterritoriality principle, i.e. individual definition of nationality irrespective of residence.[88]

Bauer's suggested concept of national-cultural autonomy aimed to preserve the multinational state, transform the monarchy into a democratic state with a federal structure, abolish special privileges, and in this way secure the equality of nations. It was by far the most progressive suggestion to solve the nationalities question in Austria at the time, even if it did not meet the expectations of the oppressed peoples that had been fighting for independence for years. Its objective was similar to that of Renner's model: reform rather than transformation of the class structure in the bourgeois state. According to this plan, the preservation of the multinational state was a precondition for waging the class struggle under the leadership of the Social-Democratic party. As Mommsen points out, the problem with the internationalist ideology that Austrian Social Democracy, including Bauer and Renner, had to wrestle with 'lay, of course, in that it presupposes that national interests are essentially limited to the cultural and linguistic

---

87   As Hanisch writes: 'This major, long-term project demanded radical constitutional reform, a complete reconstitution of Austria. The "centralist-atomic" regulation, as Bauer called the December constitution of 1867, was to be replaced by an "organic regulation"' – Hanisch 2011, p. 101.

88   Bauer rejected the territorial principle on the grounds of migration movements, the division of economic territories, and the danger of minorities being 'swallowed up'. In 1908, he identified technical and legal difficulties as standing in the way of the personal principle. In *Die soziale Gliederung der österreichischen Nationen* (*The Social Structure of the Austrian Nations*), he supported the territorial principle.

realm, while economic questions have an international character by nature'
(our translation).[89] Although questions of language and education played an
important role in the Habsburg monarchy, the assumption that national ambitions could be confined to the cultural realm was illusory. Similarly, Bauer and
Renner's belief that the economic community of interests uniting the peoples
of Austria-Hungary could offset their separatist tendencies was wishful thinking.

Voices from the Marxist camp did not spare the concept of national-cultural
autonomy from criticism. It was approved neither by the SDAP nor by the
nationalist parties, where Ignaz Seipel was one of many who viewed it with
contempt. The policy was criticised for disregarding the socio-political conditions of Austria and Europe, or else for its conservative stance towards the
independence movements. Stalin reproached Bauer for failing to explicitly
mention the right of nations to self-determination, while Lenin accused him
of German nationalism.[90] Kautsky took a particularly critical view in a series
of articles printed in *Die Neue Zeit* (1908) and a pamphlet, *Nationalität und
Internationalität* (*Nationality and Internationality*, 1908). While conceding that
autonomy was crucial for working-class organisation in the struggle against
nationalism, he disagreed that one could achieve it in a multinational state.[91]
In Kautsky's opinion, Bauer underestimated the strength of the movements
for self-determination. As early as 1908, Kautsky predicted the demise of the
monarchy. In his critique of autonomy, he considered two factors: economic differences and language. Kautsky emphasised that autonomy would not suspend
national conflicts. He believed that they resulted from the unequal economic
development of nations, which necessarily upset the equal distribution of financial means for cultural and educational purposes. Conversely, he presumed
that language was a basic criterion for a nation's development – he saw the
future of nations in communities of language. In his reply to Kautsky, Bauer
accepted that national-cultural autonomy was only a half-solution, given that
the principle of legal equality for self-administration did not revoke economic

89   Mommsen 1963, p. 10.
90   Stalin 1953, p. 338.
91   Kautsky wrote on Austria-Hungary: 'Austria itself will then become superfluous to those
      nations that still today think that they need it. If the whole of Europe were structured
      according to nations and economic areas – what place would there then be for a federal
      state in a federal state? And if all nations of contemporary Austria join together with their
      fellow language speakers outside of the existing territory of the Empire to form entities
      that are autonomous for the purpose of language culture, what elements remain for a
      specific multinational state?' – Kautsky 2010, p. 163.

divergences and national conflicts of interest. Nonetheless, he defended it as a principle that would guarantee the preservation of the state. In response, Kautsky accused Bauer of fetishising the state as a goal in itself instead of regarding it as a tool in the class struggle.

The SDAP majority also judged the model of national-cultural autonomy negatively. The prevailing view was that no suggestions for reforming the state should be made in parliament. In light of strong national antagonisms, and because each respective country aspired to extract more concessions at the expense of others, such reforms might lead to a disaster and the fall of the monarchy. This outcome, in turn, would render the party's strategic line invalid. One should not forget that the SDAP, which was embroiled in the struggle for universal suffrage at the beginning of the twentieth century, did not yet represent a serious political counterweight to the Christian Social and Greater German camps. Arguments about the liberation of the Slavic peoples emerging in the ranks of Social Democracy only complicated matters further. As Mommsen states, even the suggestion to divide the state into districts to protect the rights of Czech Germans was strongly opposed by Social Democrats.[92] The Czechs disapproved of the proposal to increase the state budget for culture contained in Bauer's model. In their view, this would primarily benefit the German population. Conversely, they were eager to get subsidies from Austria. The government successfully suppressed their efforts, as did the German-Austrian Social Democrats. One might even speak of a certain alliance between Social Democracy and the crown during the period leading up to Word War I. In contrast to the peoples of the monarchy, they both represented centralist trends. Centralist tendencies were also manifest in both autonomy models, even if they doubtlessly had a progressive character in Austria at the time. In 1920, Hans Kelsen harked back to one of their suggestions: ethnically homogeneous autonomous regions were to become a fundamental element of the national federation and the federation of national states. His texts inspired the co-founders of Austrian statehood.

2.2.3 Remarks on National Assimilation

The assimilation process, which comprised all ethnic groups equally, was a significant phenomenon of the Habsburg state. The slogan of 'national assimilation' became a cause of disagreement between German-Austrian and Czech Social Democrats especially after 1897. At the turn of the nineteenth century, increasing levels of Czech economic migration to Vienna and Lower Austria

---

92   See Mommsen 1963, p. 209.

provoked fears of slavicisation of ancient German territories among ethnic Germans. The Czechs watched the trend of migration with displeasure, quite justifiably regarding it as a cause for the economic and political weakening of their nation. The notion that national-cultural autonomy was a tool to increase migration of non-German groups was an important reason as to why the Czech Social Democrats viewed it with caution.[93]

Understandably, Bauer's conception of assimilation and the conclusions he drew from it only reinforced the Czech socialists' fears. Bauer gave assimilation a distinctly German flavour and made it part of his programme to preserve the monarchy. While he did not dedicate much theoretical attention to it, many of his statements at party congresses testified to his great hope of overcoming national conflict through assimilation. He tied this not only to autonomy as a programme for today, but also to the merging of nations in the future.

Bauer only undertook a sociological analysis of the assimilation process in a 1912 article entitled 'Die Bedingungen der nationalen Assimilation' ('The Conditions of National Assimilation'). It is where his differences with Kautsky became apparent. Kautsky depicted the foundations of assimilation in a simplified manner, i.e. a relatively straightforward process whereby the language of an ethnic majority is adopted. In contrast to Kautsky, Bauer emphasised the complexity of assimilation. For him, it was a long and complicated historical process during which diverging national characteristics, personality types, culture and customs had to be considered. Bauer was aware that there was no clear dividing line between assimilating and surrendering one's national identity. Hence, he wrote that 'national assimilation, as we have demonstrated in our fifth assimilation law, is always assimilation only to fellow members of the same class. National coercion is the subjugation of one class to the will of another, regardless of whether the ruling class uses economic or state power to do violence to a minority' (our translation).[94] Bauer based his sociological assimilation laws on the relations in Austria-Hungary: they testified to the singular, one-dimensional character of the assimilation process, which amounted to the incorporation of an ethnic minority into the majority in each respective class.

---

93   Compare Mommsen 1979b, p. 211.

94   'Die nationale Assimilation ist, wie wir in unserem fünften Assimilationsgesetz gezeigt
      haben, immer nur Angleichung an Klassengenossen, die nationale Nötigung ist Unter-
      werfung einer Klasse unter den Willen einer anderen Klasse, sei es nun, dass sich die
      herrschende Klasse ihrer wirtschaftlichen Macht oder dass sie sich ihrer Staatsgewalt
      bedient, um der Minderheit Gewalt antun' – Bauer 1980d, p. 621.

Bauer cited demographic aspects such as small size and dispersal, but particularly cultural features such as similarity in language, religion and culture as factors that accelerated this process. He attached crucial importance to the latter. His analysis was especially valuable insofar as he highlighted the degree of differentiation that existed within the respective classes and social groups during the process of assimilation. He found that the assimilation process in oppressed countries primarily involved the propertied classes, which merged with the ruling classes of the oppressor nation provided that they could benefit from their economic and political position. As to the peasantry and proletariat of the oppressed countries, their economic and cultural levels determined the pace of the assimilation process: peasants assimilated faster and with less difficulty if their economic and cultural levels were more advanced. The exact opposite was true for the working class.

We can conclude from our observations thus far that Bauer regarded assimilation in a multinational state as a desirable process. Therefore, he suggested integrating the slogan for *national assimilation* into the nationalities programme of Social Democracy. Although it contradicted the personal principle that he supported, Bauer bypassed this inconvenient fact for political reasons. As a politician defending the concerns of Austrian Social Democracy, he hoped that assimilation would proceed in one direction only: he expected that non-German peoples would assimilate to Germany due to its economic and cultural superiority. When German and Czech Social Democrats fought over the latter group's proposal to open Czech minority schools, it should therefore come as no surprise that Bauer opposed the idea. He claimed that it would upset the peaceful assimilation process and would aggravate the nationalities conflict between Germans and Czechs, who made up 26 percent of the Vienna population. Notably, this did not stop him from establishing middle schools for the German population in Czechia.[95] A similar inconsistency is apparent in Bauer's position on Czech workers. On the one hand, he opposed their forced Germanisation, fearing that it might put the German minority in Czechia at risk. In contrast, he called on Social Democrats

---

95   The following picture emerges from Bauer's discussion of the school system: minorities that assimilate (non-historical nations) should not have their own schools, while minorities that assimilate (historical nations, in this case the Germans) should have the right to national schools. On mixed territories, minorities that do or do not assimilate should have the right to form national and bilingual schools – in the Sudetenland, for instance, there should be both German and Czech schools. This education system model was clearly biased towards Germans. As to Bauer's suggestion to establish German schools in Czechia, compare Mommsen 1963, p. 211.

to support professional training and raise the cultural level of Czech workers in Austria, arguing that it would accelerate the process of their assimilation with Germany. It is justified to say that Bauer's entire line of argu-
mentation with respect to national assimilation testified to his vivid aversion towards the oppressed peoples' decentralist aspirations. What is more, it
marked the transition of Austrian Social Democracy towards nationalist positions.

2.3   *The Programme of the Left and the Demise of the Monarchy*

The conflict between Austria and Serbia that followed the annexation of Bosnia
and Herzegovina made the Austrian Social Democrats aware that the unresolved nationalities question might lead to a world war in the near future. With
the exception of a tiny group of imperial officials and a number of state-loyal
Social Democrats, few had doubts that a world war would result in the disintegration of the Habsburg Empire. Bauer was one of the few who anticipated
such a historical development as early as 1908: he believed that the outbreak of
the war would trigger a wave of revolutions across Europe, inevitably leading
to the demise of multinational states.[96] In 1911, he warned:

> Austria, too, will be caught up in these upheavals. The national struggles
> and the relationship to Hungary push for the whole of the imperial struc-
> ture to be overturned. Either Austria will be transformed into a federal
> state comprising of autonomous nations, or it will cease to exist.[97]

The outbreak of war weakened the party-internal bonds of the SDAP and
deepened the differences between Bauer's and Renner's nationalities policies.
In his wartime texts, *Österreichs Erneuerung* (*Austria's Renewal*) and *Marxismus, Krieg und Internationale* (*Marxism, War and the International*), Renner
continued to defend the principle of the multinational state. This was, on the
one hand, an expression of his old belief that Social Democracy could successfully continue its politics within the existing constitutional framework.
But on the other hand, it also betrayed his opposition to changing the socio-
political order and his affirmative stance towards the capitalist state – an attitude that Bauer harshly criticised. The task of Social Democracy in wartime,
Bauer argued, was to prepare the masses for the forthcoming revolution, not
to defend a state that would disintegrate due to the decentralist efforts of the

---

96   See Bauer 1996, pp. 5–6.
97   Bauer 1975d, p. 940.

Slavic nations.[98] The victorious 1917 socialist revolution in Russia further polarised positions in Social Democracy. Renner continued to defend his old point of view, while Bauer inspired a left group to proclaim a nationalities programme. For the first time, the SDAP – or rather, a faction of the party – pleaded for the right of nations to self-determination. Even so, the programme of 1917 did not have the slightest significance: as early as January 1918, it emerged at a delegates' congress of the Austrian, Czech and Polish left in Vienna that the Austrian Social Democrats, including Bauer, never fully supported the right to self-determination. The left adopted a new nationalities programme at this conference. Although it endorsed Czech and Polish aspirations to independence and conceded the right to self-determination to the Slavic peoples, it did not represent a significant turn in the nationalities policy of Social Democracy.[99] Rather, it was the old federalist idea dressed up in new garb – an attempt to preserve the great economic territory either through union or through the Greater German solution. The programme envisioned the following points:

1. Austria-Hungary would be divided into seven territories according to the language principle: German, Czech, Polish, Ukrainian, South Slavic, Italian, and Romanian regions; these communities would decide their national identity in a plebiscite.
2. In each territory, the national assembly would decide what type of constitution to adopt and what neighbourly relations to pursue by virtue of universal suffrage.
3. Political autonomy would not imply complete independence of the formerly Austro-Hungarian peoples; new organs would be convened to regulate economic questions in co-operation.[100]

The programme upheld the idea of a Social-Democratic party that would unite national parties in a federal structure and on an equal footing. To justify this

---

98 As Leser writes, the majority of the party did not find Bauer's 1917 speeches credible. Many Austrian workers regarded the Slavic peoples' struggle for independence as a betrayal of class interests. See Leser 1964, p. 20.

99 My assessment is mirrored in Mommsen 1979, p. 216; Panzenböck 1985, p. 83; Kulemann 1979, p. 210; Hautmann 2007, p. 93. As Hautmann demonstrates, the programme factually meant that the nations of the Austro-Hungarian monarchy would be granted the right to decide their future, which included the right to create sovereign countries. In Hautmann's opinion, the left's agreement on this question was the only way to justify its programmatic demand to annex the German-speaking territories to democratic Germany.

100 See Bauer 1980g, p. 951. Compare Panzenböck 1985, p. 83.

model, it stressed the international character of the class struggle and the necessity of the working class joining forces for the right of nations to self-determination.[101] Ten months later, Bauer referred to it in the *Arbeiter-Zeitung*, conceding to the Slavic peoples the right to choose their own future. However, it is noteworthy that Bauer did not emphasise the principle of national self-determination. The idea of Austria's annexation to the German Reich (the *Anschluss* idea) represented an obstacle in this respect: it was inconsistent with national independence and the democratic institutional solutions contained in the left's proposed model.[102] The only significant modification to Bauer's 1918 position on the nationalities question was his break with the notion that only socialism could realise the right of nations to self-determination – this also testified to his non-doctrinaire approach. From then on, Bauer linked this right with the victory of democracy in Europe.[103]

The 1918 nationalities programme of the left intensified the polemics between Renner and Bauer, with Max Adler taking Bauer's side. Renner attacked the programme, arguing that the formation of new nation states after the fall of the monarchy was a 'reactionary utopia'. Convinced that the proletariat would gain the most by backing the policies of the existing imperialist state instead of getting embroiled in national struggles, he supported the war drive of the party leadership. According to Renner, the future of Western Europe lay in establishing vast economic territories, whereas that of Eastern European peoples lay in territorial and economic union under German patronage. Renner defended this idea as late as 1922, when he conceded sovereignty to the middle and East European states yet continued to advocate economic and cultural attachment to Germany. Although he rightly reproached Bauer and the left for their Greater German orientation, Renner failed to acknowledge nationalist elements in his own thinking. His main argument for preserving the unity of the Austria-Hungarian Empire was that it would preserve the interests of national minorities, especially the German minority in Czechia. Bauer was far more realistic in evaluating the possibilities of saving the Habsburg state in 1918. In view of Austria's weakened position, the changing political balance of forces in Europe, and the revolutionary wave moving west, he expected the imminent fall of the monarchy. This is not to imply, however, that he gave up all hope in

---

101 The Hungarian Social Democrats did not accept the programme of the left. Instead, they defended Hungary's integrity against the nationalities it oppressed. This led to a war against Czechoslovakia and Romania and contributed to the defeat of the Hungarian workers' movement.

102 Compare Mommsen 1963, p. 215.

103 Ibid.

Austria-Hungary's potential salvation. On the contrary, he claimed as late as 1918 that, as long as German imperialism prevailed, the only alternative was to preserve the old structural framework of the party and work out a reform programme for the multinational state. Towards the end of the war, his position was close to the right wing of the party. The sole difference between the two leading Social Democrats was that Bauer accepted the fall of the monarchy, while Renner believed in its rebirth until the end.

As expected, the war led to the disintegration of Austria-Hungary. Investigating the causes of its demise in *The Austrian Revolution* (1923), Bauer conceded that 'the great old Empire, the great old economic unity was not destroyed by the social revolution of the German-Austrian and the Magyar proletariat, but by the national revolution of the Czech, the Polish, and the Jugo Slav bourgeoisie'.[104] In accordance with his own definition of the nation, he attributed the fall of Austria-Hungary mainly to a psychological factor, 'the old tribal feud between the nations', rather than to the economic causes of the nationalities conflicts.[105] On 3 October 1918, the parliamentary fraction of the SDAP under Bauer's leadership adopted the right of the Slavic nations to self-determination. In its appeal, it demanded the unification of all German territories in Austria into one state that would self-determine its relations to neighbouring countries, especially Germany.

After the demise of the monarchy, the question for Austria's national identity amounted to whether Austria should maintain its national independence or join the Reich.[106] Austria had always been a country characterised by much stronger German influences than the sheer size of its German populace suggested. An *Anschluss* to Germany was in the interest of the German population, which was the decisive aspect for German-Austrian Social Democracy when it accepted the *Anschluss* proposal at the plenary assembly on 6 June 1917.[107] Of all party leaders, Bauer advocated it with the greatest passion. He argued that

---

104   Bauer 1925, p. 73.

105   Kulemann 1979, p. 48.

106   The demand for Austria's annexation by Germany appeared in Austrian Social-Democratic thought as early as 1880 – See Konrad 1978, p. 25.

107   According to Fröschl and Zoitl 1985, p. 242, Austrian attitudes towards the *Anschluss* idea varied across different social classes. During the times of the monarchy, sections of the bourgeoisie were in favour of annexation by Germany, while other sections pleaded for national independence. The division became greater after 1918. The peasantry and petty bourgeoisie loathed the Protestant Prussians. The working class was generally opposed to German chauvinism and imperialism, yet parts of it came out in favour of annexation. The intelligentsia was overwhelmingly the mouthpiece of German nationalism.

three German countries should be created – an Inner Austrian, German Czech, and a Sudeten German territory – and returned to the home country.[108] Indeed, a proposal for this type of reorganisation already appeared in *The Question of Nationalities* as an alternative to national autonomy. For Bauer – as for Renner – the idea of *Anschluss* had a national dimension (community of culture, blood ties), but also political, economic, and revolutionary aspects. It is mainly for these reasons that he would obsessively revisit this idea – even after the *Anschluss* proposal had been rejected in the Treaty of Saint-Germain-en-Laye of 1919. In 1923, Bauer continued to see two possibilities: 'Supranational federation of the Danubian peoples or national unity of the Germans; restoration of the Hapsburg Monarchy or fusion [*Anschluss*] with the German Republic'.[109]

A brief comment might serve to sum up these observations. The proposals put forward before World War I (national-cultural autonomy, cultural assimilation) and during the war (*Anschluss*) reflected the transformation of Austrian Social Democracy towards nationalist positions. Because these positions effectively meant a denial of the right to national self-determination, they did not meet the expectations of the subordinate nations of Austria-Hungary. Ultimately, the solution to the nationalities question was decided by the respective countries' long-time efforts to rebuild their statehood, the defeat of the Austrian army on the war front, and the desire of the masses to end the war and national conflicts.[110]

It is worth shedding light on a particular belief that was intrinsic to Bauer's position: national objectives, when pursued by the proletariat, can become the proletariat's overriding objectives (we will examine this in more detail in

---

108 It is necessary to emphasise the fundamental difference between Bauer's and Hitler's understanding of *Anschluss*, the annexation of Austria to Germany. Bauer did not propose a simple incorporation of Austria into the Reich, but rather the creation of a body of German states (based mainly on common economic and financial policies) in which all states would retain far-reaching autonomy in domestic questions.

109 Bauer 1925, p. 282.

110 As anticipated by Bauer, independent nation states were formed. Yet questions of peaceful co-operation between these states in the capitalist era of competition over sales and labour markets have lost none of their relevance. Today, there is no doubt that Bauer's suggestions for reconciling the nations are mainly of historical interest. However, I maintain that national-cultural autonomy remains the most effective way to defend minorities against the centralisation of power in a nation state. The demands of Hungarian politicians in Slovakia, who in 1996 called for the introduction of autonomy in the spheres of culture and education, testify to this. The same is true for Silesians in Poland who do not identify with the Polish nation.

Chapter 7). The vision of a 'United States of Europe',[111] which informed *The Question of Nationalities and Social Democracy*, is certainly close to the hearts of Europeans today. In Bauer's theory, it is true, this vision was intrinsically linked to a socialist future – yet that does not diminish its grandeur.

---

111   See Bauer 1996, p. 414.

CHAPTER 5

The 'Third Way' to Socialism

Bauer's philosophical, economic, and sociological inquiries, which were covered in Chapters 1–4, held crucial elements to the fundamental political trajectories of Austromarxism: peaceful social transformation and corresponding practical activities required of Austrian Social Democracy to democratise the capitalist order. The way in which Bauer approached matters of the state, including its different forms (democracy and dictatorship) and the state of the future, was entirely theoretical. It also drove Social-Democratic politics in the bourgeois state in a specific direction. The notion of a 'third' way to socialism only faded with fascism's victory, preceded by a crisis of democracy. At the time, the Social-Democratic party's struggle against fascist reaction became the central question. These issues form the subject matter of Chapters 5–8.

1   The Vision of Peaceful Revolution and Its Realisation

Perspectives and possibilities of proletarian revolution, including the potential for a revolution in Austria, and the relationship to the Russian Revolution and Bolshevism preoccupied Bauer's mind. Crucially, statements made by SDAP leaders on possible ways of transformation from capitalism to socialism were purely theoretical up until 1917, as were remarks on perspectives of socialist revolution. With the victory of the October Revolution in Russia and the revolutionary wave in Europe, this became a practical, distinctly political, issue. That does not mean that the theoretical aspects of revolution – its form, the changing class content of the bourgeois state, and the speed of change – lost significance for Bauer. On the contrary, his views matured there and then. Nonetheless, potential roads to socialism and corresponding measures were not central during the period of social upheaval in Austria – the Austrian socialists had already elaborated these, which allowed Bauer to define ideological and theoretical solutions more closely. What instead became important were the Social-Democratic party's perspective and strategy for the revolutionary situation and for the event of a bourgeois counter-attack.

Bauer's overall concept of revolution was borne of theoretical reflections on the perspectives, conditions, aspects, forms and development mechanisms of socialist revolution. Equally tantamount was the question of allies: what social forces could potentially be won for socialism? A part of this complex situation were tactical solutions based on analysis of the political and class balance in Austria and across Europe. The theory had its strong and weak points. Bauer's assessment of socio-political conditions was certainly not without ideological considerations, and as a result, it not only bore many unconvincing elements, but also weakened the overall strategic line of the SDAP. The strong point was Bauer's emphasis on the socio-technical form, namely the method of seizing and maintaining power during the transitional period, mechanisms to win the middle classes over to proletarian revolution, and tools for transforming capitalist society. The fact that his theory proved ineffective under conditions of a modern bourgeois state, and the fact that it cannot be applied in today's circumstances, do not diminish its value.

1.1   *Parliamentarism and the Revolution*

The vision of proletarian revolution in Bauer's work was representative of the Marxist centre of the Second International and hugely popular outside Austria, including in Poland. Bauer had created the model of a parliamentary-democratic, peaceful road to socialism.[1] Since the late nineteenth century, this revolutionary theory had become manifest in the European socialist movement to varying degrees, yet it took shape within Austromarxism and remains an important contribution to socialist theory to the present day.

Crucially, the suggestion to use parliamentary institutions in the struggle for socialism derived from a specific theoretical and philosophical paradigm, the deterministic-economic conception of history.[2] The anticipation of the inevitable collapse of capitalism justified the belief in the historical necessity of socialism and was easily reconciled with the reformist orientation of the workers' parties. The vision of a gradual revolution – the working class taking control of economic and political institutions by piecemeal – was a logical and natural consequence of the deterministic-economic conception of socio-historical processes. The fact that Renner and others relied heavily on this to back their theory of 'growing into socialism' and effectively supported the capitalist order were further consequences of the historical philosophy adopted at the outset. It was based on Bernstein's notion, popularised in the Austrian Social-Democratic movement, that any revolutionary seizure of power must

---

1   For the influence on Polish socialist thought – i.e. the views of Niedziałkowski, Perl, Czapiński, Próchnik, Dreszer, Lange and others, compare Jeliński 1994, pp. 130–56; Śliwa 1980, pp. 191–280; Czerwińska 435, pp. 418–35.

2   Note that the theory of peaceful revolution contradicts this paradigm on several questions, e.g. the evaluation of the role of politics in state economic affairs. This was often overlooked in discussions at the time.

be rejected. This was derived from the antinomical view of history. At the heart of it were two premises. The first was that the reformist and revolutionary roads were two sides of the same social process. Secondly, in the changed economic, political, and social circumstances of the early twentieth century, only parliamentarism and democratic legislation could safeguard and advance the interests of the working class. A more thorough discussion of the philosophical, historical and political premises of the Austromarxist peaceful road to socialism would require wider analyses that would exceed the scope of this text. However, it is important to acknowledge that the premises emerged in a climate of scepticism towards Marx's revolutionary perspective. Bernstein and his co-thinkers, who grew increasingly influential in the course of the Second International, did not agree with Marx on this. Similarly, the greatest Marxist authority of the time, Kautsky, also did not acquiesce to it. Even during his revolutionary period, he wrote:

> The Socialist party is a revolutionary party, but not a revolution-making party. We know that our goal can be attained only through revolution. We also know that it is just as little in our power to create this revolution as it is in the power of our opponents to prevent it. It is no part of our work to instigate a revolution or to prepare the way for it.[3]

It is common knowledge that the rejection of the revolutionary perspective was largely inspired by the classical Marxists, even if that had not been their intention (and indeed, it would be difficult to blame Marx for this). The Social Democrats took Marx's 1872 statement to heart: in highly industrialised, democratic countries such as Britain and the United States, he argued, a peaceful socialist transformation would be possible.[4] Engels's 1895 statement that the workers' parties could adopt peaceful democratic strategies was met with even more enthusiasm – the Social Democrats took it as legitimising their reformist practice.[5] The fact that Engels's rejection of the revolutionary tactics of 1848 did not imply a radical break with the idea of proletarian revolution was overlooked.[6] The Social Democrats, especially the Germans and Austrians, took Engels's hint for a change of strategy and made it the basis for their political activity. They believed that their outlook was objectively supported by changing economic conditions such as rapid industrial development, improving social policies,

---

3 Kautsky 1909b, p. 50.
4 See Marx 1872.
5 See Engels 1990, pp. 520–2.
6 Hans-Josef Steinberg writes about this in Steinberg 1972, p. 71.

and a growing standard of living for the working class. The programmes of the respective parties provided theoretical justification for the concept of peaceful revolution – i.e. reforming the capitalist system through parliament – which was prevalent particularly in Austrian socialism.[7] From its inception, the following basic positions were its touchstones:

- Under democratic conditions, the working class struggle for state power will assume legal forms, and will be carried out in parliament.
- A parliamentary majority for the Social Democrats is the precondition for the beginning of the revolutionary process. To achieve this majority, it will be necessary to win the middle classes to the socialist idea.
- The revolution will be an extended process. It will culminate in the transformation of the economic and political system of capitalism into a socialist state order. Hence, it will not be necessary to break up the old economic and political apparatus.
- The success of the parliamentary-democratic revolution will be determined by the political, social, and cultural maturity of the working class, which can only be achieved through a long-term educational process.[8]

All of these elements were part of Bauer's theory of socialist revolution. He defined them more closely and complemented them with theory and tactics that were specific to Austrian conditions and reflected the international balance of forces during the revolutionary period.

Like many ideologists of Western Social Democracy at the time, Bauer saw no possibility of a Bolshevik-style revolution under Western European conditions. There were both theoretical and axiological reasons as to why he rejected it. Theoretically, he dismissed it as a voluntaristic experiment at odds with Marxism. From an axiological standpoint, he considered it an economic and cultural disaster, and a tragedy for the individual. Bauer presented two arguments against revolutionary methods of action and proletarian dictatorship in Western European countries. Firstly, he cited the necessity to preserve demo-

---

7 It represented a middle ground between Bernstein's camp of radical reformism and that of radical communists.

8 Elements of this conception were also present in German Social-Democratic thought – first among the revisionists, and later with Kautsky. The fact that they never evolved further might be because they merged many contradictory orientations. That the Austromarxists chose the parliamentary-democratic way to socialism was down to psychological and social reasons. The party leaders hailed from bourgeois circles with democratic traditions, which is why Austria never produced a revolutionary 'type'.

cracy as an organisational form of economic and social life even under socialism, and secondly, he referred to the lack of objective and subjective conditions
for socialist revolution. In most of his texts and speeches, Bauer argued for the
reformist path, the exception being his works and statements from the period
of fascisisation. Even if they did not contain any evidence for the inevitability
of socialism, he personally believed in its victory.[9] This was rooted in the belief
that reforms were a necessary stage in the struggle against capitalism, because
they shook its economic and social foundations, thus accelerating socialism's
victory. Over the years, Bauer's faith in the effectiveness of reformist politics
under capitalism faded – which, however, did not stop him from defending
reformism as a necessary step in the development of the workers' movement
until the end of his life.[10] His rationalism and pragmatism prevailed over ideology, and it is difficult to deny that the working class must attain its day-to-day
interests in whatever state it lives in.

The rationale behind Bauer's insistence on the reformist path was primarily
his evaluation of the role and level of maturity of the objective and subjective
conditions for revolution. Even if he was no orthodox Marxist, he shared Marx's
view that the victory of proletarian revolution depended on objective and subjective conditions for revolution. The objective prerequisites, for Bauer, were
all the conditions defined by Marx's law of development of socio-economic
formations, i.e. the development level of productive forces, intensity of social
antagonisms, and the economic and numerical strength of the proletariat. He
regarded the psychological factor as the most important subjective prerequisite of revolution: the will to abolish capitalism and the development structures
of political-ideological consciousness of the revolutionary class.

What appears particularly challenging in Bauer's theory is his definition of
the interrelationship between objective and subjective conditions for revolution. This predicament is rooted in Bauer's interpretation of Marxism. In Chap-

---

9   Albers shares my view – see Albers 1983, p. 49. On this question, Bauer's polemic against
     Kautsky's theses from *The Road to Power* appears symptomatic. In the latter, Kautsky poin-
     ted to the immiseration of the proletariat and austerity measures in welfare legislation
     as consequences of the imperialist stage of capitalism; he highlighted the necessity of
     struggle for political power as a basic prerequisite for changing the condition of the pro-
     letariat. In his reply, Bauer not only contradicted Kautsky's thesis of powerlessness and
     growing immiseration of the proletariat – he rejected his demand to struggle for power,
     justifying his stance with the masses' insufficient maturity and lack of faith in revolution.
     Furthermore, he highlighted the role of democracy for mitigating class antagonisms and
     the importance and possibilities of reformist politics. See Bauer 1976g, p. 957.
10   See Bauer 1976p, p. 253.

ter 2 (section 2.2), I assessed the naturalist, positivist and evolutionist layers of his theory, yet without fully considering his mechanic understanding of the relationship between economic and conscious spheres of social being. I furthermore polemicised against those interpretations of Bauer's historiosophy that highlighted the economic element and pointed to a dilemma: the question of human social practice blending in with the objective mechanism of historical development.

Bauer's writings on revolution give the impression that he overestimated the role of objective factors. There is no other way to describe his stubbornly upheld thesis – which Norbert Leser draws particular attention to – that the development of the capitalist system gradually paves the way for revolution, i.e. that the inner contradictions of the system in themselves lay the groundwork for the replacement of capitalist production.[11] Nor is it possible to find a different explanation for his claim that the lack of objective conditions could bring forth results different from those expected by the working class or lead to the reestablishment of the old political order in a different form. To vindicate his opinion on the role of the objective factor in the social revolution, Bauer cited Russia as an example: there, the lack of favourable objective conditions for revolution forced the victorious working class to reintroduce the capitalist economy and install elements parallel to the socialist mode of production.

However, a more thorough look at the relation between the two factors in Bauer's revolutionary theory reveals that the role of the objective factor was not as clear as one might assume. Without a doubt, Bauer was convinced that socio-economic conditions would already change under bourgeois rule and lead to socialism. It was the core of his economic theory. However, his belief that the revolutionary process was objectively determined was not neutral; it was strictly subordinated to its ideological function. Its role was to reinforce the masses' belief that socialism would inevitably come to pass and validate the politics of 'wait and see' held dear by the leadership. One is led to believe that Bauer was aware – if not fully – that the theory of a parliamentary-democratic road to socialism was tied to the assumption that social consciousness, ideology and politics were relatively autonomous from the economic base – an element that he accentuated in his theory of state formation. He clung to Marx's notion that the base determines the superstructure in a purely declarative manner. It would be justified to state this was a relic of orthodox thinking, caused primarily by his fear of betraying the doctrine. In reality, Bauer understood

---

11   Leser placed strong emphasis on this thesis of Bauer's in his major work on Austromarxism – see Leser 1969, p. 33.

the significance of subjective conditions in the revolutionary process. The fact that he placed great emphasis on developing the political consciousness of the proletariat and its allies testifies to this. In addition, he stressed that both conditions must be present: an objective tendency and a social will to transform the political order.

Bauer's belief in the active role of political consciousness and human action in terms of social development was directly linked to his blueprints of the structure of revolution. Bauer shared Kautsky's view that every revolution has a political and a social aspect – the two aspects differed in duration, objectives, and social reach. Political revolution can be achieved in a day; its aim is to seize state power either through social insurrection or by winning the majority in parliament. The change of political rule is a necessary precondition for the beginning of socialist transformation, but not the only one. In contrast to political revolution, the term social revolution describes an entire historical epoch. It is a prolonged process, occurring at many different levels, during which the socio-economic structure is transformed. Its side effects include wars, the decline and emergence of states, and the demise of political systems and governments. It is a result of many years of educational and ideological work. Notably, for Bauer, revolution meant social revolution, i.e. a period during which the working class in power attempts to transform the socio-economic order. In other words, revolution is the transitional period between capitalism and socialism. Capitalist property relations are maintained, yet political power is in the hands of the working class. To be precise, Bauer's theory of social revolution was based on a programme of education and socialisation.

Bauer decisively rejected a notion upheld by Marxists such as Lenin, Luxemburg and Trotsky, which was deeply rooted in the international workers' movement – namely that the proletarian revolution involved a radical break with existing economic and political relations. Drawing on his own 'balance of class forces' theory, he claimed that a so-called 'transitional period' marked by equilibrium of political and class forces (e.g. a coalition government or subordination to a state apparatus that has become autonomous) and socio-economic balance (coexistence of different economic forms) was a necessary stage in every revolution. It is hard to deny that Bauer's interpretation of revolution called into question the basics of Marx's theory, to which he referred consistently. His unorthodox reading of the classics did not escape the attention of those who were close to Bauer and supported his integral revolutionary concept.[12]

---

12   Otto Leichter was among several socialists to polemicise against Bauer on this. His pos-

In view of the above, it is evident that Bauer understood the transformation of the socio-economic order as a transitional development stage of capitalist society towards socialism that would last many years. He concurred with Marx that this stage would only begin once the bourgeoisie had been deprived of political power, although he in no way supported his doctrine of armed revolutionary uprising. What form a revolution might take remained controversial for Bauer – he strongly focused on it during both the revolutionary period (1918–21) and the fascist counter-revolution (1926–38). Because this topic will be subject to closer examination later on, a few general remarks will suffice here.

Bauer understood dictatorship as a total negation of both democracy and socialism, but, above all, as a threat to the civil rights and liberty of the individual, a restriction on the realm of productivity, and a source of alienation and dehumanisation of societies. Like Renner, he identified the dictatorship of the proletariat not just as a new type of class state, but as a distinct form of power. Yet, for Bauer, the peaceful road to socialism was much more than an issue of tactics for the workers' movement or a purely theoretical question. Analysing the forms that a socialist revolution might take, he concluded that they would depend on the conditions under which revolution took place. In his earlier works and public appearances, he did not take into account the option of employing dictatorial measures during or after the struggle for power. He summed up his position thus: 'It is barely possible to maintain a soviet dictatorship here [in Western and Central Europe] in the longer term, albeit the proletariat does not need it in order to seize power'.[13] According to Bauer, the parliamentary route was the most appropriate way, especially in a situation where the proletariat constituted a minority. Thus, he recommended at the party congress of 30 October–1 November 1918 that the working masses consider winning full political democracy in the bourgeois state their strategic goal, and only then taking up the struggle for socialism.[14]

---

ition on proletarian revolution being close to Marx's, Leichter defended the notion that there were differences between bourgeois and proletarian revolutions. See Leichter 1924, p. 179.

13   Bauer 1976c, p. 349.

14   I would like to stress that from 1918–19, many activists and ideologists of European Social Democracy adopted Bauer's perspective and proclaimed that the highly industrialised countries of Europe boasted neither political nor economic preconditions for a socialist state order. The Social Democrats believed that the struggle for socialism would assume peaceful and legal means. Parliamentary work would protect the state against the destruction of its foundations and simultaneously facilitate the modification of its functions in the interest of all social classes. Contradicting his own earlier statements, Kautsky

Indeed, Bauer thought it impossible to predetermine the means and methods by which the proletariat would seize power – hence, he did not consider this to be a pertinent question for Social-Democratic politics. What counted was defining the procedures and measures that would facilitate the transition from capitalism to socialism. *De facto* this amounted to creating a mechanism of permanent reforms in a democratic liberal spirit. Bauer may have stressed in his propaganda speeches that one should not lose sight of the overall goal, yet in reality, theory and strategy took less of a priority than tactics.[15] Precisely this habit of assessing the situation from a tactical mindset led Bauer to believe that it was possible for the working class, under conditions of political democracy, to win all progressive and democratic social forces for revolution and gain the necessary majority in parliament.[16] It also led Bauer to one of his fundamental conclusions: preparing the working class to administer the apparatuses of the state and economy was no less imperative for the transformation from capitalism to socialism than the seizure of political power. Bauer found it equally essential to ensure ideological commitment to socialism by preparing the masses ideologically, intellectually and morally for the struggle for the future social order – a sentiment informed by the influence of ethical socialism.[17] One may add that the significance that Bauer imputed to the

---

claimed that the contemporary capitalist state represented the interests of the whole nation, rendering the struggle for the interests of only one class unnecessary. Operating under the democratic conditions offered by the bourgeois state, the revolution ought to assume a peaceful, democratic form, especially since the future rule of the working class was to have such a character. See Kautsky 1927, pp. 44–52; compare Waldenberg 1972, p. 377.

15   As Ernst emphasises, the struggle for a parliamentary majority, accompanied by talk of the revolutionary goal, was geared to drive fear into the hearts of the bourgeoisie. See Ernst 1979, p. 90. Gulick points out that the Social Democrats very consciously utilised the growing radicalism of the masses during the Austrian revolution in order to scare the bourgeois parties and obtain their own political goals. See Gulick 1948, p. 114.

16   Compare Leser 1968, p. 33. Bauer was not alone in this belief. At the turn of the nineteenth and twentieth centuries, most activists and theorists of the European workers' movement, including Rosa Luxemburg, shared it. She claimed that of all revolutions, the proletarian revolution had the best chances to assume a cultural model: 'A revolution can also take place on a cultural level, and if ever there were any prospect of that, it would be in the proletarian revolution, since we are the last to take up violent means, the last to wish a brutal, violent revolution on ourselves' – Luxemburg 1899.

17   Max Adler and Gramsci integrated these ideas into revolutionary theory, as did Niedziałkowski, Czapiński, Próchnik, and Dreszer in Poland. Bauer's emphasis as well as theirs on the subjective aspect of the social process was a form of polemic against politicians

socio-economic and cultural dimensions of socialist revolution was due to Austromarxism's immanent belief in the immaturity of the working class, as well as a critical assessment of the October Revolution in Russia.

The concept of socialisation will be assessed elsewhere, since it was of great importance for the process of democratisation of economic and public life, just as it was for transforming the middle classes into advocates of socialist revolution. It is necessary to focus on the concept of 'education towards socialism', a crucial element of Austromarxist revolutionary theory, including Bauer's contribution to it. While Chapter 2.1 contained an objective critique of this theory, its objectives and functions in the revolutionary process will be further examined here.

Bauer's hypothesis of a 'revolution under the majesty of law' marked the beginning of a perspective oriented towards the legal struggle for a parliamentary majority. The cultural and ethical hegemony of the working class in society was to constitute its foundation, with socialist education serving as a means to this end. This idea was deeply rooted in German philosophy. It was reminiscent of Kant and Schiller's glorification of self-improvement through individual political education as a precondition for the political emancipation of the nation. It also had roots in Hegel's interpretation of history, according to which progress went hand in hand with an increase in freedom and developments in science and culture.[18] These motives entered the German and Austrian labour movements via Ferdinand Lassalle, who was one of the first to identify the worker's movement as a cultural movement.[19] After Lassalle, Karl Liebknecht and Max Adler, Engelbert Pernerstorfer and Otto Bauer popularised this concept in German and Austrian Social Democracy respectively. The Austrian socialists placed particular importance on educational activities, as they assumed the implementation of socialism would be built on the intellectual and moral maturity of the proletariat. The ripening of socio-economic relations, in contrast, was a secondary factor. Max Adler was the main advocate of 'education towards socialism'; the Social Democrats regarded his work, *Neue Menschen* (*New Men*, 1924), as a guide for educational development. The programme for a 'reform of consciousness' as outlined in the text was based on the premise that classes fighting for socio-economic liberation drive ethical progress in human history.

---

who accused Marx's theory of automatism and fatalism in its conception of the laws of history.

18   Also compare Seidl 1989, p. 29.

19   Ibid.

Bauer agreed with Adler that there was a need to transform capitalist society at the level of consciousness, though he linked this more explicitly to the democratic revolution than Adler did. That is to say, he argued that conquering the parliamentary majority would only be possible once three conditions had been fulfilled. Firstly, the middle classes are enticed to the socialist idea thanks to Social Democracy's attractive programme for socio-economic transformation. Secondly, there exists a proletarian mass party with a socialist, yet not necessarily Marxist, programme, which subscribes to a pluralist worldview, and which, through its inclusiveness, unites the working class under the banner of Social Democracy (this premise depended on weakening the Christian wing of the workers' movement and extinguishing Communist influence). Thirdly, taking away the bourgeois parties' hegemony over the middle layers and assuming intellectual leadership over them. To be precise, Bauer thought that intellectually 'disarming' the bourgeoisie and destroying its ideological authority would decide over the seizure of power by the working class. The fundamental role of 'education towards socialism', then, was not so much to prepare workers for the administration of workplaces and local government, but instead to entrench socialist ideals and patterns in the consciousness of broad social layers, raise workers' intellectual and cultural levels, and raise their political consciousness. Aiming to abolish the monopoly of bourgeois culture and education, it sought to educate through art, music, sports and self-education.[20] This model of 'education towards socialism' was, according to Bauer, a means for the proletariat to gain cultural hegemony, which in turn was a revolutionary factor. The concept of 'cultural hegemony' in Bauer's model was close to that of Gramsci, even if they had arrived at their conclusions independently and had political differences. Gramsci's revolutionary theory foregrounded the role of cultural and ideological phenomena and educational activity, which would ideologically unify society. He argued that this was the basis for merging society's economic and political structures. Ideological questions were important for Gramsci, yet

---

20   Weidenholzer states that Austromarxist educational theory focused on the following: a
      rejection of neutral education, a subordination of education to the interests of the class
      struggle, an upbringing in solidarity, political activity, and intellectualism. From 1904–10,
      about 1,500 lectures were given in the 'workers' university', which had been established
      upon the suggestion of the educational society, Die Zukunft. The lecturers included Max
      Adler, Bauer, Renner, Fritz Winter and Adolf Braun. The curriculum of the two-semester
      course (256 lessons) contained general political and social theory, political economy,
      Austrian law, and the history of socialism. In 1926, the party school, established on Bauer's
      initiative, took over the tasks of the 'workers' university'. See Weidenholzer 1981, pp. 54–
      69.

he expanded his concept of hegemony to include the economic and political spheres as well. Moreover, he recognised the role of force in seizing and maintaining power. In contrast, Bauer confined the concept of cultural hegemony to the intellectual sphere. 'The hegemony of the working class over the working people', he claimed, 'can therefore not be a dictatorship of the proletariat over the petty-bourgeois and petty peasant masses, but merely the intellectual leadership of these masses by the party of the proletariat' (our translation).[21] In spite of this difference, Gramsci's and Bauer's understandings had several elements in common, especially the belief that all revolutionary forces had to be united under the rule of the working class and that a new type of society had to be established once political power had been seized. Furthermore, they both conceived of hegemony as a process that would take place before and after the seizure of power and was more akin to leadership than domination.

Of course, Bauer was aware that the political power of the proletariat in the parliamentary democratic system was not synonymous with class rule. In his view, democracy as a form of political order allowed the working class to govern by virtue of legal entitlement. However, working-class rule would only truly begin once the proletariat had seized economic sovereignty. This approach, which was consistent with Marx, led Bauer to conclude that the implementation of socialist democracy – i.e. political and social democracy – would determine the end of the socialist revolution. Bauer's construction programme for a new social order (to which we shall return when we discuss his theory of the state more thoroughly) was clearly apparent in this hypothesis. For now, it is imperative to state that Bauer's attempt to define the programmatic foundations of socialism was an ambitious and unique effort in the Second International. Quite irrespective of how one judges its contents, it is still remarkable – more so because the classical Marxists had not made any such effort.[22]

Bauer remained faithful to his belief in the parliamentary-democratic road to socialism up until the victory of fascism. This was shaped not only by his political beliefs, but also by news about the totalitarian facets of the Soviet Union. Bauer never accepted the Russian form of proletarian revolution as a universal model. Like Gramsci, he believed that the Soviet Russian model was not applicable to Western Europe, and that many different ways led to

---

21   'Die Hegemonie der Arbeiterklasse über das arbeitende Volk kann hier also nicht eine Diktatur des Proletariats über die kleinbürgerlichen und kleinbäuerlichen Massen bedeuten, sondern nur die geistige Führung dieser Massen durch die Partei des Proletariats' – Bauer 1976g, p. 957.

22   Compare Leszek Nowak's interesting observations in Nowak 1997, pp. 14–15.

socialism.[23] However, Bauer only accepted them under the condition that the
working class would not destroy the gains of political democracy. He extolled

---

23   Bauer's belief in the availability of multiple roads to socialism is inconsistent with his
      remarks on world revolution contained in a series of 1919 articles (collected in the pamph-
      let, *Die Weltrevolution* [*World Revolution*], published later that year). Because they main-
      tained the core elements of his parliamentary-democratic conception of revolution, we
      shall briefly explain his attitude to world revolution here.
          In his letter to Bela Kun of 16 June 1919, Bauer defended the notion that world revolu-
      tion would assume a variety of forms determined by the respective socio-economic con-
      ditions. He wrote: 'I believe that we're in the first or second stage of world revolution; but
      I view revolution as less linear, lengthier, more diverse, more differentiated according to
      time and location than most of your closer friends do ...' – Bauer 1980n, p. 1057. Analysing
      changes in the international balance of forces after World War I, Bauer concluded that
      only Great Britain or the United States could become the focal point of the revolutionary
      movement. This view was based, on the one hand, on his assessment of the levels of indus-
      trialisation in these countries and, on the other, on his loyalty to Marx's prophecy that
      the revolution would be victorious in the most industrialised countries. Another notion
      widespread in both Marxist and liberal doctrine at the time also played a role: namely
      the idea that technological and industrial progress is a prerequisite for the progressive
      humanisation of societies. Despite his positive assessment of the industrialisation pro-
      cess in Great Britain and the United States, Bauer far from admitted that the objective
      and subjective prerequisites for revolution had already matured in these countries. On
      the contrary: given the strengthening of parliamentarism and the trade-union movement
      in Great Britain and the US, he hoped for a continuation of the democratisation process
      and socialisation of the economy, i.e. the victory of peaceful revolution. Bauer did not
      agree with the Communists that the national revolutions in Russia, Germany and Austria
      might spread and grow into a world revolution. Instead, he viewed these revolutions as
      effects of specific socio-political circumstances (defeats at the front, unemployment, and
      starvation) and denied them any historical significance. The increasing economic crisis in
      Germany and Austria made him worry as to whether a peaceful revolution would be pos-
      sible. He feared that the crisis might have consequences for the parliamentary revolution,
      provoking either counter-revolution or driving the masses to push for a dictatorship of the
      proletariat. In this respect, he maintained his resistance against the proletarian dictator-
      ship and his sharp criticisms of revolution modelled on Soviet Russia. In World Revolution,
      he wrote: '... Bolshevism is ... nothing but the political form of national bankruptcy' –
      Bauer 1976, p. 174.
          Ten years later, he returned to the question of world revolution at the third congress of
      the Labour and Socialist International on 5–11 August 1928 – see Grünberg 1966, pp. 150–
      3. In *Manifest an die Arbeiter der ganzen Welt* (*Manifesto to the Workers of the World*), he
      called upon the workers' party and trade unions to strengthen the political and economic
      positions of the working class in the capitalist state. In 1928, Bauer was convinced that
      capitalism had already achieved a high level of organisation and standardisation at a
      global level (rationalisation, social legislation, labour and trade agreements, assimilation

the superiority of the democratic road to socialism over armed uprising and force directed against the economy. He regarded two consequences of this route as particularly valuable. Firstly, its fulfilment would not obstruct existing socio-economic conditions, but would instead benefit them. Secondly, the idea of a peaceful revolution would unite all potential supporters of the working class in its power struggle for the socialist programme.

1.2   *Practice in the Service of Theory*

The question of revolution was purely theoretical up until 1918, as stated at the beginning of this chapter. It was not until the victory of the Russian Revolution that it became practical. Bauer's position found expression in the politics of Austrian Social Democracy during the revolutionary wave that gripped the country from 1918–20. Since I have already illustrated this period in my text, *Nurt mediacji* (*The Current of Mediation*, 1991),[24] only events directly linked to Bauer's theoretical thought and political activity will be discussed here.

The October Revolution in Russia had a significant impact upon the revolutionary and anti-war temperament among the Austrian working class, particularly information about gradual workers' and soldiers' autonomy passed on by deserters from the front. At first, Bauer and the SDAP leadership only passed cautious judgement over the events in Russia while remaining distinctly sceptical. On 9 November 1917, the *Arbeiter-Zeitung* ran an article tellingly entitled 'A revolution for peace', which praised the struggle for freedom and bread.[25] On 12 November 1917, the SDAP leadership sent a telegraph to the Congress of Soviets of Workers' and Soldiers' Deputies lauding the demand to lay down arms and take up peace negotiations.[26] Nonetheless, in their numerous public appearances, Victor Adler, Renner, Seitz, Adelheid Popp, and Bauer warned workers against adopting the methods of the Russian Revolution.

---

of working conditions), which would directly lead to socialist transformations. In line with these beliefs, he maintained that the working class would assume economic and political power in the state by peaceful means. For Bauer, peace and the unification of the European labour movement were preconditions for successful socialist revolution. The only new element in Bauer's revolutionary theory was his support for independence struggles in China, Egypt and India, including a favourable view of the Russian Revolution as a factor that might accelerate the process of revolution in the colonial countries.

24   See Czerwińska 1991, pp. 87–111.

25   The party's peace efforts found expression in the 86,000-strong peace demonstration in front of Vienna Concert Hall on 11 November 1917. However, neither Seitz nor Renner or Adler, who took to the platform to speak, was able to pacify the protesting workers. Compare Kropf and Hautmann 1974, p. 44.

26   See *Arbeiter-Zeitung*, 13 November 1917, p. 2.

The Austrian government rejected Russia's proposals for peace. In protest against this decision, the Austrian workers took to the streets in what became the biggest mass event of the Austrian workers' movement, the strike commencing on 15 January 1918.[27] Given the obvious revolutionary situation, it became clear that Austria lacked a party capable of leading the strike: the SDAP leadership did not approve of it and vehemently expressed its opposition.[28] Victor Adler, Hilferding, and Bauer's adverse attitudes to the general strike were part of the reason. For them, it was a form of protest and political pressure, and Bauer argued that economic forms of struggle were ineffective. All the same, the economic nature of the strikers' demands could not conceal the true character of the strike – it was no less than a political and revolutionary protest of the proletariat. The party leadership limited itself to stating that a 'pacification of the working masses' was only possible if the following conditions were met: (1) improvements in the food supply; (2) a guarantee from the government that it would preserve the national borders in negotiations; (3) suffrage reform; (4) demilitarisation of the workplaces.[29] The SDAP leaders supported the demands of the workers, hoping the strike would soon end. Meanwhile, the discrepancy between the struggling masses' demands for state power and the party leadership's passive reaction did not escape the attention of Social Democracy's opponents. Trotsky in particular sharply attacked Bauer and Renner for failing to take advantage of the revolutionary situation at the end of World War I and erect a dictatorship of the proletariat.[30]

---

27   The workers' protests began with an industrial strike in Wiener Neustadt on 14 January. On 17 January, 93,000 participated in Vienna alone, and over the next days, 100,000 in Lower Austria and 25,000 in Styria. On 18 January, the workers of Budapest supported the strike (150,000), and on 20 January, the workers of Prague followed suit (50,000). In the whole of Austria, some 700,000 workers went on strike. Source: Notes of the Imperial and Royal Ministry of the Interior, State Police Bureau from 19–21 January 1918, Vienna 1918, PA I, p. 818.

28   On 17 January 1918, the party leadership explained in the *Arbeiter-Zeitung* that the strike had begun without its agreement or that of the trade unions. On 18 January 1918, the *Arbeiter-Zeitung* published an appeal from the SDAP leadership calling upon the workers to end the strike. For more details on the role of the party leadership in stifling the protests and its collaboration with the government, compare Rosdolsky 1973.

29   See *Arbeiter-Zeitung*, 17 January 1918.

30   See Trotsky 1929. It was a characteristic feature of the Austrian workers' movement that the Left, which represented the positions of the party majority, supported the party leadership. Three groups originating in the left wing of the Social-Democratic Party of Germany (SPD) led the strikes of January 1918 in Germany: the Spartacus League, the *Lichtstrahlen* group, and the *Arbeiterpolitik* group, the latter two named after their respective journals.

In 1918, as the Habsburg Empire collapsed, spontaneously emerging revolutionary groups set about building workers' and soldiers' councils, with revolutionary fervour spreading into the ranks of the army.[31] The socio-political conditions of the moment were favourable to the formation of a soviet republic. As state power was waning, the bourgeois parties showed scarce willingness to take control. The loss of raw material and foreign markets, which were now located outside the Austrian state borders due to the disintegration of the empire, weakened the bourgeoisie.[32] In late October 1918, workers took to the streets demanding a definitive decision with respect to the political status of the Austrian state.[33] The bourgeois parties had no choice but to form a government capable of bringing the revolutionary movement under control. The Social Democrats, on the other hand, had the option to either implement a proletarian dictatorship or vouch for a bourgeois-democratic republic. Remaining true to the Austromarxist political doctrine, the Social Democrats accepted the proposal to form a coalition government submitted by a group of Austro-German delegates of the provisional national assembly of 21 October 1918.[34]

All three groups proved too weak to lead the German working class to victory. In contrast, the Austrian left called upon workers to go back to work.

31 Compare Duczyńska 1975, p. 25.

32 See Löw, Mattl and Pfabigan 1986, p. 21.

33 On 29 October 1918, a violent protest of radical-democratic bourgeois groups demanding the Anschluss to Germany took place in Vienna. In response to an SDAP appeal, a 10,000-strong crowd demonstrated for the proclamation of the republic in the town centre of Vienna on 30 October. Soldiers joined the demonstration; red flags were flying from houses.

34 The first coalition government consisted of delegates from the three most important political groups, i.e. the Social Democrats, Christian Socials, and Greater Germans – see *Stenographische Protokolle* ... 1919, p. 8. On 12 November 1918, some 150,000 people waited in front of parliament and in the town centre for the Provisional National Assembly's decision concerning a new state. When the president of the Provisional National Assembly, Franz Dinghofer, stepped before the crowd at 4 pm to proclaim the republic, and red, white, and red banners were hoisted outside the parliament building, Communist leaders urged the crowd to reject the proclamation and introduce the dictatorship of the proletariat. Communists and Red Guardists attacked the parliament building, the police opened fire, and the crowd dispersed. According to Botz, the skirmishes left some 10 people with heavy injuries and 32 with light injuries – see Botz 1976, p. 35. The Communist putsch did not succeed.

Let us add a few brief comments here. The First Republic emerged as a result of mass pressure from below, although even the masses were overwhelmingly unenthusiastic about the necessity to form a new country. Nor was the establishment of the republic desired by any of the three big political parties. The Greater German party wished for

By doing so, they came out in favour of a bourgeois-parliamentary republic.[35] Although they declared that they were ready to fight to transform Austria into a 'democratic republic', they mainly did so in order to pacify the working class. In the minds of the party leadership at the time, the republic was a distant goal – according to Renner's draft of a provisional constitution of 30 October 1918, the direct participation of the masses in government was out of the question. Although this draft hardly lived up to the expectations of the working class, it did not result in a split in the Austrian labour movement. Two reasons for this were the weakness of the Communists and the special role of Austromarxism. The doctrine of Austromarxism in particular, defined mainly by Bauer during the revolutionary period, and the political decisions he made when the danger of a proletarian dictatorship based on the 'Bolshevik model' was acute, were able to counteract the rising revolutionary tide. Whether there were any real chances for the introduction of a soviet republic in 1918 is a separate question, which must be set aside for now.

The SDAP, whose leadership Bauer took over following Victor Adler's death in the first days of the republic, assumed key offices in the newly established state: aside from providing the chancellor (Renner) and three secretaries of state (Bauer, Ferdinand Hanusch, and Julius Deutsch), it occupied strong positions in the government and local administration. The new state confronted two main issues: the status of the hitherto ruling dynasty and the soviet republics that emerged in Hungary on 21 March 1919 and in Bavaria on 5 April 1919. The act of 3 April 1919 solved the first question by depriving the houses of Habs-

---

an annexation of Austria by Germany, the Christian Socials continued to believe in the restoration of the monarchy, and the SDAP had not given up its hopes for political reforms within the framework of the Habsburg monarchy, considering the *Anschluss* to Germany as an alternative. The aforementioned attempt at a Communist coup had no political relevance, nor did the people of Vienna approve of it. In the given context, the banner with the inscription 'long live the socialist republic' displayed in front of parliament was a peculiar paradox, given that only radical factions of the working class and the rural poor desired a dictatorship of the proletariat in November 1918. Whether the SDAP – had it been a revolutionary party rather than one merely talking about revolution – would have been able to lead the discontented masses of workers, peasants, and soldiers into revolution is a separate question. The regime change in Austria was peaceful – it was not even a revolutionary change in the Austromarxist sense. For them, after all, revolutionary change meant winning the majority in parliament and ruling independently, neither of which conditions applied.

35   Out of fear that the radicalism of the masses might escalate, the following principle was integrated into the constitution: 'German Austria is a democratic republic. All public authorities are appointed by the people' – see Deutsch 1947, p. 71.

burg and Lorraine of any claims to power. Attending to the second issue, Bauer used all of his authority to prevent revolution and soviet rule in Austria.

Bauer knew his country's domestic and foreign situation well. According to Steiner, his insight extended far beyond the basic international conditions and expectations of the working masses.[36] Bauer was equally alert to sentiments held by the peasants: he knew of their hostility to the war-prone military apparatus and war profiteers, and he knew how much they loathed the defeated generals. He was also aware that the soldiers of the dissolved army hated their officers. What is more, Bauer was well informed about the newly established workers' councils, and he knew that soldiers were arming the working class with the intention of pitting themselves against the remnants of state power.[37] During this very tense period for Bauer, he was convinced that the workers could not bring their own demands to fruition and take power – he would later confirm as much at the SDAP congress in October 1922. Almost all of his texts held arguments against a proletarian dictatorship in Austria. His evaluation of the historical situation and political balance of forces provided the basis for these, as did his axiological position.

Bauer cited more precise and concise arguments against the creation of a soviet republic in the aforementioned letter to Bela Kun, appealing to aspects of domestic and foreign policy. His arguments might be summarised in three categories:

1. Economic reasons: Vienna and the industrial areas, which were economically dependent in terms of material and food supply, had no chance of economic development without the financial help of the Entente powers. For as long as states could not provide evidence for their efficiency in production and finances, they had no chance of receiving any credit from Western countries – nor could they count on help from Russia. The country's weak domestic production capacity would lead to currency devaluation, a rise in inflation, scarcity, and thus a decline in living standards and starvation. These conditions were fertile ground for mass demonstrations against the workers' and peasants' government. Bauer concluded that the revolution could not change international economic relations; however, revolutions occurring in countries that had emerged the strongest from the war would decide over the victory of socialist revolution for the whole of Europe.

---

36   See Steiner 1967, p. 10.

37   In *The Austrian Revolution*, Bauer depicted the situation as follows: 'Thus, actual control of arms was not only passed over from the Emperor to the people, but also from the propertied classes to the proletariat' (our translation) – Bauer 1923, p. 100.

Bauer's line of argument evidently displaced responsibility for the impossibility of a successful revolution in Austria onto the economic centres, Britain and the United States.

2. Political reasons: an Austrian soviet republic might provoke armed attacks by capitalist countries, mainly Germany and France, as it would stand in the way of their trade relationships with Italy, Yugoslavia, Czechoslovakia and Poland. Politically isolated, lacking the strong military force of the past, and only having a republican army at its disposal, Austria would soon lose its independence.[38]

3. The evaluation of the socio-political situation in Austria: in reaction to a proletarian dictatorship, the rural areas would separate from Vienna and Austria's industrial territories. This would not only confine the power of the workers' councils to Vienna, Lower Austria and Upper Styria, but it would also exacerbate antagonisms between town and country. In a situation of this type, food deliveries from the anti-socialistically minded clerical peasantry were likely to stop, and a civil war was probable. A victorious counter-revolution would deprive the working class of the dividends of the pre-revolutionary period, leaving the proletariat in a worse position in the capitalist state.

In the aforementioned letter to Bela Kun, Bauer withheld a number of reasons for his opposition to a radical crackdown against the ruling classes. Some of them were every bit as relevant as those he stated openly, even if they were of a different – that is, ideological and ethical – nature, and based on an evaluative approach to politics. Before the end of the war, Bauer dismissed soviet dictatorship – a proletarian form of power – as an expression of Russian backwardness.[39] He expected the victory of counter-revolution in Russia and did not approve of importing Russian revolutionary strategy to Austria – not least because he wanted to spare the working class the bitter consequences of civil war. At the same time, the identification of socialism with democracy, conceived from a perspective of general humanist values, implied that the acute

---

38   Bauer explicitly voiced his worries thus: 'The Entente cannot allow to have its connection to Czechia and Poland via Vienna blocked, because then its whole power political system would collapse. For them, Vienna is an incomparably more important post than Budapest. At the same time, it would be far easier for them to defeat us than defeat Hungary. They would occupy us before we had the chance to form a red army ... It is therefore most likely that we would provoke an occupation by proclaiming the dictatorship' (our translation) – Bauer 1980n, p. 1058.

39   See Bauer 1918.

task of the working class was not to establish its own rule, but to strengthen existing democracy. The concept of a peaceful road to socialism was one consequence of this perspective. During the revolutionary period, all main theoreticians of Austrian Social Democracy shared Bauer's view, including Renner, Max Adler, and leftist Friedrich Adler.[40]

Historians agree that the chances of establishing a dictatorship of the proletariat would have been high in the early days of the republic. The Social-Democratic party still had the trust of the working class and enjoyed support in revolutionary industrial centres, radical towns, and from the urban poor. It is difficult to judge after such a long time to what extent Bauer and the other SDAP leaders' diagnosis of the situation was accurate based on an assessment of the actual balance of forces. Likewise, it is difficult to answer whether their rejection of soviet rule was a political decision – a straightforward response is impossible, and historians disagree on the issue.[41] There is much to suggest that the rejection of proletarian dictatorship in favour of parliamentary democracy in the watershed year of 1918 was largely a political decision rooted in the theory of peaceful revolution. That said, one should not play down the socio-political balance of forces in Austria or overestimate the revolutionary potential of the Austrian working class.[42] There are two ways to determine whether the choice of methods was ideological rather than merely circumstantial or tactical: (1) by contrasting Bauer's arguments with the political and economic conditions of Austria and Europe at the time; and (2) by analysing his attitude toward the soviets.

Let us first consider which domestic and external political factors might have moved the SDAP leaders to refrain from assuming leadership over the revolutionary masses. It should be made clear from the outset that it was an exaggeration to claim that Austria had no economic chances of survival. True, Austria had lost industrial territories in the North, Northwest, and South due to the war and the demise of the empire, and Vienna lost its status as capital of an empire of 54 million inhabitants to become the capital of a state comprised of no more

---

40   Adler claimed that the most pressing task of the workers' party was not the realisation of socialism, but rather finalising the bourgeois revolution, abolishing absolutism, and introducing an absolute democracy. See F. Adler 1919.

41   See also the works of other authors: Duczyńska 1975; Leser 1968; Kulemann 1979; Löw, Mattl and Pfabigan 1986; Saage 1986; Hanisch 2011 and 2007.

42   Hanisch also views the fate of revolutionary Austria pessimistically: 'Contrary to all revolutionary romanticism, it is fair to say that a soviet republic in Austria would have inevitably ushered in a civil war, intervention by the Allies, and unavoidable defeat of the left forces – perhaps even an authoritarian regime' (our translation) – Hanisch 2007, p. 12.

than six million. It is also true that energy and gas supplies were reduced and bread rationed due to weak productivity at the beginning of the First Republic. Nonetheless, the republic inherited 90 percent of transportation, 34 percent of agricultural machines, 35 percent of steel production, 75 percent of rubber production, and 40 percent of leather production.[43] In addition, it had platinum, zinc, magnesium, and copper stock. Contrary to Bauer's claims, Austria's economic situation in 1918 was no worse than that of bordering countries: indeed, its per capita income was 8 percent higher than that of its neighbours. It was also quite common for a postwar country not to have independent foreign trade. As Stiefel writes, neighbouring countries differed from Austria in that they attempted to develop the industries in which they were lacking, while Austria embraced the role of a client state unable to survive of its own accord. There were political objectives behind this voluntary beggar status – including certain associations' drive to instigate a union with Germany.[44] Indeed, 1919 saw an improvement in deficient economic branches; industrial output increased, and the unemployment rate lowered. Only in early 1921, a period during which the revolutionary uproar had calmed, did the neighbouring countries impose high tariffs on Austrian industrial products, leading to a lack of foreign currency to buy raw materials abroad. Consequently, reserves of capital destined for production were used up and the currency devalued.[45] Only in 1922, rather than in 1918, would Austria became dependent on British, French and German capital.

Bauer's secession argument does not stand up to scrutiny either. The French prime minister, Georges Clemenceau, and the Italian representative in Versailles, Tommaso Tittoni, were opposed to a bloody suppression of the revolution in central Europe – a fact of which Bauer was well aware.[46] As his letter to Renner of 8 June 1919 proves, Cunningham had admitted to him that he saw no possibility of an armed intervention by the Entente powers, which focused on Germany, in Hungary in 1919. Likewise, the victorious powers did not consider an intervention in Austria in 1918–19.[47]

Nevertheless, Bauer was right in his assessment of the domestic situation. The economic, geographic, and demographic structure of the country was important for the future of the revolution. The First Republic was predominately an agrarian country in which the peasantry made up some two thirds of the population. The industrial centres reached from Vienna through Wiener

43   Compare Slavik 1928, p. 9.
44   Compare Stiefel 1978, p. 6.
45   Stiefel 1978, p. 25.
46   See Löw, Mattl and Pfabigan 1986, p. 22.
47   See Bauer 1980s, p. 1054.

Neustadt and the industrial and mining areas of Upper Styria to the south; Graz and Linz were industrial areas in the countryside that were surrounded by agrarian areas.[48] As to Austria's revolutionary potential from 1918–20, it is evident that the working class was the only revolutionary force, yet its revolutionary zeal was not as pronounced as to allow it to sacrifice the social gains of the preceding period.[49] At the time of struggle, the middle classes formed a progressive bloc, yet when the working class consolidated its position, anti-proletarian tendencies increased amongst the petty bourgeois. Since the Social Democrats neglected political work in the countryside, the peasantry was subject to the influence of clerical forces. It was not the Social Democrats, but the Christian Socials who paved the way for new legislation and reforms concerning rural property relations.[50] At the beginning of the Republic, a part of the peasantry supported the workers' demonstrations because they opposed the war, bureaucracy, and economic austerity – yet their attitude to revolution changed radically as the workers' councils enforced food supply contingents. The fear that the peasants would not support the councils proved fully justified. What is more, the aims of the peasantry were incompatible with socialist revolution – they were landowners, and a triumphant revolution could not increase the size of their estates, as large estates in Austria primarily comprised grasslands and woods. A workers' government would not have the support of the agrarian provinces. Bauer's conclusion that the Social Democrats had to conduct coalition politics with the Christian Socials was indeed justified.[51]

This does not change the fact that a tendency to avoid conflict prevailed in the SDAP, while the party simultaneously strove to cultivate both the trust of the working class and its status as the only significant workers' party. Bauer and his party comrades' attitude toward the councils confirms this. It is worth noting that the classic Marxist texts did not use the term workers' councils, i.e. there was no talk of the council system as an organisational form of workers' rule during the period of proletarian dictatorship. Marx only once mentioned the commune as a political model that served economic emancipation in *The*

---

48   According to Volpi, the employment rate in the agrarian provinces was higher in agriculture than in the industries. It was 53 percent in Upper Austria, 56 percent in Tirol, and 57 percent in Styria. Botz interprets this structure as containing low potential for revolutionary mobilisation despite spontaneous mass movements. See Botz 1987, p. 50.

49   Tálos confirms this assessment in Tálos 1981, p. 147.

50   Bauer himself admitted this in Bauer 1976g, pp. 15–23 and 1925b, pp. 146–63.

51   Leser also attempts to justify the SDAP's coalition work and renunciation of struggle by citing the existing isolation of the working class and impossibility of winning the peasantry as revolutionary allies. See Leser 1968, p. 311.

Civil War in France. This form of workers' rule was to consist of town councils emerging from general elections.[52] Workers' councils were formed during the Russian revolutions of 1905 and 1917 as organs of proletarian struggle. In Austria, the first workers' councils emerged in 1917 and gained importance during the January strike of 1918 when taking control over administration and food supply. In the early days of the First Republic, they were a political factor in the state, demanding that the SDAP cease co-operation with the bourgeois parties and restore unity within its ranks. The sympathies for the workers' councils present in the party, though limited to its left wing, strengthened the Hungarian and Bavarian soviet republics.[53]

Remaining true to the basic premises of Austromarxist revolutionary theory, the SDAP's view of the council (soviet) system was unequivocally negative: it considered it a threat to the democratic system of government, an expression of despotism and terror, and a rejection of its objectives of a peaceful road to socialism. In Austromarxist theory, the workers' council model is not related to the perspective of seizing power. A few months later, Braunthal cited the reasons for introducing councils: 'Above all, the purpose of the workers' councils was to maintain immediate contact between the working masses in the factories and the party, trade unions, and parliamentary delegates of the proletariat'.[54] The most common concept in contemporary discussions of Social-Democratic activists was the coexistence of the council system and parliamentarism. It is precisely this form of political power struggle that Max Adler referred to as the 'third way' to socialism in 1919. His proposal, submitted at the first council congress from 1–2 March 1919, represented the most radical vision in the ranks of the SDAP, allocating a relatively broad realm of activity to the councils. Adler thought that they should function in parallel to the national

---

52   See Marx 1977, p. 70. Also Katsoulis 1975, p. 311.

53   In 1919, the Social-Democratic Committee of Revolutionary Workers' Councils (SARA) came into existence, which referred to itself as the 'new left' to distinguish itself from the left gathered around Friedrich Adler. Its leaders – Paul and Elfriede Friedländer, Joseph Frey, Teresia Schlesinger and Franz Rothe – demanded a dictatorship of the councils/soviets (in 1920, the SARA moved closer to the Communists, and then joined the Communist Party of Austria when expelled from the SDAP). The Communists also called to attend the 15 July 1919 demonstration to demand the introduction of a soviet dictatorship. It was to have a purely proletarian character and take over legislation and jurisdiction. Compare Kreissler 1970, p. 70. Prior to this, a protest called by the Communist Party took place on 17 April 1919 in front of the parliament building – six people were killed and 56 injured. See Kulemann 1979, p. 224. The SDAP denounced the actions of the Communists at the 28–9 April 1919 congress.

54   Braunthal 1919, p. 4.

assembly and have the following functions: (1) monitor the work of officials and consider the demands of the working class in all areas of administration; (2) educational work. At the time, Adler believed that a hybrid of councils and bourgeois institutions instead of a proletarian dictatorship would secure the working class a similar status as the proclamation of a soviet republic.[55] In Löw and Pfabigan's view, Adler feared the radicalism of the masses far more than he feared the consolidation of the national assembly and parliamentarism.[56] In his mind, the councils were no revolutionary force that could lead to the seizure of power; instead, they were just instruments to aid the process of 'growing into socialism' without any constitutional status.

Bauer fully shared the SDAP's unfavourable attitude towards the council system.[57] The congress of councils, which lost the support of the party, adopted a resolution in 1919 that rendered the councils mere appendages of the party and trade unions. The leaders' revolutionary proclamations did not alter the fact that the councils were subordinated to state administration. They were no more than subsidiary bodies aiding to enforce the party line.[58]

---

55   See Adler 1919, p. 31.

56   See Löw, Mattl and Pfabigan 1986, p. 71.

57   His attitude towards the Hungarian soviet republic was exemplary for his ostensibly revolutionary politics. He welcomed its establishment only because of Austrian political interests. Like the Hungarian government, Bauer feared that Austrian counter-revolutionary forces might gain strength and the Entente countries put pressure on Austria if it joined the alliance of Danube states. As to the Hungarian revolution itself, he did not want to consider objective and subjective factors, but only saw bloody terror. In his letter to Bela Kun, he thus energetically spoke out against the introduction of a soviet republic in Austria and turned down his invitation to visit the Hungarian soviet republic. See Bauer 1980n, p. 1056. Note that as foreign minister Bauer secretly agreed to arms deliveries for Czechoslovakia against the Hungarian republic, which earned him accusations of being a traitor to the revolution – see Haas 1985, p. 134. This accusation was unjustified insofar as Bauer had never been an advocate of Russian-style revolution. Hence, he did not even attempt to defend himself, merely stating that he did not believe in the endurance of the Hungarian government and expected that a parliamentary system and mixed economy would soon replace it.

58   Because they were under the influence of the Social-Democratic leaders, the Austrian workers' councils rejected the idea of a proletarian dictatorship. Although they assumed responsibility for some administrative functions and took over the roles of self-administration and control points, they never became independent administrative organs of the state. While they allowed workers for relatively far-reaching participation in economic and social decision-making processes at company level, their influence upon general political decisions was simultaneously eliminated. A law concerning industrial councils weakened the significance of the workers' councils in political life. These organs became

During the revolutionary period, the question of *Anschluss* of the Austrian part of the country to Germany received more attention in the SDAP than did the council question. Bauer made it part of his revolutionary theory – it would remain a component of his vision of proletarian revolution until the end of his life – and pushed for it with unusual persistence. Bauer was partly driven by his wariness that Austria might become a provincial country and his disbelief that it could be an autarky. There is much to suggest, however, that his belief in Germany's special role in the socialist revolution was pivotal. There were two underlying elements to this: (1) profound social change of a socialist nature is possible only when state power is strong; and (2) the strength of the German proletariat will facilitate the seizure of power by democratic means. For Bauer, these were the preconditions that a successful revolution in Austria must meet, one of which was the maturity and revolutionary potential of the German workers' movement.[59] Max Adler and Renner equally advocated an *Anschluss* to Germany, though their motivations differed. For Renner, the economic aspect was the primary concern: the notion of *Anschluss* was consistent with his programme of creating vast economic territories and exposed his support for the expansionist aims of German imperialism. In contrast, Bauer and Adler were more preoccupied with maintaining a revolutionary perspective.[60] Bauer's vision of an all-German proletarian revolution was one of the greatest illusions in his struggle for socialism. Not only did he overestimate the revolutionary potential of the German workers' movement – by 1919, the German revolution was defeated – he was also mistaken about the attitude of the international and domestic working class towards his proposals. Much to his disappointment, the workers of France, Britain, Yugoslavia, Romania and Czechoslovakia did not

---

connecting channels between workers and the local organisations of the SDAP. In June 1922, the Communists left the industrial councils. The soldiers' councils proclaimed themselves the armed forces of the working class, subordinated themselves to the SDAP leadership, and in 1923 agreed to join the Schutzbund. In November 1924, the central committee made a formal decision, effective as of 31 December, to dissolve the workers' councils, arguing that the tasks and responsibilities of the councils were identical to those of the workers' party. This decision is contained in the appendix to the Salzburg 1934 party congress protocols – see pp. 253–6. Hanisch evaluates the role of the councils in the Austrian revolution thus: 'The workers' and soldiers' councils were instruments to pacify the masses. Every now and again, the councils stepped out of line, but, when all is said and done, they served to stabilise the situation' – Hanisch 2011, p. 146.

59   See Bauer 1976b, p. 131.
60   Even bourgeois publicists admitted that Bauer's pushing for *Anschluss* was driven by his desire to link Austria to the revolutionary transformations taking place in Germany. See *Morgenblatt*, 6 July 1927, p. 1.

support the idea of *Anschluss*, and it found little support from the Austrian proletariat. Nonetheless, Bauer's attempts to win the SDAP majority were rewarded: on 1 November 1918, the party assembly declared Austria's *Anschluss* to
the German empire as one of its objectives and a necessary component for the
success of revolution in Austria. Given the defeat the party leaders had suffered
against the Entente countries in their struggle for *Anschluss* enshrined in the
Treaty of Saint-Germain-en-Laye signed on 21 October 1919, it is unsurprising
that revolutionary enthusiasm cooled off in the Social-Democratic sections.
According to Bauer, the ban on *Anschluss* was synonymous with weakening the
position of the Austrian working class – granted, he was not wrong on this.[61]

Bauer never resigned himself to the idea that Austria might remain outside
of Germany. The *Anschluss* question was more enshrined in his revolutionary
theory than one might assume based on his statements alone. His polemic
against a proponent of the 'new left' in 1920 is telling in this respect: Bauer
attempted to prove that the revolution had not yet fulfilled the targets of a
bourgeois revolution and could therefore not set itself any socialist goals.[62]
He gave *Anschluss* the special, missionary task of consolidating the democratic political system that had been established with the proclamation of the
republic. This was precisely the political objective that the Social Democrats
set for the revolution in Austria.[63] As a case in point, the party congress of the
SDAP declared that preserving peace and the struggle for democracy were the
primary objectives of the workers' party. The position of the Social Democrats
at the time did not deviate from official statements made by representatives
of the parties that belonged to the Second International. At the 1920 congress,
they adopted a resolution which condemned the Bolshevik experiment and the
introduction of the proletarian dictatorship. The resolution spoke of a necessity to win political power by democratic means and parliament was anointed
a pivotal role in the struggle.[64]

This tactic had no realistic chance of success in the socio-political situation
at the time. The year 1919 signalled the beginning of an era: the bourgeois
parties pushed the proletariat onto the defensive, the petty bourgeoisie and
peasantry mobilised against the working class, the influence of Social Democracy in the military evaporated, and paramilitary organisations were founded.
The fall of the Communist governments in Bavaria and Hungary had no small

61   See Bauer 1920b, p. 253.
62   Ibid.
63   Löw shares this point of view – see Löw 1980, p. 43.
64   See Congress protocols of the Second International, Vol. 2, in Documents, Programmes,
      Protocols, pp. 38–9.

impact on the course of events, as did the consolidation of the political and
economic position of the bourgeoisie in the whole of Europe and Russia. After
15 June 1919, the revolutionary wave died down in the wake of mass arrests and
rising death tolls at street protests. After the suppression of a strike by the police
on 21 July 1919, a revolutionary takeover by the proletariat of Austria was out of
the question.

2   The Theory of Social Upheaval During the Post-Revolutionary
       Period

2.1   *The Programme of Linz*
Since the ruling class had destroyed the democratic foundations of the Republic, the programmes of Hainfeld and Vienna were rendered obsolete. The SDAP
leadership saw itself forced to arrive at new ideological, programmatic and
tactical principles to meet the conditions of struggle for socialism during the
period of fascisisation. These were formulated at the party congress in Linz
from 30 October–3 November 1926 and remained valid in Austrian Social
Democracy until 1958. The new programme, commonly referred to as a 'classical document of Austromarxism', went down in history as Bauer's programme – after all, he had played a decisive role at the party congress. The
programme of Linz also became known as a programme for power: more so
than the programmes that had gone before, it prioritised the prognosis that
the proletariat would seize state power soon and with absolute certainty. This
was based on the SDAP leadership's delusion that the working class would rapidly acquire a parliamentary majority through the adopted tactics. The only
real novelty in the programme was the introduction of a formula according to
which the proletariat would apply 'defensive violence' if democracy were under
threat from reactionary forces.

    The authors of this programme aimed to outline a clear strategy of party
activity for the workers, hoping this would strengthen their class consciousness
and win allies of socialism among peasants, officials, and the progressive intelligentsia. The thesis of socialism as a historical necessity was pushed to the rear,
and instead, emphasis shifted to courses of action.[65] Two primary issues arose
from these tactics: how would the working class take and maintain power, and

---

65   The neatly composed programme, 17 pages in length, begins with an analysis of the
      development of capitalism during the postwar period. Based on this analysis, it devises
      the goals and methods of the proletarian struggle against the capitalist state order, the
      road to seizing state power by the working class, the transitional forms from capitalism

what tangible advantages of Social-Democratic politics might be presented to the middle classes. The specific proposals for middle-class-friendly policies will be touched upon when discussing the question of alliances. For now, the turn to the struggle of the working class for state power takes precedence. It is important to emphasise that at the outset the change in tactics announced by the party was not commensurable with the politics of Social Democracy. The two main points in the programme demanded to educate the working class to be faithful to parliamentary democracy and to instigate a proletarian dictatorship if the foundations of the republic were under threat. These demands effectively rendered the document a programme for the protection of the republic rather than a fighting programme for state power. Worse still, in practice the programme of Linz was not at all beneficial for the working class, but instead paved the way for the political enemies of Social Democracy and their anti-democratic activities. Further weaknesses were erratic analyses and assessments, especially of the social composition and strength of the working class.[66]

The tactic contained in the programme of Linz referred back to a couple of earlier works of Bauer's, namely *Die Grundlagen unserer Taktik* (*The Principles of Our Tactics*, 1913) and *Der Kampf um die Macht* (*The Struggle for Power*, 1924), which were influenced by Engels's essay 'Socialism in Germany' (1892) and Kautsky's *The Road to Power* (1909). Their basic ideas are best summed up as follows: 'The proof is in the numbers: within a few years, we can conquer the majority by ballot and thus power in the republic, the rule over the republic' (our translation).[67] In 1924, despite the failed socialisation programme, Bauer believed that the possibility of captivating the middle classes was absolutely certain. This was also expressed in the programme of Linz. Its strategic principle was that working-class power would be seized democratically through parliament, i.e. there would be a struggle 'for the hearts of the majority' conducted by the two main social classes against each other by parliamentary means. Instead of regarding the simultaneous existence of objective and subjective factors as the condition for revolution, the delegates of Linz thought that gaining social legitimacy through the support of progressive and democratic forces for socialism would suffice. This section in the programme also justified the parliamentary practice of the SDAP in retrospect.

---

to socialism, and the future tasks of Social Democracy focusing on winning the middle classes. See Berchtold 1967 in Documents, Programmes, Protocols, pp. 248–56.

66   Compare Leser 1968, p. 386.

67   'Die Zahlen beweisen es: Wir können in wenigen Jahren mit dem Stimmzettel die Mehrheit und damit die Macht in der Republik, die Herrschaft über die Republik erobern' – Bauer 1976g, p. 25.

Bauer's statements at the party congress testified to his illusion of proletarian strength and the unjustified belief that capitalism would soon be overcome. Winning political power was a task that the present generation of the working class had to complete.[68] With great conviction, he remained faithful to the theory that the bourgeois republic had to be preserved as the most advantageous platform of working-class struggle for the socialist state order. He argued in favour of preserving democratic principles of struggle, citing a sociological analysis of the composition of the proletariat and his belief in the 'hegemony of the proletariat'. Drawing on Marx's model of society's polarisation into two main social groups, Bauer employed, as Leser writes, a broad definition of the term 'working class'. According to Bauer, agricultural workers, officials, and the working intelligentsia – all of whom the SDAP needed to win for its strategy – belonged to the working class.[69] He deduced another incorrect conclusion from Marx's thesis of social polarisation: according to Bauer, the whole of the bourgeois class was a reactionary mass lording over the proletariat by virtue of its political and cultural hegemony – he bypassed the economic aspect. In his view, these conditions would be met once the socialists had obtained most of the seats in parliament and excluded the bourgeoisie from the political stage. Bauer was confident that the chosen strategy would succeed, and nearly all members of the SDAP leadership shared his assurance. Only Max Adler, who had warned of democratic illusions, was sceptical. At the congress, he decisively opposed the 'path of the voting card' as ideologically harmful and chimerical in practice. For Adler, it seemed unfeasible given the social, economic, and political circumstances and of no prosperity to the proletariat given the balance of class forces.[70] Yet his contribution was ignored.

The programme of Linz bolstered the reformist orientation of the party. It furthermore contained a proposal of co-operation between the SDAP and the bourgeois parties. One might perceive the ethos of the new programme as a warning of bourgeois counter-revolution and armed conflict. Its orchestrator knew that the bourgeoisie would reject all democratic forms if they found that democracy had become inopportune. It would then strive to either establish

---

68   In 1925, the party was 592,346 members strong (of which 324,525 were in Vienna). It published six daily papers, 31 weekly magazines, and many monthly journals. The Social-Democratic Free Unions comprised 807,515 members and published 54 trade magazines. See Reimann 1968, p. 340.

69   Compare Leser 1968, pp. 386–7.

70   His critique was part of a broader argument about attitudes towards democracy and dictatorship led by Adler against the other SDAP ideologists.

its own dictatorship or seek protection in the bosom of a fascist dictatorship.[71] This was acknowledged in the programme, in the following reservation:

> The bourgeoisie will not surrender its power voluntarily ... Only if the working class is sufficiently capable of defending the democratic republic against any kind of monarchist or fascist counter-revolution ... only then will the bourgeoisie not dare to rebel against the republic ... If the bourgeoisie succeeds in smashing democracy despite the efforts of the Social-Democratic Worker's Party, then the working class will only be able to conquer state power by means of civil war.[72]

This was merely an early caution that the methods of struggle would change from peaceful to armed, yet it did not define the political rule or type of state that would be established after the proletarian revolution. The tentative attitude of the congress on this question was a consequence of polarisation within the SDAP leadership itself – its members did not agree on the function and role of democracy and dictatorship in state formation. Whether or not to cite the dictatorship of the proletariat in the programme proved the most contentious question. The right wing around Renner rejected the thesis of 'insurmountable class contradictions' and was against incorporating this into the programme. Renner insisted that the party eschewed Marxian phraseology and instead designed a political compromise which would facilitate a peaceful continuation of reformist politics. The party left under Max Adler's command stood in opposition: Adler objected to the dichotomy between democracy and dictatorship put forward by Renner, reminding him that every political democracy has, in fact, the function of a dictatorship. Adler's depiction of the First Republic as a bourgeois state met with strong resistance from Bauer, Renner, Friedrich Adler and Austerlitz.

---

71   The prognosis that counter-revolution would be the bourgeoisie's answer to a potential victory of the proletariat can be found in Engels's introduction to *The Civil War in France* – see Engels 1895.

72   'Die Bourgeoisie wird nicht freiwillig ihre Machtstellung räumen ... Nur wenn die Arbeit-erklasse wehrhaft genug sein wird, die demokratische Republik gegen jede monarch-istische oder faschistische Gegenrevolution zu verteidigen ... nur dann wird es die Bour-geoisie nicht wagen können, sich gegen die Demokratie aufzulehnen ... Wenn es aber trotz allen diesen Anstrengungen der Sozialdemokratischen Arbeiterpartei einer Gegen-revolution der Bourgeoisie gelänge, die Demokratie zu sprengen, dann könnte die Arbeit-erklasse die Staatsmacht nur noch im Bürgerkrieg erobern' – Berchtold 1967, pp. 248–56.

Bauer's position in the argument on dictatorship was less than clear. When protesting against Adler's suggestion to integrate the demand for a proletarian dictatorship into the programme, he argued that 'one should not try to tell us that dictatorship and terrorism are two entirely different things'.[73] Appealing to Engels's renowned critique of the Erfurt programme of 1891, he emphasised that democracy and dictatorship were not opposites in principle, yet they had become opposites due to Bolshevik political practice (we shall assess to what extent he believed in this statement later). In any case, the debate about terms was secondary for Bauer – he was far more preoccupied with finding a compromise that would unite the right and left wings of the party. By way of such a compromise, he confined himself to stating that in the transitional phase between capitalism and socialism, the proletarian dictatorship ought to assume the form of a dictatorship of all working people, i.e. the rule of the working majority over the bourgeoisie, exercised democratically.

When arguing against the use of force, Bauer reminded the party left of the Russian Civil War. For him, the only legitimate form of violence was defensive violence to protect the democratic foundations of the state.[74] The reasons as to why he demanded that the rhetoric of 'defensive violence' be adopted into the programme were, firstly, his desire to reconcile the two opposing positions so as to not jeopardise party unity. Secondly, he feared the rise of anti-democratic forces which, in fact, had begun to undermine Austrian democracy since 1923.[75] The phrase 'defensive violence' communicated that the party would not abandon the struggle for state power during peaceful periods – and if the bourgeois parties attacked democracy, it would introduce a proletarian dictatorship.[76] The formula justified the use of force only for the case that the bourgeois government jeopardised the reformist road. Dictatorship was

---

73   See SDAP 1926 in Documents, Programmes, Protocols, p. 271.

74   Karl Popper also espoused this view. See Popper 1945, p. 152.

75   Volpi and Pfabigan pointed out that the formula of 'defensive violence' had been present in Bauer's work long before the party congress of Linz. According to Volpi, it was already implicit in his text, 'Die Grundfrage unserer Taktik' ('The Fundamental Question Concerning Our Tactics') and, according to Pfabigan, in his 1920 polemic against Bolshevism. See Bauer 1913; Volpi 1977, p. 184; Pfabigan 1985, p. 46.

76   The programme contained the following statement: 'But if the bourgeoisie resists the social transformation that will be the task of the working class through planned sabotage of economic life, violent insurgency, or conspiracy with foreign counter-revolutionary forces, then the working class would be compelled to break the resistance of the bourgeoisie by means of dictatorship' – see SDAP 1926, p. 176. The enemies of Social Democracy often cited this sentence in their political propaganda.

considered only a purely defensive measure, not as a method of struggle for power. It would therefore be inaccurate to compare the theory of 'defensive violence' to Marx's premise of a violent seizure of power and introduction of a proletarian class state. Bauer's motto was 'democratically if we can, by means of dictatorship only if they compel us, and only to the extent they compel us'.[77] It was down to the notion that the working class would not employ force in the struggle for power as long as counter-revolutionary forces did not destroy formal democracy.

Renner and Ellenbogen were convinced of the political realism of the programme, while Bauer attempted to prove that it buried democratic illusions. In truth, the programme was evidence that the workers' party was too confident in its own strength. The theory of 'defensive violence' amounted to underestimating the extent of resistance the bourgeois organisations would exhibit, as well as ignoring that the balance of forces in Austria had shifted in the bourgeoisie's favour since 1919. The expectations that it would scare off the bourgeoisie were not met, even remotely. As Kluge writes, the threat of dictatorship articulated in the programme of Linz rested on a false prognosis, leaving all political initiative to the enemy and limiting the working class to a purely defensive struggle for a legality that had long since been under attack.[78] It is therefore unsurprising that the socialist camp viewed the programme of Linz with mixed feelings, ranging from enthusiastic applause to biting criticism. Otto Jenssen, who belonged to the left wing of the Social Democratic Party of Germany, lauded the programme. Paul Levi and Arcadius Gurland issued cutting rebuttals. In their view, the programme disregarded the actual situation of the working class, put too much faith in democracy, and overestimated the defensive role of violence in the struggle for autonomy. Furthermore, it misrepresented dictatorship as a tactic in struggle rather than a form of state during the transitional period.[79] Trotsky, likewise, subjected the concept of 'defensive violence' to a sharp critique.[80]

The question arises as to whether the bourgeois parties themselves perceived the programme as a significant change to the orientation of the Social-Democratic party and as a threat to their own position. Most likely, this was not the case – after all, the reduction of the dictatorship of the proletariat to the status of a weapon to defend democracy stripped it of its revolutionary potential. Nonetheless, the bourgeois parties immediately jumped at the opportunity

---

77   SDAP 1926, p. 272.
78   See Kluge 1984, p. 30.
79   See Strom and Walter 1984, p. 11.
80   See Trotsky 1929.

to use the programme as a pretext to fulfil their own political goals, i.e. implement an authoritarian government. There is no doubt that Bauer's attitude to the use of violence, and the readiness to go on the offensive implied in the programme, was met with approval from the working class. The elections of 1927, which gained the SDAP the highest number of votes in the First Republic, testified to this. Alas, SDAP leaders responded to the working class's support with false displays of action. The concept of defensive violence present in the programme of Linz proved a mere manoeuvre: in political practice, the party never made any use of it. After a bloody battle involving the working class in 1927, Bauer tenaciously pursued the usual reformist strategy, limiting the role of the party during the offensive of anti-democratic forces and fascist battalions to monitoring the opposition. At the party congress that year, he claimed that initiating a revolution would amount to collective suicide, as the reactionary forces had gained strength across Europe and the peasantry was scarcely interested in changing the existing social order.[81]

While it is true Bauer publicly declared the necessity of radicalising the party's ideological and strategic premises during the fascist offensive, he himself was not convinced of it. His attitude towards the 1933 manifesto drafted by a group named 'Neu beginnen' ('Start Anew'), which accommodated a critique of reformist politics, was evidence of this. Rejecting their proposition, Bauer accused them of displaying an overly revolutionary character which was unjustifiable given the socio-historical conditions, but also of deepening the rift in the workers' movement. Even in view of imminent disaster in his own party, Bauer remained true to his belief that the working class must set itself achievable goals in capitalist society. He ignored the critics who lambasted his political line. One such critique was that of Käthe Leichter, who in 1931 demanded a revision of the party programme, sharply disapproving of its possible outcomes such as the mobilisation of bourgeois forces and passive position of the SDAP leadership. What is more, she warned of overestimating the effectiveness of democratic methods – for her, an armed revolution was the only effective means to defend democracy.[82] Suffice to say, her suggestions were rebuffed by Bauer, Ellenbogen and Renner. At the same congress, Bauer protested that the question of armed struggle had been raised at all.

The period of fascist dictatorship plainly demonstrated to Bauer and the SDAP that the use of force was necessary to win against capitalism. In *Zwischen zwei Weltkriegen* (*Between Two World Wars*), he wrote:

---

81   See Bauer 1976k, p. 7.
82   Compare Steiner 1973, p. 67.

The construction of socialism in the Soviet Union is more complete than I had expected in 1931. In central Europe, fascism has defeated democracy. We would have to be blind to world historical facts if these two great events did not influence our views concerning the road to socialism.[83]

our translation

2.2   'Integral Socialism'

Bauer regarded co-operation between both wings of the workers' movement as the primary task in fascist Europe rather than the introduction of dictatorship. The theory of 'integral socialism', ardently supported by Max Adler in his public speeches, was to serve him for this purpose. It was an attempt to transform the split of the international workers' movement into reformist and revolutionary currents. For this, new theoretical and strategic principles had to be established specifically to facilitate the struggle for socialism under conditions of fascist dictatorships and authoritarian governments. While these efforts testified to the author's ideological evolution and his broadening political consciousness, they did not represent a profound or significant change. After all, they did not contain any critique of the strategy of Social Democracy hitherto, nor were they, contrary to all assurances, an appeal to take up armed struggle against the ruling regime in the literal sense. Rather, Bauer aspired to overcome the rift between Social Democrats and Communists, and design a common platform to fall back on in the event of war. It was a progressive and democratic premise, even if it only insufficiently considered the ideological barriers that divided the two camps, as it did the difficult socio-economic and political conditions under which the working class was to abolish its own enslavement and bring a new social order to pass.

The objective conditions that conceived of this concept are worth considering. The idea of 'integral socialism' was the result of an economic, political, and sociological analysis of the interwar period. The economic crisis led to a rise in unemployment and impoverishment of both the working and middle classes. One effect was the radicalisation of a considerable segment of the working masses; the other was that all social classes became more receptive to fascist ideology. At the same time, the consolidation of authoritarian regimes and dictatorships in Europe invoked the threat of war, which led both Social Democrats and Communists to feel powerless. Bauer's theory was rooted in his fear that

---

83   'Der sozialistische Aufbau in der Sowjetunion ist vollkommener, als ich es im Jahre 1931 erwartet habe, gelungen. Die Demokratie ist in Mitteleuropa dem Faschismus erlegen. Wir müßten blind sein für weltgeschichtliche Tatsachen, wenn diese beiden großen Erlebnisse unsere Ansichten über den Weg zum Sozialismus nicht beeinflußten' – Bauer 1976p, p. 270.

fascism would win indefinitely, that the working class would lose its position, and that the consequences of war would be fatal.

Bauer's idea of 'integral socialism' was by no means unfamiliar – it accompanied the founding of the Vienna International in 1921, and indeed Max Adler had long since advocated it in his writings. Bauer only gradually adopted this position from 1921 onward, although the degree of his radicalism was inconsistent. In this author's view, Bauer's 1922 positions were more radical than those he advocated in 1936, when his programme for co-operation between both wings of the workers' movement reached its full maturity. When the executives of the three internationals met at the April 1922 congress, Bauer did not, unlike in the later period, think of the ideological differences between Social Democrats and Communists as fundamental. Instead of blaming the divisions within the workers' movement solely on different theoretical premises, strategic goals and resultant decisions by the party leaders, he identified different socio-political conditions in the East and west as part of the reason. Because of these, he argued, the methods adopted by the working class in the struggle for socialism differed too. Characteristically for Bauer's perspective, his congress thesis concerning co-operation between the two tendencies did not speak of unity, but of coexistence and division of spheres of influence. The west was to remain the Social Democrats' ideological sphere of influence, the East the dominion of the Communists.[84] To be precise, Bauer did not think that there was a space for the Communist parties in the Western countries, nor for the Menshevik opposition in the East. One cannot but notice that Bauer contradicted himself, even if he was unaware of it: his demand for a division of spheres of influence implied, after all, that the Social-Democratic and Communist parties were ideologically different. However, Bauer adopted a different tone for the congress of the three internationals, defending the Russian Revolution from critique in his own camp and attacks by the bourgeois groups. Despite the undeniable role of Russian conditions, it is surprising that Bauer did not recognise the influence of Lenin's doctrine on the shape that Bolshevism took in practice. After all, Lenin had outlined the doctrine, which clearly defined the role of the party after the revolution, as early as in 1902 when he wrote *What Is To Be Done?*

In 1934, Bauer admitted in the journal, *Der Kampf*, that the main subject of dispute between Social Democrats and Communists had been vanquished with the fall of democracy.[85] Nonetheless, he thought that the contradictions between reformist and revolutionary socialism, which in his view resulted

---

84   Compare Merchav 1978, p. 35.
85   See Bauer 1934c, p. 110.

from different objective and subjective living conditions of the working class, could be overcome based on socialist theory.[86] According to Bauer, this did not exclude a co-operation of both currents at a political level. As a condition for such co-operation, the Social Democrats' pessimistic assessment of the Soviet Union would have to be readdressed. In 1936, he formulated the second condition: Social Democracy had to adopt his programme of 'integral socialism'.[87]

Bauer assumed that the struggle against fascist dictatorships and authoritarian regimes was a matter concerning not just the working class, but all progressive and democratic social forces. He was convinced that only the unification of different classes and social layers could save democracy, and this goal remained a priority for him. Bauer did not want to work out a programme for merging both sides. He desired co-operation, but not in a united front as advocated by the Communists. He expressed his tense relationship to their united front idea thus: 'It is important for the future of the world proletariat to bridge the gap that divides the socialist parties of west and central Europe from the Russian Revolution. But it is equally important not to sever the ties that link the socialist parties of west and central Europe' (our translation).[88] Rather, Bauer was concerned with establishing a platform for co-operation between the Social-Democratic and Communist movements that might gain strong support from the trade unions, co-operatives, and cultural institutions. It was not his intention to propose platforms of communication between Social Democrats and Communists which could have forced either side to give up its ideology. Instead, he sought a synthesis of values; for this purpose, it would be sufficient to recognise that the capitalist system had to be reconstructed in the spirit of socialist aims and ideals. The Social-Democratic movement would contribute its tradition of fighting for freedom and democracy, respecting the freedom and rights of the individual, and taking responsibility for cultural heritage. The Communists, meanwhile, would contribute their radicalism and revolutionism of action, i.e. the belief that the working class could only achieve complete liberation with the introduction of a proletarian dictatorship and destruction of the capitalist order.

---

86   See Bauer 1976p, p. 302.

87   Detlev Albers outlines this concept in Albers 1979, pp. 90–6.

88   'Es ist für die ganze Zukunft des Weltproletariats wichtig, dass die Kluft überbrückt werde, die die sozialistischen Parteien West- und Mitteleuropas von der russischen Revolution scheidet. Aber es ist ebenso wichtig, daß die Bande nicht zerrissen werden, die die sozialistischen Parteien West- und Mitteleuropas untereinander verbinden' – Bauer 1980bb, p. 589.

The concept of 'integral socialism' essentially came down to the idea of uniting the two main tendencies of the workers' movement in the struggle against counter-revolutionary and fascist forces. This unit must assemble under a banner of defending mutually accepted values. It was intended as a process of dialogue and mutual learning curve to mitigate antagonisms between the reformist and Communist wings and prepare the working class for united action in the case of war. Bauer attached further hopes to it: that the Social Democrats recognise the limits of reformist socialism and the Communists learn to appreciate democratic values. In addition, he hoped that terror in Russia would be reduced and democratic principles of social coexistence introduced as an effect of his idea. Bauer firmly believed that his suggestion could be put into practice. As an example, he cited the collaboration between socialists and Communists in France, although he depreciated the difference between the situation in Austria and that in a country where two legal political parties engaged in common activities under conditions of parliamentary democracy. For the sake of precision, one should add that, irrespective of his long-term perspectives, Bauer linked more humble practical goals to his concept: he wanted to win communist parties that had distanced themselves from the dogmatism of the Communist International to the Social Democrats. The suggestion contained in his theory of 'integral socialism' to dissolve small communist parties in the west so its members might bolster the ranks of the Social-Democratic mass parties is evidence of this. However, his hope proved misguided. To justify Bauer's strategic concept, it is important to state that he devised it half a year before the Moscow Trials. These trials extinguished any hope for the unification of Social Democrats and Communists for good.

What did Bauer's programme of 'integral socialism' actually represent? Moreover, was its glorification by researchers from Bremen University and Eurocommunist theorists in the 1970s–80s, who considered it a premise for potential collaboration between contemporary Communists and social democrats, justified? In 1984, Ernst Wimmer, a member and theorist of the Communist Party of Austria, argued that it embodied the old Austrian idea of working-class unity.[89] However, its content, value, and political usefulness were weak. The reason why it was so popular before the fall of really existing socialism in the Eastern Bloc states is that left socialists had not worked out their own programme for co-operation with the Communists.

---

89   See Wimmer 1984, p. 4.

3   The Question of Revolutionary Allies for the Working Class

The relationship of the middle classes to the working class and bourgeoisie, including its position during democratic and socialist transformations, occupied a special place in the concept of gradual revolution. This question was of great importance insofar as peaceful revolution would only be possible if the working class won these social layers to the socialist idea. Indeed, the neutral position of the non-proletarian classes undermined hopes of winning the parliamentary majority and commencing an era of social revolution. Both theory and revolutionary practice determined Social-Democratic positions concerning allies. Hence, it appears justified to approach the question of revolutionary allies by contrasting theoretical insights with the experience of the revolutionary period. The fact that the Social Democrats' proposals to win the middle classes only emerged in the years 1920–6 is not the only factor that would suggest such an approach.

While debates about the middle classes were ongoing in the SDAP for many years, they were not based on much theoretical analysis. Only the sociological aspect was touched upon due to Bauer's writings – and this was limited to defining the place and function of the middle classes within the bourgeois state's socio-economic structure and balance of class forces. Bauer identified two problems. First, Marx's prognosis that the middle classes would disappear and become proletarianised in the course of capitalist development had not come true; second, the degree to which the petty bourgeoisie and peasantry are politically organised increases under the ideological leadership of the bourgeoisie as these groups tie their class interests to big capital. From this, Bauer concluded that the petty bourgeoisie, peasantry and intelligentsia were politically dependent, and that the proletariat, on account of its economic condition, was the only consistent political opponent of the bourgeoisie. While considering it the sole revolutionary class in Austria, Bauer did not exclude the possibility that the working class might gain support from poor peasants in its struggle. For such a situation, he reserved the role of hegemon concerning the process of social transformations for the proletariat. Notably, neither Bauer nor the other SDAP theorists, in contrast to Lenin, raised the question of a worker and peasant alliance for socialist revolution. This is easily explained in that the Bolsheviks wanted an armed uprising, which would only be possible with unified forces. The Social Democrats' objective, meanwhile, was to acquire legal legitimacy for workers' rule, and that did not require a permanent alliance. More crucial than tactical differences, however, were differences in position held by the working classes in the social structures of their respective countries. In Russia, peasants were natural allies to the proletariat due to their socio-economic position. In Austria, on the other hand, the interests of the proletarian and peasant classes overlapped only marginally.

Austromarxist revolutionary theory for a long time lacked a genuine interest in the middle classes question. The first reason for this was that the middle classes were seen as partial subjects of the revolutionary process – i.e. social groups to be won to the aims of socialist politics, yet without an active role in history. The second was that their participation in the struggle for socialism was deemed a question of Social-Democratic party strategy and tactics rather than a theoretical one. This tactic focused on finding mechanisms that might destroy the economic, political and cultural hegemony of the bourgeoisie. The Social Democrats knew that hegemony was not just the result of the economic position of the bourgeoisie – the power of finance capital, the system of credits, tariff policies – but also resulted from the fact that bourgeois government relied on mass parties which united the majority of society, made up of the petty bourgeoisie and peasantry. For this reason, they saw it as their duty to liberate the middle classes from bourgeois influence and convince them that the Social-Democratic party did not just represent one class, but that its social policies considered all those selling their labour power for a living.

To achieve this, the party's theory of socialist revolution had to undergo a modification. Its inadequate tendency was that it declared the seizure of political power by the proletariat as the condition *sine qua non* for the first stage of social revolution. Seizing power within the democratic system, in turn, was not possible without winning a parliamentary majority, and that was not achievable without prior Social-Democratic efforts to transform the capitalist state for the benefit of the broad masses. Only a formula envisioning a revolution in two stages could help the party out of this dilemma. The programmes drafted by Bauer, who composed *The Road to Socialism*, offered such a formula in the form of his socialisation and agricultural programmes. Bauer hoped that the realisation of these programmes would accelerate the process of democratising social relations under capitalism. This would, according to the understanding of Social Democracy, amount to transforming the capitalist system in a socialist spirit. He also thought that the programme would garner sympathies for socialism from broad social layers. One important aspect should not be overlooked: neither the concept of socialisation, which was understood as a transitional stage between capitalism and socialism, nor the draft agricultural programme were revisions of Austromarxist revolutionary theory, but rather were mere supplements resulting from the necessity to subordinate theory to the needs of political practice. Nevertheless, they had far-reaching consequences for Austromarxist theory: efforts to find socialist solutions under capitalism diverted the party's attention from the struggle to accrue state power for the working class. Both programmes framed the question of class allies in the revolution in a new light. Whether the middle classes could become potential allies for the working-class revolution became of secondary concern; rather, convincing these layers that the process of democratising the capitalist state, inaugurated by the proletariat and its party, was in its own interest.

Bauer's projects for winning over broad social layers for the socialist idea will be examined further; however, it is necessary to make a general observation in advance. Bauer's notion was an overall concept of struggle for socialism, according to which, however, socialism could not be introduced due to the economic, political and social factors of the time. Simultaneously, it was a model that allowed Social Democracy to substantially improve the living conditions not only of the working class, but also of other social groups.

3.1 The Socialisation Programme

The working class of Austria entrusted a specific hope to the proclamation of the Republic and seizure of power by the Social Democrats: that their party would make every effort to transform the old social system. Among their demands to this effect, socialisation occupied a central place. The newly formed Communist Party of Austria (KPÖ) was the first political party to adhere to this: the programme it introduced was one of full socialisation – i.e. nationalisation – of the industries, banks, land, and woods.[90] Likewise, the 28 December 1918 election manifesto of the SDAP contained the demand for socialisation. Its prime motivation was the fear that the masses might commence spontaneous action to transform the state order – in 1918, the slogan of 'socialisation' featured in the party programme was a mere tactical manoeuvre, not a serious programmatic demand.[91] The Social Democrats, like the Communists, had no real idea of how a functioning socialist economy might be organised at the time.

It is necessary to elaborate the content of the term 'socialisation' as interpreted by the Social Democrats, not least because it was fundamentally different from the way the Communists understood it. For the Social Democrats, 'socialisation' was opposed to socialisation in Marx's interpretation. They

---

90   See Hautmann 1970, p. 60.

91   Bauer's position was crucial for adopting the demand for socialisation into the programme of the SDAP. He defended the stance in his text, 'Bolschewismus oder Sozialdemokratie?', as follows: 'In west and central Europe, one cannot do as in Russia, first leaving social organisation to the destructive force of instinctive mass movements for half a year, and then use state power controlled by a small minority to impose a fundamentally different state order upon the popular masses' (our translation) – Bauer 1976c, p. 318.

instead adhered to the same connotation that the president of the Belgian
Labour Party, Emile Vandervelde, had ascribed to the term at the end of the
nineteenth century: it denoted a process by which workers' organisations,
such as co-operatives and trade unions, would gradually supersede capitalist
institutions. Marx's concept required a radical change in the balance of class
forces in the capitalist state and its replacement by a socialist state. The Social-
Democratic project, in contrast, implied economic and political modifications
of social life that would leave capitalist class relations intact. In the minds of
Social Democrats, laws and regulations for socialisation represented an early
stage of full socialisation and were prefigurative of revolutionary solutions. It
is easy to see that this type of 'socialisation' was closely related to the notion of
'growing into socialism' and had much in common with the practice of reformism.

The appeal, 'socialisation is the slogan of the day', became increasingly popular in Austria after the publication of a pamphlet by *Arbeiter-Zeitung* editor,
Alexander Täubler.[92] On 14 March 1919, parliament passed a law on commencing the preparations for socialisation: industrial enterprises sufficiently ripe
for socialisation were to be socialised by the state, federal or municipal government. As an aside, socialisation according to this law was the responsibility
of the government – hence bourgeois forces were able to sabotage it from its
infancy. In order to implement the law, a national socialisation commission
with Bauer at the helm was set up.[93] The election results of 16 February 1919, the
national conference of workers' and soldiers' councils on 1 March 1919, and the
numerical growth of the Communist Party all helped to hasten the socialisation project. These events all testified to the radical mood among the working
masses. In the spring of 1919, the bourgeois bloc assumed a conciliatory attitude
toward the socialisation programme – evidently, it feared that any resistance on
its part might escalate social upheavals.

Bauer took upon himself the task of drafting a socialisation programme.
As early as January 1919, he outlined the central ideas of the socialisation

---

92   See Täubler 1919. Compare Albers 1979, p. 32.
93   The commission largely consisted of politicians rather than economic experts, which
      would have negatively affected the content and practice of socialisation. Among their
      members were five national assembly representatives, two delegates from the SDAP, two
      from the Christian Socials, and one from the Greater Germans. A socialisation commission
      had been convened in Germany prior to that, yet the German Social Democrats and
      government were unable to work out a clear socialisation programme. In contrast to
      Austria, the socialisation programme in Germany mainly interested the Independent
      Social Democratic Party of Germany (USPD).

concept in a number of articles in the *Arbeiter-Zeitung*.[94] As a theorist, Bauer was not in an easy position: the socialist movement offered him no ready-made models to fall back on. Hence, he saw himself compelled to look for inspiration in other political currents. These were, as Bauer himself noted in the introduction to *Der Weg zum Sozialismus*, British guild socialism and the Russian model adopted at the convention of national economy councils in May 1918.[95]

Bauer's socialisation theory was intended as a negation of the national-isations that the Bolsheviks implemented after the October Revolution. His justification for this was twofold: firstly, he claimed that the rationalisation of production, the allocation of resources, and the process of modernisation required profound changes in consciousness and the economy. These could not simply be obtained by decree.[96] Secondly, he argued that the Russian model was impractical for the west European countries because their mutual economic networks were far more advanced. For industrialised countries, Bauer crafted a plan of gradual horizontal socialisation.[97]

The programme contained the outline of a partial socialisation against compensation: large estates, woods, big industrial enterprises and banks would be passed into common ownership. Primarily, the plan was to nationalise branches of the economy that were strategically significant and had evolved towards forms of planned economy due to a high degree of concentration – i.e. steel, iron, coal and electricity works. According to the programme, these represented foundations of centralised production management.[98] The process of nationalising these industries was to proceed under the control of the capitalists and in co-operation with them. The sum of compensation payments for the expropriated assets of heavy industry would be collected through taxes on all capitalist property. Bauer envisioned the possibility to expand nation-

---

94   They were compiled in the pamphlet, *Der Weg zum Sozialismus* (*The Road to Socialism*).

95   See Bauer 1976b, p. 712.

96   Bauer wrote: 'Thus, raising the living standard of the masses requires not only the *legal* act of expropriating the expropriators, but also the *economic* process of streamlining the social apparatus of production and distribution ... Dictatorship cannot accelerate the economic process of socialisation' – Bauer 1976d, p. 338.

97   For more on this concept and its further evolution, see März and Weber, pp. 77–89.

98   Although Bauer worked out a plan for a planned economy, he was nonetheless a decis-ive opponent of completely abolishing the market. Unlike the Bolsheviks, he argued that a planned economy should be introduced once socialisation was completed. In Aus-tria, Otto Neurath, who was favourable to Social Democracy, formulated the notion of a planned economy that went hand in hand with abolishing the market.

alisation gradually onto other branches of the economy. As a stopgap solution for branches of industry that were not ready for socialisation, he suggested cartels similar to the industrial associations modelled on the centres and associations developed in the First World War. The peak of the socialisation process would be the expropriation of banks and establishment of a central bank.[99] Bauer excluded individual farming and small industrial and trading enterprises, citing the detrimental consequences of expropriation decrees in the Hungarian Soviet Republic, such as the disruption of the economic cycle, growing expenses of trading transactions, and a lack of skilled managers in the working class.

Bauer's programme provided a clear blueprint as to how the mixed model would function during the transitional stage of nationalisation. One might wonder how socialist industries could be maintained in a capitalist environment. Bauer cites two essential conditions for this: (1) division of labour, an increase in productivity through lower production costs and increased work efficiency; (2) implementing socialisation at an international level rather than in political and social isolation as had been the case in Russia.[100] This process was to occur initially in economically autarkic countries, and later spread to less developed lands. A worldwide planned economy was to emerge from the subsequent stages of socialisation. As März and Weber observed, an inner contradiction was immanent to Bauer's project: on the one hand, it was designed exclusively for postwar Austria; on the other, the *Anschluss* of Austria to Germany was mandatory for it to succeed.[101] The economic aspect of the *Anschluss* was decisive, as Germany fulfilled the required criteria for socialisation cited by Bauer to a far greater degree. As a bigger economic territory, its production was additionally more concentrated than in Austria. One particular virtue of Bauer's programme was not the notion of gradual socialisation, but his specific standard for nationalised industries.[102] Bauer categorically rejected the nationalisation of property and production management by the state

---

99   Bauer was referring to Hilferding here. Note that he had doubts about nationalising the banks, as he feared that this act might infringe upon international capital relations. His project of nationalising the banks was met with approval from Käthe Leichter and Renner. See Steiner 1973b, p. 423; Renner 1924, p. 372.

100 Karl Kautsky, who in his works stressed the link between socialisation and increasing productivity, exerted great influence over Bauer's views of socialist economy. Compare Bauer 1919, p. 664.

101 See März and Weber, p. 81.

102 This project found the most support in the international workers' movements' discussion on socialisation.

as insisted upon by Marx as a condition for the development of a socialist economy. Rather, he shared with Hilferding and Weber the belief (later also passionately defended by Popper) that state socialism would reinforce bureaucratic tendencies and exclude the main component of true socialisation, namely social control. However, with regards to Bauer's ideas on the role of the state in the socialisation process, it is paramount to distinguish between two different aspects. For Bauer, 'the state' was 'the worst economist', and socialisation was not to be confused with nationalisation (a thesis fully confirmed by the development of the economy under 'really existing socialism'). Nonetheless, he did not entirely renounce the state as a factor in the socialisation process, but apportioned a concrete significance to it: it was to liquidate big property, pay compensations, and, ultimately, act as a mediator in the new system of production management. Thus, Bauer favoured democratic solutions over bureaucratic economic structures, yet without going so far as to advocate economic liberalism. It is from this perspective that he criticised syndicalism: he believed it represented a system that prioritised the ambition of individual production firms to assert their own economic interests at the expense of producers. As an alternative to both state socialism and syndicalism, he proposed a 3/3 principle for socialised workplaces and production co-operatives – i.e. the creation of collective administration boards consisting of an equal number of delegates from three interest groups: producers, consumers and the state. Common economic interests and a comprehensive economic plan would guide them.[103] Rather than representing the interests of the state in these collective boards, state delegates would assume a mediator role between producers and consumers. Industrial councils would be formed in all workplaces with more than 20 workers and control each collective administration board. Doubtlessly, it was an interesting proposal – yet it had a flaw that went unnoticed by its founder: the impossibility of reconciling the intrinsically opposing interests of the different groups. Workers are always interested in high wages, consumers in low prices, and the state demands the biggest revenue possible.

What expectations did Bauer tie to his socialisation programme? Before a response can be formulated, it is crucial to address the fact that, for Bauer, socialisation meant transformation not only of property relations, but also of the organisational structure of production, the process of profit distribution,

---

103 This administrative structure would bear responsibility for distributing the income of the socialised workplace: one third was to be paid to workers and other employees, one third was to cover capital expenditure, and one third paid over to the state treasury.

allocation, and the introduction of a new works constitution. The foremost objective of socialisation was the implementation of industrial democracy.[104]

Bauer's socialisation programme served to reinforce the argument that transformations of a socialist character could be realised in a capitalist system. It painted an image of a working class that peacefully assumes power over the economy bit by bit, as well as that of a state that rules in the interest of all classes and social groups. Its discreet objective was to suppress the revolutionary mood of the working class and divert their attention away from the workers' councils. The radicalism of the masses, after all, was inimical to the interests of a party that sought to seduce the middle classes and change their political views. The programme contained many interesting points that continue to engage theorists to the present day. They were also reflected in documents of postwar social democracy – yet back in their time, they were premature and not consistent with the economic, social and political conditions in Austria. The programme insufficiently considered the immanent mechanisms of the economy, such as dependency on foreign capital, the low educational level of the working masses, and their underdeveloped ability to think in economic and political terms. In 1919, Bauer's socialisation plan became the official programme of the SDAP, and it continued to be upheld at the party congress in Linz.[105] Party-internal resistance only came from representatives of the consumer co-operatives. They feared that workers' co-management in the co-operatives would stifle production, and they rejected the suggestion to create industrial councils because of their social character.[106] Renner, though scep-

---

104 For more on this concept, compare Chapter 6, second heading.

105 The programme of Linz preserved the central ideas of the 1919 socialisation programme: The socialisation process would take a long time to accomplish. Socialism could only be achieved in great economic territories that provided fertile ground for a planned economy. Various forms of mixed economy would be necessary. Trading and consumer co-operatives would need to be formed, petty property protected and guaranteed, industrial democracy strengthened, co-management alongside industrial councils introduced, unemployment insurance extended, laws concerning workplace health and safety regulations improved, birth control introduced, abortion legalised, and free education offered. The fact that Bauer reiterated the basic premises of the old programme testifies to his low political sense of reality. While the spring of 1919 still offered favourable conditions for implementing the socialisation programme (the revolutionary crisis, the clear ascendancy of Social Democracy, insecurity and splits in the bourgeois camp, pro-revolutionary attitudes in the intelligentsia and peasantry), the demand for socialisation scarcely inspired the sympathies of the middle classes in 1926. They were becoming increasingly reactionary. See Berchtold 1967, pp. 248–56.

106 See März and Weber 1979.

tical, did not raise any objections officially. Outside of Austria, the programme was recognised among Social Democrats.[107] Likewise, it was well received by the bourgeois.

Indeed, the programme complemented the broad social reforms that the Social-Democratic government, with Ferdinand Hanusch at its helm, had already attempted to push through parliament since autumn 1918.[108] These bylaws were nothing unique. On the contrary, they had been present in the programmes of the SDAP for decades. Even representatives of the Christian trade unions suggested comparable measures, although the balance of forces in Austria had been unfavourable to putting them into practice. In this respect, the revolutionary period offered a unique opportunity. The Social Democrats used it to pass laws which changed the living and working conditions for broad layers of the working population to a degree that cannot be overstated. The bulk of these laws continue to be in place today. They are rightly regarded as the greatest successes of Social-Democratic reformist politics. The period of social legislation was a genuine social revolution not only for activists, but also for masses of ordinary people. The following laws, drafted by the socialisation commission and passed from 1918–19, were among the most important new regulations:

- Public unemployment insurance, passed on 6 November 1918. This insurance applied to all industrial and agricultural workers.[109] Due to this, arbitration commissions helping workers to find employment and providing protection against unlawful dismissal were set up in all districts.
- The eight-hour workday, passed on 19 December 1918. This was consistent with the demand put forward at the big demonstration of the international workers' movement on 1 May 1890. Rules outlawing child labour and night work by women and minors were also included (passed on 14 May 1919).

---

107 Karl Kautsky and a member of the German socialisation commission, Robert Wilbrandt, were among those who lauded the programme – see Euchner 1979, p. 32. The congress of the Second International in Geneva from 31 July–5 August 1920 upheld a socialisation programme in the spirit of Otto Bauer and Austromarxism. In Poland, Mieczysław Niedziałkowski, Adam Próchnik, Bronisław Ziemięcki, Zygmunt Żuławski, Oskar Lange, and Kazimierz Czapiński further developed Bauer's ideas of socialisation – see Czerwińska 1991, pp. 431–2.

108 The ministry of welfare work was established as early as 22 December 1917. See Steiner 1967.

109 According to Kreissler, the number of unemployed claiming benefits rose every year: 46,203 on 1 December 1918; 162,104 on 1 February 1919; 178,553 on 1 April 2015.

- Public compensation for disabled war veterans, war widows and war orphans (25 April 1919).
- The creation of industrial councils (15 May 1919).
- The right of workers to paid holidays (30 July 1919).[110]
- Regulations of overtime pay (17 December 1919).

Among other great achievements of this period were laws on journalists, the protection of domestic servants, the right to claim war compensation, and the creation of employees' associations ensuring that industrial law and social legislation were implemented (26 February 1920). All of these laws were passed despite the protest of the Christian Social and Greater German parties, which objected to the social costs involved. The 1918–20 social reforms peaked with the transformation of public health insurance – now extended to include family members – and the pensions system.[111]

The Social Democrats regarded the adopted social legislation as representative of an early form of the legal system that would prevail in the socialist state. They had strong hopes for the law concerning the formation of industrial councils in the enterprises, trade, and agriculture; for them, this was the first step on the road to socialisation.[112] However, they also expected that a thorough democratisation of workplaces would lead to increased productivity, teach workers how to manage the production process, and train them up to improve their general skills. The responsibilities of the industrial councils were as follows: controlling the implementation of social legislation, maintaining labour agreements, securing workers' participation in determining wages, protecting workers from unlawful dismissal, maintaining discipline in the workplaces and monitoring the technological aspects of production. In big enterprises, responsibilities were extended to monitoring the finances and wage statistics of the company. The law obliged bosses to summon meetings between the company management and industrial council at the bequest of the latter at least

---

110   Only state employees enjoyed this right under the monarchy.

111   As to social legislation during the first days of the Republic, see Kaufmann 1978, pp. 134–40, and Tálos 1990, pp. 353–61.

112   On 14 April 1919, Bauer wrote in the *Arbeiter-Zeitung*: 'The introduction of industrial councils in itself ... does not yet amount to socialisation, it merely means that the works constitution is democratised. However, the industrial councils provide a basis for socialisation, which can then proceed' (our translation). Original: 'Die Einführung von Betriebräten ... bedeutet an sich noch keine Sozialisierung, es ist nur eine Demokratisierung der Betriebsverfassung, aber es ist eine Grundlage für die Sozialisierung, auf der diese dann aufgebaut werden kann'.

once a month.[113] The concessions granted by the bourgeoisie were relatively far-reaching when it came to defining the tasks of the industrial councils, not least because they did not fundamentally change the existing social order. Soon enough, life would crush the Social Democrats' expectations that the industrial councils would play a fundamental role in bringing about socialist relations in the workplaces and lead to the breakdown of capitalist monopoly over the economy. In truth, the industrial councils helped to dispel the revolutionary atmosphere as they acted in opposition to arbitrary socialisation. After 1921, their responsibilities were confined to regulating occupational safety, defending the social legislation, looking after technical problems, and monitoring wages and piecework. Soon, they simply merged with the trade unions.[114]

Even though the industrial councils law did not meet the expectations of their founders,[115] the Social Democrats' attempts to apply social legislation, alongside their housing and education policies, contributed to international discussion of a 'red Vienna'.[116] The actual implementation of key ideas from

---

113   The 1947 law concerning industrial councils and the 1973 labour constitution regulations only marginally differed from the 1919 law.

114   Max Adler warned that the industrial councils might be co-opted by the existing capitalist system. He was aware that the council members were insufficiently theoretically prepared and demanded that they undergo an intense educational period. The SDAP leadership did not approve his proposal.

115   In 1919, Bauer argued that 'as an agency of proletarian self-government in the processes of production, the works' committees form a preliminary stage to the to the socialistic mode of production' – Bauer 1925, p. 145.

116   Before 1919, 73 percent of all apartments had 0.5–1.5 rooms judging by modern standards. 58 percent of working-class family members had to share their bed with another person, and 22 percent of working-class families were subletting in order to stump up their rent. The miserable living conditions were fertile ground for tuberculosis, which was referred to as the Vienna disease. Compare Anreiter 1985–6, p. 35. Housing was the most serious social problem that the Social Democrats had to attend to in order to convince the working masses of the superiority of their politics over the bourgeois parties. Soon enough, the Social-Democratic local government of Vienna turned the city into one big construction site. The treasurer of Vienna, Hugo Breitner, worked out a progressive tax system that made the rich pay high taxes for luxury apartments, racing horses, domestic servants, even pet dogs and theatre and cinema tickets. The money was used to build some 60,000 flats with en-suite bathrooms and toilets – an almost unimaginably high standard at the time. Schools, orphanages, sports facilities, and cultural institutions for children were erected en masse. The professor of anatomy, Julius Tandler, introduced medicine as a subject of study in schools and offered relevant courses for mothers. In 1919, the Social-Democratic minister of education, Otto Glöckel, reformed the school system permitting women to study at university. See Kreissler 1970, p. 137; compare Konrad 2008, pp. 229–36.

Bauer's socialisation programme – expropriations and the creation of socialised enterprises – appeared much worse in practice. The preparatory programme for socialisation passed in parliament on 14 March 1919 announced
expropriations in the spirit of Bauer's programme – yet Ignaz Seipel, head of
the socialisation commission, sabotaged its implementation from the start,
even going so far as to introduce an alternative socialisation programme in
the name of the Christian Social Party in order to forestall the SDAP.[117] The
extent in which processes of the socialisation commission went their separate ways was not only a sign of inter-party strife and programmatic differences,
but also brought the brittleness and forced character of working in a coalition to
the fore. The coalition government contented itself with introducing a socialisation programme for coalmines, steel mines, electricity works, large woodlands, and the wood industry in May 1919 – yet even these programmes never
really took shape. Likewise, laws passed in parliament – such as the expropriation law of 30 May 1919 or the law concerning the formation of municipal
enterprises of 29 July 1919 – had little effect. Because of the resistance of the
bourgeois bloc, the law regulating the expropriation of industrial enterprises
was, in practice, a procedural principle without any relevant basis and point
of reference.[118] It could not be applied for a number of reasons: the state cof-
fers were empty, foreign credit to help pay the compensation was lacking, and
individual federal states, primarily Styria and Carinthia, resisted the planned
changes.[119] Socialisation plans were stunted further by economic crisis, the
sectional interests of the federal states and arguments among the parliamentary fraction as to how best to proceed when building socialised enterprises.
Only a small number of militarised workplaces without any great economic
significance were successfully socialised. As a result, the following had become
community-controlled enterprises: the textiles factory of Steyr, the Sollenau
chemical plant, the German-Austrian dress production factories, a number of
shoe manufacturers, pharma producers, a loan office in Vienna, and an old
arms factory in the old Vienna armoury in the third district. Some of these
enterprises went bankrupt during the 1922 crisis, while the rest were shut down

---

117   The Christian Social Party's proposal confined itself to industries where monopolisation
        had long advanced, i.e. transport companies, mines, and factories manufacturing mass
        consumer goods. Compare Weissel 1976, p. 262.
118   Compare Leser 1968, p. 322.
119   The minister of economy and theorist of economics, Joseph Schumpeter, energetically
        opposed Bauer's plan to gain financial means for compensation by taxing assets and
        inheritances.

in 1934.[120] Heavy industry suffered a blow when the majority shares of Alpine Montangesellschaft – the only complex whose socialisation had a practical meaning for the success of the whole effort – were sold to the Italians on 22 May 1919.[121]

Two factors decided the untimely fate of the socialisation effort. The first was the international situation in 1919: the revolutionary wave in Western Europe ebbed as the Bavarian and Hungarian soviet republics were defeated and bourgeois governments were consolidated in Poland and Czechoslovakia. The second factor was the domestic situation in Austria. That is to say, its dependency on the Entente powers, inflation, the growing resistance of the propertied classes, continuous agitation conducted by the Christian Social Party and peasantry against the socialisation project, and a lack of pressure on the part of the SDAP leadership.[122] Once the socialisation policies, however partially implemented, had served their purpose in damping the revolutionary mood of the working class, the Christian Social Party could scarcely conceal its aversion to any further collaboration with the Social Democrats. In September 1919, the socialisation commission discontinued its operations, with no further meetings taking place thereafter. In October 1919, Bauer consequently resigned from his position as chair of the commission. In his opinion, two factors crucially contributed to the project's failure: the ban on *Anschluss* and economic dependency on the Entente.[123] While the aforementioned factors were just as

---

120   Compare März 1965, p. 65 and Leser 1968, p. 322.

121   Compare März 1975, p. 420. Alpine Montangesellschaft was Austria's biggest iron and steel corporation. Joseph Schumpeter decided to sell off the majority shares in order to source money for coal and food.

122   The Entente powers threatened to deny the Austrian government any further credit if parliament were to pass socialisation laws. At the same time, foreign shares in the banks of Vienna increased:

1913	1923	
17.8 percent	46.0 percent	Boden-Creditanstalt
31.4 percent	70.0 percent	Länderbank
3.0 percent	55.6 percent	Anglo-Bank
3.4 percent	60.0 percent	Mercurbank

SOURCE: MÄRZ 1981, P. 443.

123   In his unpublished speech, Bauer wrote: 'We were unable to socialise because we could not sever our international ties ... Our payments balance was unfavourable, and we were

influential, Bauer's overall assessment of the economic, political, and social situation in Austria was accurate. One might well ask whether Bauer and the SDAP leadership would have had any alternatives to their chosen strategy. The only truthful answer is yes, but only if they had gone the way of revolutionary violence. As this was not the SDAP strategy, they saw themselves forced to commence socialisation efforts to pacify the angry masses in order to maintain their credibility. Furthermore, prevalent economic and political conditions limited any room for manoeuvre.

Postwar Austrian social democracy drew lessons from the socialisation programme debacle. In the Second Republic, the textile and energy industries, machine engineering and big banks were nationalised very quickly. However, it is impossible to ignore the fact that the Social-Democratic Party of Austria's (SPÖ) 1946–7 programmes demanded socialisation in addition to nationalisation. The criteria for socialisation – i.e. size and economic significance of prospective enterprises – represented a continuation of the criteria defined in 1919. Not unlike the original socialisation plans, the postwar programmes outlined an economic model that would coalesce a planned economy with workers' co-management in the workplaces, as well as demand the restoration of pre-1934 social legislation. Further analogies to Bauer's socialisation programme can be found in the SPÖ programme of 1958, which demanded the expropriation of big landowners for compensation, continued inviolability of petty production enterprises and agriculture, and the introduction of an administration system according to the 3/3 principle in socialised workplaces. The aims of these proposals, too, were the same as those of Bauer's project in 1919.[124]

3.2   The Agrarian Programme

The ongoing war and fall of the monarchy upset the traditional structure of class relations in the countryside and revolutionised the peasant masses. From 1918–20, a wave of peasant uprisings against officials who upheld wartime policies in administration and trade broke out. Agricultural and silvicultural workers also proclaimed their discontent. They had hoped that the fall of the Empire would bring changes in rural property relations, and that the Social-Democratic government would introduce an agricultural programme to improve working conditions and raise wages. These groups were receptive to

---

not able to acquire the necessary foreign financial means to import bread and coal. There was only one way to get them, namely by selling off assets ... We had to pass our factories into the hands of foreign capitalists' (our translation) – Bauer 1920, in Archival Sources.

124   On the 1946–59 programmes of the SPÖ, see Kozub's interesting depiction in Kozub 1982, pp. 56–69.

Communist agitation for nationalisation and demanded that land be equally distributed (especially so in Lower Austria).[125] In the early days of the Republic, the countryside welcomed the democratisation of the Austrian state – especially the suffrage reforms, which resulted in changes to the representations of class forces in regional governments. For the first time in its history, the Social-Democratic movement faced the opportunity to acquaint socialist ideas to rural parts of the country, which it had largely neglected. The struggle was aided by the spontaneous emergence of socialist peasant organisations and growing membership numbers in the association of agricultural and silvicultural workers.[126] In April 1919, this association submitted a draft for agricultural reforms that envisaged the expropriation of large rural landholdings by the state, federal governments, and communes, and their socialisation according to the co-operative principle. The association counted on the SDAP's support. Likewise, the smallholders' union sided with the Social Democrats, hoping that independent agricultural enterprises would be set up. However, the SDAP paid no great attention to agitation in the countryside. True, Bauer had already discussed these issues in *The Road To Socialism*, and his 'Leitsätze zur Agrarpolitik' ('Principles of Agricultural Policy', 1921) provided the basis for a debate held in *Der Kampf* in June 1921. But the SDAP leadership did not consider any close co-operation with the socialist peasant movement at the time. What is more, during the revolutionary period, when there was a genuine opportunity for the peasant parties and Social Democrats to work together, the SDAP leaders sought compromise with the bourgeois parties instead of approaching the Social-Democratic peasants' movement. The Christian Social Party readily exploited the SDAP's passive stance with respect to the countryside, consolidating its position when it established the Christian Peasants' Union. From a historical point of view, it is justified to ask whether the co-operation proposal submitted to the SDAP in 1918–20 had any real chances of success and whether it could have strengthened the party's position in the countryside. For some,

---

125   For more details about the situation in the countryside, see Mattl 1985b, p. 219.

126   In Lower Austria, for instance, a regional organisation of smallholders was created in 1920. In Vienna, a national association called 'Union of Smallholders, Winegrowers and Crofters' emerged and joined the Association of Agricultural and Silvicultural Workers as an autonomous section. In 1925, smallholders split from the Association of Agricultural and Silvicultural Workers and formed the Association of Free Working Peasants of Austria. See Winkler 1976, pp. 31–2. According to Mattl, the Social-Democratic agricultural and silvicultural workers' association grew from 700 to 30,000 members in the years 1918–20 – compare Mattl 1985b, p. 220b. In his writings, Bauer passionately supported the emerging workers' movement.

the Social Democrats' distrust of the peasant movement emerging under their aegis was justified: the socialist peasants' movement was a perfunctory trend. The peasant leaders neither managed to agree on a platform of co-operation between various rural groups, nor did they make inroads into the middle-class layers of the peasantry, which were hostile to the growth of the agricultural workers' movement. In addition, the leaders of the peasant organisations were indiscreet about the fact that their support for the SDAP was a tactical manoeuvre to prevent the rise of workers' councils.[127]

In 1923, objective factors drew the attention of the SDAP to the agricultural question. Economically, the situation in agriculture was poor: due to low productivity, the needs of the cities could not be met. The other factor was of a political nature: because of their dispersed existence and low class consciousness, the Social Democrats still did not consider the peasantry an independent political force. On the other hand, they could no longer ignore the political advantage that the Christian Social Party and Landbund, which in 1920 had forced the SDAP to resign from the coalition government, had secured from organising the rural population. When in 1923 votes for the SDAP increased by 300,000, the party's appetite for seizing power of its own accord awakened. In order to achieve this, it had to take the professional and social structure of Austria's populace into account, i.e. appeal not only to the industrial working class, but also to the peasantry. For the majority of the party, it was evident that the SDAP could only consolidate its power and implement a socialist order by enticing the peasants from the bourgeois parties' grasp. The direction in which Social-Democratic politics would move was significant for the peasants too, if they were to support the SDAP and contribute to their success.

European Social-Democratic thought on the agrarian question since the advent of World War I was characterised by orthodox Marxist positions, especially those expounded in Kautsky's early writings: the development of capitalism would go hand in hand with the process of concentration in agriculture, leading to the demise of small farms and rise of big agricultural enterprises. In the long-term, these enterprises would become links in the chain of a planned socialist economy, and in the short-term, they would modify property relations in the countryside based on property relations in the cities – capitalist landowners versus the proletarianised peasantry. The logical conclusion from this position was that peasants were the natural allies of workers in the socialist revolution. For the Social Democrats – with the exception of the theorists around Bernstein who looked into the agrarian question – this served as a

---

127   See Mattl 1985b, p. 221.

justification for neglecting the peasant question and failing to work out any programmes for the countryside.

The SDAP was the first Social-Democratic party that delivered such a programme. In the 1920s, Austrian Social Democrats were aware that the development of agriculture had not vindicated Marxian prognoses. Moreover, they did not believe that one should wait for history to catch up and vindicate them. In their view, a party wishing to change property relations in the countryside required a programme which took into account not the projected but the actual development tendencies of agriculture. Furthermore, it should be attractive to the divided countryside. The agricultural committee summoned at the party congress in Salzburg on 2 November 1923, with Bauer at its head, was entrusted with the responsibility to draft such a programme. Bauer's profound and extensive study, *Der Kampf um Wald und Weide* (*The Struggle for Woods and Pastures*), served as a basis. The draft was unanimously adopted at the 1925 party congress and incorporated into the programme of Linz. It represented the quintessence of Social-Democratic politics concerning the countryside, and at the same time reflected the social policies of the SDAP. Disregarding to what extent it was genuinely a socialist programme, its authors' effort to precisely define its basic features and carefully consider detailed solutions cannot be rated highly enough.

Marxist theory served as a source of inspiration for the agrarian programme. It is difficult not to recognise the influence of classical Marxists on the agrarian question reflected in its pages. For instance, the notion that the productivity of big agricultural enterprises is greater than the productivity of smaller ones prevailed. According to the programme, this was the reason why big enterprises objectively contributed to the rationalisation of production. Nonetheless, the programme departed from the premise that small agricultural enterprises would disappear, a premise that had remained in the European Social-Democratic movement since the adoption of the 1891 Erfurt programme. Instead, the necessity to preserve the private property of peasants, even under socialism, was accentuated.[128] This echoed analyses based on experiences of the October Revolution that Bauer had expressed in earlier texts. He argued that it would be wrong to impose collectivisation on Austrian peasants from above, because social relations were more advanced in the Austrian countryside than in Russia. Hence, the emphasis of his agrarian programme was on the question as to whether it was possible – or, indeed, desirable – to introduce socialist relations into the countryside without infringing the interest of peas-

---

128   See SDAP 1926b in Documents, Programmes, Protocols, p. 23.

ants. His views on the fundamental question for Social-Democratic agrarian policy were also shaped by his party's fear of anti-socialist boycott in the countryside, social discontentment in the cities, and a subsequent weakening of Social Democracy. Bauer himself reinforced this anxiety in numerous speeches.

The Social Democrats directed their proposal chiefly at small peasants, agricultural and silvicultural workers. The short-term and long-term objectives of the agrarian policy were summarised in two parts. The first part outlined efforts to be achieved under capitalism, whereas the second focused on defining the development of agriculture during the transitional period between capitalism and socialism. In the first part, increasing productivity and expanding the reach of social legislation to the countryside took precedence. The vital component of the second part was the nationalisation of woods and large estates for the benefit of communes and federal states to ensure that broad layers of the rural population had access to natural goods. Both parts were moulded by contributions by the co-operative movement. After all, the Social Democrats had been supporting the co-operative movement – in their eyes, the third pillar of the workers' movement alongside the party and trade unions – from the beginning.[129]

Improvements in the economy and conditions of life in the countryside were the centre of interest and determined the planned course of action:

1. Increased productivity – this demand was regarded as the most important programmatic requirement.[130] The following measures were to be taken: raising educational levels (i.e. expanding and reforming elementary schools in the countryside, scholarship funds, widening the advice and courses network), raising agricultural standards (developing infrastructure in the countryside, improving the quality of soil through melioration systems and aquifers, passing decrees which would oblige peasants to use high quality seeding materials and breeding animals). If the advisory networks and system of regulations did not provide effective means of rationalising agricultural production, the programme implied legal statutes that would convert the land of rebellious property owners into community property. The Social Democrats had no doubt that it was legitimate to infringe the prop-

---

129 Leser discusses this in Leser 1968, p. 380.

130 The reasons for priorities being set thus go back to Bauer's remark that the peasantry should declare not pricing policies, but an increase in industrial farm productivity its main objective; only this would secure an expansion of sales markets for industrial production. Increasing productivity was, according to him, the common interest of peasants and workers. See Bauer 1978b, p. 346; compare Mattl 1985b, p. 222.

erty rights of farmers if these rights stood in contradiction to the interests of the community. However, they did not forget the damage done in Russia and tried to prevent the danger of creating a command economy by passing the responsibility for landlord expropriation to the chamber of agriculture.

2. Improving the situation of the smallholders – in this part of the programme, regulations to abolish the exploitation of agriculture by commercial capital were brought to the fore. A decree that obliged farmers to form agricultural marketing co-operatives, which were to co-operate with urban consumer co-operatives according to plan, was considered the most important bill. Aside from this proposal, the programme aimed to introduce a state monopoly on agricultural products in order to protect the interest of peasants, price regulations by the state, and tariffs policies to protect the domestic market. These changes were to guarantee domestic sales and protect peasants from the competition of the employment market. Further measures to support smallholders included granting favourable credits, setting up state controlled agricultural banks, expanding leaseholder protection, and launching an insurance system against the effects of natural disasters.

3. Eliminating rural poverty – this point in the programme deserves special attention: it demanded that the living conditions of agricultural and silvicultural workers be raised to the level of the industrial working class. The existing social welfare system – industrial safety regulations, the right to paid holidays, health insurance and pensions, wage agreements, arbitration committees, industrial tribunals and official representation in the chamber of labour – was to be extended to include these groups.

It is difficult to ascertain from all of these demands, irrespective of how justified and undeniably progressive, just how they served to conduct specifically socialist policies in the countryside.[131] The second part of the programme did not meet this criterion either: even if its demands stressed the economic benefits arising from conglomerating all estates within a municipality, they were not necessarily heading in the direction of socialisation. Rather, they represented a cluster of legislations enforced to prevent the contamination of capitalism into rural relations.

---

131 Bauer himself admitted as much when he wrote: 'there is no argument between the Social Democrats and bourgeois parties about the necessity of all these regulations. Quite true, but the parties differ in the extent to which they dare to promote the development of agriculture by introducing binding, compulsory regulations' – Bauer 1976i, p. 294.

In a section entitled 'The transition to the socialist social order', the SDAP demanded that all private property and estates belonging to the church, as well as all private woodlands and pastures, be nationalised, and the right to hunt for the sake of private profit abolished for the benefit of the state and communes. The communes were to become the basic economic units and centres of creating socialist relations in the countryside. In reality, the role of the commune was programmatically limited to deciding the usage rights to appropriated land, regulating harvest work and cattle breeding, and drawing up wood and pasture management plans for the benefit of the village population. The programme explicitly stressed that the smallholders' and urban proletariat's appetites for land could not be satisfied as long as capitalist relations persisted in the countryside – that would only be possible with the introduction of socialism. Hence, it demanded neither the distribution of nationalised land, nor the capitulation of private agricultural enterprises. Instead, it implied a different solution: big agricultural enterprises would be founded on nationalised land and administrated just like regular industrial workplaces (although the programme did not state who would be employed). This proposal was consistent with the Social Democrats' confidence in the superiority of big enterprises over smaller ones, as well as the notion that they were the arbiters of technical progress in the countryside.[132] In the event that conditions were not ripe for establishing a new, common economic unit, the programme recommended to lease the newly established enterprises to competent peasants or, alternatively, leave the land to the previous owners while simultaneously subjecting them to state leadership and control. This solution was conducive to three aims, of which the Social Democrats considered the last to be the most important. The supply of land could be raised, prices for land rising above the value of revenue generated could be counteracted, and agriculture could be integrated into the planned economic process.

Without a doubt, the agricultural programme of the SDAP contained many ideas that were attractive from a social perspective. Among the guarantees it offered, there was equal access to education, limits to individual privileges and rights if they conflicted with the common good of the rural population, the utilisation of community property, and protection of the weak. The overarching principle that inspired the creators of the programme was not the expropriation or nationalisation of land as such, but rather that the administration of land would be taken up by immediate producers in the form of individual enterprises, co-operatives, and production plants. The role of the

---

132   See Bauer 1978b, p. 243.

state in the countryside was reduced to that of an auxiliary organ for the transition to self-administration. Despite all its virtues, the Social-Democratic agrarian programme did not meet with a lot of response among the rural popu-lation.[133] Peasants, traditionally ill disposed toward statism, were not enthusi-astic. Those organised in the Christian Social Party were reluctant about estab-lishing big agricultural enterprises and industrial councils. The programme could not inveigle the peasantry because it scarcely offered them more than they already had: peasants had been using woods and pastures held in com-mon since the fourteenth century, while co-operatives had been successfully operating in the Austrian countryside since the late nineteenth century. A sec-ondary factor, which nonetheless co-determined the fate of the programme, was the peasantry's strong anti-Semitism, manifesting itself in mistrust towards the SDAP. The rural proletariat, in turn, was aware that the SDAP proposals could only become reality if the party seized state power – and from 1925 to 1926, the chances of depriving the bourgeois parties of power were decidedly low. Although it was highly appraised by some, it is fair to say that the agrarian programme laid bare the deficiency of the Social-Democratic strategy. It rep-resented a theoretical model that lacked the experience of working within a coalition, including the failed socialisation of the industry. What is more, it truly existed in a vacuum. As the Social Democrats failed to co-operate with the socialist peasant movement, they gambled away their chances of realising their programme in the countryside. The programme did play a positive role in Social-Democratic politics, which essentially relied on convincing the peasants that the Social Democrats did not represent a 'red threat' to the countryside. All the same, it was not enough to stop the corporatist ideology gaining ground in rural areas.

As an aside, the 1925 agrarian programme was taken up again in Austria after World War II, when social democrats returned to models of agricultural education, loans to agricultural enterprises, and market regulation for key agricultural products and social policies.

---

133   Hanisch cites Hänisch 1995, p. 499, as follows: 'When the SDAP became the strongest
       individual party at the National Assembly elections in 1930, it received only six percent
       of the votes from those working in agriculture; in contrast, the Christian Socials received
       59 percent' (our translation) – Hanisch 2011 p. 228.

4   The Gradual Development of Attitudes toward Revolution and
     Bolshevik Practice

The victory of the October Revolution in Russia posed a challenge to European
Social Democracy. For decades, socialist revolution had been the centre of
discourse in Europe as either an inevitable result of the development of modern
societies (the determinist version) or, alternatively, an act of the working class
determined by that development (the activist-determinist version). Contrary to
these expectations, a social revolution took place in a country that European
Social Democracy had completely disregarded in its calculations. Its theorists
faced what appeared to be a vital complication for the fate of the international
workers' movement: how to evaluate the Russian experiment theoretically and
practically. As to the former, the most pressing dilemma was how to integrate
it into Marxist theory, and, with respect to practice, whether it was legitimate
to adopt the Russian revolutionary model and its relevant methods. Leading
Social Democrats were absorbed in this debate for years. As a result, splits in
the Second International intensified (although elaborating this in detail would
go beyond the scope of this work).

The SDAP's internal debate about the legitimacy of the Russian Revolution,
its perspectives and consequences for international socialism, corresponded
with a succession of political events in Soviet Russia and the Soviet Union.
It is worth considering that the Austrian party followed the developments in
Russia more attentively than was the case with its Social-Democratic sister
parties. The reasons were that, by and large, the SDAP faction of the Second
International had cultivated a friendly attitude towards the Bolsheviks, and,
with Vienna being a centre of Russian emigration, had a close relationship to
the Russian Social-Democratic movement. It was due to these circumstances
that the SDAP enthusiastically welcomed the outbreak of revolution and the
first strides towards Soviet power in Russia, the nationalisation of land and
banks.[134] When the Bolsheviks dissolved the constituent assembly, attitudes
in the SDAP radically changed, although they did not deny the progressive
character of the October Revolution. The Austrians distanced themselves from
the Bolsheviks. This ambivalent attitude towards the events in Russia and
the methods the Bolsheviks adhered to in order to construct a socialist state
influenced Bauer's position to the same degree.

Bauer was one of a small number of Marxist theorists who analysed the October Revolution and its historical consequences for years, meticulously keeping

---

134   See *Arbeiter-Zeitung* of 11 December 1917 and 1 January 1918; compare Löw 1982, p. 10.

up-to-date about Bolshevik politics. There were at least a few reasons as to why his voice in this debate was decisive for the entire Social-Democratic movement: Bauer was the only leading Western Social Democrat who had experienced the February Revolution first-hand between 1918–23, and was therefore able to base his judgement on direct observations. He kept in touch with the Mensheviks, spoke Russian and, what is more, drafted a theory concerning the development of the Soviet Russian state.[135] Frankly, his historical analyses of the Russian situation and Bolshevik endeavours were often fairly uncritical and inadequate – albeit this was partly due to a lack of detailed information and Russia's isolation from the international arena.

With respect to the whole of his revolutionary theory, Bauer's attitude towards the October Revolution and Bolshevism could be interpreted as rather secondary and complementary. It did not add to his theory of social revolution, nor did it lead Bauer to abandon his adopted theses. This attitude appears relevant with respect to another aspect: it accurately reflects the tensions between loyalties to Marxist theory, Bauer's own basic ideological stance, and his anticipations of the Soviet experiment. Leser describes these contradictions as follows:

> Among the Marxist theorists who spent their lifetimes engaging with the October Revolution and its historical consequences ... the Austromarxist, Otto Bauer, occupies a special place ... because his standpoint during the main period of his activity and work took up a middling ground between total identification and complete rejection. It thus satisfied a widespread desire not to submit to the new masters of the Soviet state, and on the other hand not to fully deny them socialist intentions nor a Marxist legitimisation of these intentions and actions.[136]

Bauer's positions on Soviet Russia, and later the Soviet Union, were so controversial that even Social Democrats who otherwise accepted his views and

---

135   His knowledge of historical conditions (three years spent in the POW camp in Russia, four weeks spent in St Petersburg in 1917), language skills, and status as a leading theorist of the Labour and Socialist International earned him the reputation of being an outstanding and competent expert on the situation in Russia. He was given the role of main speaker on the Russian question at LSI congresses starting in Hamburg (1923) and ending in Vienna (1931). Aside from Kautsky, he was also the Social-Democratic theorist most frequently attacked by Lenin and the Comintern – compare Lenin 1974, pp. 228–30; Löw 1981, p. 51.

136   Our translation. Leser 1979b, p. 95.

general political line were critical of them.[137] However, his position was not consistent – it evolved with the trajectory of Communism in Russia and the USSR. It is possible to loosely identify three stages:

1. From 1917–21, when Bauer recognised the historical necessity of the October Revolution, predicted its defeat, and at the same time endorsed despotism as an instrument of historical progress;
2. From 1921–9, when he supported the introduction of the New Economic Policy while criticising the dictatorship as an impediment to Russia's economic development;
3. From 1930–8, when he was fascinated by the Five Year Plan, and hoped for a democratisation of political life and considered Stalinism a necessary step in this process.[138]

It is possible to visualise Bauer's changing attitude toward Bolshevism as a curve that first goes down, only to go up again.[139] In its ascendancy, this curve was one of growing hope and illusion in the socialist character of Russia's internal transformations. What characterised his standpoint during this phase was Bauer's attempts to justify Bolshevik practice by citing economic and social factors, which he proclaimed to be crucial in the process of democratic change. This type of rationale, rooted in Marxist orthodoxy, was hard to reconcile with actual Bolshevik practice, where political goals and the will of the Communist leaders determined the boundaries of economic and social change, as well as defined the political order.

4.1   The Doctrinaire Perspective: Chances of Socialist Revolution in Russia

Bauer was concerned with this issue before the October Revolution and devoted himself to it during the first three years of Bolshevik rule. His assessment, based on an analysis of the economic structures and balance of class forces in Russia, was contained in two works: a pamphlet published under the pseud-

---

137 Kautsky, Mensheviks Dan and Abramovich, and all theorists of Austrian Social Democracy polemicised against Bauer's position.
138 Löw proposed this periodisation in Löw 1981. I believe it to be the most accurate outline of the evolution of Bauer's views.
139 From 1917–19, Bauer primarily depicted the economic and social differences between Russia and the West European countries. In the later periods, he formulated conclusions from his own assessment of developments in Russia. This led him to errors of judgement and inaccurate prognoses later on.

onym Heinrich Weber just before the October Revolution, entitled *Die russische Revolution und das europäische Proletariat* (*The Russian Revolution and the European Proletariat*, 1917), and a book published three years later, *Bolschewismus oder Sozialdemokratie?* (*Bolshevism and Social Democracy*). In both of these early treatises, the author cast doubt on the legitimacy of a socialist revolution in a politically backward country from a classical Marxist perspective. At the time, Bauer echoed the sentiments found within the work of the 'father of Russian Marxism', Georgi Plekhanov, also held by most Social Democrats of his time: In Russia, capitalist development must precede revolution. Secondly, the weakness of the domestic bourgeoisie, a repercussion of Russia's dependency on foreign capital, implied that it should be led by the proletariat in alliance with the peasantry. Thirdly, the result of the Russian Revolution can only be a democratic republic with the bourgeoisie in power. After his return from imprisonment in Russia, shortly after the outbreak of the October Revolution, Bauer wrote:

> Russia is an agrarian country where the workers are a minority of the population. The Russian Revolution cannot culminate in a dictatorship of the proletariat; it cannot establish a socialist social order. Even if the Russian Revolution overcomes all the dangers it will have to deal with, the result cannot be anything but a bourgeois democratic republic.[140]
>
> our translation

Bauer critically evaluated Lenin's *April Theses* starting from this basic position. In contrast to Lenin, he maintained that it was necessary for the soviets to cooperate with the provisional government and that the parliamentary platform must be sustained. As is evident from his 28 September 1917 letter to Kautsky, he essentially adopted the same position as the Menshevik-Internationalists (Fyodor Dan, Julius Martov) who emphasised the limitations of the working-class struggle in a semi-feudal country.[141] This struggle was directed against both the Mensheviks' coalition with the bourgeoisie and the Bolsheviks' proletarian dictatorship. Furthermore, the workers demanded that the Social Revolutionaries engage in a pact with different Social-Democratic trends and entrust the strongest party in the constituent assembly.

---

140 'Russland ist ein Agrarland, in dem die Arbeiter eine Minderheit der Bevölkerung sind. Die russische Revolution kann nicht mit der Diktatur des Proletariats enden, sie kann nicht eine sozialistische Gesellschaftsordnung aufrichten. Auch wenn die russische Revolution alle ihr drohenden Gefahren überwindet, wird ihr Ergebnis nichts anderes sein können als eine bürgerliche demokratische Republik' – Bauer 1917, p. 26.

141 Letter from Otto Bauer to Karl Kautsky, 28 September 1917.

It becomes obvious from the remarks cited above that Bauer predicted the defeat of the Russian Revolution even before its commencement. Nonetheless, he declared that the victory of the October Revolution was a historical necessity. For Bauer, the determination of the revolutionary leaders and whatever theory they adhered to were not decisive. What counted were changes in the balance of class forces (the working class gained strength after the February Revolution) and how the socio-political conditions differed from those in highly developed countries (i.e. how to win the economically exploited, culturally backward and politically unenlightened peasantry for socialism, among other issues).[142] Bauer was inclined to believe that the alliance of workers and peasants had been enforced primarily by economic factors and was therefore ephemeral. It is imperative to remember that he dissociated himself from the markedly nullifying evaluation emanating from the right wing of the party around Renner. Bauer regarded the processes occurring in Russia as crucial for the victory of socialism in Europe and prophetically predicted that they would inspire the revolutionary spirit and will of the Western European working class.

At the time, Bauer's praise for the accomplishments of the Russian Revolution did not yet amount to revising his position on the fate of building socialism in Russia. In this period, he held fast to his conviction that building socialism in Russia was doomed to failure if not aided by the world revolution – in this, the Bolsheviks agreed with him. Secondly, he did not believe that seizing power and introducing a proletarian dictatorship was anywhere close to the final goal. He considered it a political misjudgement of far-reaching consequences, including the acute danger of civil war and economic breakdown, for the working class to seize power in a country where objective conditions were insufficiently ripe – his prognosis would soon be validated. Bauer blamed both the Bolsheviks and the Mensheviks for the course of events. He accused the Bolsheviks of revolutionary voluntarism and transgressing the boundaries of bourgeois revolution. Conversely, he criticised the Mensheviks for collaborating with the bourgeoisie, supporting the imperialist war, and insufficiently taking the economic life of workers and peasants into account. In truth, Bauer expected that after the seizure of power, a constitutional assembly and the establishment of a democratic government would follow. When the constituent assembly was dissolved in early 1918, he viewed this as an early sign of defeat for the Russian experiment, which he would go on to anticipate for many years. He cited several reasons in support for his 1917–20 prognosis concerning the defeat of the Octo-

---

142   See Bauer 1976c, pp. 274–5.

ber Revolution: low levels of industrial development in Russia, an undeveloped agriculture, and the immaturity of the working class with respect to governing a state – especially the diminishing social base for the proletarian dictatorship and its degeneration into a party dictatorship.

However, the fact that Bauer constantly stressed the different economic, social and political conditions in Russia and Western Europe was also motivated by the objectives of SDAP policy. This way he could justify the validity of the Social-Democratic concept of revolution. By implying that the 'theory and practice of the Bolsheviks represent an adaptation of socialism to a country where capitalism is still undeveloped, the proletariat therefore only constitutes a minority of the nation, and socialism adapts to Russia's economic backwardness' (our translation), he vindicated his thesis that there were different roads to socialism, and that the Russian revolutionary model should not be implemented in highly developed countries.[143] This also served to convince workers infatuated with the victory of socialism in the East that it was impossible to repeat the Russian scenario at home. At the time, Bauer stood in full solidarity with Kautsky, who proclaimed that the Social Democrats must distance themselves from Bolshevik strategy if they were to preserve the credibility of Social-Democratic politics and save international socialism. Bauer foresaw the consequences of the Bolsheviks' strategy and realistically assessed the proletarian dictatorship's chances of success:

> Bolshevism cannot improve the condition of the proletariat because it can only destroy, not raise, production. Ultimately, the 'dictatorship of the proletariat' will stand in opposition to the proletariat. For this reason, it must fail. However, if socialism does not sharply dissociate itself from Bolshevism, then the defeat of Bolshevism will become the defeat of socialism as such.[144]
>
> our translation

---

143 '... Theorie und Praxis der Bolschewiki die Anpassung des Sozialismus an ein Land sind, in dem der Kapitalismus noch unentwickelt ist, das Proletariat daher noch eine Minderheit der Nation darstellt und sich der Sozialismus an die wirtschaftliche Rückständigkeit Russlands anpasst' – Bauer 1980h, p. 928.

144 'Der Bolschewismus kann die Lage des Proletariats nicht verbessern, weil er die Produktion nicht heben, sondern nur zerstören kann. Er muß daher das Proletariat enttäuschen. Die "Diktatur des Proletariats" muß schließlich in Gegensatz zum Proletariat geraten. Darum muß sie scheitern. Aber wenn sich der Sozialismus vom Bolschewismus nicht scharf scheidet, dann wird die Niederlage des Bolschewismus zur Niederlage des Sozialismus überhaupt' – Bauer 1919, p. 666.

The thought expressed in the final sentence represented Bauer's anticipation of the eventual fate of socialist doctrine. Socialism only remained effective in Western European social-democratic parties because they explicitly dissociated themselves from the Leninist version of Marxism in the Frankfurt Declaration adopted by the Socialist International in 1951, adhering to Kautsky's concept of 'democratic socialism' thereafter. In contrast, socialism lost social recognition in the countries of 'really existing socialism', which were forced to reiterate the Bolshevik models for decades.

Of course, Bauer's theses were subject to caustic criticism from the Bolsheviks, who had been hoping for the outbreak of world revolution since 1920. In a sense, Bauer contradicted himself in assuming that the Russian Revolution might provide a blueprint for other Asian countries. Kautsky, who, unlike Bauer, did not believe that Bolshevism was merely the product of an economically undeveloped agrarian country, but specifically of Russian conditions after World War I, objected to this.[145]

The most interesting – and at the same time most surprising – aspect of Bauer's *Bolshevism or Social Democracy* is the notion upon which the author's prognosis of the defeat of socialism in Russia rested; namely, a positive assessment of the proletarian dictatorship in its totalitarian form. The essential question here pertains to the assumptions on which Bauer based his thesis. The first might be summed up thus: Russian conditions – economic underdevelopment, the low cultural level of the masses, the inner developmental mechanisms of dictatorship – unavoidably led to degeneration into a party dictatorship over the proletariat and peasantry. That is to say, the consolidation of power by a minority coincides with the centralisation of power, which, in turn, results in the bureaucratisation and increasing autonomy of the state apparatus. 'Despotic socialism', Bauer wrote, 'is the necessary product of a development that triggered a social revolution at a stage of development when Russian peasants were not even mature enough for political democracy and Russian workers were insufficiently mature for industrial democracy' (our translation).[146] The second assumption is reminiscent of his unswerving belief that it was impossible to build socialism in a country like Russia without employing a 'proletarian' apparatus of coercion. Understood literally, this view

145   See Kautsky 1920, p. 262.

146   'Der despotische Sozialismus ist das notwendige Produkt einer Entwicklung, die soziale Revolution heraufbeschworen hat, auf einer Entwicklungsstufe, auf der russische Bauer noch nicht einmal zur politischen, der russische Arbeiter noch nicht zur industriellen Demokratie reif war' – Bauer 1976c, p. 293.

of Bauer's would amount to a revision of his theory on the integral link between democracy and socialism.

In fact, Bauer was convinced of the progressive character of the Bolshevik dictatorship, even if he criticised its political terror and its repression of Mensheviks and Social Revolutionaries. As if foreshadowing his later positions in 1931, Bauer claimed that under Russian conditions, despotism could offer a road to socialist development. In his view, Russia might thus be able to overcome its economic stagnancy and lay the groundwork for a future bourgeois democracy. One consequence of this was that Bauer endorsed Bolshevik policies, including Trotsky's concept of a 'militarisation of labour', and permitted the possibility of socialism without democratic premises. It is imperative to note that Bauer only condoned despotic methods in an undeveloped country because he based his perspective on an understanding of democracy as the highest stage of historic development.[147] What is more, in this case he instrumentalised democracy as a means to an end, depriving it of its intrinsic value. He expressed this as follows:

> The principles of democracy, likewise, are not *eternal truths*. Even democracy is an evolutionary product and stage. Democracy is only possible when the productive forces, class struggles, and cultural maturity of the masses have reached a particular stage of development. Where these preconditions are absent, the despotism of a progressive minority is a *transitional necessity*, a temporarily indispensable tool of historical progress.[148]
>   our translation

Bauer presumed that under economically and politically backward conditions, socialism had to take a shape that differed from traditional models, according to which socialism corresponded with democracy. Bauer referred to this variation as 'despotic socialism'.[149]

It is questionable as to whether Bauer, a democrat and humanist, truly believed that one could build a new society on the renunciation of elementary rights and liberties. Rather, he endeavoured to accentuate the role of com-

---

147   Compare Leser 1979b, p. 98.
148   'Auch die Prinzipien der Demokratie sind keine ewigen Wahrheiten. Auch die Demokratie ist Entwicklungsprodukt und Entwicklungsphase. Nur auf bestimmter Entwicklungsphase der Produktivkräfte, der Klassenkämpfe, der kulturellen Reife der Masse ist die Demokratie möglich. Wo diese Voraussetzungen nicht gegeben sind, ist der Despotismus einer vorgeschrittenen Minderheit eine transitorische Notwendigkeit, ein zeitweilig unentbehrliches Instrument des historischen Fortschritts' – Bauer 1976c, p. 293.
149   Compare Leser 1979b, p. 98.

pulsion as an accelerator of economic and socio-political transformations. His position was informed by the determinist conception of history, from which he concluded that the methods of economic compulsion created economic foundations for socialism.[150] These, in turn, provided the democratic foundations for the political and legal superstructure. However, Bauer did not essentially revise his view that socialism and democracy were inseparable. Rather than being a long-term programmatic perspective, his support for separating the two on Russian soil was a temporary tactic for the Russian Revolution. This is evidenced by the expectations that Bauer tied to 'despotic socialism': creating the foundations for the development of bourgeois democracy. Bauer engaged in a polemic with the Bolsheviks, who hoped that their revolutionary model would be adopted in Western Europe:

> The dictatorship of the proletariat in Russia does not amount to overcoming democracy, but represents a phase in its development. The despotism of the proletariat has the historical mission to liberate the Russian peasant masses from the lack of culture to which Tsarist despotism has confined them, elevate them, and thus create the conditions for democracy in Russia. Contrary to what the theory of Bolshevism assumes, the dictatorship of the proletariat in Russia is therefore not the final, ultimate form of the Russian state ... [r]ather, it only represents a transitional stage in the Russian development that will, at most, last until the Russian popular masses are sufficiently culturally mature for the democratic state.[151]
>   our translation

From 1918 to 1920, Bauer was deeply convinced that the Russian system would soon undergo democratisation and liberalisation, and individual rights and

---

150 As previously referred to in this chapter, Bauer wanted to avoid the determinist conception of history. Nonetheless, it strongly characterised his general view of history.

151 'Die Diktatur des Proletariats in Russland ist nicht die Überwindung der Demokratie, sondern eine Phase der Entwicklung zur Demokratie. Der Despotismus des Proletariats hat die geschichtliche Aufgabe, die bäuerliche Masse des russischen Volkes aus der Kulturlosigkeit, in der sie der zaristische Despotismus gehalten hat, emporzuheben und dadurch erst die Voraussetzungen der Demokratie in Russland zu schaffen. Die Diktatur des Proletariats in Russland ist also nicht, wie die Theorie des Bolschewismus annimmt, die letzte, endgültige Form des russischen Staates ... sie ist vielmehr nur eine Durchgangsphase der russischen Entwicklung, die bestenfalls so lang dauern wird, bis die Masse des russischen Volkes kulturell reif wird für den demokratischen Staat' – Bauer 1976c, p. 300.

THE 'THIRD WAY' TO SOCIALISM

liberties be restored.[152] His assessment of despotic socialism bore, in fact, the anticipation of the imminent end of Bolshevik dictatorship. Bauer fell victim to idealism that had more to do with his emotional relationship to the Russian Revolution than it did with a rational assessment of reality. In his text, *Der 'neue Kurs' in Sowjetrußland* (*Soviet Russia's 'New Policy'*, 1921), he cited the two most likely scenarios for the demise of the dictatorship: from above (a process of democratisation initiated and directed by the Communist Party) and from below (forced by the revolutionary resistance of the working masses).[153] In case both prognoses turned out to be wrong, he outlined the following scenario:

> Out of the chaos that will be the harvest of dictatorship, a bloody counter-revolution will arise, robbing the Russian workers not only of all revolutionary gains, but giving international counter-revolution a strong boost and serving it as a powerful pillar.[154]
>
> our translation

Only one position that Bauer tenaciously upheld until the end of his life was accurate, although it only came to fruition after a long historical period, i.e. the undoing of the dictatorship by the oppressed masses. However, Bauer was not alone among Western European Social Democrats, who generally underestimated the Bolsheviks' ability to remain in power. Many theorists of European Social Democracy, such as Rosa Luxemburg, concurred with Bauer's positions, including his belief that the dictatorship was digging its own grave.

4.2   *A Doctrinaire-Pragmatic Perspective: The New Economic Policy*

At the 1925 congress of the Labour and Socialist International in Marseille, Bauer proclaimed, 'Hands off Soviet Russia' – a succinct reflection of his attitude toward the policies of the Bolsheviks after the October Revolution. The slogan was preceded by a radical change in Bauer's convictions about the process of social transformation occurring in the Soviet republic. A major consideration was his fascination with the New Economic Policy introduced by Lenin in 1921.

---

152   According to Hanisch, Bauer's hope for democratisation of the Communist dictatorship was the key element of his ambivalent attitude towards the Soviet Union, often leading to alarming errors of judgement. See Hanisch 2011, p. 346.

153   See Bauer 1976e, p. 456.

154   'Aus dem Chaos, das der Diktatur Erbe sein wird, wird dann die blutige Konterrevolution hervorgehen, die nicht nur die russischen Arbeiter aller revolutionären Errungenschaften berauben, sondern auch der internationalen Konterrevolution starken Antrieb und eine mächtige Stütze geben kann' – ibid.

Bauer was well aware that the new turn in Russia had not resulted from a change in the Bolsheviks' programmatic line, but was forced upon them by economic and political circumstances.[155] He took Lenin's decision as validation of his earlier theories, especially his view that the attempt to build socialism in a backward country by means of compulsion would result in an utter fiasco.[156] In an assessment of Russia he constructed in the early 1920s, he narrowed his focus to three aspects: the dependency of the country on foreign capital, the creation of a capitalist framework to preserve the transitional character of the state, and, most importantly, the necessity to adapt socio-political relations to the new economic conditions. These remarks were all based on the notion that the dictatorship had served its historical purpose and was harmful to the development of productive forces. As an aside, Bauer's statement caused uproar in the Bolshevik camp. In his reply to Bauer at the Fourth Congress of the Comintern, Trotsky made it clear that he considered the persistence of the Bolshevik party dictatorship as a key bulwark against the unfettered growth of capitalism.

As late as 1925, Bauer remained faithful to his position on the New Economic Policy, yet he limited his judgement to the NEP's economic effects. In this, he markedly strayed from the path of Marxist orthodoxy, as well as revised his own 1921 thesis of the necessity of capitalist development in Russia, proposing instead a mixed economic model that might assist the country in overcom-

---

155   The civil war in Russia claimed countless lives and caused heavy economic losses. The economic crisis, exacerbated further by the peasants' resistance against war communism policies such as forced food deliveries, increased the discontent in the cities and countryside. The Bolshevik rule lost popular approval. Furthermore, the subordination of the trade unions to the state led to political controversy in the party itself and threatened to split it. Against the background of strikes and unrest in the countryside, a sailor uprising occurred in Kronstadt in March 1921. The sailors demanded the restoration of political liberties, new elections, the abolition of war levies in the countryside, and the introduction of a free market. The economically and politically conditioned tensions constituted a serious threat to the Bolshevik model of rule. The party saw itself as forced to discontinue war communism policies and restore mechanisms of market economy. When Lenin introduced the New Economic Policy, he did not hide the fact that the Bolshevik Party thus admitted to its defeat (the policy essentially came down to replacing food confiscation by contingents, restoring free trade, privatising small enterprises, granting concessions to foreign capital, and developing co-operatives). He regarded the retreat as a necessary tactical change rather than a matter of programmatic principle. Even so, the liberalisation of the economy was not accompanied by any relaxation of the political framework (freedom of the press, rule of law).

156   See Bauer 1979, p. 280.

ing its economic stagnation. In numerous articles written from 1921 until 1928, Bauer did not fail to mention the uncompromising side effects that accompanied the reversal of Bolshevik policies: the strengthening of the bureaucracy (he now referred to socialism in Russia as a dictatorship of the bureaucracy), political terror against former allies in the struggle against Tsarism, an escalation of social tensions, and struggles between different party factions since Lenin's stroke.[157] Nevertheless, Bauer, while criticising these phenomena, objected to the demand issued by Trotsky in *The Revolution Betrayed* for a political revolution in order to eradicate the dictatorship. In Bauer's view, such a revolution would shatter the unstable condition of the USSR and strengthen counter-revolutionary forces within and outside of Russia.

Bauer thought that the Soviet government itself could dispose of bureaucracy and put an end to violence and political and economic terror by introducing a democratic national constitution and democratic regulations for workplaces. He argued in this vein at congresses of the Labour and Socialist International. While criticising the methods of Bolshevism, he sided with the embattled USSR and argued that the Soviet state must be protected against imperialist intervention. His position was manifest in the resolution adopted at the LSI congress in Hamburg and was maintained at the LSI congress in Marseille and Brussels.[158] In 1929, the LSI executive rejected a motion submitted by Dan and Abramowicz that spoke of the inevitability of civil war and victory of the counter-revolution in the Soviet Union.[159]

These resolutions by no means implied that Bauer was prepared to collaborate with the Communist International, even temporarily. On the contrary, along with most of the LSI leaders, he was hostile to the Comintern. Amongst other denunciations, he objected to the rapprochement between British and

---

157 In the autumn of 1923, the group around Trotsky came into conflict with the triumvirate of Stalin, Zinoviev and Kamenev. The Trotskyist opposition demanded an end to party dictatorship, internal elections instead of appointed functionaries, and freedom of criticism and debate in the party. See Trotsky 1965. Trotsky's group found itself in the minority at the Thirteenth Congress of the Russian Communist Party (cited in Löw 1980. p. 83). In 1927, Trotsky was expelled from the party.

158 The participants of the Hamburg congress passed a resolution that expressed solidarity with the victims of Bolshevik terror and at the same time called upon the working class to resist the intervention of capitalist states in the Soviet Union. It furthermore demanded that these governments take up economic and diplomatic co-operation with the USSR. Compare Protocol of the International Socialist Workers' Congress in Hamburg, 21–5 May 1923, pp. 86–7. This was also the position that the Socialist International advocated until 1939.

159 See LSI archive, 348/12–13, II.S.G.

Soviet trade unions in 1925, the Comintern executive committee's call on the LSI to engage in united front action to protect the Chinese revolution in 1925, and the British Labour Party's 1926 suggestion to enter into negotiations regarding unification with the Comintern. It was also symptomatic that he, as Austrian foreign minister, did not take up diplomatic relations with Moscow and, furthermore, warned Austrian trade-union delegates travelling to Moscow in 1926 not to co-operate with the Communists.[160] Actually, Bauer was undecided about the political and social processes in the USSR. As chair of the 'committee against the danger of war in the East' at the Marseilles congress, he called upon delegates to reject a demand made by Kautsky and the Georgian Social Revolutionaries that the LSI support spontaneous national uprisings in the USSR; he argued that the party should not intervene in the internal affairs of the Soviet republic. At the same congress, he criticised Bolshevik endeavours to gain control of revolutionary movements in Asia and use them to trigger a world war that would realise the Communists' desire for world revolution.[161] The question arises as to why relations between the Austrian socialists and the USSR were so tense. Bauer expected two outcomes: first, the swift democratisation of the Soviet system; second, the Comintern's recognition that the Social-Democratic party type was the most desirable model for organising the working class under conditions of advanced capitalism, and its programmes the only valid strategy for action. However, in light of the Third International's challenging attacks against the Labour and Socialist International, and because of permanent mutual criticism, co-operation between the two groups was out of the question from the outset.

4.3   A Pragmatic Perspective: Stalinism

At the end of the 1920s, the politics of Joseph Stalin changed significantly. This turn had been preceded by a conflict of interests between industrial workers, the petty peasantry, and kulaks, as well as disputes and factional struggles in the Communist Party leadership from 1925 onward. These were centred on two aspects: the possibility of building socialism in an isolated country and the question of peasants, who had become rich due to the New Economic Policy.[162]

---

160   The delegation stayed in Russia from 28 January–1 April 1926. In this time, it visited Minsk, Moscow, Leningrad and Charkov, and reported to the shop steward meeting in Vienna on 17 April. At the time, Bauer was ambiguous. On the one hand, he recommended drawing lessons from the Russian experience, and on the other, he sharply criticised the Communist regime. See Böröcz 1985, p. 37.

161   See Bauer 1980p, p. 101.

162   As to the former concern, two trends emerged in the Communist Party. Stalin, Bukharin,

The victory of Stalin's line within the party heralded a break with its Leninist past and the liquidation of the left (Trotsky, Zinoviev, Kamenev) and right (Bukharin) oppositional factions in 1928. In 1929, the New Economic Policy suffered a defeat, leading to forced collectivisation. The first Five Year Plan, adopted in 1929, outlined a perspective of rapid industrialisation, electrification, new methods of planned economy, and forced collectivisation – the price the Soviet people would have to pay was a tougher political line and a rise in political terror.

With the introduction of the first Five Year Plan, Bauer's attitude underwent another transformation. His former repudiation that it was possible to build socialism in an economically underdeveloped country mutated into its extreme opposite. Paradoxically, his newfound positive view of the socio-economic events in Russia coexisted with his continued hope for imminent democratisation of the political system. Particularly Bauer's last works, *Rationalisierung – Fehlrationalisierung* (*Rationalisation and False Rationalisation*, 1931) and *Zwischen zwei Weltkriegen* (*Between Two World Wars*, 1936) were proof that he had increasingly surrendered to the illusion that the social transformations in the USSR bore a socialist character.

As early as 1926, in numerous articles Bauer supported Stalin's abandonment of the Bolshevik conception of world revolution and intention to build socialism in one country. In *Rationalisation and False Rationalisation*, he referred to the Five Year Plan as the shortest road to transforming the USSR into a modern industrial country. His approval of this policy and emphasis on its economic and social gains – such as increased productivity, falling levels of unemployment, and migration of peasants into the cities – had an objective: capitalism's recession in Germany and the United States. It is true that Bauer was aware of some of the negative consequences of Stalin's policies, e.g. the development of the means of production at the expense of consumer products, increasing bureaucratisation of the industry, hasty collectivisation, and the escalating conflict between the cities and the countryside. Still, he saw this as the price Russian society had to pay so that the countryside might overcome its long-standing

Rykov, and the majority of the Politburo took the side of socialism in one country, while Trotsky, Zinoviev, and Kamenev defended the thesis that socialism must be accelerated by the advent of a world revolution (1924). As to the peasant question, a different divide emerged in the party ranks: Bukharin, Tomsky, and Rykow advocated the introduction of market relations in agriculture and guaranteed state loans for peasants. Stalin's faction, which represented the party majority, demanded a confrontation with the kulaks and forced collectivisation (1928). Stalin based this on the assertion that 'the class struggle will intensify as socialism advances'.

economic and social backwardness. This line of argument led him to the logical conclusion that the industrialisation and collectivisation of the Soviet republic had laid the foundations for the future socialist social order. Note that this did not amount to any profound evolution of his theoretical views. Yet, even so, there was only an ostensible contradiction between his denial that a noncapitalist Russia could exist in the mid-1920s and his concession that socialism took national forms and could be realised in one country. Bauer looked at the new stage of development in Russia as a 'progressive form of state capitalism' and believed that the Communist Party's drive to fast industrialisation represented its capitulation to the line established by the classical Marxists, who had coupled the emergence of socialism with the rising tide of productive forces.

Bauer's evaluation of the endurance and necessity of Stalin's dictatorship represented a significant change of position. In the 1930s, Bauer not only maintained his constructive view of the role of the party dictatorship for the process of industrialisation that he had developed in the 1920s, he virtually paid deference to Stalin's regime. In 1931, he wrote:

> This unprecedented transformation is occurring under a terrorist dictatorship, and it can only occur under such circumstances. Only a terrorist dictatorship can force a nation of 150 million people to accept such hardship in the present for the sake of a greater future.
> our translation[163]

He was even more explicit in 1933 when justifying his position with fear of reactionary counter-revolution: 'Democracy is certainly unthinkable in today's Russia'.[164] In fact, Bauer's attitude towards the Stalinist dictatorship was ambivalent. On the one hand, he stressed its efficacious role in furthering the transformation of social and property relations in Russia. On the other, he condemned its distinct ways of exercising power.[165]

---

163   'Diese ganze beispiellose Umwälzung vollzieht sich unter einer terroristischen Diktatur und kann sich nur unter ihr vollziehen. Nur eine terroristische Diktatur kann ein Volk von mehr als 150 Millionen Menschen zwingen, um einer größeren Zukunft willen so schwere Entbehrungen in der Gegenwart auf sich nehmen' – Bauer 1931, p. 218.

164   Bauer 1980v, p. 328.

165   Bauer's comparison of fascist and Stalinist dictatorships served as a succinct reflection of this dissonance in evaluating the historical significance of Stalinism. In 1936, he contrasted the two dictatorships as follows: 'Of course, there is an essential difference between the two modern forms of dictatorship. The fascist dictatorship destroys the results of the political emancipation of the individual in order to prevent the social emancipation of the

Reading Bauer's works on Russia, one cannot fail to notice that he recognised the ossification of Stalin's system and resulting dangers. In the 1930s, he based his standpoint on two elementary assumptions. Firstly, the sentimental belief that a socialist society would arise from the process initiated by Lenin and the Bolshevik Party, which was not validated by the actual events occurring in the Soviet republic. Secondly, that the existence of the USSR offered hope for the international working class. At the SDAP party congress of 1932, when commenting on the situation in Russia, he stated that the demise of the Soviet regime would 'strengthen reaction all over the world. The breakdown of the great experiment would shatter the belief in the possibility of a socialist mode of production everywhere in the world for a long time' (our translation).[166] Were such statements exclusively motivated by propagandistic reasons as well as Bauer's personal orientation towards the East? This was most definitely not the case, yet there is an explanation for his emphasis on socialist transformations in the USSR: the Social Democrats' fallacious belief in a peaceful road to socialism was destroyed by the defeat of the workers' movement in Western Europe from 1933 until 1934. Consequently, prospects for international socialism looked increasingly miserable. In this situation, the Communist-ruled country appeared to him as the only force capable of preventing the forward march of fascism. Bauer was convinced that the future of the international working class depended on whether '... it will be able to defend the great world-historic gains of the great Russian revolution, beat the mortal enemy of the working class, fascism, take advantage of the great convulsion that a new war will bring to the capitalist world, and overcome the

---

popular masses. The dictatorship of the proletariat, meanwhile, suspends the results of the political emancipation of the individual in order to force the social emancipation of the popular masses. But regardless of how profoundly and fundamentally they differ in this respect, they nonetheless have in common that they destroy the liberties and humanity that the age of bourgeois revolutions won' (our translation). Original: 'Selbstverständlich besteht ein wesentlicher Gegensatz zwischen den beiden modernen Formen der Diktatur. Die faschistische Diktatur zerstört die Resultate der politischen Emanzipation des Individuums, um die soziale Emanzipation der Volksmassen zu verhindern. Die Diktatur des Proletariats hebt die Resultate der politischen Emanzipation des Individuums auf, um die soziale Emanzipation der Volksmassen zu erzwingen. Aber so tief und wesentlich dieser Gegensatz auch ist, so haben beide doch gemein, dass sie zerstören, was das Zeitalter der bürgerlichen Revolution an Freiheit und Menschlichkeit erobert hat' – see Bauer 1976p, p. 196.

166   '... die Reaktion in der ganzen Welt stärken. Der Zusammenbruch des großen Versuchs würde den Glauben an die Möglichkeit einer sozialistischen Produktionsweise in der ganzen Welt für geraume Zeit erschüttern' – Bauer 1931, p. 908.

capitalist barbarism of exploitation, unemployment, and class rule' (our translation).[167] Hence, it should come as no surprise that Bauer cohered to the hope of an anti-fascist revolution to the USSR and, from 1934 onward, regarded socialist development in Russia not as a possibility, but as reality.[168]

The progression of Bauer's views with respect to revolution, dictatorship and building socialism in the USSR was fundamental. From denying that revolution in non-capitalist countries had any chance of success and recommending that the proletarian dictatorship be abandoned, he had come a long way as he recognised the socialist character of the USSR, extolled the necessity of dictatorship, and cited domestic relations in the Soviet republic to venerate the Stalinist bureaucracy. It is worth contemplating whether the aforementioned reasons sufficiently explain the great divergence between his successive positions. Largely, they were driven by his deterministic view of Soviet development. As Schöller succinctly notes: 'Even he [Bauer] is prone to distort his justified interest in reducing political phenomena to their economic background by referring to them as unavoidable or inevitable'.[169] Bauer believed with absolute certainty that the economic consequences of the Five Year Plan would precede the cultural emancipation of the working class, which, in turn, would transform the Communist regime into a democratic republic ruled by law. That is why until 1936 he maintained against all evidence that Stalin's dictatorship was a necessary step on the road towards de-totalitarianising the system.

Bauer's optimistic prognoses for the Five Year Plan and demise of the dictatorship were not accepted by Social Democrats. The majority of participants at the Labour and Socialist International congress in Vienna objected to his positions. Kautsky, Friedrich Adler, and Dan criticised the SDAP leader harshly.

---

167   '... imstande sein wird, die großen weltgeschichtlichen Resultate der großen russischen Revolution zu verteidigen, den Faschismus, den Todfeind der Arbeiterklasse zu schlagen und die Erschütterung der kapitalistischen Welt durch einen neuen Krieg zur Überwindung der kapitalistischen Barbarei der Ausbeutung, der Arbeitslosigkeit, der Klassenherrschaft, des Krieges auszunutzen' – Bauer 1980z, pp. 559–60.

168   In 1935, Bauer wrote that the USSR had laid the economic foundations for socialism – see Bauer 1980l, p. 477. In 1936, he added: 'If the USSR is granted peace for a few more years, it will, thanks to its rapidly increasing productivity, be able to *match* the living standards of the most advanced capitalist countries, and even *surpass* them'. Original: 'Bleibt der Sowjetunion noch wenige Jahre der Friede erhalten, wird sie dank der überaus schnell steigenden Produktivität der Arbeit die Lebenserhaltung der Volksmassen der vorgeschrittensten kapitalistischen Länder *einholen* und *überholen* können' – Bauer 1976p, pp. 224–5.

169   See Schöller 1979, p. 115.

Max Adler was alone in siding with Bauer.[170] Yet Bauer was deaf to criticism: he refused to revise his position even when information about mass deportations and growing repression against the old power apparatus culminating in the infamous Moscow trials reached to Vienna.[171] With respect to the conflict between Stalin and the socialist opposition in the USSR, Bauer's sympathies before the defeat of the workers' movement in Austria were with Stalin and his supporters. His stance on the Moscow trials was ambiguous. He considered them a backward retreat on the road towards democratisation, criticised the arrests and denunciations of Bolsheviks as counter-revolutionary, and referred to Stalin's methods of fighting the Trotskyists as 'repulsive and dangerous'.[172] However, he also blamed the Trotskyists for the Moscow trials, claiming they were planning a second revolution. Although he castigated Trotsky's politics as sectarian, he objected to the idea of an official LSI motion in protest at the Zinoviev and Kamenev trials, demanding that the International dissociate itself from their views.[173] The Moscow trials did not make him revise the expecta-

---

170 In his book, *Der Bolschewismus in der Sackgasse* (*Bolshevism in the Impasse*, 1930), Kautsky countered Bauer's claims, emphasising the ossification and counter-revolutionary orientation of Bolshevism. Friedrich Adler, meanwhile, objected to Bauer's appreciation of the planned economy and collectivisation as elements of socialism. He thought that Stalin's decisions were motivated not by a political but an economic rationale and referred to his policies as a 'move of doubt' – see Adler 1932, p. 7. Dan cast doubt over Bauer's thesis that the proletarian dictatorship was a necessary intermediate stage. He viewed Bauer's claim that the Russian Communists could soon develop production and raise consumption as utopian – see Dan 1932, pp. 64–5. Only Max Adler stressed the revolutionary character of the Stalinist dictatorship, justified the terror against the kulaks as an economic necessity of the proletarian revolution, supported the attempt at building socialism in one country, and called upon the Mensheviks to side with Stalin's party. See Adler 1932, p. 215 and p. 301.

171 In the Soviet Union, spectacular purges and trials took place, initially in scientific and Menshevik circles, under the pretext of eliminating 'saboteurs'. These trials were intended to show the masses the alleged agents behind the economic failures of the Five Year Plan. When the party secretary, Sergey Kirov, was murdered in Leningrad, Stalin took this as a pretext to settle scores with the 'old Bolsheviks'. In July 1936, trials against Zinoviev, Kamenev, and 13 further members of the Central Committee were initiated. In January, trials against Radkov, Pyatakov, and 15 further Bolsheviks followed. In March 1938, the infamous Trial of the Twenty-One, during which Bukharin and Rykov were sentenced, took place. In June 1936, the generals, with Tukhachevsky at their helm, were accused of treason. The official justifications for the Great Purge, in the course of which 70 percent of Central Committee members were executed, were accusations of sabotage, plans for a political coup, and espionage on behalf of Western states.

172 See Bauer 1980ee, p. 716.

173 See 'Letter from Otto Bauer to Friedrich Adler of 19 August 1936', in Archival Sources.

tions he had of the Soviet Union. Throughout the trials, his attitude remained cautious and reserved. According to Löw, this was because he saw no alternative to Stalin's dictatorship in light of the imminent confrontation with fascism and defeat of the workers' movement in the west.[174] The criminal nature of this dictatorship escaped Bauer's attention.

Bauer's positive assessment of the political changes in the USSR proved devoid of any basis in reality when the consequences of political terror (paralysis of mass activism) and collectivisation (famine and millions of deaths) became public. Although details of the effects of Stalin's policies – such as the full extent of repression – were unavailable in the West, the general situation in the USSR was well known due to reports from the Russian diaspora, Social Revolutionaries, Social-Democratic trade-union activists, and Austrian Communists who were in touch with the Comintern. Bauer felt betrayed by Stalin's politics – in 1937, he expressed his disappointment when admitting that the Russian Communists were incapable of governing democratically despite the uncompromising threat of war.[175] One might ask why Bauer attempted to minimise the gap between the reformist and revolutionary wings of the workers' movement instead of radically dissociating himself from Communist politics like other Social Democrats. Aside from the aforementioned first rationale – fear of fascism – another factor motivated him: after the defeat of the revolution in the West and the ebbing of support for a world revolution, the USSR remained the only country in which classical Marxian theory was put to practical use. Bauer was not the only Western theorist to justify force as an instrument of historical progress. One can find similar views in the writings of Lukács.[176] None of these thinkers recognised the autonomous mechanism of political terror for what it was, nor its immanent tendency to subject all classes, social groups, and aspects of life to totalitarian rule. Only one of Bauer's prognoses was confirmed: the power of dictatorship is based not on formal institutions, but on the ability to influence the masses ideologically. Totalitarianism as a form of rule is impossible to reconcile with the human desire for freedom. A state of total indoctrination of society is impossible to achieve, and the moment when people demand their freedom back is inevitable. It was in Bauer's analyses and statements regarding the Soviet Union that a determ-

---

The Communist press in Austria harshly attacked Bauer's article on the Moscow trials – compare *Rundschau* of 3 September 1936: 'Otto Bauer im Chor der Antisowjethetzer' ('Otto Bauer Joins the Choir of Anti-Soviet Agitators').

174 See Löw 1980, p. 61.

175 See Bauer 1937, p. 107.

176 See Lukács 1971, pp. 502–3.

inistic conception of history was at its most pronounced, more so than in his other theories. Here, he viewed all relations – social and especially political – as subordinated to economics. From this, he concluded that transformations in the economic structure of society inevitability predetermine political phenomena, which can all be predicted.[177] His conclusion had little to do with the reality in the Soviet Union.

---

177 For Leser and Löw, this understanding of history was the greatest weakness of Bauer's concept. See Leser 1968, p. 126; compare Löw 1980, p. 279. With respect to Bolshevism, I agree with their judgement.

CHAPTER 6

State, Democracy, Socialism

The 'third way' to socialism was complementary to the Austromarxists' reflections on the state and the direction that Social-Democratic politics aspired to take within the bourgeois-democratic framework. The idiosyncratic quality of these analyses was that they understood the state, law, and forms of political order (democracy, dictatorship) as mutually independent forms: they distinguished between a formal and a sociological order – i.e. they abstracted the form of phenomena from their content and social function. The views of Hans Kelsen, a moderate liberal theorist on law and the state and founder of the 'pure theory of law', provided the basis for this differentiation.[1] Three fundamental theses of legal normativism were most influential in the Austromarxists' theory of state formation. The first was of a purely formal character of political and legal categories, which granted them the status of *a priori* ideas. The second served to justify the dualism between being and ought, form and content, facts and values, causality and normativity, and, ultimately, law and politics. The third was the assumption that the state was synonymous with the law, and as such the territorial order was identical to the coercive order. Owing to the fact that they drew on Kelsen's 'pure theory of law', the Austromarxists developed perspectives on democracy and the state which are still discussed today.[2]

The Austromarxian theory of law and the state was devised mainly by Karl Renner and Max Adler. Renner in particular focused on the formal aspects of the categories under investigation, while Adler researched both normative and sociological functions. Despite the considerable differences between their positions, Renner and Adler agreed, along with Bauer, that the working class could

---

1 The 'pure theory of law' was devised under the influence of neo-Kantianism and legal positivism. Kelsen adopted two methodological guiding principles from neo-Kantianism: formalism and the dualism of being and ought. He amalgamated ahistoricism, criticism and relativism with legal positivism. Furthermore, Kelsen's normativity of law drew on positivism's notion that the origins of law were not scientific, since the essence of law consists of a formal order of norms. According to the 'pure theory of law', norms are acts of will, and the basis of the legal system, the *Grundnorm* (fundamental norm), is a logical precondition for legal recognition in the Kantian sense. The specific character of legal science lay in the fact that legal norms are investigated only on the basis of legislation, while social conditions are not taken into account.

2 See, for example, Sartori 1987.

take control of the institutions of the capitalist state by democratic means and give them new class content. Their belief that it was not necessary to eradicate the old state apparatus, as it could automatically be made to serve proletarian rule, was one of the factors that determined the Austrian Social Democrats' favourable attitude toward parliamentarism. This perspective stood in stark contradiction to Lenin, who argued that the permanence of revolutionary processes depended on the abolition of the bourgeois state.

Unlike Max Adler and Renner, Bauer paid little attention to theories of law and the state prior to World War I. Instead, he concentrated on sociological analyses of the social content and function of the state, arriving at resolutions consistent with Marxist theory: the state had to be understood as a ruling instrument of the economically dominant classes. Consequently, the bourgeois state was radically counterposed to the proletarian state. This conception corresponded with Bauer's historic-philosophical proclivity, according to which the working class and the bourgeoisie were the primary antagonistic agents in the historical process.

In reference to the perception of the state as a class state, Bauer stressed the superiority of the socialist over the capitalist state in all dimensions of social life, including in the economic, political and moral domains. One cannot avoid the impression, however, that many of his statements on the state and society of the future were not strictly theoretical, but propagandistic – as was also the case with his temporary criticisms of the bourgeois state.

Bauer's statements on state socialism drew on a variety of assertions common in Marxist literature, but which played no part in the political practice of Social Democracy. They were essentially prognoses about the emergence of a classless society in which a democratically appointed government would replace the coercive state apparatus and self-manage production, exchange and administration. What specific forms government would take in the proletarian state after a successful socialist revolution was a question that was approached very cautiously. Had it been raised programmatically, for instance as a demand for proletarian dictatorship, the party might have no longer found it possible to win the middle classes as voters, and thus the Social Democrats' preferred strategy and tactics would then fail. Secondly, Bauer thought that the concentration and centralisation of capital represented an early stage of the socialist planned economy. Tied into this was the idea that the social process had an evolutionary disposition, and that the legal and political institutions of the bourgeois state would 'grow into' institutions of the socialist state. This idea provided some of the basis for the SDAP's focus on short-term tactics rather than distant, strategic objectives. Thirdly, Bauer decidedly distinguished between two dimensions of the state: the state as a formal organisation of society, and the state as a specific legal and political order. Like Max Adler, he saw the bourgeois-democratic state as a tool of bourgeois rule, stressing that its legal system only served to fortify economic and class subjugation. Like other Austromarxists, however, he prioritised the formal rather than the class facet. Hence, as a mature politician, he ratified a notion borrowed from Lassalle, a view also present in the beliefs of Renner and Kelsen – under capitalist property relations, he argued, the state had a neutral character and was beneficial to the working class.[3] Despite his criticisms, Bauer's theory of the state as 'balance of class power' testified to his respect for the bourgeois state and democracy as formal institutions. Democracy was not only the overriding category in his state theory; it was also the cardinal value in his perception of democratic socialism.

1   The State as 'Balance' of Class Power

This theory can be found in Bauer's works from 1923–4, *Die österreichische Revolution* (*The Austrian Revolution*) and *Das Gleichgewicht der Klassenkräfte* (*The Balance of Class Power*). The fact that he revisited the theory in his 1934–6 texts, *Demokratie und Sozialismus* (*Democracy and Socialism*) and *Zwischen zwei Weltkriegen* (*Between Two World Wars*) demonstrates how significant he considered it to be. The aims it intended to serve culminated from sociohistorical conditions: initially, 'balance' theory provided the antecedent for the practice of democratically transforming capitalism into socialism. Later, he used it to explain the mechanisms by which fascism could obtain power.[4] Its constitutional thesis was that the capitalist state would enter a period during which the balance of antagonistic classes was practically equal.[5] Bauer based

---

3   In the 1920s, Renner stated that in the contemporary bourgeois state, there is a growing tendency for 'the economy ... to exclusively serve the capitalist class, and for the state to predominately serve the proletariat' (our translation). Original: 'die Ökonomie ... immer ausschließlicher der Kapitalistenklasse, der Staat immer vorwiegender dem Proletariat dient'. This was based on Kelsen's thesis from Kelsen 1923, p. 105.

4   For interesting commentary on both aspects of Bauer's theory of the 'balance of class power', see Saage 1986, pp. 83–5 and Saage 1990, pp. 67–76.

5   The concept did not refer to arithmetic equality between the bourgeoisie and the proletariat, but rather to the political strength of both. This is echoed in Kautsky's *Die proletarische Revolution und ihr Programm* (*The Proletarian Revolution and its Programme*, 1922), where he finds that a state of balance between the bourgeoisie and the proletariat can be achieved. With universal suffrage at its disposal and because of its increased electoral potential, the working class can defend itself against being pushed onto the defensive. Kautsky concluded

this on Marx's periodisation of the 1848 revolution in France and his own analysis of the socio-political dynamics in Austria after World War I.[6]

When analysing the revolutionary period in Austria, Bauer distinguished between three stages: the dominance of the working class after 1918, the balance of class power from 1919–22, and the restoration of bourgeois power after 1922. He argued that between the years of 1919 and 1922, neither the bourgeoisie nor the proletariat were strong enough to rule on their own. Unlike in France or Italy, the state apparatus did not become independent of class forces, but rather state power was shared between the classes. As Bauer argued, disjuncture occurred as state organs had been replaced by the organisations of the working class. This development allowed for an extraordinary type of state to emerge, which Bauer christened 'balance of class power' or, alternatively, a people's republic. Characterising this type of state, he wrote with reference to the First Republic, which existed until 1922:

> Thus the Republic was neither a bourgeois nor a proletarian republic. In this phase, the Republic was not a class State, that is, not an instrument for the domination of one class over other classes, but the outcome of a compromise between the classes, a result of the balance of class power. Just as the Republic arose in October, 1918, upon the basis of a social contract, a political treaty between the three great parties which represented the three classes of society, so it was only able to survive by means of daily compromises between the classes.[7]

The affinity between his findings and the traditional concept of the state advocated by the right wing of the party was remarkable. The latter were influenced by Bernstein, according to whom the modern bourgeois state was an instrument to obtain the common interests of society and, consequently, represented a transitional stage between capitalism and socialism.

---

that upsetting the balance of class power would lead to a civil war and destroy the domestic economy.

6   It was not without genuine bases, the first of which was the existing economic, geographical, and demographic situation in the country – i.e. tensions between industrial Vienna and the dispersed agrarian and relatively sparsely populated provinces. The second was the socio-political situation of Austria during the revolutionary period: the workers had gained considerable control over the army and police, which put certain limits on the bourgeoisie. See also Saage 1986, p. 86.

7   Bauer 1925, p. 246. This depiction was inaccurate. Bauer conveniently overlooked the fact that, in 1920, the bourgeois parties had assumed state power on their own.

Bauer also strove to consider the premises on which the hypothesis of a gradually changing bourgeois state depended. He was convinced that the balance of class power had allowed for the emergence of an 'ultra-democratic' form of state, a people's republic. Its essence was supposedly a variation of the parliamentary system modified and adjusted by a functional democracy. The political order proposed by Bauer was defined by the subordination of the executive to parliamentary control, additionally reinforced by social organisations. Bauer assumed that the government would not be able to rely solely on an elected parliament due to strong, extra-parliamentary and primarily working-class pressure groups. It would have to seek approval from autonomous citizens' organisations to legitimise its conduct. For Bauer, the shifting paradigms of exerting power implied that the function of the state was changing too. It would transition from acting as watchman of the capitalist economic and social order to mediator between the sectional interests of different social groups. According to 'balance of class power' state theory, maintaining that equilibrium was a condition for the development of reformist socialism. In reality, concessions granted to the working class by the bourgeoisie were measures to stabilise capitalism, even if they served the temporary interests of the working masses. The belief that the bourgeoisie and the proletariat could permanently and amicably share political power in any state proved to be an illusion. Even Bauer was conscious that underneath the temporary balance of class power, there was a tendency for class antagonisms to thrive. In his polemic with Kelsen, he acknowledged that the 'balance of class power' was a transitional phase in the development of the state, and that it could evolve in two opposite directions. It would either lead to the working class confiscating state power or result in a situation where bourgeois dominance was restored and the proletariat driven to the peripheries.[8] As chair of the workers' party, he wanted to sustain the masses' faith in reformist practice. Hence, he optimistically declared that a state based on the 'balance of class power' could be remodelled into a proletarian state. This was based on the notion – *de facto* underappreciated in Marxism – that legal institutions could regulate the economy. Bauer accorded great significance to the project of changing consciousness. He wanted the working class to achieve hegemony in the immaterial world. For him, these projects were the means by which to transform the bourgeois state democratically. Concerning the basic conditions in West European democracies as opposed to, say, Soviet Russia, he was inclined to believe that the political and legal superstructure was relatively independent of the economic structure. To conceive

---

8   Compare also Saage 1986, p. 146.

of the relation between politics and the economy in this way is now custom-
ary, yet it was novel in Marxist thinking at the time. However, Bauer's idea of
a far-reaching autonomy of politics led him to overestimate the role of superstructural political forms at the expense of economic relations.[9] Consequently,
his overall assessment of the people's republic was misguided.

Bauer's references about the emergence of the First Republic imply that during the revolutionary period, it was a class-neutral state. The two most important social classes allegedly possessed similar strength in the power struggle. It is
difficult to see the veracity of this. After all, the 'balance of classes' in the First
Republic was based on capitalist property relations. Maintaining these property relations was synonymous with preserving the rule of the economically
dominant classes, even if their political strength was temporarily weakened.
The participation of delegates of the workers' party in government did not vis-
ibly change the socio-economic structure. Without wanting to depreciate the
merit of Bauer's analyses, nonetheless what he glorified as a people's republic
was in actuality a class state of the bourgeoisie. For all its rational and positive
assets, workers' participation in production and superstructural institutions in
this state was limited.

Similarly, another idea in Bauer's analysis also falls short. Namely, his analogy between the political emancipation of the bourgeoisie in the feudal state
and the political emancipation of the proletariat in the people's republic.
According to Bauer, a provisional balance between the class of feudal landowners and the bourgeoisie gradually allowed the latter to conquer the state apparatus. Moreover, Bauer saw an analogy between the mechanisms by which the
bourgeoisie took power and the position of the working class in the bourgeois
state. That is to say, it would gradually amass control over all institutions until it
ruled on its own. Legally guaranteed forms of co-operation between the bourgeoisie and proletariat would secure the full emancipation of the proletariat.
For many, the mechanical analogy between the bourgeois rise to power and the
working-class struggle for the same ends was unfounded then, and remains so
today. In feudal society, the bourgeoisie first solidified its economic position
and then used it to gradually ascend to power. A comparable path is unavailable for the working class in capitalist states. Social reforms, trade unions, co-
operatives and industrial councils achieved meaningful social change in the
political and economic capitalist order, yet they have still not shaken the foundations of capitalist relations of production to any degree.

---

9   Kelsen voiced the same objection to Bauer's theory. See Kelsen 1965, p. 273. Further criticism
    of Bauer's theory can be found in Kelsen 1924, pp. 50–6.

As a politician well acquainted with the socio-political dynamics within the state, Bauer knew that the bourgeoisie would fight to rule exclusively as soon as it had buttressed its political standing. He also realised that it would attempt to push the working class out of all political, administrative and economic bodies that limited bourgeois economic power. Prophetically, he predicted in the 1920s that the bourgeoisie would abandon democratic positions the moment democracy was no longer able to safeguard its economic interests. Bauer came to experience this first-hand after 1922, when the bloc of bourgeois parties, emboldened by the fact that Seipel's plans for the Geneva Protocol had been successful, repealed some of the concessions achieved by the working class during the revolutionary period. In practice, abstracted from socio-economic realities, the 'social balance' theory of the state assumed the concrete forms of the bourgeois democratic republic in the 1920s and the authoritarian regime after 1934.

Bauer's 'balance of class power' theory provoked ire from Lenin[10] – understandably so, from a Communist perspective – and was dismissed as a petty-bourgeois delusion on the part of the Social Democrats.[11] Nor was it spared criticism from bourgeois theorists. Kelsen accused Bauer of revising the Marxist theory of class struggle and abandoning Marxist positions, claiming that he had forsaken revolutionary perspectives.[12] This charge would have been justified had Bauer ever endorsed Marx's theory of armed revolution. In truth, his concept of the state as 'balance of class power' was an integral part of his overall vision of a democratic road to socialism. Bauer's theory of the state allowed him to provide a common ground of cross-class understanding and co-operation. Its sincere actual purpose was to vindicate the SDAP's strategies and legitimise the coalition policies in which it had engaged since the beginning of the First Republic. The idea that it was necessary for the workers' party to forge coalitions and co-operate with bourgeois parties was the result of a specific assessment of bourgeois democracy and a corresponding strategic approach.[13]

---

10   Lenin unabashedly attacked it as being harmful for the working class – see Lenin 1965, pp. 460–80.
11   See Adler 1981, pp. 198–203.
12   See Kelsen 1924.
13   Kautsky shared this perspective – see Kautsky 1922, p. 106.

2   Parliamentary and Social Democracy

The rapid transformation of Austria from a monarchy into a republic shaped public opinion on democracy and predetermined its fate. As Pelinka notes, the new republic lacked a parliamentary tradition. In its early days, the citizens of the new republic felt no loyalty towards the state, and consequently, society did not respect the principles of the political order.[14] Nor did the existing bourgeois parties have any aspirations to reinforce democratic political structures; after all, the proclamation of the republic had not been the culmination of their political struggles, but was forced upon them by the postwar situation in Austria. The masses entrusted their loyalty to their respective political affiliations before pledging any allegiance to the democratic republic. Since there was no universal interpretation of democracy, an established way for the party to function within the system of political democracy was equally non-existent.[15] Thus, Austrian parliament became a site of struggle between competing political elites.[16] In contrast to other political groups, the Austrian Social Democrats occupied a distinct place: from the earliest days of the republic, they defended bourgeois democracy.

Attitudes towards democracy varied within the SDAP, and this state of affairs persisted until the party congress of Linz. The fact that various definitions of the contentious concept coexisted within the party further sharpened the existing polarisation. Depending on who one talked to, democracy could mean, for instance, a system for the common good, the rule of a homogeneous people, a way to peacefully reconcile opposing interests, or the rule of the majority.[17] Party comrades agreed only on foregrounding universal humanist aims and democratic values manifest in the protection of civil rights and human dignity, and on democracy's vital role in the decentralisation of state power and the political education of the masses. The wide range of interpretations inspired the party's main ideologists to discern the theoretical foundations of democracy. As a result of their efforts, however, three different theories of democracy existed within Austromarxist political theory: Bauer's, Renner's and Max Adler's.[18] In contrast to the other two, Bauer's theory centred on the axiological

---

14   See Pelinka 1982, p. 82.
15   On the shortcomings of democracy in Austria, compare Reimann's insightful disquisition
      in Reimann 1968, p. 154.
16   See Pelinka 1982, p. 84.
17   Compare Pfabigan 1982, p. 221.
18   I wrote on their similarities and differences in *Nurt medjacji* – see Czerwińska 1991,
      pp. 283–97.

dimension of democracy and its role in establishing the *bürgerliche Gesellschaft* (civil society). Bauer unified both aspects – the evaluative and the political – in his model, which he based on political and functional democracy.

Indeed, it is evident from Bauer's writings that political democracy played a fundamental role in his theory. Drawing on Kelsen's arguments, his analysis distinguished between democracy's formal and social content. In all statements on democracy as a principle that shaped the political order, Bauer consistently pointed out its ahistorical, class-neutral qualities. With reference to Jean-Jacques Rousseau, he proclaimed that popular sovereignty was the core principle of this form of state organisation – i.e. the free will of the people to decide whom to entrust with governing the state. Here, 'the people' were understood as a political rather than class order. Again with reference to Kelsen, Bauer designed a distinct model of representative democracy, which became one of several competing theories of democracy.

According to Bauer, the essential component of democracy was the formal majority principle, with universal suffrage as the benchmark that decided whether the majority really had a say. Bauer argued that the proletariat was not yet politically mature enough to acquire power because it did not enjoy the support of the majority of society. Secondly, he concluded from this that the state performed its duties on behalf of the whole of society. Bauer was convinced that the majority had to strive for the common good instead of enforcing sectional objectives if it wanted to remain in power. For him, equal opportunities to obtain power and the right to change one's political views were intrinsic to the majority principle, and to consent to this principle was crucial for a healthy democracy. These traits allowed democracy to survive crises in the most effective manner: opposing interests were brought to the surface and reconciled through legally defined regulatory mechanisms. Therefore, preserving social peace by means of political compromise was a hallmark of democracy, which Kelsen also conceded. No doubt, a liberal thinker such as Thomas Vernor Smith, according to whom the term political democracy denoted a process of resolving collective conflicts through legislative bodies, would fully subscribe to this interpretation.[19]

For Bauer, freedom was the second fundamental principle of the democratic political order, the right of the people to elect their own government, and both to entrust it with authority and to deprive it of authority.[20] An important aspect of his theory was that he connoted freedom with democracy and socialism.

---

19   See Smith 1942, p. 2.
20   See Bauer 1976p, p. 194.

Unlike Max Adler, however, he was far removed from associating the achievement of freedom in the collective sense with the socialist order. Rather, he
advocated ethical individualism: democracy's aim was to secure for individuals a right to privacy and protect inalienable rights, interests, and opinions.
The state, even one founded on the principle of popular sovereignty, should
not encroach upon these. Nonetheless, freedom under democratic conditions
was not to be understood as individualist anarchism, but as a principle that
facilitated unified, collective action within the framework of the adopted legal
order. Freedom understood in this way, Bauer argued, secured legal protection
for minorities and granted them free expression. It therefore offered minorities ample opportunity to become the majority and allowed for power to be
reassigned. Bauer based his assumption that the Social Democrats would eventually gain command of the levers of power on this premise. In his early texts,
he typically neglected the principles of social and economic equality as basic
prerequisites for democracy. This not only betrayed the influence of Kelsen's
thought, but also testified to the classical Austromarxist proclivity for favour-
ing the political over social emancipation.

One may wonder whether Bauer was not wary that certain excesses of
the democratic state order, toward which both Kelsen and Max Weber were
vigilant, might pose a threat to political democracy itself. That is, its tendency towards bureaucratisation (political representatives losing touch with
the electorate), party leaders striving to increase their influence in the executive sphere, and ultimately, the propensity of delegates to put their own party
interests above the interests of voters. In reality, Bauer had no such reservations,
since he overestimated the potential of the democratic political order. The first
reason was that in the early stages of modern democracy, these threats were
not as pronounced as they are now. The second was that Bauer, like Karl Popper many years later, thought that political democracy allowed the governed to
fully regulate the government and thus prevent abuses of power.[21]

There was also a sociological logic to Bauer's approach to democracy, albeit a
latent one. In his view, prioritising formal categories – for example, the majority
and freedom principles as formally understood – above class did not imply that
the largest concern for the social content of power was brushed aside. Marx's
theory one-sidedly equated political democracy with bourgeois democracy,
which it regarded as an apparatus of class rule and oppression. According to
Marxian doctrine, the economy thwarted the autonomy of politics. In light
of Western democracies, Bauer far from reduced himself to such simplistic

---

21   See Popper 1945, p. 119.

limitations on the dependency between economic conditions and the political system, even if by doing so he contradicted some of his own statements on the function of objective historical factors. He was inclined to agree with Marx on one point: democracy remained an instrument of class rule, and because it preserved the rule of capital, the bourgeois democratic republic was a class state of the bourgeoisie. Yet essentially, Bauer upheld that legal forms and institutions were relatively independent from the economic base, believing it possible to regulate the economy through legal institutions. According to Bauer, the social content of power under democracy was determined by the existing composition of class forces. This composition, in turn, was determined by not only economic but also social factors, such as the strength of the class, degree of organisation, strength of its ideology, and political maturity. From this he made two observations, both of which illustrated the decisive necessity of political democracy in political practice. The first, in short, is as follows: political democracy facilitated the democratic control of economic power – even in the capitalist state, it could already become an instrument to limit exploitation based on capital. The second reiterated a fundamental conviction of Austromarxist revolutionary theory. It determined that political democracy enabled the proletariat to emancipate itself economically because it offered the possibility of winning social hegemony 'by intellectual means'. It was therefore a sufficient condition for the seizure of power by the proletariat.

For Bauer, parliament was significant in political democracy, yet it would be simplistic to claim that he identified democracy with the system of parliamentary representation. Bauer explained the difference as follows: 'Democracy – that is more than parliamentarism, more than the voice of legal institutions. For me, the state constitution offers the best possible guarantee for individual intellectual freedom' (our translation).[22] This argument was informed by his aspiration to extend the democratic principle of popular sovereignty to all areas of social activity, especially the economic and political realms. Admittedly, Bauer equated parliamentarism and political democracy whenever he referred to it. His position was a faithful reiteration of Kelsen's ideas – for Kelsen, parliamentarism manifestly represented the only political form 'in which the idea of democracy can be fulfilled within today's social reality. Thus a decision about parliamentarism is at the same time a decision about democracy'.[23] Bauer and

---

22   'Die Demokratie – das ist mehr als der Parlamentarismus, mehr als eine Stimme juristischer Institutionen. Sie ist mir die Staatsverfassung, die die bestmöglichen Bürgschaften der individuellen, der geistigen Freiheit gibt' – Bauer 1980j, p. 487.

23   Kelsen 2000, pp. 95–6.

Kelsen both believed that true freedom could only be obtained through parliamentary democracy. Moreover, both theorists considered parliamentarism the
only tool that could keep class antagonisms within certain limits.

Bauer was sceptical towards parliamentarism during the early period of his
political activity. Certainly, the reason was that at the beginning of the twentieth century, the working class could not look back on many successes on
the parliamentary stage.[24] The slur 'parliamentary cretinism', which, already
present in Marx's work and used by Bauer in 1910, heaped scorn on the notion
that the capitalist class system could be transformed through parliament and
was a popular phrase amongst workers. All the same, Bauer's critique of parliamentarism had an ideological character. He confined himself to stating that the
balance of forces in parliament was a reflection of the social and class order, and
that only a social revolution could change it. Notably, this verdict did not stop
him from endorsing Victor Adler's choice of parliament as the main weapon of
class struggle.

Bauer's critique of parliamentarism, which he voiced mainly in public appearances, intended to cultivate the working masses' belief in the revolutionary
nature of the party. In fact, Bauer had always been convinced that parliament
would decisively assist in granting the working class power. This belief was
based on the idea that parliament was by nature class-neutral. Given the actual
parliamentary dynamics, it is fair to say that this was misleading. The supremacy of the bourgeois over Social Democracy was a permanent condition, and
the bourgeois government possessed not only the means of state repression,
but also ideological influence, which Bauer himself acknowledged. His evaluation as to the degree that the proletariat could use parliament for the purpose
of class struggle is worth further examination. Frankly, Bauer argued on more
than one occasion that the proletariat was not politically mature enough.[25] It is
difficult to argue with this. At the time, the political consciousness of the working class was not sufficiently advanced for it to act as an independent political
force. The Bolsheviks, confident in the veracity of their theory, were alone in
their assumption that seizing power, building a new political order by decree,
and proclaiming the party to be the leading force of the nation could accomplish a sufficient level of working-class political sophistication to efficiently

---

24   At the end of the nineteenth century, both wings of the Austrian workers' movement –
      moderate and radical – were opposed to leading the political struggle in parliament. The
      situation changed following the unification of the workers' movement in Hainfeld, when
      Victor Adler declared that parliament was the crucial site of struggle for the working class
      to win social reforms and extend political liberties.
25   For example, in Bauer 1976n, p. 483.

administer a state. As is well-known, these hopes were already squandered in
the early stages of the Russian experiment. History has shown that the position
of moderate Social Democrats, who had a realistic picture of the working class
and viewed bourgeois democracy precisely as a tool of political education, was
justified.

Likewise, Bauer's work was shaped by the belief in the progressive character of bourgeois democracy, even if this was a tense relationship. For many
years, he stressed democracy's benefits for the political emancipation of society, yet at the same time pointed to its deficits, which were rooted in capitalist
property relations. While claiming that bourgeois democracy was a prop that
supported the economic and ideological power of the propertied classes, he
did not go as far as to consider the capitalist-friendly status quo as a permanent condition. Economic and extra-economic means of repression, he argued,
would only remain in the hands of capitalists as long as they were able to
present their interest as the interest of all classes. They dominated the bourgeois political parties, and therefore the middle classes and part of the working
class, only because they claimed that this interest had to be pursued for the
sake of the economy. Bauer's polemics against Marx and particularly Lenin's
arguments require some attention. For both thinkers, every government, be it
democratic or not, was a dictatorship of the ruling class over the ruled classes.
Consequently, bourgeois democracy was synonymous with a dictatorship of
the bourgeoisie. In his defence of bourgeois democracy, Bauer admonished
Adler's belief that the Austrian bourgeois governments were essentially dictatorial in the political sense of unrestricted power. According to Bauer, the
minority rule of capital was secured by a majority rule of bourgeois parties that
accepted the rule of capital – this, for him, was the specific character of bourgeois democracy.[26] Although Bauer held bourgeois democracy in high esteem,

---

26   'The point is precisely that the rule of the capitalist class in democracy is not an unrestric-
      ted rule of the capitalist. One denies oneself the recognition of historical particularity if
      one ... regards every class rule as a class dictatorship ... [I]t is precisely the specific features
      of democracy that get lost in the process: that bourgeois democracy does not yet repres-
      ent majority rule, but a minority rule of the big bourgeoisie through the majority rule
      of the bourgeois mass parties. On the other hand, the requirements of majority govern-
      ment place limits on the class rule of the big bourgeoisie, thus distinguishing democracy
      from the unlimited rule known as dictatorship' (our translation). Original: 'Die Herrschaft
      der Kapitalistenklasse in der Demokratie ist eben nicht eine unbeschränkte Diktatur
      der Kapitalistenklasse; man macht sich selbst die Erkenntnis der geschichtlichen Beson-
      derheit der einzelnen Staatsformen unmöglich, wenn man ... jede Klassenherrschaft für
      eine Klassendiktatur ansieht ... Dabei geht gerade das Spezifische der Demokratie ver-

he was aware of its intrinsic contradiction between economic power and political equality of all classes. Because it tied in with his vision of a future state, he dedicated most of his attention to this until the late 1920s.

Bauer admitted on more than one occasion that the victory of bourgeois democracy was also beneficial for the working class because it expedited its political, if not social, emancipation. Like Marx, he believed that democracy could only be fully realised in a classless society, where economic factors could no longer compromise the freedom and equality of all. Even in his earliest writings, Bauer spoke of the necessity for the proletariat to use democracy for its advantage and, by extension, for the liberation of humanity. Many theorists of Western Social Democracy, such as Kautsky and Renner, but also Mieczysław Niedziałkowski and other Polish Social Democrats, agreed that bourgeois democracy was the most favourable platform for the proletarian liberation struggle. They believed that parliament was a training ground for the working class to prepare for power, a propaganda platform for socialist ideas, a means of political education, and, above all, a tool for garnering support from beyond the remit of the working class. In Bauer's opinion, the latter two aspects were particularly important. According to his idea of revolution, winning the parliamentary majority would prelude the autonomous seizure of power by the working class and usher in an era of social revolution.

For most of his life, Bauer's political activity was defined by his conviction that parliamentary democracy would allow the proletariat to transform the capitalist system into a socialist order peacefully. This is certainly why Leser believes that, for Bauer, parliamentary democracy was nothing more than a transitional stage on the road to socialism.[27] One should exercise some caution with this assessment, however. Bauer, who also wrote a pamphlet entitled 'Um die Demokratie' ('For the Sake of Democracy'), primarily recognised political democracy as an objective in its own right, yet at the same time valued its relevance for the Social-Democratic strategy. Bauer's confidence in the valu-

---

loren: dass die bürgerliche Demokratie eben noch nicht Mehrheitsherrschaft, sondern Minderheitsherrschaft der Großbourgeoisie mittels Mehrheitsregierung der bürgerlichen Massenparteien ist, und dass anderseits gerade die Notwendigkeiten der Mehrheitsregierung der Klassenherrschaft der Großbourgeoisie Schranken setzen und dadurch die Demokratie von der Diktatur, der schrankenlosen Herrschaft unterscheiden' – Bauer 1980r, p. 208.

27   See Leser 1968, p. 84. It is an undisputed fact that the party leadership under Bauer opted for a peaceful road to socialism in the most important historical moments of the First Republic, i.e. July 1927, March 1933, and February 1934. In these situations, differences of opinion between party wings were irrelevant.

able functions of democracy in the proletarian struggle for a new social order prompts a query: how did he reconcile his parliamentary hopes with the inevitability of socialism? In fact, the answer is far simpler than the question itself. The inevitability of socialism due to objective historical laws was a dogma of the Second International. With the passage of time, it degenerated into rhetoric, though admittedly some Social Democrats, including Bauer, unflinchingly believed in it until the end. Even so, faith did not prevent them from focusing on specific duties in their political practice, including using parliament as a platform. The Social Democrats regarded reforms that helped to improve the condition of the working class in the bourgeois state as necessary steps to overcome the capitalist system. Consequently, all reforms achieved through parliament were regarded as stepping-stones on the path to socialism – no distinction between short-term and long-term objectives was made. The postwar social-democratic movement preserved this sentiment, believing there was no need to discontinue capitalist property relations or attack bourgeois democracy, but rather to take advantage of the legal framework of the state to win economic and political reforms in the interest of the broadest social layers.

As it was Bauer's belief that bourgeois democracy represented a transitional stage between capitalism and socialism, it is necessary to assess the three central premises upon which Bauer based his idea of democracy's inevitable development towards socialism. The first was that the democratic forms of the capitalist state were relatively enduring. The second was based on a sociological argument: the number of employees grew as members of the middle classes became declassed, and this affected their political consciousness. To advance their own interests, Bauer thought, they would endorse the programme of Social Democracy, which would lead the workers' party to victory. Up until 1932, Bauer offered no explanation as to why the economic crisis saw the working masses bolster the ranks of the fascists rather than the Social Democrats.

The third premise decisively shaped the idea that bourgeois democracy was a prerequisite for socialist transformation. It contained an important idea of Bauer's unique position in the socialist movement. He assumed that it was possible to deepen democracy by associating the principle of popular sovereignty with the social and economic realms. In his texts, he developed the concept of functional democracy to substantiate this. The core idea of functional democracy was that the democratic social structures that made up a political system evolved from below.

The concept of functional democracy was an integral component of Bauer's dynamic model of democracy – one might say a supplement to political democracy. His understanding of functional democracy and its special variation, industrial democracy, requires some explanation. In layman's terms, functional democracy comprised two types of micro-democracy: democracy at the level of groups or organisations, and democracy in the workplace. In relation to democracy as state order and political principle, these two types of democracy played a subordinate role, and it is not possible to define them conclusively because Bauer's statements were imprecise. Even so, it is feasible to attempt to describe them by looking at the constitutive traits of functional democracy and the tasks they were designed to serve.

Bauer employed the term 'industrial democracy' when discussing the socialisation programme for the society of the future and outlining its economic structure. His models were largely based on writings by Sidney and Beatrice Webb and the guild socialists, particularly George Douglas Howard Cole.[28] For Bauer, the term had not only an economic but also a political dimension. He understood it primarily as workers' direct involvement in the administration of production through self-management in the factories, and ancillary participation through democratically organised trade unions, industrial councils, professional associations for public servants, workers' and peasants' co-operatives, and consumer associations. Moreover, the term was associated with producer self-management in the industries.[29] As to the structure of industrial democracy, Bauer implied a transition from democratic internal regulations in the

---

28   The term 'industrial democracy' was popularised at the turn of the nineteenth and twentieth centuries by Sidney and Beatrice Webb – see Webb 1897. The creators of guild socialism, GDH Cole, Samuel George Hobson, Alfred Richard Orage and Arthur Penty, adopted it. They elicited the ideas of Marxism, syndicalism and Fabianism. The emergence of guild socialism refers to the architect Arthur Penty's book, *The Restoration of the Guild System* (1906) – popularised in *New Age* magazine from 1908 onwards. The core principles of this were the organisation of the domestic system of co-operative production, changing the form of remuneration, and transforming the trade unions into organs of production self-management. The trend gained influence due to Cole's 1913 book, *The World of Labour*, which aimed to put the medieval idea of guilds at the service of the modern workers' movement. Cole presented a model that would exclude the capitalists from the production process and reconcile the interests of the immediate producers and consumers. It was to be based on a decentralised form of economic organisation: guilds – i.e. trade unions converted into production associations – were to regulate the economy autonomously. Meanwhile, a central political organisation would own the means of production as a unitary state power and represent the interests of consumers. At consumer request, it would also control the economic policies of the guilds. The principles of internal democratisation, social control, and self-management were intrinsic to this model.

29   Bauer did not conceal the fact that full industrial democracy could only be achieved if the working class assumed state power or at least significantly participated in government. He was also aware that the workers were neither prepared nor mature enough to manage production. This was the reason why he stressed the extra-economic significance of the

factories towards an integrated system where groups of workers would be represented by profession. These forms of representation would serve as organs of social control and organisation to protect workers' interests. In Western democracies after World War II, these suggestions were essentially revived as demands to create strong union centres and establish co-management in workplaces.

It appears far more difficult to assess what Bauer meant by 'functional democracy'.[30] It is comprised of two aspects. Firstly, it required democracy on a basic level, i.e. as broad as possible popular participation in local administration and self-administration bodies to influence communal, environmental, cultural and educational policies. Secondly, the working class and its pressure groups as a mass would need to compel the government to make decisions beneficial to all social layers. In other words, the executive would be subjected to the control of parliament and social organisations. If strong extra-parliamentary interest groups, mainly workers' associations, were established, then the government would not only require support in parliament for the duration of its legislative period, but additionally seek the approval of autonomous citizens' organisations to legitimise its actions. He did not go into more detail about the principles and criteria for such citizens' organisations. Their purposes, however, were clear: decentralise state power by assigning part of the legislative and executive responsibilities to power holders at local and self-administration levels; increase social control; preserve the interests of the working masses and ensure that their goals are met. Bauer believed that functional democracy would allow citizens to influence government and administrative decisions as a form of extra-parliamentary authority, as well as transform bourgeois rule into working-class rule within the framework of parliamentary democracy. Most of all, it would encourage citizens' initiative, change their attitude towards the state, and develop their awareness of shared responsibility and social commitment. Core elements of Bauer's concept of functional democracy have become fundamental components of contemporary socio-political practice in the West.

---

socialisation programme so rigorously. For him, industrial democracy was a means to prepare workers for the administration of the state and production in the future, as well as raise their political and class consciousness. With regard to the question of industrial democracy, Bauer went so far as to deny the necessity of carrying consciousness into the working class 'from outside'. This can be explained by his belief that the working class could develop political consciousness of its own accord if it were in possession of a tool such as industrial democracy.

30   Drawing on Bauer, Ernst Fraenkel introduced this category in the discussion about the political order in the Weimar Republic. See Butterwege 1981.

The demand to expand democracy is one of Bauer's most valuable ideas and deserves to be popularised in countries that aim to reinforce their democratic structures. The principle at the heart of Bauer's plea was that he wished to continue prioritising political democracy as a prerequisite for the existence of extra-parliamentary forms of democracy.

3   Democratic Socialism

Bauer developed his concept of democratic socialism during the second half of the 1930s. It was based on a sociological analysis of the ways in which parliamentary forms of rule functioned in the bourgeois state under given sociopolitical conditions. Considering the experience of the counter-revolutionary period, Bauer saw himself forced to admit that in practice, democracy did not necessarily respect popular sovereignty. The bourgeoisie had means of material and immaterial violence at its disposal. Moreover, it succeeded in using pettybourgeois and peasant parties, which had the support of broad masses, as tools to enforce its overriding political and economic objectives. Towards the end of the 1920s, Bauer surrendered his duty to democratise the bourgeois political order. Instead, he began to express his belief in the class character of bourgeois democracy, a conviction that had been present in his texts since before World War I, in definitive terms. He now acknowledged that formal safeguards of freedom did not offer protection from economic and political ruling-class pressure: if its class rule was under threat, the bourgeoisie was quite prepared to renounce democratic principle and resort to dictatorship. When the autumn of 1930 came, the dissolution of the bourgeois bloc, which effectively meant the demise of the bourgeois republic, confirmed Bauer's predictions. The Social Democrats' delusions that it was possible to engage with the bourgeois camp at a parliamentary level had been destroyed.[31]

Bauer became increasingly sceptical about bourgeois democracy as the fascisisation of Austria advanced. The experience of fascist counter-revolution convinced him that the capitalists had to be fundamentally deprived of economic power if true democracy was to be achieved. However, Bauer's ideological evolution was not particularly profound. His criticisms of bourgeois democracy by no means implied that he endorsed the dictatorship of the proletariat as an alternative. One contention which had arisen from his philosophical perspective that defined a specific axiological option was the fundamental

---

31   Compare Saage 1985, p. 28.

difference between democracy and dictatorship. This difference was the degree to which basic freedoms were realised under these two forms of government. Dictatorship, for him, meant the abolition of the principle of freedom, the basis of the socialist idea. A state of dictatorship where all the power to make decisions was, by definition, in the hands of a small group, excluded the initiative of the proletariat, without which socialism was impossible. Like Kautsky, who had coined the term, Bauer advocated democratic socialism – a form of social organisation based on the socialisation of production and a democratic political order. According to Bauer, socialism was inseparable from democracy. Its core value was the freedom of the individual, by which he referred to a freedom that individuals are able to use consciously.

The antagonism between democracy and dictatorship asserted by Bauer must also be assessed. As many of his statements attest, he shared Max Adler's belief that the two concepts were not contradictory in Marx and Engels's doctrine and had only become opposites with the practice of Bolshevism. Privately, however, it appears that Bauer was not entirely sure if this was accurate. In fact, Bauer's idea of dictatorship and Marx's were clearly divergent. Firstly, Bauer used the term 'dictatorship of the proletariat' to describe a form of government based on the rule of a minority. Consequently, he saw no possibility to reconcile this state form with the democratic organisation of social and political life. Moreover, he was well aware of the true meaning behind Marx's formulation: Marx used it to describe a stage in the construction of a classless society, a declaration of intent to change property relations and abolish classes. Without doubt, the use of force was part of this project. It would be naive to expect that such radical social changes might be achieved by peaceful democratic means, and one can hardly suspect Marx of such naivety. Thirdly, Bauer noticed the ambiguity with which Marx employed the term 'dictatorship' when referring to the new type of state. To the extent that socialism would allow the working class to exercise power by democratic means, Bauer argued, the term 'dictatorship' would become superfluous. A dictatorship subjected to democratic control, after all, would lose its dictatorial character. This interpretation of dictatorship, according to Bauer, was practically identical to the concept of popular rule. In light of Bauer's insights, it is important to draw a line of distinction between a working-class government and a dictatorship of the class. There is no such thing as a dictatorship of the working masses, as it inevitably degenerates into a dictatorship of their elected representatives. There is no way to prevent the democratically elected leadership from transforming itself into the dictatorship of a group or individual. In short, it is impossible to make a dictatorship subject to social control as the mechanism of dictatorial rule precludes such an option.

In the 1930s, under the impression of historical events such as the defeat of the Austrian workers' insurrection, the demise of the party, and the establishment of an authoritarian state, Bauer modified his view of the dictatorship of the proletariat. Even so, he consistently opposed the implementation of a proletarian dictatorship, merely accepting it as a provisional measure in the working-class struggle for state power. Bauer wrote:

> The dictatorship of the proletariat is not and must not be an end in itself. It is only a means that the working class must use on its historical road to abolish class divisions in society and thus create the conditions for a socialist democracy. The dictatorship of the proletariat can therefore only be the constitution of a transitional stage in the development towards socialist democracy.[32]
>
> our translation

Bauer's notion of a 'democratic dictatorship' was not indistinguishable from Lenin's theory of dictatorship. Violence is permitted as a means to initiate the transformation of the political order, yet such measures are only tactical. Once the task of depriving the capitalists of power has been achieved, the dictatorship must be immediately abolished and replaced by the foundations of full democracy. Bauer opposed the dictatorship of the proletariat as a system of government until the end of his life. What is more, the only political order that he wished to defend was bourgeois democracy. As late as 1936, he stressed:

> For as long as the balance of class power in Europe does not confront the peoples with a choice between bourgeois democracy and proletarian dictatorship, the proletariat in its historical practice must defend bourgeois democracy against fascism in the democratic countries and attempt to win back the most basic democratic freedoms in the fascist countries. Until then, the struggle for democracy in these countries – that is to say, bourgeois democracy – is the real, daily practice of the workers' move-

---

32   'Die Diktatur des Proletariats ist nicht Selbstzweck und kann nicht Selbstzweck sein. Sie ist nur das Mittel, dessen sich die Arbeiterklasse auf ihrem geschichtlichen Wege bedienen muss, um die Klassenscheidung der Gesellschaft zu beseitigen und damit die Voraussetzungen einer sozialistischen Demokratie zu schaffen. Die Diktatur des Proletariats kann also nur die Verfassung einer Übergangsepoche zur sozialistischen Demokratie sein' – Bauer 1980w, pp. 391–2.

ment. The dictatorship of the proletariat, in contrast, is merely a vision of the future based on socialist theory.[33]

our translation

Bauer's tireless opposition to the dictatorship of the proletariat begs the question as to what 'state of the future' he envisioned. In this respect, it is worth pointing out that Bauer was one of the few Marxists to formulate the programmatic principles of a new political and economic order. Although these were essentially no more than basic outlines of a social organisational model, this did not diminish the value of Bauer's effort. Rather than educing the classical-Marxist texts, which offered but the faintest, utopian outlines, he based his outline on his own theories of democracy and the state. When reconstructing Bauer's vision of a 'state of the future', the basic assumption at its core should be the starting point of analysis: Bauer saw the necessity for democracy to evolve internally from bourgeois via proletarian and onwards to socialist democracy. The logical conclusion from the 'three phases model' is that the capitalist state evolves into a workers' state during the first phase and only becomes socialist during the second. This evolutionary model of transformation already contains the rudiments of the polemics Bauer would later wage against Lenin's interpretation of Marxism. For Lenin, who tended to avoid the term 'socialism', communism was a socio-economic formation that would follow immediately after capitalism in the form of a classless and stateless society based on horizontal self-management. Bauer, on the other hand, strictly rejected such an interpretation. His vision was firmly rooted in a perceived necessity to preserve the political dimension of the state. Unlike Lenin, Bauer did not believe that the seizure of power by the proletariat would immediately lead to the abolition of the class state. If the workers acquired control over the leadership of the state, he argued, this would effect a change in its class structure, but not its abolition. To be precise, a proletarian state built on democratic foundations would emerge during the first phase – one that has nothing to

---

33   '[S]olange die Machtverhältnisse der Klassen in Europa die Völker nicht vor die Wahl zwischen bürgerlicher Demokratie und proletarischer Diktatur stellen, sondern vor die Wahl zwischen der bürgerlichen Demokratie und dem Faschismus, solange muss das Proletariat in seiner geschichtlichen Praxis in den demokratischen Ländern die bürgerliche Demokratie gegen den Faschismus verteidigen, in den faschistischen Ländern die elementarsten demokratischen Freiheiten wiederzuerobern suchen. So lange bleibt also in diesen Ländern der Kampf um die Demokratie, die bürgerliche Demokratie, die reale, tägliche Praxis der Arbeiterbewegung, die Diktatur des Proletariats nur eine Zukunftsvorstellung der sozialistischen Theorie' – Bauer 1976p, p. 213.

do with Lenin's 'dictatorship of the proletariat', which represented the superior
might of the victorious working class. Its political form would be proletarian
democracy, i.e. the rule of the working class emerging from general elections
which accounted for the will of the majority and guaranteed civil rights such as
freedom of speech, science, faith, assembly and association.[34] However, Bauer
did not regard this phase of development as fully-fledged democracy, which
he believed would only come to fruition under socialism and its respective
political order, namely socialist democracy. This type of democracy demands
further explanation, after all, the term 'socialist democracy' was liberally used
in the Eastern Bloc states and might therefore be confused with Communist practice. For Bauer, socialist democracy was politically synonymous with
representative democracy. Economically, it was synonymous with a classless
community of producers based at the local level (factories, communes, towns)
on the principle of self-management. At the time, Bauer intended his concept
as a counterweight to the Bolsheviks' theory. It contradicted a majority of
their theses, particularly Lenin's argument in *State and Revolution*, according to
which democracy would wither away in a classless society. His argument was
also obliquely directed against Lenin's assertion that the Communist Party had
a leading role during the process of social and economic transformation. While
Bauer remained quiet on the question of political representation in the socialist state, his understanding of 'socialist democracy' precluded the authority of
any single political organisation. Indeed, the very fact that Bauer forwent any
detailed description of the forms that a socialist political system might take was
a hallmark of his excellence. He thus avoided making the kind of prophecies for
which the Bolsheviks were known.

It is worth citing another issue associated with the theory of socialism
outlined above. In his economic theory, Bauer echoed Marx's insistence that
a planned economy should be maintained under socialism. This was by no
means at odds with Bauer's call for decentralised self-management in the economic realm. Bauer never conflated the planned economy with authoritarian
state regulation in production. Rather, he spoke of a political order based on
democratic planning, which would be preceded by debate and thus receive
society's consent. This model envisioned the role of the state as being limited to
coordinating the actions of economic subjects and ensuring equal opportunities in the course of economic development. Bauer's concept bore no similarity
to the Leninist-Bolshevik notion of planning, which required the centralisation
of economic decisions. The two solutions were, in fact, opposites: the relation-

---

34   Compare Gransow and Krätke 1985, p. 116.

ship between them was roughly analogous to the relationship between the integral concept of socialist democracy and the Bolsheviks' theoretical outlines for a future political order.

4   Coalition Work

Among Marxist theorists, only Lenin entertained the illusion that capitalism could be abolished and communism built in its ruins during his lifetime.[35] His contemporaries, the Social Democrats in Western Europe, were far more cautious about the historical moment at which the transformation of the political order was to unfold. Accordingly, the vision of a future state order merely had theoretical and propagandistic value in Bauer's doctrine, whereas for the political practice of Social Democracy, it was irrelevant. The distant strategic goal was obscured by day-to-day politics, whose objective, according to Austromarxist revolutionary and state theory, was to gain a strong position for the working class in the capitalist state. This would serve the class as a foundation for a future seizure of power. Parliament was designated as the place where the fate of the proletariat would be decided.

As this is precisely what the party regarded as its core strategy since the Hainfeld party congress, it accepted the limitations that this choice demanded in the struggle for socialism. In the parliamentary arena, the party had a choice between two tactics: it could either continue the struggle for its programme in isolation, aware that its chances of success depended upon the number of voters it could win. Alternatively, it could negotiate with other groups in parliament and seek to come to an understanding on less controversial questions. From its inception up until 1914, the SDAP did not collaborate with bourgeois parties at all. There were several reasons for this. For one, the existing parties lacked common purposes: suffice it to say, the Christian Socials and Greater Germans were not interested in SDAP-led campaigns for universal suffrage and the creation of strong trade unions to protect the interests of workers against despotic bosses. Positions on the national question also differed. Some features of the Austrian empire's party system need to be considered. Firstly, each party had its own electorate, and each electorate had distinct expectations of their politics. Secondly, the Social Democrats, although increasingly a mass party commanding an ever-greater number of seats in parliament, were no match

---

35   However, he grew increasingly sceptical about the possibility of building communism quickly in the Soviet Union in the 1920s.

for the united forces of the bourgeois-peasant camp. In addition, any potential collaboration between different political groups was thwarted by the Marxist dogmatism that prevailed in the SDAP: any co-operation with the class enemy was rejected on ideological grounds. The 1917 resolution of the left and the 1918 national programme of the left are informed by very similar sentiments.

After the demise of the monarchy, the SDAP leadership reconsidered its stance on collaboration with other parties. In October 1918, the Austrian Social Democrats were inclined, much like their German sister party, towards coalition policies, even if the decision of the party leadership was not supported by rank and file members.[36] The theoretical assumptions and socio-political conditions that convinced SDAP leaders to adapt their attitude to coalitions are worthy of investigation. In the theoretical domain, the desire to uphold the concept of peaceful revolution was crucial, which corresponded with the party's fear of a violent attempt by the indignant masses to usher in a proletarian state. Joining the coalition was understood as a necessary step towards defending the early democratic gains of the republic, a guarantee for the continuation of the reformist road, and a safeguard against Bolshevisation.[37] The Social Democrats' belief that the transformation of the political order had been premature led to a novel situation. For the first time in the history of Austrian parliamentarism, inter-party quarrels were secondary to the concern for a common objective. To summarise, the theory of a historical necessity to engage in coalition work, unanimously supported by the leadership at the dawn of the republic, was entrenched in their desire to protect bourgeois democracy. Bauer and Renner's theories of democracy and the state provided justifications for this.

Nonetheless, it is hard to entirely deny Bauer's 1919 assertion that the decision to engage in a coalition was forced upon the party by the socio-political balance of forces.[38] True enough, no party actively desired a coalition, nor

---

36   No one spoke resolutely against a coalition at the 1918 congress. When the coalition government was formed with the participation of the SDAP on 30 October 1918, this caused outrage among workers, as they were hostile towards collaboration with bourgeois parties. Renner stressed this a few days later at a state council meeting. See Pfabigan 1982, p. 146.

37   At the first meeting of the provisional national assembly, Victor Adler claimed that Social Democracy would not abandon its political goals when entering the coalition – see Berchtold 1967, p. 32. This proclamation did not change the reality that both the Social Democrats and Christian Socials regarded the coalition as the only way to prevent the emergence of a proletarian dictatorship. Compare Leopold Kunschak's speech of 30 May 1919, cited by Leser 1986, p. 280; and Bauer 1920b, p. 255.

38   At the October 1919 party congress, Bauer explained that 'the coalition is a bitter necessity

did any of them wish for the division of state power to remain a permanent condition. Not so much the intention or ideological orientation of the party, but the real social and political circumstance was decisive. The bourgeois parties could have formed their own government, but they capitulated in the face of revolutionary threat. Similarly, it would have been impossible for the Social Democrats to form a government on their own, given the anti-socialist resistance in the regions. The necessity of coalition, then, was the result of cool calculation: just as the Christian Socials could not have governed Vienna on their own, so the Social Democrats could not have ruled all of Austria without Christian Social support.

As far as the socialists were concerned, the coalition government embodied the first stage of revolution, although this conviction had more to do with the expectations they attached to the coalition than the actual results. Its objectives were to consolidate the state and implement reforms in the interest of broad social layers. In practice, the coalition was active in three areas: constitutional, socio-economic, and foreign affairs. Aside from legislative issues, its policies had little to do with socialist aims. Especially from the second half of 1919 onward, when the bourgeois bloc no longer felt threatened by the domestic situation and brazenly began to consolidate its power, Bauer's prophetic words of 1907 had come true as far as the working masses were concerned. Back then, he had argued:

> If the Social Democratic movement ... one moment [joins] forces with this and the next moment with that political group, perhaps even forming a part of the governmental majority and participating in government itself ... it appears itself to be an institution of the capitalist state; it shares responsibility ... for all the misery and exploitation endured by the working people in capitalist society.[39]

During the autumn of 1919, the SARA faction defended the workers who were dissatisfied with the political direction in which the SDAP leadership was heading. It demanded more radical measures, more power to the left wing of the SDAP, and that the party leave the coalition. On 14 September 1920, Joseph Frey commented during the meeting of the Vienna SDAP executive:

---

for us all, yet for the moment, it is a necessity nonetheless' – quoted in Reimann 1968, p. 335.

39   Bauer 1996, pp. 445–6.

The only means to achieve this is the unification of the Social-Democratic and Communist parties. However, the coalition stands in the way of unification. I prefer a coalition even with the worst, dirtiest Communist to a coalition with the Christian Socials and Greater Germans.[40]

our translation

A majority of the working class endorsed the demand to withdraw from the coalition, which the left at the party congress of 1920 repeated. The workers urged the leadership – Bauer in particular – to take a firm stand.

In 1918, Bauer did not particularly desire a coalition with bourgeois parties and had reservations about its stability.[41] In spite of this, neither he nor his closest associates managed to present a clear position on co-operation with other political groups during the entire period of the First Republic. It is difficult to blame them. Their perspectives evolved on the balance of class forces, and the arguments they offered the working class intended to validate party policies. Bauer's stance at the 1920 SDAP congress illustrates this. He admitted that permanent co-operation with bourgeois parties inevitably involved a change of the party line. As an aside, there was a far more significant problem behind his statement, which, even if the socialists did not fully realise it at the time, became paramount after World War II. The 1920 discussion was not so much about revising the current party line as it was about changing the very character of the party. As it were, the question was whether the SDAP should remain a class party, or whether the experience of coalition work militated for it to become a party of the entire populace. Incidentally, the postwar social democrats of Western Europe unequivocally solved this question when renouncing the myth of the class character of their parties, which they considered of little use given the changed social and political circumstances. Bauer protested that the party must withdraw from the coalition at the 1920 party congress. To rationalise this, he drew on the Marxist notion that class contradictions in capitalist society would steadily increase. He argued that 'the governing of the bourgeois state, for as long as it remains a bourgeois state naturally falls to the bourgeois class. The stance of the proletariat towards the bourgeois state even in its republican form is one of opposition'.[42] In reality, Bauer realised that

---

40   'Das einzige Mittel hierzu ist die Vereinigung der Sozialdemokratischen Partei mit der Kommunistischen. Das Hindernis dieser Einigung ist aber die Koalition. Mir ist die Koalition mit dem letzten, dreckigsten Kommunisten lieber als mit den Christlichsozialen und Deutschnationalen' – quoted in Raming 1979, p. 16.

41   See Bauer 1979i, p. 20.

42   See SDAP 1921, in Documents, Programmes, Protocols.

the SDAP was losing its hegemony and feared rising Communist influence and a potential split in the party. While none of this was unjustified, the Social Democrats' political practice and their logic for rejecting any further collaboration with bourgeois parties were not the same as the reasons they offered to the masses. In addition, the bourgeois parties did not desire further SDAP participation in government any more than the Social Democrats did. A Christian Social and Greater German bloc could very well do without the Social Democrats. The latter, meanwhile, were aware of their powerlessness and were thus forced to abandon the idea. When the elections on 17 October 1920, the first after Renner's resignation, resulted in an unexpected ascendancy of the bourgeois parties, the Social Democrats joined the opposition using a dispute on military legislation as a pretext.[43] The exit from the coalition did not shake the party leadership's faith in the democratic road to socialism, despite the fact that engaging with the coalition was one of the pivotal aspects of this strategy. The SDAP leaders dismissed the affair as a temporary exclusion from power. In 1920, they firmly believed that new fertile ground for resuming coalition work would soon be created. Without a doubt, this was partly due to the deterministic view of history prevailing among Social Democrats.[44] On a more trivial level, the Social Democrats' hope to re-enter a coalition was also due to their expectation that the victorious parties' policies in government would soon end in disaster.

Yet their hopes were never actualised. The bourgeois bloc consolidated its power in the state. What is more, in 1922, after having declined Bauer's offer to participate in government, it managed to navigate the country out of the economic crisis without the Social Democrats' co-operation. Meanwhile, the Social-Democratic party, which on Bauer's advice had remained in opposition, was debilitated to such a degree that it was completely at the mercy of the bourgeois parties' paramilitary formations when the wave of terror escalated after 1927.[45] After 1920, there was only one real opportunity for the Social

---

43   The Social Democrats demanded replacing the standing army with a popular militia. This
      suggestion provoked vehement resistance from their coalition partners – see Leser 1986,
      p. 281. The election results played a far greater role in the SDAP's decision: in 1919, the
      Christian Social Party increased its number of mandates by 19 and the Greater German
      People's Party by two, while the SDAP lost seven seats in parliament. This change in
      balance reflected the gradual dissipation of the revolutionary wave and consolidation of
      bourgeois dominance.

44   Compare Leser 1979, p. 33.

45   Bauer wrote about the suggestion he had made to Seipel on the front page of the *Arbeiter-
      Zeitung* of 24 August.

Democrats to participate in government, namely when Ignaz Seipel offered to form a coalition. They declined.

With regard to their rejection of the offer, it is important to remember that the position of the SDAP leadership in 1931 resulted from a 1927–30 discussion about Social-Democratic participation in coalitions. The discussion came to the fore at the 1927 party congress, where two contending positions emerged. Bauer's group was against coalition work, while Renner's faction supported it. At the time, Bauer discussed three different situations under which coalitions were formed: working-class dominance, balance of class power, and bourgeois dominance. He categorically rejected coalitions in the last case. The weakness of the workers' party, he argued, would lead to inefficient action on the part of Social-Democratic ministers, and the masses would ultimately lose confidence in their leaders.[46] Moreover, he claimed that coalition work was only beneficial for the working class in a situation when it was in the ascendancy.[47] Subsequently protesting against a coalition at the congress, he offered the dubious argument that there was little point in sharing power with bourgeois parties since electoral support for Social Democracy was on the rise. This, according to him, gave the socialists hope for their own government in the near future. Bauer's optimism was completely unfounded. Renner, Oskar Helmer and Heinrich Schneidmadl accused the party leader of spreading illusions as to the power and significance of the party. Contrary to Bauer's convictions, the party was so weak from 1927–30 onward that the bourgeois bloc ceased to consider Social Democracy a political factor in the Austrian state. After 1931, Bauer made an effort to obscure this state of affairs from the working class. He vindicated the exclusion of Social Democracy from the political arena by claiming that coalition work only served to buttress the foundations of the capitalist state.[48]

---

46   See Bauer 1928, p. 335 and Bauer 1930, p. 193.
47   Ibid.
48   In 1930, Bauer wrote: 'under favourable conditions, the participation of Social Democrats in government can be beneficial, even necessary. It can protect the working class against threats and be to its advantage. It can significantly strengthen the resistance of the democratic state against the pressures of the capitalist plutocracy. However, leaving aside revolutionary periods such as 1918–20, it cannot abolish the bourgeois character of the state' (our translation). Original: 'Die Teilnahme der Sozialdemokratie an der Regierung kann unter günstigen Voraussetzungen nützlich, notwendig sein. Sie kann die Arbeiterklasse vor Gefahren bewahren und kann der Arbeiterklasse manchen Vorteil bringen. Sie kann die Widerstandskraft der demokratischen Staatsgewalt gegen den Druck der kapitalistischen Plutokratie wesentlich stärken. Aber sie kann – von revolutionären Zeiten, wie

Similarly, Seipel's offer did not mean that he recognised the Social Democrats as equal partners. Nor did it imply that the Christian Socials were revising their political line, even if certain factions of that party were prepared to co-operate with the Social Democrats at the end of the 1920s. According to Staudinger, the leadership of the Christian Socials' parliamentary club did not intend to grant the SDAP proportional representation in a future coalition government.[49] Seipel's motivations for the offer of a coalition were prompted by the Christian Socials' anxiety that the state could progress in an increasingly authoritarian direction. In light of electoral losses and economic crisis, they were worried that they might not be able to salvage democracy on their own. The Social Democrats offered two reasons for declining the offer. Firstly, the position granted to the Social-Democratic party in a coalition government would have been far too weak. Secondly, participation in such a government went against the wishes of the party majority.[50] Bauer's crowning argument was his claim that 'the sheer act of Social Democrats entering government when capitalism is subject to the heaviest turmoil ... would put us at the great risk of merely co-administering the affairs of collapsing capitalism as part of this government, while not being able to adequately serve the interests of the working class and ideals of socialism' (our translation).[51] The Social Democrats wanted

---

1918 bis 1920 abgesehen – den bourgeoisen Charakter des Staatswesens nicht aufheben' - Bauer 1930b, p. 310.

49   See Staudinger 1984, p. 12.

50   Julius Deutsch was the only member of the party leadership to speak in favour of entering a coalition. Renner, who had been waiting for such an opportunity for years, agreed with Bauer. Modern historians disagree over whether the Social Democrats should have joined the government in 1931 – see Staudinger 1984, p. 6; Simon 1984, p. 12; Maimann and Mattl 1984, pp. 6–7. As Haas states, a partial collaboration between Social Democrats and Christian Socials existed from 1932–3 in some provinces, e.g. Lower Austria, despite the SDAP's rejection of the coalition offer. After 15 March 1933, the SDAP leaders were prone to a politics of compromise. They offered Dollfuss a co-operation against the Nazis, for instance, which the chancellor declined. See Haas 1990, p. 422 and p. 424.

51   '... [D]er bloße Eintritt von Sozialdemokraten in die Regierung in dieser Zeit der schwersten Erschütterung des Kapitalismus ... würde uns in die große Gefahr bringen, dass wir in dieser Regierung nur die Geschäfte des zusammenbrechenden Kapitalismus mitadministrieren sollten und nicht in der Lage wären, wirklich den Interessen der Arbeiterklasse und den Idealen des Sozialismus in ihr entsprechend zu dienen' - SDAP 1931, in Documents, Programmes, Protocols, p. 29. It seems justified to assume that the Social Democrats' participation in government would have involved a joint effort to save the bankrupt banks and therefore inevitably would have led to cutting unemployment allowances. As Renner mentioned in light of Bauer's strong resistance, joining the coalition would have only been

to evade the responsibility for the deteriorating economic situation in Austria and the economic crisis. In 1931, their calculations did not consider that the introduction of socialism was probably not a realistic alternative for Austria at the time. In all likelihood, the choice was one between defending bourgeois democracy and facing a fascist dictatorship.

Many Austrian scholars agree that Bauer was adverse to a collaboration with bourgeois-peasant parties.[52] While this is essentially justified, a few complementary remarks are necessary. Bauer's attitude towards coalitions was influenced by his struggle to preserve the unity of the workers' movement and protect its immediate interests. Considering deteriorating economic conditions for the working class, such as rising unemployment and a relapse into inflation, this was no easy task. What is more, it bore the real danger, which would partly come true, that the workers might leave the ranks of the Social Democrats and join the Communists and fascists instead. Bauer was neither an advocate nor an adversary of coalitions.[53] For him, judging the expediency of forming a coalition depended on the balance of political and class forces across the country. Depending on the occasion, he was in favour of coalition to balance opposing class forces, which logically resulted from his theory of a 'balance of class power'.[54] Given the domestic situation in Austria in 1931, to decline a coalition offer was not a thoroughly considered decision. Following Susanne Miller in her essay, 'Politische Führung und Spontanität in der österreichischen Sozialdemokratie' ('Political Leadership and Spontaneity in Austrian Social Democracy', 1985), one may wonder whether collaboration between the SDAP and Christian Socials would have been a viable option. It is equally debatable as to whether it could have averted the danger of fascism at home.[55]

The historical fate of the coalition in the First Republic laid bare the contradictions of the 'third way' under bourgeois-democratic conditions. The political structures only allowed the Social Democrats marginal room for man-

---

possible at the cost of splitting the party – a price no Social Democrat wanted to pay. See Renner 1952b, p. 41.

52 See Kulemann 1979, p. 238; Reimann 1968, p. 336; Leser 1986, p. 281; Hanisch 2011, p. 167.

53 Many scholars share this assessment of Bauer's legacy. Leser, for instance, writes: 'He was not an opponent of coalition governments as a matter of principle' (our translation) – Leser 1964, p. 70.

54 Likewise, Hanisch argues, 'for the phase of relative stability, it is possible to sum up as follows: Bauer did not reject coalitions as a matter of principle, but the conditions were determined exclusively by the interests of the working class, not by the interests of the whole of society' (our translation) – Hanisch 2011, pp. 211–12.

55 Compare Miller 1979, p. 73.

oeuvre when the bourgeoisie was weak during the post-revolutionary period. It also offered the class enemies of Social Democracy a legal framework for their rebirth and instigations of extra-parliamentary means of violence. These groups managed to eliminate the workers' party from political prominence without great difficulty. In opposition, the party was unable to resist the forces that annihilated democracy. Nor could it construct the tactical prerequisites for an effective struggle to reclaim its position in the state. The Social Democrats' strategic objective of defending bourgeois democracy remained unfulfilled, wishful thinking.

CHAPTER 7

The Question of War in Bauer's Thought in Light of SDAP and LSI Policies

For Austromarxists, war was not an object of philosophical or ethical reflection, nor was its political aspect of major interest. They did not deny that there was a political dimension to war, yet as faithful disciples of Marx, they believed it had an instrumental role (as an aside, I have previously pointed out the peculiar inversion of this relationship with respect to Bauer's theory on the state and the national question). As was the case with most of their positions, the Austromarxists were prone to overestimate the economic (class) factor at the expense of the non-economic (legal, political, cultural). Consequently, their view of the war phenomenon was defined by a deterministic, strictly economic perception of history, which strongly accentuated class relationships. It is also notable, however, that for Bauer and his tendency, the war question was only relevant as a matter of political practice.[1] For this reason, he analysed the causes, objectives, and perspectives of war, as well as the ways in which one might prevent it, only at congresses of the SDAP, Second International, and Labour and Socialist International. Hence, it is pivotal to assess his attitudes in consideration of the politics of the SDAP and the two internationals, all of which he helped to shape.

1   The SDAP Position Until the Outbreak of World War I

Under the shadow of war in the Balkans and the outbreak of World War I, the Austrian Social-Democratic movement was forced to merge its politics with what was unfolding in reality, and confront the traditions of the party. Deeply rooted in the organisation was the disbelief in the possibility of war and illusions as to the power of Social Democracy to prevent it from happening. As Leser writes:

---

1   What is more, Bauer and the Austromarxists regarded war merely as armed conflict between nation states, which further limited their understanding of it. On war in the broader and narrower sense (as armed action, uprising, and revolution), see Jeliński 1996, p. 160.

This optimism was not based on any analysis of the real balance of forces or sober assessment of available options to resist or intervene. Nor was it based on a realistic self-assessment of one's own, fundamentally non-revolutionary – one might say, not even eager – attitude, but on a romanticism informed by the over-estimation of one's own abilities. That is how reality was approached.[2]

> our translation

This faith in the power of the workers' movement and the revolutionary rhetoric that came with it, neither of which reflected the actual political and social balance of forces under capitalism, was by no means an Austrian peculiarity. It regularly materialised at the congresses of the Second International whenever the war question was on the agenda (Brussels 1891, Zurich 1893, London 1896). It was particularly apparent at the 1907 congress in Stuttgart, which put forward a resolution committing all Social-Democratic parties to '... make every effort to take advantage of the economic and political crisis brought about by war for the purpose of awakening the popular masses and accelerating the demise of capitalist class rule'.[3] It was clear from this motion that any potential war was to be transformed into a social revolution. At the same time, it was a purely declamatory call to arms – none present at the congress seriously contemplated the necessary means to obtain this, nor did they take into account the obstacles they would face. One need only consider that nationalism was on the rise within the working class.

The Austrian Social Democrats failed to recognise the objectives thus outlined at the Stuttgart congress. Does this mean they were more realistic than the leaders of the Second International? Not by any stretch. Their reasons were, firstly, a typical SDAP politics of 'patience' – there had been persistent talk of revolution since the Hainfeld congress, yet the talk never came to fruition. Secondly, the party believed that possibilities for the Social-Democratic party to prevent war without taking radical measures were practically unlimited – a conviction that was perspicuous in Victor Adler's contributions in Stuttgart.[4]

---

2   Leser 1968, p. 263.

3   International Socialist Congress in Stuttgart, in Documents, Programmes, Protocols, p. 16. The resolution, authored by Luxemburg and Lenin, represented a compromise incorporating war as part of the nature of the capitalist state.

4   At the time, Adler said: 'we do not need to wait until war is declared in order to fight the war. All our actions, all our party work serves to prevent the war – that is the true anti-militarist activity' – International Socialist Congress in Stuttgart, in Documents, Programmes, Protocols, p. 95.

As late as 1907, the SDAP leadership did not deem it necessary to draft a plan for war prevention, despite the fact that the Austrian government had been preparing to invade Serbia for some time. Nor did it fully fathom the mechanisms that the Austrian workers' party could use to prevent the annexation of Bosnia and Herzegovina. On the one hand, the party leaders were unable to win the national movements to the fight against the ruling classes and monarchy. On the other, they were increasingly reluctant to engage in protests against the government. They rejected demands made at Second International congresses to disseminate anti-war propaganda amongst the armed forces, as well as other measures that could have weakened the influence of militaristic ideas. More importantly, though, the party's attitude toward the Habsburg monarchy's imperialist policies was ambivalent in form. True enough, Bauer and Renner attacked imperialist aggression in their speeches in parliament – yet the majority of the German-Austrian Social-Democratic movement firmly believed in Austria's cultural mission in the Balkans. At the 1910 congress in Copenhagen, the Austrian delegates did not form a united front on the question of militarism, even as the conflict in the Balkans drew precariously close. Renner put forward a motion on behalf of the Austrian section, calling for general disarmament, the creation of international arbitration courts, and the publication of secret pacts between parties.[5] However, this did not mean that the Austrian Social Democrats were prepared to subordinate national interests to the interests of the international proletariat. Their refusal to rally for a general strike in the case of war was symptomatic of this.[6] The Austrian leadership's only response to the war was an appeal passed by the executive committee on 15 October 1912, which put forward the slogan, 'No intervention in the Balkans war! The Balkans for the Balkans people! Maintain peace!' as a slogan of the proletariat, thus leaving the weight of responsibility to Tsarism and international imperialism.[7] The Balkan peoples' right to self-determination was a controversial question, given that these were not historical nations, and therefore had, according to Marxist dogma, no right to exist independently. The demand for preserving peace in the Balkans was not grounded in any efficient war preven-

---

5   See International Socialist Congress in Copenhagen, in Documents, Programmes, Protocols, p. 104. Renner's demands were an arsenal of measures typical of bourgeois pacifist ideology.

6   The French delegation issued to call a strike. The Austrian, German, and Italian delegates argued that calling a general strike would give the party an illegal character and lead to heavy repercussions. See International Socialist Congress in Copenhagen, in Documents, Programmes, Protocols, p. 104.

7   See SPD 1912, pp. 107–24.

tion programme – understandably so, considering the SDAP was not a political force that may have resisted the bourgeois bloc and its politics in 1912. Victor Adler acknowledged the feeling of powerlessness that swept through the party at the 1912 congress of the Second International in Basel.[8] The party leader's congressional statement supported Otto Bauer's notion of the inevitability of war in antagonistic societies, principally within the framework of imperialism, due to the inadequacy of economic working-class struggle as an instrument of war prevention.[9]

For many European states, the assassination in Sarajevo on 27 July 1914 was a precursor to war.[10] Not so for the Austrian socialists, who, on Victor Adler's insistence, not only denied the imminent outbreak of war, but also misapprehended the connection between the assassination and Austro-Hungarian imperialism.[11] They assumed that the perpetrators would be punished and order restored.[12] After the ultimatum given to Serbia, it would have been possible to coordinate the activities of all Social-Democratic parties of the empire. Yet the only outcome of the meeting between German, Czech and Polish activists on 29 July 1914 was a manifesto formulated by the German delegates. They proffered support for the Austrian Social Democrats, who in their view were not at fault for the outbreak of war. The SDAP leadership reiterated this protest on the first day of war. It was not the monarchy, they argued, who were to blame for the war, but Serbia.[13]

The outbreak of World War I and confrontation with the tangible political balance was a rude awakening for the misled Social Democrats. At that time, few among them were aware that a politics based on false Marxian dogma would inevitably prove fatal for Social Democracy. As Leser writes, among these

---

8　Adler expressed this as follows: 'Unfortunately, it does not depend on us Social Democrats whether the war is coming or not. We are well aware that the working class of all countries grows more powerful every day ... But let us not overestimate our own power, and let us especially not overestimate the rational thinking of our governments' – Extraordinary International Socialist Congress in Basel from 24–25 November 1912, p. 17.

9　Ibid.

10　A day after the assassination, hundreds of workers in Germany and Britain staged an anti-war demonstration.

11　Ardelt shares this view – see Ardelt 1979, p. 63.

12　By way of testimony to the Social Democrats' deep conviction that there was no imminent danger, Friedrich Adler wanted to set the date for the socialist congress in Vienna for August.

13　Kulemann notes that the Social Democrats' negative stance on the Austro-Hungarian empire's nations' right to self-determination was but one step away from supporting the annexation of Serbia. See Kulemann 1979, p. 167.

dogmas was their belief that the masses would spontaneously jump into action if class contradictions intensified, as well as their hope for the international solidarity of workers. The latter was based on the notion that the interests of the working class as a whole were stronger than the common national interests of different classes.[14] These and other basic ideological and theoretical premises of Marxism were fertile ground for one of the gravest illusions of the workers' movement – that is, the notion that the Second International could prevent war. One of the few socialists to recognise the discrepancies between Social-Democratic theory and practice was Max Adler, who in 1915 wrote:

> That is why the International did not actually fail. The war only made apparent that it did, in fact, not yet exist, that it had no existence aside from being a mere ideology of the proletariat, a noble desire without any guarantee of fulfilment.[15]
>
> our translation

The war clearly exposed the miscalculations of Marx's theory on historical materialism. For one, it revealed the limits of society's class structures, demonstrating that national, political, and cultural cross-class bonds played a far greater role in politics than class ties. What is more, it proved that social and political interests are not clearly determined by economic matters. To no lesser degree, cross-class interests within communities stem from their various political and national histories. Legal advantages offered by the state played a dominant role. That is precisely why the Social-Democratic parties of Germany, France and Britain advocated, in spite of the arrangements made at the congresses of the Second International, a politics of 'defending the fatherland'. The Social-Democratic Party of Germany was the first to vote for war credits, arguing that democracy and Western culture had to be defended against the totalitarianism of Tsarism. The other Social-Democratic parties of Europe also took the side of their respective governments, a move decisively influenced by the nationalist mood of the masses.[16] Consistent with their politics

---

14   Compare Leser 1968, p. 266.

15   'Die Internationale hat darum eigentlich auch gar nicht versagt, sondern der Krieg hat nur offenbar gemacht, dass sie überhaupt noch gar nicht bestanden hatte, dass sie noch keine andere Existenz führte als die einer bloßen Ideologie des Proletariats, als eines edlen Wunsches ohne irgendwelche reale Garantie seiner Erfüllung' – Adler 1915b, p. 47.

16   The war cabinets boasted well-known socialists, e.g. Emile Vandervelde in Belgium and Jules Guesde and Marcel Sembat in France. The decision to join the war was supported by Henry Hyndman and Ernest Belfort Bax in Britain and Plekhanov in Russia.

of preserving the multinational state, the SDAP assumed a government-friendly position, citing fear of Russia as justification. The stance of the party leadership was partly down to the enthusiasm of the masses, who participated in a pro-war demonstration on the streets of Vienna.[17] The right wing of the party (Victor Adler, Austerlitz, Renner, Pernerstorfer, Leuthner), who represented the major-ity, sympathised with this patriotic turn and did not attempt to hide its German nationalist sentiments. The delegates were only able to avoid a compulsory vote on war credits due to the dissolution of parliament. The party press were apo-logetic, publishing articles that served to prove the SDAP's ideological support for the war. In a special issue of the *Arbeiter-Zeitung* of 1 August 1914, Russia was deemed solely responsible for imperialist endeavours. In the 2 August 1914 issue, Austerlitz absolved Germany and Austria from any responsibility for the outbreak of war in his article, 'Der Weltkrieg des Zaren' ('The Tsar's World War'). On 5 August 1914, Austerlitz's famous comment, 'Der Tag der deutschen Nation' ('Day of the German Nation') was published: it endorsed the SDAP position on war credits and conceded the right of self-defence of every country. Austerl-itz referred to the day when the interests of the Social Democracy movement merged with those of the ruling apparatus as 'a day of the proudest and mighti-est revolt of the German spirit'.[18] Well aware that the Social Democrats' support for the government at the outbreak of war had exposed, to the working class, the hitherto well-concealed defensive position of the party, Bauer wrote at the end of his life:

> The 4 August 1914 exposed all for what it was. For decades, the revolu-tionary socialist movement expected that a European war would allow the proletariat to take advantage of the shock administered to capitalist society by war and the arming of the masses. It would use it to conquer state power by revolutionary means and thus transform the social order. Had the socialist movement really stuck to a revolutionary perspective, it would have immediately had to blame the capitalist classes and their governments for the war when it broke out ... It would have had to pre-pare, even if forced into illegality, to exploit the revolutionary situation that would have inevitably presented itself during the war or at its end. In

---

17   For more on the enthusiasm of the masses, see Wandruszka 1954, p. 438; Wereszyski 1975, p. 258. According to Burian, a majority of the population of the Austro-Hungarian Empire supported the war not out of loyalty to the Habsburg monarchy, but because of its own national interest. See Burian 1974, p. 11.

18   '... Tag der stolzesten und gewaltigsten Erhebung des deutschen Geistes' – Austerlitz 1914b.

reality, however, the socialist parties, frightened by the war, abandoned the struggle against their capitalist governments.[19]

2   Bauer's Opposition to the SDAP Position on World War I

Bauer later went on to substantiate the position taken at the last congress of the Second International more thoroughly in two articles written in 1912, both of which were published under the Heinrich Weber moniker: 'Der Sozialismus und der Krieg' ('Socialism and War') and 'Balkankrieg und die deutsche Politik' ('War in the Balkans and German Policies'). He viewed war from a historical class perspective, overemphasising economic factors at the expense of the political. His notion of the causes of war was one-sided: he cited the social conditions based on private ownership of the means of production, as well as the class character of the capitalist state. In the era of imperialism, Bauer argued, war had become necessary, resulting from an immanent expansionist tendency that made any enduring peace impossible. Bauer linked the nature of the Balkan war to the politics of the propertied classes. When describing the negative consequences of imperialist war – such as economic collapse, destruction, and loss of human life – he conceded that they affected all social classes. Nonetheless, he was inclined to see war as a factor of historical development. For him, the destruction of old social structures and existing political relations counted as progress. Bauer did not go as far as the left of the Second International (Vaillant, Luxemburg, Lenin), which demanded that imperialist wars between nations be transformed into wars against the governments of their respective countries. Although he wanted Social Democracy to support the revolutionary forces in Russia and the Balkan countries in their struggle against

19   'Der 4. August 1914 hat demaskiert, was war. Jahrzehnte lang hatte der revolutionäre Sozialismus erwartet, ein europäischer Krieg werde es dem Proletariat ermöglichen, die ... unmittelbar revolutionäre Aktion wiederaufzunehmen, die Erschütterung der kapitalistischen Gesellschaft durch den Krieg und die Bewaffnung der Volksmassen durch den Krieg zu revolutionärer Eroberung der Staatsmacht und damit zur Umwälzung der Gesellschaftsordnung auszunutzen. Hätte der Sozialismus tatsächlich die revolutionäre Zukunftsperspektive festgehalten, so hätte er am Beginn des Krieges die kapitalistischen Klassen und ihre Regierungen für den Krieg verantwortlich machen müssen ... Er hätte, sei er auch in die Illegalität gedrängt, die Ausnützung einer revolutionären Situation vorbereiten müssen, die im Verlaufe des Krieges oder am Ende des Krieges kommen musste. In Wirklichkeit aber haben die sozialistischen Parteien, vom Kriege erschreckt, den Kampf gegen die kapitalistischen Regierungen eingestellt' – Bauer 1976p, p. 251.

Tsarism, this demand existed in a historical vacuum. Bauer did not indicate the ways in which it could be put into practice, and in 1912 the Western countries were far from declaring war on the Tsarist Empire.

When contemplating measures suitable for the working class and Social Democracy during wartime, Bauer, who authored *Der Sozialismus und der Krieg* (*Socialism and War*), warned of placing false hope in the effectiveness of a general strike, claiming that '... under present circumstances, stopping a war through general strike is a utopia'.[20] According to Zimmermann, Bauer's position on war was ambiguous. On the one hand, he was convinced of the inevitability of war under capitalism and the pointlessness of Social-Democratic anti-war propaganda. On the other, he attempted to prove that the working class would transcend national interests, support international anti-war policies, and commence a struggle against imperialism.[21] The weapons he suggested for this struggle – anti-war propaganda, speeches in parliament, street demonstrations – were hardly effective measures to protect the proletariat from the imperialist governments and their policies. Indeed, Bauer himself did not believe that the anti-war sentiments of the party and working class would amount to much.

Bauer's position on the breakout of World War I and its potential consequences was far more realistic than that of Renner and the party majority. This led to the cooling of the relationship between the two politicians, and condemned Bauer to political isolation within the party. Renner not only justified the government's acts of war; he even established a connection between war and economic progress. For him, it contained the possibility to create great economic territories and thus preserve the multinational Habsburg state. In contrast, Bauer realised that the war would stimulate the political activity of the various nations of the Empire. Consequently, he warned of the misconceptions escalated by Renner – he expected that the independence movements in the Slavic countries would receive a boost leading to the breakup of the empire. From 1914–16, this possibility was hardly ever considered in the party. Rather, there prevailed a belief that the pre-war political line must be maintained, i.e. agitating for political reforms and defending all nations of the Austro-Hungarian Empire from Tsarism. A veil of silence was cast over the Austrian imperialist war aims that these policies served to further.[22] During the war

---

20   '... unter den heute gegebenen Umständen die Verhinderung eines Krieges durch den Generalstreik eine Utopie ist' – Bauer 1980e, p. 743. According to Steiner, the majority of Social Democrats shared Bauer's position – see Steiner 1967, p. 5.

21   Compare Zimmermann 1976, p. 448.

22   This does not at all mean that the leaders of Austrian Social Democracy misapprehended

years, the SDAP declared as its foremost tasks the preservation of party unity
and the rescue of national organisations. When assessing the state of the party
towards the end of the war, including the relationship to shop stewards, Julius
Deutsch noted that 'they were almost exclusively interested in the struggles
of the day and immediate organisational tasks. As they rushed from election
campaign to publicity campaign, their political work evaporated' (our translation).[23] In 1915, the SDAP leadership took up an anti-war initiative organising a
peace demonstration – yet for fear of repercussions, the demonstration never
took place.

During the same period, left oppositional forces hostile to the war gained
strength among Social-Democratic parties. At international congresses in Zimmerwald (August 1915) and Kienthal (April–May 1916), they subjected the pro-
war politics of the party majorities to sharp criticism. In Germany, where they
failed to arrive at a joint position, the opposition split the newly formed Independent Socialist-Democratic Party of Germany (USPD) away from the SPD in
April 1917. In Austria too, an opposition led by Friedrich Adler surfaced the
moment war was declared. Adler expressed defiance for the first time in his
letter to the party leadership of 7 August 1914, where he questioned the necessity of defence as a war demand of the Social-Democratic party, albeit taking
care not to allow his theoretical critique to transcend the boundaries of party
unity. A group of critical party members gathering around him from 1915–16
held similar positions – among them were Max Adler, Leon Winarsky, Gustav
Proft, Theresia Schlesinger, Robert Danneberg, Gustav Eckstein and Rudolf Hilferding. The Social-Democratic parties' vote for war credits and the pro-war
policies of the SDAP leadership being the main targets of their criticism, they
supported the anti-war programme of the German USPD and demanded peace
without conquered territories or war reparations. The left group was organisationally and numerically weak, counting only some 120 members – mainly
intellectuals – who did not dare leave the party even though their critique met
with no significant resonance in the SDAP. Lively debate now took place on the
platform legally provided by the 'Karl Marx debating society', which the left had

---

the expansive politics of the government. On the contrary, they stood in solidarity with
the government: at a secret party leadership meeting on 19 November 1915, Victor Adler
stated that to divide Poland further between Austria and Germany would be a fortunate
solution. Compare Kulemann 1979, p. 168. At the party congress in March 1916, the SDAP
restated its will to preserve the unity of the Austro-Hungarian Empire.

23   'Ihr Interesse war fast ausschließlich auf die Tageskämpfe und die unmittelbaren organ-
     isatorischen Aufgaben gerichtet. Zwischen Wahlkampf und Werbeaktion verlief ihr polit-
     isches Wirken' – Deutsch 1918, p. 608.

reconvened in December 1915 in order to propagate 'Zimmerwald left' ideas.[24] The peace resolutions that the members of the society submitted to the 1915 and 1916 party congresses found no support. The SDAP leadership had no desire whatsoever to drop its pro-war policies. Furthermore, it feared an increase in the influence of left-wing agitators on war-weary workers, and that the same fate which befell the German sister party could develop once again – that is, that the workers' movement might split and thus lose strength. Bauer, who at the time was a prisoner of war in Russia, wrote letters to the SDAP leadership in which he endorsed the split in the German workers' movement, considering it a result of the distorted proportionality between reformist and revolutionary trends. He did not take the ideological and theoretical arguments raging in the SDAP during the wartime seriously. Rather, he claimed that the party had preserved its revolutionary character, and that its unity was not in jeopardy. He was only right on the latter point. Despite its protests against the party leadership and the patriotic endeavours of the centrist forces behind it, the left did not want a repetition of the German scenario. It feared the powerful repercussions that the ruling apparatus might unleash against the workers' movement if the latter were significantly weakened.

Divergent positions on war, though manifest since its outbreak, were most vociferous at the SDAP congress from 19–24 October 1917. Otto Bauer, newly released from a POW camp, took over the leadership of the opposition, which numbered 51 out of 283 delegates. Upon his initiative, the opposition introduced its own programme, the so-called 'Declaration of the Left'. Acting as representatives of the class interests of the workers' movement, the opposition attacked the coalition between Social-Democratic and bourgeois parties, the SDAP's vote for war credits, and the nationalism of the party leadership. It expeditiously demanded to work towards a swift end to war.[25] Note that the

---

24   The second Zimmerwald congress from 5–8 August 1915 saw sharp polemical exchanges between Lenin's group of radicals and the moderate reformists under Robert Grimm's leadership. The draft brought forward by the so-called Zimmerwald left founded by Lenin was rejected by 19 to 12 votes; yet the adopted manifesto demanding unity of the workers' movement to defend peace was a serious step on the path towards uniting all socialist forces against the war. Friedrich Adler, impressed by the Zimmerwald manifesto, published an article, 'Die Internationalen in Österreich und die Internationalen aller Länder' ('The Austrian Internationalists to the Internationalists of All Countries'), directed against the politics of the party right. See Hautmann 1971, p. 22.

25   The 'Declaration of the Left' states: 'Social Democracy can only fulfil its historical task in the class struggle ... Reformism necessarily leads to ministerialism. We reject every permanent alliance with bourgeois parties, every bloc politics. We stick to the old principle,

class position of the left was not wholly consistent: as mentioned earlier, it supported the centrist project of conceding national autonomy while maintaining the existing ties between all nations of the empire. Because it did not want to cause a split, the left advocated, quite irrespective of the slogans expressed, an overall position closer to the right than the left wing of the Zimmerwald conference, and supported the SDAP leadership in a vote of confidence. The latter amounted to the opposition subordinating itself to the party leadership, and therefore agreeing to reject its demand for peace without conquered territories or war reparations. In late 1917, the Social Democrats still hoped the Austro-Hungarian Empire would escape the clutches of war with nothing more than a slap on the wrist, and that the party might continue its reformist policies.[26] Bauer did not quite agree with this, yet he did not openly oppose the political line adopted by the SDAP. It was only a few years later, when critically revisiting the positions of the party, that Bauer admitted their character had been pro-war – during the first years of the conflict, the Social Democrats supported the war apparatus simply because they feared the overwhelming might of Tsarism.[27]

"Not one man and not one penny for the capitalist state"' (our translation) – Protocol of negotiations at the congress of the German Social-Democratic Workers' Party in Austria from 19 October, in Documents, Programmes, Protocols, p. 116. Max Adler was the main left speaker at the war congress of the SDAP. In his critique of the war, he shifted emphasis from the political to culture and consciousness. He assumed that the Social-Democratic party could stop the war by weakening the masses' psychological and moral preparedness to participate in it. See M. Adler 1981b, p. 282.

26   Towards the end of the war, minister president Max Hussarek von Heinlein brought forward a draft for the establishment of national cantons that would allow the preservation of the federal state. The draft found encouragement from the German part of the SDAP leadership, yet the delegates from the Slavic countries supported the sectional interests of their respective nations. On 4 November 1918, foreign minister Count Ottokar von Czernin turned to US president Wilson requesting help for the peace mission. Emperor Charles I of Austria's manifesto of 17 November, proposing to treat Austria as a federation of free nations, found no support. A note sent by Wilson on 19 November 1918 recognising the independence of Poland, Yugoslavia, and the Czech Republic also meant the end of the monarchy.

27   See Bauer 1925, p. 27.

3   Bauer on a Future Armed World Conflict: Fears, Hopes, and Plans

By the early 1920s, the living conditions of the Austrian working class had heavily deteriorated: inflation, prices, and unemployment rates all rose. At the same time, Michael Mayr's government, newly formed in the autumn of 1920, stopped all social and political reforms. From 1921 onwards, there was an increase in terrorist activities conducted by so-called 'movements for the defence of the fatherland' against the 'red peril'. Their orientation was recognisably fascist. In Italy, the fascist movement that would soon seize power consolidated itself. In this political climate, the centrist circles in the workers' movement strove to reunite the Social-Democratic parties in order to preserve the gains that had been won and prevent another war. At the 1923 congress in Hamburg, the Social Democrats brought the Labour and Socialist International (LSI) into being, which continued the reformist orientation of the Second International. This organisation came about through the unification of the so-called Geneva and Vienna internationals and comprised more than 40 parties with over 6 million members. Like the Second International, it was a loose association of parties intending to construct the socialist movement as a place where information and experience might be shared. Rather than having an absolute character, the resolutions it passed were mere suggestions for the activities of the individual parties. Discussion in Hamburg focused on the danger of war and the possibility of preventing it. A resolution passed by congress, 'The imperialist peace and the tasks of the working class', demanded that vigorous steps be taken in order to preserve peace and stop imperialist policies and military alliances. Even by that period, the LSI had already repeated the same mistakes as the former international: it did not proffer any guidance on how to fulfil the agreed demands, and there was a miscalculation on the actual strength of the workers' movement, its ability to co-operate in the case of war, and chances to put the demands into practice. When appearing at the Hamburg congress, Bauer reminded delegates of the inglorious past of the Second International and argued that it was impossible to conduct true anti-war politics by passing resolutions. Instead of mere verbal declarations, he suggested convening a special foreign office staffed by experts to analyse the political situation in the respective countries and to establish measures to prevent international conflicts from escalating into a world war. Against Bauer's warning, the LSI confined itself at subsequent congresses to passing anti-war resolutions.

In the meantime, the offensive of bourgeois and fascist forces had gathered strength in Austria. Paramilitary Heimwehr units assumed control over enterprises, while its battalions attacked workers at demonstrations. Attaining increasing influence in the Christian Social and Greater German parties, they gradually worked towards seizing state power. Further to constituting the greatest threat to democracy, they were generally believed to entertain alliances with imperialist circles in Germany and Italy. This suggested that they might implicate Austria in a war. From 1927–9, the SDAP focused on the question of whether peace could be preserved in Europe. Bauer reproached Max Adler, who had set the tone of this debate, with a harsh rebuttal. Within the SPD, the discussion around the Social-Democratic movement's position on the German army (*Reichswehr*) and protracted armament plans (e.g. the new battleship Panzerkreuzer A) inspired this particular disagreement. Much like the left opposition in Germany, Max Adler protested against further militarisation, advocating a standpoint close to Lenin's: every imperialist war should be used to awaken the revolutionary consciousness of the masses and turn them against their respective governments.[28] For him, 'socialist education' already provided a sufficient impediment to imperialist war policies, as well as an instrument for transforming an ongoing war into a socialist revolution. Interestingly, Adler did not consider any legal or institutional process for his theory, and as such Bauer's accusations of idealism were quite justified. Bauer highlighted the impracticality and utopian nature of the Social-Democratic war programme drafts. Yet at the same time, he fell victim to a different extreme, which could be ascribed to his unflinching loyalty to Marx's theory. Like Marx, he regarded politics as merely instrumental in comparison to economics. This was based on the understanding that the entire politics of the workers' party had to do justice to economic, social, historical, and class conditions. For him, it was these elements – rather than the *raison d' état* or national interests – that determined the war character. It would be fair to say that Bauer differentiated, even if he did not mention this explicitly, between 'just' and 'unjust' wars – a dichotomy harking back to the classical Marxists and assumptions widespread in the Labour and Socialist International. What is more, he seconded Jean Jaurés's view that the working class should participate in wars to defend their own national territories and resist imperialist wars of conquest. This is implicit in his negative view of a paper exploring the function and role of the German army submitted by the SPD left – or, more specifically, the Klassenkampf (Class Struggle) group around Max Seydewith, Kurt Rosenfeld, Paul Levis and Max Adler. Stressing the imperialist quality of all wars, the paper advocated Germany's full disarmament. Bauer objected to this, convinced instead that Social Democracy had to establish its positions on analyses of the international and political balance of forces. In addition, the disarmament of one side alone would render defending

---

28   See Adler 1981b, p. 41.

the country against a potential invasion impossible. Concretely, he feared that French and British troops might potentially march through German territory in a war against Russia.

As an advocate of the preservation of Germany, Bauer gave a speech entitled 'The situation in Germany and central Europe and the working class struggle for democracy' at the 1931 congress of the Labour and Socialist International in Vienna, in which delegates from 32 countries participated. In his analysis of the crisis in Germany, he cautioned that it would lead to the rise of Nazis and Communists in the state – as both groups intended to destroy the democratic foundations of the Weimar Republic, provoke a civil war, and introduce a dictatorship. Bauer demanded that the Western countries grant credits to Germany and annul her war debt in order to prevent the latter becoming reality. The majority of the Vienna congress adopted a resolution based on Bauer's suggestions.

By then, however, the German Social Democrats had already been losing votes to the National Socialists since 1931. There were no forces left with whom they could have allied in order to defend democracy, considering that the Communists were arch-enemies of Social Democracy at the time. Hence, they supported the bourgeois government as a 'lesser evil'. When Adolf Hitler assumed the post of chancellor on 30 January 1933, the Weimar Republic was still in a deep sleep. Hitler's reprisals and ban on the SPD, the leading party of the Labour and Socialist International, reinforced fears stirring in the socialist camp of the fascist peril. In light of the disagreement as to the measures that the working class should instigate in the case of war, the LSI convened an international socialist congress in Paris from 21–5 August 1933. Bauer, one of the leading speakers, pointed out that the Nazis' seizure of power by constitutional means had shattered the masses' faith in the bourgeois democratic system. In his resolution entitled 'Strategy and Tactics of the International Workers' Movement', he recommended that the Social-Democratic parties employ different methods of struggle against reaction depending on the conditions in each respective country.[29] In fascist countries, the working class should organise revolutionary uprisings to bring down the regimes and introduce socialist democracy. In bourgeois democratic countries, it should preserve the existing democratic liberties by expanding political democracy. The adoption of the resolution by congress testifies to how intently Social-Democratic leaders believed that mere formal measures could stop the bourgeois counter-revolution. Bauer soon

---

29   It was adopted with 291 to 18 votes. Five members abstained. This document would become the basic LSI programme for the struggle against fascism.

became aware that this was a gross misapprehension. Two months later, at the last SDAP congress in October 1933, he admitted:

> Today, we certainly do not have the time, leisure, or maturity to discuss which path socialism will take to prevail in the world. Today at this congress, we are facing the far more urgent and pressing task of elaborating the ways in which we can defend ourselves against the immediate fascist threat in Austria ... Then we have to go into battle, but with full awareness of what this battle means. Then we need to know ... that there can be no other decision than to win or perish and disappear for a long time.[30]
> our translation

Despite this solid assessment of the threat posed by fascism, the party leadership, with Bauer at its helm, continued to pursue a conciliatory pact with the Dollfuss government. As late as 1933, Bauer inaccurately assumed that the bourgeoisie would join forces with the working class in order to defend bourgeois democracy against fascisisation.

The defeat of the workers' uprising in February 1934, the dissolution of the Communist Party of Austria and SDAP, and the newly established corporative state in Austria were the central justifications as to why Bauer assumed a similar approach to the LSI left, which had been calling for a united front of Communists and Social Democrats against fascism since the Paris congress.[31] In the summer of 1935, Bauer, Jean Żyromski and Teodor Dan worked out the so-called war theses, which were published in the form of a pamphlet, *Die Internationale und der Krieg* (*The International and the War*). The text contained both short-term and long-term tasks for the LSI and working class in the struggle against fascism.[32] Furthermore, it contained an assessment of

---

30   'Heute haben wir sicher nicht die Zeit, nicht die Muße und nicht die Reife, zu diskutieren, auf welchem Weg sich der Sozialismus in der Welt durchsetzen wird. Heute stehen wir auf dem Parteitag vor der ungleich unmittelbareren und dringlicheren Aufgabe, zu erörtern, in welcher Weise wir uns der unmittelbar drohenden faschistischen Gefahr in Österreich erwehren können ... Dann in den Kampf gehen, aber mit der Erkenntnis, was dieser Kampf bedeutet. Dann muß man wissen ... dass es keine andere Entscheidung gibt, als zu siegen oder unterzugehen und für lange Zeit zu verschwinden' – Bauer 1976k, p. 701 and p. 723.

31   This position was advocated by the representative of the Italian Socialist Party, Petro Nenni, the members of the French Section of the Workers' International, Marceau Pivert and Jean Żyromski, and the delegate from the Belgian Workers' Party, Paul Spaak, among others.

32   Compare Löw 1980, p. 219.

the political situation and a prognosis as to how this situation would affect the international workers' movement. While in 1935 many Social Democrats had their doubts as to whether the course of history would flow as such, the manifesto's authors firmly believed war between Germany and the USSR was inevitable, and that Germany's potential victory in this conflict would be synonymous with the subjugation of the whole of Europe to the brutality of fascism. The manifesto insisted upon the following political efforts for the proletariat during the war: (1) the destruction of German fascism by an anti-Hitler coalition comprised of the allied nations and the Soviet Union; (2) support for the Soviet Union in its endeavour to defeat the capitalist social order; (3) taking advantage of the war in order to seize power and commence building socialism, particularly since transfiguring the war in Germany into a proletarian revolution would be a prerequisite for a successful revolution across Europe.[33] The manifesto's originators regarded the following as short-term tasks for the LSI: (1) support for capitalist governments in creating a system of collective security; (2) support for armament policies; (3) defending all countries threatened by Hitler's aggression while simultaneously warning the working class of their respective governments' imperialist policies; (4) urging neutral countries to place sanctions on Germany. Of particular interest for Bauer and his collaborators were the war doctrines of the Soviet Union. Considering a USSR victory as a factor that could revolutionise conditions in Western Europe, they incited the whole working class to stand in solidarity with the Soviet Union in case of German aggression. What is more, they appealed to anti-Bolshevik oppositional forces in Russia to join in defending the fatherland, while expecting the Soviet government to release the opposition in order to strengthen the country's anti-fascist potential. Without a doubt, Bauer was one of the key figures to inspire these demands. After all, he had idealised the process of building socialism in Russia for a long time.

Beside the nonsensical demand pointed out by Hanisch, it is impossible not to notice the three great illusions on which Bauer's theses were based. The three authors of the 1935 anti-war manifesto failed to recognise the connection between the war objectives of the Soviet Union and its imperialist ambitions, underestimated the enormous impact of the realities created by Nazism on the German working class, and therefore erroneously anticipated the outbreak of

---

33   Commenting on the latter of Bauer's aims, Hanisch writes: 'One must try to imagine this: in the midst of World War II, the "popular masses" are supposed to unleash a proletarian revolution in France and Britain against their own governments – i.e. start a civil war before defeating fascism. In light of the experience of World War II, a downright crazy idea' (our translation) – Hanisch 2011, p. 347.

proletarian revolution in Germany. Ultimately, they believed that the divide in the international workers' movement could be overcome despite existing differences. Their position was not met with approval within the LSI. Friedrich Adler, who was the LSI secretary at the time, rejected the war theses, as he did not consider the LSI ready for a unified statement on the imminent war. Léon Blum and the 'Neu Beginnen' group likewise criticised the theses. Bauer directly responded to this in his December 1935 article in *Der Kampf* and in the book *Zwischen zwei Weltkriegen*, where he outlined three distinct working-class attitudes towards war: (1) patriotism, which aims to keep the peace and involves the subordination of the proletariat to the government (Germany and Austria during World War I); (2) revolutionary deviationism, which aims to transform the war into a socialist revolution under any socio-political circumstances, even the defeat of one's country (the Zimmerwald left); and (3) defending the fatherland and attempting to use the masses' readiness for war in order to seize political power (the left wing of the LSI).[34] Bauer identified the following main reasons for war: in the foreground, the interests of American, British, French and Japanese imperialism in Africa, the Middle East, Far East and China; national conflict involving minorities that result for the new division of Europe after World War I to a secondary degree; and lastly, the economic crisis as the reason for the victory of fascism in Germany and Italy. Bauer was convinced that the capitalist countries' war objectives were directed firmly against the socialist countries – i.e. the Soviet Union and China – irrespective of any signed agreements, such as that between the Soviet Union and France. In addition, he believed that the coming war would be a conflict between two different socio-political systems. Therefore, he maintained that it would be necessary for the Social Democrats to co-operate with the Communists if war were declared, and called on the French, British and Russian proletariat to unite. However, due to mutual feelings of disregard, the LSI had no interest whatsoever in forming a united front with the Comintern. True, it passed a resolution upon Bauer's request (17 November 1935) that granted every affiliated party the right to co-operate with the Communists – but even so, co-operation did not materialise due to insurmountable mutual prejudice. Likewise, Bauer's attempts to entice the Social Democrats into supporting the popular front in Spain (February 1937) and allowing the Russian trade unions to affiliate to the International Trade Union Confederation remained fruitless. Disappointed with the stance of the LSI, Bauer accurately observed at the end of his life that the isolation of the Soviet Union significantly weakened the international proletariat in the

---

34 Compare Löw, p. 219.

struggle against fascism. We will address this question in more detail when discussing fascism in the following chapter. For now, let us conclude with a brief statement: concrete analyses, assessments or conclusions were not what made Bauer's stance on war valuable against the backdrop of European Social Democracy. The crucial element was his critical attitude toward the illusions of the international workers' movement: its misapprehension of the workers' organisations' willingness to engage in anti-war activities, and its misguided belief in the efficacy of their actions.

The Spectre of Fascism

1 Harbingers of Fascism

A critical assessment of Bauer's theory of fascism is only understandable in its historical and political context. It is important to remember that since the beginning of the First Republic, the fascist movement was split into two wings fighting each other with increasing vehemence: Austrofascism, also known as 'black' fascism, and National Socialism, also known as 'brown' fascism.[1]

From the mid-1920s onward, the two groups shared the following aims: exclusion of the Social-Democratic Party from the political stage, abolishment of the social gains of the working class, and replacement of the bourgeois democratic political order with a fascist dictatorship. Both movements had a similar social base – in 1929, it mainly consisted of the peasantry, the intelligentsia, declassed officers, and aristocratic landowners. As the economic crisis dawned, the impoverished petty bourgeoisie, industrial workers, the unemployed, and students joined the factions. Austrofascism and National Socialism were primarily divided over their respective attitudes towards the Catholic Church and their foreign policies. In the Heimwehr (Home Defence, a far right paramilitary organisation), which was led by imperial officers, clerical tendencies prevailed. The National Socialists, in contrast, adhered to the slogan, 'Away from Rome!', and pinned their hopes on Hitler's Germany.[2] The political and economic foundations of the two varieties of fascism also differed. In Austria, on the one side, it consisted of the Heimwehr, backed by the church, aristocratic landowners, and big capital. On the other, there were the bourgeois parties. Outside of this balance of forces were the National Socialists.

All historical sources confirm that the Austrian Nazi party, the so-called German National-Socialist Workers' Party (DNSAP), did not become a mass move-

---

1 Austrian authors, such as Gerhard Botz, Ernst Hanisch, Anton Pelinka, and Erich Zöllner, have extensively researched their inception and development. As such, we will not investigate this matter too intensely. However, we should note that most Austrian historians also differentiate between the two different varieties of fascism. Francis L. Carsten, meanwhile, offers an opposing view. Beside the National-Socialist movement, he argues, there were two different trends within the Heimwehr: German nationalist and authoritarian fascist. See Carsten 1982, p. 190.

2 Compare Braunthal 1967, p. 403.

ment or exert any significant influence upon political life before Hitler's annexation of Austria on 11 March 1938.[3] Notably, the National-Socialist movement in Austria was never strong enough to exist independently. Until 1926, it hid under the wings of the Greater German People's Party, and on 29 August 1926, it changed its name to National-Socialist German Workers' Party and was incorporated into the structures of its German sister party, Hitler's NSDAP. Hence, the word 'fascism' did not carry the same weight in Austria as it did in Germany. It stood for the Austrian clerical variety of fascism known as Austrofascism and the political power held by the Heimwehr and politicians from the Christian Social and Greater German camps allied to it – i.e. an authoritarian rule rather than the totalitarian rule in Germany.

How do we explain the success of this paramilitary organisation, and how did it manage to seize power? Bauer offered thorough explanations in his insightful analysis of fascism. Before any further discussion can take place, it is important to identify some key facts of Austrian political life from 1927–34 that are linked to his position as an author of the SDAP's political line.

When the bourgeois coalition government ruled from 1920–9, the Social Democrats were an important oppositional movement. After the July 1927 events, they were pushed onto the defensive. Members of the SDAP bureaucracy, who were so content with economic reforms and electoral successes that they failed to notice the party's weaknesses, were chiefly to blame for the ineffectiveness of Social-Democratic politics. The Schutzbund also lost touch with the masses and gradually turned into a bureaucratic organisation – a development that the leader of the workers' detachments, General Theodor Körner, had cautioned against.

In the autumn of 1927, all Heimwehr forces united into a single organisation. In 1927, Ignaz Seipel – whose foremost aim was to destroy the democratic republic and Social-Democratic movement in order to establish an authoritarian corporative state (*Ständestaat*) in its ruins – asked the Heimwehr for aid. On 16 July 1929, Seipel held a speech at Tubingen University, exposing the vulnerability of the state's parliamentary structures and glorifying the Heimwehr as defenders of the state against the power of political parties. From 1927–30, the number of Heimwehr members rose from 10,000 to 350,000. Most of

---

3   Braunthal concurs with this. According to him, there was no danger of Nazism flooding Austria in the early 1930s. Unlike the case in Germany, the National-Socialist movement had no hopes of broad support in Austria. The big capitalists sided with the Heimwehr in the struggle against brown fascism. The Catholic part of the petty bourgeoisie and the peasants, who were under the influence of the church and loyal to the Christian Social Party, were not very susceptible to National-Socialist slogans. Compare Braunthal 1967, p. 404.

them were peasants. However, members of different social classes and political parties were also among them – for instance, sections of the working class tied to the Christian Social Party, the Jewish bourgeoisie, radical anti-Semites, proponents and opponents of an annexation to Germany, and Christian Social and Greater German party members.[4] In the late 1920s, the Heimwehr became a political force and mass movement. When several unions joined – in 1929, for instance, 100,000 members of the Austrian Peasant Association and 250,000 members of the Austrian Trade Association – it founded its own Association of Independent Trade Unions.[5] Since the Social-Democratic Free Unions (SFG) recognised the fascist trade unions, its own ranks diminished rapidly as former members began to join the fascist unions *en masse* – until 1933, the number of its members declined by half.[6] From 1928–9, the ranks of the Heimwehr swelled, and it enjoyed military and financial support from Mussolini and Austrian finance capital. It staged marches and demonstrations largely in Tyrol and Styria, which claimed many casualties – e.g. 12 November 1928 in Innsbruck, 18 July 1929 in St. Lorenzen, and 20 August 1929 in Vösendorf. The leader of the Styrian section of the Heimwehr, W. Pfirmer, openly called for the destruction of parliamentary democracy and the creation of an 'anti-Marxist coalition'.[7] At the time, Bauer and Renner still underestimated the role and importance of the Heimwehr. At the 1929 party congress, Bauer denied that the Heimwehr was an independent political force, as he believed it to be a tool of the bourgeois parties. In the ranks of the SDAP, Leichter was the only one to take to the pages of *Der Kampf* to warn of the acute danger. He pointed out that the economic crisis was driving the workers and petty

---

4 See Wandruszka 1954, pp. 362–3.

5 See Schöpfer 1929, p. 1033.

6 From 1922–32, many members of the Social-Democratic party and Social-Democratic Free Unions joined the ranks of the fascist groups. The available data proves that this process was slower in parties that were more effective at spreading illusions about their own strength to the masses. Data cited from Leichter 1964, p. 31.

	SDAP members	SFG members
1922	553,000	1,080,000
1929	718,000	737,000
1930	698,000	655,000
1932	649,000	520,000

7 See Oberkofler 1979, p. 210.

bourgeoisie into the arms of the fascists, who intended to bring about their dictatorship at all costs.[8]

Seipel's 'strongman' politics led to another governmental crisis.[9] In Johann Schober's government (26 September 1919–25 September 1930), the personal and ideological influence of the Heimwehr was very weak as the new chancellor proved to be, against all expectations, a defender of the democratic foundations of the state. He did not consider the Heimwehr as having the potential to seize power. While the Heimwehr was very disappointed with his politics, the Social Democrats gained new hope. In 1929, they began to co-operate with Johann Schober's government on an amendment to the constitution that Ernst Streeruwitz's cabinet had initiated. The new draft was introduced to parliament on 18 October 1929. As Renner rightly pointed out, it was an attempt to reintroduce emergency laws against the socialists.[10] Bauer allowed himself to be duped, believing the law was to be a barrier against the fascisisation of the country. Naturally, the church and Christian Social Party had different hopes for the amendment entirely: they expected that it would strengthen the power of the Federal President and transform the Federal Assembly into an assembly representing the estates (*Stände*). The Heimwehr also supported the amendment, anticipating that it would increase the authority of the state and finally allow it to settle scores with Social Democracy.[11]

In 1930, the fascist programme ratified at the meeting in Korneuburg on 18 May 1930 was consolidated. Othmar Spann, a philosopher and professor at Vienna University, provided its philosophical formula, the 'oath of Korneuburg'. Its principles included the rejection of democracy as a threat to culture and the demand for a hierarchical power structure. The 'oath of Korneuburg' was an early warning for the planned abolition of parliamentarism, seizure of power, and creation of an authoritarian state modelled on the principles of Italian Fascism. The ambivalent attitude of the Christian Social Party toward Heimwehr activities at the time is worthy of attention. The right wing of the party supported the ideology expressed in the 'oath of Korneuburg', while

---

8   See Pelinka 1984, p. 56.

9   Seipel did not agree to an amnesty for the participants in the riots of 15 July 1927, which led to many Catholics leaving the church in protest. In 1927 alone, 21,857 Catholics abandoned the church, and in 1929, Seipel had to resign as chancellor. Compare Leichter 1964, p. 62.

10   Renner 1965, p. 301.

11   The new constitution strengthened the position of the federal president and gave the government the right to pass emergency decrees. On 15 March 1933, Dollfuss made use of this right, dissolving parliament and applying 'full war and industrial authorisation' dating back to 1917.

the more left-leaning leaders of Leopold Kunschak's Christian trade unions wanted to defend democracy.[12]

A brief digression before we assess the standpoint of the Christian Socials. In the early 1930s, the Heimwehr was a significant but not decisive state power. The Social Democrats made up the parliamentary majority, and the government formed by delegates of the Christian Socials, the Heimwehr, and the Landbund had only received one more vote. An alliance between the Christian Social and Social-Democratic parties to avert the threat of Austrofascism was theoretically possible. However, it is fair to say without engaging in speculations that co-operation between clerical and democratic forces was not a realistic proposition in Austria, not just on the basis of their programmatic and political differences. The increasing influence of the Heimwehr in the Christian Social Party was far more important. As evidenced by the rapprochement of the Christian Socials and Heimwehr after the elections of 9 September 1930, pro-fascist tendencies gradually prevailed in this party. One of the ministers of Karl Vaugoin's minority government, Ernst Rüdiger Starmhemberg, became the leader of the Heimwehr. This election – the last freely held general election of the First Republic – granted the Heimwehr a partial success: it only received eight seats in parliament.[13] Even so, this signified a shift of forces in the bourgeois camp. The Christian Social Party was losing its influence to the Heimwehr, while the SDAP, which had scored an electoral success, had ostensibly consolidated its power – after all, it had become the strongest party in parliament for the first time since 1919. However, the election victory blinded the SDAP to its own critical state. The ideology that held it together had lost strength. The divide between the party leadership and factions, trade unions, and groups of intellectuals was expanding. In light of the fascists' growing power, the masses'

---

12 In the Christian Social Party, the democratic current (represented by the chair of the Christian trade-union movement, Leopold Kunschak) faced anti-democratic traditions (Seipel, Vaugoin, Dollfuss). From 1900 onward, nationalist thinking prevailed. It emphasised the superiority of Germans in Austria and anti-Marxism. These aspects were also dominant in the Christian Social Party's programmes of 1923, 1926 and 1928. They were expressions of the German character of the party and the close relationship between Austria and the German Reich. See Berchtold 1967, in Documents, Programmes, Protocols, pp. 356–63; Lüer 1987; and Simon 1984b, p. 122.

13 In the elections, the Social Democrats won 72 mandates (41 percent of votes), the Christian Socials 66 mandates (36 percent), the Greater Germans and Landbund 19 mandates (12 percent), and the Heimwehr 8 mandates (6 percent). It was also characteristic that the Nazi party, having only received 100,000 votes (3 percent) did not manage to secure a parliamentary seat, while the National Socialists in Germany won 107 mandates (18.5 percent) in the elections of 14 September 1930. See Zöllner 1979.

willingness to accept the party leaders' purely defensive administration was
waning. On Bauer's recommendation, the SDAP remained in opposition despite its election victory.

Given the escalating economic crisis from 1931–2, Otto Ender's government
attempted to save the economic situation by agreeing on a tariff union with
Germany – yet this was never actualised due to resistance from France and the
Little Entente. As the Christian Social and Greater German coalition fell apart,
both the Heimwehr and NSDAP took advantage of the intensifying economic
and political crisis. Although a putsch attempt by the Styrian commander of the
Heimwehr, Walter Pfirmer, failed on 13 September 1931, the perpetrators were
not brought to justice. It was a sign that the balance of forces within the Heimwehr was changing: the conservative-legitimist trend prevailed over the nationalist, and its exponent, Emil Fey, was appointed vice chancellor of the government. In the regional elections on 24 April 1932, the National Socialists scored
their first electoral success, winning 336,000 votes (17.4 percent) at the expense
of the Christian Social Party. The Social Democrats still expected to win over
the working masses, petty bourgeoisie and unemployed, as they falsely believed
that impoverishment and hardship were revolutionising factors (Kautsky had
already warned against this during World War I).[14] In reality, unemployment
led to resignation and drove the affected into the arms of fascists of both factions. Nazi propaganda skilfully exploited this phenomenon by declaring Germany as the country where an economic miracle had occurred. If one considers
the methods that Bauer forced on the party at the time – remaining in opposition, constantly attacking Karl Buresch's government and demanding elections – then it is fair to wonder, as Leser does, how a party leadership actively
weakening the shaky foundations of the bourgeois state and unwilling to use
force against the fascists intended to save democracy.[15] Bauer only recognised
the fact that the Social Democrats' position had been a tactical error, caused
by the leaders' stubborn clinging to Austromarxist theory, in the wake of the
total defeat of democracy in 1934. Earlier, at the party congress in the autumn
of 1932, he finally became aware of the fascist peril, stating the following:

---

14   In his commentary on the election results of 24 April 1932, Bauer arrived at the wrong
        conclusion regarding the growing fascist trend. He believed the Social Democrats could
        win the petty-bourgeois masses that the crisis had put at risk for socialism. See Bauer
        1932, p. 192. As Leser points out in Leser 1968, p. 457, Bauer did not realise that the petty-
        bourgeois masses did not wish for socialist equality and a classless society, but – on
        the contrary – rescuing from being declassed. They wanted to preserve their position in
        society at the price of general inequality of classes.
15   Compare Leser 1968, p. 458.

The question today is not one of capitalism or socialism ... [R]ight now, we are facing a different question entirely. Surrounded by reactionary states – fascism in the south, south-east, east, and west – it is the big, but also glorious, task of the Austrian proletariat to preserve the country as an island of democratic freedom.[16]

our translation

This aspiration would soon die when Dollfuss introduced the corporative state on 1 May 1934 (as will be further explained in the fourth section). Austria was then subjected to changes that paved the way for Hitler's annexation, even if this was not done consciously or intentionally. In the year 1931, Schober and Curtius signed the draft for a tariffs union between Austria and Germany; however, as mentioned earlier, international political factors prevented this from being put into practice. Another step which helped create the conditions for the annexation was the agreement signed between the Greater German People's Party and the Austrian section of the NSDAP in 1933 – a rude awakening for left and right groups alike. In the autumn of that year, the leadership of the SDAP and SFG adopted a resolution on defending Austria against Nazism. For the same purpose, the Christian Social Party and Heimwehr jointly formed the Fatherland Front on 20 April 1933 (it became a legal party in 1934). Kunschak identified the growing significance of brown fascism and impending civil war. In a speech held at the Vienna local council on 9 February 1934, he appealed to the SDAP leaders to join forces to defend the country against National Socialism. Alas, his call fell on deaf ears.[17] The third and fourth sections of this chapter are dedicated to the consequences of the approaches of Bauer and the other SDAP leaders.

---

16 'Das Problem steht heute nicht zwischen Kapitalismus und Sozialismus; (...) sondern im Augenblick stehen wir hier vor einer ganz anderen Frage. Umzingelt von den reaktionären Staaten rings um uns, vom Faschismus im Süden, Südosten, im Osten und im Westen ist es die ungeheuer große, aber auch ungeheuer ruhmvolle Aufgabe des österreichischen Proletariats hier eine Insel demokratischer Freiheit zu erhalten' – SDAP 1932, p. 39, in Documents, Programmes, Protocols.

17 Shortly after, on 25 July 1934, Chancellor Dollfuss was killed during a failed Nazi putsch attempt. After his death, Schuschnigg's government arrested numerous Nazis, yet this was only an ostensible defeat for National Socialism. Nazi propaganda increased, Nazis employed in the police or judiciary joined the Fatherland Front, anti-Semitic members of the Christian Social Party still held Nazi sympathies, and members of the government and Heimwehr maintained their secret contacts to the Nazis. See Hindels 1981, p. 35.

2   Bauer's Theory of Fascism

European history bears the imprints of two varieties of fascism in particular: German National Socialism and Italian Fascism, which relevant literature refers to as classical fascism. Fascist movements with specifically national characteristics also emerged in other countries, such as Bulgaria, Romania, Portugal, Spain, France, Hungary and Austria. As Czubiński aptly observed, the fascist parties 'grew fastest in countries threatened by revolutionary upheaval, where the governing social forces were already too weak to preserve the old order and revolutionary forces were too weak to seize power and establish a new social order'.[18] There is no doubt that the weakness of the Social-Democratic parties was one of the factors that benefitted the fascists in their rise to power. In most cases, these parties downplayed the threat of fascism and did not devise any effective strategy for combating fascist reaction.

In the 1920s and 30s, enlightened scholars, publicists, and some politicians were conscious of the danger emanating from fascism and the power it held – in contrast to political parties, whether proletarian or bourgeois. The most serious interpretations of the phenomenon emerged from three circles: bourgeois intellectuals, Marxist thinkers, and fascists themselves. In general, they agreed on only two impressions: they deemed fascism to be a result of social changes in European society resulting from the war and its long-term consequences, such as the economic and moral crisis. Nobody had doubts about its anti-liberal, anti-democratic, anti-socialist, anti-pacifist and nationalist nature, nor was there any controversy as to its primary objectives: the destruction of democracy and the workers' movement. A wide range of answers and explanations was offered with respect to other questions: What social forces does fascism represent? Can one speak of fascism in a general sense, or must every strain of fascism be assessed separately as a local, national phenomenon? What social forces and mechanisms allowed fascism to seize power? What is fascism as a mass movement, and what is it as a system of government? How does fascist rule compare to other totalitarian and authoritarian regimes? It is not our intention to examine all of these queries in detail – Ernst Nolte and Renzo de Felice, as well as a number of Polish authors, have accomplished this thoroughly.[19] Because of

---

18   Czubiński 1985, p. 7.
19   See Nolte 1967; De Felice 1977; Czubiński1985; Filipiak 1985; and Zmierczak 1988. De Felice identifies three basic interpretations of fascism: (1) fascism as a moral disease taking hold of Europe (an expression of moral values being thrown into crisis), thus understood by Croces, Meinecke, Ritter, and Mann; (2) fascism as a logical and inevitable consequence of the historical development of some countries, thus understood by Vermeil,

the special place occupied by Bauer's analysis in the Marxist bloc, however, we cannot refrain from outlining the differences between Communist and Social-Democratic views of fascism. Within the framework of our observations, these differences are merely comparative rather than constitutive – the reader will therefore find a brief explanation in the footnote.[20]

McGovern and Viereck; (3) fascism as a product of capitalist society and anti-proletarian reaction, thus understood by authors from Comintern circles, e.g. Thalheimer, Labriola, Dobb, Baran, Löwenthal, Sweezy, and at the time Bauer. Compare De Felice 1977, pp. 37–82.

20 Two brief remarks before we cite the main Communist and Social-Democratic assessments of fascism in the 1920s and 30s. Firstly, this is a very rough outline that only serves to demonstrate the essential characteristics of both interpretations. More thorough and complex readings of fascism can be found in both camps. Secondly, the scientific value of these interpretations is of no interest to us in this context. In their analyses of fascism, the Communists – Dimitrov, Radek, Koszucka, Zetkin, Zinoviev, and others – looked mainly at two social classes: the bourgeoisie and the proletariat. When they did mention the petty bourgeoisie, it was of lesser significance. In the 1920s, they regarded fascism as a counter-revolutionary threat, a method of the bourgeoisie to defend itself against the revolutionary danger emanating from the proletariat. Their position only marginally changed in the course of the 1930s. When identifying the social carriers of fascism, they no longer spoke of the bourgeoisie as a whole, but specifically singled out the finance oligarchy, believing that the destruction of the workers' movement was merely its short-term objective – in the long-term, it was planning another imperialist war and a new division of the world. Dimitrov's definition of fascism, as formulated at the 13th enlarged plenum of the executive committee of the Comintern and reiterated at the eighth congress in Moscow in August 1935, would be pivotal for the Communists for years to come. According to this definition, which persisted even after World War II, fascism was the 'open terrorist dictatorship of the most reactionary, most chauvinistic and most imperialist elements of finance capital' – see Dimitrov 1935. The Communists did not shy away from accusing the Social Democrats of periphrastically assisting fascism or even directly collaborating with it. Until 1935, they bandied the phrase 'social fascism' based on the 'theory of fascism' coined in 1928, against the Social Democrats. It nipped in the bud any attempts to build a united anti-fascist front. In their attacks against parliamentarism and bourgeois democracy, the Communists even went so far as to equate democracy with fascist dictatorship. *Dokumenty z historii III Międzynarodówki komunistycznej*, in Documents, Programmes, Protocols, pp. 275–465; compare Sobolev et al. 1971.

The Social Democrats' attitude towards fascism in that period was more complex than the Communist position because many different interpretations coexisted within Social Democracy. See e.g. Deutsch 1926; Hilferding 1932; Breitscheid 1977; Rosenberg 1934; Bauer 1976p and 1939. It is, however, possible to outline the basic premises of the Social-Democratic interpretations. Unlike the Communists, the Social Democrats regarded the petty bourgeoisie and declassed members of all social layers and classes as the social

In the socialist camp, the Austromarxists Deutsch, Renner, Ellenbogen, Leichter, Max Adler and Bauer decisively contributed to investigating the fascist anomaly. For the sake of precision, we hasten to clarify that they only began to excel in this area in the 1930s, as before that time, the Austrians failed to recognise the fascist threat for what it was. According to Botz, two beliefs that were widespread in the Austrian Social-Democratic movement further hampered their analysis. Many Social Democrats dismissed the fascist movements as armed gang activities, painting the perpetrators as thugs who served the capitalists as foot soldiers against the working class; others believed that the government had voluntarily handed power to the fascists.[21] The 1920s literature of Deutsch and Braunthal, in addition to Renner's postwar writings, served to reinforce this perspective.[22]

Bauer's dissertations from the 1920s contained more profound theses on the rise of fascism than most Austrian socialist texts. However, one can only speak of mature theories of fascism with respect to his 1930s writings. In a complex and meticulous manner, *Zwischen zwei Weltkriegen* (*Between Two World Wars*, 1936) and *Die illegale Partei* (*The Illegal Party*, posthumously published in 1939) depict fascism's genesis, social base, and mechanisms of seizing power, as well as investigating the social forces which facilitated a fascist dictatorship in Italy. What is more, the author differentiated between fascism as a mass movement and fascism as a form of rule. Bauer interpreted fascism as a product of economic crisis and the consequences of war in Europe. Even so, he did not go so far as to consider it a historical necessity or inevitable developmental tendency in all capitalist countries.[23] For him, the primary reasons why fascism proved

---

basis of fascism. They traced the mechanisms by which fascism seized power with greater attention to detail than the Communists, foregrounding the thesis – shared by the Communists – that the bourgeoisie handed power to the fascists to defend the existing social order in case the proletariat underwent radicalisation. Some socialists considered fascism a tool used by big capital and aristocratic landowners to put pressure on the working class. At the same time, Bauer's theory that fascism in power had become autonomous of both bourgeoisie and proletariat was very popular among Social Democrats. Note that this thesis was sharply criticised by the Communists. In addition, even though the tone of Bauer, Breitscheid, Deutsch, Hilferding, de Mans, Löwenthal, Tasca, Turati, and Rosenberg was not as harsh as the polemics offered by the Communists, they still denounced the Communists for supporting the Bolshevik model of rule, arguing that the bourgeoisie had resorted to fascism because it feared that Bolshevism might spread to the West.

21   Compare Botz 1980, p. 178.

22   See Deutsch 1926; Braunthal 1922; Renner 1932, pp. 89–90; Renner 1953, p. 78.

23   He claimed, for instance, that there could be no talk of fascism in Poland, Bulgaria and

immensely popular – particularly in Italy and Germany – were political rather than economic: the Italians were disgruntled by the fact that British, French and American capitalism had deprived the country of its war loot. The Germans were bitter over the lost war and unjust Treaty of Versailles, and the parliamentary democratic system in both countries was immature and fragile. Bauer also thought that the self-inflicted defeat of the German revolution and splitting of the workers' movement had paved the way for fascism. A particularly important aspect of his understanding was that he thought of fascism as a supranational phenomenon, even if the rhetoric contained in his texts provoked a lot of misunderstanding.[24] He qualified his assessment by linking it to historical reality and the national varieties of fascism, especially Austromarxism. Rather than being a scholarly construct, Bauer's comprehensions of fascism were that of an active politician.[25] They were deeply rooted in the experience of the international, but especially the German, workers' movement, and were intended as a weapon in the anti-fascist struggle. It would be a mistake to look at them as a coherent whole, considering that they evolved along with the European political situation and the workers' movement itself. According to Pelinka, Bauer's interpretations contain three different – if overlapping – theories of fascism reflecting three periods in the European and Austrian workers' movement:[26]

Yugoslavia. According to him, the governments that had emerged in these countries were merely counter-revolutionary, lacking elements that were crucial for the development of fascism, such as a mass basis and a petty-bourgeois ideology. See Bauer 1976p, p. 136.

24   Bauer frequently used the term 'fascism' without specifying whether he meant German or Italian fascism.

25   This resulted in contradictions between the three theories. Hanisch demonstrated this in Hanisch 1974.

26   Pelinka depicts the three phases of Bauer's theory of fascism as corresponding to three chapters in the history of Austrian Social Democracy. Compare Pelinka 1985, p. 26. In contrast, Botz identifies six distinct theories of fascism in Bauer's writings – a view I do not share: (1) an early theory based on Bonapartism (1923); (2) a simplified theory of Bonapartism; (3) the fascism theory of the Linz programme (1926); (4) the assessment of Austrofascism; (5) an expanded theory of Bonapartism (1936); and (6) fascism theory as a theory of imperialism. See Botz 1985, p. 161. In my view, the 'three theories' model is more accurate on two counts. First, because in the 1920s, the Bonapartism model only served Bauer as an aid to explain the victory of fascism; later, it remained an integral component of his theory, which he consistently developed until 1936. Second, one can hardly call the references to the social basis of fascism and strategy of 'defensive violence' in the Linz programme, which was drafted by Bauer, a theory.

1. A theory of fascism drawing on the notion of Bonapartism in light of the situation in Europe after the victory of fascist regimes and concurrent defeat of Social Democracy (1924–36);
2. A theory of Austrofascism that settled scores with the corporative state (*Ständestaat*) and Dollfuss's and Schuschnigg's authoritarian governments from the point of view of Social Democracy (1934–8);
3. A theory of fascism drawing on imperialism theory and linked to the socialist movement's anti-fascist struggle in the face of looming war (1939).

Two pressing questions emerge. Firstly, do these theories contain elements that link them together – and if so, what are they? Secondly, how do they differ from each other? We shall precede further analysis with a brief statement: only Bauer's insights into the ideology and social base of fascism remained consistent in his three aforementioned theories, especially in the first and second. They differed in the most important aspects when explaining the phenomenon of fascism. In the first and second theories, sociological, political, and historical components prevailed. In the third, the emphasis shifted to economics.

2.1   Fascism Theory Based on the Notion of Bonapartism

The theory put forward in the chapter, 'Fascism', in *Between Two World Wars* – which went on to become Bauer's best-known text on fascism when published separately – was his first attempt at a thorough explanation of fascism. Elements of this were already present in the author's earlier essay, *Gleichgewicht der Klassenkräfte* (*Balance of Class Forces*), and in the Linz programme of 1926. In 'Fascism', he outlined the processes that provided fertile ground for fascism, the character of its ideology, its social base, and its social and political consequences. However, the two most fundamental aspects were: firstly, his investigation of the social forces and mechanisms that allowed fascism to usurp power from the republicans; secondly, the question as to how fascism as a mass movement differs from fascism in power, and the differences between the dominant and the ruling class within this system. We will refer to this theory as the theory of Bonapartism because it was based on the sociological scheme from Marx's *The Eighteenth Brumaire of Louis Bonaparte* (1852).[27]

Bauer clearly differentiated between the fascist movement and fascist rule. The integral element in his analysis of fascism's genesis was his identification of the sociological factors that allowed fascism to merge divergent social interests

---

27   Botz also used this term in the aforementioned articles.

into one apparently unified force. In *Between Two World Wars*, he demonstrated that the birth of fascism was the result of a synthesis of three different, yet coherent, social processes:

1. The creation of fascist militias from declassed former war combatants. In the main, they were members of the intelligentsia and officers. The war had torn them away from their quiet lives, confined them to the margins of civil society, and imbued them with a militaristic and anti-democratic ideology. Hoping that they would regain the posts and social prestige they held during the war, they came out in favour of militaristic nationalism.
2. The pauperisation of a majority of the petty bourgeoisie and peasantry due to the economic crisis. From these layers, disenchanted with the government and bourgeois democratic parties, emerged a nationalist, petty-bourgeois ideology. They were the social basis of fascism as a mass movement, yet the movement could only grow with support from the capitalist class.
3. Factual constraints: the economic crisis affected the capitalists' profits, which could only grow through increased exploitation. Hence, the capitalists saw themselves as forced to seek fascist assistance against the working class. In order to increase exploitation to satisfying levels, parliamentary democracy would have to be destroyed and the trade unions and workers' organisations dissolved.[28]

For Bauer, these processes led to the emergence of an eclectic fascist ideology rooted in German Romanticism, the writings of Vilfredo Pareto and George Sorel, and race theorists. It denied its class character and presented itself as speaking for the entire nation. It made its supporters believe that they were participating in a general revolution that would meet whatever hopes and expectations the respective social groups attached to it. It was militaristic (based on discipline and the cult of the *Führer*), nationalist (glorifying one's own nation and race), anti-democratic (breaking with the sovereignty of the people and formal democracy), but especially anti-bourgeois (opposed to bourgeois and civic values, and the bourgeois way of life in terms of freedom, individualism and pluralism). Bauer rightly accentuated two characteristics of this ideology: its ability to assume a national colouration (in Germany, it merged with racism and anti-Semitism, in Austria with clericalism, and in Italy with anti-rationalism), and its hostility towards the proletariat and monopoly capital,

---

28 A similar understanding can be found in a text by the Italian Social Democrat Filippo Turati, *Fascismo, Socialismo, Democrazia* (1928). Compare De Felize 1977, p. 197.

which reflected the social and political condition of the middle classes. It directed its attacks particularly against the workers. Because of their class solidarity and organisation, Bauer argued, workers were better equipped to defend themselves against the effects of economic crisis than the petty bourgeoisie. Its psychological basis was the middle classes' fear of being declassed and proletarianised. According to Bauer, the fascist ideology prevailed in countries with a weak parliamentary tradition, an unstable capitalist economy, and a social structure subject to unexpected fluctuations in the wake of war and revolution.

The ideology of fascism was by no means the principle focus of Bauer's writings. He was far more interested in the attitudes of different social groups and classes towards fascism – and, to be precise, the question of which social forces fascism relied on to gain momentum prior to assuming power. Bauer pointed out that the big capitalists and aristocrats felt nothing but contempt for Hitler and rejected the fascist ideology and movement. Nor did the bourgeoisie convert to National Socialism. Initially, it did not even consider that the movement might seize power; rather, it viewed it as a useful tool to break the resistance of the working class against its own deflationary politics and attacks on social and political legislation, as well as curb the influence of the workers' organisations and trade unions. The bourgeoisie naively imagined that it could effortlessly exclude fascism from the political stage once it had engaged with it in order to stabilise bourgeois political and economic rule. However, it turned out to be the other way round, as the 'third force' held the bourgeoisie captive instead. Analysing the social consistency of the fascist movements, Bauer concluded that fascism, while winning support in all social groups, derived its specific strength and development from the middle classes, i.e. the petty bourgeoisie, artisans, intelligentsia, youth and bankrupted peasants. Contemporary research confirms this.[29]

In an article entitled 'Der 24. April 1932', Bauer wrote after the 1932 elections that the cause of fascism was a rebellion of the petty bourgeoisie, yet he did

---

29   Research conducted by Bendix proves that in 1921, 61.6 percent of the members of the fascist party came from the middle classes. In Germany in 1933, members of the middle classes also prevailed in Hitler's party. See Bendix 1966, pp. 596–609. The relationship between fascism and the middle classes is one of the key questions in sociological and historical literature on fascism. The following authors focused on the role of the middle class: Harold Lasswell, David Joseph Saposs, Sven Ronulf, Talcott Parsons, Nathaniel Preston, Seymour Martin Lipset, and Luigi Salvatorelli. Compare De Felice 1977, p. 129. Compare also Saage's depiction of the relationship between Nazism and the middle classes in Saage 1977, chapters 5 and 6.

not go so far as to credit the middle class as an independent political force. Rather, he thought of it as a mere instrument in the hands of the fascists and *de facto* big capital. The elite of the fascist party hailed from the grande bourgeoisie and landowners, whose interests opposed those of the middle classes. Bauer was right in asserting that the fascist dictatorship emancipated itself from the fascist movement the moment it seized power, which occurred at the expense of the ambitions of the middle classes. His other conclusion was no less accurate: Social Democracy in power had disappointed the hopes of many, and during the period prior to fascism taking full control, it was unable to use the discontent and revolutionary potential of the middle classes to reinvigorate itself. The programmes of the workers' parties had insufficiently taken into account the interests of the middle classes – the SDAP programmes of the 1920s came too late in this respect. Because of this misstep, the left-leaning sections of these classes deserted in favour of fascism.

The main issue that preoccupied Bauer in his works on fascism from 1924–36 was the mechanism by which fascism could obtain dominance. In order to discern it, he had to address a couple of questions. First, in what way did the rebellion of the middle classes lead to the introduction of fascist dictatorships? Second, which social forces *de facto* allowed the fascist movements to assume power and consolidate their rule? Bauer was not the only one to make use of Marx's theory of Bonapartism as a blueprint to answer these questions.[30] August Thalheimer, then a member of the Communist Party of Germany (Opposition), and Leon Trotsky employed much the same mode of explanation, and even non-Marxist theorists such as Ernst Fraenkel, Franz Neumann, Friedrich Pollock, Alfred Sohn-Rethel, Timothy Mason and Gert Schäfer referred to Marx's theory of Bonapartism in their work on fascism. This theory provoked numerous controversies amongst socialists and did not find the approval of Social-Democratic parties.[31]

---

30   In *The Eighteenth Brumaire of Louis Bonaparte*, Marx analysed the historical sources and social content of Bonapartism. For him, the historically conditioned class constellation of French society provided the prerequisites for Bonaparte's coup. The most valuable achievement of Marx's analysis was not so much that he identified the actual social basis (the peasantry whose land had been divided into parcels) and class content of Bonapartism (the economic power of the finance oligarchy), but his emphasis on the socio-political balance of forces that gave rise to Bonapartism: a bourgeoisie that aimed to protect its economic interests and a proletariat that was unable to gain, let alone maintain, power in the state in light of the crisis. See Marx 1852.

31   The critical reader should not fail to notice that Bauer's and Thalheimer's analyses – and, to a lesser extent, Trotsky's – rather mechanically applied Marx's conclusions to

The basic premise of Bauer's interpretation of fascism as Bonapartism, even during the year of 1924, was as follows: fascism was not a form of rule by the propertied classes that one could explain through the imperialist developmental stage of capitalism. Rather, an analogy could be drawn between fascism's seizure of power in both Italy and Germany and Louis-Napoleon Bonaparte's coup of 1851, to which all social classes subordinated themselves due to the balance of class forces at the time. According to Bauer, the comparable conditions between Germany and Italy resulted from economic crisis. In these countries, a relative equilibrium of class forces had emerged that was politically and socially specific, i.e. based on the weakness of both main classes in capitalist society – the bourgeoisie and proletariat.[32] On one side, the crisis-shaken bourgeois class had lost the support of the middle classes, who felt disenchanted with bourgeois democracy. Hence, it was also too frail to subordinate the working class and rule the state by democratic means. It was, however, strong enough to arm fascist militias as their auxiliary troops. On the other side, there was the working class, which was still too weak to initiate the socialist revolution and seize power. Because of their weakness, both classes were unable to act independently, which created fertile ground for a fascist victory. In the meantime, fascism matured and, unlike the old classes, was able to maintain the balance of class forces. The only prerequisite for its assumption of rule in the state was the seizure of executive power and enforcement of a dictatorship over all classes.

In 1924, Bauer explained the complex relationship between the bourgeoisie and fascism by additionally differentiating between the political and economic power of the bourgeois class. At the time, he still held the simplistic idea that the bourgeoisie had voluntarily handed power to the fascists in order to defend

---

fascism; Marx would have most certainly disapproved of this methodology. The positive side was their effort to explain fascism in relation to the social and political structure of capitalist society at the time and identify their contradictions. However, their attempt at applying an analysis based on free market-era capitalism to capitalism in its imperialist stage, as well as scarce consideration of the relationship between economic and political power, inevitably led to astonishing, one-sided speculation. See Thalheimer 1930; Trotsky 1971.

32   Note that Bauer considered the balance of class forces to be a normal state in bourgeois society – see also Saage 1977, p. 128. In addition, maintaining the balance of class forces based on the strength of the bourgeoisie and working class was, according to Bauer's theory of a 'state of balance of class forces', a precondition for the further development of capitalism as a political and economic system, as well as a precondition for reformist socialism.

its interests and economic position in the face of the radicalisation of the workers' movement. In his book, *Gleichgewicht der Klassenkräfte* (*The Balance of Class Forces*), he wrote:

> The Italian Fascism of 1922 is the equivalent of the French Bonapartism of 1851. In both cases, an adventurer backed by gangs of armed adventurers managed to disperse the bourgeois parliament and thus overthrow the political rule of the bourgeoisie and erect his own dictatorship over all classes. This occurred as the bourgeoisie abandoned its own political representatives and threw itself into the arms of the force that rebelled again its own state power. In exchange for its political rule, it saved its property against the proletarian threat.[33]
>
> our translation

Bauer was evidently incorrect. At no point was fascism a reaction to the victories of the working class; after all, the working class had already been driven onto the defensive by the bourgeoisie in the early 1920s. In fact, the opposite was the case: the shortcomings of the workers' movement, the hollowness of its words, and the sluggishness of its leaders drove the petty bourgeois and workers into the arms of the fascists, allowing them to build a social base for their success.[34] This was not the only deficiency in Bauer's analysis. In the aforementioned text, the author recognised that fascist Bonapartism was a specific form of counter-revolution rather than a dictatorship of the bourgeoisie. Yet Bauer did not take into account the role of fascist mass organisations and conflicts between the petty bourgeoisie and big bourgeoisie.[35] It is important to remember that he disregarded the threat of fascism during that period, and it was in this spirit that he made his statements at the 1927 congress of the SDAP.[36] His nonchalance might be ascribed to the belief

---

33   'Der italienische Faschismus von 1922 ist das Gegenstück des französischen Bonapartismus von 1851. In beiden Fällen hat ein Abenteurer, auf Banden bewaffneter Abenteurer gestützt, das bürgerliche Parlament auseinanderjagen damit die politische Herrschaft das Bourgeoisie stürzen und seine Diktatur über alle Klassen aufrichten können, weil die Bourgeoisie selbst ihre politische Vertretung im Stich ließ, ihre eigene Klassenherrschaft preisgab, sich der gegen ihre eigene Staatsmacht rebellierenden Gewalt in die Arme warf um, gegen Preisgabe ihrer politischen Herrschaft ihr vom Proletariat bedrohtes Eigentum zu retten' – see Bauer 1980o, p. 66.

34   Compare Heimann 1985, p. 136.

35   See Pelinka 1985, p. 60.

36   At the time, he stated: 'one should not try to scare us with the Italian example ... The

that it would suffice for the workers to refrain from any defensive activities in order to restore social peace, as well as an underestimation of the influence of fascist ideology upon the petty-bourgeois masses and peasantry. It is not hard to agree with Kösten, who claims that Bauer's approach to fascism, based as it was on the blueprint of Bonapartism, was not a strategy to mobilise the working class against fascism, but rather a pious hope to strengthen democratic bourgeois forces as a counterweight to fascisisation.[37] It is also difficult to rationally explain how Bauer could overlook the growing influence of the Heimwehr in the Christian Social and Greater German parties. There is simply no logical explanation for why Bauer demanded in 1929 that the Schutzbund be disarmed, in the hope that this would avert the threat of fascism.

It was not until Hitler's victory in Germany and the defeat of his own party in 1934 that Bauer revised his assessments from the late 1920s and early 1930s, developing and heightening his analyses. In 1936, he returned to his earlier theory of fascism as Bonapartism and its basic premise of a balance of class forces. He modified his standpoint in three respects: the position and role of the working class, the social and class content of fascism, and the separation between power apparatus and ruling class under fascism.

Bauer abandoned the idea that fascism was a defensive reaction of the bourgeoisie to the system's readiness for social revolution. He conceded that it amassed power at a time when the working class was powerless. In contrast, he interpreted fascism's successes and its support from the bourgeoisie as a result of the crisis of bourgeois hegemony, which coincided with the crisis of the workers' movement. Bauer's tense relationship to reformism is an interesting aspect in this. On the one hand, he accused reformism of impotence. It had proved incapable of protecting the working and middle classes from the effects of economic crisis. On the other, he gave too much weight to the bourgeoisie's struggle against the gains of reformist socialism in attempting to explain the fascist victory. For Bauer, fascism superseded the old order because the bourgeoisie sought the help of illegal fascist squads to protect its profits dur-

---

Austrian working class, which is a far greater part of our population and far more geographically concentrated than is the case in Italy, would put up much stronger resistance. In general, dictatorships – both fascist and Bolshevik – have only emerged in the agrarian states of east and south Europe. In the industrial countries, democracy has always prevailed' – Protocol of the Social-Democratic congress 1927, in Documents, Programmes, Protocols, p. 120.

37   See Kösten 1984, p. 152.

ing economic upheaval – it could not suppress reformist socialism by means of
state coercion, as it was too weak and hindered by democratic institutions.[38]

---

38   Bauer wrote: 'The fascist dictatorship thus emerges as the result of a peculiar balance
      of class forces. On one side stands a bourgeoisie that is the master of the means of pro-
      duction and circulation and executive state power. However, the economic crisis has des-
      troyed the profits of this bourgeoisie. The democratic institutions prevent the bourgeoisie
      from imposing its will upon the proletariat to a degree the bourgeoisie deems necessary
      to restore its profits. This bourgeoisie is too weak to continue enforcing its will by the
      same ideological means it employs to rule the masses in bourgeois democracy. The demo-
      cratic legal order restricts it, and it is too weak to crush the proletariat by legal means.
      However, it is strong enough to bankroll a lawless, unconstitutional private army, equip
      it with arms, and unleash it upon the working class. Reformism and trade unions have
      become stronger than the bourgeoisie can tolerate. Resistance against it raising the degree
      of exploitation stands in the way of deflation. It can no longer be broken other than by
      force. Yet even though reformist socialism is being attacked because of its strength and
      the greatness of its successes, it is at the same time too weak to defend itself against the
      violence. Because it operates within the framework of the existing bourgeois democratic
      system, holding on to it as its battleground and source of strength, it appears like a "party
      of the system" to the broad, petty-bourgeois, peasant and proletarian masses – a parti-
      cipant and beneficiary of the same democracy that is incapable of protecting them from
      pauperisation by economic crisis. It is therefore not able to draw in the masses that the
      crisis radicalises. They flock towards its mortal enemy, fascism. The result of this bal-
      ance of forces – or rather, weakness of both classes – is the victory of fascism, which
      crushes the working class in the service of the capitalists. However, while paid by the
      capitalists it gets so out of hand that the capitalists end up helping it to seize unlim-
      ited power over the whole people, including themselves' (our translation). Original: 'Die
      faschistische Diktatur entsteht so als das Resultat eines eigenartigen Gleichgewichtes der
      Klassenkräfte. Auf der einen Seite steht eine Bourgeoisie, die Herrin der Produktions- und
      der Zirkulationsmittel und der Staatsgewalt ist. Aber die Wirtschaftskrise hat die Profite
      dieser Bourgeoisie vernichtet. Die demokratischen Institutionen hindern die Bourgeoisie
      ihren Willen dem Proletariat in dem Ausmaß aufzuzwingen, das ihr zur Wiederherstel-
      lung ihrer Profite notwendig erscheint. Diese Bourgeoisie ist zu schwach um ihren Willen
      noch mit jenen geistigen ideologischen Mitteln durchzusetzen, durch die sie in der bürger-
      lichen Demokratie die Wählermassen beherrscht. Sie ist, durch die demokratische Recht-
      sordnung beengt, zu schwach, um das Proletariat mit gesetzlichen Mitteln, mittels ihres
      gesetzlichen Staatsapparates niederzuwerfen. Aber sie ist stark genug, eine gesetzlose,
      gesetzwidrige Privatarmee zu besolden, auszurüsten und auf die Arbeiterklasse loszu-
      lassen. Auf der anderen Seite steht eine von dem reformistischen Sozialismus und von den
      Gewerkschaften geführte Arbeiterklasse. Reformismus und Gewerkschaften sind stärker
      geworden, als es die Bourgeoisie erträgt. Ihr Widerstand gegen die Hebung des Grades
      der Ausbeutung steht der Deflation im Wege. Er kann nicht mehr anders, als durch Gewalt
      gebrochen werden. Aber wird der reformistische Sozialismus gerade um seiner Stärke wil-

Thus, fascism was granted support as a 'gift' from bourgeois hands, and, once it held power, it did not intend on relinquishing it. Thereafter, fascism took specific measures. Firstly, it turned against the social base thanks to which it had grown and which it no longer required – i.e. the middle classes, whose resistance it now brutally suppressed. Secondly, it proceeded to destroy the parity of classes that had allowed fascism to be elevated to power, and which had been one of the main reasons for the republic's defencelessness.[39] The victim of this attack was the entire existing apparatus of parties and political institutions of parliamentary democracy – that is to say, fascism had not lost sight of its main objective, namely dictatorship. Bauer understood the transition to fascist dictatorship as a process in which state power became gradually autonomous of class relations under conditions of crisis and took on a life of its own. He was the first to establish the thesis, based on the model of Bonapartism and later repeated by Thalheimer, of the fascist state apparatus as a construct standing above all classes.

It is possible to query, as Bauer did, whether the transformation of the bourgeois democratic political order into the fascist order meant essential changes to the hitherto existing capitalist system. Without a doubt, this was the case, the most fundamental modification being the shift of class power. As long as the power of the capitalists is maintained, bourgeois democracy facilitates peaceful solutions to social conflicts. Its limitations result from the temporary nature of the class balance. It cannot be turned into the unlimited power of one particular class because the interests of voters, represented by political mass parties, have to be taken into account. Fascism's liquidation of parliamentary democracy drained power from most of the bourgeoisie and remaining classes,

---

len, um der Größe seiner Erfolge willen, um der Kraft seines Widerstandes willen gewaltsam angegriffen, so ist er andererseits zu schwach, sich der Gewalt zu erwerben. Auf dem Boden der bestehenden bürgerlichen Demokratie wirkend, an der Demokratie als seinen Kampfboden und seiner Kraftquelle festhaltend, scheint er breiten, kleinbürgerlichen, bäuerlichen, proletarischen Massen eine "Systempartei", ein Teilhaber und Nutznießer jener bürgerlichen Demokratie, die sie vor der Verelendung durch die Wirtschaftskrise nicht zu schützen vermag. Er vermag daher die durch die Krise revolutionierten Massen nicht an sich zu ziehen. Sie strömen seinem Todfeind, dem Faschismus zu. Das Resultat dieses Gleichgewichtes der Kräfte oder vielmehr der Schwäche beider Klassen ist der Sieg des Faschismus, der die Arbeiterklasse im Dienste der Kapitalisten niederwirft, aber im Solde der Kapitalisten diesen so über den Kopf wächst, dass sie ihn schließlich zum unbeschränkten Herren über das ganze Volk und damit auch über sich selbst machen müssen' – Bauer 1976p, pp. 148–9.

39   Not unlike Thalheimer and Trotsky, Bauer linked the shift in the balance of forces to the emergence of the NSDAP as a mass party.

instead granting unlimited power to big capital and big landowners.[40] Hence, fascism transferred its social basis from the middle classes to monopoly capital.[41] Bauer explained this state of affairs through the fascist dictatorship's dependency on big capital, which continued to hold economic power in the fascist state and thus maintained its influence upon political decisions. In other words, the fascist state left property relations untouched – class power always remained in the hands of the capitalists, even if their personnel changed. Bauer concluded that fascism was a totalitarian dictatorship of the pro-war sections of the big bourgeoisie and big landowners. Its establishment completed the process of bourgeois counter-revolution, which had begun in 1920. The victory of fascism was evidence of the importance of the middle classes in the class struggle between big capital and the working class.

Another fundamental component of Bauer's 1936 analysis of fascism deserves mention – namely its understanding of fascist rule as a division between the economic rule of big capital and the political rule of the fascist bureaucratic caste, which consisted of declassed elements of all classes.[42] According to Bauer, this division had far-reaching consequences both for fascism itself and for the potential direction in which the history of Europe would evolve. Conflicts of interest between the ruling and the dominant class are inevitable in a fascist regime – the 'command economy' developed by fascism forces the fascist bureaucracy to make decisions that contradict the interests of the respective groups of capitalists. It thus becomes an opponent of these groups and reinforces state power over all social classes. On the other hand, pro-war fractions of big monopoly capital gain the upper hand under fascism and build the armaments industry at the expense of other branches of the economy. Militarism and expansionism, according to Bauer, inevitably culminate in war.

This analysis is neither entirely accurate nor convincing. Of course, one might agree with Botz that the analogy between fascism and Bonapartism is a stage in Bauer's analyses of fascism – if only because *Between Two World Wars*, of which 'Fascism' was but a fragment, contained a series of statements on the imperialist roots of fascism.[43] If one, however, treats 'Fascism' as an autonomous text, it becomes truly questionable. From a historical standpoint,

---

40   The SPD leadership upheld the belief that fascism serves the interests of big capital from
       1934 onward. Compare Zmierczak 1988, p. 88.

41   Botz argues that Bauer's differentiation between the role of big capital and that of the
       petty bourgeoisie in the fascist movement served a political purpose, namely to extend
       the influence of Social Democracy to the middle classes. See Botz 1980, p. 171.

42   See also Tasca 2010; compare Bloch 1972, p. 189.

43   Compare Botz 1980, p. 174.

fascism was not a result of the balance of class forces in either Italy or Germany, as by 1920 the working class in both countries was already too weak to be able to resist a bourgeois counter-revolution. After 1920, the bourgeoisie had no reason to fear a revolution – even Bauer conceded this in 1936. Nor is it possible to explain the fascist offensive simply by citing the economic crisis, given that fascism in both countries only seized power when the effects of the crisis had waned. To this day, many different theories are offered as to why fascism managed to captivate millions of people and prevail. It is certainly not a terrible mistake to assume that fascism was the result of a cacophony of economic, political and social factors, of which economic crises, the crisis of bourgeois values and bourgeois culture, and the crisis of the parliamentary democratic system were decisive.

2.2   Austrofascism as a Special Sub-Variety of Fascism

In the early 1930s, Austria's Marxist organisations did not initially pay any great attention to the fascisisation of its own country. One can put this down to objective political and ideological conditions: for the broad masses, the polar-isation between the two fascist currents was barely recognisable, and the inter-ference of the Heimwehr in the state apparatus increased gradually. The lack of interest in fascism was an ideological weakness that undermined the program-matic positions of both Communists and Social Democrats. The Communists did not undertake any theoretical analysis of the fascist phenomenon. Instead, they confined themselves to the thesis of 'social fascism', according to which the opportunist politics of Social Democracy were partly to blame for the fascisisa-tion of Austria. Although there is no doubting the one-sided, narrow nature of their positions, the Communists' evaluation of the Social Democrats' strategies was nevertheless accurate. Bauer's concept of the 'defensive role of force', which in 1926 became official party policy, permitted the use of revolutionary violence only when civil rights and political liberties were drastically infringed. Violence was reserved for the worst-case scenario – i.e. an ultimate attack on democracy in the course of which basic rights were abolished. How the working class and its party should approach a situation in which anti-democratic forces gradually conquered state power did not form part of Bauer's reflections.

Bauer's views on the fascisisation of Austria from 1926–32 are characterised by his unswerving belief in the ability of democracy to defend itself and pre-vail through its intrinsic mechanisms. As mentioned earlier, his statement at the 1927 congress concerning the possibility of a fascist dictatorship in Austria and the ability of the working class to resist was optimistic. By no means do we wish to imply that Bauer failed to take notice of the growing influence of the Heimwehr in the state apparatus. On the contrary, in 1927, he spoke out against wildcat strikes and workers' demonstrations initiated without official endorsement from the party and trade unions in order to avoid confrontations with the Heimwehr. It did not escape the attention of Social Democracy's opponents that this was motivated by Bauer's characteristically fearful politics and aversion to radical phenomena. It is hardly surprising that they felt intensely relaxed about the SDAP's election victory in 1930; after all, they were aware that the Social Democrats would not use the historical opportunity that they had, once again, been given. The election result only inspired Bauer to an even more confident assessment of the possibilities to preserve the democratic foundations of the state. In 1930, he presented conclusions on the unlikelihood of a fascist dictatorship in Austria on economic grounds. For example, he surmised that Austria's dependency on foreign capital was a *de facto* guarantee against the fascists rising to power.[44] Evidently, this was a wrong assumption – Bauer did not consider that German and Italian capital in fact bankrolled the Heimwehr and the National Socialists. Bauer's other economic prognosis, based on Hilferding's theory of organised capitalism, was just as inaccurate. According to this theory, finance capital would be transformed into state capital because of the crisis, i.e. it would assume the form of a centrally planned economy and pave the way for socialism.

It follows that Bauer still did not yet fear a fascist threat in early 1930s Austria. His statements at the LSI congress in 1931, where he cited the possibility of defeating fascism and saving democracy, are further evidence of this. So too are his remarks at the SDAP congress in 1932, where he proposed a struggle against anti-democratic tendencies waged by parliamentary means. Until 1932, Bauer was convinced that Austria did not contain a social basis for fascism, and that fascism overestimated its own abilities. He continued to underestimate fascism's impact, even when it became startlingly apparent due to the progressive fascisisation of the Christian Social Party and ever-closer links between conservative forces and fascists of both varieties.

When Dollfuss dissolved parliament in March 1933, Bauer was forced to admit that he had introduced an authoritarian regime, even if he rightly did not refer to it as totalitarian. He also observed that the Heimwehr had consolidated its position in the bourgeois government and believed it possible that it would evolve towards fascism. He identified both the landed gentry, the Jewish bourgeoisie who sought protection from the anti-Semitism of the Nazis, and the urban and peasant middle classes under the influence of the Christian Social Party as the social vehicles of fascism. In 1933, Bauer was still wrong

---

44   See Bauer 1980t, p. 253.

in his appraisal of fascism and was weighed down by contradictions. His article, 'Um die Demokratie' ('For Democracy'), was an example of this: on the one hand, he admitted that the crisis had pushed the weary working class onto the defensive and had incapacitated it from defending democracy.[45] On the other, he expected the proletariat to win over the petty bourgeoisie and peasantry, who were divided between the democratic and conservative wings of the Christian Social Party, to the defence of the democratic state order.[46] Moreover, the article testified to his erroneous diagnosis of the political situation, including his misjudgement of the two fascist movements.[47] There is no other way to explain why he feared that the two currents might merge. Similarly, Bauer's support for Dollfuss's emergency regulations against the Nazis was not particularly well thought out. Given that the government's plans in 1933 were not exactly a secret, it would have been easy to predict that the same laws would soon also be used against Marxists. We shall refrain from focusing on Bauer's publications from 1933–4 in detail, as they are rather unfruitful for our purposes. To summarise, Bauer did not believe that Austrofascism could win, right up until the defeat of the February uprising.[48] Without wishing to provide a justification for his neglect, it is certainly the case that the fascist phenomenon, which was not one of Bauer's main areas of study at the time, caught him by surprise.

From 1934–8, after the demise of democracy, Bauer attempted an analysis of Austrofascism that contained theoretical elements. It is therefore justified to call it a theory of Austrofascism. Ahead of our appraisal, let us recall that Bauer consistently viewed fascism as a national phenomenon, and that there were two main reasons for his hostility towards Austrofascism: first, Dollfuss's insistence on Austrian independence, which was irreconcilable with Bauer's

---

45 See Bauer 1980u, p. 304.

46 Commenting on this proposal, Hanisch writes: 'What he [Bauer] overlooked, however, is how deeply imbued the aversion against parties, parliament, and therefore against democracy had already become in the mentality and collective feelings of the population' – Hanisch 2011, p. 293.

47 The Heimwehr aspired to gain a political position in the state. The main goal of the National Socialists, on the other hand, was the annexation of Austria to the German Reich. Kösten pointed out the naivety of Bauer's approach at the time in Kösten 1984, p. 203.

48 He put his position very clearly: 'In the long term, the situation of the Austrofascist dictatorship is therefore forlorn. It will either dismantle itself, seek to come to an understanding with the working class, capitulate before the working class, or the working class will overthrow it. The objective conditions of its overthrow will be created by the mechanism of its development' (our translation) – Bauer 1980y, p. 418.

desire for union with Germany, and second, Bauer's opposition to any political systems which infringed individual liberty and aimed to abolish its legal guarantees.

When approaching Austrofascism, Bauer aimed to reveal the economic, social and political basis of this phenomenon, especially the differences between Austrian, German and Italian fascism. The core of his conclusions was as follows: Austria is the first country in which clericalism with fascist tendencies conglomerated to form a dictatorship.

Bauer identified a number of causes for the victory of Austrofascism. The first was the fall of the Habsburg monarchy, which included the costs of the lost war and loss of foreign markets. The second was the economic situation of the First Republic – that is to say, dependency on foreign capital, the decline of exports, the banks' loss of independence and subordination to state control, and the workers' loss of purchasing power resulting from the crisis and unemployment. Bauer considered it less important to investigate the economic conditions that allowed fascism to grow than to study the mechanisms by which it seized power, its class content, and its nature and social base.

Indeed, it was not that easy to explain how fascism had come to power, especially since conditions in Austria were different from those in Germany or Italy. In Austria, fascism did not enjoy support from the masses and did not produce its own ideology or charismatic leaders. Nor is it possible to ignore the longstanding, relentless struggle between the two fascist trends. When analysing the mechanism due to which Austrian fascism had emerged, Bauer's conclusions were similar to the works of contemporary historians:[49] fascism rested on the illegitimate assumption of power by a coalition of governing forces, the representatives of the Christian Social Party and the Heimwehr, supported by the church. Bauer's words succinctly reflected the situation in Austria:

> So the clerical, Austrian-patriotic faction of the bourgeoisie hostile to union with Germany resolved to use the state power to establish a dictatorship which was intended to suppress by force German-nationalist Fascism and the working class at the same time. On the surface it imitated Fascist methods, adopted Fascist ideology, and linked it with Catholic clericalism. In reality, however, its 'Fatherland Front' did not arise from a popular mass movement, as did the Fascist party in Italy and the National

---

49   Compare the writings contained in Tálos, Emmerich and Wolfgang Neugebauer 1984. Matthes, who offers a somewhat divergent assessment that is no less historically accurate if one considers the long-term process of fascisisation, argues that Austrofascism seized power by gradually conquering the state apparatus. See Matthes 1979, p. 259.

Socialist Party in Germany, but was invented and established by the government, and was imposed on the mass of the people by the coercive
power of the state. In this case Fascism is not the natural product of grass
roots movements and class struggles, but an artefact which the constitutional state power has imposed upon the people.[50]

In light of the above, it was essential to define the social base and class content of the Austrofascist dictatorship. Bauer had to determine which social
forces had elevated Dollfuss and the circle of politicians around him to the
levels of power, and whose interests the new regime represented. Once again,
Bauer returned to the theoretical framework of Bonapartism, which impeded
him from identifying the actual agents of fascism in Austria, where democracy had been abolished not by forces outside of the bourgeois parties, but
by a right-wing government. Once more, Bauer reiterated the thesis of a 'third
force' standing above the bourgeoisie and proletariat. The two classes both
appeared incapable of coordinating their political activities. The 'third force'
supposedly comprised the aristocratic landowners and church hierarchy, who
used the Heimwehr to seize power. Meanwhile, the declassed peasants, petty
bourgeoisie and unemployed workers were not aware of the true aims of the
political struggle and were therefore mere tools of the aristocracy. Bauer conceded that the aristocracy initially had to share power with representatives of
the major industries, yet it emerged victorious from its struggle for leadership
against big capital, which was inclined towards National Socialism.

As to the class content of the Austrian fascist state, Bauer's view was not
entirely thought-through. His point that the Austrofascist dictatorship represented the concerns of the capitalists against the defeated working class coexisted with permanent denials of bourgeois class rule under Austrofascism and
an emphasis on the regime's clerical-feudal character. Bauer referred to it as a
'historical anomaly' and thought of it as a feudal relic. For him, Austrofascism
embodied the rule of classes whose historical time had passed – an anachron-
ism in the capitalist epoch.

Let us examine the corporative state, the *Ständestaat*, to determine whether
a fascist dictatorship was introduced in Austria. To stick with the terminology
proposed by Bauer, we need to establish whether the dictatorship he described
really did have a feudal character. The short answer is no – the 'historical anomaly' described by Bauer never existed. Not realising that the aristocracy and
church had lost their pre-capitalist character in the era of monopoly capital-

---

50   Bauer 1978e, p. 184.

ism, he envisaged a distorted image of Dollfuss's political system. Likewise, his evaluation of the role of the church in Austrofascism was wide of the mark. Contrary to his claims, it did not aspire to introduce a Catholic fascist dictatorship.[51] As Hanisch demonstrates, the Austrian church was the absolute guardian of the authoritarian state and, as such, an obstacle for the fully developed fascist orientation of the government.[52] It is true, however, that Dollfuss granted the church cultural and social privileges, and that the church used its influence upon the middle classes to foster support for the Dollfuss government.

Bauer distinguished between three phases of the Dollfuss-Schuschnigg dictatorship. He referred to the first phase of the Austrofascist system from 1934–6 as a coalition between clerical fascism and Heimwehr fascism. The church, the bureaucratic layer of officials, and the bourgeois-peasant organisations on the one hand, and the aristocracy and imperial officers on the other, supported it. Bauer was convinced that this system would soon collapse as it had a narrow social base, no charismatic leader, and was economically unstable – i.e. dependent on Italian capital.[53] In 1935, Bauer saw a new danger arising from these factors. It has to be said that it was illusory: he feared Austrofascism's alleged ambitions to consolidate its power by restoring the Habsburg monarchy.[54] This belief was rooted in the fact that some elements in the church and Christian Social Party held monarchist sympathies. Yet the notion that the church would want to restore the monarchy was not based on fact, considering the 1855 concordat had not even granted the church half as many privileges as Dollfuss's government was prepared to. Bauer's suspicion that France, Britain and Italy had an interest in restoring the monarchy was equally unfounded: after Hitler's victory in Germany, the Dollfuss government's resolve to preserve Austrian independence coincided with British and French political interests, while the type of government in Austria was of little relevance to these countries. If the facts spoke for themselves, Bauer was scarcely inclined to acknowledge them. Instead, he dreamt up the nonsensical vision of a victorious working-class revolution in alliance with pro-German elements against the res-

---

51 See Bauer 1980x, p. 449.

52 See Hanisch 1974, p. 253.

53 See Bauer 1980cc, p. 227.

54 In 1935, Bauer wrote: 'Habsburg stands at the gates. The Austrofascist dictatorship is paving the way for the Habsburgians ... Not the Nazis, but the Habsburgians are the immediate, most pressing danger at the moment'. Original: 'Habsburg steht vor den Toren. Die austrofaschistische Diktatur bahnt den Habsburgern den Weg ... nicht die Nazis, sondern die Habsburger sind im Augenblick die nächste dringendste Gefahr' – Bauer 1980aa, p. 505.

322

CHAPTER 8

toration of the monarchy. In 1935, he was prepared to enter an agreement with the National Socialists to avert a restoration of the Habsburg monarchy and *de facto* jointly combat the Dollfuss government, even though he was fully aware that the potential German partner represented a deadly threat to the party and the working class.[55] Botz sardonically notes in his comment on Bauer's proposal that it was a rather surprising turn, given that from late 1933 to early 1934 he had still lent support to the establishment of the corporative state.[56] To sum up Bauer's secondary theory of Austrofascism, it is worth noting that he feared the restoration of the monarchy primarily because it might squander his hopes for Austria's union with Germany.

It is critical that Bauer did not dedicate a great deal of attention to the second and third phases of Austrofascism that he had outlined. In his view, the second period from 1935–8 was characterised by the exclusion of the Heimwehr by clerical fascism, the effective autonomy of the state power, and its evolution in an autocratic-bureaucratic direction.

Bauer referred to the third period from February 1938 onward as a coalition between clerical fascism and National Socialism, backed by big industry, the petty bourgeoisie, the intelligentsia, and the state bureaucracy. In 1938, he was convinced that the National Socialists would establish their own dictatorship in Austria.[57]

As Hanisch notes, Bauer was ultimately not sure about his views on Austrofascism.[58] This is confirmed in the way he fluctuated between defining it as a fascist dictatorship and an autocratic regime. Although he repeatedly employed the term 'fascist dictatorship', Bauer still acknowledged that Austrian fascism was weaker than its German and Italian counterparts – it lacked popular support, its ideology was less 'refined' compared to Nazism, and its leaders were undecided as to its political direction. This dictatorship was not as comprehensive or brutal as others. In the last months of his life, Bauer revised his position and referred to the three phases of the Dollfuss-Schuschnigg dictatorship as 'semi-fascism', also using the term 'small state fascism'.[59]

---

55   Compare Hanisch 1974, p. 257.
56   See Botz 1985, p. 176.
57   According to Kösten, Bauer identified 'fascisating' factors in various forces, such as monarchists (1923), the Heimwehr (1930), the National Socialists (1932), and in the Dollfuss government (1933). See Kösten 1984, p. 270. Note that Bauer courted all manner of forces, hoping to come to some understanding, according to his subjective view of the political situation in Austria rather than a realistic assessment.
58   See Hanisch 1974, p. 256.
59   See Bauer 1980ff, p. 889.

Let us conclude by citing Botz, who pointed out that Bauer's definition of 'Austrofascism' had little to do with the definition the author proposed for fascism in a broader sense. Botz assumes that Bauer coined the term for the purpose of political struggle rather than political analysis.[60] It is more likely that the opposite was the case. Bauer aimed to establish a scientific distinction between Austrian fascism and other varieties. However, his lack of distance from the political events of the day, and the fact that he only knew the corporative state from an emigrant's perspective, made it impossible for him to formulate an appropriate theoretical diagnosis of the Dollfuss-Schuschnigg system.

2.3 The Theory of Fascism as Imperialism

Shortly before his death, Bauer prepared the last, unfinished chapter of *The Illegal Party* for publication as a separate book.[61] It contained his third theory of fascism, which linked the phenomenon with the economic development of capitalism and the changing role of the capitalist state in a more pronounced manner. It was similar to Hilferding's premise of 'organised capitalism', which also attributed to the state a growing role in the economy and highlighted planning as a characteristic element of the capitalist economy. The theory was certainly not new. Although Bauer foregrounded the economic foundations of fascism, he denied this time around that the balance of class forces and class apparatus were a precondition for the fascist movement to seize power. At the same time, echoes of his first fascism theory still lingered: Bauer argued that under fascist rule, the executive power of the state became gradually autonomous. Furthermore, he emphasised the inner contradictions of the fascist system, which are expressed in the conflict of interests between the state apparatus and the respective social classes and groups.

The basic premise of Bauer's third theory was his insistence that fascism was a form of aggressive, bellicose, imperialist capitalism. On this, he concurred with GDH Cole.[62] One of the typical characteristics of aggressive capitalism, according to Bauer, was its tendency to increase the exploitation and oppression of the working class domestically while at the same time waging a struggle for markets abroad. It follows that Bauer considered capitalism's development towards imperialism to be a general and fundamental condition for the rise of fascism. However, he realised that this general account was insufficient as an

---

60 See Botz 1985, p. 177. Hanisch shares this view – see Hanisch 1984, p. 53.

61 It appeared after Bauer's death as 'Der Faschismus' in *Der sozialistische Kampf*.

62 See Cole 1953, p. 60.

explanation in understanding the reasons as to why fascism had prevailed in Germany and Italy, while fascist movements in other countries did not threaten the bourgeois democratic state order at all or merely resulted in the advent of semi-dictatorships or autocratic governments. To explain this phenomenon, he pointed to additional historical and social conditions that had paved the way for bellicose imperialism, including different democratic traditions and the effects of World War I.[63] He cited as one of the effects of war the weakening of young democracies, which had occurred in the course of revolutionary and counter-revolutionary processes after the war and the inauguration of the parliamentary era in the victorious countries. In these countries, the bourgeoisie was bolstered by its success and maintained its position. Another consequence of the war, decisive for the political development in Europe, was the new division of the world, which had borne two kinds of imperialism: on the one hand, the conservative and peaceful imperialism of France and Britain, which continued to live off their colonies as well as at the expense of defeated Germany and Italy. On the other, an aggressive, pugnacious imperialism reigned supreme in Germany and Italy, which were particularly affected by the economic crisis and had ambitions to overrule it through territorial expansion.[64] Fascism was – so went Bauer's conclusion – a weapon in the struggle to revise the division of the world.

When fascism succeeded, it envisaged a new economic and political order which reflected the changes to which the structure of monopoly capitalism had been subjected. The most fundamental of these changes was a tendency to intensify the statist organisation of the economy while keeping property relations intact. This tendency became stronger in the wake of World War I and the 1929 economic crisis. According to Bauer, it found its fullest expression in the command economy of the fascist state, which he regarded as its essence and its totalitarian character: the state regulated all areas of life and had full power over the economy. Bauer referred to the state control over the economy as 'fascist etatism' (or, alternatively, 'war economy' or 'dirigist economy') and regarded it as a new development phase of capitalism, a qualitatively new form of imperial-

---

63   Compare Botz 1985, p. 180.

64   Bauer wrote: 'Since then, British and French imperialism have been defending the dominant position they won in the world war. Britain's and France's imperialism is the imperialism of the satisfied, a full stomach imperialism. It is therefore conservative and peaceful' (our translation) – Bauer 1980ff, p. 874. Note that unlike in his earlier writings, Bauer refrained from criticising the expansionist and militarist aims of French and British colonialism in this text. He probably did so in order to highlight Germany and Italy's aggressive war drive, and to stress the more threatening character of their imperialism.

ism. At the same time, he was inclined to acknowledge positive effects achieved by the war economy and its imposed control over the labour and wage market and planned economy, including a lowering of the unemployment rate, an increase in work productivity, the development of new economic branches due to armament policies, and technological progress. Naturally, this does not mean that Bauer overlooked the unfavourable sides of imperialism's evolution. On the contrary, he stressed that labour legislation disadvantageous to the working class had preceded the statist economy. Indeed, fascist labour legislation ushered in many negative changes for workers: the trade unions were dissolved, strikes prohibited, wage agreements annulled, forced labour introduced, and wages determined by the state. Nevertheless, reflecting on his conclusions in *Rationalisierung*, Bauer recognised the superiority of fascist statism over free market capitalism, even though he was fully aware of the restrictions imposed by 'war economy'. Granted, he did not consider statism to be a cure for all of capitalism's ills. For instance, he did not think that it could overcome crises – he merely believed they would be different under fascism. According to Bauer, crises caused by an undersupply of goods for peaceful purposes were inevitable.

Bauer drew attention to the fact that the war economy served the state military rather than the immediate interests of social classes. The war imperialism of the fascist states forced other countries to raise their armaments expenses. The contradictions between the capitalist countries led to economic fluctuation as the fear of war restricts the flow of capital towards peacetime production. Bauer's conclusion was correct: the fascist command economy would meet its limits and precede war. For Bauer, there was an integral link between the imminence of war and the development of imperialism. This was not a completely novel insight, but rather reiterated the theses contained in Bauer's articles on imperialism and his first theory of fascism. According to Botz and Butterwegge, Bauer's prognosis that the synthesis of fascism and imperialism would inevitably lead to conflict was not too distant from Communist assessments of fascism from the 1920s and 30s.[65] Note, however, that Bauer's analysis was far more profound than the Communists' rhetoric, which ignored the historical, political, and economic factors that allowed fascism to grow – e.g. the weakness of parliamentary democracy, the consequences of World War I, the command of politics over the economy, and the effects of economic crisis.

In 1938, Bauer made two prognoses with respect to the fate of fascism – one was of a purely political nature, the other was sociological-political. According

---

65   See Botz 1985, p. 189; compare Butterwegge 1990, p. 556.

to his political prognosis, the fascist dictatorships in Italy, Poland, Estland, Bulgaria and Yugoslavia were weakened; yet on the other hand, he predicted that Hitler would attack Eastern Europe. The sociological-political prognosis was far more complex. It was based on the incoherence of class rule and political power under fascism. Let us note that the manner in which this fascism theory illustrated the relationship between the two powers was nebulous. Aside from claiming that the fascist dictatorship reinforced the economic power of the bourgeoisie, Bauer asserted that the fascist government is thrown into conflict with the big bourgeoisie in particular. The governing fascist caste turns on various fractions of the capitalist ruling class, uniting with them in common struggle only to keep the working class at bay. Bauer's emphasis on the tensions and instability of the fascist system served one particular purpose: to reinforce the vision of an anti-fascist revolution. Pointing out the conflict of interests between the political and economic powers served to buttress the notion that this would lead to a radical transformation of the social conditions, and thus to a loss of fascism's social base. At the end of the manuscript, Bauer cited three enemies of fascism: the working class, the disappointed petty bourgeoisie, and the bourgeoisie at odds with fascism for economic reasons. These classes would wage a common struggle to abolish the totalitarian regime. The notion of cross-class struggle directly referred to Bauer's concept of the anti-fascist united front, according to which the proletariat would lead the middle classes and parts of the capitalist class into struggle. In 1938, Bauer was convinced of the following:

> If the working class gets moving, if big mass strikes shake the fascist system of rule and the statist command economy to its foundations, then broad masses of petty bourgeois, peasants, and intellectuals will coalesce around the working class to bring down the hated fascist bureaucracy, its totalitarian rule, and its dictatorship over economic life.[66]
> our translation

It was, of course, another misguided prognosis. The conclusions Bauer drew from the concept of a 'dirigist economy', however, were not as idealistic as his previous verdicts in his theory of 'organised capitalism' – i.e. he did not think of it as a phase that heralded the socialist economy. This does not mean that he relinquished his fatalist perspective. Rather, he now supported his notion of the inevitability of socialism by citing the dialectical unity of the objective and

---

66   Bauer 1980ff, p. 895.

subjective development tendencies of fascist imperialism, i.e. the centralised economy and the anti-fascist, socialist revolution.

3   The Anti-Fascist Uprising of Austrian Workers

The primary objectives of fascism of the Austrian variety were to eliminate political parties, including the Social-Democratic party, from the political stage, abolish the republic, and establish the corporative state. On its way to achieving these goals, Austrofascism encountered an unexpected obstacle: a spontaneous and dramatic workers' uprising in defence of the beleaguered and suppressed democracy lasting from 12–18 February 1934.

The outbreak of the February uprising poses a number of questions. We have already addressed in points 1 and 2.2 as to whether fascism in Austria lived up to its own ambitions in the same way as German fascism did. Further questions still need to be addressed: Were fratricidal struggles inevitable in the democratic republic that Austria had become after the fall of the monarchy? Why could a political compromise agreed in parliament not resolve the escalating conflict? Finally, why was the Social-Democratic leadership unable to stop the course of events and live up to the challenges posed by both Austrofascism and the working class?

All Austrian political forces, including the Social Democrats, were clear that the warning accommodated in the programme of Linz, according to which force would be used if fascism seized power, was not a credible threat. When parliament was dissolved, the Social-Democratic party was deprived of the democratic conditions for struggle that had been its strategic premise – it was synonymous with the party's exclusion from the political arena. The only trajectory still possible for the party was that of active resistance. Alas, Bauer lacked the self-assertion and decisiveness that so distinguished Dollfuss. In light of the constitutional crisis, the SDAP leadership failed to call for the strike that the working masses were expecting for fear of civil war. Instead, it announced that it was prepared to co-operate with the government on the imminent constitutional reform that aimed to strengthen the executive power. What is more, the SDAP offered the Dollfuss government the support of the Schutzbund and agreed with the decision to grant the government extraordinary powers – this, it hoped, would be the harbinger for co-operation in the struggle against Nazism. The tactical misjudgements committed by the party leadership resulted not only from its erratic assessment of the political situation; they were also the product of Social Democracy's ideological and programmatic assumptions, i.e. its belief in the inevitability of historical progress.

It was precisely this belief that additionally reinforced the party's unrealistic evaluation of its own strength and of the situation.[67] Other political factors also played a significant part in its choice of tactics – that is, the party's long-standing and loyal adherence to democratic methods, its lack of faith in the workers' fighting spirit, and the notion that the country was isolated and under threat from the fascist powers that had grown abroad. These were accompanied by moral considerations, such as the aversion to fratricidal struggle, and individual temperaments, such as the fear of taking responsibility for radical political decisions and unwillingness to act consequently displayed by Social-Democratic politicians. These various factors led to the SDAP leadership's passivity, which undermined the workers' militancy, which had still been alive and full of promise in 1933. Consequently, the winner in the struggle against fascism was predetermined, as it were, and the demise of democracy in Austria accelerated.[68]

The fascist dictatorships of Italy and Germany were no less interested in the destruction of Austrian democracy than Dollfuss was. They differed only in their ultimate objectives: Dollfuss aspired, in the name of banishing the 'red peril', to abolish the democratic and social successes of the working masses, dissolve the Marxist parties and trade unions, and strengthen the position of the church by exterminating the influence of anti-clerical Social Democracy. For Italy and Germany, in contrast, expansionist aims were paramount.[69] When Dollfuss's attempts to come to an understanding with Hitler failed,[70] Italy offered to help him to introduce dictatorial powers in Austria, but made the offer dependent on Dollfuss's hastening of the process of combating Social Democracy. The Heimwehr, having won such a strong ally, decided to proceed in radical fashion.[71] These were truly decisive moments for the republic, yet the SDAP leadership failed. It lacked gumption, and the fear of civil war and its

---

67   Over years, the party leadership's waiting for a favourable historical moment instead of going on the offensive inevitably led to an eternal 'wait and see' politics in practice, as Leser writes. Consequently, the party was not taken seriously as a political partner. Compare Leser 1986, pp. 296–7.

68   In 1933, Dollfuss still had to consider democratic forces in the Christian Social Party and state apparatus.

69   Germany wanted to annex Austria to make its invasion of Czechoslovakia easier. Italy aimed at establishing a union of fascist states (Italy, Hungary, Austria) to counterbalance Nazi Germany.

70   The failed negotiations between Dollfuss and Hitler were decisive in Dollfuss's resolve to preserve Austrian independence and his hostility towards Nazism.

71   The leader of the Heimwehr and minister of domestic security, Emil Fey, ordered to search party buildings for arms, destroy Social-Democratic printing presses, and arrest mem-

aftermath left it paralysed. Aware of the anti-fascist sentiments of the workers, it decided on 8 February to postpone the outbreak of civil war and on 12 February 1934 it restricted the role of the Schutzbund to purely defensive measures. Yet the party's apparent willingness to fight turned out to be false – the contrast between words and deeds not only threatened to fatally undermine the leadership's credibility in the party ranks, but also cost several hundred human lives. This was the price paid for years of bandying revolutionary phraseology – alas, Bauer and his close circle of comrades realised this too late.

On 12 February 1934, the Schutzbund troops of Linz initiated, against the decision of the party leadership, a skirmish against the Heimwehr and armed police, thus firing the starting shot for the outbreak of the workers' uprising.[72] The ensuing street battles ravaged Upper Austria, Styria, and Vienna in particular.[73] The desperate Schutzbund troops recognised the hopelessness of their situation from the start.[74] Their leaders, Ernst Fischer and Ernst Draskowitsch, noted as early as 12 February: 'This struggle is lost from the outset. One cannot capitulate for a whole year and then win'.[75] Neither did the chair of the Schutzbund, General Theodor Körner, see any chances of success – and both the right wing (Kautsky) and left wing (Béla Kun) of the international workers'

---

bers of the Schutzbund. On 5 January 1934, the Heimwehr occupied the headquarters of the *Innsbrucker Volkszeitung* newspaper. The following day, it occupied the Social-Democratic printing presses in Linz, Graz and Eisenstadt, and on 9 February 1934 arrested ten Schutzbund leaders. According to Renner's recollections, Fey boasted after the deployment of Heimwehr units in Langenzersfort on 11 February 1934: 'This week, we will do a thorough job'. See Renner 1952b, p. 137. Ernst Starhemberg reportedly made a comment in the same spirit – ibid. In Tyrol and Styria, the Heimwehr occupied government buildings.

72   According to Konrad, 'by 19 February, all regional and local leaders of the Schutzbund, numbering almost 200, had been arrested' – Konrad 2004. In the night from 11–12 February, the Heimwehr unit commander of Linz, Richard Bernaschek, informed Bauer in a letter about the decision to resist a planned raid of the local party building with firearms. In his reply, Bauer did not approve of the decision. See Rabinach 1989, p. 173; compare Braunthal 1961, p. 35.

73   About 20,000 Schutzbund members, joined by some Communists, fought against better armed and better organised units: the 4,200-strong army, the 7,500-strong police, and 9,600-strong bourgeois paramilitaries. There is no agreement among Austrian historians as to how many combatants were wounded and killed. According to Gulick, there were 118 dead and 486 injured on the pro-government side, and 196 dead and 319 wounded on the rebel side. See Gulick 1948; Peball 1974, p. 38.

74   See also Kulemann 1979, p. 400.

75   Ibid.

movement agreed that the uprising was a belated affair.[76] Aside from the political determinant, the psychological aspect was no less decisive in the heroic struggle of the Schutzbund troops. Not only did they defend democracy, they also defended the reputation of a party many identified with, and whose willingness to fight they trusted.

Reacting to the unwelcome uprising, the SDAP leadership restricted itself to proclaiming a general strike. For a number of reasons, this strike turned out to be a fiasco lacking mass support. Economic limitations, such as the fear of losing one's job in a time of economic crisis, played a role. So too did sociological and political aspects: the masses did not believe they could win, and the party had imbued them with the superiority of legal struggle for many years. What is more, there were organisational issues: there was no real defence plan and scarce information with respect to arms and coordination of actions. Contradictory decisions and irresponsible conduct on the part of the SDAP leaders further contributed to the debacle.[77] The lone Schutzbund fighters, abandoned in struggle by the party leadership, laid down arms on 18 February 1934.[78] As the conflict was still ongoing, the government dissolved the Social-Democratic party, arrested its leaders, and sent 10,000 people to concentration camps.[79]

---

76   See Kautsky 1934, p. 18; compare Kun 1934.

77   Some telling facts testify to the poor organisation of the uprising: turning off the electricity – a pre-arranged sign to commence the strike – made it impossible for Bruno Kreisky to print Bauer's fighting appeal. When the strike was called, Danneberg and Renner went to join a meeting with Christian-Social politicians, thus exposing themselves to immediate arrest. Due to bad organisation, Bauer and Deutsch faced an army cordon in front of them instead of joining the fighting members of the Schutzbund as intended. As Hanisch writes, Bauer and Deutsch were transferred to Czechoslovakia on the second day of the uprising. The combatants were outraged at the flight of their leaders. See Hanisch 2011, p. 305.

78   After 1934, numerous Schutzbund members joined the Communist Party of Austria and newly formed socialist groups. Some of them established an illegal faction named 'Autonomous Schutzbund' that was disconnected from the party in the same year. A significant percentage of them emigrated to Czechoslovakia and the Soviet Union, and then to Spain in 1936. See West 1978, p. 44. Konrad confirms this depiction of events, adding that in 1934 many Social Democrats joined the Nazis, who were regarded as the main opponents of the corporative state. See Konrad 2004, p. 96. Hanisch states more precisely that some fighters (mostly from the big cities and industrial areas) joined the Communists and others joined the Nazis (mostly from the provinces), while most simply went into 'inner exile'. See Hanisch 2011, p. 306.

79   Seitz and Hugo Breitner were arrested, and some leaders were executed. The uprising

At that point, the party numbered more than 700,000 members, enjoyed the support of 1.5 million voters, had an 80,000-strong paramilitary organisation at its disposal, occupied 71 of 165 parliamentary seats, and had 25 delegates in regional governments and 387 town mayors. The defeat of the uprising and the party became the subject of numerous assessments, analyses, and controversies, especially in the Social-Democratic movement. After all, its leaders had an interest in denying any responsibility for the defeat. Even observers not directly involved in Austrian political life agreed that the February uprising amounted to a conscious act by a section of the working class not only against the government's actions, but also against the reformist line of the SDAP leadership. At the same time, it was synonymous with the defeat of Bauer's political line. It was Bauer who was chiefly responsible for reinforcing the masses' illusions in the party's willingness to fight.[80]

Numerous 1934 articles and his pamphlet *Der Aufstand der österreichischen Arbeiter* (*The Austrian Workers' Uprising*) testify to the fact that Bauer felt more responsible for the course of events than any of the other SDAP leaders. They also prove that he was unable to understand the essential elements which led to the party's downfall – that is, the contradiction between its revolutionary rhetoric and passive political practice (its opponents recognised this contradiction and knew how to take advantage of it). Furthermore, Bauer's writings prove that his basic theoretical premises had been wrong, leading to erratic judgement and inaccurate decisions in response to given socio-political conditions. In *The Austrian Workers' Uprising*, Bauer did admit to tactical errors, yet he did not subject the actual political line of the party to any criticism. In his view, a range of factors that could be blamed on the SDAP leadership

---

had a huge impact abroad. By 12 February, the first demonstrations in solidarity with the Austrian workers took place in Czechoslovakia. The British Labour Party set up a fund to support the families of workers killed in the uprising. Anti-fascist activities in France, Italy and Spain followed in the wake of the Austrian uprising. About 2,000 of the combatants later joined the Republican side in the Spanish Civil War. They also formed a battalion named '12 February', which in 1938 became the first Austrian military formation fighting for Austria's independence. The workers' uprising had awakened Austrian national consciousness.

80   On this question, I concur with Leser, who states: 'The 12 February uprising was not only a heroic sacrifice on behalf of the working class of Vienna that had remained loyal. It was also the day when an unconstitutional regime employed force against the defenders of democracy. It was the collapse of a politics on which Bauer had already stated the following in 1911, unaware that he would thus describe his own politics: "The worst politics is a politics of illusions. In the end, it can only ever lead to mass disappointment, discouragement, and ineffective outbreaks of desperation"' – Leser 1968, p. 483.

contributed to the defeat of the party: for instance, the inefficient organisation of the struggle, the failed general strike, the Schutzbund troops being
abandoned, and allowing the government to spread propaganda according to
which the party leadership had fled – the latter, it must be added, was undeniable with respect to Bauer and Deutsch. On the other hand, also conducive
to the SDAP's defeat was the general economic and political situation that
the party was in no position to influence, i.e. economic crises that subjected
the petty-bourgeois and peasant masses to poverty, the defeat of the German
working class in the struggle against Nazism, and the fading out of the revolutionary wave in Europe.[81] Bauer cited the following as mistakes, if only *tactical* mistakes: the SDAP's refusal to co-operate with Karl Buresch's government
after the 1932 elections, which strengthened the advance of both the Heimwehr and NSDAP; and the failure to proclaim a general strike in response to
Dollfuss's dissolving parliament and introducing emergency measures. Bauer
openly discussed whether the Dollfuss dictatorship could have been prevented and denied that this could have been achieved. Objectively, he argued, the
economic crisis drove the masses into the arms of the fascists. Undoubtedly,
one cannot blame Bauer and the party leadership for the conscious destruction
of Austrian democracy, for which the two fascist groups and the conservative right wing of the Christian Social Party bear responsibility. I concur with
Pelinka on this point: 'February 1934 was neither a tragedy that came over Austria solely through "objective circumstances", nor the result of "shared responsibility" or a "renunciation of democracy" for which all parties were equally
responsible. February 1934 saw the dramatic conclusion of a development consciously pushed forward, for which Dollfuss, Starhemberg, and Fey were openly
prepared to take responsibility' (our translation).[82] However, one should add
that Bauer's misguided policies, based on the Austromarxist doctrine, were a
factor that fostered and accelerated this development. If one draws strategic
and tactical premises for the working-class struggle from a theory that had long
been detached from reality, the inadequacy of these premises is transparent
from the outset.

81   See Bauer 1934, p. 24.
82   Pelinka 1984, p. 12.

4   Austrian Social Democracy and the Triumph of Fascism

4.1   *Austrian Social Democracy's Relationship to Strategic and Tactical*
        Concepts of the Workers' Movement During the Period of Fascist
        Reaction

We shall now assess the statement, at the end of our previous section, according
to which a theory out of touch with reality led to inadequate strategic premises.
It implies that the means and methods Bauer proposed for the anti-fascist
struggles were unfit for purpose, even with respect to his own evaluation of
fascism. It does not, however, fully explain the motives that determined Bauer
and his party comrades' decisions during the February uprising. In truth, the
strategy and tactics that the party had adopted for the working-class struggle
against fascism drove their decisions. These, in turn, were based not on a
realistic assessment of the social and political situation, but rather on the
values that the Social Democrats were willing to defend.

Let us take a closer look at Bauer and the SDAP leadership's anti-fascist
strategy and the goals to which it was subordinated. Between the Hamburg
congress of the LSI in 1923 and the last SDAP party congress in 1933, Bauer's
accounts on the general strategic premises of the anti-fascist struggle of the proletariat were characterised primarily by their purely declarative revolutionary
nature and his aversion to co-operating with the Communists. These sentiments were typical for the parties that belonged to the LSI. Another prominent
aspect was the fact that the individual parties championed their respective
national interests over the interests of the international workers' movement
as a whole. This made it impossible to arrive at a shared line of action against
fascism and weakened the practical meaning of resolutions adopted at the LSI
congresses.[83] Since the beginning of the organisation's existence, Bauer set the
tone of official LSI documents, and it was largely his views that determined
their form. At the founding congress of the LSI, he warned of the international
dimension of the fascist phenomenon. In a rather one-sided fashion, he blamed
the Bolsheviks for its emergence. In his opinion, they had contributed to its rise
by splitting the international workers' movement and trade unions, as well as
introducing terror. For fear that red terror might spread, he argued, the bourgeoisie called the fascists to its aid. Bauer rightly criticised the Communists'
dogmatic thinking – for them, the working-class struggle against fascism could
be used to rapidly herald the world revolution. He conceded with the Communists, however, that the available democratic institutions were not enough

---

83   Compare Zmierczak 1988, p. 78.

CHAPTER 8

to stop the fascisisation of the country.[84] He pleaded for coupling parliamentary action with street demonstrations. He issued the following tasks to the Social-Democratic movement: maintaining the proletariat's readiness to fight, providing military training for the youth, and reinforcing democratic values in society, particularly in areas subordinated to the state apparatus.

The resolution Bauer authored and put to the fifth LSI congress in Paris in 1933 reflected the enormous importance he attributed to preserving democracy (this document was previously discussed in Chapter 7, which pointed out the two different strains of working-class anti-fascist struggle it advocated, which depended on the degree to which democracy was threatened). Bauer acknowledged the theory of 'organised capitalism' in defence of democracy, demonstrating that due to the arms economy, monopoly capitalism had achieved a level of organisation it had predicted. According to Bauer, this would lead to a transformation of the system into a socialist state in the near future, i.e. the fall of the fascist dictatorships. Bauer's resolution bore the demand for preserving the neutrality of the LSI if any constituent parties took up negotiations with the Comintern concerning the creation of a united front of the working class against fascism. However, the Paris congress did not adopt this postulate.

Not for nothing did Bauer insist, in both congress speeches, that the main goal of the working-class struggle against fascism was not a socialist revolution, but rather the defence of bourgeois democracy and its political and social gains. This hierarchy of priorities was also consistent with the speeches of other LSI party leaders. It found a passionate advocate in the secretary of the LSI, Friedrich Adler, who argued that surrendering the struggle for democracy would be tantamount to admitting that Social Democracy had chosen the wrong path.[85] The Social Democrats defended bourgeois democracy on two bases: as a value in itself, and as a necessary premise for the struggle for social change. One is inclined to agree with Zmierczak's argument that the Social Democrats were so preoccupied with the necessity of defending democracy that they rarely ever contemplated a course of action for the case that the democratic system was under threat.[86] When fascism seized power in Germany and Italy, the lack of a clear programme paralysed the Social Democrats. Distinct examples for this were the passive attitude of the SPD in light of the

---

84   See Protocol of the International Socialist Workers' Congress in Hamburg, 21–25 May 1923, in Documents, Programmes, Protocols, p. 26.

85   Replying to the Austrian left socialists' demand to adopt the slogan of a 'dictatorship of the proletariat', Friedrich Adler stressed in his letter that the fundamental interest of the working class was to defend democracy. See Zmierczak 1988, p. 89.

86   See Zmierczak 1988, p. 93.

dissolution of Prussian parliament (1932) and the appointment of Hitler's government in 1933, as well as the disengaged stance of the SDAP during the events of February 1934.

The defeat of the Austrian workers' uprising led Bauer to reconsider his position on bourgeois democracy, even if he effectively only modified his earlier standpoint to the slightest degree. Fatalist optimism still prevailed. For Bauer, the February defeat was but a step towards the final victory of the proletariat.[87] Indeed, Bauer continued to advocate bourgeois democracy and resisted all criticism from within the socialist camp, which blamed parliamentary democracy for the defeat of the workers' movement. The true cause of defeat, according to Bauer, had been the susceptibility of the petty bourgeoisie, peasantry, and part of the working class to Dollfuss's fascist ideas. Like many other socialists of his time, Bauer failed to realise that fascism had exploited the disappointment of these layers, who had been let down by the Social-Democratic party's failure to put its proclaimed programme of social transformation into practice. What is more, Bauer was deeply convinced that the working class had to defend bourgeois democracy even if this implied that the working class would be perceived as a conservative force. The first reason was that bourgeois democracy was the result of working-class struggle, and its contemporary form was decisively shaped by the proletariat. Secondly, the bourgeois-democratic state form guaranteed, unlike fascist dictatorship, legally enshrined liberty. Only towards the end of his life did Bauer admit that this legal freedom was a source of passive reformism.

The victory of fascism was synonymous with the end of the legal Social-Democratic movement. In light of the consolidation of the fascist regime, Bauer suggested during the second half of 1934 the abandonment of the reformist tactic, having concluded that the fascist dictatorship could only be abolished by revolutionary means. Bauer spoke from the perspective of a revolutionary fanatic rather than a politician soberly evaluating available options for the workers' movement. Proof of this can be found in his denial that it would be possible to return to bourgeois democracy once fascism was defeated. The new programme combined the struggle against fascism with the struggle for socialism. On this, Bauer was clear:

> There is now only one task left: the overthrow of the fascist dictatorship. There is no other means to overthrow it than revolutionary force. However, the revolution against fascism cannot be a bourgeois revolu-

---

87   See Bauer 1934b, p. 8.

tion that the working class might attempt to drive forward and transform into a proletarian revolution at a later point. It can only be a proletarian revolution from the outset, for there are no more bourgeois revolutions in Europe. The task of overthrowing fascism thus coincides with the task of the working class to conquer state power. The struggle against fascism therefore becomes synonymous with the struggle for socialism.[88]

In 1934, Bauer did not shy away from using the term 'dictatorship of the proletariat' when defining the type of state and methods for the proletariat to seize power, even if he was motivated by tactical considerations rather than his true beliefs. Nonetheless, he acknowledged the need for the working class to garner allies in the struggle against fascism, namely the petty bourgeoisie, peasantry, and intelligentsia. Hence, he insisted that the proletarian dictatorship was merely a brief transitional stage during which society would evolve towards classlessness. Bauer was convinced that a section of the middle classes would turn away from fascism and be so discouraged by its restriction of civil liberties and evident failure to realise its economic programme that it would instead give the workers' movement its support. He ignored one important aspect: the middle classes sought protection under the wings of fascism because they feared being declassed. The notion of a classless society filled them with more anxiety than the totalitarian goals of fascism.

Bauer revised his aforementioned views on the correct anti-fascist strategy for the working-class movement after the February events. Did he, however, also change his attitudes towards collaboration with the Communists in this struggle? In the mid-1930s, his relationship to the Communist Party of Austria was no less ambivalent than his perspective on the Soviet Union. While he did stress the difference between fascist and Bolshevik dictatorships, he remained sceptical towards the Communists. His incredulity was due to divergent views on the forms of power struggle, the character and shape of proletarian force, democracy and dictatorship. Furthermore, his failure to comprehend the position of the KPÖ, which had gained in power after the defeat of Social Democracy, as well as its justified critique of the SDAP leadership, reinforced his aversion to the Communists. When fending off their objections, Bauer accused the Communists of having made it easier for the fascists to seize dominance.[89] He persevered in his opposition to the united front of the working class created by both wings of the labour movement. Bauer justified his reluctance by point-

---

88   Bauer 1934b, p. 9.
89   More details in Hanisch 1974, p. 259.

ing to the legacy of the Russian Revolution, the weak position of Communist parties in Western countries, and, ultimately, his fear that Social Democracy might lose its middle-class support. Towards the end of his life, Bauer drew closer to the Communists on many issues. Some Communists believed that the evolution of his views amounted to Bauer's recognition of the united front, yet this was an oversight. It is certainly the case that, in 1937, Bauer called on the working class of the West to support the Soviet Union in the struggle against fascism, and was buoyant towards the united front established in 1936. Yet he did not go so far as to consider it a true force in the struggle against fascism. It is also necessary to state that Bauer did not employ the term 'popular front' in the hope for an alliance between Communists and Social Democrats, but the united movement of the proletariat and middle classes against the common enemy. Bauer was aware that the conditions for such a movement did not exist in Western Europe at the time. Hence, he confined his advocacy of the Communist appeal for a bilateral struggle against fascism to the theory of 'integral socialism', which did not exceed the expectations of either side.

To reiterate, Austrian Social Democracy based its strategic premises for a working-class-led anti-fascist struggle on an inaccurate assessment of the socio-political situation in the country. From the observations outlined above, it follows that this resulted in the resolution to defend democracy, and later, in the period after the defeat of the Social-Democratic movement, the suggestion to start a revolution in isolation from the Communists. In Social-Democratic hands, this manoeuvre could not provide an effective means to combat fascism. From 1926 onward, the party leadership did not engage in any radical activities to protect democracy. On the contrary, it often behaved in a way that was counterproductive to these ends. Bauer's attempts to broach an understanding with bourgeois parties in 1932 came too late – pro-fascist tendencies had already aligned themselves with the bourgeois bloc. After the defeat of the February uprising, the rallying cries for revolution lacked any basis in actuality, as scarcely any forces on which one might base such an endeavour remained. No working-class strategy against fascism had any chance of success in the Austria of the late 1920s and early 1930s. After all, the working class under the leadership of the SDAP had been in retreat since 1927. Meanwhile, the sections of the working and middle classes that had found protection in the ranks of the Christian Social Party supported the Heimwehr, and declassed members of all classes strengthened the ranks of the NSDAP.

4.2   *Oppositional Activity of the Social-Democratic Movement at Home and in Exile after the* SDAP *Ban*

The establishment of the corporative state on 1 May 1934 after Dollfuss had secured control of the government amounted to the definite triumph of Austrofascism. What was the 'corporative state', Austrian style? How did it establish its supremacy, and what did it mean for democracy and the Social-Democratic movement? What role did the Heimwehr play?

The vision of a harmonious social structure based on the principles of corporatism already existed as an ideology in Austria since 1918.[90] However, it only found passionate advocates during the second half of the 1920s – initially in academic circles (e.g. the philosopher Othmar Spann, the legal historian Karl Hugelman, the historians Hans Hirsch and Heinrich von Srbik, the geographer Hugo Hassinger, the Germanist Josef Nadler, and the palaeontologist Othenio Abel),[91] and later among politicians embittered by the crisis (e.g. Karl Lugmayr and Leopold Kunschak). Its supporters aspired to abolish the bourgeois democratic system and replace it with a corporative state equipped with a strong apparatus of power. Sectional interests of individuals and social groups were to be subordinated to the common interest of state and community. The intention was to establish an authoritarian state whose social structure would be based not on classes, but on professional sectors (corporations, interest groups) functioning in a hierarchical order (federal state, region, commune, borough and village – all sectors were to be equal). This was based on the utopian premise that it was possible to achieve a unity of interests between producers and capitalists within every professional sector and use the goals of the respective sectors for the common good. This, it was hoped, would end class struggle.

In consideration of the above, it is necessary to draw attention to 1930s Austria, the ideology of Austrofascism, and the 'corporative state' led by Dollfuss and Schuschnigg. Anti-democratic tendencies were already on the rise from 1926, when the 'iron chancellor', Ignaz Seipel, ruled the country with an iron fist. Seipel believed that all political parties ought to be dissolved – he considered them obstacles impeding the smooth functioning of government.[92] Accomplishing this depended on two factors, the main factor being the existence of a political and military force interested in the destruction of democracy. The secondary factor was the need for an ideology that would justify such a venture.

---

90   Compare Kluge 1984, pp. 46–7.

91   For the influence of Austrofascist ideology on academic circles, compare Staudinger 1984b, p. 289.

92   Compare Pelinka 1972, p. 26.

Indeed, the Heimwehr precisely constituted such a force from its conception. Major capitalists and large estate holders endorsed it. The church also helped to suppress any symptoms of liberal tendencies in politics and the economy. To protect its own economic and political investments, the Heimwehr supported the idea of the 'corporative state' as chartered by Dollfuss and became a pillar of his government as the fascist system was fortified. The 'corporative state' was the most extensive, but not the sole, aspect of Austrofascist ideology. Autocracy, elitism, anti-democratism, anti-Marxism, clericalism and nationalism were further components. Zöllner writes:

> One has to hand it to Dollfuss that the professional sector orientation was consistent with his actual beliefs. It did not simply draw on fascist ideology, but rather also drew on a socially conservative tradition adopted from Seipel – although Dollfuss was fond of stressing its basic consistence with the ideas contained in the papal encyclicals, *Rerum novarum* by Pope Leo XIII and *Quadragesimo anno* by Pius XI.[93]
>
> our translation

What this ideology shared with classical fascism was the construction of the state's overriding role with respect to the nation, social groups, and individuals. It assumed that the state was 'omnipotent' in economic and political life, if not in intellectual life. It was a reactionary, conservative ideology, which served to validate government suppression of the opposition – the SDAP, KPÖ, and NSDAP, to name but a few of the organisations that were subjected to persecution. As Staudinger observes, its nationalism was its only positive component, considering the political balance of forces in Europe. It protected Austria's political sovereignty against Germany's annexation pledges.[94] All the same, this aspect of Austrofascist ideology did not amount to any significant social transformations because the popular masses were excluded from public life when parliament was dissolved. There was another reason as to why Austrofascist nationalism could not fulfil its intended duties. As Staudinger writes:

> This German ideology of 'Austria' was unsuitable for reinforcing existing Austrian patriotic trends in their own ranks. The complicated intellectual stylisation of the corporative 'Austria' ideology alone did not exactly further its broad reception. What is more, its insistence on Austria's belong-

---

93   Zöllner 1979, p. 514.
94   See Staudinger 1984b, p. 311.

ing to the German nation not only failed to encourage an emerging formulation of Austrian national consciousness (Ernst Karl Winter), it virtually
suppressed it.[95]

> our translation

On 19 August 1933 in Riccione, Dollfuss, who was hoping for a future congru-
ous with Italy, broached an agreement with Mussolini that committed him to a
corporative constitution.[96] During the period in which the authoritarian constitution was finalised, a feat that lasted almost a year, only four important
organisations prevailed on Austria's political stage; the Christian Social Party,
the Fatherland Front set up by the government (which merged with associations which supported Austrian independence), the Greater German People's
Party, and the Heimwehr. The May constitution (30 April–1 May 1934) supported by these groups introduced the following reforms: professional sectors were
subject to strict state control, authoritarian virtues granted to the chancellor,
the government became the central authority in political decisions, bans on
plebiscites, strikes, and demonstrations.[97] There was no place for the Heim-

---

95   Ibid. Staudinger cites another important factor which weakened the influence of the
     'Austria' ideology: 'Without a doubt, the corporative "Austria" ideology was intended to
     play a defensive role against trends that desired a union with National Socialist Germany.
     Evaluating the defensive power of this ideology, however, one must note that it had no
     such effect. The weakness of its defensive power cannot be explained merely by citing
     the phenomenon of the National Socialist *Anschluss* policy's success, but primarily by
     pointing to the "Austria" ideology's inadequate character given the effect it aspired to have.
     Its weakness is found in the very attempt to compete with National Socialism to achieve
     similar goals – i.e. to establish and organise a great empire, lead German culture, and
     cultivate "German folk traditions", including abroad. To obtain these aims, the political
     power basis held by Germany had an incomparably stronger appeal than the Austrian
     position' (our translation) – Ibid.

96   Mussolini's influence in Austria became more significant after the signing of the 'Rome
     protocols' on 17 March 1934. The Italian leverage was unpopular among Austrians. Mus-
     solini's fascist decrees received no applause, and the *Duce*'s policies in South Tyrol pro-
     voked aversion and fear.

97   The 'Constitution 1934' was unanimously decreed by the council of ministers on 30 April
     1934. It was ratified by the provisional parliament (76 of 165 delegates). The constitution
     was to transfigure the democratic republic, Austria, into an authoritarian corporative
     state. It was published in the 'Federal Law Gazette for the State of Austria' as no. 1 on 1 May
     1934. Wereszycki points to the illegal character of this measure, explaining that according
     to the existing constitution of 1929, a constitutional change could only be decided by
     referendum, not by parliament.
         The new constitution changed the official name of the country from 'Republic Aus-

wehr in the new corporative state – once an indispensable aid in the struggle for power; it now stood in the way of authoritarian rule. Following a government decision in 1935, the Heimwehr was co-opted by the Fatherland Front and subjected to state control. On 9 October 1936, it was dissolved. Once the Heimwehr had been abolished and the NSDAP dissolved (1935), the process of implementing the Austrian dictatorship was accomplished.[98] A question that Bauer himself posed in his analysis of Austrofascism arises: did the Dollfuss dictatorship have a truly fascist character comparable to Hitler's and Mussolini's? This was definitely not the case, even if, as Steiner points out, answers to this

---

tria' to 'Federal State of Austria'. The organised professional sectors of the authoritarian state replaced the democratic republican form. The organisational principle was that the organs of the state were not appointed 'from below' in general elections, but 'from above' by higher bodies. Unlike in parliamentary democracy, it was not the legislative organs, but the highest executive bodies that exerted definite influence over the actions of representative bodies in the federal states. The executive bodies were subordinate to the government led by the chancellor, and the constitution gave the chancellor the power to decide over the political line.

With regard to state legislation, four advisory bodies were created (the state council, state economy council, state council of culture, and district council). Their purpose was to assess laws prepared through these organs and pass their assessment on to the government. The assessment was not binding for the government; it could make its own decisions. Furthermore, the constitution envisaged the appointment of a parliament consisting of 49 members of the advisory bodies (in reality, however, this parliament never met). Parliament had the right to vote on laws, yet this right was limited to either accepting or rejecting proposals submitted by the government in its unadulterated form.

The legislative sections of the individual federal states (the state parliaments or *Landtage*) consisted of the elected representatives of cultural communities and professional sectors (however, no elections ever materialised). The federal state governments and mayor of Vienna were appointed and recalled by the federal president, who, in turn, was to be elected by an assembly of all mayors. The federal president had the right to appoint and recall the chancellor.

The reality was that no federal president elections took place during the entire period of corporative state power from 1934–8 because the president's term of office was extended (he had been elected in 1934). The federal president had no authority over the chancellor, who exercised his power in a dictatorial fashion. Compare Adamovich and Spanner 1957, pp. 33–5. See also Zöllner 1979, p. 515.

98 Botz distinguishes three phases of this dictatorship: (1) the phase of the late parliamentary government (May 1932–March 1933); (2) the phase of authoritarian semi-dictatorship and increasing fascisisation (until January 1934); (3) the phase of advanced semi-fascist authoritarian dictatorship (until October 1935 or mid-1936); before (4) the final phase of partial defascisisation and bureaucratically ossified corporatism. See Botz 1984, pp. 320–7.

question are polarised.[99] It was an authoritarian dictatorship that disregarded any rule of law; it was based on a narrow group of powerful individuals supporting each other and employing means of force (police and the army), yet it was doubtlessly not a totalitarian dictatorship. It never degenerated into one ruler's power over the minds and souls of the population, nor was this its purpose. Rather, the regime was interested in keeping individuals and social groups in line for the price of restricting and infringing their political, social, and civil liberties. It is worth highlighting that the 'corporative state' was unable to function in practice and did not abolish the existing social antagonisms. As Kluge also stated, the system saw the professional sector groups sharply collide with the government and Fatherland Front.[100] The Catholic Church sustained its position and organisation, and the Catholic workers' movement enjoyed freedom in the corporative state. The Nazis too influenced the state's political and economic silhouette. The real victim of the authoritarian regime was, consistently with the intentions of its founders, the socialist workers' movement, which it deprived of all and any legal institutions to defend its interests. Among other reasons, this was possible because the parliamentary democratic system in itself does not offer sufficient protection from attacks by anti-democratic forces if political parties are not genuinely willing to democratise social life. The example of Austrian Social Democracy, which was influential in 1930 and lost any practical significance in 1934, illustrates this point succinctly.

The liquidation of the legal party fundamentally weakened the workers' movement, even if it did not mean a complete abandonment of struggle on the part of the Austrian Social Democrats just yet. An illegal organisation named Revolutionary Socialists (RS) was formed on the initiative of the former editors of the *Arbeiter-Zeitung*, Pollack and Leichter.[101] In spite of existing programmatic and generational differences, it considered itself the successor to the old party.[102] That being said, it was unable to win the support of the masses

99   See Steiner 2004, pp. 33–133, where the author illustrates various classifications of the Austrian regime reflected in the works of many postwar and contemporary historians and political scientists – such as Botz, Hanisch, Bracher, Gulick, Clemenz, Holtmann, Talos, Hozer, Carsten, Nolte, Payne, Ludwig, Reichhold, and his own (2004, pp. 133–293) – and points out their differences.

100   See Kluge 1984, p. 87.

101   In 1933, Communist underground circles influenced by 'Neu Beginnen' emerged, e.g. the groups Funke, Rote Front, and Weissel were born.

102   Renner was particularly hostile to the emergence of the party. He was convinced that illegal resistance was futile and dismissed the RS as a merger of left socialists and Communists as opposed to the SDAP's heirs. See Hannak 1965, p. 625.

and become a significant political bulwark.[103] During the first phase of the organisation's development, the 'time of revenge and romanticism', according to Gulick,[104] the Revolutionary Socialists were striking in their verbal radicalism and undue faith in the imminent outbreak of the anti-fascist revolution.[105] In reality, their activity was confined to three duties: helping the families of combatants who had fallen in the uprising; anti-fascist propaganda; and training new recruits – none of which weakened the Austrofascist dictatorship. Lack of decisiveness with respect to programmatic lines and positions on the February 1934 uprising defined the leaders of the new party in the Bauer-led foreign office in Bern.[106]

From the dawn of the party's existence, Bauer's standpoint was as follows: 'Political emigration can only flee from this fate ... [I]t can only become anything other than the flotsam and jetsam of history to the extent it is capable of serving the illegal movement at home and fulfil functions that can only be fulfilled from abroad'.[107] That is to say, Bauer recognised the new leadership and refrained from overseeing the organisation himself. It also meant that aid for the socialists at home would be limited to financial dividends and advocacy.[108] Behind this was not simply Bauer's belief that an illegal movement could not be directed from an outside agent, but also a self-critical assessment of his own failed politics, and a partial change in his views on the role of the workers' party in the age of fascism. His posthumously published text, *The Illegal Party*, attested to the fact that Bauer had lost faith in a rebirth of the old party, advoc-

---

103 'Despite important successes, organisational consolidation, and ideological stabilisation, the Revolutionary Socialists' immobility in relation to forming alliances rendered them incapable of playing any political role in the struggle for Austria's future' (our translation) – Butterwegge 1990, p. 534.

104 Information according to Botz 1978b, p, 363.

105 The illegal paper of the RS was named *Die Revolution*. According to Holtmann, it was published irregularly – twice a month at most – and its circulation was an estimated 10,000–15,000. See Holtmann 1996, p. 1996.

106 Its vacillations were a symptom of attempting to define the relationship between the old and new party, especially with regard to questions of leadership and the degree of collaboration.

107 Bauer 1939, p. 512.

108 His attitude towards the new party was transparent: 'We, the old guard, cannot take up this task from them. However, we have a duty to pass on the experience, knowledge, and values that we acquired through our work and our struggles. We need to pass it on so it may merge with the new knowledge and values that come out from the life and struggles of the new movement that emerged under the pressures of fascism' (our translation) – Bauer 1976p, p. 325.

ating instead the emergence of a new organisation with a different structure and ideology.[109] He recommended forming a party of a proletarian character similar to the Leninist model: a narrow, disciplined, hierarchic cadre organisation based on democratic centralism. Much like Lenin, he aspired to grant this party the monopoly of leading the working class. Unlike the Bolshevik leader, however, he did not go so far as to conflate this task with lawlessness and lack of accountability to the masses. However, Bauer's position within party activity was not entirely clear. Aside from employing Leninist phraseology when, for instance, referring to the party as a combat organisation, he also spoke of the momentous historical importance and continuity of the old ideas in the new movement. According to Maimann, Bauer's ambiguity followed a certain logic: he wanted to nurture the revolutionary character of the new party to prevent former SDAP members from drifting towards Communism; at the same time, by acquainting the party with its tradition, he wanted to create a premise upon which the old and new wings could co-operate.[110] Bauer attempted to overcome the split in the party at a convention of confidantes in Blansko near Brünn in the autumn of 1934.[111] Although it succeeded in the short-term, long-term cooperation between the two factions proved impossible because of divergent programmatic positions. In 1935, the leadership of the RS relinquished the radicalism it had cultivated in its early stages, speaking critically of Léon Blum's popular front in France, which the 'old guard' supported. It also expressed scepticism over the changes in the Soviet Union and the possibility of unifying the international workers' movement. Likewise, the party's initial confidence in the triumph of the anti-fascist struggle was soon dispelled.[112] The Revolutionary Socialists' trajectory inspired impassioned protest from Bauer, who accused their leaders of spreading pessimism and fatalism in the ranks of the working class.[113] Bauer felt personally hurt when the Revolutionary Socialists criticised

---

109 Marschalek depicts Bauer's model of the illegal party engagingly in Marschalek 1990, pp. 41–4.

110 Compare Maimann 1985, p. 232.

111 For a few months, the party adopted the name United Socialist Party Austria. See Wandruszka 1954, p. 468.

112 The relationship between the two parties soured after the congress in Brünn, which Bauer and Friedrich Adler attended. 28 congress attendees were detained for treason and convicted in 1936. Among those condemned to 25 years in prison was Kreisky, who was, however, soon released.

113 See Bauer 1980dd, p. 209. Goller elaborates on the conflict between Bauer and Buttinger over programmatic and tactical differences between the old and new parties in Goller 2008, pp. 96–100. Otto Leichter supported Bauer's position – see Leichter 1937, p. 342.

him for his indecisive politics and contradiction between words and deeds. For him, the new party was a sect, and he demanded that the illegal movement refrain from critically examining the party's past. He could never bring himself to pass honest judgement of the SDAP leadership or acknowledge its fatalist nature.

During his time of emigration, Bauer remained adamant about the concept of 'integral socialism', which intended to unite the Social-Democratic and Communist tendencies. Hence, he attentively followed the tense relationship between the RS and the Communist Party of Austria (KPÖ). There were controversies primarily concerned with the creation of a popular front within both organisations. The KPÖ had approached the SDAP as early on as 1933 with this proposal, and it renewed its offer when approaching the Revolutionary Socialists following the February events. After its ban, the KPÖ vastly shifted its emphasis and modified its strategic and tactical paradigms. Party members forewent their accusations that Social Democracy had collaborated with the fascists. After the uprising was vanquished and a section of SDAP and Schutzbund members had joined the Communists, the KPÖ commenced efforts to unite the workers' movement.[114] What the KPÖ and RS had in common was their struggle against fascism and the illegal character of their activities, yet the suggestion to form a united front under Communist leadership did not receive corroboration from the Revolutionary Socialists.[115] The Revolutionary Socialists rejected the principle of a unified organisational structure for all countries, vying instead for the unity of all classes and social groups within the respective nation. From 1934–6, Bauer agreed with this and accused the Communists of spreading centralist tendencies. He was conscious that the majority of parties affiliated to the LSI did not desire any co-operation with the Comintern.[116] The second half of the 1930s did not see a formal alliance or even loose coordination of activities between the two groups. Bauer, who regarded this as

---

114   See Kolenig 1934, p. 185.

115   The popular front question was brought up once again at the seventh congress of the Comintern in 1935, where Dimitrov justified the necessity of forming a united anti-fascist front. See Dimitrov 1960.

116   This was confirmed in September 1935. The Comintern advocated united action against Italy's imminent attack on Ethiopia. The French, Italian, Spanish, Swiss and Austrian parties, the Mensheviks and the Jewish Bund accepted the invitation. The British, Dutch, Swedish, Danish and both Czechoslovak parties rejected it decisively. However, Bauer's suggested solution – namely that the parties calling for co-operation with the Communists should go ahead of their own accord – was not accepted. No united actions were undertaken as the LSI executive rejected Moscow's offer. See Brügel 1978, p. 12.

positive, distanced himself from any efforts to create a united front. He did so not least under the impression of the Moscow show trials of 1936.

Simultaneously, Schuschnigg's policies had weakened the Austrian middle classes. After the dissolution of the Heimwehr, a shift of power took place in the Christian Social Party benefiting the Fatherland Front and Greater German party. Because of his aversion to democracy and social pluralism, Schuschnigg adhered to the 'German path', thus decisively, if unintentionally, paving the way for National Socialism. Schuschnigg's 11 July 1936 agreement with Hitler was an important milestone on this path. Ostensibly, the leaders signed to reinforce friendly relations between the two countries.[117] Yet in fact, Austria, which had not received any support from Italy since 1936, had to grant serious concessions to Nazi Germany – essentially, the agreement handed the country over to Nazi jurisdiction. After the failed 12 February negotiations with Hitler, Schuschnigg made a final attempt to save Austria's independence by decreeing a referendum for a 'free, independent, German, and Christian Austria'.[118] The two illegal parties, the KPÖ and RS, announced their support for the referendum, even if they did not believe that the clerical-fascist government's resistance against German Nazism would be successful, given that Schuschnigg eschewed the support of the working class and the state power rested solely on the police. The anticipated plebiscite, to which Bauer attached great hope, never had a chance to take place. On 11 March 1938, German troops marched into Austria and forced Schuschnigg to surrender unconditionally. The National-Socialist government formed on 13 March with German consent appealed to the 'extraordinary powers' implemented in 1934 and introduced a new constitution, according to which Austria was incorporated into the German Reich. No lawful act legitimised Austria's occupation – it was a forceful annexation. That said, the majority of Austrian society welcomed the *Anschluss* with enthusiasm.[119] It is important to remember that this stage in the history of the country was the result of many years of passive Social-Democratic politics, the counter-revolutionary offensive

---

117   By virtue of this agreement, Germany recognised Austria's full independence, while the Austrian government proclaimed that its principle was to build Austria as a German state. It furthermore committed itself to counter anti-Hitler propaganda and liquidate Heimwehr units hostile to Hitler and Nazism.

118   See Adamovich and Spanner 1957, p. 35.

119   The citizens of Graz, who welcomed Hitler's annexation with great warmth, may serve as an example. The Third Reich awarded Graz the title, 'the city of the people's uprising'. However, there is no clear record as to how many Austrians supported Hitler's annexation – not least because some of those hostile to the NSDAP nonetheless supported the *Anschluss*.

of the bourgeois parties, and the weakness of the parliamentary system. It was these factors which allowed the 'black fascists' to seize power years before the annexation, thus creating a broad framework for the development of Nazism, which could then effortlessly erase the competition from the political arena.

Following Austria's annexation to Germany, Bauer's writings in emigration focused on apologia for the anti-fascist revolution, which he saw as a consequence of the accomplished annexation.[120] As has been previously mentioned, the demand for *Anschluss* was an integral part of the programme of Austrian Social Democracy. True, the political situation forced the Social Democrats to expunge this point from their programme in 1933; but this by no means amounted to an end to the party's Germanophilia. For some Austrian socialists, Bauer included, Hitler's *Anschluss* was a 'tragedy of history'[121] – but that did not stop them from viewing it as historical progress, as well as considering German revenge for the Allied dictates of St. Germain and Versailles politically justified.[122] Bauer supported this assessment, which was ambivalent in a manner that is typical of the Austrian mentality. It is not unreasonable to state that Bauer's take on Hitler's *Anschluss* was ambiguous. Emotionally, he genuinely perceived it as an assault on Austria's independence. As a politician, he anticipated its consequence: war. One may not ignore, however, that Bauer's anxieties, resulting from being a minority in isolation and coupled with a loss of faith in the ability of his country to survive, had only amassed following the defeat of national revolutions and the rise of fascism in Europe. These factors had already preoccupied his socio-political thinking in the 1920s, and their presence thrived in emigration. They certainly had a crucial impact on his support for Austria's *Anschluss* to Germany in the form of an anti-fascist and socialist revolution in the final period of his life.

If one wants to understand the meaning of the appeal Bauer made in his articles, 'Kann Österreich noch gerettet werden?' ('Can Austria Still Be Saved?'), 'Nach der Annexion' ('After the Annexation'), and 'Österreichs Ende' ('Austria's End'), which were also the author's political testament, then it is important to take his motives into consideration. The most important of them, based on the political situation after World War I, was his desire to transform the war into an anti-fascist revolution from which a new, united, socialist Europe would emerge. Like a few other German Social Democrats in exile and the left wing

---

120   As Maimann also acknowledges, 'The hope for an anti-fascist revolution is a recurring theme throughout [Bauer's] entire history of political exile during Nazism' (our translation) – Maimann 1985, p. 234.

121   See 1980gg, p. 834.

122   See 'Interview mit Karl Renner', *Neues Wiener Tagblatt*, 3 April 1938.

of the British Labour Party, he was still convinced that Germany would be a revolutionary hotbed. According to Bauer, 'the German revolution will have to defend the unity of the German people and Reich not only against capitalist counter-revolution in Germany, but also against counter-revolutionary intervention by imperialist powers' (our translation).[123] Based on this, on 31 March 1938, the KPÖ and RS called for an armed uprising against Hitler's annexation, which Bauer dismissed as a counter-revolutionary threat against the socialist revolution. In opposition, he declared annexation the main premise of the all-German revolution. He sharply criticised the Communists and their ambitions for independence in 'After the Annexation', and the Revolutionary Socialists and theirs in 'Austria's End'. He wrote:

> We cannot turn back the wheel of world history. Only Germany's defeat in war could tear Austria away from the German Reich again, but any German defeat in war would unleash the German revolution, and socialism would not tear Austria away from the German revolution. The future of the Austrian working class, then, is not in any kind of Austrian separatism. The German-Austrian working class can only be liberated if the whole German working class is liberated. The future of the German-Austrian working class is in the future of the German revolution.[124]
>
> our translation

These words of Bauer's were vehemently rebuked by Ernst Bloch, who accused the Austrian socialist of being unable to tell the difference – self-evident to national-minded Austrians – between voluntary union to a democratic Germany and Hitler's annexation.[125] It is difficult to fully concur with the philosopher's view.[126] A more appropriate assessment would be that the interpretations of *Anschluss* by both Bauer and Hitler were by no means the same, even if Bauer rated Hitler's annexation of Austria as historically and socially progress-

---

123   Bauer 1980hh, p. 858.
124   Bauer 1980gg, p. 844. In this article, Bauer argued that while it was an economic necessity to preserve Austria within the framework of the Reich, as it would end structural unemployment, this aspect was secondary.
125   Bloch, in *Neue Welttribüne*, 7 July 1938.
126   In the article, 'Austria's End', Bauer referred to the annexation as the 'German union in fascist slavery' – see Bauer 1980gg, p. 9. In 'After the Annexation', he wrote: 'The union we all wanted was Austria's incorporation into the German Reich by Austrian people's free will. The annexation we have seen is the violent subjugation of the Austrian people by a superior armed power' (our translation) – Bauer 1980hh, p. 855.

ive when confronted with the accomplished fact. What is more, the difference between his position and that of Renner on this question was minimal despite their divergent theoretical justifications.

The pathos and self-assuredness with which Bauer spoke about the imminent revolution in his final articles raise a number of questions. Firstly, on what did Bauer base his assumption of an anti-fascist insurrection in Germany, what did he fail to take into account, and what did he overestimate? Secondly, did he truly believe in his own vision of Europe's future, given the Schuschnigg-Hitler agreement, mass arrests of Communists and socialists, deportations of Jews, and concentration camps? Did he really believe that the hypnotic power of socialism could compete against fascist propaganda and expansion?[127]

Like most European Social Democrats, Bauer spent a lifetime overestimating the German workers' movement's capabilities of organisation, its possibilities, and its willingness to act. The theoretical and political leadership of the Social-Democratic Party of Germany obliquely conditioned this. One can hardly blame him, but from the perspective of exile, he was unable to make a realistic analysis of the illegal organisations' room for manoeuvre under the conditions of fascism. The same is the case for the working class's susceptibility to fascist rhetoric. Furthermore, his perspective blinded him to the reality that fascism had solidified itself and sent its political opponents to camps or had them assassinated. On the other hand, it is difficult to believe that an experienced politician and expert on the national question such as Bauer would be uninformed about the growing nationalism in the German and Austrian working classes and Social-Democratic parties. Likewise, it is improbable that he was inattentive to the causes of lost national revolutions and the resulting legacies. His misrecognition of these factors and their consequences was psychological. Bauer was a fanatical revolutionary, even if his fanaticism was of a different variety to Lenin's. It was the fanaticism of a man obsessed with the idea of freedom, who dogmatically and one-sidedly conflated it with socialism, and therefore also with revolution as a tool with which to realise the ideal. What is more, Bauer was incapable of critically assessing his own perception of history, and he could not come to terms with the demise of the SDAP's political vision and the end of the Austromarxist doctrine. Likewise, he was unable to forgo his revolutionary rhetoric, which accompanied him his entire life and consistently contained hollow formulas, something that he failed to acknowledge.

---

127   Maimann poses similar questions in the aforementioned article and answers in the negative. See Maimann 1985, p. 235.

The recollections of his party comrades and his dispersed notes are evidence that Bauer never lost his faith in socialism's appeal. This was the case even though he lived to see the demise of his lifetime achievements, i.e. the defeat of the party, growing pessimism in the illegal movement, and Stalin and Hitler's intensifying terrorism. That he suddenly died after all his hopes had been squashed seems to confirm that he truly embodied his beliefs. It is difficult to tell whether he would have stuck to these had he lived to witness the Hitler-Stalin pact, the annexation of Polish territories to the Soviet Union, and the forceful creation of the bloc of countries on which 'really existing socialism' was imposed. It is not the task of historians to indulge in such speculations. Hence, it is fitting to conclude this analysis of Bauer's thought where death put an end to it.

Closing Remarks

I do not intend to end this book with a synthesis of Austromarxist theory and practice as understood by Otto Bauer. The most important reasons are the following. Firstly, Bauer's theoretical legacy comprises a number of different scientific disciplines. In his work, they maintain a relatively autonomous character. Consequently, I treated them as self-contained areas of study in my reconstruction, while striving to flesh out the motifs they had in common – that is, the defence of individual freedom, and democracy as an autotelic value of paramount importance for the entire organisation of social and political life. Secondly, it is impossible to reveal the epistemological value of individual theories by analysing the theses they encompass. This can only be done by relating these ideas to the influential intellectual and political tendencies of the time. Wherever Bauer's ideas were linked to the political practice of the Social-Democratic movement, I presented their connection to concrete socio-political issues and the relevant historical and social conditions. Thirdly, but no less importantly, I ended each chapter of this book with conclusions and appraisals.

Instead of a summary, I will therefore offer a few general remarks on Bauer's contribution to socialist theory. That is to say, I will highlight where he contradicted Marxian ideas that could no longer be applied to the socio-political realities of Bauer's lifetime. I will also briefly comment on the political strategy and tactics he adopted for the SDAP.

Otto Bauer, a legend when he was still alive, remains a controversial figure posthumously. His work is distinguished by his outstanding personality and intense, critical mind. Literature dedicated to Bauer tends to emphasise his great achievements as a historian, sociologist, and political scientist in four areas: the social and economic history of Austria, studies on the nation and nationalism, the analysis of the Russian Revolution and Bolshevism, and interpretations of fascism.[1] Although this appraisal is entirely justified, I would like to complement it further by drawing attention to a number of issues that were essential to Bauer's contribution:

– In light of the dominant positions in the Second International, his proposals for the national question and socialist revolution, the state, and especially democracy, were innovative. Bauer's emphasis on the axiological value of democracy and its role in civil society appears especially valuable to me.

---

1 See, for example, Hanisch 1985, p. 195.

- Bauer determinedly settled scores with Lenin's interpretation of Marx's historical materialism and the Bolshevik method of building socialism.
- His vision of a future state, his programme for cultural autonomy, his socialisation and agrarian programme, and his theory of 'integral socialism', which are associated with him today, were all original contributions to the evolution of Marxist and socialist theory.
- His proposals concerning the socio-political and democratic system were remarkable.

There is yet another aspect to Bauer's theoretical input which usually escapes the attention of historians and political scientists. Although he invariably asserted his loyalty to Marxism, Bauer remained an independent thinker who was far from blind to changing realities. Hence his texts contain ideas strongly rooted in Marxist dogma, but also attempt to break free from such strictures. This tension in Bauer's thinking was particularly manifested in his consistent attempts to incorporate the subjective and evaluative aspect into the determinist perspective. He favoured the latter outlook in the historiosophical, ethical, and political realms, and he employed it whenever he wanted to stress the autonomy of politics from economics.[2] The same tension was present in his now controversial attempts at solving the contradictions between individual freedom and freedom in a community, and the antinomy between power and voluntary compromise.

Many writers are critical of Bauer's political activism. Ellenbogen, Wandruszka, and Butterwegge explain the schisms of his politics by way of a conflicted personality – that is, the divergence between thought and action, apparent in his attitude toward revolution, coalition, democracy, and dictatorship.[3] Leser accuses Bauer of acting in a politically half-baked manner, which, according to him, became apparent during periods of increasing social pressures and conflicts, e.g. war, revolution, and the fascist offensive. Moreover, he criticises Bauer for consciously oscillating between programmatic minimalism and maximalism. Finally, he blames Bauer for the SDAP's erratic political line.[4] In my view, these charges do a disservice to Bauer. Ultimately, they subjectively presume an

---

2   Of all analysts of Bauer's thought, only Saage developed this aspect of his historiosophy. I wish to stress, however, that we arrived at our convergent conclusions independently. Saage writes: 'In fact, no Marxist of the Second International before or after World War I emphasised the importance of the "subjective factor" as strongly as Bauer did' – Saage 1990b, p. 56.
3   See Ellenbogen 1980, p. 1095; Wandruszka 1954, p. 451; and Butterwegge 1981, pp. 61–71.
4   See Leser 1968, p. 304.

individual's freedom of political action, while leaving aside the complex socio-historical reality in which Bauer had to make decisions.[5]

It is not easy to pass judgement on Bauer's strategy and tactics. It seems more likely to me that the inadequacy of his theoretical and practical answers resulted from his excessive dependency on Marxian discourse and thought patterns, many of which did not correspond to social realities of Marx's time. A good example (and here I agree with Leser) was Bauer's belief in the mechanisms of history and the automatism of capitalist development, from which he concluded that socialism was historically inevitable.[6] Hanisch's appraisal of Bauer as a politician comes closest to mine when he writes in his Otto Bauer biography:

> The central problem of Bauer's politics was not so much the contradiction between theory and practice ... as a politics of 'on the one hand / on the other' ... In other words, the difference between the sharp analyst and the political practitioner who was frequently incapable of acting.[7]
> our translation

Without a doubt, Bauer's political indecision and supposed incapability to act were greatly influenced by his exceptionally strong sense of moral responsibility, his unquestioned humanism, and his ability to foresee the course of events. His truthful assessment of the workers' activism in 1927 serves as a case in point: their anticipation of mass support for a general strike proved baseless.

Given all the criticism voiced by Austrian researchers, it is justified to wonder whether Bauer as strategist and tactician only ever committed mistakes. If one seriously considers the balance of political forces in Austria and Europe, one has to reply that he did not – the hard political realities of 1918, 1931 and 1933–8 sufficiently prove this. Let us look at the issues that provoke such severe criticism of Bauer's behaviour. In the first instance, his refusal to instigate a revolution in 1918 was based on a realistic evaluation of the political climate across Europe. Short of a victorious revolution in the West, the fate of a proletarian dictatorship in Austria would have most likely resembled that of the Hungarian and Bavarian Soviet republics. In the second instance, a Christian-Social and Social-Democratic coalition in 1931 might have been able to prevent the ascent

---

5 Saage holds similar views on this – see Saage 1985, p. 11.

6 See Leser 1968, p. 33.

7 Hanisch 2011, p. 13.

of the Heimwehr. However, it is questionable whether it could have smashed Nazism and countered the rise of German nationalism and anti-Semitism.

When assessing Bauer's political conduct, it is necessary to draw a line between what was advocated and what was day-to-day practice determined by socio-historical conditions and the political situation. Bauer's policies were designed to create mechanisms that would push the bourgeois state in a democratic-liberal direction. Before the rise of fascism, he succeeded in this to a considerable extent. The overriding strategic goal, socialism, never made him blind to the short-term advantages that reformist policies could bring the working class in a bourgeois state. Success came in the form of social legislation and institutions that changed the living and working conditions of the masses for the better. The living standard of the lower social classes in today's Austria is a permanent achievement of the Social-Democratic movement of the First Republic.

None of this fully absolves Bauer from responsibility for the political defeat of Austromarxism. As the SDAP's key strategist, he is chiefly at fault for stoking the masses' illusions as to the power of the workers' movement. He can also be blamed for his excessive belief in democracy's defensive mechanisms and the stability of the democratic form of government. Moreover, his belief in the superiority and cultural and political mission of the German nation led him to overrate the revolutionary strength of the German workers' movement. Bauer's revolutionary pathos was also politically harmful.[8] Not that it was of any

---

8   Bauer's emotionally loaded speeches in parliament provoked heckles such as 'Jewish lackey' and 'Bolshevik'. Some did not stop short of physical attacks. His verbal radicalism was the reason for polarised attitudes towards him in the press. Social-Democratic papers deemed Otto Bauer the theoretical inheritor of Victor Adler. The bourgeois press – especially the *Reichspost, Neue Freie Presse*, and *Deutschösterreichische Zeitung* – painted a damning portrait of a politician out of touch with socio-political reality, capable only of viewing the world through the prism of class struggle. We might add to this a few words on Bauer's attitude to life. He was a passionate and uncompromising speaker – but only when speaking from the platform. In private, he was extraordinarily humble, timid, and not very social. When speaking to peasants and workers, he suffered from an inferiority complex typical for the bourgeois intelligentsia. Because of this, Bauer approached workers and intellectuals in different ways. Full of patience and understanding when in conversation with the former, he was far more morally demanding of the latter, and he kept them at arm's length. His contemporaries' recollections describe Bauer as someone alien to the salons, using the tram to commute to the Baroque Palace on Ballhausplatz in worn-out clothes every day. Although he was a well-known and wealthy politician, he continued to live in a modest one-bedroom flat in Kasernengasse 2, a street that still bears his name. Bauer possessed two qualities that people highly valued in Social-Democratic politicians: he did not attach any

significance for the leaders of hostile political factions, who were well aware that there was no genuine will to act behind the revolutionary rhetoric. It did, however, mislead potential supporters of Social Democracy: a considerable part of society believed that Bauer's politics would herald civil war in Austria. This fear resulted in widespread hostility towards the SDAP and allowed the bourgeois parties to consolidate their power.

Bauer placed great importance on the moral value of his politics, and his fate incontestably demonstrates the extent to which this both drove and incapacitated his politics. His failure as a politician does not diminish the value of the ideas he served: the realisation of social partnership and the unity of progressive and democratic forces. To accomplish these ideas, one needs to extend democracy and civil liberties and abide by ideological pluralism – principles that were close to Bauer's heart.

Austromarxism, including Bauer's theory and practice, is a fragment of the history of Marxism, a part of the history of the international workers' movement, and an essential piece of the political history of Europe. The value of Austromarxist philosophical, sociological, economic, political, and cultural ideas remains the subject of research and debate. Even if history thwarted the vision of Austromarxism, this does not diminish its real gains as a political movement.[9] Bauer's contribution to these gains cannot possibly be overestimated.

---

  importance to titles, wealth, or personal advantage, and he lived according to the values he preached.

9 Some of the Austromarxists' achievements include: encouragement of theoretical and scientific interest, cultural and sport activity, education in the spirit of ideological and religious tolerance, the introduction of intellectualism into working-class and petty-bourgeois milieus, school and health reforms, social legislation, and housing and recreational facilities.

References

1   Archival Sources

A   *Adler Archive, Vienna*
Letter from Victor Adler to Karl Kautsky, 14 Nov 1917, file 74.
Letter from Ludo Hartmann to Otto Bauer, 24 Jun 1919, file 85.
Letters from Otto Bauer to Victor and Friedrich Adler, 1909–37.

**B   *General Administration Archive (Allgemeines Verwaltungsarchiv),
Vienna***
Bauer, Otto 1920, *Vortrag vom 24/25.08.1920*, S.D. Parl. Klub, Karte 113. Sozialdemokrat-
ische Parteistellen 121, 123.

C   *Old Party Archive, Verein für Geschichte der Arbeiterbewegung, Wien*
Adler, Friedrich 1923, 'Rede auf der Sitzung der Roten Garde' (speech at the meeting of
the Red Guards), 21 Nov 1923, Arbeiterräte.
Meeting protocols of the party leadership 1913–33.

D   *Arberrörelens Arkiv, Stockholm*
Letter from Victor Adler to Hjalmar Branting, 7 May 1917.

E   *Archive of the Republic, Vienna*
'Rede L. Kunschak vom 9 Februar 1934 im Gemeinderat Wien' (Kunschak's speech on
9 Feb 1934 at Vienna town council), file 174.

**F   *Family, Court and State Archive (Haus-, Hof- und Staatsarchiv),
Vienna***
Political department I – 818, 958, 959.

**G   *Kautsky Archive, Internationaal Instituut voor Soziale Geschiedenis,
Amsterdam***
Letter from Otto Bauer to Karl Kautsky, 3 Jan 1913, D. II, SG.
Letter from Otto Bauer to Karl Kautsky, 28 Sep 1917, D. II, SG.
Letter from Ludo Hartmann to Otto Bauer, 24 Jun 1919, file 85.

H   *LSI Archive, Internationaal Instituut voor Soziale Geschiedenis,*
       Amsterdam
Letter from Otto Bauer to Friedrich Adler, 19 Aug 1936, 26/16/11/S.G.
file 348/12–13, II, S.G.

2   Documents, Programmes, Protocols

Activities of the association of Social-Democratic delegates in the Constituent National
    Assembly and National Council of the Republic of German-Austria, Vienna 1919–
    26.
Berchtold, Klaus 1967, *Österreichische Parteiprogramme 1868–1966*, Munich and Olden-
    burg.
Congress Protocols of the Second International (Kongress-Protokolle der Zweiten
    Internationale), Vol. 2, Stuttgart 1907–Basel 1912, Appendix, Protocol of the meeting
    of the International Bureau from 29–30 Jul 1914 in Bruxelles, Darmstadt.
Congress Protocols of the Second International, Berlin–Bonn 1979.
Dokumenty z historii III *Międzynarodówki komunistycznej*. z. 1. [Documents from the
    history of the Third Communist International], Warsaw 1962.
Extraordinary International Socialist Congress in Basel from 24–25 Nov 1912, Berlin 1912.
International Socialist Congress in Copenhagen from 28 Aug–3 Sep, Berlin 1910.
International Socialist Congress in Stuttgart from 18–24 Aug, Berlin 1907.
Protocol of the International Socialist Workers' Congress in Hamburg, 21–25 May 1923,
    Berlin 1923.
Reports of the Imperial and Royal Interior Ministry, Political Police Department, 19–21
    Jan 1918, Vienna 1918.
SDAP 1892, Third Austrian Social-Democratic Party Congress in Vienna Proceedings,
    5–9 Jun 1892.
SDAP 1894, Fourth Austrian Social-Democratic Party Congress in Vienna Proceedings,
    25–31 Mar 1894.
SDAP 1896, Fifth Austrian Social-Democratic Party Congress in Vienna Proceedings, 5–
    11 Apr 1896.
SDAP 1897, Sixth Austrian Social-Democratic Party Congress in Vienna Proceedings, 6–
    12 Jun 1897.
SDAP 1899, All-Party Congress of Austrian Social Democracy, 24–29 Sep 1899, Vienna:
    Brand.
SDAP 1901, Protocol of the SDAP aggregate of 2–6 Nov 1901, Vienna.
SDAP 1902, Congress of the German SDAP in Aussig proceedings, 15–18 Aug 1902, Vienna.
SDAP 1903, All-Party Congress in Vienna Proceedings, 9–13 Nov 1903, Vienna 1903.
SDAP 1909, Protocol of the SDAP Congress of 19–24 Sep 1909, Vienna.

SDAP 1912, Protocol of the SDAP Congress of 31 Oct–4 Nov 1912, Vienna.

SDAP 1913, Protocol of the SDAP Congress of 31 Oct–4 Nov 1913, Vienna.

SDAP 1917, Protocol of the SDAP Congress of 19–24 Oct 1917, Vienna.

SDAP 1920, Protocol of SDAP Negotiations (Austria, German-Austria) 1905–20.

SDAP 1921, Protocol of the SDAP Congress of 5–7 Nov 1920, Vienna.

SDAP 1926a, Protocol of the SDAP Congress in Linz of 30 Oct–3 Nov 1926, Vienna.

SDAP 1926b, The Agrarian Programme of German-Austrian Social Democracy, Vienna.

SDAP 1927, Protocol of the SDAP Congress of 19 Oct–1 Nov 1927, Vienna.

SDAP 1931, Protocol of the SDAP Congress of 13–15 Nov 1931, Vienna.

SDAP 1932, Protocol of the SDAP Congress of 13–15 Nov 1932 at the Working Men's Club in Ottakring, Vienna.

SDAP 1934, Protocol of the SDAP Congress in Salzburg.

Second Congress of the Labour and Socialist International in Marseille from 22–27 Aug 1925, Marseille 1925.

SPD 1905, Aggregate of All-German Party Delegates from 23–25 Jan 1905.

SPD 1912, Protocol of Negotiations at the Congress of the German Social-Democratic Workers' Party in Austria, Vienna 31 Oct–4 Nov 1912.

Stenographic protocols of Provisional National Assembly of German-Austria sessions in Vienna, 1918–19.

3 Works and Secondary Literature

Abendroth, Wolfgang 1965, *Sozialgeschichte der europäischen Arbeiterbewegung*, Frankfurt am Main: Suhrkamp.

Adamovich, Ludwig Karl and Hans Spanner 1957, *Handbuch des österreichischen Verfassungsrechts*, Fifth Edition, Vienna: Springer.

Adler, Friedrich 1914, 'Der Tag der deutschen Nation', *Arbeiter-Zeitung*, 5 Aug 1914, Vienna.

———— 1918a, *Ernst Machs Überwindung des mechanischen Materialismus*, Vienna: Verlag der Wiener Volksbuchhandlung.

———— 1918b, *Die Erneuerung der Internationale, Aufsätze aus der Kriegszeit*, edited by Robert Danneberg, Vienna: I. Brand.

———— 1919, *Friedrich Adler vor dem Ausnahmegericht. Die Verhandlungen vor dem 14. Gericht am 18. und 19. Mai 1917 nach dem stenographischen Protokoll.* Berlin: P. Cassirer.

———— 1932, 'Das Stalinische Experiment und der Sozialismus', *Der Kampf*, 25: 4–16.

Adler, Max 1901, 'Zur Revision des Parteiprogramms. Über den Wert eines sozialdemokratischen Parteiprogramms. Zum Kapitel: Verelendungstheorie', *Arbeiter-Zeitung*, 22 Nov.

———— 1913, *Marxistische Probleme. Beiträge zur Theorie der materialistischen Geschichtsauffassung und Dialektik*, Stuttgart: J.H.W. Dietz Nachf. G.m.b.H.

———— 1915a, 'Was ist die Notwendigkeit der Entwicklung?', *Der Kampf*, 8: 173–232.

———— 1915b, *Prinzip oder Romantik. Sozialistische Betrachtungen zum Weltkrieg*, Nuremberg: Fränkische Verlagsanstalt & Buchdruckerei.

———— 1919, *Demokratie und Rätesystem*, Vienna: Brand.

———— 1925, *Marx als Denker*, Berlin: J.H.W. Dietz Nachf.

———— 1932, 'Zur Disskusion über Sowjetrußland', *Der Kampf*, 5: 215–24.

———— 1964, *Grundlegung der materialistischen Geschichtsauffassung*, Vienna: Europaverlag.

———— 1978 [1904], 'Causality and Teleology', in *Austro-Marxism*, edited by Tom Bottomore and Patrick Goode, Oxford: Clarendon Press.

———— 1981a, 'Das Gleichgewicht der Klassenkräfte', in *Ausgewählte Schriften*, Vienna: Österreichischer Bundesverlag.

———— 1981b, *Ausgewählte Schriften*, Vienna: Österreichischer Bundesverlag.

Albers, Detlev 1979, 'Otto Bauer und das Konzept des "integralen Sozialismus"', in *Otto Bauer und der 'dritte' Weg. Die Wiederentdeckung des Austromarxismus durch Linkssozialisten u. Eurokommunisten*, edited by Detlev Albers, Frankfurt and New York: Campus Verlag.

———— 1983, *Versuch über Otto Bauer und Antonio Gramsci. Zur politischen Theorie des Marxismus*, Berlin: Argument-Verlag.

———— 1985a, 'Über den Marxismus Bauers und Gramscis', in *Otto Bauer (1881–1938): Theorie und Praxis*, edited by Erich Fröschl and Helge Zoitl, Vienna: Europaverlag.

———— (ed.) 1985b, *Otto Bauer: Theorie und Politik*, (*Argument* special edition), AS 129, Berlin: Argument-Verlag.

Anreiter, Fritz 1986, 'Wohnbaupolitik und Wohnverhältnisse im Roten Wien. Ein didaktischer Versuch', *Zeitgeschichte*, 13: 28–37.

Ardelt, Rudolf G. 1979, 'Die österreichische Sozialdemokratie und der Kriegsausbruch 1914. Die Krise einer politischer Elite', *Jahrbuch für Zeitgeschichte 1979*: 59–130.

Austerlitz, Friedrich 1914a, 'Der Weltkrieg des Zaren', *Arbeiter-Zeitung*, 2 Aug 1914, Vienna.

———— 1914b, 'Der Tag der deutschen Nation', *Arbeiter-Zeitung*, 5 Aug 1914, Vienna.

Barczyk, Ryszard and Zygmunt Kowalczyk 1985, 'Teoria kryzysów i cyklu koniunkturalnego Karola Marksa', in *Marks, Marksizm, Współczesność*, edited by Seweryn Dziamski, Poznan: Wydawnictwo Naukowe UAM.

Bauer, Otto [as Heinrich Weber] 1909, 'Nationale und internationale Gesichtspunkte in der auswärtigen Politik', *Der Kampf*, 2, 12: 535–42.

———— 1913, 'Die Grundfrage unserer Taktik', *Der Kampf*, 7: 49–63.

———— 1917, *Die russische Revolution und das europäische Proletariat*, Vienna: Brand.

———— 1918, 'Das Selbstbestimmungsrecht der österreichischen Nationen, die Bolschewiki und wir. Voraussetzungen der Internationale', *Der Kampf*, 11: 201–15.

———— 1919, 'Karl Kautsky und der Bolschewismus', *Der Kampf*, 28: 661–7.

———— 1920a, 'Referat Bauers im Vorstand der sozialdemokratischen Partei, 20. Mai 1920', Leadership Protocols Supplement, Vienna: Verein für Geschichte der Arbeiterbewegung.

———— 1920b, 'Die alte und die neue Linke', *Der Kampf*, 20, 3: 249–60.

———— 1923, *Die österreichische Revolution*, Vienna: Wiener Volksbuchhandlung.

———— 1925a, *The Austrian Revolution* (abridged translation of *Die österreichische Revolution*), London: Leonard Parsons.

———— 1925b, *Der Kampf um Wald und Weide. Studien zur österreichischen Agrargeschichte und Agrarpolitik*, Vienna: Wiener Volksbuchhandlung.

———— 1927, 'Nach dem Parteitag', *Der Kampf*, 12: 545–51.

———— 1928, 'Klassenkampf und Ideologie', *Der Kampf*, 21: 281–8.

———— 1930a, 'Die Bourgeoise-Republik in Österreich', *Der Kampf*, 23: 193–202.

———— 1930b, 'Ein Brief an Karl Renner', *Der Kampf*, 23: 305–11.

———— 1931, *Kapitalismus und Sozialismus nach dem Weltkrieg*, Volume 1: *Rationalisierung – Fehlrationalisierung*, Vienna: Wiener Volksbuchhandlung.

———— 1932, 'Der 24. April', *Der Kampf*, 25: 189–93.

———— 1934a, *Der Aufstand der österreichischen Arbeiter. Seine Ursachen und seine Wirkungen*, Prague: Verlag der Deutschen Sozialdemokratischen Arbeiterpartei in der Tschechoslowakischen Republik.

———— 1934b, 'Die Strategie des Klassenkampfes', *Der Kampf*, 27: 3–12.

———— 1934c, 'Kommunisten und Sozialisten in Österreich', *Der Kampf*, 7: 104–20.

———— [as Heinrich Weber] 1937, 'Das Wesen der Volksfront', *Der Kampf*, 4: 169–77.

———— 1939, *Die illegale Partei. Aus dem unveröffentlichten Nachlass*, Paris: Éditions 'La lutte socialiste'.

———— 1961 [1937], 'Max Adler. Ein Beitrag zur Geschichte des Austromarxismus', in *Otto Bauer. Eine Auswahl aus seinem Lebenswerk: Mit einem Lebensbild Otto Bauers von Julius Braunthal*, edited by Julius Braunthal, Vienna: Verlag der Wiener Volksbuchhandlung.

———— 1975a [1907], 'Deutschtum und Sozialdemokratie', in *Werkausgabe*, Volume 1, Vienna: Europaverlag.

———— 1975b [1910], *Die Teuerung. Eine Einführung in die Wirtschaftspolitik der Sozialdemokratie* in *Werkausgabe*, Volume 1, Vienna: Europaverlag.

———— 1975c [1911], *Großkapital und Militarismus. Wem nützen die neuen Kriegsschiffe?*, in *Werkausgabe*, Volume 1, Vienna: Europaverlag.

———— 1975d [1911], *Geschichte Österreichs*, in *Werkausgabe*, Volume 1, Vienna: Europaverlag.

———— 1976a [1919], *Die Weltrevolution*, in *Werkausgabe*, Volume 2, Vienna: Europaverlag.

———— 1976b [1919], *Der Weg zum Sozialismus*, in *Werkausgabe*, Volume 2, Vienna: Europaverlag.

———— 1976c [1920], 'Bolschewismus oder Sozialdemokratie?', in *Werkausgabe*, Volume 2, Vienna: Europaverlag.

———— 1976d [1920], 'Probleme der europäischen Revolution', in *Werkausgabe*, Volume 2, Vienna: Europaverlag.

———— 1976e [1921], *Der neue Kurs in Sowjetrußland*, in *Werkausgabe*, Volume 2, Vienna: Europaverlag.

———— 1976f [1924], 'Das Weltbild des Kapitalismus', in *Werkausgabe*, Volume 2, Vienna: Europaverlag.

———— 1976g [1924], 'Der Kampf um die Macht', in *Werkausgabe*, Volume 2, Vienna: Europaverlag.

———— 1976h [1925], '*Die Wirtschaftskrise in Österreich. Ihre Ursache – ihre Heilung*', in *Werkausgabe*, Volume 3, Vienna: Europaverlag.

———— 1976i [1926], *Sozialdemokratische Agrarpolitik*, in *Werkausgabe*, Volume 3, Vienna: Europaverlag.

———— 1976j [1927], *Sozialdemokratie, Religion und Kirche*, in *Werkausgabe*, Volume 3, Vienna: Europaverlag.

———— 1976k [1927], 'Die politische Lage. Referat auf dem Parteitag von Oktober 1927', in *Werkausgabe*, Volume 3, Vienna: Europaverlag.

———— 1976l [1928], 'Die wirtschaftliche und soziale Lage Österreich', in *Werkausgabe*, Volume 3, Vienna: Europaverlag.

———— 1976m [1928], *Revolutionäre Kleinarbeit*, in *Werkausgabe*, Volume 3, Vienna: Europaverlag.

———— 1976n [1907–8], *Parlamentarismus und Arbeiterschaft*, in *Werkausgabe*, Volume 4, Vienna: Europaverlag.

———— 1976o [1931], 'Die Lage in Deutschland und Zentraleuropa und der Kampf der Arbeiterklasse um die Demokratie. Vierter Kongreß der Sozialistischen Arbeiter-Internationale, Wien 25. Juli bis 1. Aug 1931', in *Werkausgabe*, Volume 4, Vienna: Europaverlag.

———— 1976p [1936], *Zwischen zwei Weltkriegen? Die Krise der Weltwirtschaft, der Demokratie und des Sozialismus*, in *Werkausgabe*, Volume 4, Vienna: Europaverlag.

———— 1976q [1952], *Einführung in die Volkswirtschaftslehre*, in *Werkausgabe*, Volume 4, Vienna: Europaverlag.

———— 1978 [1912–13], 'Zum Innsbrucker Parteitag', in *Werkausgabe*, Volume 5, Vienna: Europaverlag.

———— 1978b [1925], 'Das Agrarprogramm', in *Werkausgabe*, Volume 5, Vienna: Europaverlag.

——— 1978c [1933], 'Ausserordentlicher Parteitag', in *Werkausgabe*, Volume 5, Vienna: Europaverlag.

——— 1978d [1937], 'Max Adler: A Contribution to the History of Austro-Marxism', in *Austro-Marxism*, edited by Tom Bottomore and Patrick Goode, Oxford: Clarendon Press.

——— 1978e [1936], 'Fascism', in *Austro-Marxism*, edited by Tom Bottomore and Patrick Goode, Oxford: Clarendon Press.

——— 1979 [1921], 'Tagung des Reichsarbeitsrates', in *Werkausgabe*, Volume 6, Vienna: Europaverlag.

——— 1979b, *Werkausgabe*, Volume 7, Vienna: Europaverlag.

——— 1979c [1904], 'Marx' Theorie der Wirtschaftskrisen', in *Werkausgabe*, Volume 7, Vienna: Europaverlag.

——— 1979d [1905], 'Die Kolonialpolitik und die Arbeiter', in *Werkausgabe*, Volume 7, Vienna: Europaverlag.

——— 1979e, 'Marxismus und Ethik', in *Werkausgabe*, Volume 7, Vienna: Europaverlag.

——— 1979f [1908], 'Die Geschichte eines Buches', in *Werkausgabe*, Volume 7, Vienna: Europaverlag.

——— 1979g [1913], 'Die Erklärung des Imperialismus', in *Werkausgabe*, Volume 7, Vienna: Europaverlag.

——— 1979h [1913], 'Die Akkumulation des Kapitals', in *Werkausgabe*, Volume 7, Vienna: Europaverlag.

——— 1979i [1918], 'Arbeiter-Zeitung 24.11.1918', in *Werkausgabe*, Volume 7, Vienna: Europaverlag.

——— 1979j [1921], 'Wenn Kapitalisten uns loben', in *Werkausgabe*, Volume 7, Vienna: Europaverlag.

——— 1979k [1924], 'Die Wirtschaftskrise im Ausland und in Österreich', in *Werkausgabe*, Volume 7, Vienna: Europaverlag.

——— 1979l [1936], 'Der Moskauer Prozess', in *Werkausgabe*, Volume 7, Vienna: Europaverlag.

——— 1980 [1908], 'Krise und Teuerung', in *Werkausgabe*, Volume 8, Vienna: Europaverlag.

——— 1980b [1908–9], 'Der Staat und die Kartelle', in *Werkausgabe*, Volume 8, Vienna: Europaverlag.

——— 1980c [1909–10], 'Das Finanzkapital', in *Werkausgabe*, Volume 8, Vienna: Europaverlag.

——— 1980d [1912], 'Die Bedingungen der nationalen Assimilation', in *Werkausgabe*, Volume 8, Vienna: Europaverlag.

——— 1980e [1912], 'Der Sozialismus und der Krieg', in *Werkausgabe*, Volume 8, Vienna: Europaverlag.

——— 1980f [1913–14], 'Kapitalsvermehrung und Bevölkerungswachstum', in *Werkausgabe*, Volume 8, Vienna: Europaverlag.

————— 1980g [1918], 'Das Nationalitätenprogramm der Linken', in *Werkausgabe*, Volume 8, Vienna: Europaverlag.

————— 1980h [1918], 'Die Bolschewiki und wir', in *Werkausgabe*, Volume 8, Vienna: Europaverlag.

————— 1980i [1923], 'Marx als Mahnung', in *Werkausgabe*, Volume 8, Vienna: Europaverlag.

————— 1980j [1932], 'Wir Bolschewiken. Eine Antwort an Dollfuss', in *Werkausgabe*, Volume 8, Vienna: Europaverlag.

————— 1980k [1914], 'Brief an Helene', in *Werkausgabe*, Volume 9, Vienna: Europaverlag.

————— 1980l [1917], 'Brief an Karl Kautsky, 8.09.1917', in *Werkausgabe*, Volume 9, Vienna: Europaverlag.

————— 1980m [1918], 'Brief an Karl Kautsky, 4.01.1918', in *Werkausgabe*, Volume 9, Vienna: Europaverlag.

————— 1980n [1919], 'Brief an Bela Kun, 16.06.1919', in *Werkausgabe*, Volume 9, Vienna: Europaverlag.

————— 1980o [1924], 'Das Gleichgewicht der Klassenkräfte', in *Werkausgabe*, Volume 9, Vienna: Europaverlag.

————— 1980p, 'Der Kongress in Marseilles', in *Werkausgabe*, Volume 9, Vienna: Europaverlag.

————— 1980q [1928], 'Klassenkampf und Ideologie', in *Werkausgabe*, Volume 9, Vienna: Europaverlag.

————— 1980r [1928], 'Kapitalsherrschaft in der Demokratie', in *Werkausgabe*, Volume 9, Vienna: Europaverlag.

————— 1980s [1930], 'Ein Brief an Karl Renner', in *Werkausgabe*, Volume 9, Vienna: Europaverlag.

————— 1980t [1930], 'Die Bourgeoisierepublik in Österreich', in *Werkausgabe*, Volume 9, Vienna: Europaverlag.

————— 1980u [1933], 'Um die Demokratie', in *Werkausgabe*, Volume 9, Vienna: Europaverlag.

————— 1980v [1933], 'Der deutsche Faschismus und die Internationale', in *Werkausgabe*, Volume 9, Vienna: Europaverlag.

————— 1980w [1934], 'Demokratie und Sozialismus', in *Werkausgabe*, Volume 9, Vienna: Europaverlag.

————— 1980x [1934], 'Die Gegenrevolution und die Kirche', in *Werkausgabe*, Volume 9, Vienna: Europaverlag.

————— 1980y [1934], 'Der Austrofaschismus nach dem Naziputsch', in *Werkausgabe*, Volume 9, Vienna: Europaverlag.

————— 1980z [1935], 'Einheitsfront in der Weltpolitik', in *Werkausgabe*, Volume 9, Vienna: Europaverlag.

———— 1980aa [1935], 'Habsburg steht vor den Toren', in *Werkausgabe*, Volume 9, Vienna: Europaverlag.

———— 1980bb [1936], 'Probleme der organischen Einheit', in *Werkausgabe*, Volume 9, Vienna: Europaverlag.

———— 1980cc [1936], 'Starhembergs Sturz', in *Werkausgabe*, Volume 9, Vienna: Europaverlag.

———— 1980dd [1937], 'Optimismus und Pessimismus in der illegalen Arbeiterbewegung', in *Werkausgabe*, Volume 9, Vienna: Europaverlag.

———— 1980ee [1937], 'Der Trotzkismus und die Trotzkistenprozesse', in *Werkausgabe*, Volume 9, Vienna: Europaverlag.

———— 1980ff [1938], 'Der Faschismus', in *Werkausgabe*, Volume 9, Vienna: Europaverlag.

———— 1980gg [1938], 'Österreichs Ende', in *Werkausgabe*, Volume 9, Vienna: Europaverlag.

———— 1980hh [1938], 'Nach der Annexion', in *Werkausgabe*, Volume 9, Vienna: Europaverlag.

———— 1986 [1913], 'Accumulation of Capital', *History of Political Economy*, 18, 1: 87–110.

———— 1996 [1907], *The Question of Nationalities and Social Democracy*, edited by Ephraim J. Nimni, Minneapolis and London: University of Minnesota Press.

Bębenek, Marian 1987, 'Innowacja i tradycja w refleksji klasyków marksizmu nad zjawiskiem narodowym', *Studia Filozoficzne*, 4: 23–39.

Bendix, Reinhard and Seymour Martin Lipset 1966, *Class, Status, and Power: Social Stratification in Comparative Perspective*, New York: Free Press.

Bernstein, Eduard 1899, *Die Voraussetzungen des Sozialismus und die Aufgaben der Sozialdemokratie*, Stuttgart: J.H.W. Dietz.

Bloch, Ernst 1972, *Vom Hasard zur Katastrophe. Politische Aufsätze aus den Jahren 1934– 1939*, Frankfurt am Main: Suhrkamp.

Böhm, Hermann 1974, *Theorie und Praxis des Austromarxismus bei Otto Bauer*, Vienna: unpublished dissertation.

———— 2000, *Die Tragödie des Austromarxismus am Beispiel von Otto Bauer. Ein Beitrag zur Geschichte des österreichischen Sozialismus*, Frankfurt: Lang.

Böröcz, Vinzenz 1985, 'Otto Bauers Haltung zur ersten österreichischen Arbeiterdelegation in der Sowjetunion', *Weg und Ziel*, 1: 36–8.

Botz, Gerhard 1978a, 'Otto Bauer im Ersten Weltkrieg', *Die Zukunft*, 7: 32–5.

———— 1978b, *Bewegung und Klasse. Studien zur österreichischen Arbeitergeschichte*, Vienna, Munich and Zurich: Europaverlag.

———— 1980, 'Austromarxistische Theorien über den Faschismus als Massenbewegung und als Herrschaftssystem', in *Studia nad Faszyzmem i Zbrodniami Hitlerowskimi*, Volume 6, edited by Kazimierz Dzialocha, Karol Jonca, Franciszek Ryszka and Wojciech Wrzesinsk, Wroclaw: Wydawnictwa Universytetu Wroclawskiego.

────── 1984, 'Faschismus und "Ständestaat" vor und nach dem 12. Februar 1934', in *Ursachen, Fakten, Folgen. Beiträge zum wissenschaftlichen Symposion des Dr.-Karl-Renner-Instituts, abgehalten vom 13. bis 15. Februar 1984 in Wien*, edited by Erich Fröschl and Helge Zoitl, Vienna: Verlag der Wiener Volksbuchhandlung.

────── 1985, 'Faschismustheorien Otto Bauers', in *Otto Bauer 1881–1938: Theorie und Praxis*, edited by Erich Fröschl and Helge Zoitl, Vienna: Europaverlag.

────── 1987, *Krisenzonen einer Demokratie. Gewalt, Streit und Konfliktunterdrückung in Österreich seit 1918*, Frankfurt and New York: Campus.

Braunthal, Julius 1919, *Die Arbeiterräte in Deutschösterreich*, Vienna: Sozialistische Bücherei.

────── 1922, 'Der Putsch der Faschisten', *Der Kampf*, 15: 320–33.

────── 1961, *Otto Bauer. Eine Auswahl aus seinem Lebenswerk. Mit einem Lebensbild Otto Bauers von Julius Braunthal*, Vienna: Verlag der Wiener Volksbuchhandlung.

────── 1964 [1948], *Auf der Suche nach dem Millenium*, Vienna: Europaverlag.

────── 1967 [1963], *History of the International 1914–1943*, Volume 2, London: Thomas Nelson and Sons.

────── 1975, 'Introduction', in *Werkausgabe*, Volumes 1–4, by Otto Bauer, Vienna: Europaverlag.

────── 1976a, 'Anstatt einer Einleitung', in *Werkausgabe*, Volume 3, by Otto Bauer, Vienna: Europaverlag.

────── 1976b, 'Statt einer Einleitung', in *Werkausgabe*, Volume 4, by Otto Bauer, Vienna: Europaverlag.

Braunthal, Julius and Robert Peiper 1975, 'Preface', *Werkausgabe*, Volumes 1–4, by Otto Bauer, Vienna: Europaverlag.

Breitscheid, Rudolf 1977, *Antifaschistische Beiträge 1933–1939*, Frankfurt am Main: Verlag Marxistische Blätter.

Brügel, Johann Wolfgang 1978, 'Spaltung und Untergang. Die Sozialistische Arbeiter-Internationale und die Komintern', *Die Zukunft*, 11: 29–33.

Bukharin, Nikolai 1972 [1925], *Imperialism and the Accumulation of Capital*, London: Penguin Press.

Burian, Wilhelm 1974, *Reform ohne Massen. Zur Entwicklung der Sozialdemokratie seit 1918*, Vienna: Jugend & Volk.

Butterwegge, Christoph 1981, 'Gramsci und/oder Bauer?', *Marxistische Blätter*, 5: s. 67–72.

────── 1990, *Austromarxismus und Staat. Politiktheorie und Praxis der österreichischen Sozialdemokratie zwischen den beiden Weltkriegen*, Marburg: VA & G.

Cackowski, Zdzisław 1974, *Główne pojęcia materializmu historycznego*, Warsaw: Książka i Wiedza.

Carsten, Francis L. 1984, 'Zwei oder drei faschistische Bewegungen in Österreich?', in *Februar 1934. Ursachen, Fakten, Folgen. Beiträge zum wissenschaftlichen Symposion des Dr.–Karl-Renner-Instituts, abgehalten vom 13. bis 15. Februar 1984 in Wien*, Vienna: Verlag der Wiener Volksbuchhandlung.

Chaloupek, Günther 2009, 'Otto Bauers Theorie der Krise des Kapitalismus im Kontext der Zeit', in *Die Ökonomik der Arbeiterbewegung zwischen den Weltkriegen*, Volume 2, edited by Günther Chaloupek, Graz: Leykam.

Chałasiński, Józef 1966, 'Zagadnienie narodu', *Przegląd Socjologiczny*, 10: 35–52.

Cohen, Hermann 1910, *Kants Begründung der Ethik. Nebst ihren Anwendungen auf Recht, Religion und Geschichte*, Berlin: B. Cassirer.

———— 1921 [1904], *Ethik des reinen Willens*, Berlin: B. Cassirer.

Cole, George Douglas Howard 1960, *A History of Socialist Thought Vol. 5: Socialism and Fascism 1931–1939*, London: MacMillan.

Cunow, Heinrich 1903, 'Kartellfragen', *Die Neue Zeit*, 14: 420–7, 21: 645–52, 22: 689–95.

Czerwińska, Ewa 1991, *Nurt mediacji. Automarksizm w Polsce*, Poznań: Instytut Filozofii UAM.

Czubiński, Anton 1985, *Faszyzm niemiecki z perspektywy półwiecza. Materiały i studia*, edited by Antoni Czubiński, Poznań: Wydawn.

Dan, Fyodor 1932, 'Tua res agitur', *Der Kampf*, 2: 59–71.

De Felice, Renzo 1977, *Interpretations of Fascism*, Cambridge, MA: Harvard University Press.

Deutsch, Julius 1918, 'Zu neuer Arbeit', *Der Kampf*, 11: 607–12.

———— 1926, *Antifaschismus! Proletarische Wehrhaftigkeit im Kampfe gegen den Faschismus*, Vienna: Verlag der Wiener Volksbuchhandlung.

———— 1947, *Geschichte der österreichischen Arbeiterbewegung. Eine Skizze*, Vienna: Wiener Volksbuchhandlung.

Dimitrov, Georgi 1935, 'The Fascist Offensive and the Tasks of the Communist International in the Struggle of the Working Class against Fascism', available at: http://www.marxists.org.

Duczyńska, Ilona 1975, 'Theodor Körner und der 12. Februar 1934', *Weg und Ziel*, 4: 61–5.

———— 1975b, *Der demokratische Bolschewik. Zur Theorie und Praxis der Gewalt*, Munich: List.

Ellenbogen, Wilhelm 1980, 'Wille und Intellekt', in *Werkausgabe*, Volume 9, by Otto Bauer, Vienna: Europaverlag.

———— 1983, *Ausgewählte Schriften*, Vienna: Österreichischer Bundesverlag.

Engels, Friedrich 1895, 'Introduction', in *The Class Struggles in France*, by Karl Marx, available at: http://www.marxists.org.

———— 1975 [1848], 'The Beginning of the End in Austria', in *Marx and Engels Collected Works*, Volume 6, London: Lawrence & Wishart.

———— 1977 [1849], 'Democratic Pan-Slavism', in *Marx and Engels Collected Works*, Volume 8, London: Lawrence & Wishart.

———— 1983 [1859], 'Marx to Engels in London', in *Marx and Engels Collected Works*, Volume 40, London: Lawrence & Wishart.

Ernst, Werner 1979, *Sozialdemokratie. Versuch einer Rekonstruktion.* Vienna, Cologne, and Graz: Böhlau.

Euchner, Walter 1979, in *Otto Bauer und der 'dritte' Weg. Die Wiederentdeckung des Austromarxismus durch Linkssozialisten u. Eurokommunisten*, edited by Detlev Albers, Frankfurt and New York: Campus Verlag.

Filipiak, Teodor 1985, *Polityczna i społeczna doktryna faszyzmu. Główne założenia i interpretacje*, Warsaw: Wydawnictwo Uniwersytetu Warszawskiego.

Flis, Andrzej 1990, *Antynomie wielkiej wizji*, Krakow: Towarzystwo Autorów i Wydawców Prac Naukowych Universitas.

Fröschl, Erich and Helge Zoitl (eds.) 1985, *Otto Bauer (1881–1938). Theorie und Praxis*, Vienna: Europaverlag.

Goller, Peter 2008, *Otto Bauer – Max Adler. Beiträge zur Geschichte des Austromarxismus (1904–1938)*, Vienna: Alfred Klahr Gesellschaft.

Gransow, Volker and Michael Krätke 1985, 'Thesen zur politischen Theorie im Austromarxismus', in *Otto Bauer: Theorie und Politik (Argument* special edition), AS 129, edited by Detlev Albers, Berlin: Argument-Verlag.

Grossman, Henryk 1929, *Akkumulations- und Zusammenbruchsgesetz des kapitalistischen Systems*, Leipzig: Verlag C.L. Hirschfeld.

———— 1992 [1929], *The Law of Accumulation and Breakdown of the Capitalist System. Being Also a Theory of Crises*, Abridged translation of the German original, London: Pluto Press.

Grünberg, Karl 1966, *Archiv für die Geschichte des Sozialismus und der Arbeiterbewegung*, Graz: Akademische Druck- u. Verlagsanstalt.

Gulick, Charles 1948, *Österreich von Habsburg zu Hitler*, Volume 1, Vienna: Danubia-Verlag.

Haas, Hanns 1982, 'Sozialer Konflikt und politisches System', *Zeitgeschichte. Beiträge zur Lehrerfortbildung*, 22: 43–61.

———— 1985, 'Otto Bauer als Außenpolitiker', in *Otto Bauer 1881–1938: Theorie und Praxis*, edited by Erich Fröschl and Helge Zoitl, Vienna: Europaverlag.

———— 1990, 'Das Ende des Austromarxismus. Sozialdemokratische Politik 1933/34', in *Die Bewegung. Hundert Jahre Sozialdemokratie in Österreich*, edited by Erich Fröschl, Vienna: Passagen.

Hänisch, Dirk 1995, 'Wahlentwicklung und Wahlverhalten in der Ersten Republik', in *Handbuch des politischen Systems Österreichs. Erste Republik 1918–1933*, edited by Emmerich Tálos, Herbert Dachs, Ernst Hanisch and Anton Staudinger, Vienna: Manzsche Verlags- und Universitätsbuchhandlung.

Hanisch, Ernst 1974, 'Otto Bauers Theorie des Austrofaschismus', *Zeitgeschichte*, 1: 251–63.

———— 1978a, 'Die Marx-Rezeption in der österreichischen Arbeiterbewegung', *Südost-Forschungen, Internationale Zeitschrift für Geschichte, Kultur und Landeskunde Südosteuropas*, Volume 37, Munich: Oldenbourg Wissenschaftsverlag.

———— 1978b, *Der kranke Mann an der Donau: Marx und Engels über Österreich*, Vienna: Europaverlag.

———— 1984, 'Der politische Katholizismus als ideologischer Träger des Austrofaschismus', in *'Austrofaschismus'. Beiträge über Politik, Ökonomie und Kultur, 1934–1938*, edited by Emmerich Talos and Wolfgang Neugebauer, Vienna: Verlag für Gesellschaftskritik.

———— 1985, 'Otto Bauer als Historiker', in *Otto Bauer (1881–1938): Theorie und Praxis*, edited by Erich Fröschl and Helge Zoitl, Vienna: Europaverlag.

———— 2007, 'Der revolutionäre Diskurs in Österreich 1918–1920', in *Niederösterreich 1918–1922*, Volume 39, edited by Willibald Rosner and Reinelde Motz-Linhart, St. Pölten: Niederösterreichisches Institut für Landeskunde im Selbstverlag.

———— 2011, *Der große Illusionist. Otto Bauer (1881–1938)*, Vienna, Cologne and Weimar: Böhlau-Verlag.

Hannak, Jacques 1965, *Karl Renner und seine Zeit. Versuch einer Biographie*, Vienna: Europaverlag.

Haug, Fritz Wolfgang 1985, 'Der Entwurf einer neuen Einheit in der Unterschiedlichkeit bei Otto Bauer', in *Otto Bauer: Theorie und Politik* (*Argument* special edition), AS 129, edited by Detlev Albers, Berlin: Argument-Verlag.

Haussmann, Robert 1979, *Die Entwicklung des Kapitalismus in der österreichisch-ungarischen Monarchie und die Entstehung des 'Austromarxismus'*, Osnabrück: Univ. Diss.

Hautmann, Hans 1970, *Die Anfänge der linksradikalen Bewegung und der Kommunistischen Partei Deutschösterreichs, 1916–1919*, Vienna: Europaverlag.

———— 1971, *Die verlorene Räterepublik. Am Beispiel der Kommunistischen Partei Deutschösterreichs*, Vienna: Europaverlag.

———— 2007, 'Die Sozialdemokratie in der "österreichischen Revolution"', in *Niederösterreich 1918 bis 1922*, St. Pölten: NÖ-Institut für Landeskunde.

Heimann, Horst 1985, 'Otto Bauers Theorieansatz als Revision oder Weiterentwicklung des Marxismus', in *Otto Bauer: Theorie und Politik* (*Argument* special edition), AS 129, edited by Detlev Albers, Berlin: Argument-Verlag.

Hilferding, Rudolf 1915, 'Europäer, nicht Mitteleuropäer', *Der Kampf*, 8, 11: 356–65.

———— 1932, 'Unter der Drohung des Faschismus', *Die Gesellschaft. Internationale Revue für Sozialismus und Politik*, 9, 1: 1–12.

———— 1981 [1910], *Finance Capital: A Study of the Latest Phase of Capitalist Development*, edited with an introduction by Tom Bottomore, London, Boston and Henley: Routledge & Kegan Paul.

Hindels, Josef 1981, *Otto Bauer ist jung geblieben. Anlässlich des 100. Geburtsjahres von Otto Bauer*, Vienna: SPÖ, Bildungsausschuss.

———— 1984, '50 Jahre nach dem Naziputsch', *Die Zukunft*, 7/8: 33–5.

Hofmann, Werner 1971, *Ideengeschichte der sozialen Bewegung des 19. und 20. Jahrhunderts*, Berlin: Walter de Gruyter & Co.

Holtmann, Everhard 1996, *Die Organisation der Sozialdemokratie in der Illegalität 1934–1945*, in *Die Organisation der österreichischen Sozialdemokratie 1889–1995*, edited by Wolfgang Maderthaner and Wolfgang Müller, Vienna: Löcker.

Horwitz, Maksymilian Henryk 1907, *W kwestii żydowskiej*, Krakow: Drukarnia Narodowa.

Jedlicka, Ludwig and Rudolf Neck (eds.) 1975, *Vom Justizpalast zum Heldenplatz. Studien und Dokumentation*, Vienna: Österreichische Staatsdruckerei.

Jeliński, Edward 1994, *Myśl a rzeczywistość. O pewnych osobliwościach polskiej myśli socjalistycznej w II Rzeczypospolitej*, Poznan: Wydawnictwo Naukowe UAM.

Kaff, Sigmund 1931, *Der Austrobolschewismus als Hüter der 'Gesetzlichkeit'. Ein Kapitel aus der innerpolitischen Krankheitsgeschichte Österreich*, Zurich: Amalthea-Verlag.

Kann, Robert Adolf 1973, *Renners Beitrag zur Lösung nationaler Konflikte im Lichte nationaler Probleme der Gegenwart*, Vienna: Österreichische Akademie der Wissenschaften.

Katsoulis, Ilias 1975, *Sozialismus und Staat. Demokratie, Revolution und Diktatur des Proletariats im Austromarxismus*, Meisenheim am Glan: Hain.

Kaufmann, Fritz 1978, *Sozialdemokratie in Österreich. Idee u. Geschichte einer Partei von 1889 bis zur Gegenwart*, Vienna and Munich: Amalthea.

Kautsky, Karl 1899, *Bernstein und das sozialdemokratische Programm*, Stuttgart: J.H.W. Dietz.

———— 1902, 'Krisentheorien', *Die Neue Zeit*, 20, 2: 37–143.

———— 1906, *Ethik und materialistische Geschichtsauffassung*, Stuttgart: J.H.W. Dietz.

———— 1908, *Nationalität und Internationalität*, Stuttgart: Verlag und Druck von P. Singer.

———— 1909a [1906], *Ethics and the Materialist Conception of History*, Chicago: Charles H. Kerr & Company.

———— 1909b, *The Road to Power*, Chicago: Samuel A. Bloch.

———— 1910, *Vermehrung und Entwicklung in Natur und Gesellschaft*, Stuttgart: J.H.W. Dietz.

———— 1911, 'Finance-Capital and Crises', *The Social Democrat*, 15: 326–30, 368–71, 423–7, 470–3, 517–23, 556–60 (partial translation of 'Finanzkapital und Krisen: Rudolf Hilferding, *Das Finanzkapital*', *Die Neue Zeit*, 29, 1: 764–72, 797–804, 838–64, 874–83), available at: http://www.marxists.org.

———— 1916, *Die Vereinigten Staaten Mitteleuropas*, Stuttgart: Dietz.

———— 1917, *Serbien und Belgien in der Geschichte. Historische Studien zur Frage der Nationalitäten und der Kriegsziele*, Stuttgart: J.H.W. Dietz.

———— 1920, 'Eine Schrift über den Bolschewismus', *Der Kampf*, 8: 260–5.

———— 1922, *Die proletarische Revolution und ihr Programm*, Stuttgart and Berlin: J.H.W. Dietz Nachfolger.

———— 1927, *Die materialistische Geschichtsauffassung*, Vol. 2, Berlin: Dietz.

———— 1934, *Grenzen der Gewalt. Aussichten und Wirkungen bewaffneter Erhebungen des Proletariats*, Karlsbad: Graphia.

———— 1983 [1906], 'Life, Science and Ethics', in *Selected Political Writings*, edited and translated by Peter Goode, London: Macmillan.

———— 2009 [1908], 'Nationality and Internationality', *Critique: A Journal of Soviet Studies and Socialist Theory*, 37, 3: 371–89.

———— 2010 [1908], 'Nationality and Internationality', Part 2, *Critique: A Journal of Soviet Studies and Socialist Theory*, 38, 1: 143–63.

Kelles-Krauz, Kazimierz 1903, 'Program narodowościowy socjalnej demokracji austriackiej a program PPS', *Przedświt*, 7: 276–83.

Kelsen, Hans 2000 [1920], 'On the Essence and Value of Democracy', in *Weimar: A Jurisprudence of Crisis*, by Arthur J. Jacobson and Bernhard Schlink, Berkeley, CA: University of California Press.

———— 1923, *Sozialismus und Staat. Eine Untersuchung der politischen Theorie des Marxismus*, Leipzig: C.L. Hirschfeld.

———— 1924, 'Otto Bauers politische Theorien', *Der Kampf*, 17: 50–6.

———— 1965 [1924], 'Marx oder Lasalle', in *Archiv für die Geschichte des Sozialismus und der Arbeiterbewegung*, Volume 9, edited by Carl Grünberg, Graz: Akademische Druck- u. Verl.-Anst.

Kende, Richard 1977, *Die austromarxistische Praxis und die Theorie Otto Bauers*, Berlin: unpublished dissertation.

Kernbauer, Hans 1990, 'Das ökonomische Erbe des Ersten Weltkrieges', in *Die Bewegung. Hundert Jahre Sozialdemokratie in Österreich*, edited by Erich Fröschl, Maria Mesner and Helge Zoitl, Vienna: Passagen-Verlag.

Kluge, Ulrich 1984, *Der österreichische Ständestaat 1934–1938*, Munich: Oldenburg.

Kluza-Wołosiewicz, Zenona 1963, *Teoria rozwoju kapitalizmu w dyskusjach socjaldemokracji niemieckiej 1891–1914*, Warsaw: Państwowe Wydawnictwo Naukowe.

Kołakowski, Leszek 2005 [1978], *Main Currents of Marxism*, New York and London: W.W. Norton & Co.

Konrad, Helmut 1976, *Nationalismus und Internationalismus. Die österr. Arbeiterbewegung vor dem Ersten Weltkrieg*, Vienna: Europaverlag.

———— 1977, 'Nationale Frage und Arbeiterbewegung in Österreich um die Jahrhundertwende', *Österreichische Zeitschrift für die Politikwissenschaft*, 2: 193–203.

———— 1978, *Sozialdemokratie und Anschluss: Historische Wurzeln, Anschluss 1918 u. 1938, Nachwirkungen. Eine Tagung des Dr.-Karl-Renner-Instituts, Wien, 1. März 1978*. Vienna: Europaverlag.

———— 1981, 'Otto Bauer und die nationale Frage', *Wiener Tagebuch*, 10: 18–21.

———— 2004, '12. Februar in Österreich', in *Österreich 1934. Vorgeschichte – Ereignisse – Wirkungen*, edited by Günther Schefbeck, Vienna: Verlag für Geschichte und Politik.

———— 2008, 'Das Rote Wien. Ein Konzept für eine moderne Großstadt?', in *Das Werden der Ersten Republik ... der Rest ist Österreich*, Vienna: Gerold.

Koplenig, Johann 1934, *Referat auf dem 12. Parteitag*, Vienna: Zentral-Kommittee der KPÖ.

———— 1963, *Izbrannye proizvedenija, 1924–1962 gody.*, Moscow: Gos. Izd-vo polit. Litry.

Kösten, Ingrid 1984, *Darstellung und kritische Reflexion der Faschismusanalysen Otto Bauers: Ihre Grundgedanken und inneren Widersprüchlichkeiten*, Vienna: unpublished dissertation.

Kotlarski, Grzegorz 1987, *Myśl społeczna Róży Luksemburg. Próba rekonstrukcji historiozofii*, Poznań: Wydawn. Nauk. Uniwersytetu im. Adama Mickiewicza w Poznaniu.

Kozub 1982, *Socjaldemokracja w Austrii współczesnej, 1945–1966*, Poznań: Instytut Zachodni.

Kozyr-Kowalski, Stanisław and Jarosław Ładosz 1974, *Dialektyka a społeczeństwo. Wstęp do materializmu historycznego*, Warsaw: Państwowe Wydawnictwo Naukowe.

Krätke, Michael R. 2008, 'Über die Krise der Weltwirtschaft, Demokratie und Sozialismus. Eine unveröffentlichte Untersuchung Otto Bauers über die Weltwirtschaftskrise der dreißiger Jahre', in *Otto Bauer und der Austromarxismus. 'Integraler Sozialismus' und die heutige Linke*, edited by Walter Baier, Lisbeth N. Trallori and Derek Weber, Berlin: Karl Dietz.

Kreissler, Felix 1970, *Von der Revolution zur Annexion, Österreich 1918 bis 1939*. Vienna: Europaverlag.

Kropf, Rudolf and Hans Hautmann 1974, *Die österreichische Arbeiterbewegung vom Vormärz bis 1945. Sozialökonomische Ursprünge ihrer Ideologie und Politik*, Vienna: Europaverlag.

Kulemann, Peter 1979, *Am Beispiel des Austromarxismus. Sozialdemokratische Arbeiterbewegung in Österreich von Hainfeld bis zur Dollfuss-Diktatur*, Hamburg: Junius.

Kun, Béla 1934, *The February Struggle in Austria and Its Lessons*, New York: Workers' Library Publishers.

Lange, Oskar Ryszard 1929, 'Wzrastanie w socjalizm czy nowa faza kapitalizmu', *Robotniczy Przegląd Gospodarczy*, 3: 69–74.

Lasalle, Ferdinand 1892, *Ferd. Lasalle's Reden und Schriften. Neue Gesammt-Ausgabe*, edited by Eduard Bernstein, Berlin: Verlag der Expedition des 'Vorwärts' Berliner Volksblatt.

Lederer, Emil 1956, 'Von der Wissenschaft zur Utopie', in *Archiv für die Geschichte des Sozialismus und der Arbeiterbewegung*, Volume 7, edited by Carl Grünberg, Graz: Akademische Druck- und Verlagsanstalt.

Leichter, Otto 1924, 'Zum Problem der sozialen Gleichgewichtszustände', *Der Kampf*, 17: 179–87.

———— 1937, 'Der Pessimismus – eine politische Theorie?', *Der Kampf*, 4: 338–44.

———— 1964, *Glanz und Ende der Ersten Republik. Wie es zum österreichischen Bürgerkrieg kam*, Vienna: Europaverlag.

———— 1970, *Otto Bauer. Tragödie oder Triumph*, Vienna: Europaverlag.

Leiße, Olaf 2012, *Der Untergang des österreichischen Imperiums: Otto Bauer und die Nationalitätenfrage in der Habsburger Monarchie*, Marburg: Tectum.

Lenin, Vladimir Ilyich 1993 [1920], *'Left Wing' Communism. An Infantile Disorder*, London, Chicago, Melbourne: Bookmarks, available at: http://www.marxists.org.

———— 1963 [1913], 'Theses on the National Question', in *Collected Works*, Volume 19, London: Lawrence & Wishart, available at: http://www.marxists.org.

———— 1964a [1901], 'Lessons of the Crisis', in *Collected Works*, Moscow: Progress Publishers, available at: http://www.marxists.org.

———— 1964b [1899], 'A Draft of Our Party Programme', in *Collected Works*, Volume 4, Moscow: Progress Publishers, available at: http://www.marxists.org.

———— 1965 [1906], 'How Comrade Plekhanov Argues About Social-Democratic Tactics', in *Collected Works*, Volume 10, Moscow: Progress Publishers, available at: http://www.marxists.org.

———— 1972 [1897], *A Characterisation of Economic Romanticism. Sismondi and our native Sismondists*, in *Collected Works*, Volume 2, 4th English Edition, Moscow: Progress Publishers, available at: http://www.marxists.org.

———— 1974 [1920], 'Report On The International Situation and the Fundamental Tasks of the Communist International, July 19', in *The Second Congress of the Communist International*, Moscow: Progress Publishers, available at: http://www.marxists.org.

———— 1977 [1914], *The Right of Nations to Self-Determination*, in *Collected Works*, Moscow: Progress Publishers, available at: http://www.marxists.org.

Leonhard, Wolfgang 1979 [1978], *Eurocommunism: Challenge for East and West*, New York: Holt, Rinehart, and Winston.

Leser, Norbert 1964, *Werk und Widerhall. Grosse Gestalten des österreichischen Sozialismus*, Vienna: Verlag der Volksbuchhandlung

———— 1968, *Zwischen Reformismus und Bolschewismus. Der Austromarxismus als Theorie und Praxis*, Vienna: Europaverlag.

———— 1979a, 'Was bleibt vom Austromarxismus?', *Die Zukunft*, 11/12: 30–6.

———— 1979b, 'Otto Bauers Haltung gegenüber dem Bolschewismus', in *Otto Bauer und der 'dritte' Weg. Die Wiederentdeckung des Austromarxismus durch Linkssozialisten u. Eurokommunisten*, edited by Detlev Albers, Frankfurt and New York: Campus Verlag.

———— 1986, *Genius Austriacus. Beiträge zur politischen Geschichte und Geistesgeschichte Österreich*, Vienna: Böhlaus.

Leser, Norbert und Richard Berzeller 1977, *Als Zaungäste der Politik. Österreichische Zeitgeschichte in Konfrontationen*, Munich: Jugend & Volk.

Lüer, Andreas 1987, 'Nationalismus in christlichsozialen Programmen 1918–1933', *Zeitgeschichte*, 14: 147–66.

Lih, Lars 2005, *Lenin Rediscovered: 'What Is To Be Done?' in Context*, Leiden and Boston: Brill.

Löw, Raimund 1980, *Otto Bauer und die russische Revolution*, Vienna: Europaverlag.

———— 1981, 'Otto Bauer, die russische Revolution und der Stalinismus', in *Otto Bauer 1881–1938: Theorie und Praxis*, edited by Erich Fröschl and Helge Zoitl, Vienna, Europaverlag.

———— 1982, 'Otto Bauer und die "Arbeiter-Zeitung" zur Oktoberrevolution', *Wiener Tagebuch*, 10: 10–13.

Löw, Raimund, Siegfried Mattl and Alfred Pfabigan 1986, *Der Austromarxismus. Eine Autopsie. Drei Studien*, Frankfurt am Main: ISP-verlag.

Löwenthal, Richard 1946, *Jenseits des Kapitalismus. Ein Beitrag zur sozialistischen Neuorientierung*, Nuremberg: Nest-Verlag.

Lukács, György 1971 [1923], *History and Class Consciousness*, Cambridge, MA: MIT Press.

Luxemburg, Rosa 1899, 'Speech to the Hannover Congress. Oct 1899', available at: http://www.marxists.org.

———— 1976 [1908–9], *The National Question: Selected Writings by Rosa Luxemburg*, edited by Horace B. Davis, New York and London: Monthly Review Press.

———— 2004 [1898–9], 'Social Reform or Revolution', in *The Rosa Luxemburg Reader*, edited by Peter Hudis and Kevin B. Anderson, New York: Monthly Review Press.

Maderthaner, Wolfgang 2004, 'Die Krise einer Kultur', in *Österreich 1934. Vorgeschichte-Ereignisse-Wirkungen*, edited by Günther Schefbeck, Vienna: Verlag für Geschichte und Politik.

Maimann, Helene 1985, 'Otto Bauer und das Exil', in *Otto Bauer (1881–1938)*, edited by Erich Fröschl and Helge Zoitl, Vienna: Europaverlag.

Maimann, Helene and Siegfried Mattl 1984, '12. Februar 1934 – Nur mehr ein Gedenktag?', *Die Zukunft*, 12: 6–9.

Marschalek, Manfred 1990, *Untergrund und Exil. Österreichs Sozialisten zwischen 1934 und 1945*, Vienna: Löcker.

Marx, Karl 1872, 'La Liberté speech', available at: http://www.marxists.org.

———— 1852, *The Eighteenth Brumaire of Louis Bonaparte*, available at: http://www.marxists.org.

———— 1959 [1894], *Capital, Volume 3: The Process of Capitalist Production as a Whole*, edited by Frederick Engels, London: Lawrence & Wishart.

———— 1972 [1893], *Capital: A Critique of Political Economy, Volume 2: The Progress of Circulation of Capital*, edited by Frederick Engels, London: Lawrence & Wishart.

———— 1977 [1871], *The Civil War in France*, Beijing: Foreign Languages Press.

———— 1982 [1860], *Herr Vogt*, London: New Park.

———— 1990 [1867], *Capital*, Volume 1, London: Penguin.

———— 1985 [1860], 'Marx to Engels', in *Marx and Engels Collected Works*, Volume 41, London: Lawrence & Wishart.

März, Eduard 1965, *Österreichs Wirtschaft zwischen Ost und West. Eine sozialistische Analyse*, Vienna and Frankfurt: Europaverlag.

———— 1975, 'Soziale Reform und Sozialisierungsdebatte in Österreich', in *Wissenschaft und Weltbild*, Vienna: Europaverlag.

———— 1981, *Österreichische Bankpolitik in der Zeit der grossen Wende 1913–1923. Am Beispiel der Creditanstalt für Handel und Gewerbe*, Vienna: Verlag für Geschichte und Politik.

März, Eduard and Fritz Weber 1979, 'Otto Bauer und die Sozialisierung', in *Otto Bauer und der 'dritte' Weg. Die Wiederentdeckung des Austromarxismus durch Linkssozialisten u. Eurokommunisten*, edited by Detlev Albers, Frankfurt and New York: Campus Verlag.

Matthes, Reinar 1979, *Das Ende der Ersten Republik Österreich: Studien zur Krise ihres politischen Systems*, PhD Thesis, Berlin: Free University.

Mattl, Siegfried 1985a, 'Krise, Politik und Krisenpolitik bei Otto Bauer', in *Otto Bauer 1881–1938: Theorie und Praxis*, edited by Erich Fröschl and Helge Zoitl, Vienna, Europaverlag.

———— 1985b, 'Theorie und Praxis sozialdemokratischer Agrarpolitik – Otto Bauer und das Agrarprogramm 1925', in *Otto Bauer 1881–1938: Theorie und Praxis*, edited by Erich Fröschl and Helge Zoitl, Vienna: Europaverlag.

Mendelson, Lev Abramovich 1959, *Teoria i historia kryzysów i cykli ekonomicznych*, Warsaw: Państwowe Wydawnictwo Naukowe.

Menger, Carl 1981 [1871], *Principles of Economics*, New York and London: New York University Press.

———— 1985 [1883], *Investigations into the Method of the Social Sciences with Special Reference to Economics – Studies in Economic Theory*, New York: New York University Press.

Merchav, Peretz 1978, 'Otto Bauer und Max Adler', *Die Zukunft*, 1: 34–8.

Miller, Susanne 1979, 'Politische Führung und Spontaneität in der österreichischen Sozialdemokratie', in *Otto Bauer und der 'dritte' Weg. Die Wiederentdeckung des Austromarxismus durch Linkssozialisten u. Eurokommunisten*, edited by Detlev Albers, Frankfurt and New York: Campus Verlag.

Mommsen, Hans 1963, *Die Sozialdemokratie und die Nationalitätenfrage im habsburgischen Vielvölkerstaat*, Vienna: Europaverlag.

———— 1979a, *Arbeiterbewegung und nationale Frage. Ausgewählte Aufsätze*, Göttingen: Vandenhoeck & Ruprecht.

———— 1979b, 'Otto Bauer, Karl Renner und die sozialdemokratische Nationalitäten-politik in Österreich 1905–1914', in *Arbeiterbewegung und nationale Frage. Ausge-wählte Aufsätze*, Göttingen: Vandenhoeck & Ruprecht.

Moringer, Wolfgang 1978, 'Die bürgerlich-idealistische Position des "Austromarxismus" in der nationalen Frage', *Weg und Ziel*, 4: 152–5.

Mozetič, Gerald 1983, *Austromarxistische Positionen. Klassische Studien zur sozialwis-senschaftlichen Theorie, Weltanschauungslehre und Wissenschaftsforschung*, Vol. 2, Vienna: Böhlau.

———— 1987, *Die Gesellschaftstheorie des Austromarxismus. Geistesgeschichtliche Vor-aussetzungen, Methodologie und soziologisches Programm*, Darmstadt: Wissen-schaftliche Buchgesellschaft.

Niedziałkowski, Mieczyslaw 1922, 'Szkice o polityce socjalistycznej', *Trybuna* 12: 133–5.

———— 1926, *Teorja i praktyka socjalizmu wobec nowych zagadnień etc*, Warsaw and Kraków: Nakladem Spółdzielni Wydawniczo-Księgarskiej 'Nowe Życie'.

———— 1943, 'Theory and Practice of Socialism in the Face of New Problems' [abridged translation], in *For Your Freedom and Ours: Polish Progressive Spirit Through the Centuries*, edited by Manfred Kridl, Władysław Malinowski and Józef Wittlin, New York: Frederick Ungar Publishing Co.

Nolte, Ernst 1967, *Theorien über den Faschismus*, Cologne and Berlin: Kiepenheuer u. Witsch.

Nowak, Leszek 1997, 'Marksizm versus liberalizm. Pewien paradoks', in *Marksizm, lib-eralizm, próby wyjścia*, Poznan: Zysk i S-ka Wydawnictwo.

Oberkofler, Georg 1979, *Die Tiroler Arbeiterbewegung*, Vienna: Europaverlag.

Pannekoek, Antonie 1912, *Class Struggle and Nation*, available at: http://www.marxists .org.

Panzenböck, Ernst 1985, *Ein deutscher Traum. Die Anschlußidee und Anschlußpolitik bei Karl Renner und Otto Bauer*, Vienna: Europaverlag.

Pawlak, Józef 1979, *Filozofia społeczna Mikołaja K. Michajłowskiego*, Toruń: UMK.

Peball, Kurt 1974, *Die Kämpfe in Wien im Februar 1934* (*Militarhistorische Schriftenreihe*), Vienna: Österreichischer Bundesverlag.

Pelinka, Anton 1972, *Stand oder Klasse? Die Christliche Arbeiterbewegung Österreichs 1933 bis 1938*, Vienna, Munich and Zurich: Europaverlag.

———— 1982 [1979], 'Von der Konkurrenz zur Konvergenz', in *Zeitgeschichte*, edited by Leopold Rettinger, Kurt Scholz and Ernst Popp, Vienna: Österreichischer Bundes-verlag.

———— 1984, 'Der Bürgerkrieg als Ende und als Anfang', *Die Zukunft*, 2.

———— 1985, 'Die Faschismusanalyse Otto Bauers und der antifaschistische Abwehr-kampf der SDAP', in *Otto Bauer: Theorie und Politik*, edited by Detlev Albers, Berlin: Argument-Verlag.

Pernerstorfer, Engelbert 1907, 'Protocol', in *Internationaler Sozialisten Kongreß zu Stut-tgart, vom 18. bis 24. August*, Berlin: Buchhandlung Vorwärts.

Pfabigan, Alfred 1977, 'Die Rezeption der Marxschen Methode im Austromarxismus', *Österreichische Zeitschrift für Politikwissenschaft*, 1: 39–53.

———— 1982, *Max Adler. Eine politische Biographie*, Frankfurt: Campus.

———— 1985, *Otto Bauer 1881–1938: Theorie und Praxis*, edited by Erich Fröschl and Helge Zoitl, Vienna, Europaverlag.

———— 1990a, 'Das ideologische Profil der österreichischen Sozialdemokratie vor dem Ersten Weltkrieg', in *Die Bewegung: 100 Jahre Sozialdemokratie in Österreich*, edited by Erich Fröschl, Maria Mesner and Helge Zoitl, Vienna: Passagen-Verlag.

———— 1990b, 'Das Konzept des austromarxistischen Intellektuellen', *Österreichische Zeitschrift für Geschichtswissenschaften*, 1, 3: 49–66.

Popper, Karl R. 1945: *The Open Society and its Enemies. Volume 2: The High Tide of Prophecy*, London: Routledge & Sons.

Przestalski, Andrzej 1981, 'Naród i charakter narodowy w teorii Otto Bauera', *Ruch prawniczy, ekonomiczny i socjologiczny*, 2: 205–25.

Rabinbach, Anson 1989, *Vom roten Wien zum Bürgerkrieg*, Vienna: Löcker.

Raming, Walter 1979, *Von Marx bis Kreisky. Wege und Ziele des Sozialismus 1888–2000*, Vienna: Reichsbund, Landesverlag Niederösterreich.

Rauscher, Walter 1995, *Karl Renner. Ein österreichischer Mythos*, Vienna: Ueberreuter.

Reimann, Viktor 1968, *Zu gross für Österreich. Seipel und Bauer im Kampf um die Erste Republik*, Vienna, Frankfurt and Zurich: Molden.

Renner, Karl 1902, *Der Kampf der österreichischen Nationen um den Staat*, Leipzig and Vienna: F. Deuticke.

———— 1906, *Grundlagen und Entwicklungsziele der österreichisch-ungarischen Monarchie. Politische Studie über den Zusammenbruch der Privilegenparlamente und die Wahlreform in beiden Staaten, über die Reichsidee und ihre Zukunft*, Vienna and Leipzig: F. Deuticke.

———— 1913, *Was ist die nationale Autonomie? Was ist soziale Verwaltung? Einführung in die nationale Frage und Erläuterung der Grundsätze des nationalen Programms der Sozialdemokratie*, Vienna: Brand.

———— 1914, *Die Nation als Rechtsidee und die Internationale*, Vienna: Brand.

———— 1915, 'Sozialistischer Imperialismus oder internationaler Sozialismus', *Der Kampf*, 8: 104–58.

———— 1916, *Österreichs Erneuerung*, Vienna: Brand.

———— 1917, *Marxismus, Krieg und Internationale. Kritische Studien über offene Probleme des wissenschaftlichen und des praktischen Sozialismus in und nach dem Weltkrieg*, Stuttgart: Dietz.

———— 1924, *Die Wirtschaft als Gesamtprozeß und die Sozialisierung*, Berlin: Dietz.

———— 1932, *Novemberverbrecher? Die Anklagen der Hitler-Bewegung gegen die 'Novemberverbrecher' wegen nationalen Verrats*, Vienna: Verlag der Wiener Volksbuchhandlung.

――――― 1952a, *Mensch und Gesellschaft. Grundriss einer Soziologie*, Vienna: Verlag der Wiener Volksbuchhandlung.

――――― 1952b, *Österreich von der Ersten zur Zweiten Republik*, Vienna: Verlag der Wiener Volksbuchhandlung.

――――― 1953, *Wandlungen der modernen Gesellschaft; zwei Abhandlungen über die Probleme der Nachkriegszeit*, Vienna: Verlag der Wiener Volksbuchhandlung.

――――― 1964 [manuscript dated 1937], 'Die Nation. Mythos und Wirklichkeit', in *Geist und Gesellschaft. Texte zum Studium der sozialen Entwicklung*, Vienna: Europaverlag.

――――― 1970, *Porträt einer Evolution*, Vienna, Frankfurt and Zurich: Europaverlag.

――――― 2005 [1899], 'State and Nation', in *National Cultural Autonomy and Its Contemporary Critics*, edited by Ephraim Nimni, London: Routledge.

Rosdolsky, Roman 1973, 'Die revolutionäre Situation in Österreich 1918 und die Politik der Sozialdemokratie. Der österreichische Jännerstreik 1918', in *Studien über revolutionäre Taktik. Zwei unveröffentlichte Arbeiten über die II. Internationale und die österreichische Sozialdemokratie*, West Berlin: Verlag für das Studium der Arbeiterbewegung.

Rosenberg, Arthur 1934, *Der Faschismus als Massenbewegung. Sein Aufstieg und seine Zersetzung*, Karlsbad: Verl.-Anst. 'Graphia'.

Rosner, Peter 1987, 'Der moderne Kapitalismus. Die Vorstufe des Sozialismus', in *Quellen und Studien zur österreichischen Geistesgeschichte im 19. und 20. Jahrhundert*, Volume 6, Vienna: Österreichischer Bundesverlag.

Rudziński, Roman 1975, *Ideał moralny a proces dziejowy w marksizmie i neokantyzmie*, Warsaw: Ksiąka i Wiedza.

Saage, Richard 1977, *Faschismustheorien: Eine Einführung*, Munich: C.H. Beck.

――――― 1985, 'Restriktionsanalysen Otto Bauers', in *Otto Bauer: Theorie und Politik* (*Argument* special edition), AS 129, edited by Detlev Albers, Berlin: Argument-Verlag.

――――― 1986, *Solidargemeinschaft und Klassenkampf. Politische Konzeptionen der Sozialdemokratie zwischen den Weltkriegen*, Frankfurt: Suhrkamp.

――――― 1990a, 'Restriktionsanalysen Otto Bauers am Beispiel der Ersten österreichischen Republik', in *Das Ende der politischen Utopie?*, Frankfurt: Suhrkamp.

――――― 1990b, 'Zum Sozialismusbegriff Otto Bauers', in *Das Ende der politischen Utopie?*, Frankfurt: Suhrkamp.

――――― 2009, 'Zur Rezeption und Aktualität des Austromarxismus. Das Beispiel Otto Bauer', *Zeitschrift für Geschichtswissenschaft*, 57, 1: 51–63.

Sandkühler, Hans Jörg 1974 [1970], *Marxismus und Ethik. Texte zum neukantianischen Sozialismus*, Frankfurt am Main: Suhrkamp Verlag.

Sartori, Giovanni 1987, *The Theory of Democracy Revisited*, Chatham: Chatham House Publishers.

Say, Jean-Baptiste 2000 [1803], *A Treatise on Political Economy*, New Brunswick, NJ: Transaction Publishers.

Schippel, Max 1888, *Das moderne Elend und die moderne Übervölkerung*, Stuttgart: Dietz.

Schlesinger, Rudolf August Joseph 1950, *Marx: His Time and Ours*, London: Routledge & Kegan Paul.

Schöller, Uli 1979, *Otto Bauer und der 'dritte' Weg. Die Wiederentdeckung des Austromarxismus durch Linkssozialisten u. Eurokommunisten*, edited by Detlev Albers, Frankfurt and New York: Campus Verlag.

Schöpfer, Ämilian 1929, 'Österreich vor dem Bürgerkrieg', *Das Neue Reich*, 28 Nov: 7.

Seidel, Jutta 1982, 'Zu einigen Aspekten der Beziehungen zwischen der deutschen und österreichischen Sozialdemokratie in den ersten Jahren des 20. Jahrhunderts', in *Die deutsche und die österreichische Sozialdemokratie zur Zeit der II. Internationale*, edited by Helmut Konrad, Vienna: Europaverlag.

Seidl, Johann Wilhelm 1989, *Musik und Austromarxismus. Zur Musikrezeption der österreichischen Arbeiterbewegung im späten Kaiserreich und in der Ersten Republik*, Vienna: Böhlau.

Simmel, Georg 2009, *Sociology: Inquiries into the Construction of Social Forms*, Leiden and Boston: Brill.

Simon, Walter 1984a, 'Drei Fragen zum 12. Februar 1934', *Die Zukunft*, 2: 16–17.

——— 1984b, *Österreich 1918–1958. Ideologien und Politik*, Vienna, Graz and Cologne: Böhlau.

Singer, Ladislaus 1979, *Marxisten im Widerstreit. 6 Porträts*, Stuttgart: Seewald.

Siwek, Bronisław 1921, 'Sprawa narodowa czy socjalizm', *Trybuna*, 35: s. 6–8.

Slavik, Gerhard 1928, *Der Außenhandel und die Handelspolitik Österreichs 1918 bis 1926*, Klagenfurt: Kleinmayr.

Śliwa, Michał 1980, *Myśl polityczna Mieczysława Niedziałkowskiego (1893–1940)*, Warsaw: Państwowe Wydawnictwo Naukowe.

Smith, Thomas Vernor 1942, 'Compromise: Its Context and Limits', *Ethics* 53, 1: 1–13.

Sobolev, Aleksandr Ivanovich et al. 1971, *Outline History of the Communist International*, Moscow: Progress Publishers.

Sobolewski, Marek 1956, *Rola austromarksizmu w rewolucji 1918 r. w Austrii*, Warsaw: Państwowe Wydawnictwo Naukowe.

Sombart, Werner 1909 [1896], *Socialism and the Social Movement*, London: J.M. Dent & Co.

Sporrer, Maria and Herbert Steiner 1983, *Rosa Jochmann. Zeitzeugin*, Vienna: Europaverlag.

Stalin, Joseph 1953 [1913], *Marxism and the National Question*, in *Works*, Volume 2, Moscow: Foreign Languages Publishing House, also available at: http://www .marxists.org.

——— 2003 [1936], *Marxism and the National and Colonial Question*, Honolulu: University Press of the Pacific.

Stammler, Rudolf 1896, *Wirtschaft und Recht nach der materialistischen Geschichtsauffassung*, Leipzig: Veit & comp.

——— 1920, *Sozialismus und Christentum. Erörterungen zu den Grundbegriffen und den Grundsätzen der Sozialwissenschaft*, Leipzig: Verlag von Felix Meiner.

Staudinger, Anton 1984a, 'Konzentrationsregierung, Bürgerblock oder Präsidiales Minderheitsregime? Zum angeblichen Koalitionsangebot Ignaz Seipels an die Sozialdemokratie im Juni 1931', *Zeitgeschichte*, 12: 1–18.

——— 1984b, 'Austrofaschistische Österreich-Ideologie', in *Austrofaschismus. Beiträge über Politik, Ökonomie und Kultur 1934–1938*, edited by Emmerich Tálos and Wolfgang Neugebauer, Vienna: Verlag für Gesellschaftskritik.

Steinberg, Hans-Josef 1972, 'Sozialismus und deutsche Sozialdemokratie', in *Sozialdemokratie zwischen Klassenbewegung und Volkspartei*, edited by Hans Mommsen, Frankfurt am Main: Athenäum-Fischer-Taschenbuch-Verlag.

Steiner, Guenther 2004, *Wahre Demokratie? Transformation und Demokratieverständnis in der Ersten Republik Österreich und im Ständestaat Österreich 1918–1938*, Frankfurt am Main: Lang.

Steiner, Herbert 1967, 'Am Beispiel Otto Bauers – die Oktoberrevolution und der Austromarxismus', *Weg und Ziel*, summer 1967 special edition: 3–22.

——— 1973a, 'Auseinandersetzungen innerhalb der Sozialdemokratie vor dem 12. Februar 1934', *Weg und Ziel*, 5: 67–8.

——— 1973b, *Käthe Leichter. Leben und Werk*, Vienna: Europaverlag.

——— 1984, in *Ursachen, Fakten, Folgen. Beiträge zum wissenschaftlichen Symposion des Dr.-Karl-Renner-Instituts, abgehalten vom 13. bis 15. Februar 1984 in Wien*, edited by Erich Fröschl and Helge Zoitl, Vienna: Verlag der Wiener Volksbuchhandlung.

Strasser, Josef 1912, *Der Arbeiter und die Nation*, Reichenberg: Runge.

Stiefel, Dieter 1978, Stiefel: *Konjunkturelle Entwicklung und struktureller Wandel der österreichischen Wirtschaft in der Zwischenkriegszeit*, Vienna: IHS.

Strom, Gerd and Franz Walter 1984, *Weimarer Linkssozialismus und Austromarxismus. Historische Vorbilder für einen 'Dritten Weg' zum Sozialismus?*, Berlin: Verlag Europäische Perspektiven.

Sweezy, Paul 1964 [1942], *The Theory of Capitalist Development: Principles of Marxian Political Economy*, New York: Monthly Review Press.

Szyszkowska, Maria 1970, *Neokantyzm. Filozofia społeczna wraz z filozofia prawa natury o zmiennej treści*, Warsaw: Pax.

Tálos, Emmerich 1981, *Staatliche Sozialpolitik in Österreich. Rekonstruktion und Analyse*, Vienna: Verlag für Gesellschaftskritik.

——— 1990, 'Sozialpolitische Reformen in der Ersten Republik', in *Die Bewegung. Hundert Jahre Sozialdemokratie in Österreich*, edited by Erich Fröschl, Maria Mesner and Helge Zoitl, Vienna: Passagen-Verlag.

Tálos, Emmerich and Wolfgang Neugebauer 1984, 'Austrofaschismus'. Beiträge über Politik, Ökonomie und Kultur 1934–1938, Vienna: Verlag für Gesellschaftskritik.

Tasca, Angelo 2010, The Rise of Italian Fascism 1918–1922, London and New York: Routledge.

Täubler, Alexander 1919, Die Sozialisierung und der neue Geist der Zeit. Den Arbeiter-, Soldaten- u. Bauernräten Deutschösterreichs gewidmet, Vienna: Brand.

Thalheimer, August 1930, On Fascism, available at: http://www.marxists.org.

Tönnies, Ferdinand 2003 [1887], Community and Society, New York: Dover Publications.

Trotsky, Leon 1929, 'The Austrian Crisis And Communism', available at: http://www.marxists.org.

——— 1945 [1924], The First Five Years of the Communist International, New York: Pioneer Publishers, available at: http://www.marxists.org.

——— 1965 [1923], The New Course, edited by Max Shachtman, Ann Arbor, MI: University of Michigan Press.

——— 1971 [1934], 'Bonapartism and Fascism', in The Struggle Against Fascism in Germany, New York: Pathfinder Press.

——— 2011 [1920], Terrorism and Communism, New York: Union Books.

Tugan-Baranovsky, Mikhail 1923, Periodicheskie promyshlennye krizisy, Smolensk: Literary Cooperative Society of the Smolensk Government-Committee.

Unfried, Berthold 1988, 'Arbeiterschaft und Arbeiterbewegung im 1. Weltkrieg. Wien und Niederösterreich', in Sozialdemokratie und Habsburgstaat, edited by Wolfgang Maderthaner, Vienna: Löcker.

Volpi, Shelley 1977, Otto Bauer und sein Weg zur politischen Macht, Vienna: university paper.

Vorländer, Karl 1920, Kant, Fichte, Hegel und der Sozialismus, Berlin: P. Cassirer.

——— 1926 [1911], Kant und Marx. Ein Beitrag zur Philosophie des Sozialismus. Tübingen: Mohr.

——— 1955 [1908], Geschichte der Philosophie. Band 2: Die Philosophie der Neuzeit bis Kant, Leipzig: Meiner.

Waldenberg, Marek 1972, Wzlot i upadek Karola Kautsky'ego. Studium z historii myśli społecznej i politycznej, Volume 2, Krakow: Wydawnictwo Literackie.

——— 1976, Kautsky, Warsaw: Wiedza Powszechna.

Walicki, Andrzej 1995, Marxism and the Leap to the Kingdom of Freedom: The Rise and Fall of the Communist Utopia, Stanford, CA: Stanford University Press.

Wandruszka, Adam 1954, Österreichs politische Struktur. Die Entwicklung der Parteien und politischen Bewegungen, Vienna: Verlag für Geschichte und Politik.

Wasilewski, Leon 1907, Austrja spółczesna, Warsaw.

——— 1929, Sprawy narodowościowe w teorii w życiu, Warsaw and Kraków: J. Mortkowicz.

Webb, Sidney and Beatrice 1897, *Industrial Democracy*, Volumes 1 and 2, London: Longman.

Weber, Fritz 1984, 'Weltwirtschaftskrise und das Ende der Demokratie in Österreich', in *Der 4. März 1933. Vom Verfassungsbruch zur Diktatur*, edited by Erich Fröschl and Helge Zoitl, Vienna: Verlag der Wiener Volksbuchhandlung.

Weidenholzer, Josef 1981, *Auf dem Weg zum 'neuen Menschen'. Bildungs- und Kulturarbeit der österreichischen Sozialdemokratie in der Ersten Republik*, Vienna: Europaverlag.

Weikart, Richard 1993, 'The Origins of Social Darwinism in Germany 1859–1895', *Journal of the History of Ideas*, 54, 3: 469–88.

Weinzierl, Erika 1982, 'Hauptprobleme der Ersten Republik', *Zeitgeschichte. Beiträge zur Lehrerfortbildung*, 22.

Weinzierl, Ulrich 1984, *Österreicher im Exil: 1934–1945*, Vienna: Österreichischer Bundesverlag.

Weissel, Erwin 1976, *Die Ohnmacht des Sieges. Arbeiterschaft und Sozialisierung nach dem Ersten Weltkrieg in Österreich*, Vienna: Europaverlag.

Wereszyski, Henryk 1975, *Pod berłem Habsburgów. Zagadnienia narodowościowe*, Krakow: Wydawn. Literackie.

West, Franz 1978, *Die Linke im Ständestaat Österreich. Revolutionäre Sozialisten und Kommunisten, 1934–1938*, Vienna, Munich and Zurich: Europaverlag.

Wiatr, Jerzy J. 1973, *Narod i panstwo. Socjologiczne problemy kwestii narodowej*, Warsaw: Książka i Wiedza.

Wimmer, Ernst 1984, 'Gramsci und Bauer', *Weg und Ziel*, 3 and 4: 113–16 and 141–4.

Winkler, Ernst 1976, '50 Jahre Agrarprogramm', *Die Zukunft*, 15/16: 5–9.

Woltmann, Ludwig 1974 [1900], 'Die Begründung der Moral', in *Marxismus und Ethik. Texte zum neukantianischen Sozialismus*, edited by Hans Jörg Sandkühler and Rafael de la Vega, Frankfurt am Main: Suhrkamp Verlag.

Zimmermann, Helmut 1976, *Sozialgeschichtliche und organisatorische Entwicklungsbedingungen der österreichischen Arbeiterbewegung bis 1914 unter besonderer Berücksichtigung des Austromarxismus*, Marburg/Lahn: Dissertation.

Zmierczak, Maria 1988, *Spory o istotę faszyzmu. Dzieje i krytyka*, Poznań: Wydawn. Nauk. Uniwersytetu im. Adama Mickiewicza w Poznaniu.

Znaniecki, Florian Witold 1952, *Modern Nationalities: A Sociological Study*, Urbana, IL: University of Illinois Press.

Zöllner, Erich 1979, *Geschichte Österreichs. Von den Anfängen bis zur Gegenwart*, Vienna: Verlag für Geschichte und Politik.

4   Letters

Adler, Victor 1929, *Aufsätze, Reden und Briefe, Wien 1922–1929*, I–IX, Vienna.

———— 1954, *Briefwechsel mit August Bebel und Karl Kautsky, sowie anderen deutschen Sozialdemokraten*, Vienna.

Bauer, Otto 1913, *Brief an Kautsky*, 3 Jan 1913.

———— 1914, *Brief an Helene*, 6 Dec 1914.

———— 1918, *Brief an Kautsky*, 4 Aug 1918.

———— 1919, *Brief an Béla Kun*, 16 Jun 1919.

———— 1930, 'Brief an Karl Renner', *Der Kampf*, 23.

———— 1949, 'Geheimer Briefwechsel Mussolini – Dollfuss' (Secret letter exchange between Mussolini and Dollfuss), Vienna.

Trotsky, Leon 1972 [1933], 'On The Difficulties of Our Work – A Letter To An Austrian Comrade, Jun 17 1933', in *Writings of Leon Trotsky, 1932–33*, New York: Pathfinder Press.

5   Selected Speeches

Ackermann, Manfred 1969, *Rede über Otto Bauer*, Vienna: Bund Sozialistischer Freiheit-skämpfer.

Hilferding, Rudolf 1971 [1927], 'Referat von R. Hilferding auf dem Kieler Parteitag der SPD, 1927' (Hilferding's speech at the 1927 Congress of the Social-Democratic Party of Germany), Berlin.

Renner, Karl 1927, 'Auf dem Parteitag', Vienna.

'Zum Tode Otto Bauers', in *RS Korrespondenz. Mitteilungen der Auslandsvertretung der österreichischen Sozialisten*, 3, 3 Aug 1938: 3–7.

Index